MULTI-NATIONAL CORPORATIONS AND THIRD WORLD DEVELOPMENT

International Development Resource Books
Pradip K. Ghosh, editor

Industrialization and Development: A Third World Perspective
Urban Development in the Third World
Technology Policy and Development: A Third World Perspective
Energy Policy and Third World Development
Population, Environment and Resources,
and Third World Development
Health, Food, and Nutrition in Third World Development
Economic Policy and Planning in Third World Development
Development Policy and Planning: A Third World Perspective
New International Economic Order: A Third World Perspective
Foreign Aid and Third World Development
Multi-national Corporations and Third World Development
Economic Integration and Third World Development
Third World Development: A Basic Needs Approach
Appropriate Technology in Third World Development
Development Co-operation and Third World Development
International Trade and Third World Development
Disarmament and Development: A Global Perspective
Developing South Asia: A Modernization Perspective
Developing Latin America: A Modernization Perspective
Developing Africa: A Modernization Perspective

MULTI-NATIONAL CORPORATIONS AND THIRD WORLD DEVELOPMENT

Pradip K. Ghosh, *Editor*

Foreword by Gamani Corea, Secretary-General of UNCTAD

Prepared under the auspices of the Center for International Development, University of Maryland, College Park, and the World Academy of Development and Cooperation, Washington, D.C.

International Development Resource Books, Number 11

Greenwood Press
Westport, Connecticut • London, England

Library of Congress Cataloging in Publication Data

Main entry under title:

Multi-national corporations and Third World development.

    (International development resource books, ISSN 0738-1425; no. 11)
    Bibliography: p.
    Includes index.
    1. International business enterprises. 2. Inter-
national business enterprises—Developing countries.
3. International business enterprises—Information
services. I. Ghosh, Pradip K., 1947–   . II. Title:
Multi-national corporations and Third World development.
III. Series.
HD2755.5.M8335   1984   338.8'881724   83-26680
ISBN 0-313-24147-3 (lib. bdg.)

Library of Congress Catalog Card Number: 83-26680
ISBN: 0-313-24147-3
ISSN: 0738-1425

First published in 1984

Greenwood Press
A division of Congressional Information Service, Inc.
88 Post Road West, Westport, Connecticut 06881

Printed in the United States of America

10 9 8 7 6 5 4 3 2 1

TO

THE RESEARCHERS AT THE INTERNATIONAL LABOR ORGANIZATION

IN GRATEFUL RECOGNITION OF THEIR LEADERSHIP ROLE
IN THIRD WORLD DEVELOPMENT RESEARCH

"THE ULTIMATE OBJECTIVE OF DEVELOPMENT MUST BE TO BRING ABOUT A SUSTAINED IMPROVEMENT IN THE WELL-BEING OF THE INDIVIDUAL AND BESTOW BENEFITS ON ALL. IF UNDUE PRIVILEGES, EXTREMES OF WEALTH AND SOCIAL INJUSTICES PERSIST, THEN DEVELOPMENT FAILS IN THE ESSENTIAL PURPOSE"

- UNITED NATIONS GENERAL ASSEMBLY RESOLUTION 2626 (XXV), 24 OCTOBER 1970.

Contents

LIST OF TABLES

THE TRANSNATIONAL CORPORATION AS AN AGENT FOR INDUSTRIAL
RESTRUCTING

MULTINATIONAL CORPORATIONS, SOCIO-CULTURAL DEPENDENCE AND
INDUSTRIALIZATION: NEED SATISFACTION OR WANT CREATION?

MULTINATIONAL CORPORATIONS, THE INDUSTRY TECHNOLOGY CYCLE
AND DEVELOPMENT

PART II

STATISTICAL INFORMATION AND SOURCES

LIST OF FIGURES

MULTINATIONAL CORPORATIONS, ECONOMIC POLICY AND NATIONAL
DEVELOPMENT IN THE WORLD SYSTEM

The Third World

Afghanistan
  Republic of Afghanistan
Algeria
  Democratic and Popular
  Republic of Algeria
Angola
  People's Republic of Angola
Argentina
  Argentine Republic
Bahamas
  Commonwealth of the Bahamas
Bahrain
  State of Bahrain
Bangladesh
  People's Republic of
  Bangladesh
Barbados
  People's Republic of
  Barbados
Benin
  People's Republic of Benin
Bhutan
  People's Republic of Bhutan
Bolivia
  Republic of Bolivia
Botswana
  Republic of Botswana
Brazil
  Federative Republic of Brazil
Burma
  Socialist Republic of the
  Union of Burma
Burundi
  Republic of Burundi

Cambodia
  Democratic Kampuchea

Cameroon
  United Republic of Cameroon
Cape Verde
  Republic of Cape Verde
Central African Empire
Chad
  Republic of Chad
Chile
  Republic of Chile
Colombia
  Republic of Colombia
Comoro Islands
  Republic of the Comoros
Congo
  People's Republic of the
  Congo
Costa Rica
  Republic of Costa Rica
Cuba
  Republic of Cuba
Dominican Republic
Ecuador
  Republic of Ecuador
Egypt
  Arab Republic of Egypt
El Salvador
  Republic of El Salvador
Equatorial Guinea
  Republic of Equatorial
  Guinea
Ethiopia
Fiji
  Dominion of Fiji
Gabon
  Gabonese Republic
Gambia
  Republic of the Gambia

Ghana
  Republic of Ghana
Grenada
  State of Grenada
Guatemala
  Republic of Guatemala
Guinea
  Republic of Guinea
Guinea-Bissau
  Republic of Guinea-Bissau
Guyana
  Cooperative Republic of
  Guyana
Haiti
  Republic of Haiti
Honduras
  Republic of Honduras
India
  Republic of India
Indonesia
  Republic of Indonesia
Iran
  Imperial Government of Iran
Iraq
  Republic of Iraq
Ivory Coast
  Republic of Ivory Coast
Jamaica
Jordan
  Hashemite Kingdom of Jordan
Kenya
  Republic of Kenya
Kuwait
  State of Kuwait
Laos
  Lao People's
  Democratic Republic
Lebanon
  Republic of Lebanon
Lesotho
  Kingdom of Lesotho
Liberia
  Republic of Liberia
Libya
  People's Socialist
  Libyan Arab Republic

Madagascar
  Democratic Republic
  of Madagascar
Malawi
  Republic of Malawi
Malaysia
Maldives
  Republic of Maldives
Mali
  Republic of Mali
Mauritania
  Islamic Republic
  of Mauritania
Mauritius
Mexico
  United Mexican States
Mongolia
  Mongolian People's Republic
Morocco
  Kingdom of Morocco
Mozambique
  People's Republic
  of Mozambique
Nepal
  Kingdom of Nepal
Nicaragua
  Republic of Nicaragua
Niger
  Republic of Niger
Nigeria
  Federal Republic of Nigeria
Oman
  Sultanate of Oman
Pakistan
  Islamic Republic of Pakistan
Panama
  Republic of Panama
Papua New Guinea
Paraguay
  Republic of Paraguay
Peru
  Republic of Peru
Philippines
  Republic of the Philippines
Qatar
  State of Qatar

Adopted from THE THIRD WORLD: PREMISES OF U.S. POLICY by W. Scott Thompson, Institute for Contemporary Studies, San Francisco, 1978.

Rhodesia
Ruanda
  Republic of Ruanda
Samoa
Sao Tome and Principe
  Democratic Republic of
  Sao Tome and Principe
Saudi Arabia
  Kingdom of Saudi Arabia
Senegal
  Republic of Senegal
Seychelles
Sierra Leone
  Republic of Sierra Leone
Singapore
  Republic of Singapore
Somalia
  Somali Democratic Republic
Sri Lanka
  Republic of Sri Lanka
Sudan
  Democratic Republic of
  the Sudan
Surinam
Swaziland
  Kingdom of Swaziland
Syria
  Syrian Arab Republic
Tanzania
  United Republic of Tanzania

Thailand
  Kingdom of Thailand
Togo
  Republic of Togo
Trinidad and Tobago
Tunisia
  Republic of Tunisia
Uganda
  Republic of Uganda
United Arab Emirates
Upper Volta
  Republic of Upper Volta
Uruguay
  Oriental Republic of Uruguay
Venezuela
  Republic of Venezuela
Vietnam
  Socialist Republic of Vietnam
Western Sahara
Yemen
  People's Democratic Republic
  of Yemen
Yemen
  Yemen Arab Republic
Zaire
  Republic of Zaire
Zambia
  Republic of Zambia

Countries which have social and economic characteristics in
common with the Third World but, because of political
affiliations or regimes, are not associated with Third
World organizations:

China
  People's Republic of China
Cyprus
  Republic of Cyprus
Israel
  State of Israel
Kazakhstan
Kirghizia
Korea
  Democratic People's Republic
  of Korea
Romania
  Socialist Republic of Romania

South Africa
  Republic of South Africa
South West Africa
  Namibia
Tadzhikistan
Turkmenistan
Uzbekistan
Yugoslavia
  Socialist Federal Republic
  of Yugoslavia

Abbreviations

ADC	Andean Development Corporation
AsDB	Asian Development Bank
ASEAN	Association of South-East Asian Nations
CARIFTA	Caribbean Free Trade Association
DAC	Development Assistance Committee (of OECD)
ECA	Economic Commission for Africa
ECE	Economic Commission for Europe
ECLA	Economic Commission for Latin America
ECOWAS	Economic Commission of West African States
EDF	European Development Fund
EEC	European Economic Community
EFTA	European Free Trade Association
ESCAP	Economic and Social Commission for Asia and the Pacific
FAO	Food and Agriculture Organization of the United Nations
GATT	General Agreement on Tariffs and Trade
GDP	gross domestic product
GNP	gross national product
IBRD	International Bank for Reconstruction and Development (World Bank)
IDA	International Development Association
IDB	Inter-American Development Bank
IFC	International Finance Corporation
IIEP	International Institute for Educational Planning
ILO	International Labour Office
IMF	International Monetary Fund
LAFTA	Latin American Free Trade Association
ODA	official development assistance
OECD	Organisation for Economic Co-operation and Development
OPEC	Organization of Petroleum Exporting Countries
UNDP	United Nations Development Programme
UNEP	United Nations Environment Programme
UNESCO	United Nations Educational, Scientific and Cultural Organization
UNHCR	Office of the United Nations High Commissioner for Refugees
UNITAR	United Nations Institute for Training and Research
UNICEF	United Nations Children's Fund
UNIDO	United Nations Industrial Development Organization
WFP	World Food Programme
WHO	World Health Organization

Foreword

I am pleased to know of the International Development Resources Book project. The 20 resource books which are published under this project, covering the whole spectrum of issues in the fields of development economics and international co-operation for development, and containing not only current reading materials but also up-to-date statistical data and bibliographical notes, will, I am sure, prove to be extremely useful to a wide public.

I would like to commend the author for having undertaken this very ambitious and serious project and, by so doing, rendered a most valuable service. I am confident that it will have a great success.

Gamani Corea

Secretary-General
United Nations Conference on Trade and Development

Preface

Stimulus for the publication of an international resource book series was developed in 1980, while teaching and researching various topics related to third world development. Since that time, I have built up a long list of related resource materials on different subjects, usually considered to be very important for researchers, educators, and public policy decision makers involved with developing country problems. This series of resource books makes an attempt for the first time to give the reader a comprehensive look at the current issues, methods, strategies and policies, statistical information and comprehensive resource bibliographies, and a directory of various information sources on the topic.

This topic is very important because within the framework of the current international economic order, developing an effective multi-national corporations and third world development policy is envisaged as a dynamic instrument of growth essential to the rapid economic and social development of the developing countries, in particular of the least developed countries of Asia, Africa and Latin America.

Much of this work was completed during my residency as a visiting scholar in the Center for Advanced Study of International Development at Michigan State University. Suzanne Wilson, Mary Ann Kozak, Kathy White and Susan Costello, students at the University, provided much needed assistance with the project. I am thankful to the M.S.U. Sociology department for providing necessary support services and Dr. James T. Sabin, Vice President, editorial of Greenwood Press who encouraged me in pursuing the work and finally agreeing to publish in book form.

I would also like to gratefully acknowledge the encouragement given to me by Dr. Denton Morrison to pursue this project and Dr. Mark Van de Vall who has been an inspiration to me since my graduate school days.

Finally, preparation of this book would not have been completed without the contributions from Joseph LaPalombara, Stephen Blank, Volker Bornschier, Frederick F. Clairmonte, John

H.   Cavanagh, Arghiri Emmanuel, S.   C.   Jain, Y.   Puri, Susumu
Watanabe, Stephen J. Kobrin, Stephen P. Magee, Dimitri Germidis,
Mikoto Usui, Arturo Nunez del Prado, Rolf Jungnickel and Georg
Koopmann.   I am also gratefully indebted to Journal of Economic
Literature, U.N. Documents and World Bank Publications for the
much needed annotations, and a very special thanks to Tom and
Jackie Minkel for their assistance in the preparation of this
book in camera ready form.

PART I

CURRENT ISSUES, TRENDS, ANALYTICAL METHODS, STRATEGIES AND POLICIES, COUNTRY STUDIES

Introduction

This resource book has two multifaceted purposes. Firstly, to document and analyze the current trends in the role of multinational corporations in the development of the third world countries--and to evaluate the progress made by them during the past decade in attaining long term objectives of a sustained economic growth and improvement in the quality of living future populations.

We are all very much familiar with the problems of Third World countries, usually described by Latin America (excluding Cuba) the whole of Africa, Asia (excluding its socialist countries, Japan and Israel) and Oceania (Australia and New Zealand). They are plagued by poverty, very high rates of population growth, low growth rates of gross domestic product, low rates of industrialization, extremely high dependence on agriculture, rate of unemployment, and uneven income distribution. Although the expression "Third World countries" no longer has a clear meaning, majority of the international development experts would consider the poor developing countries to belong in the third world irrespective of their affiliation as aligned or non-aligned characteristic.

Secondly, major purpose of this volume is to provide the researchers with the much needed knowledge about the different sources of information and available data related to the objectives and goals of multinational corporations in Third World development. Multinational corporations' programs in the developing countries have raised many complex issues. While these issues are largely dependent on national policies and priorities, their solution is of international concern.

The pace and pattern of development have varied widely among the developing countries partly because of differences in the availability of natural, human and capital resources and in factors such as size and location, and partly because of differences in objectives, strategies and policies related to MNC's that countries have pursued. The issues affecting strategies and policies differ considerably at the present time from those that were important a decade ago and policy design is thus now more complex and difficult than before.

The dramatic transformation of the climate surrounding relations between rich and poor nations since the OPEC oil embargo in 1973 has faised new hopes that MNC's (Multinational Corporations) may be made to energize development in the Third World. Improved information about the vulnerability of the rich nations and about techniques for dealing with MNC's, some writers argue, will enable underdeveloped countries to ensure that foreign investment serves as an "engine of development." This view exaggerates the strengths of Third World states. A lack of information about opportunities and techniques is a small part of the burden which underdevelopment imposes on pocr countries in their dealings with MNC's. A case study of Japanese MNC's in Southeast Asia raises doubts concerning the likelihood that the poor countries will be able to harness MNC's for their development. Southeast Asia's growing dependence on Japan in the fields of trade, offical development aid, and private investment tends to impose constraints on efforts to influence the behavior of MNCs. A more basic problem resides in the "softness" of underdeveloped states, which renders ineffectual regulations intended to control MNCs. Because MNCs in certain important respects inhibit the process of building viable indigenous institutions and even contribute to the perpetuation of soft states, they may do more to impede than to stimulate development, at least in the softer Third World states. It may well be that more serious attention should be paid to studies of how Third World states might develop if the role of MNCs were circumscribed.[2]

The question of whether foreign investment, specifically that of MNCs, actually alleviates or perpetuates underdevelopment has, of course, long been a matter of debate. But the dramatic transformation of the climate surrounding relations between the rich and poor nations since the OPEC oil embargo in 1973 has raised new hopes that MNCs may indeed be made to energize development efforts in the Third World. Since 1974 there has been talk of a major shift in power from industrialized to underdeveloped nations. It is argured that Third World countries (except for the most impoverished, now relegated to the "Fourth World") are just now becoming aware of their capacity, through both individual and collective action, to compel MNCs to adjust their operations to serve the needs of the host nations.

There is increasing international emphasis upon the role of science and technology in the development process and the need for greatly expanded research on the technological needs of the Third World. This stems not merely from the appreciation of the major contribution of technological change to the aggregate growth of every economy in which measurements of the various factor contributions have been attempted, but also, and increasingly, from the perception that new technologies, adapted or developed to suit the peculiar resource and factor endowments, market sizes, and sonsumption patterns and needs of poor countries, are required if development aspirations of the type now considered appropriate in the Third World are to be realized.

The bulk of the literature concerning the role of the multinational enterprise in the transfer of technology to the less developed countries has been addressed to two issues: (1) the 'appropriateness' of the technology being transferred; (2) its availability and cost to the purchaser, both absolutely and relative to the available alternatives. Both of these issues must be addressed simultaneously, since achievement of progress with one, without any change in the other, may generate negligible or even harmful results for the less developed countries.[3]

This volume examines the experience of a substantial number of the Third World countries in implementing development plans during approximately the 1970's and draws some general conslusions for policy action during the years ahead.

Attention has been focussed on some of the major problems faced by hard core developing countries and policy issues posed by those problems. However, the development needs of hard-core developing countries are very large and call for much greater interest and attention from world community than has been the case for. A systematic attack on the acute problems of countries facing extreme poverty and underdevelopment should therefore now be at the center of the policies designed to usher in a new international economic order.

It is hoped that this resource book will be of use not only to those directly involved in the formulation and implementation of development policies but also will help to acquaint a wide reading audience with the thrusts planned by developing countries for accelerated progress. In addition, the intercountry comparative analysis may be cf use to planners and policy makers in developing countries, especially from the viewpoint of harmonizing national plans in order to strengthen economic co-operation with respect to multinational corporations among interested countries.

The plan of the reading materials in Part I of the book and the selection of the fifteen pieces represents a specific orientation, or bias. They present current international issues and trends affecting MNC's in third world development, analytical methods, strategies and policies regarding MNC's development and selected third world country studies.

Part II includes statistical information and a descriptive bibliography of information sources related to industrialization and development in the third world countries.

Part III is a select bibliography of bocks, documents and periodical articles published since 1970, relevant to MNC's and development of the developing countries. Annotations for the different titles have been compiled from The Journal of Economic Literature, International Social Sciences Index, U.N. Documents Index, World Bank Publications, Finance and Development, Bock Publisher's promotion brochures and the IMF-IBRD Joint Library Publications.

Part IV consists of a directory of information sources. This section is in four parts, directory of United Nations Information Sources, listing of bibliographic sources, titles of selected periodicals published around the world and a directory of institutions involved in research relevant to MNC's in the third world countries.

[1] Rodwin Lloyd, "Regional Planning Perspectives in Third World Countries," in TRAINING FOR REGIONAL DEVELOPMENT PLANNING: PERSPECTIVES FOR THE THIRD DEVELOPMENT DECADE, ed. by, Om Prakash Mathur, UNCRD, 1981.
Thompson, W. Scott, THE THIRD WORLD: PREMISES OF U.S. POLICY Institute for Contemporary Studies, San Francisco, 1978.

[2] Weinstein, Franklin B., "Multinational Corporations and the Third World" INTERNATIONAL ORGANIZATION, Vol. 36, No. 3, Summer, 1976.

[3] Helleiner, G.K., "The Role of Multinational Corporations in The Less Developed Countries' Trade in Technology, WORLD DEVELOPMENT, Vol. 3, No. 4, Apr. 1975, pp. 161-189.

Multinational Corporations and Developing Countries

JOSEPH LaPALOMBARA
STEPHEN BLANK

Few issues have generated more rhetoric in recent years than the relations between multinational corporation (MNCs) and developing nations. Extensive debate has resulted in little agreement among the defenders and opponents of the MNCs is the developing world. For some, like former Secretary of State Henry Kissinger, the multinational corporation is seen as "one of the most effective engines of development"; for others, such as Ronald Muller, co-author of Global Reach, the MNC is "one of the most powerful impediments to Third World development."[1]

The purpose of this article, which draws upon research conducted by the authors for The Conference Board in 1976-78, is to throw light on an important dimension of international relations that is likely to affect increasingly the foreign policy framework in many developing nations. While the scope and nature of private multinational corporate involvement varies greatly throughout the developing world, governments in almost every developing nation have been active in establishing guidelines for these companies that seek to enhance benefits provided to host countries. As issues of economic development and national security become less distinct, analysts of foreign policies of developing countries must give closer attention to how governing elites view the role of MNCs. Before turning to this topic, however, we want to look briefly at the general pattern of foreign direct investment in the developing world.

From **JOURNAL OF INTERNATIONAL AFFAIRS**, 34, Spring 1980, (119-136), reprinted by permission of the publisher.

I. FOREIGN DIRECT INVESTMENT IN THE DEVELOPING COUNTRIES

Most MNC activities are located in the developed, not the developing world. This is so notwithstanding the proliferation of developing nations since World War II, and notwithstanding the location of natural resources and population growth in the Third world. In fact the imbalance seems to be increasing. Table 1 depicts the global distribution of foreign direct investment (FDI) of the developed market-economy nations. In 1975, more than 40 percent of all developed-nation foreign direct investment was located in four host countries: the United States, the United Kingdom, Canada and the Federal Republic of Germany.

The share of the global stock of foreign direct investment located in the developing nations fell from 31 percent in 1967 to 26 percent in 1975. Three percent of the investment going to the developing nations in 1975 was directed to tax-haven countries such as Bermuda and the Netherlands Antilles, and was often routed back to the developed nations; six percent went to the OPEC nations -- leaving only 17 percent of the global stock of foreign direct investment in all of the other developing nations.

Data gathered by the United Nations in 1972 indicate that in 1967 about three-quarters of the affiliates of MNCs headquartered in the developed nations operated in the developed world. The UN data show that between 65 and 75 percent of US-based MNC affiliates were located in the developed market economics, as were 68 percent of the British, 82 percent of the German, and 60 percent of the French.[2] Japan is the exception to this rule in that more than half of its direct investment stock was in developing nations in 1975, although this proportion, like that of other developed nations, was lower than in 1967.[3]

Research carried out by the Harvard Comparative Multinational Enterprise Project confirms the United Nations' findings. The Harvard group found that 60 percent of the foreign manufacturing subsidiaries of large US MNCs are sited in the developed nations and in the less-developed nations of Europe (which the UN counts as developed). For Britain, the share is 55 percent; for Germany, 62 percent; and for France, 57 percent.[4]

In 1957, 41 percent of the book value of US direct investment overseas was in the developing nations; by 1973, the figure was only 24 percent (see Table 2). The British pattern is similar: 28 percent of British foreign direct investment was sited in the developing Commonwealth nations in 1962 and only 15 percent in 1974 (see Table 3).

Latin America has by far the largest regional stock of foreign direct investment from the developed nations, although its share of the global stock of FDI dropped slightly between 1967 and 1972. Asia's share increased significantly during this period, while the African and Middle Eastern proportions both declined marginally.

Working with OECD data, an International Labor Organization research team analyzed the distribution of foreign direct investment in the developing nations (including Southern Europe) by type and region of investment (see Table 4). Three basic types of

TABLE 1:
Stock of Direct Investment Abroad of Developed Market Economies, by Host Country, 1967–1975

Host Country and Country Group	1967	1971	1975
Total value of stock (billions of dollars)	$105	$156	$259
Distribution of stock (percentage)			
Developed market economies	69%[a]	72%[a]	74%
Canada	18	17	15
United States	9	9	11
United Kingdom	8	9	9
Germany (Federal Republic)	3	5	6
Other	30	32	33
Developing countries	31	28	26
OPEC countries[1]	9	7	6
Tax havens[2]	2	3	3
Other	20	17	17
Total	100%	100%	100%

Source: United Nations Economic and Social Council, *Transnational Corporations in World Development: A Re-Examination*, E/C. 10/38, March 20, 1978, p. 237.

1 Algeria, Ecuador, Gabon, Indonesia, Iran, Iraq, Kuwait, Libya, Nigeria, Qatar, Saudi Arabia, United Arab Emirates, and Venezuela.

2 Bahamas, Barbados, Bermuda, Cayman Islands, Netherlands Antilles, and Panama.

a Details do not add to 100 percent because of rounding.

TABLE 2:
U.S. Direct Investment Position Abroad at Year-end (Million US$)

Country or Area	1957		1962		1967		1973		1978	
	Amount	Percent	Amount	Percent	Amount	Percent	Amount	Percent	Amount	Percent
All Countries	$25,262	100%	$37,226	100%	$56,583	100%	$100,675	100%	$168,100	100%
Developed Countries	13,905	55	22,618	61	38,708	69	72,214	70	120,700	72
Developing Countries	10,316	41	12,960	35	14,928	26	25,266	24	40,500	24
Other	1,041	4	1,647	4	2,947	5	6,195	6	6,900	4

Sources: 1957, *U.S. Business Investment in Foreign Countries,* US Department of Commerce, 1960
1962, *Survey of Current Business,* US Department of Commerce, August 1964
1967–73, *Revised Data Series on US Direct Investment, 1966–1974,* US Department of Commerce, 1974.
1978, *Survey of Current Business,* US Department of Commerce, August 1979

10

TABLE 3:

United Kingdom Overseas Direct Investment, Location and Growth, 1962–1974[a]

Book Values (£ million)

Country or Area	1962		1970		1974		Average Annual Percent Increase	
	Amount	Percent	Amount	Percent	Amount	Percent	1962–1969	1970–1974
Developed Commonwealth (including Canada)	£1,470	43%	£2,759	43%	£3,961	37%	12%	9%
Developing Commonwealth	936	28	1,300	20	1,633	15	4	7
United States	301	09	762	12	1,678	16	16	32
EEC (the six)	272	08	808	13	2,095	20	24	37
EFTA (the seven)	82	02	182	03	373	04	14	25
Other	344	10	593	09	883	08	10	11
Total	£3,405	100%	£6,404	100%	£10,623	100%	11%	15%

Source: John M. Stopford, "Changing Perspectives on Investment by British Manufacturing Multinationals," *Journal of International Business Studies,* Fall–Winter, 1976, p. 15.

a Excludes oil, banking, insurance

TABLE 4:

Developing Countries, 1970—Breakdown of Foreign Private Investment (by region and type)

Region	Type of Foreign Investment			Total	
	Exploitation of basic products (percent)	Penetration of protected markets (percent)	Exploitation of cheap labour (percent)	Million US Dollars	Percent
Africa	60%	34%	6%	$ 7.9 m.	20.8%
Latin America	33	62	5	20.8	54.6
Middle East	91	9	–	3.6	9.4
Asia	30	36	34	5.8	15.2
Totals (in million U.S. dollars)	$16.6	$18.0	$3.5	$38.1 m.	
Percent of overall total	44%	48%	9%		100%

Source: Computed from Y. Sabdo and R. Trajtenberg in collaboration with J.P. Sajhau, *The Impact of Transnational Enterprises on Employment in the Developing Countries.* Geneva, Switzerland: International Labour Organisation, 1976, p. 2.

investment are categorized: exploitation of basic products; penetration of protected markets; and exploitation of cheap labor. Table 4 shows that overwhelmingly the largest share of FDI in the Middle East and the largest share in Africa was of the the basic product variety. In Latin America, important substitution programs provide the incentives for FDI. Although the three types of incentives are evenly distributed in Asia, it is noteworthy how relatively important the incentive of cheap labor is for that region.

Available data may underestimate the amount of foreign investment flowing into the developing countries, and into the OPEC nations in particular. For one thing, data on investment flows from several major developed nations -- Germany, for example -- are probably incomplete. Secondly, through the use of management contracts, licenses and other similar arrangements, the presence of the multinationals in developing countries undoubtedly is greater than figures on direct investment alone suggest.

These data also omit the rising flow of foreign direct investment within the developing world. Nations such as India, Mexico, Argentina, Taiwan, Hong Kong and Singapore are growing sources of foreign investment, and multinationals headquartered in developing nations are increasingly active in their own regions and even globally.[5] Brazilian investors are found throughout Nigeria, for example, and Singapore remains the leading source of foreign investment in Malaysia.

These additional sources of investment notwithstanding, investors in the developed nations by and large have been progressively less attracted to the developing nations since World War II, relative to their enormously increasing interests in other developed nations. The attitude of many MNCs toward the developing world is well summarized by Peter Drucker. He observes that in a group of 45 major multinationals he has studied, "75 to 85 percent of all growth, whether in sales or profits, in the last 25 years, occurred in the developed countries." He argues that

> for the typical twentieth century multinational, that is a manufacturing, distributing or financial company, developing countries are important neither as markets nor as producers or profits.[6]

II. INCREASING DIFFERENCES WITHIN THE DEVELOPING NATIONS

Even where by global standards the amount of investment, the size of MNC affiliates, and the scale of their operations are small, foreign direct investment is still frequently a critical factor in a developing nation's economic life. What may be a small investment in a relatively minor operation by New York or London boardroom standards can be of crucial importance to the economy of the host nation. Peter Drucker, in the article previously cited, emphasized that the discrepancy can be a key source of tension between MNCs and developing country governments:

> Within the developing country the man in charge of a business
> with 750 employees and eight million dollars in sales has to
> be an important man. While his business is minute compared to
> the company's business in Germany, Great Britain, or the
> United States, it is every bit as difficult -- indeed it is
> likely to be a good deal more difficult, risky and demanding.
> And he has to be treated as an equal with the government
> leaders, the bankers, and the business leaders of his
> country -- people whom the district sales manager in Hamburg,
> Rotterdam or Kansas City never even sees. Yet his sales and
> profits are less than those of the Hamburg, Rotterdam, or
> Kansas City district. And his growth potential is, in most
> cases, even lower.

That foreign investment or the activities of foreign companies
often give rise to severe tensions between home and host company
governments, or between host countries and foreign firms, is no
surprise. Nor are such tensions a recent phenomenon.
Expropriation, nationalization and armed intervention to protect
foreign-owned property were not uncommon long before the era of the
multinational corporation. But the rapid emergence of so many
politically independent countries (in 1950, 37 developing countries
were members of the United Nations; in 1977, there were 110); the
growing concern in these nations with economic development and with
the economic aspects of independence; and the expansion of the
multinational corporation in the world economy have all focused
attention on the role -- positive and negative -- of the MNC in
national development and internal economic relations.

Tensions between multinational corporations and developing
nations often reflect the deep feeling of ambivalence regarding
industrialization in the developing nations. Almost all are
committed to the goal of industrialization, even as they
acknowledge the social and political cost of development. Leaders
in these nations are unsure about the means of economic
development. Does external assistance -- through foreign aid or
the participation of multinational corporations -- lessen or
increase social costs?

Differences of opinion such as these frequently lead to
ambivalent responses to the presence of foreign corporations. On
the one hand, Charles Kindleberger observes, "...'uncompromising
nationalism and economic populism' and the aim to 'terminate
dependence on the United States' or the developed world seem...to
characterize the environment in which the multinational corporation
has had to operate vis-a-vis developing governments in the last
decade or so."[7] On the other hand, governments of the developing
nations (especially in the corridors of their own ministries) urge
greater MNC participation and investment. MNC executives complain
that leaders of developing countries take a different line on
foreign investment for each audience, and policies toward the
foreign investor becomes stakes in host country politics.

Although the share of the world stock of foreign direct
investment located in the developing nations has declined, the

absolute amount of investment in these nations, has increased
substantially, according to UN data, from $32.8 billion in 1967 to
$68.2 billion in 1975.[8] Aggregate figures such as these, however,
obscure more fundamental changes taking place within the developing
world -- in particular, the increasing differentiation within the
group according to the rate and structure of economic development.
The fact is that a relatively small group of Asian and Latin
American countries can no longer be considered "less developed" at
all. These are the NICs, the newly industrializing countries,[9]
which while heterogeneous with regard to geography, per capita
income and development policies are all "characterized by rapid
growth in the level and share of industrial employment, expansion
of export market share in manufactures and real per capita income
levels which are approaching those of some of the advanced
industrial countries."[10]

The NIC role is especially prominent in industrial production
and in the worldwide export of manufactured goods. Between 1963
and 1977, the developing countries' share of world industrial
production increased from 14 to 19 percent, and between 1965 and
1974, the developing countries' manufactured exports rose from five
to eight percent of the world trade in manufactured goods. Even in
aggregate terms, these apparently modest LDC gains include some
remarkable achievements. In 1977, for example, 49 percent of the
US and 34 percent of EEC imports of miscellaneous manufactures,
including clothing and shoes, came from developing countries; with
regard to manufactures based on raw materials, 22 percent of US and
24 percent of EEC imports were produced in the developing world.[11]

A disaggregation of these statistics by source of exports is
still more impressive. They are heavily concentrated in a few
nations. Bradford, in the paper cited, calculated that the 22
second-tier developing nations exported only 20 percent of the NIC
total in manufactured goods in 1976. While the real growth in
manufactured exports from North America was about nine percent per
year between 1965 and 1974, from Western Europe ten percent and
from Japan, 16 percent, Korea's exports of manufactures grew by 37
percent a year in this period, Taiwan's by 29 percent, Brazil's by
25 percent and Mexico's by 21 percent.

One result of the widening gap between the NICs and poorer
developing nations has been to strain the unity of the developing
world on many key issues in the global economy. The developinn
nations have struggled to maintain a common front in recent
negotiations with the developed nations, although they have adopted
more moderate positions on several key issues than in the past.
Efforts by the developed nations to split off the non-oil producing
developing nations from the OPEC countries have not been
successfull (See Mossavar-Rahmani and Rothstein in this volume).
Wealthier developing nations, such as Brazil, have taken a line,
possibly to demonstrate their solidarity with the poorer members of
the developing world. But despite heroic efforts by the Group of
77 to maintain a common front, and the concern of the richer
developing nations to keep in step, the heterogeneity of the
nations of the developing world and the variety of their interests
and needs are increasingly evident.

Much of this heterogeneity rests on basic "givens." Some of

the developing nations are plentifully endowed with natural resources; petroleum, minerals, and of growing importance, soil and climate suitable for extensive agricultural production.

The history and experience of a developing nation constitutes another crucial "given." Because colonial power drew borders between countries without reference to ethnic, tribal, religious or linguistic factors, every African nation today embodies an inherent source of instability as an element of its colonial heritage. The British predilection for "indirect rule" provides one legacy; the

Asian cultures seem to have been more resilient than African in the face of European domination, while the Indian cultures of South America all but disappeared. Colonial systems altered entire social structures. The British brought Chinese to work in the tine mines of what is now Malaysia and also carried the seeds for the rubber tree from Brazil to Malaysia. European and American slavers mined the west coast of Africa for human cargoes and violently altered social, economic and political structures there.

The level of political and economic development at the time of independence constitutes another "given." Were there cadres of trained local administrators? Had there been some experience with local self-government? How well-developed was the economic infrastructure? Were there railroads, ports, communications? Had efforts been made to develop the entire local economy, or merely one sector--or none of it as all?

What did the country face to win its independence? A long and violent struggle or a more gradual process? Were patterns of trade with the former colonial nation maintained or sharply interrupted? Were long-term economic and assistance agreements laid down at independence, or was the newly independent nation determined (or forced) to fend for itself? Did the new nation plunge immediately into internal strife; rebellion, civil war, partition? What about external pressures? Rapacious neighbors? Did it become a pawn in the Cold War?

The effect of these "givens" has been heightened by policy choices for development. The public sector's role in the economy is substantial in all developing countries, given the demands of modernization and industrialization. But while some nations have opted for a high degree of centralization, administrative discretion, and a large segment of public ownership in the economy, others seek to lessen the role of government and to emphasize private sector growth. While few nations have chosen a Chinese model of development -- excluding foreign corporations -- the degree of acceptance of foreign corporations varies considerably. All developing nations would like to have the technology, capital and managerial skills multinational corporations provide -- but not all are willing to pay the cost involved in terms of providing stable investment regulations, provisions for rapid remittance of profits and capital, and so on. Developing countries are more or less capable of exploiting the growing competition among MNCs, particularly as they come increasingly from different home countries. They also differ in their capacity to negotiate favorable terms with foreign corporations.

Resources are a necessary but not sufficient element of success. Countries with substantial natural resources have failed to develop coherent national resources have failed to develop coherent national development policies and programs and have squandered their wealth. Others with less natural endowment (for example, Singapore and the Ivory Coast) have devoted intense efforts to development and to the maintenance of a favorable investment and business climate.

Development is self-reinforcing; success breeds success. Critical managerial and entrepreneurial skills acquired in one sector are spun off to another; lessons learned become guidelines for the future. As Bradford observed, "Once Korean manufacturers learned how to penetrate the US market for electronic calculators in a major way, they could move on to color television sets with greater ease than other countries who have been marginal exporters.[12] Success also attracts external interest. International banks and multinational corporations are primarily interested in those countries with the best track records. Indeed, there is a further self-reinforcing characteristic of this interest: once foreign banks and companies commit themselves heavily to a particular country -- such as Brazil -- it is even more difficult for them to decrease their involvements (see Leeds in this volume).

A recent study of the NICs carried out by the Royal Institute of International Affairs lists several factors which support the recent rapid economic development in these nations.[13] The first is the educational revolution: several NICs now have literacy rates very close to levels in developed nations. Even where literacy rates are still lower, as in India or Mexico, large numbers of highly trained (often in the US) public and private sector managers staff key positions throughout the economy.

Improvements in global communications, secondly, have given the NICs access to the developed nations' economies. Third is the improved planning capabilities in the NICs, as well as the commitment of leaders in most of the NICs to effective economic planning systems. Another factor listed in the Chatham House study is the improved access of the NICs to international finance. "In the past," Turner and his associates observe, "Third World countries had to rely on foreign direct investment or aid to finance large industrial projects. Now, the expansion of the Eurocurrency markets means that leading Third World countries can borrow directly from the international banking system."

Finally, technology is now far more readily available than in the past. In few industries do a small number of companies now effectively control key technical processes. Rising levels of skills in the NICs, together with heightened competition among multinational corporations from different nations, mean that for the most part no effective limits exist to the spread of technology in most mainstream industries.

The impressive economic gains recorded by the NICs in no way suggests that all problems of development have been solved. Indeed, initial stages of economic development may, in fact, be easier to achieve than later stages that are closer to self-sustaining growth. As development proceeds, the easy decisions have all been taken and the early, high-return investments (basic communication systems or port development, for example) all made. Profit margins are narrower and the social costs of mistakes may be higher. Development targets can no longer be framed in terms of such general goals as miles of road completed or number of elementary schools constructed. Choices made at this stage with regard to policies which favor import substitution or the development of export capacities, which channel manpower development in one or another direction, or which put in place this or that technology will determine whether or not development aspirations are achieved.

Governments at this stage must also begin to confront some of the social costs of development. Development strategies must be reformulated to include policies to create a better distribution of income; to deal with imbalances in rural and urban development; to establish more effective social welfare protection for newly urbanized workers and their families; and to regulate local business practices. As certain nations approach the goal of self-sustaining growth, their economic policies may become more conservative. They are playing the game and beginning to win. They now have much more to lose by seeking to change the rules.

For some of the developing nations, the achievement of political and economic stability seems within reach. For others, even some with great natural resources, it is a goal that cannot be obtained. Nations of South America, which have been independent since the early 19th century, may experience continuing political turmoil, but their existence as nations is not in doubt. But many delegations now sitting at the United Nations represent countries without historic or cultural identities. Some of these new nations may never achieve adolescence, let alone maturity. Strife between ethnic groups in a developing nation, even open internal warfare, might create fissures in society so wide that they can never be bridged, or it might be the catalyst for national unification. Success in coping with these problems underlies further achievements; failure decreases confidence in existing institutions and political arrangements and leads contending groups to seek alternative solutions all the more vigorously.

III. PATTERNS OF DEVELOPING COUNTRY POLICY TOWARD MULTINATIONAL CORPORATIONS

If leaders of developing nations are hesitant, even fearful, about industrialization, momentum in that direction is too strong to halt. The pressures of population and poverty often impel governments to be less discriminating than they might be where there is an overwhelming need for capital, technology, managerial know-how, and access to foreign markets.

The capacity of these governments to negotiate with multinational corporations has increased sharply as the skills of their administrative cadres have improved and as competition among multinationals from different countries has increased. In addition, after a period of intense preoccupation with the multinationals, in the mid-1970s many leaders in developing countries saw that the multinational corporation was only one -- and not the most important -- dimension of the problems that confronted their nations. Critical problems of the global economy, of North-South relations, and of economic development were not caused by the multinationals and, while the MNCs remain a convenient symbol of these problems, hammering the multinationals has done little to provide solutions.

In all countries in which MNCs operate, the network of regulation and control has become more and more dense. National legislation relating to multinational corporations (reports a recent United Nations survey) focuses on four broad areas.[14] The first is foreign-investment decision making. This includes procedures for the selection of foreign investment and the screening of foreign investment proposals, control of takeovers, establishment of sectors reserved for local firms or in which foreign participation is restricted, and incentive schemes designed to attract foreign investment interest, particularly in certain regions of the country or in certain sectors of the economy.

The second focus of national foreign investment legislation is ownership, management and employment: restrictions on foreign ownership involving either specific local participation requirements or a requirement for eventual divestment; requirements regarding local participation in management; and restrictions relating to employment creation and the use of expatriates. The third area is taxation and financial transactions. This includes the determination of taxable income (often in the form of bilateral double-taxation agreements) and the regulations of corporate financial transactions -- particularly the repatriation of capital and profits and debt financing by foreign enterprises.

The fourth area of regulation deals with the administration and supervision of national foreign investment legislation. The report suggests that in the developing countries such legislation is increasingly administered by interministerial investment boards or commissions, or by special agencies established for the purpose of coordinating all matters relating to foreign investment. This is one dimension of a tendency among the countries studied toward the coordination and integration of legislation relating to private investment in general -- and foreign direct investment in particular.

The United Nations report surveys the foreign investment laws and regulations of 37 developing countries. It states that, in nearly all of these countries, major investment proposals are thoroughly scrutinized either at the time the foreign enterprise is established or in connection with an application for incentive benefits. It notes, however, that criteria for screening investment or incentive applications, although numerous, are often not precise enough to serve as a fixed standard for evaluation. Although there is a tendency in developing countries to encourage local equity participation in foreign enterprises, the proportion of those countries studied that require majority local ownership is still small (6 out of 37). The movement toward increased local equity participation is nevertheless apparent.

In most countries, foreign direct investment in certain

sectors of the economy is prohibited or restricted. Such sectors
include defense-related production, nuclear power, public
utilities, inland transportation, telecommunications, radio,
television and the press. Commercial banking and insurance are
increasingly included among the closed sectors, and wholesale and
retail trade are often reserved for local entrepreneurs.

Investment incentives constitute an important part of most
developing nations' private investment policies. In a few cases,
regulation may be limited to foreign firms receiving incentive
benefits. Elsewhere, benefits may be designed to encourage local
equity participation by being limited to joint ventures or to
enterprises with a minority foreign participation. Investment laws
tend to deal with the financial aspects of investment in general
terms. When they are more specific, they frequently take the form
of a limitation on the proportion of profits that can be
repatriated. In most financial aspects of foreign investment and
in the determination of taxable income, host country regulations
are vague and general.

Arrangements for supervision and control after the
establishment of a foreign enterprise are frequently
unsatisfactory, the UN report concludes. Disclosure requirements
may vary among government departments, and coordination of
ministerial or departmental regulations is normally poor. Problems
also tend to arise in connection with registration or licensing,
the expansion of an enterprise or its merger with another company.
The settlement of disputes between host countries and foreign
enterprises constitutes one of the most sensitive areas of the
relationship. Virtually all Western hemisphere developing nations
(and some in Asia and North Africa) insist on local jurisdiction
for investment disputes, membership in the International Centre for
Settlement of Investment Disputes notwithstanding. Some regional
agreements (such as the Andean Common Market, ANCOM) also cover the
settlement of disputes.

The UN report suggests that while foreign investment
legislation is too complex to permit generalizations beyond these,
three general patterns of foreign direct investment regulation are
discernible. One general pattern prevails in most African and
certain Asian nations, as well as in the Central American Common
Market (CACM), and is characterized by relatively few regulations
and restrictions and a greater number of incentives. The pattern
found in the Asian Middle East and North Africa is similar, except
that most of these countries have established local participation
quotas. The South American pattern is characterized for the most
part by greater restriction and control. The three patterns are
summarized in Exhibit 1.

IV. THE BRAZILIAN MODEL

Our research suggests that there are good grounds for
believing that another pattern or model of MNC-host country

EXHIBIT 1:

Patterns of Foreign Direct Investment Regulation in Selected Developing Countries

Parameter	Pattern 1 (mostly Asia – excluding India – Africa, CACM)	Pattern 2 (mostly Middle East, North Africa)	Pattern 3 (mostly South America)
I. Administration	Case-by-case screening largely restricted to award of incentives (non-discriminatory).	Case-by-case screening at establishment (degree of discrimination varies).	Separate administration for foreign investment. Screening at establishment.
II. Investment screening criteria	Emphasis on functional contributions of investment. Little indication of extensive cost/benefit analysis. Screening largely for award of incentives.	Emphasis on functional contributions and conditions of investment. Little indication of extensive cost/benefit analysis.	Criteria formulated for cost/benefit analysis, often extensive. Includes social cost criteria in some cases.
III. Ownership	Few requirements. Few sectors closed to foreign investment.	Joint ventures prevalent.	Strict regulations on ownership and investment (exc. Brazil). A large number of closed sectors.
IV. Finance	Few repatriation limitations.	Few repatriation limitations.	Repatriation ceilings in most areas (exc. Mexico). Screening of foreign loans. Special control of payments to parent company.
V. Employment and training	Announced indigenization policies but little headway in practice.	Local quotas for work force. Few local quotas for management.	Specific across-the-board indigenization requirements.
VI. Technology transfer	No controls.	No controls.	Screening and registration of all technology imported.
VII. Investment incentives	Long-term tax incentives for establishment.	Establishment incentives limited to five years – in most cases non-renewable.	Incentives tied to specific contributions, but incentives may be curtailed for foreign-owned firms.

Source: U.N. Commission on Transnational Corporations, *National Legislation and Regulations Relating to Transnational Corporations.* (Report of the Secretariat) (NY: United Nations. 1976; E/C. 10/8–12.1.76), pp. 21–22.

relationship is now coming into existence, particularly in the most industrially advanced developing nations. We call this the Brazilian model, and suggest that, within limits, one can think of Brazil as constituting a model of the kinds of demands, bargaining posture, and regulations multinational corporations will encounter in other developing nations. The model cannot be generalized even to all of the NICs. Hong Kong and Singapore, for example, cannot gain the leverage Brazil has with its size and muscle in the world economy. Few developing nations can aspire to be in Brazil's class. Most will never weigh as heavily as Brazil in their dealings with multinationals.

Despite such obvious caveats, the concept of the Brazilian model is appealing. In its basic posture toward foreign investment, Brazil seems to fit what many observers would expect from nations as they develop economically and politically. The Brazilian case makes it perfectly clear that a developing nation can introduce a wide range of stringent policies and regulations without turning off the flow of foreign direct investment. Brazil seems also to represent a novel middle ground between laissez-faire capitalist and socialist assumptions about the need and value of foreign investment -- and what form such investment should take.

The Brazilian model is usefully considered along the following major dimensions:

Ideology

Preconceptions are less rigid about capitalism and socialism, or about the relative superiority of private or public ownership of the instruments of production. However, most leaders agree that the state constitutes a major factor in the economy -- as a source of investment capital, as entrepreneur and producer, as planner and regulator of industrial and agricultural enterprise.

Some degree of centralized planning is accepted. The need for coordinating the Brazilian public and private sectors, as well as the private foreign investment sector, is widely acknowledged. Also the need to bring into harmony developmental plans and policies of governmental units throughout the federal system is conceded.

Attitudes Toward FDI

Attitudes are favorable but no uncritical. The basic commitment is to encourage a continuous flow of foreign capital, to treat the foreign investor fairly, and to accept modes of resolving conflict typical of the industrial world. A growing commitment is that the kind and levels of FDI should be more consciously attuned to the developmental needs and priorities of the nation.

The multinationals are seen as major factors regarding a range of problems of great concern to Brazilian interest groups, political leaders, and policymakers. These include the balance of payments, servicing foreign debt, import substitution, exports, rationalization of national industry, and so on. Because of this, regulation and control of the multinational is considered a prime requisite of effective internal economic management.

Significant Actors

In the normal negotiations and day-to-day operations carried on by the multinationals in places like Brazil, the most significant host-country actors are found in the upper reaches of the military and civilian bureaucracies. Key figures in these sectors seem to be permanent; they generally manage to survive many changes of presidents, cabinets and governments. They also probably account for most of the policies directed toward the multinationals and their administration. Among the strategic elite categories of host countries, this one is the most important.

These actors in Brazil are tecnicos -- well-trained professionals who, by and large, know what they are doing. Their internal economic and political managerial capability is high. They approach multinationals with self-confidence. Their praise and criticism of the foreign direct investor, their demands and concessions are, more often than not, likely to be based on direct experience.

Significant actors are not limited to the military or civilian bureaucracies. As the political system is liberalized, they will appear increasingly at the head of labor unions, the mass media, and political parties. Within the universities and other intellectual circles, there are always those whose views about the foreign direct investor are more than marginally important. It must be taken for granted that actors from the these categories will often make the multinationals the objects of much of their criticism of society. On the whole -- and for a variety of reasons -- such criticisms are likely to remain circumscribed within bounds that will not seriously threaten the foreign investor.

Indigenous industrialists and entrepreneurs are also significant actors. They are neither merely potential "sleeping partners" for foreign companies nor necessarily natural allies of the multinational corporation. They are also potential competitors, often highly influential, who may try to keep some foreign investors out; and they are potential partners in joint ventures who will want to share management control. By and large, the impact of these groups is favorable both to the preservation of the private sector and to the encouragement of a continuing but regulated flow of FDI.

Bargaining Style

Because the stakes are high, Brazilians seek to drive hard bargains. As the world's tenth largest economy, Brazil will no doubt escalate the demands its makes not only on foreign investors, but also on international banks whose offshore lending practices are considered demeaning or offensive.

Brazilians are also pragmatic negotiators. This means that, despite what may appear as formal legislation or regulation, they prefer to deal with issues on a day-to-day, case-by-case basis. They prefer not to stand too rigidly on legalistic formulations. Their bargaining style is indirect, opaque, nuanced and polite.

Bargaining Strategies

The basic strategy is to keep the other side off balance, but to do so within a context that clearly implies a rational and pragmatic approach to negotiations. Beyond pragmatism, Brazilians are empiricists; they want to gather and analyze the relevant facts. They are likely to be as capable at arranging data to suit their own arguments and purposes as those they deal with.

They emphasize that their policies and their implementation will be coherent, predictable and efficient. In exchange for this, Brazilians will demand much greater efforts by foreign investors to integrate their business plans into Brazil's developmental schemes.

Managerial Capability

As the foregoing suggests, managerial capacity is high, and no doubt much higher than in many Third World countries. There is also extensive interaction and collaboration among elites in government and in the private economy. Brazil has undoubtedly been a leader in this development -- what some have called the "new corporatism." For this reason, the kind of authoritarian political system that exists there today must not be confused with the more historically typical form of military or authoritarian political systems. Brazil, many feel, is in this basic sense very much the wave of the future.

Political Stability

High-level managerial skills may reduce the probability of
explosive political developments but they will not entirely remove
it. This is especially so where economic development brings about
extreme levels of inequality, as it has in Brazil. Indeed, the
history of nations since World War II suggests that the more open
the political system, the greater the probability of economic
turmoil, political fragmentation, and political repression
(military or otherwise).

Levels of current inequality in Brazil, measured by class,
geography and race, are acknowledged to be excessive. If the real
wages of industrial workers in the cities have been steadily
decreasing for some years, their income, on average, is still four
times that of the agricultural peasant. If inflation has battered
purchasing power in Brazil's industrialized Southwest, rising
prices of food and other necessities have been devastating in the
countryside. If Brazil can boast the largest black population
outside Africa and many truly remarkable achievements in racial
integration, it cannot escape the fact that groups at or below the
poverty line are overwhelmingly black or Indian.

Brazil's political leaders acknowledge that better wage, price
and taxation policies would reduce existing extremes of inequality.
Some effort to develop such policies is under way. On the other
hand, the leadership wants to resist populism or falling into the
easy trap of thinking that the level of inflation can be reduced
without austerity,

Brazil's leaders believe the way to resolve current economic
problems is through continued economic growth. They say that if
they are to succeed in this mission, they will require a high
degree of understanding and cooperation from the international
banking community and from the multinational firms operating there.

Brazilians, in short, understand the implications of
integration into the world market and the interdependence this
implies. They wonder whether those who provide capital and direct
investment from the developed nations also understand these
implications. The dialogue they want to pursue, as well as the
policies they put in place, will certainly attract imitators
throughout the developing world.

V. CONCLUDING THOUGHTS

The fate of foreign-owned multinational enterprise is guided
or influenced for the most part by the attitudes and behavior of
the host country's strategic elites.[15] With variation from country
to country, these elites are the leaders of political parties and
trade unions, influential industrialists and educators, opinion
makers in the mass media, highly placed officials in the executive

and legislative branches of government and, above all, the civilian and military managers who occupy the commanding heights of public bureaucracies. Not riots or revolutions but the attitudes, policies and behavior of these elites toward the multinationals is what affects most of these companies in most countries most of the time.

Strategic elites in almost every developing nation tend to be ambivalent toward multinational corporations. This is true even of those who wish to encourage foreign direct investment, and who acknowledge that its continuing flow is a necessary condition for economic growth. Essentially all national leaders would prefer that a nation be able to move forward under its own power. When dependence on the outside world is focused on them by the nature of the international economy, it is unrealistic to expect that they will be unqualifiedly grateful.

The following patterns and tendencies summarize our findings with regard to elite attitudes toward multinationals in the developing world:

(1) The most generalized suspicions of the MNCs are likely to exist in countries at the lower levels of economic development, especially those that have only recently become independent. Here foreign capital has been traditionally associated with extractive industries and has dominated the cash economy. Their leaders will typically have had limited experience with the multinational firms, and it is predictable that the foreign investor will be viewed as essentially exploitative.

(2) Almost by definition, the least developed countries are also in greatest need of outside inputs of capital and managerial, organizational and technological know-how. Thus, suspicion is matched by felt need. The frustration this engenders will sometimes lead to aggressive policies and behavior toward the foreign investment community.

(3) Where developing countries possess significant capital resources of their own, it is natural to expect more demanding and stringent regulation of the foreign investor. Nigeria is a good example and Mexico, visibly flexing its new-found economic muscles, is another.

(4) It would be premature to suggest, however, that as Third World countries discover new resources, or reach higher levels of economic development, their attitudes toward the multinationals will become more hostile. An equally plausible hypothesis is that the development of the economy will lead to more integration of these nations into the world economy, to more economic and financial interdependence, and, therefore, to a mature and sophisticated approach to the foreign investor.

(5) Brazil provides strong evidence that the latter is the more probable tendency. The Brazilian case suggests that more sophisticated approaches to the multinationals should not be equated with a more liberal or permissive climate of regulation. Brazilians have a precise understanding of how the multinational firm works, and what place it should have in the economy. One result is that foreign investors in Brazil are spared not only sweeping negative judgements, but also the kinds of general laws that raise anxiety levels among those investors. Another result is

that the more knowledgeable and experienced Brazilian elites have produced a wide array of specific regulations designed to cope with the multinational-related problems they have pinpointed for attention.

(6) Far from causing high anxiety or panic among investors, policies and regulations of this kind might be welcomed. They suggest not only that governmental elites know what they are doing, but also that, within limits, they perceive foreign investment problems as predictable and manageable. Moreover, insofar as regulations result in unanticipated consequences for either side, they are open to further discussion and negotiation -- although administrative elites in all of the countries studied claim to be more rational and pragmatic than they believe they are judged to be by multinational corporate managers.

(7) Although host-country knowledge of industrial enterprise varies by sector and country, it is apparent that the knowledge gap is narrowing almost everywhere. Horror stories about bureaucratic corruption of inefficiencies should not be too readily generalized for all of the Third World, or reported as if they do not find counterparts in the West. It is generally a mistake to assume that one's business is so complex that no one in the host country can understand it.

(8) Elites in these nations are not of one mind regarding the role of the public sector in the ownership and management of enterprise. Many are committed to maintaining a dual economy in which the market and the private sector remain fundamental. Even in those cases where leaders advocate direct public ownership in certain sectors, there is usually recognition that private property, free markets, and profitability are necessary to attract foreign direct investment. Nevertheless, these same leaders do not anticipate that state-ownership trends will be reversed; and they believe that central planning of economic development is not only desirable but essential.

(9) Bureaucratic elites in particular defend the entrepreneurial role of the public sector. Those who manage state-owned enterprises will not passively accept efforts to return these firms to the private sector. In tomorrow's world, they will find allies at many points in the political and interest-group spectrum. The multinational firm must, therefore, be prepared to deal with the public managers not only in their traditional regulatory roles, but also as potential competitors, joint-venture partners, and so on.

(10) Nationalism should not be confused with xenophobia. It means nothing more than greater self-consciousness on the part of elites of host countries that they can -- and should -- secure the greatest benefits for their countries that bargaining circumstances will allow.

It is doubtful that in dealing with governmental officials abroad multinational firms will be able to overpower them with the underlying logic -- the so-called imperatives -- of industrial enterprise conducted on a global scale. These and other local leaders will resist accepting truncated subsidiaries; they will insist on full-scale production, on production for export, on a wide range of conditions that restrict the freedom of the corporate center to optimize its worldwide operations.

(11) When elites think about the benefits multinationals bring, the transfer of technology tops almost everyone's list. There is no way around this issue with host-country leaders who are increasingly able to tell whether the "black box" has anything of value in it. The problem of discussing technological value added becomes exceedingly complicated where host-country pressures are high and where, as in Brazil, local joint-venture partners intend to share in the management and control of the firm. More than ever in the past, negotiations will center on this issue and, therefore, may well require modified corporate negotiating strategies and skills.

NOTES

[1] Address by Henry R. Kissinger on "Global Consensus and Economic Development"; delivered by Daniel P. Moynihan, US Representative to the United Nations, Seventh Special Session of the UN General Assembly, September 1, 1975; Ronald Muller, "The Multinational Corporation and the Exercise of Power: Latin America," in Abdul A. Said and Luiz R. Simmons, Eds., The New Sovereigns: Multinational Corporations as World Power, Englewood Cliffs, N. J., 1974, p. 55.

[2] United Nations, Multinational Corporations in World Development, St/ECA/190, 1973, p. 147.

[3] See United Nations, Transnational Corporations in World Development: A Re-Examination, E/C. 10/38, March 20, 1978, p. 40.

[4] Lawrence G. Franko, The European Multinationals: A Renewed Challenge to American and British Big Business, Stamford, Conn., 1976, p. 108.

[5] See articles by Louis Wells and Carlos F. Diaz-Alejandro in Agmon and Kindleberger, eds., Multinationals from Small Countries, Cambridge, Mass., 1977.

[6] Peter F. Drucker, "Multinationals and Developing Countries: Myths and Realities", Foreign Affairs, October 1974, pp. 121-122.

[7] Charles P. Kindleberger, "The Multinational Corporation in a World of Militant Developing Countries," in George W. Ball, ed., Global Companies: The Political Economy of World Business, Englewood Cliffs, N. J., 1975, p. 71.

[8]UN, <u>Transnational Corporations in World Development, op. cit.</u>, p. 254.

[9]Those considered to be NICs include Brazil, Hong Kong, Mexico, Singapore, South Korea and Taiwan; Argentina and India are also often included in this group.

[10]Helmut Fuhrer, "The Industrialisation of the Third World", <u>OCED Observer</u>, January 1980, p. 24.

[11]Fuhrer, <u>op. cit.</u>, and Colin I. Bradford, Jr., "The Newly Industrialising Countries in Global perspective", unpublished paper, June 1980.

[12]Bradford, <u>op. cit</u>., p. 28.

[13]Louis Turner <u>et al.</u>, "Living with the Newly Industrialising Countries", The Royal Institute of International Affairs, London, 1980, pp. 3-5.

[14]United Nations Centre on Transnational Corporations, <u>National Legislation and Regulations Relating to Transnational Corporations</u>, New York, 1978.

[15]For a brief overview, see Joseph LaPalombara and Stephen Blank, <u>Multinational Corporations and National Elites: A Study in Tenisons,</u> New York: The Conference Board, 1976, Appendix.

Multinational Corporations, Economic Policy and National Development in the World System

VOLKER BORNSCHIER

I. INTRODUCTION

The empirical findings reported in this article are derived from the research project on Multinational Corporations, Economic Policy and National Development[1] at the University of Zurich. Only marginally will comparisons be made with other findings, for a more systematic review of the literature see [8,9].*

Furthermore, for reasons of space, it is not possible to comment on the theoretical propositions underlying the research. The theoretical framework which organizes the various propositions is conceived as world system analysis which I like to call a °social science world conception'. One must note that this theoretical framework has not yet achieved the status of a theory in the strict sense. Many theoretical statements are scattered through the references, but for a more systematic presentation the reader may be referred to certain books [13, 14, 16].

Further, a note of caution. The findings are often presented in causal language, though they are based on correlation (also if multiple regression with time lags or path analysis is used). While causality can never be observed empirically the modern techniques of social science can, if properly used, avoid false causal influences. Though many appropriate tests have been performed to achieve this, not all the theoretically and logically possible controls were exhausted. Thus, the causal language relates to the underlying theoretical propositions which must not be changed unless solid contradictory empirical evidence is found.

The main findings can be arranged around three major questions. First, what is the effect of Multinational Corporation (MNC) presence on (a) economic growth, and (b) social inequality in

From **INTERNATIONAL SOCIAL SCIENCE JOURNAL**, Vol XXXII, No. 1, 1980, (158-172), reprinted by permission of the publisher.

host countries? Second, how can such effects be explained
empirically? Third, how do host countries distribute according to
(a) various types of economic policy; (b) which determinants have
such economic policies; and (c) what are the consequences of
different economic policies?

II. THE EFFECTS OF MNC PRESENCE

Economic Growth

One must distinguish between the short- and long-term consequences
for economic growth of the presence of MNC's. This is taken into
account through two measures of MNC presence, MNC-investment[2] (for
the short-term effect) and MNC-penetration[3] (for the long-term
effect). On the basis of cross-national comparisons over the
period 1960-75 with samples of up to ninety-one countries[4] the
following results have been suggested by multiple regression, path
analysis and analysis of covariance:
MNC-investment has the short-term effect of increasing the economic
      growth rate [2, 3, 5, 8, 9, 10, 11]. The same holds true for
      the growth rate of the stock of capital controlled by MNCs
      [6].
The higher the cumulated investment of MNCs in relation to the
      total stock of capital and population, that is to say the
      greater MNC penetration, as a structural feature of the host
      countries, the lower the subsequent growth rate of per capita
      income as well as total income [2, 3, 5, 6, 8, 9, 10, 11, 15,
      17]. MNC penetration thus has long-term negative consequences
      (a period of up to twenty years has been considered) and fresh
      investment by MNCs has short-term positive consequences
      (during the period in which it occurs). Although MNC
      investment has been found to make short-term positive
      contributions to growth, one must note that such investment
      increases MNC penetration and therefore contributes in the
      long run to the negative effect associated therewith.[5]
MNC activity resulting in technological dependence for host
      countries (as measured by foreign control over patents) also
      has clearly negative long-term effects on economic growth [10,
      11].
Various dependencies created or maintained mainly by MNCs in the
world economy, with regard to technology, trade, capital and
organizational networks, are generally positively correlated, and
their negative consequences for economic growth in the longer run,
are similar [7, 10, 11]. With regard to the relationships between
different forms of economic dependence further research is
necessary, since the operationalization of trade dependency and
technological dependence in the literature, if applied to explain
growth and inequality within countries, suffers from theoretical

short-comings.[6]

The headquarter status represents the importance of an MNC's business abroad for the home country. Headquarter status and MNC penetration have no symmetrical effects on economic growth, of the kind: advantage for the headquarter country spells disadvantage for the penetrated country. But they are both related to a lower economic growth rate [6].

A logically possible alternative explanation of the finding that MNC penetration is inversely related to long-term economic growth could be that °there is a tendency for countries with poor growth prospects to devote greater efforts to building up a stock of foreign investment in intended compensation' [17, p. 18]. This hypothesis, however, can be ruled out empirically since it implies a positive correlation between poor growth performance and MNC investment. This is clearly not substantiated by the findings: MNC investment is high where income growth is also high. This, as well as the fact that the relationship holds after controlling for several factors that might be of relevance to economic growth, i.e. level of income at the beginning of the growth period, income distribution, capital formation, investment growth, population growth, level and growth of urbanization, and relative weight in the world market position with regard to natural resources, suggest support for the causal interpretation of the finding that penetration by MNC's retards long-term economic growth.

The lowering of the economic growth rate through high MNC penetration is more pronounced for less developed countries (LDCs) than for a world sample of countries. For the rich countries analysed separately no significant relationship exists [5, 6, 9].

It was investigated whether variations in the sectoral locations of MNC capital have a different impact on the aggregate growth of income per capita [6, 9]. Four of the ten sectors in which MNC penetration was studied for eighty-eight LDCs account for slightly more than three-quarters of the total penetration, these being: manufacturing, agro-business, mining and smelting, and the integrated petroleum business. MNC penetration in manufacturing has a clearly significant negative impact on subsequent growth of aggregate income per capita. The same holds for MNC penetration in mining and smelting. Both effects are of about equal strength. The effect of MNC penetration in the agro-business is smaller and statistically insignificant, whereas there is no effect at all for integrated petroleum. One can add that the measures of MNC penetration in these four major sectors are statistically rather independent when all LDCs are studied.

The short-term growth-promoting effect of MNC investment is of similar strength in various subsamples of LDCs. The same is true for the long-term growth-retarding effect of MNC penetration. Earlier results have suggested stronger negative effects for wealthier LDCs [8]. More detailed research has shown, however, that this was a spurious finding. It could be demonstrated that the negative effect is of about equal importance for all subsamples of LDCs, except for those with an extremely circumscribed monetized market segment [9]. For this comparatively small group of very small countries, which are amongst the poorest in the world, no statistically significant relationship exists; the association, however, is positive [9]. Including a larger number of such very small countries in the analysis of subsamples explains smaller negative effects [5, 6, 8]. Furthermore, detailed analyses have revealed that the effects on growth hold independently of the geographical location of LDCs [8, 9].

That the growth-reducing consequence of MNC penetration has to date aroused rather mild scholarly and public concern is especially due to two factors. First, so long as overall MNC investment remains high, the negative effect of penetration is partly neutralized. Second, the most important negative effect concerns those countries for which growth potential is above average. Thus, the slowing down of economic growth in the long run, in general does not imply economic stagnation, but a markedly lower growth rate than one would expect against the background of the growth potential. This important finding is illustrated in Figure 1 by use of a regression model with a curvilinear function of the level of economic development [5].

The solid line in Figure 1 is the prediction of the income per capita growth rate 1965-75 with the multiple regression on the logged initial income per capita 1965, for average MNC penetration and average MNC investment. The broken line refers to high MNC penetration (one standard deviation above the mean) and average MNC investment, while the dotted line refers to low MNC penetration (one standard deviation below the mean) and average MNC investment. The variation of MNC penetration graphically presented does not exhaust the empirical one. For example in the case of larger LDCs, one-fifth of countries score higher on MNC penetration than one standard deviation above the mean, and one-tenth of countries are below one standard deviation below the mean.

The regression results are graphically presented for three subsamples. The MNC penetration effect differs among the subsamples. For small LDCs (according to the size of the modernized sector of the economy) which are centered more on low levels of income, the effect is smaller (-0.7 per cent for one standard deviation) than for larger LDCs (-1.35 per cent for one standard deviation). Both effects are statistically significant (the same applies to the opposite effect of MNC investment: +0.7 and +0.9 per cent for one standard deviation). For rich countries the MNC penetration effect is small and insignificant. (One can add that the correlation between MNC penetration and MNC investment differs across subsamples. It is 0.5 for the small LDCs, 0.18 for the larger LDCs and 0.62 for rich countries.)

The empirical findings with regard to the growth effects of MNCs based on samples of up to 103 countries have been checked carefully and compared with the results of all available cross-national studies [8, 9]. However, the relationship of MNC capital penetration with other forms of economic dependence whether or not they are mainly the result of the actual behaviour of MNCs as institutions, needs further research. It is recommended to construct an indicator for MNC penetration which is not only based on one aspect (namely capital) but on all aspects of dependence resulting from the MNCs as institutions.

One may conclude that the results reported here seem to attain the status of social facts in the world system after the Second

TABLE 1. Types of policy directed against MNCs

	General interventions	Transfer restrictions	Incentives
Advantageous for MNCs ↑			
Promoting liberalism	Low	Low	High
Laissez-faire liberalism	Low	Low	Low
Stop-and-go liberalism	Low	High	High
Restrictive liberalism	Low	High	Low
Promoting interventionism	High	Low	High
Non-specific interventionism	High	Low	Low
Stop-and-go interventionism	High	High	High
Restrictive interventionism	High	High	Low
Disadvantageous for MNCs			

World War. We suggest, therefore, that any empirically relevant
theory of development, whatever its perspective, must be able to
explain these findings.

Social inequality

The analysis also revealed relationships between the level of MNC
penetration and indicators of social inequality. Personal income
inequality has been used as the most important indicator.
    The level of MNC penetration as a structural feature of host
countries was associated in the 1960s with a more unequal
distribution of income among households or income recipients [1, 4,
6, 7, 8, 9]. This relationship holds for a world sample and is
stronger for LDCs. By contract MNC penetration is accompanied by
less income inequality in rich countries [6, 13]. The headquarter
status of countries is related to greater equality in income
distribution which, however, is not significant once the level
of income per capita is taken into account [7].
    Inequality among economic sectors with regard to labour
productivity (sectoral income inequality), associated with
corresponding differences in capital intensity, is more pronounced
if MNC penetration is high [5, 15]. This holds only for LDCs.
    The established relationship between MNC penetration and
personal income inequality is fairly consolidated, rests on large
samples (up to seventy-two cases) and is consistent with other
findings in the literature using different indicators for MNC
penetration [8, 9].
    Since time series for income distribution measures are
lacking, the causality remains open. The possibilities for testing
the theoretically assumed two-way causation between MNCs and
inequality in LDCs are limited. In general, what has been tested
is whether and through which variables MNC penetration affects
income distribution [1, 4, 7]. Existing income inequality in LDCs
is, however, one theoretical prerequisite for opportunities for
MNCs oriented towards domestic LDC markets. Preliminary findings
suggest that both directions of influence seem to be empirically
relevant [6].

III. EMPIRICAL EXPLANATIONS OF THE EFFECTS OF MNC PRESENCE

Economic growth

Important findings with regard to variables linking MNC penetration
and economic growth are presented here, which together can explain

a large part of the observed negative effect.

Since MNC penetration goes together with higher income inequality, and since the latter is significantly related to lower capital formation and lower economic growth in larger LDCs (where the domestic market is of importance), part of the negative effect of MNCs on economic growth can be explained through personal income inequality [6, 13]. This finding also helps to explain why the negative effect is present only for LDCs, since MNC penetration is associated with more income inequality only in LDCs.

The decapitalization thesis maintains that host countries lose more capital in the long run through outflows due to MNC activities than has ever flowed into the country through investment inflows of MNCs. Thus, it is argued that the funds available for investment in the host country are, on balance, reduced. Empirical findings suggest cross-national support for this thesis. MNC penetration determining subsequent MNC investment is significantly related to lower investment growth in the host country. Since investment growth is an important determinant of income growth, the lowering of subsequent investment growth due to high MNC penetration helps to explain another component of the negative effect on income growth [5]. Again, one can add that the effect is not significant for rich countries.

Empirical results suggest that MNC penetration is frequently associated with a substitution of labour by machines to an extent not dictated, in cross-national comparison, by labour supply shortages [7]. Thus the presumed intensification of structural unemployment, to which MNCs add, may also have negative implications for economic growth.

Unequal labour productivity and capital intensities both between and within economic sectors (as indicated by sectoral income inequality) are accentuated if MNC penetration is high [5, 15]. Such disparities imply a low level of integration and linkage effects, and thus are likely to contribute to a lower level of overall productivity, so that a given capital input results in comparatively lower economic growth. This may also explain part of the negative effect on growth in LDCs because only there does MNC penetration accompany and presumably intensify the disparities.

Findings further suggest that MNC penetration is compatible with a host country's orientation towards a more pronounced °elite' model of education, rather than orientation towards vocational training. Since an educational orientation towards the expansion of vocational training is favourable to fast economic growth (especially in LDCs) one can hypothesize that MNCs also exert an influence by lowering the possible positive contribution of special types of education for economic growth. These conclusions are posed in the yet unpublished work of Thanh-Huyen Ballmer-Cao.

Technological dependence due to control of MNCs over patents can explain a further part of the consequences of MNC penetration on economic growth [11]. MNC control over patents can be regarded, in addition, as part of a comprehensive pattern of restrictive business practice and monopolistic behaviour which is reported to be frequent, especially in LDCs, and which contribute to a non-competitive and therefore less efficient industrial structure.

The negative effect of MNC penetration may also find an explanation in that it is associated with a particular foreign trade structure (partner concentration, commodity concentration, low position within the vertical structure of foreign trade) which is unfavourable for economic growth [10].

Lastly, MNC penetration is associated with a higher level of internal social conflict and lower executive stability [1]. This contributes to lowering the possible economic growth rate. It is also likely to affect negatively the ability of the state to pursue a policy of growth, independently of the class interests created by foreign capital.

Personal income inequality

The empirical explanation of the influence of MNC penetration on personal income inequality investigated the extent to which the links to the world economy through the MNCs affect the power distribution within host countries. Apart from the land-tenure structure in agriculture, the power distribution within the aggregate organizational system outside agriculture (occupational structure variables), the power distribution in the labour market and the steering power of the state have been considered. It must be noted that the results are not based on time series; the causal ordering is therefore preliminary and has to be substantiated by further tests with time series.

Since, on the one hand, concentration of land tenure in agriculture is related to rural and total income distribution, and since, on the other hand, MNC penetration is accompanied by higher land concentration, part of the relationship between MNCs and personal income inequality thus finds an explanation [4, 7].

Empirical evidence further suggests that, in accordance with hypotheses relating to the organizational structure and division of labour of MNCs on a world scale, MNC penetration affects the organizational structure variables of society at large. It lowers the degree of power-sharing with expertise in society and reduces in the aggregate the shift of the labour force towards bureaucratic jobs [4, 7]. At the same time, the superimposed organizational stratification of MNCs contributes to an intensification of the hierarchy of authority. Thus, MNCs contribute to a disparate development of organizational parameters, resulting in a more unequal distribution of organizational power and hence of personal incomes.

This also contributes to disparities among (and within) economic sectors, as reflected in wider sectoral income inequality [5, 15]. Since this represents a major source of personal income inequalities, the impact of MNCs on income inequality in LDCs is further corroborated.

Concerning hypotheses relating to the steering power of the state (for example, impact via secondary income distribution), what has been analysed is the extent to which MNC penetration affects government revenue and the pattern of public expenditures relevant to income distribution. Governments' share in total income has not been found to be significantly affected through MNC penetration; the association is mildly negative [7]. Empirical support is, however, suggested for the hypothesis that MNCs do have an impact on income distribution by their connection with internal conflict and executive instability [1], and their relations to specific dominant political power constellations, which seem to be created or supported by high MNC penetration. According to the available evidence such political power constellations seem not only to oppose income redistribution to the poor, but favour an even more unequal distribution of income [7]. This is seen as due to policies and priorities in public expenditure that favour the dominant power constellation, including MNCs, but is restricted to situations of general resource scarcity or to those of LDCs [7]. Since it is only in LDCs that the statistical interaction between high MNC penetration and the government share of total income results in higher income inequality--whereas in general, a higher government share is associated with lower inequality--this finding contributes to an explanation why MNCs ceteris paribus, exacerbate income inequality only in LDCs.

IV. POLICIES AND THEIR EFFECTS

Types of economic policy

The major theoretical components of a content analysis to establish data for economic policies were, first, an intervention dimension (with the two poles: liberalism--interventionism) as a representation of the quantitative extent of state intervention in the economy and in the sphere of corporate property, and, secondly, a restriction dimension (with the two poles: promotion--restriction) which examines the qualitative aspect of the extent to which policies are directed against MNCs or are favourable to them [2, 3].

The most important economic policy variables (i.e. general intervention and nationalization, capital transfer and import restrictions, and investment incentives) have been used to construct typologies of economic policy [2, 3]. The most differentiated typology consists of eight types which have been analysed separately as well as in combination, in the form of a rank-scaled variable expressing an intensification of policy directed against MNCs which implies increasing restriction and an unfavourable milieu for them (see Table 1).

An analysis of the distribution of seventy-three countries among the different types of economic policy leads to the following findings for the period between 1960 and 1975 [2, 3].

All eight types of policy towards MNCs are empirically

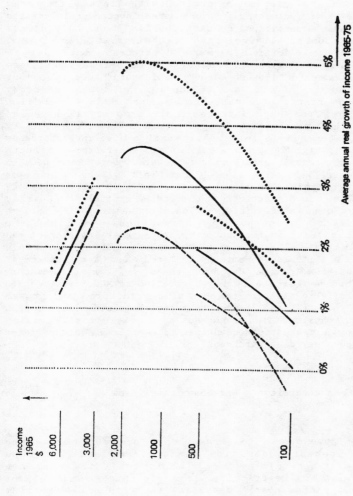

Fig. 1. Income per capita growth regressed on level of income per capita, MNC penetration and MNC investment [5]. Results for subsamples: 15 rich countries, 34 larger LDCs and 41 small LDCs (according to the size of the modernized sector of the economy). Curves for the actual range within subsamples.

relevant for the period considered. In the earlier years, however, basically liberal economic policies prevailed, while more recently interventionist policies have become prevalent.

In the period up to 1975 a clear polarization has developed: one large group of countries concentrates on °promoting liberalism' and another larger groups on °stop-and-go interventionism'. The reason for the shifts over time is that both disadvantageously liberal and interventionist countries (with imposed transfer restrictions) have increasingly incorporated investment incentives for MNCs in their economic policy package. In 1960, only 38 per cent of the countries ranked high on the variable investment incentives, but by 1975 this figure was 89 per cent.

°Stop-and-go interventionism' has become markedly more frequent over time. In 1960 no country represented this type, but by 1975 30 out of 73 did so. It consists of a contradictory combination of restrictive measures against MNCs (including interventions with regard to corporate property rights) and promotion in the form of incentives for fresh investment by MNCs.

Rising °stop-and-go interventionism' can be interpreted as follows. Due to high MNC penetration, negative structural effects appear and the economic growth rate is lowered; both contribute to increasing social and political problems. This is seen as a major source of restrictive legislation against MNCs in many countries, especially LDCs. Such restrictions on foreign capital, especially in the context of a general interventionist economic policy, affect the propensity to invest negatively and thus are likely to contribute, at least in the short run, to further lowering of the economic growth rate. This makes the economic and social crisis more acute. A shift in economic policy, represented by investment incentives for MNCs, can be considered to be an attempt to maintain the short-term positive growth contribution of MNC investment in order temporarily to mitigate the negative structural and growth effect of MNC penetration. Since the positive growth effect of MNC investment is transitory MNC investment adds to their penetration and hence to increased subsequent negative effects, such policies can only be considered as patch-ups.

Determinants and concomitants of economic policies [2, 3]

The level of development (as measured by per capita income) occupies a prominent position among the determinants and concomitants of economic policy. The lower it is, the more interventionist and restrictive vis-a-vis foreign capital the economic policy of a host country is likely to be. A similar finding applies, with increasing importance over time, to another aspect of development, namely the level of secondary school enrolment: the higher it is the lower the degree of intervention and restriction imposed on MNCs by economic policy.

Among the concomitants or framework variables for economic policy, which are rather independent of the level of development,

one can point to the voting behaviour within international
organizations (east-west and north-south cleavages) and the degree
of integration into international organizations. The relationship
of such variables with economic policy suggest that--although they
are structurally rooted within host countries--their implementation
may be supported by increased political participation and
synchronization within the system of international organizations.
This might explain why international organizations have become
increasingly important, especially for LDCs.

The higher the level of MNC penetration, the less
interventionist and restrictive is economic policy generally. This
linkage, which would normally be expected is, however, weakened
over the course of time. Increasingly, countries are able to adopt
an unfavourable policy towards MNCs, despite high MNC penetration.
Contrary to this negative, though considerably weakened,
relationship with MNC penetration as measured on the basis of
capital invested, the association between patent penetration and
restrictive policy is somewhat positive. Although one can assume
that restrictive policies towards MNCs are frequently accompanied
by regulations concerning the use and abuse of patents
(monopolistic practices), the positive correlation would suggest
that such regulations have remained generally ineffective because
of absent or insufficient control. This permits MNCs to react
with alternative strategies towards a changing political climate in
the world: they can penetrate countries either on the basis of
capital and organization and/or by technology, i.e., by control
over patents.

Consequences of economic policy [2, 3]

The long-term consequences of economic policy cannot be adequately
analysed since there has been an intensification of measures aimed
against MNCs only in the second half of the 1960-75 period. The
following findings refer, therefore, only to the period studied and
the lags are in general no longer than five years. Moreover, we
wish to point out that no analyses employing statistical
interaction have been performed so far concerning economic policy,
investigating, for example, the impact of MNC penetration on
structure and growth under different conditions. This can easily
be done in the future by analysis of covariance. Furthermore, the
relationship between economic policy and income distribution has
not yet been studied because the observations for the latter
variable scatter over a rather wide range of years.

The policy variable that has been built as a scale of types of
policy ranked by intensification of measures to counter the MNCs
acts negatively on investment stocks and flows of MNCs. The
association with flows is, as one would expect, more significant,
but the impact on stocks is clearly accentuated with longer lags.
The individual policy types also act in the expected directions.

Although one can observe that high MNC penetration has to some extent inhibited policies against the MNCs, especially in the earlier half of the period under study, one must observe that such policies MNCs, once implemented, can in fact lessen dependence on foreign capital provided by MNCs. This would reduce the future negative impact of MNCs on structure and growth. However, one cannot conclude that these restrictive policies have themselves had an immediate positive impact on economic growth. Quite the opposite is suggested by the findings.

The more interventionist and restrictive the economic policy, against MNCs, the lower the subsequent economic growth. This has been controlled for the level of MNC penetration and cannot be explained by relation to prior growth, since the relation between this and subsequent policy formulation is not significant. The same effect as for the scaled policy variable holds also for the degree of general interventions in the economy, whereas investment incentives (due to their positive effect on MNC-investment) have positive growth consequences.

The negative impact of interventionist and restrictive policies for economic growth can largely be explained by the fact that the propensity to invest is reduced.

Since capital formation, in general, has a strong positive influence on average economic growth, while foreign investment has a negative impact in the long run, it can be suggested that an economic policy for growth should restrict foreign capital formation and compensate, or even over-compensate, by promoting indigenous capital formation. The available empirical evidence suggests that restrictive policy against MNCs has not succeeded in doing this, at least not in general and in the short run.

It remains, therefore, an open question to what extent policy measures unfavourable for MNCs increasingly implemented recently have resulted in or initiated a real reconstruction of underdeveloped economies, towards greater satisfaction of basic needs, including a wide redistribution of income and a reduction of economic and regional disparities, and actually led to more self-sustaining development. Such a reconstruction would be decisive in order for an approach countering forces in the world economy to result in a more even and equitable growth in the long run, despite the short-term intensification of the social and economic crisis suggested by the results.

Yet our available findings point to severe difficulties for such reconstruction. That interventionist and restrictive policies have a negative impact on subsequent growth, at least in the short run, is likely to imply limited popularity for such policies and the regimes that implement them; this strengthens the hands of those supporting the status quo. This can be seen as a stabilization mechanism built into dependence on the world economy. It frequently seems to leave no choice other than a patch-up policy. The contradictory combination of restrictions upon and incentives for the MNCs which has suddenly arisen in recent time is a case in point; it might be interpreted as one of the results of the stabilization mechanism of the status quo. Therefore, it would be rather misleading to consider the increase in investment incentives for MNCs as a host-country policy basically in favour of MNCs, as apologists have frequently asserted in recent discussions.

V. CONCLUDING REMARKS

Investment by MNCs in LDCs could contribute to faster economic growth if it did not add to, or actually produce structural imbalances in the longer run, so that the short-term growth contributions are compensated and reversed. The experience of the last two decades leaves but little hope that there are self-sustaining mechanisms mitigating or even overcoming these structural imbalances of dependent industrialization over time. The economic policy of states seems not to have counteracted them, either, whether owing to a lack of options or will remains open.

The empirical findings do not lend support to the frequently advanced position that high income inequality in the course of development is a necessary sacrifice for faster economic growth. Such sacrifice would make sense only if the lower social strata could also derive advantages in absolute terms, though they would have to content themselves with a smaller relative share. MNCs accompany higher income inequality and do not make for greater, but for less economic growth over the long run. And income inequality, quite apart from MNC presence, results in slower economic growth for the majority of LDCs. Therefore, a strategy of industrialization relying heavily on inequality and MNCs is not one designed to satisfy the needs of the majority of the population in LDCs, not even in regard to faster absolute gains.

The growing dependency on MNC investment, as well as on foreign credits, which numerous less developed states suffer in order to mitigate in the short run the long-term structural defects that have appeared, as a result of dependent industrialization is likely to prove a major structural hindrance for a development policy directed towards the needs of the masses. This constellation is especially likely to frustrate the redistribution of income in LDCs, because it would weaken the short-term opportunities of MNCs in the domestic market.

In a broader perspective one may conclude that a fundamental contradiction is obviously built into the functioning of the world economy, which threatens the working of the system in the long run. Whereas, in the short run, the maximization of the goals of private enterprises requires a large part of the produced surplus to be withheld from immediate consumption by the majority of the population, an effective mass demand is the precondition for balanced and continuous economic growth. This can only be achieved by redistributing a significant part of the surplus to those from whom it is withheld by the normal functioning of the economic system. Since such indispensable redistributions in LDCs do not occur to any appreciable extent, and since, at the world level, there are no independent redistributing agents, the contradiction is assuming dimensions that threaten world society.

NOTES

[1]Directed by Volker Bornschier and Peter Heintz at the Sociological Institute of the University of Zurich. The collaborators were Thanh-Huyen Ballmer-Cao, Gottfried Berweger, Jean-Pierre Hoby, Alexandros Kyrtsis, Peter Meyer-Fehr and Jurg Scheidegger. Laurence R. Alschuler is working on six single case studies of countries in the framework of the project. The funding from the Deutsche Gesellschaft fur Friedens- und Konfliktforschung (DGFK), Bonn-Bad Godesberg, is gratefully acknowledged.

[2]This is a flow concept. The indicator is: change in the total stock of foreign direct investment over a period in relation to total domestic product. Beside the change in stocks, another indicator has been used, namely foreign direct investment inflows. The results are similar [5].

[3]This is a stock concept. It theoretically represents the degree to which MNCs control the economy of a host cuontry. The indicator is: total stock of foreign direct investment in relation to total capital stock and total population. Partial penetration indicators have been used for different sectorial location of MNC capital, too [6]. The results have been checked with an alternative indicator based on completely independent data, namely the number of subsidiaries of the largest 400 industrial MNCs weighted by their average size (capital invested) in the given host country. The results are similar [1,5].

[4]A more recent version of the review of findings in the literature considers 103 countries in a reanalysis from 1965 to 1977 [9].

[5]The indicators used to date are not weighted according to the size of the country. It is rather problematic to relate, for example, a trade structure indicator to economic growth without considering whether foreign trade as a percentage of total product is, let us say, 10 or 50. The same problem does not apply to MNC-penetration indicators.

[6]All results relating to economic policy are based on a world sample of seventy-three countries. No subsample analysis has yet been undertaken.

REFERENCES

1. Ballmer-Cao, Thanh-Huyen. Systeme politique, repartition des revenus et penetration des entreprises multinationales. Annuaire Suisse de Science Politique, 1979.

2.   B e r w e g e r ,   G o t t f i e d ;   H o b y ,   J e a n - P i e r r e .
      Wirtschaftspolitik gegenuber Auslandskapital. Bulletin
      of the Sociological Institute of the University of
      Zurich, No. 35, December 1978, p. 1-136.

-- Nationale Wirtschaftspolitik und multinationale Konzerne.
      In: V. Bornschier (ed.), Multinational Konzerne,
      Wirtschaftpoliti-- un nationale Entwicklung im
      Weltsystem (in preparation).

4. B o r n s c h i e r, Volker.   Einkommensungleichheit innerhalb
      von Landern in komparativer Sicht. Schweizerische
      Zeitschrift fur Soziologie, No. 4, March 1978, p. 3-45.

5. Bornschier, Volker, Multinational Corporations and
      Economic Growth: A Cross-National Test of the
      Decapitalization Thesis. Journal of Development
      Economics (in preparation).

6.   B o r n s c h i e r e ,   V o l k e r ;   B a l l m e r - C a o ,   T h a n g - H u y e n .
      Multinational Corporations in the World Economy and
      National Development. An Empirical Study of Income per
      capita Growth 1960-75. Bulletin of the Sociological
      Institute of the University of Zurich, No. 32, January
      1978, p. 1-169.

7. Bornschier, Volker; Ballmer-Cao, Thanh-Huyen, Income
      Inequality. A Cross-National Study of the Relationships
      between MNC-penetration, Dimensions of the Power
      Structure and Income Distribution. American
      Sociological Review, No. 44, June 1979, p. 487-506.

8. Bornschier, Volker; Chase-Dunn, Christopher; Rubinson,
      Richard. Corss-National Evidence on the Effects of
      Foreign Investment and Aid on Economic Growth and
      Inequality: A survey of Findings and a Reanalysis.
      American Journal of Sociology, No. 84, November 1978, p.
      651-83.

9. Bornschier, Volker; Chase-Dunn, Christopher; Rubinson,
      Richard. Auslandskapital, Wirtschaftswachstum und
      Ungleichheit: Ueberblick uber die Evidenzen und
      Reanalyse. In: V. Bornschier (ed.), Multinational
      Konzerne, Wirtschaftpolitik und nationale Entwicklung im
      Weltsystem (in preparation).

10.   Meyer-Fehr, Peter. Bestimmungsfaktoren des
      Wirtschaftswachstums von Nationen. Komparative
      empirische Analyse unter Berucksichtigung
      Miltinationaler Konzerne. Bulletin of the Sociological
      Institute of the University of Zurich, No. 34, December
      1978, p. 1-105.

11.   Meyer-Fehr, Peter. Technologieabhangigkeit und

Wirtschaftswachstum. Schweizerische Zeitschrift fur Soziologie, No. 5, March 1979, p. 79-96.

12. Bornschier, Volker; Heintz, Peter (eds.). Compendium of Data for World System Analyses. A Sourcebook of Data Based on the Study of Multinational Corporations, Economic Policy and National Development. Reworked and extended by Thanh-Huyen Ballmer-Cao and Jurg Scheidegger. Bulletin of the Sociological Institute of the University of Zurich, March 1979. (Special issue.)

13. Bornschier, Volker (with contributions by Ballmer-Cao, Berweger, Chase-Dunn, Hoby, Meyer-Fehr and Rubinson). Multinational Konzerne, Wirtschaftspolitik und national-Entwicklung im Weltsystem (in preparation).

14. Bornschier, Volker, Wachstum, Konzentration und Multinationalisierung von Industrieunternehmen. Frauenfeld/Stuttgart, Huber, 1976.

15. Bornschier, Volker. Abhangige Industrialisierung und Einkommensentwicklung. Schweizerische Zeitschrift fur Soziologie, No. 1, November 1975, p. 67-105.

16. Bornschier, Volker; Chase-Dunn, Christopher. Core Corporations and Underdevelopment in the World-System (in preparation).

17. Stoneman, Colin. Foreign Capital and Economic Growth. World Development, No. 3, 1975, p. 11-26.

Transnational Corporations and Global Markets: Changing Power Relations

FREDERICK F. CLAIRMONTE
JOHN H. CAVANAGH

I. INTRODUCTION

The principal object of this article is not merely to present facts and figures illustrating the dominance of transnational corporations (TNCs) in global trade, but to analyse their changing roles in reshaping the world market. It is designed as a contribution to the larger theoretical and empirical debate on the directions of global capitalism by concentrating on its key institution--the TNC[1]--which has propelled trade into novel directions and greater importance in the world economy.[2]

The analytical thrust is therefore directed at elucidating four central movements in the shifting roles of TNCs as they battle for global markets:

a) The explosive growth of conglomerate extensions of the TNCs, and further capital concentration in specific sectors to form oligopolies at national and international levels, have been conspicuous features of the last two decades.[3] The trajectory of the world market has been profoundly affected by enhanced ability of the conglomerates to undermine non-conglomerate competitors through their multi-product marketing networks, as well as through such increasingly sophisticated techniques as cross-subsidization.[4] The further surge to national and global oligopoly has not only strengthened the control of the TNCs over price formation, but has also offered an opportunity for more innovative collusive practices.

b) These changes in corporate power structures have been accompanied by the introduction of a new set of corporate priorities dictated by geopolitical realities and expectations of

From **TRADE AND DEVELOPMENT** , UNCTAD Review, Winter 1982, No. 4, (149-182), reprinted by permission of the publisher.

shifts in gains to be derived from the control of specific economic
activities. In the past two decades, there has been a marked
transformation in the approach of TNCs to the entire productive
chain. In practice, what has happened is that the extent of the
ownership of TNCs of primary commodity output has shrunk and their
control of processing, marketing, distribution and services has
expanded, a trend best epitomized by the Japanese Sogo Shoshas. In
response to internal political shifts in many developing countries
since independence, TNCs have sought to preserve amicable relations
with segments of internal oligarchies by the formal transfer of
mine and plantation ownership. In fact, however, TNCs
retained effective control of output through an ensemble of new
techniques, of which contract-growing in plantation agriculture is
but one.[5] In addition, the growing control of TNCs over the far
more profitable domains of marketing and distribution has
partially or wholly neutralized the internal oligarchies' gains
from nationalizations.

        c)   Corporate strategies in relation to the world market have
likewise been conditioned by strides in science and technology,
conspicuously in information services, transport and
communications. TNCs have seized upon innovations in ways
inconceivable a decade ago in order to fragment entire production
processes. The institutional method chosen by them for this
purpose has been to set up subsidiaries, joint ventures, licensing
and subcontracting agreements, all embodied in the theory and
practice of free trade zones (FTZs, sometimes designated as export
processing zones). In addition to increasing the volume of world
trade, and locking many developing countries more firmly into the
world market, this movement has generated certain political
repercussions. First, it has pitted local oligarchies in different
developing countries against one another in a competition to offer
the most alluring incentives to TNC investors. Secondly, it has
enabled the TNCs not only to cheapen the labour power input, but to
neutralize the strike weapon and break the labour movement by
threats and actual relocation to other countries.

        d)   These three trends have been supported by, and contributed
to, a fourth: the internationalization of finance through the
growth in the number and importance of transnational banks (TNBs).
The rise of the TNBs has led to a very close relationship at the
production and marketing levels between TNBs, TNCs, mega
multi-commodity trading companies and certain segments of State
power, with Japan once again exhibiting the most mature form of
these relations. Both the TNBs and the State (essentially through
monetary policies and a wide variety of subsidies) have promoted,
directly and indirectly, the largest TNCs on the world market, with
the consequence that the liquidation of small and medium size
business enterprises is proceeding apace.

        The growing control of the global market exercised by TNCs in
the ways described above has neither diminished the antagonistic
relations on the market, nor has it been able to counter what some
commentators have labelled the most ominous economic crisis since
the 1930s. Rather, TNCs have contributed to exacerbate the crisis
and antagonisms on the global market.

II. THE HISTORICAL BACKDROP

The role of TNCs in world trade is seen in the historical evolution of the modern capitalist corporation, schematically discernible in the following periodization: 1895–1945, the emergence and consolidation of oligopolies in key sectors in North America, Western Europe, Japan and Russia to 1917; 1946 to the mid–1960s, the rise of TNCs as a paramount force in many sectors of the world economy; and the mid–1960s to the present, the consolidation of several sectors into oligopolies dominated by transnational conglomerates linked to State power.

1895–1945

These five decades witnessed profound convulsions and economic antagonisms in the world market, including two world wars, economic stagnation and depression, and mass unemployment. A transition from relatively competitive conditions to monopolistic and oligopolistic output and market structures was effected by pooling arrangements, the modern corporation, the financial holding company, and a legal framework congenial to the concentration of corporate power.[6]

While certain North American and European corporations were extending their sales and output internationally, none approached the conglomeration of the Japanese Zaibatsu (or "financial cliques") that operated in conjunction with the State. Despite efforts by United States authorities after World War II to dismantle the Zaibatsu, a new variant evolved after 1945 that worked in easy consonance with the Ministry of International Trade and Industry (MITI) and other ministries.[7]

A. 1946 to Mid–1960s

In the three decades following the war, the growth, nature and composition of world trade and investment were revolutionized. At the epicentre of this transformation stood the TNC, now marketing roughly four-fifths of world trade, other than that of centrally planned economies (CPEs).[8]

The international oligopolies owed their ascendancy to the internationalization of output, finance[9] and commerce, aided by technical innovations in three basic sectors: revolutionary strides in containerized shipping made dispersal of production facilities profitable; improved engineering techniques provided the complex communications network crucial to the speed of operations; and

pervasive computer applications made possible the virtually
instantaneous data processing vital for maximization of global
profits and market shares. These three interlinked innovations
were instrumental in raising multi-commodity traders to their
present prominence in the entire commodity trade.

B. Mid-1960s to the Present

Since the 1960s, the driving force behind the
internationalization of certain goods and services has been the
drop of consumption in the markets of developed market economies
(DMEs), owing to a decline in population growth and to other
conjunctural forces. As from the early 1970s, this drop was
coupled with escalating costs of raw materials and petroleum (and
other energy), which impelled TNCs to export as well as to extend
their operations abroad in pursuit of growth through lower unit
costs.

The current phase has been marked by a spate of worldwide
mergers beginning in the late 1960s, a growing number of them
conglomerate.[10]   In the United States there were 711 mergers of
large firms between 1948 and 1965, of which 454 were
conglomerates.[11]   The indefatigable rhythm continued into the
1970s, with the value of conglomerate mergers and acquisitions
surpassing $1.5 billion in 1972.   By 1977, after what one expert
has called "an orgy of cannibalism which has reached unprecedented
levels", it had soared to $6 billion.[12]   In 1981, the $7.3 billion
annexation of Conoco (the ninth largest US oil company) by Du Pont
(the nation's largest chemical company) along outstripped the 1977
figure.   Merely in the United States, the dollar value of all
mergers and acquisitions during 1981 topped $82 billion, and on a
global basis was not far short of $180 billion.[13]

The worldwide drive to conglomeration, in combination with
oligopoly, has been a source of prodigious economic power for TNCs.
While different markets expand and contract, the conglomerate which
straddles several oligopolies can ride with the tide, shifting its
resources into whatever happens to be the most profitable business
at a given moment.   By means of cross-subsidization, the
conglomerate operating in many fields deploys its earnings from
various profit centres to subsidize losses in temporarily depressed
lines of business.

During this recent period, the metamorphosis of corporate
power is reflected in the soaring revenues of the top 200
companies; their share of world GDP (excluding the socialist
countries), increased from 18 per cent to 29 per cent over the last
two decades:[14]

a) The most conspicuous shift was the drop in the number of
United States TNCs from 127 to 91. Notwithstanding this slide,
these corporations still accounted for over 50 per cent of the
top 200's total sales, indicating that the average size of United
States TNCs is larger than that of its competitors;

b) A concomitant of the decline in the number of US-based TNCs has been the rise in the number of other challengers, principally firms in France and Japan. The numbers of French TNCs increased from 7 to 15, whose sales expanded from $4 to $161 billion. No less dramatic, even in the absence of the Sogo Shoshas (which, like certain giant traders, e.g. Cargill and Continental, do not figure in these totals), was the steep rise in the number of Japanese TNCs from five to 20;

c) Although the number of British TNCs dwindled by as much as a third, nonetheless their share of aggregate sales remained almost the same.

The wave of annexationism among TNCs could not have attained its present magnitude without the participation of TNBs on a scale which dwarfs that of the corporate mergers and acquisitions of the middle period (1947 to mid-1960s).[15] A perusal of the figures relating to the world's top 100 banks shows how powerful are these banks. In 1981 their combined assets of $4.4 trillion were the equivalent of more than half of global GDP; and more than double the combined sales of the top 200 industrial corporations. Big Japanese and United States banks alone control two-fifths of the top 100's total assets, with 24 Japanese banks accounting for over a quarter of total assets. This financial leverage has been crucial in the Sogo Shoshas' conquest of external markets.

Although data concerning the assets and sources of earnings of the top 200 TNCs and top 100 TNBs are indispensable for an understanding of changing power complexes in the world market, they are not sufficient in themselves to convey an idea of the sectoral specificities of transnational power. Data concerning the foreign revenues of the top 100 United States TNCs and TNBs (the only ones available to the authors) highlight both the sectoral breakdown and the breadth of transnationality:[16]

(a) The sectoral spectrum varies from the service sectors of banks and transport, where over half of the leading TNC's revenues comes from abroad at the upper end, to retailing at the lower end;

(b) Major industrial sectors range between these two extremes, but it should be borne in mind that a few of the biggest corporations derive well over half their revenues from abroad, particularly certain oil giants;

(c) These foreign revenue numbers should not be seen as indicating a static situation but rather as evidence of the extent of the penetration of foreign markets by TNCs and TNBs, specifically in the last two decades.

The transnationalization of the primary manufactures and service sectors is by no means the sole prerogative of United States corporations, but rather has become the common feature of large corporations in all DMEs, as a study of several sectors would suggest.

TABLE 1

Changing profile of the top 200 industrial corporations (1960-1980)

Country	Number			Sales (billions of U.S. dollars)			Per cent of sales		
	1960	1970	1980	1960	1970	1980	1960	1970	1980
USA	127	123	91	144.6	313.5	1 080.4	72.7	66.0	50.1
Germany, Fed. Rep. of	20	15	21	13.4	34.6	209.0	6.8	7.3	9.7
UK	24	17	16½ a	19.6	39.2	199.5	9.9	8.2	9.2
France	7	13	15	3.5	19.8	161.0	1.8	4.2	7.5
Japan	5	13	20	2.9	28.1	155.2	1.5	5.9	7.2
Netherlands	3	3	5	6.4	15.0	89.6	3.2	3.2	4.2
Italy	3	5	4½ a	1.9	9.6	69.5	0.9	2.0	3.2
Canada	5	2	5	2.6	2.4	32.5	1.3	0.5	1.5
Switzerland	2	4	4	2.0	6.4	31.9	1.0	1.3	1.5
Belgium	1	1	2	0.5	1.3	14.5	0.2	0.3	0.7
Sweden	1	1	2	0.4	1.0	11.0	0.2	0.2	0.5
Rep. of Korea	—	—	2	—	—	10.0	—	—	0.5
Others	2	3	12	1.1	4.4	91.1	0.5	0.9	4.2
Total (excl. USA)	73	77	109	54.4	161.7	1 074.8	27.3	34.0	49.9
Total	200	200	200	199.0	475.2	2 155.2	100.0	100.0	100.0
World GDP b				1 126.2	2 489.0	7 548.0			
Top 200 as per cent of GDP	. .			17.7	19.1	28.6			

Source: Calculated from *Fortune's* listings of leading industrial corporations.

NOTE: Countries were selected with more than one corporation in the top 200 in 1980, and ranked according to 1980 sales.

a Corporations owned by interests in two countries are counted as one-half.
b Excluding socialist countries.

52

TABLE 2

Profile of top 100 banks, 1981

Country/territory [a]	Number of banks	Assets ($ billion)	Per cent of total assets	Profits ($ billion)	Per cent of total profits
Japan	24	1 097.6	25.1	88.4	20.8
USA	12	650.7	14.9	91.2	21.4
France	8	509.2	11.6	35.8	8.4
Germany, Fed. Rep. of	11	464.3	10.6	45.9	10.8
UK	5	344.5	7.9	42.1	9.9
Italy	8	258.1	5.9	28.6	6.7
Canada	5	240.6	5.5	34.5	8.1
Netherlands	4	160.4	3.7	2.5	0.6
Switzerland	3	141.9	3.2	12.8	3.0
Belgium	4	100.2	2.3	12.2	2.9
Spain	3	67.5	1.5	6.7	1.6
Brazil	1	65.1	1.5	5.3	1.2
Sweden	3	64.6	1.5	3.1	0.7
Australia	3	60.0	1.4	7.1	1.7
Hong Kong	1	52.1	1.2	..	..
Islamic Rep. of Iran	1	23.9	0.6	1.1	0.3
India	1	20.5	0.5	1.9	0.5
Israel	1	19.2	0.4	4.2	1.0
Mexico	1	18.4	0.4	..	..
Austria	1	18.2	0.4	1.7	0.4
	100	4 377.0	100.0	425.1 [b]	100.0

Source: Computed from The Banker, June 1982.

[a] Countries ranked by banks' assets.

[b] Profit figures not provided for banks in the case of: France (3), Hong Kong (1), Netherlands (2), Japan (1) Italy (1), UK (1), Sweden (1), Mexico (1).

TABLE 3

Foreign revenues of top 100 United States TNCs and TNBs, 1981 [a]

Rank [b]	Company	Total revenues ($ billion)	Foreign revenue as per cent of total
Banks and non-bank financial			
13	Chase Manhattan	10.7	65.0
19	J. P. Morgan	6.8	63.3
9	Citicorp	18.3	62.0
83	Irving Bank	2.4	57.1
65	First National Boston	2.9	56.7
39	Bankers Trust New York	4.7	55.0
8	Phibro-Salomon	25.1	53.3
22	Manufacturers Hanover	7.5	53.3
12	Bank America	15.1	52.7
49	First Chicago	4.3	48.3
97	Marine Midland Banks	2.5	47.9
35	Chemical New York	5.7	47.2
41	Continental Illinois	6.3	37.8
56	American Express	7.2	26.9
	Sector average		*53.5*
Transportation			
36	Pan Am World Airways	3.8	70.0
58	Trans World	5.3	35.8
	Sector average		*50.5*
Natural resources (fuel and related)			
43	Atlantic Richfield	27.8	83.9
1	Exxon	108.1	70.1
3	Texaco	57.6	67.0
2	Mobil	65.4	62.9
4	Standard Oil California	44.2	53.9
11	Gulf Oil	28.2	36.7

TABLE 3 (Continued)

Rank [b]	Company	Total revenues ($ billion)	Foreign revenue as per cent of total
	Automotive [c]		
5	Ford Motor	38.2	48.4
26	Goodyear	9.2	41.0
71	Firestone	4.4	34.9
46	International Harvester	7.0	30.3
87	Bendix	4.4	29.6
6	General Motors	62.7	25.0
45	Chrysler	10.8	20.2
	Sector average		*32.9*
	Food and beverage		
34	CPC International	4.3	64.4
38	Coca-Cola	5.9	45.0
76	H. J. Heinz	3.6	39.9
55	Nabisco Brands	5.8	34.1
52	General Foods	6.6	30.9
32	Dart & Kraft	10.2	28.5
75	Consolidated Foods	5.6	25.6
91	Ralston Purina	5.2	24.0
50	Beatrice Foods	9.0	23.1
66	PepsiCo	7.0	22.7
	Sector average		*31.8*
	Conglomerates		
10	Intl. Tel & Tel	23.2	47.3
96	Litton Industries	4.9	24.5
89	TRW	5.3	23.9
33	Tenneco	15.5	18.8
80	Gulf & Western Inds.	7.4	18.6
	Sector average		*31.6*

TABLE 3 (Continued)

Miscellaneous

30 Colgate-Palmolive	5.3	58.7
85 Gillette	2.3	57.3
69 American Intl. Group	3.2	48.9
93 Avon Products	2.6	47.9
99 Singer	2.8	40.6
61 American Brands	4.5	40.0
40 Minn. Mining & Mfg.	6.5	39.3
23 Eastman Kodak	10.3	38.0
86 Scott Paper	3.6	36.6
100 Ingersoll-Rand	3.4	34.0
25 Procter & Gamble	11.4	32.8
57 Fluor	6.1	31.6
70 Deere	5.4	28.2
37 R. J. Reynolds	9.8	27.2
73 Continental Group	5.8	25.1
31 United Technologies	13.7	22.1
64 Caterpillar Tractor	9.2	18.6
53 General Tel. & Elec.	11.0	18.4
98 Philip Morris	8.3	14.0
Sector average		*30.7*

Electrical, electronics

95 Motorola	3.3	36.4
84 Texas Instruments	4.2	31.9
15 General Electric	27.9	20.9
77 RCA	9.0	15.7
94 Westinghouse Electric	9.4	13.0
Sector average		*20.3*

Retailing (food and non-food)

28 F. W. Woolworth	8.3	40.9
20 Safeway Stores	16.6	24.7
72 K. Mart	17.4	8.7
54 Sears Roebuck	29.3	6.9
Sector average		*15.4*

ᵇ Ranking based on foreign revenues in *Forbes'* 100 largest multinationals.

ᵉ Including rubber and tyre corporations.

TABLE 3 (Continued)

18 Occidental Petroleum	15.3	31.7
21 Sun Co.	16.0	25.6
48 Halliburton	8.5	24.7
27 Phillips Petroleum	16.0	21.3
44 Getty Oil	12.9	17.8
60 Union Oil California	10.9	16.8
17 Standard Oil Indiana	30.4	16.4
Sector average		*48.8*
Office equipment and computers		
62 NCR	3.4	52.1
63 Hewlett-Packard	3.6	48.2
7 IBM	29.1	48.1
24 Xerox	8.7	44.5
81 Burroughs	3.4	40.2
47 Sperry	5.4	39.3
92 Digital Equipment	3.2	39.1
68 Honeywell	5.4	29.0
Sector average		*44.7*
Chemicals and drugs		
59 Pfizer	3.3	56.8
16 Dow Chemical	11.9	47.9
82 Merck	2.9	46.7
42 Johnson & Johnson	5.4	44.0
74 Warner-Lambert	3.4	42.6
90 Bristol-Myers	3.5	36.0
88 American Cyanamid	3.6	35.0
79 American Home Products . . .	4.1	33.6
29 Union Carbide	10.2	31.4
51 Monsanto	6.9	29.9
14 E. I. Du Pont de Nemours . .	22.8	29.5
67 Allied Corp.	6.4	24.4
78 W. R. Grace	6.5	21.3
Sector average		*34.9*

Source : Calculated from data in *Forbes*, 5 July 1982.

ᵃ Ranked by foreign as per cent of total revenues.

TABLE 4

Corporate control of global commodity trade, 1980

Commodity	Total exports ($ million)	Percentage marketed by 15 largest transnationals [a]
Food		
Wheat	16 556	85-90
Sugar	14 367	60
Coffee	12 585	85-90
Corn	11 852	85-90
Rice	4 978	70
Cocoa	3 004	85
Tea	1 905	80
Bananas	1 260	70-75
Pineapples	440 [b]	90
Agricultural raw materials		
Forest products	54 477	90
Cotton	7 886	85-90
Natural rubber	4 393	70-75
Tobacco	3 859	85-90
Hides and skins	2 743	25
Jute	203	85-90
Ores, minerals, and metals		
Crude petroleum	306 000	75
Copper	10 650	80-85
Iron ore	6 930	90-95
Tin	3 588	75-80
Phosphates	1 585	50-60
Bauxite	991	80-85

Source : UNCTAD secretariat estimates, based on extensive research and interviews with traders and marketing specialists. The figures represent orders of magnitude only.

[a] In most cases, only 3 to 6 transnational traders account for the bulk of the market.

[b] Four-fifths consists of canned pineapples and one-fifth of fresh pineapples.

TABLE 5

British American Tobacco Co.: geographical breakdown, 1981

Region	Sales		Profits	
	(£ million)	*Per cent*	*(£ million)*	*Per cent*
North America	2 542	27	283	45
UK	2 034	22	46	7
Europe	1 979	21	77	12
Latin America	1 731	19	131	21
Asia	566	6	59	9
Africa	355	4	35	6
Australasia	58	1	3	—
TOTAL	9 265	100	634	100

Source: BAT, *Annual Report*, 1981.

[28] *Fortune*, 9 August 1982.

[29] *Fortune*, 24 August 1981; the statement takes into account sales made through foreign affiliates.

[30] These include the major military contractors: Boeing (the No. 1 US exporter); General Electric (3); United Technologies (7); McDonnell Douglas (8); Lockheed (10); and the two big auto companies: General Motors (2) and Ford (4).

[31] *Labour Research*, September 1981.

TABLE 6

Growth in international profits of leading US banks, 1970 and 1981

Bank [a]	International profits ($ million)		Per cent of total profits	
	1970	1981	1970	1981
Citicorp	58	287	40	54
Bank America	25	245	15	55
Chase Manhattan	31	247	22	60
Manufacturers Hanover . .	11	120	13	48
J. P. Morgan	26	234	25	67
Chemical New York	8	74	10	34
Bankers Trust New York . .	8	116	15	62
Total	167	1 323	22	55

Source: Calculated from data from Salomon Bros. in *The Economist*, 14 January 1978 and *Forbes*, 5 July 1982.
[a] Ranked on basis of 1981 assets.

[53] See Frederick F. Clairmonte, "World Tobacco: A Portrait of Corporate Power" in William Finger (ed.), *The Tobacco Industry in Transition* (Toronto, 1981).

[54] The first figure is derived from computer printouts supplied by the US Department of Commerce, November 1981. The latter figure is from UNCTAD, *Fibres and Textiles, op. cit.*, p. 134.

III. MORPHOLOGY OF SECTORS

A study of the morphology of major sectors illustrates even more clearly the four principal trends of the activities of TNCs noted in the introduction. In a certain sense, the conventional tripartite division of sectors into primary commodities, manufactures and services is being blurred, or rendered less useful for purposes of analysis, by one of these trends, the push to conglomeration.[17] While certain giant TNCs, through corporate expansion, straddle the three sectors, trading relations in each still retain their own distinct specificities.

A Primary Commodities

While this article is concerned mainly with corporate power relations in trade, it is difficult to separate the institutional and social forces influencing the trade of TNCs from those affecting their output. Certain vertically integrated TNCs, with mining or plantation subsidiaries, have in certain countries divested themselves of these holdings (while retaining them in others) in response to nationalist and other political pressures. Whereas the transfer of ownership may be construed as a step away from vertical integration, in reality it in no way diminishes TNC control over output. To be sure, by retaining a tight grip on global marketing (and in several cases domestic marketing) and financing, TNCs retain the power to determine the conditions under which raw materials are supplied and priced.

During the 1950s and 1960s, all primary commodity sectors witnessed the disappearance (through mergers, takeovers and bankruptcies) of small--and medium-sized trading companies to a point where, by 1980, roughly 70-80 per cent of the global primary commodity trade valued at $980 billion was accounted for by TNCs.[18] This figure includes $230 of $306 billion worth of crude petroleum exports under the control of the world's petroleum giants; and around $500 of $674 billion worth of the remainder of primary commodity trade (agriculture, minerals and other fuels) under the control of multi-commodity traders and the trading affiliates of industrial TNCs.[19] The share of a given commodity's global trade accounted for by TNCs can vary from one year to another as multi-commodity traders shift their operations into those commodities which are considered the most profitable.

In particular, in the last two decades the domination of primary commodity markets has passed from single commodity traders (e.g. the former United Fruit Company) to firms paramount in several global commodity markets. The trade in three commodities, by no means exceptional, illustrates the dimension of marketing leverage: the trade in bananas, where three conglomerates dominate 70-75 per cent of global markets; the cocoa trade, of which six corporations account for over 70 per cent; and the trade in leaf tobacco, where 85-90 per cent is under the direct control of six transnational leaf buyers.[20]

The market power of the multi-commodity traders stems from their self-reinforcing modes of conduct that contribute to enhance their bargaining stance vis-a-vis developing countries. Most multi-commodity traders are private and largely non-accountable, not only in developing but also in developed market economy countries. Many are integrated backward into plantations and forward into processing, and hence are in an even stronger bargaining position vis-a-vis national marketing institutions with which they deal.

Over the years, intimate working relations have been forged between the big traders and transnational banks. Several of the biggest have individual credit lines of up to $120 million each with one bank. In some cases, a multi-commodity trader may have as many as 12-15 such credit lines.[21] Moreover, the ties that bind multi-commodity traders to the large banks are by no means exclusively financial. In several cases, the two are imbricated through interlocking directorships. Multi-commodity traders, thanks to their economic, political and trading intelligence networks, can operate with a speed and flexibility often unmatched by national marketing institutions. Nor does competition among multi-commodity traders in the world market in any way exclude collusive deals in pricing, buying and selling when such deals are in the mutual interest of the parties concerned.

Another important feature of the primary commodity trade—that in minerals—are intra-firm transfers carried out by transnational trading affiliates of industrial TNCs. In consequence of progressive vertical integration, intra-firm trading is becoming increasingly significant.[22] This device, whereby corporations arrange "buying and selling" transactions between their own subsidiaries, has given rise to the widespread technique of transfer pricing,[23] designed to enhance corporate interests and circumvent national economic policies.

By means of this technique corporations are able to minimize their overall tax liability by manipulating prices of intra-corporation transactions, and so enhancing profits in countries with lower tax rates and trimming them in countries with high tax rates. Not only are such corporate practices widespread in and between developing countries, but they are also manifest in DMEs as well.[24] Even within the United States economy, it has been discovered that TNCs evaded state corporate income taxes by shifting profits in their financial accounts from within the United States proper to their Puerto Rican accounts, tax rates being lower in Puerto Rico.[25]

B. Manufactures and Semi-Manufactures

An important qualitative change in the world market has been a shift in the nature and composition of trade. Whereas formerly there was a relatively clear demarcation between trade in raw materials and that in end products, there is now a burgeoning trade in semi-manufactures and components under the control of TNCs, made possible by two inter-acting phenomena: one technological, the other political. Growth in trade has been facilitated by technical changes in three fields: cheaper transport, telecommunications and the entire spectrum of information technology.

Politically, such international operations have benefits from State support. Several hundred free trade zones (FTZs) and other special enclaves (e.g. industrial estates) have been set up in developing countries which offer a wide range of incentives to attract TNCs, e.g. extensive tax holidays, subsidized infrastructure, and even the elimination of militant trade unions.[26]

By contrast with primary commodity trade, global trade in manufactures is largely dominated by a different ensemble of protagonists (with the exception of the ubiquitous presence of the Sogo Shoshas). Essentially, these are trading subsidiaries of industrial TNCs which, jointly with the Sogo Shoshas, accounted in 1980 for roughly $810 billion of the $1,015 billion worth of global manufactured exports.[27] While the most impressive advance in the past quarter century has been achieved by developing countries, which doubled their share of world manufactures exports in that period, this business is still largely under the ownership and marketing control of TNCs.

The biggest revenues of manufactures, as of agricultural products, are earned by the largest TNCs. In the United States, for example, the aggregate foreign sales of the top 50 exporters exceeded $63 billion in 1981, more than a quarter of all United States merchandise sold abroad.[28] With but two exceptions, the top 50 United States exporters are among the top 200 of Fortune's 500[29] largest industrial firms. For many of these corporations, the world market is indispensable for survival; for example, four depend on exports for over a third of their sales: Boeing, Caterpillar Tractor, McDonnell Douglas and Northrop. Sectoral concentration is also observable: the top 10 exporters depend heavily on exports of military equipment and automobiles.[30]

Among British firms, an even more marked penetration of the world market has been achieved by the largest TNCs. The 50 biggest non-public sector manufacturing companies exported a full 18 per cent of their United Kingdom output in 1980, two-fifths of their aggregate sales being accounted for by goods produced overseas.[31] If exports and output through foreign affiliates are counted together it can be seen that the 50 leading British firms depend on the world market for over half their sales. One of the compelling reasons for their entry into foreign markets is seen in a geographical breakdown of the balance sheets and income statements of certain large TNCs. The British American Tobacco Company (1981 sales: 9.3 billion pounds and number three among the UK corporations), for example, earned a trifling 7 per cent of its profits on the 22 per cent of its world-wide sales recorded in the United Kingdom. Corresponding proportions for its

North American operations were 45 and 27 per cent; and for operations in developing countries 36 and 29 per cent.

Whereas the concentration of TNC control over global trade is very visible in the United States and the United Kingdom, it is most pronounced in Japan. As the prime exemplar of institutional integration of commodity and manufactures trade, the Sogo Shoshas are engaged in a plethora of industrial, financial and service operations. In the last 200 years, they have become the most dynamic machine of Japan's impressive growth--at home and abroad.[32] Ineluctably, corporate power of such magnitude has transcended the geo-political frontiers of the island empire, with banks providing financing; the Shoshas ensuring the purchasing, marketing, carrying out of inventory and market research; and industrial subsidiaries being the production arm.

Currently, there are nine giant Sogo Shoshas, whose 1981 aggregate revenues exceeded $357 billion, a figure which excludes revenues from their financial and industrial affiliates.[33] In the latter half of the 1970s, their share of Japan's foreign trade (exports plus imports) at times exceeded 60 per cent. Each Sogo Shosha handles 20,000-25,000 products--evidence of the organizational breadth of these conglomerates which have long ceased to be purely trading corporations.

The Japanese economy reveals the institutional complexity of State, finance, trade and industrial interlocking relationships, with the Sogo Shoshas often co-operating among themselves and with MITI to expand their global market shares. In view of Japan's market power and success, several countries, both developed and developing, are striving to emulate this model of global marketing. Whether their attempts will be successful, and to what extent, remains problematical.

In the last two decades a small number of developing countries have for the first time penetrated the world market for various light manufactures; these countries may be categorized into a leading group of seven and a lesser group of twelve. It would be a fallacy, however, to infer that the groups of seven and twelve constitute,or have the potential of ever becoming, an autonomous power block in the world market. Rather, much of their output is under the control of subsidiaries and joint ventures of TNCs, and the bulk of their trade is marketed by multi-commodity traders and the Sogo Shosha.

With the group of seven achieving annual GDP growth rates of 7-10 per cent in the 1960s and early 1970s, the gap between them and the rest of the developing countries has grown perceptibly wider. By 1980, these seven accounted for well over two-thirds of all manufactured exports of all developing countries, whereas their share had been 55 per cent in 1965.[34]

Their growth strategies, in tandem with TNCs, proved most effective on world markets as they succeeded in holding down unit labour costs by curbing trade union activism, currency devaluations, restraining domestic consumption and massively subsidizing export-led growth. Another trait of this export-led policy has been concentration on a relatively limited basket of manufactures, primarily apparel, textiles and consumer electronics. Among the big seven, there is also marked concentration in specific

sectors; for example, three of them account for over half of the
manufacturing exports of all developing countries in several
sectors.[35] The big seven have been emulated in the last decade by
a group of twelve which recorded yearly growth rates (1970–1979) in
manufacturing exports varying between 29 and 54 per cent.[36]

What is new about much of the export business carried on by
these developing countries is that it involves a novel strategy on
the part of the TNCs. These corporations are fragmenting the
production process by contracting out the most labour-intensive
phases to developing countries where wage costs are relatively low.
In the textile and apparel sector, for example, outward processing
involves domestic fabric design and cutting by the TNCs,
followed by shipment to a developing country for yet another
operational phase—sewing. In an ultimate phase, the partially
processed goods are then reimported for finishing and packaging.
In the major Western European countries and the United States, such
operations are encouraged by special tariff concessions by virtue
of which the TNCs concerned pay duty only on the value added to the
product abroad.[37] Likewise, in many developing countries this
practice is promoted by the setting up of free trade and other
zones where TNCs are the beneficiaries of subsidized
infrastructure, tax holidays and exemptions from duty.[38] To these
attractive incentives could be added what are now vaunted in
certain countries (including the big seven) as cheap and docile
labour forces.

Technology in this perspective cannot be viewed as
an independent variable but one which historically responds to the
direction and pull of capital accumulation. Technical
innovations, epitomized by the massive diffusion of
micro-processors and the silicon chip, make it possible to achieve
ever higher output and productivity norms, which enable the firms
concerned to break into the world market.

For instance, a robot can now complete in 11 seconds a small
plug weld which takes a human welder 9 minutes, or a ratio of 1:50.
Even in what conventionally have been labelled labour-intensive
industries (e.g. apparel) the pace of concentration is accelerating
in response to the current economic crisis, rising costs of
technical applications (even as the costs of certain microprocessor
components drop) and the imperatives of the market. Once again,
the United States offers an example of this movement. In the
course of several decades, its apparel industry, which at one time
employed thousands of small-scale sweat shops, has been gradually
replaced by one led by nine large conglomerates (e.g. Gulf &
Western and Consolidated Foods). The industry is being rapidly
automated even though certain new machines cost over half a million
dollars each.[39]

Nowhere, perhaps, has technology's imprint on the global
market been more graphically described than in the words of the
United Kingdom's Minister of State for Industry and
Information Technology: "Britain is a trading nation and heavily
dependent on exports of manufactured goods. If we want to remain
competitive and maintain and increase our share of both our
domestic and world markets we must be up with our competitors in

using the most efficient production techniques . . . The choice is
stark: Automate or liquidate."[40] Or, in the no less harsh verdict
of an article in The New York Times: "Automate, emigrate or
evaporate".[41]

While the growth of manufactures exports of certain developing
countries has undoubtedly been numerically impressive, its
foundations are by no means uniformly solid. With the same
alacrity with which they located plants in developing countries,
TNCs are able to uproot such plants as advances in technology
cancel the principal advantage of these countries—the costs
attractions of cheaper labour. Thus, in a relatively brief span,
what has become a notable but ephemeral segment of international
trade can quickly be wiped out.

C. Services

In the past decade, the services sector has grown faster than
the primary commodities and manufactures sectors, assuming a
crucial role in global capitalism.[42] Widespread applications of
microprocessor technology has once again been instrumental in
speeding up this movement. The expansion of service sectors
nationally has been matched by a rapid increase in the world trade
in services. A wide range of TNCs have moved swiftly to dominate
it, and transnational banks and a large number of financial
institutions have become the linchpin of the entire international
trade in services, as they are in the trade in goods.

Of all export sectors, the services sector remains the least
systematized in terms of data collection and comparability. From
sparse indicators, however, one can piece together the contours of
the international trade in services.

According to the World Invisible Trade Bulletin, the value of
this trade soared from $77 billion in 1969 to $551 billion in 1980,
excluding the CPEs.[43] United States exports of services, however,
totalled two-fifths of its goods exports, a ratio which, projected
on a global canvas, would suggest that total exports of services be
valued at around $800 billion.[44] It appears plausible that the
world services trade would fall within the spectrum of these two
sets of numbers, and that as in other sectors the bulk of the trade
is controlled by TNCs and TNBs. An attempt is made below to
estimate the approximate size of major sectors of the global
services trade, and to investigate the corporations which dominate
each.

Travel and transport

According to UNCTAD estimates, exports in the form of the

provision of travel, passenger and other transport services exceeded $155 billion in 1980, consisting essentially of services for tourism[45] and business travel. More than half a billion tourists spent over $80 billion worldwide in 1979[46] and the principal beneficiaries were giant TNCs in the airline and hotel business as well as corporate owners of other transport and entertainment services.

Earnings from foreign investment

This item ranks second only to travel in total earnings from exports of services. Fees and royalties are derived from licensing agreements concluded by TNCs, whereas investment income is a function of the stock of direct investment abroad.[47] In 1976, the capital value of this investment stock exceeded $287 billion, over four-fifths being accounted for by investors from six countries: the United States (48 per cent); the United Kingdom (11); the Federal Republic of Germany (7); Japan (7); Switzerland (7) and France (4).[48] Fragmentary estimates suggest that the value of the worldwide investment had increased to over $470 billion by 1980.[49] In the United States alone, $42.5 billion in income, fees and royalties was earned from direct investment and licensing (1980), a figure from which it could be inferred that worldwide earnings from these sources would exceed $94 billion.[50]

These numbers throw light on an important relationship in the world economy, namely that between trade and investment. One aspect of this relationship is that investment income is an important item in the trade balance. In certain countries, e.g. the United States, large surpluses in the international services trade contribute to offset deficits in the international goods trade.[51]

Yet another aspect of the relationship is that large-scale investment income is drained out of developing countries into DMEs, adversely affecting the former's balance of payments. In just one year (1978) Brazil and Mexico experienced a net combined outflow of investment income of $5.6 billion.[52] What aggravates the negative impact of these outflows is that they are not largely a product of capital brought into the countries, but rather represent earnings from capital siphoned from domestic savings by transnational and domestic banks: about four-fifths of manufacturing operations of United States firms in Latin America during the 1960s was financed by domestic capital.[53]

Corporations active in many different sectors shared the benefits of foreign investment earnings. In any given country, at any given time, however, a particular sector may account for a large share of the gains. In the United States (1980), the large petroleum corporations received over a third of all income derived from direct United States investment abroad, as well as two-fifths of the aggregate profits of the United States manufacturing industry.[54]

Earnings of TNCs

A considerably smaller, but none the less significant, segment
of the international trade in services consists of the foreign
activities of TNBs, the earnings from which expanded exponentially
in the 1970s. Nowhere is this expansion seen more vividly than in
the large-scale penetration of the world economy by the biggest
United States banks, in whose portfolios the former overwhelming
emphasis on domestic markets (1970) has given place to a no less
dominant position in foreign markets in 1981.
    The dual implications of this spectacular change are that TNBs
have become even more intricately involved in the fortunes of the
world market, and that they are a more powerful determinant of its
contours.
    By the end of 1981, TNBs had a stock of $1,500 billion in
loans worldwide, of which over $300 billion were loans to
developing countries.[55] TNCs, in turn, controlled around 80 per
cent of the $2,000 billion worth of trade (excluding services) and
around $470 billion worth of direct foreign investment.[56] Owing to
the interdependence of trade, investment and indebtedness, trade
can be greatly stimulated by investment flows, which provide the
means for setting up of industrial plants that at once require
imports and generate exports. Loans also boost trade by supplying
the requisite foreign exchange to finance imports.
    In the present potentially explosive economic conjuncture the
TNBs are in a strategically strong position to slow global capital
flows and hence world trade. TNBs reacted to the gravity of
Poland's debt (and of the 26 developing countries that were in
arrears in their loan repayments[57] by the end of 1980) by
decelerating loan flows to non-oil developing countries after 1979,
and by reducing loans to socialist countries in 1980 and 1981.[58]
In this setting, TNBs have become yet another aggravator of the
global crisis. Indeed, TNBs move money into and out of countries
according to the dictates of corporate, not national, policy.

The advertising phalanx

Worldwide mass advertising, now effectively controlled by
TNCs, is at once a major component of the services sector and a
stimulator of the trade in goods. An idea of the pervasive impact
of advertising by TNCs is conveyed by an analysis of global
advertising billings, which were estimated at more than $120
billion in 1981.[59] The United States accounts for fully one-half
of the advertising universe, with roughly $60 billion in
advertising outlays in 1981. The United States and five other
centres of corporate power--Japan, the Federal Republic of Germany,
the United Kingdom, France and Canada--account altogether for
four-fifths of the total.[60]

The giant advertising corporations have become an indispensable adjunct of corporate capital in all economic sectors. Led by Japan's Dentsu and the United States giants Young & Rubicam and J. Walter Thompson, 12 advertising agencies operating worldwide (each with yearly billings in excess of $1 billion) jointly account for over 17 per cent of expenditure on publicity.[61] It is these large advertising companies that secure the bulk of contracts awarded by the biggest TNCs, and whose expertise is the most sophisticated in promoting products.

The same big 12 advertising agencies are omnipresent in both developed and developing countries. In Latin America, for example, J. Walter Thompson is the leading advertising agency in Argentina, Chile and Venezuela; number two in Brazil and number four in Mexico.[62] Thus, marketing technology perfected in the DMEs is adaptively deployed in developing countries. In many cases, advertising TNCs possess a greater knowledge of consumer behaviour in local and national markets than most governments.

Shipping,[63] consulting services, insurance, telecommunications and government transactions are among the remaining group of services that are an important segment of global trade. With the exception of the last, all are no less dominated by TNCs.

The rise of TNCs and TNBs in the world market has paralleled and conditioned the revolutionizing of corporate marketing technologies and strategies that have remoulded the power complexes of international trade.

IV. STRATEGIES OF TNC's

In their most rudimentary and universal form, corporate marketing strategies and techniques are designed to separate the consumer from his money. In pursuit of this goal, the modern corporation has built up a series of interrelated techniques for packaging, advertising, promoting, selling and pricing its products in order to attain the twin goals of profit and market aggrandisement. Central to all TNC marketing strategies is the integration of each individual corporate component. No one has defined this central concern more aggressively than the chairman of the world's biggest brewer, Mr. August A. Busch III of the Anheuser-Busch dynasty:

In 1977, we installed a programme which we called "Total Marketing" which combines all of the key marketing elements into a single orchestrated thrust. Advertising was joined by sales promotion, merchandising, field sales, sales training and sports programming, enabling us to market not only on a national plan, but also at the grassroots level. This "in the trenches" capability, coupled with our national programme, will prove vital to our growth in the eighties.[64]

The national logic of such expansionist strategies becomes even more compelling as corporate power moves into the international market. Corporate expansion in the world market depends on a multiplicity of interdependent elements that only the very large corporations have at their command: far-reaching economic intelligence networks joined to distribution facilities, intimate links with TNBs and close working relations with large importers who prefer to do business with the biggest TNCs.

By no means fortuitously, corporate marketing strategies employ both the jargon and techniques of military warfare, symptomatic of the fierce competition characterising the world market. Pungently underlining the pervasiveness of this military jargon in the waging of economic warfare, Kotler and Singh observe:[65]

> The increased need of business to develop will lead managers to turn more and more to the subject of military science. The classic works of Clausewitz, Liddell Hart and other military theorists are being increasingly combed for ideas, just as economic theory and consumer behaviour theory were studied in the last two decades.
> Business people frequently use military talk to describe their situations. There are price "wars", "border clashes", and "skirmishes" among the major computer manufacturers; and "escalating arms race" among cigarette manufacturers; "market invasion" and "guerilla warfare" in the coffee market. A company's advertising is its "propaganda arm", its salesmen are its "shock troops", and its marketing research is its "intelligence". There is talk about "confrontation", "brinkmanship", "superweapons", "reprisals", and "psychological warfare".
> But the real question is whether the use of "warfare" language in business is just descriptive of whether it really aids in thinking and planning competitive strategy. We believe it does, and that principles of military strategy apply in three critical business decision areas--namely, determining objectives, developing attack strategies, and developing defense strategies.

The sums involved in such marketing warfare and in the legal takeover battles,[66] are so huge that only the largest and most transnationalized can survive.

Pricing techniques are another form of corporate warfare. Oligopolistic competition in the global market is characterized by large corporations acting as "pricemakers", as distinct from a competitive situation where the individual firm is a "price taker".[67] Despite variations due to specific historical and legal circumstances, oligopolistic pricing is in no way immutable. Rather, in times of sectoral, national and/or international crises, it is subject to erosion and recomposition in different forms under different conditions.

The traditional mechanisms of industrial oligopolistic pricing

either do not exist or operate differently in the trade in primary
commodities. Pricing policies of the multi-commodity traders are
more like highly complex exercises in which profits are earned
through secrecy, hedging, speculation, arbitrage and warehousing.[68]
Yet, despite differences between oligopolies in primary commodity
trade and industry, their similarity is that in both a tiny number
of large firms are the determinative agents in price formation.

      Certain oligopolistic firms move from tacit collusion to overt
cartels, the members of which agree on prices and occasionally on
market shares and geographical spheres of influence. As has been
pointed out by an OECD group of experts, firms sometimes:

          consolidate their economic power and draw advantages
      from it not only individually but also by means of
      agreements or concerted actions with other enterprises,
      particularly in oligopolies where most multinationals are
      to be found.   Such agreements are facilitated by the
      possibility in many countries of legalizing certain types
      of cartels: for example, rebate, rationalization, import
      and specialization cartels in which the subsidiaries of
      multinational firms may participate and which may, and in
      fact sometimes do, serve as the nucleus for an
      international system of restrictive agreements.[69]

      Although the data are not sufficiently exhaustive for a
sector-by-sector assessment of the precise role of TNCs in export
cartels, it appears nonetheless from a study by the Federal Cartel
Office that in the Federal Republic of Germany TNCs participate in
around 70 per cent of all export cartels in that country. In the
United Kingdom, an analysis of 41 international export cartels
demonstrated that 20 out of 29 cartels with transnational
participation had both British and foreign transnational members.[70]
      Oligopolistic members of an international export cartel are
often capable of "persuading" other corporations engaged in
domestic and foreign trade to adhere to the cartel's export prices.
Such cartels are often encouraged and nurtured by the State through
exemptions from anti-monopoly litigation, subsidies, tax benefits
and authorization to firms to pool their resources.[71]
      Just as the institutionalization of domestic and export
cartels harks back to the 1870s and 1880s, another corporate
strategy (which has gathered tremendous momentum over the last
decade) with deep historic antecedents is that of barter,
countertrade and buy-back deals. What differentiates it from
conventional trade is that, instead of the medium of foreign
exchange, purchases of one item are pegged to the purchases of
another, which may or may not bear a relationship to prevailing
world market prices. In the buy-back version of such deals,
technology or entire plants are exchanged for a future flow of
products.
      In the socialist and developing countries, the reason for such
deals is the dearth of foreign exchange. As debt levels rise in
many countries, the lure of countertrade also rises. TNCs enter
such deals to increase market shares in areas suffering from a
shortage of foreign exchange, and at times they barter products on

advantageous terms because of pressing financial needs of their
trading partners.   By   the   late   1970s,   government   officials,
financiers   and industrialists were   predicting that buy-back deals
would   account for   a fifth   of all   international trade during the
1980s.   However, according to General Electric,   one of the world's
largest   exporters,   the   value   of   international countertrade had
already reached $350 billion by 1979, or a   fifth of world trade.[72]
As   the crisis deepened in   1982, countertrade transactions rose to
constitute as much as 25-30 per cent of world trade.[73]

The magnitude of   certain countertrade deals   is illustrated by
the 1978 agreement between one of the world's apparel leaders--Levi
Strauss--and   the   Hungarian   Government.   The   latter   received
equipment and expertise in exchange for three-fifths of the plant's
annual output, now amounting to   around one million pairs of   jeans
yearly   which Levi Strauss   merchandises   in   Western   Europe and
Africa.   Giant TNCs,   like General   Electric[74] and General Motors,
carry   on   such   an   extensive   countertrade that special corporate
departments have been set up to develop markets in   countries where
cash deals or capital investment are not feasible.

It is a   distinguishing feature of countertrade that the value
assigned   to   goods   exchanged   is   determined   entirely   outside a
so-called "free-market"   framework.   Rather, the   exchange value of
goods bought and sold is often a function of the relative power   of
the   contending   parties.   Indeed,   as   noted by the United States
Assistant Secretary   of State   for Economic   and Business   Affairs:
"The most distorting countertrade arrangements are those which call
for the   exchange of   fixed quantities   of goods   or services   over
protracted   periods of   time without   reference to prices."[75]   What
could be added   is that distortions   of alleged free-market   prices
are   characteristic not only of countertrade   but of a good deal of
international trade as a whole.

Indubitably,   one result of the escalation of countertrade has
been to buttress larger   TNCs to the detriment of   small and medium
enterprises which   lack   the   extensive marketing and distribution
networks required for such   large volume turnovers.   Another result
linked   to the   rising indebtedness   of the   socialist countries is
that   the   latter   have   become   increasingly   integrated   into the
TNC-dominated global trading   system, albeit not on   the same level
as   developing countries.   Contrary   to a belief   widely held after
the   Second   World   War,   there   are   no   two sharply defined world
markets, each   with its   own economic   specificities, but   rather a
single   world market whose   systemic corporate connections permeate
all regions.   Poland's economic   troubles of   the early   1980s are
causing   other   socialist   countries   to   pay   attention   to   the
operational   mechanisms of these   systemic connections.   It remains
conjectural whether the relationship of socialist countries   to the
global market will remain what it was in the last two decades.

V. THE STATE/TNC POWER COMPLEX

In all the major selected sectors of global trade (primary commodities, manufactures and services), the State continues to play an important part in furthering the output and trade of TNCs. The historic antecedents of these linkages, which became so conspicuous after 1873, go well beyond the confines of this article, but it suffices here to sketch the outlines of the relationship. Both developing and developed market economy countries have long aided TNCs individually and collectively through State-sponsored cartels, subsidized input prices, research grants, government contracts and government-aided rationalization of crisis-stricken sectors. As the world market stagnates and competition becomes ever keener, the weaponry of State power is being effectively mobilized to bolster the largest TNCs in the economic fight for market shares and, in many cases, simply for survival.[76]

Of the vast armoury that the State in a developed market economy country is in a position to deploy, four of the most potent exemplify the mechanisms used for supporting the operations of TNCs: a varied range of subsidies; underwriting of research and development; generous tax, tariff and antitrust legislation; and State-authorized export cartels and rationalization measures.

During 1980, the State subsidized 18 per cent of United States, 34 of French, 35 of British, and 39 per cent of Japanese exports.[77] Even more significant, however, is that most of such export subsidies benefit the biggest exporters among the TNCs. In the United States, two-thirds of the Export-Import Bank's loans granted in 1980 were accounted for by seven giant TNCs: Boeing, General Electric, Westinghouse, McDonnell Douglas, Lockheed, Western Electric and Combustion Engineering.[78] The scale of such loans and the ease with which TNCs can obtain State financing often make the difference between success and failure in winning a foreign contract.[79] Export credits provided to foreign customers at below market rates of interest have likewise risen in recent years to unprecedented levels.[80]

Guaranteed loans have become one of the most visible external characteristics of the intimate relations linking the State, TNCs and TNBs--a commonly used "survival kit" for crippled TNCs. The subsidies in but one sector typify the specific mechanisms at work. In the steel sector, which is in crisis almost everywhere, and one of the sources of economic antagonisms among DMEs, subsidies take three forms: loans at preferential rates, government equity participation, and cash grants.[81]

Another buttress of State/TNC/TNB power relations that is reshaping the world market for technology is the subsidization of research and development, strikingly so in high technology sectors. Already, MITI finances 16 per cent of Japan's R & D, and the Pentagon almost a third of that of the United States.[82]

The repeal and amendment of antitrust, banking and tax legislation are further weapons in the armoury of economic warfare explicitly designed to accelerate the tempo of concentration, to

raise competitive capabilities in the global market. As United
States Assistant Attorney General William Baxter has said: "There
is no question [the new antitrust guidelines] are somewhat more
permissive. Their underlying philosophy is that mergers are a
very, very healthy phenomenon of the capital markets and should not
be interfered with except under exceptional circumstances."[83] What
is true of the United States, which was the world's pioneer in
antitrust legislation, now holds true for all DMEs, in varying
degrees.

A fourth method whereby the State supports TNCs is
intervention in specific sectors through export cartels--already
alluded to--and rationalization measures, of which there are many
institutional variants. Japan's MITI, for example, masterminded
the consolidation of major fibre giants in the late 1970s, reducing
their number from eight to four. In Western Europe another method
has been chosen: "crisis cartels" under EEC auspices.
Irrespective of the method employed, however, the object is to
streamline industries--invariably involving mass layoffs--and to
reinforce export capabilities.

Likewise, there are great variations in the degree and
techniques of State intervention in developing countries[84] to
underpin TNCs, ranging from the establishment of free trade zones[85]
to direct State influence on the domestic economy. In some
developing countries, the local oligarchies co-operate closely with
TNCs.

These internal oligarchies[86] become part of the TNC/TNB power
system through joint ventures and corporate kickbacks. Corrupt
practices have become an important and ubiquitous phenomenon in
international marketing and distribution, as is the partially
dissimulated recycling of these oligarchies' royalties and other
earnings--licit and illicit--into the TNB circuit. Despite
divergences in the workings of developing countries and DMEs with
TNCs, both are united in a wish to preserve the prevailing system
through a myriad of self-reinforcing strategies.

VI. LEADING DOCTRINAL CURRENTS

Any account like the preceding overview of the
interrelationship of the State, TNCs and TNBs is conspicuously and
deliberately absent from the major modern debates on world trade.
Such sedulous avoidance of the complexities inherent in the global
economy has limited the capacity of some leading theorists and
policy practitioners--designated by the authors of this article as
neo-liberals, North-South protagonists, and South-South
protagonists--to throw light on a swiftly changing reality.
Caution should be exercised in any attempt to classify individuals
exclusively into one of these categories. Quite often, an
individual would agree with one doctrine on a given issue, and with
another on other issues.

In no way can their prevailing propositions and therapies be regarded as innocuous, since they form the foundations of the prevailing international trading system, whose rules are set by GATT, the IMF, and the World Bank operating in concert with the State and TNCs.

A. The Neo-Liberals

As the 1982 Versailles summit of the leading seven DMEs showed, the dominant doctrine relating to the global market is that the eradication of trade barriers and liberalized market access constitute the panacea for the global crisis. This naive vision finds its counterpart in domestic policies propounded by monetarists and supply siders that have exacerbated the crisis in which the patient no longer responds to the therapy of high interest rates and the stimulation of mass unemployment.[87]
While the elimination of trade barriers has often been paraded as a cure for stagnating trade and crisis, in practice TNCs ignore such propositions. By the now routine practice of implanting subsidiaries, joint ventures and licensing agreements behind trade barriers, they circumvent these in order to exploit the gains of a protected market. But that is not all. For even if tariff and other trade barriers were dismantled, such a world market could in no way be construed as "free".[88]
Just as TNCs are best positioned to exploit current trade barriers, it is these same protagonists, through their dominion over world trade, who are also best poised to exploit what is embodied in the cliches of trade liberalization and freer access to markets. What neo-liberal theorizing is designed to achieve is to deflect the development and trade trajectory of those developing countries which seek to frame an independent development strategy (including tariff barriers) untrammelled by the control of TNCs.

B. North-South Protagonists

Certain international organizations could perhaps be said to have moved one stage beyond the neo-liberals' attitude to the world economy to focus attention on the future trajectories of the developing countries. Undoubtedly, the most audible and visual form of what might be called the "sentimental approach" is UNIDO's Lima target: the location of a quarter of global manufacturing in developing countries by the end of the century. Institutionally, this blueprint is commended by the World Bank and other agencies whose loans, advice and consent were instrumental in the setting up of numerous (usually light manufacturing) factories in several leading developing countries.

Such a policy drift presupposes a rapidly expanding world market that would absorb the new industrial output pouring out of the industrial plants of these developing countries. In a stagnating world market, already severely affecting the export capabilities of DMEs, it requires little imagination to perceive the devastating consequences of the inevitable competitive wars for developing countries. Even on the unrealistic assumption that world trade will resume growth at this juncture, the gains of trade will certainly not redound to workers and peasants in these countries, but rather to the familiar coalition of TNCs and segments of internal oligarchies. And the number of developing countries which may benefit is very small indeed.

C. South-South Protagonists

A third school of thought can be differentiated from the preceding two by reason of its emphasis on the slogan of collective self-reliance of developing countries in lieu of looking to DMEs for inspiration, assistance and growth. Such a stance at the formal level has won vociferous adherents in certain developing countries and United Nations agencies in consequence of the failure of commodity agreements and global negotiations. While the authors of this article recognize the minor achievements of joint marketing agencies set up by developing countries, such as UPEB's Comunbana (the banana community of the Union of Banana Exporting Countries), these achievements should not mask the grimmer realities mentioned in this article, namely that the entire global trading network is overwhelmingly under the dominion of, and geared to, the imperatives of TNCs.

The South-South idealized vision of a homogeneous developing world obscures, furthermore, the nature of those institutions in developing countries which have managed to make a few precarious inroads into the global market.[89] A first category consists of private corporations, including Tata, Birla, Samsung, San Miguel, and others, which in their institutional design and corporate motivations, are but paler carbon copies of TNCs. Although these companies and the TNCs compete in certain markets, their interests on the global economic chessboard often coincide.

A second group, commonly designated as producers associations, seldom recycle economic surpluses to development projects in the developing countries, and even more rarely to those projects which are not directly under TNC control. OPEC is an exemplar. Out of an OPEC investible surplus of $87 billion in 1980, a mere 7.6 per cent was invested in developing countries, a drop from 9.2 per cent in 1974.[90] Overwhelmingly, the remainder is recycled through TNB circuits, inevitably flowing to TNCs.[91]

Just as the bulk of OPEC's surplus is of marginal relevance to the development of developing countries, so there are no automatic mechanisms whereby the economic surpluses of other producer/marketing associations are channelled towards social formations other than the conspicuous consumption patterns of internal oligarchies. Nor can it be otherwise, for OPEC and its smaller emulators are—with few exceptions—entrapped in the TNC/TNB web.

VII. TNC's AND THE CRISIS

The irrelevance of these three leading doctrines of international trade and development is perhaps most clearly discernible in their inability to analyse the present crisis. The internationalization of goods, services and capital by TNCs, as depicted in this article, has contributed to deepen the most serious crisis in the world economy since the 1930s. While the authors do not contend that TNCs are the exclusive causes of the crisis, nonetheless certain interconnections can be traced by reference to five phenomena: unemployment, inflation, industrial stagnation, indebtedness, and mounting economic rivalries of major DMEs. Extensive research at a macroeconomic and sectoral level is needed for understanding more profoundly the causal links between TNCs and the crisis.

These five indicators should be analysed as grave underlying symptoms (as distinct from causes) of conflicts inherent in global capitalism. Although the strategies of TNCs are designed to manage the world market in a way serving their own interests, these interests, as they become more powerful and entrenched, come into conflict with the essential production and marketing needs of nations.

Merely in the OECD group of countries, the legions of unemployed already exceed the 30 million mark. The misery, which bare figures can never convey, is far worse in developing countries plagued by mass unemployment. What, it may be asked, has this suffering to do with the transnationalization of capital?[92] In their annexationist momentum, corporations are impelled to seize the newest technical innovations and adapt them to the whole range of their output and marketing operations. In this grand design, labour force liquidation becomes an overriding concern, as even a perfunctory reading of the annual reports of companies would indicate.

Inflation remains another phenomenon of the global capitalist crisis: most OECD countries were experiencing consistently high and unprecedented levels of inflation by the late 1970s. These inflationary pressures are the result of a multiplicity of factors, of which concentration and oligopolistic corporate structures and pricing strategies are contributory causes. While obviously there are sectoral variations, corporate concentration has fuelled inflation[93] through several techniques: price leadership in industrial sectors; speculation and manipulation of future markets by the large multi-commodity traders; and the mark-up practices of large-scale retailers. To this catalogue could be added the activities of those TNCs which are the major beneficiaries of the

$600 billion global arms industry which, being non-productive, remains one of inflation's classic breeding grounds.

Another component of the global crisis has been industrial stagnation in all DMEs, with certain sectors afflicted by a capacity utilization rate of less than 50 per cent. In part, this underutilization is imputable to the practice of TNCs globalizing their production, marketing and financing operations so that entire plants are transferred to developing countries, particularly to those in which labour militancy has been eradicated.

Unprecedently high and climbing debt levels, both national and personal, are another crisis index. The fragility of the debt pyramid, with borrowings of developing countries from TNBs already topping $600 billion (to which could be added borrowings from non-bank sources of another $156 billion), has already been touched on. The size of international indebtedness has long overshadowed another development, the ballooning personal debt within DMEs. In the United States, for example, personal debt exceeded $1,000 billion in 1977, and climbed beyond $1,500 billion four years later. Personal and national debts are interrelated, in the sense that the former exert tremendous upward pressure on the price of money, i.e. on interest rates, that developing countries must pay on their soaring debts to TNBs.

The depth of the crisis is further reflected in rising tariff and other protectionist bulwarks, and the deepening economic war between leading DMEs, seen in beggar-my-neighbour policies, escalating levels of protectionism, embargoes, competitive devaluations, interest rate battles, etc. Despite past liberalization efforts, nearly one-half of international trade is now under quantitative controls and the proportion is increasing. Paradoxically as it may appear, TNCs are both stimulators and beneficiaries of protectionism. Given the inherently unequal growth of the global capitalist economy, the gains among corporate contenders are no less disproportionate.

The present economic war had been foreshadowed by the relative eclipse of United States corporate power among the world's largest 200 corporations and the ascendancy of other corporate forces, notably those of Japan. Comment on this corporate _omnium bellum contra omnes_ has concentrated mainly on one of its manifestations, Japan's 1981 trade surpluses of $10.5 billion with the European Economic Community and $13.5 billion with the United States.[94] What this signalizes is the dominance--which is by no means necessarily permanent--of the Sogo Shoshas over rival corporations.

VIII. CONCLUDING REMARKS

The authors intend this article to stimulate further research and to serve as a source of reflection on the nature of power in the world market and on the manner and direction in which it continues to inflect the momentum of the global crisis. It refers to the harsh realities of the global market, which must be

seriously pondered by those social and political forces genuinely
striving to redefine their nation's relationship to State, TNC and
TNB power.

NOTES

[1]Agribusiness and industrial TNCs can be defined as corporations
with production facilities in more than one country, whereas
trading and other service TNCs may be described as business
entities that control assets in two or more countries. At
present, both sets of TNCs number around 18,000 worldwide.
Actually, the locus of TNC power is to be found in a much smaller
number. In the colourful prose of the Bangkok Bank Monthly
Review, "approximately 200 of them are the fearsome giants
clutching world business in their grip". (Bangkok Bank Monthly
Review, November 1981.)

[2]Trade's growing importance can be gauged by the rising proportion
of the major industrial countries--resources from exports of
goods and services. Between 1970 and 1980, exports as a per cent
of GNP rose from 4.4 to 8.4 in the United States; from 18.5 to 23
in the Federal Republic of Germany; from 9.5 to 12.5 in Japan;
from 12.8 to 17.8 in France;and from 15.9 to 22.2 in the United
Kingdom. (Union Bank of Switzerland, Business Facts and Figures,
September 1981.)

[3]Prominent national oligopolies exist in several countries in the
beer, distilled spirits, chemicals, pharmaceuticals, steel
and food processing sectors, to name but a few. International
oligopolies have become paramount in the past decade in
petroleum, cigarettes, automobiles and numerous primary commodity
trading sectors.

[4]Cross-subsidization is a common practice of conglomerates whereby
profits from one product line are used to subsidize the pricing
of another product below the level of long-term total costs.
This is an ideal marketing device for enlarging market shares in
a given sector by underpricing competitors.

[5]For a description of the role of contract-growing in but one
sector, see Randolf S. David, et. al., Transnational Corporations
and the Philippine Banana Export Industry (Quezon City, 1981).

[6]The pervasiveness of concentration was not confined to
corporations within the same national economy, as epitomized in
the classical merger (1902) of the American Tobacco Company (ATC)
and the Imperial Tobacco Company that created the British

American Tobacco Caompany (BAT). See Marketing and Distribution
of Tobacco; study prepared by the UNCTAD secretariat
(TD/B/C.1/205) (United Nations publication, Sales No.
E.78.II.D.14). Two major avenues of concentration were
horizontal and vertical mergers. Horizontal mergers are those
between companies producing identical or closely interchangeable
products. Vertical mergers are those between companies in a
buyer/seller relationship. See Coal Trades Review (London), 12
May 1899, quoted in J. M. Blair, Economic Concentration:
Structure, Behaviour and Public Policy (New York, 1972). See
also J. D. Bernal, Science in History (London, 1969); and H. U.
Faulkner, The Decline of Laissez-Faire, 1897-1917 (New York,
1951).

[7]In the 1940s, Mitsubishi, the second largest Zaibatsu, accounted
for over 10 per cent of Japan's production in many sectors,
including flour milling (50 per cent); aircraft engines (45);
sugar and electrical equipment (35); and shipbuilding, shipping
and iron ore (25). (Report of the Mission on Japanese Combines.
A Report to the Department of State and the War Department
Washington, D.C., March 1946, p. 133.) Despite marked
similarities between the pre-ware Zaibatsu and the modern Sogo
Shosha, there are three basic differences: the former operated
as traditional family institutions, whereas the latter are public
companies; the former controlled almost all major industries,
whereas the latter is more loosely connected to industry and
finance; the former had strong ties with the military whereas the
latter's State ties are with MITI. See Alexander Young, The Sogo
Shoshas: Japan's Multinational Trading Companies (Boulder
(Colorado), Westview Press, 1979).

[8]In different commodities, TNC control of marketing implies
different degrees of TNC market power. In commodities such as
tea, where a vertically integrated TNC buys tea from its own
plantations and sells it to its own blenders, market power (e.g.
control over pricing, contract specifications, etc.) is high.
In other commodities, where traders buy from large independent
producers and sell to large independent processors, market power
is less strong. The figure "roughly four-fifths" has been
derived from detailed studies over a period of many years of
several major commoditiy sectors, as well as numerous
discussions with traders, bankers and public sector officials in
the major OECD countries and numberous developing countries.
While the proportion handled by TNCs varies from year to year in
different commodities, "roughly four-fifths" is for the moment as
precise as the authors can get. For an elaboration of the
methodology employed in estimating TNC control of a given sector
see the report by the UNCTAD secretariat, "The marketing and
distribution system for bananas" (TD/B/C.1/162), December 1974.

[9]"One of the favourite pastimes of concentrated financial power,"
noted Congressman Wright Patman, Chairman of the US House
Subcommittee on Banking and Currency, "is promoting concentration
in non-financial industries. There is substantial evidence that

the major commerical banks have been actively fuelling the corporate merger movement." (Other People's Money", <u>The New Republic</u>, 17 February 1973.) He went on: "A 1971 congressional report, for example, found that the major banks financed acquisitions, furnished key financial personnel to conglomerates, and were even willing to clean out stock from their trust departments to aid in takeover bids. Thus Gulf and Western, one of the most aggressive conglomerates of the 1950s and 1960s (92 acquisitions involving almost a billion dollars in 11 years), expanded hand in glove with Chase Manhattan. Friendly representatives of Chase made funds available and provided advice and services that assisted Gulf and Western in its acquisitions. In return, in addition to the customary business charges for Gulf and Western's accounts and loans, Chase secured banking business generated by the newly developing conglomerate that formerly had gone to other banks, and was recipient of advance inside information on proposed future acquisitions."

[10]Conglomerate mergers are those between companies which are neither direct competitors nor in a buyer–seller relationship with one another.

[11]United States Senate, Subcommittee on Antitrust and Monopoly of the Senate Committee of the Judiciary, <u>Mergers and Industrial Concentration, Hearings before the Subcommittee on Antitrust and Monopoly</u>. <u>Acquisitions and Mergers by Conglomerates of Unrelated Businesses</u>, 12 May, 27 and 28 July and 21 September 1978, Washington, D.C., 1978, p. 151. "Large firms" refers to acquired firms with assets of $10 million or more.

[12]<u>Ibid</u>., p. 143.

[13]Hopes by curbing such annexationism through antitrust legislation are illusory, as acknowledged by U.S. Congressman Neil Smith in a contention relevant to all DMEs" "Enforcement of this nation's existing antitrust laws rests with whoever may be in power at the Justice Department; and, if and when those laws are enforced, the process is so time-consuming that the injured firms may be long out of business before a decision is reached." United States, House of Representative, Transcript Record of "Excerpts from the Testimony of Neil Smith before the Subcommittee on Livestock and Grains", 30 October 1979 (Washington, D.C.), p. 7. Likewise, Canada's Anti–Combines Branch of the Department of Consumer and Corporate Affairs is virtually powerless, as has been pointed out and elaborated by the Branch's director: "What we will have if this march of increased concentration continues is a national oligarchy in which a few dozen people will interact to bargain about the economic future of millions." (<u>New York Times</u>, 25 March 1980).

[14]These percentages are presented as indicators of the growing power of TNCs. To measure the top 200's actual share of global GDP would require precise breakdowns of value added by each firm. Such figures do not exist. Percentages are calculated from

Fortune's listing of leading industrial corporations.

[15]Both nationally and internationally, most giant TNBs are openly advertising their legal and financial expertise in the takeover field. This widespread advertising is exemplified in Commerzbank's announcement of its services for takeover and divestitures on a national and international basis. (Commerzbank, Wer gehort zu wem, Hamburg, May 1982.) The intimate connection between the largest TNCs and TNBs is clearly manifest also in the conditions of the loans that finance these acquisitions. Referring to the $3 billion credit arranged for the (eventually abortive) bid to acquire Conoco, Seagram stated that "thirty-one banks participated, an unusually small number for such a large credit, and the time in which the financing was accomplished was unusually short". (Seagram, Annual Report, 1981.)

[16]Foreign revenues are based on sales of manufacturing plants abroad. They exclude export revenues from the US and thus, in several cases, underestimate the transnational operations of firms.

[17]An illustrative case history is that of the US conglomerate R. J. Reynolds, whose subsidiaries straddle all three sectors: primary commodities (Del Monte, Aminoil); manufactures (Heublein, and cigarette operations); and services (Sea-Land, Kentucky Fried Chicken). The compulsion to diversify was the corporate expression of the dynamics of capital accumulation. "First having captured one-third of the US cigarette market," notes its centenary report, "the company could see a point of diminishing returns for growth potential." Adopting "an unrestricted approach towards diversification, Reynolds moved into entirely new areas, shipping and petroleum, on the theory that it made sense, when appropriate, to apply cash to any well-established business". (R. J. Reynolds, Our 100th Anniversary, 1875-1975, Winston-Salem, 1975.)

[18]According to Prof. Philippe Chalmin, "in fact it can be said that the bulk of international commodity trade is in the hands of about 50 companies, around which there is a great number of smaller companies dealing (physically or on paper) in one or another product, but quite irregularly". (P. Chalmin, "International Commodity Trading Companies", Journal of World Trade Law, November-December 1980, p. 539.)

[19]These figures, like those for manufactures trade, were estimated on the same basis as the figure for TNC control of global trade. See footnote 8. Another 1980 breakdown of primary commodity trade is provided by the World Bank: fuels--$535 billion; non-fuel primary products--$400 billion. (World Development Report 1981 (New York, Oxford University Press, 1981), table 3.1)

[20]UNCTAD, Fibres and Textiles: Dimensions of Corporate Marketing Structure (TD/B/C.1/219 and Corr.1) (United Nations publication,

Sales No. E.81,II.D.1), para. 138.

[21]Derived from interviews with commodity trading officers in several large TNBs in New York and London.

[22]For data concerning the growth of intra-firm transactions, see Economist Intelligence Unit, "Multinationals and world trade", Multinational Business, No. 4, 1981, pp. 16-19.

[23]For a detailed account of transfer pricing, see Robin Murray (ed.), Multinationals Beyond the Market: Intra-Firm Trade and the Control of Transfer Pricing (Sussex, The Harvester Press, 1981).

[24]Indicative of the massive sums involved are the findings of the US Securities and Exchange Commission (SEC), which revealed that between 1973 and 1980 at least $46 million in currency transaction profits were improperly shifted from Citicorp's branches in Europe, where taxes are high, to branch banks in the Bahamas, where taxes on profits are much lower. Yet such investigations, ethically desirable as they are, undoubtedly expose only a minuscule segment of these practices. See International Herald Tribune, 14 and 17 September 1982.

[25]A number of pharmaceutical companies have booked as much as two-thirds of their global profits in Puerto Rico to exploit its minimal taxes. (International Herald Tribune, 27 January 1981.)

[26]It has been estimated that in 1978 these numbered 270 operating in 66 countries. (See Marcel Barang, "La proliferation des zones franches en Asie", Le Monde Diplomatique, January 1981.)

[27]Other, albeit lesser, institutions involved in manufactures trade are large independent trading companies which are often large-scale conglomerates, e.g. Jardine Matheson and other "hongs" in Hong Kong.

[28]Fortune, 9 August 1982.

[29]Fortune, 24 August 1981; the statement takes into account sales made through foreign affiliates.

[30]These include the major military contractors: Boeing (the No. 1 US exporter); General Electric (3); United Technologies (7); McDonnell Douglas (8); Lockheed (10); and the two big auto companies: General Motors (2) and Ford (4).

[31]Labour Research, September 1981.

[32]Earlier, they were the trading muscle of the conglomerate Zaibatsu until the latters' dissolution by the United State occupation authorities after the Second World War. After the initial big antitrust drive had ebbed, the Shoshas were reconstituted to become even more powerful extensions of Japanese

industrial corporations.

[33]Calculated from Forbes, 5 July 1982.

[34]Noteworthy shifts have occurred in the percentage shares in industrial exports of developing countries accounted for by the big seven between 1965 and 1980: Taiwan (4 to 18); the Republic of Korea (2 to 15); Hong Kong (19 to 14); Singapore (7 to 9); Brazil (2 to 7); India (18 to 5); and Mexico (3 to 2). In short, merely three developing countries account for almost half of the total. (Computations of the UNCTAD secretariat.)

[35]In 1980, the top three exporters' percentage shares of total exports of developing countries in specific sectors were: footwear 85 per cent; apparel 68; leather 63; machinery and transport equipment 48; textiles 39; and chemicals 30. (Calculated by the UNCTAD secretariat, August 1982.)

[36]Growth rates estimated by O. Havrylyshyn and I. Alikhani, "Is there Cause for Export Optimism? An enquiry into the existence of a second-generation of successful exporters", World Bank Staff Working Paper January 1982. These include (ranked by 1979 manufacturing exports): Malaysia ($1,557 million); Thailand ($1,196); Philippines ($998); Colombia ($649); Tunisia ($604); Morocco ($460); Indonesia ($448); Uruguay ($295); Cyprus ($227); Peru ($214); Sri Lange ($121); and Jordan ($97). Concentration is no less marked, with the top three accounting for over half of the group's manufactures exports.

[37]In the US, for example, under tariff items 806.30 and 807.00 import duties are chargeable only on the portion of production which represents "value-added" in the exporting countries. According to figures from the US International Trade Commission, over $7.1 billion worth of manufactured goods entered the US under these tariff items in 1977.

[38]According to one observer: "The second wave of free trade zones is proceeding with full force. The huge economies of China, South Asia and Indonesia are being cajoled, tempted, or prodded into putting their labour force for hire in the international market by setting up free trade zones". (Ho Kwon Ping, "Birth of the Second Generation", Far Eastern Economic Review, 18 May 1979.)

[39]In the early 1970s, there were 22,700 producing units in the US apparel industry, averaging 59 employees per unit; by the end of the decade the number had dropped to 15,000. In the mid-1970s, the top five corporations accounted for 11 per cent of industry sales, and the top 10 for 15 per cent. Projections by Kurt Salmon Associates suggest that, by the end of the century, there will be between 75 and 100 apparel manufactures, each with annual sales exceeding $100 million and accounting for about 75 per cent of total industry sales. Ths could very well be an underestimate. (Business Week, 14 May 1979, and United States,

Department of Commerce, U.S. Industrial Outlook, 1975: with Projections to 1980, Washington, D.C., 1976, pp. 224–225.) For a thorough analysis of development in the apparel sector, see UNCTAD, Fibres and Textiles: Dimensions of Corporate Marketing Structures, op. cit.

[40]Kenneth Baker, "Speech for the International Production, Engineering and Productivity Exhibition", London, 2 March 1982, quoted in British Business, 5 March 1982.

[41]The New York Times, 4 March 1982.

[42]Between 1970 and 1979, services grew faster than both agriculture and industry in low-income countries, industrial market economies and capital-surplus oil exporters. Only in middle-income countries did industry grow slightly faster than services. (World Bank, World Development Report 1981, op. cit., Annex, table 2.)

[43]World Invisible Trade Bulletin, Committee on Invisible Exports, quoted in Financial Times, 2 August 1982. Dollar figures were calculated from "invisible trade" totals given in SDRs.

[44]Wall Street Journal, 10 February 1982.

[45]For a more extensive treatment of tourism, see Robert Wood, "Tourism and Underdevelopment in Southeast Asia", Journal of Contemporary Asia, vol. 9, No. 3, 1979: Michael Peters, International Tourism (London, Hutchinson, 1969); and A. J. Burkart and S. Medlik Tourism: Past, Present and Future (London, Heinemann, 1974).

[46]World Tourism Organization, Regional Breakdown of World Tourism Statistics, 1975–1979, Madrid, 1981. In 1964, tourists had spent a mere $10 billion.

[47]Direct foreign investments include establishment of subsidiaries and branches abroad, equity participation in foreign companies for management purposes, and loan repayments by subsidiaries. Income from direct foreign investment comprises dividends from overseas units, profits earned by branches, and interest earned.

[48]OECD, International Investment and Multinational Enterprises (Paris, 1981), p. 39.

[49]The US share of the global foreign direct investment stock was 48 per cent in 1976, having slipped gradually in the 1970s. US direct investment abroad totalled $213.5 billion in 1980. Assuming the US share had dropped to 45 per cent in 1980, the global total would have been around $470 billion. Calculated from data in ibid.

[50] From computer printouts supplied to the authors by the US Commerce Department in 1981. In the UK, earnings from direct

investment abroad rose from L718 million in 1971 to L3.6 billion
in 1981. (See Central Statistical Office, United Kingdom Balance
of Payments (HMSO, 1982), p. 32.)

51The $37 billion earned from the $213 billion US direct investment
abroad in 1980 far outstripped the foreign profits on $65 billion
of foreign direct investments in the US. This single item was
the major factor offsetting a US goods trade deficit. (Wall
Street Journal, 10 February 1982.) Likewise, in Japan, the $1.46
billion in profits from direct investment abroad far surpassed
the $596 million in profits earned by foreign business investment
in Japan, and accounted for 15 per cent of the current account
surplus during 1981. (Japan Economic Journal, 6 July 1982.)

52World Invisible Trade, Committee on Invisible Exports (London,
1980).

53See Frederick F. Clairmonte, "World Tobacco: A Portrait of
Corporate Power" in William Finger (ed.), The Tobacco Industry in
Trasition (Toronto, 1981).

54The first figure is derived from computer printouts supplied by
the US Department of Commerce, November 1981. The latter
figureis from UNCTAD, Fibres and Textiles, op. cit., p. 134.

55Bank for International Settlements, Fifty-First Annual Report
(Basle, 1981).

56Calculated from OECD and US Department of Commerce data.

57International Herald Tribune, 29 October 1981.

58Annual growth in the flow of new loans to non-oil exporting
developing countries dropped from 62 per cent (1978-1979) to 11
(1979-1980) to 6 (1980-1981). (Calculated from Bank for
International Settlements, Fifty-First Annual Report, Basle,
1981.) In the current crisis of international finance, it has
been estimated that by autumn 1983, no more than 100 TNBs—down
from 1,100 in autumn 1982—will be participating in large
syndicated loans to foreign countries. And only the very largest
(e.g. Morgan Guaranty, Deutsche Bank and Lloyds) will be actively
leading the syndications. (See Business Week, 20 September
1982.)

59It should be emphasized that these figures underestimate total
advertising outlays as they exclude other promotional gimmicks,
including sponsorship of sports events. US advertising billing
of $61.3 billion in 1981 is approximately half of the world
trade. (Advertising Age, various issues; The Economist, 20
September 1980; International Herald Tribune, 11 June 1980.) As
expected, there are huge variations between countries in the
volume of resources deployed in advertising, ranging from an
estimated 0.04 per cent of GNP in Ethiopia to over 2 per cent in
the United States. (A Survey of World Advertising Expenditures

in 1977 (Mamaroneck, New York, Starch I. Hooper, 1979, p. 11);
and J. Walter Thompson Co., Trends in Total
Advertising Expenditures in 25 Countries, 1970-1979 (London, A
report prepared by the JWT Unilever International Co-ordination
Group, 1980, pp. 3, 4.))

60The global shre of the US dropped from 54 per cent in 1977 to 51
per cent in 1979. (Hooper, op. cit., p. 5 and International
Herald Tribune, 11 June 1980).

61These include: Dentsu (1980 global billings: $2.7 billion);
Young & Rubicam ($2.2 billion); J. Walter Thompson ($2.1
billion); McCann-Erickson ($1.7 billion); Ogilvy & Mather; Ted
Bates; BBDO; Leo Burnett Co.; SSC & B; Foote, Cone & Belding;
D'Arcy-Mac Manus & Masius; and Doyle Dane Bernbach. Advertising
Age, 20 April 1981. The marketing leverage of several leading
advertising agencies, as in the case of the TNCs themselves, is
reinforced by their conglomerate reach. Within a short span,
Young & Rubicam annexed 15 corporations to become a leader in
such related fields as public relations, package design, sales
promotion, direct marketing and advertising to professional
groups. (See Wall Street Journal, 2 March 1982.) Corporate
expansion to form a more coherent corporate galaxy is but one
strategy. Another, no less effective strategy, is the build-up
of joint ventures between the largest advertising agencies in
order to further penetrate a given market. Dentsu and Young &
Rubicam (the world's two biggest advertising agencies) already
have a joint venture in Japan and similar associations are
planned for other markets. Dentsu has already appropriated
around a quarter of Japan's advertising billings. (Financial
Times, 4 June 1981.)

62Advertising Age, 25 May 1981. Over half of the billings of the
five largest US advertising agencies emanate from abroad, a
figure applicable to leading advertisers from other DMEs.
(Advertising Age, 16 February 1981.)

63Total freight costs in world trade topped $108 billion in 1980.
(UNCTAD, Review of Maritime Transport, 1981 (TD/B/C.4/251), 5
April 1982 (forthcoming United Nations publication).)

64Brewers Digest, January 1981.

65Philip Kotler and Ravi Singh, "Marketing Warfare", American
Journal of Business Strategy, winter 1981.

66As Ralph Nader observes: "The posture of two agencies (the
Antitrust Division of the US Justice Department and the Federal
Trade Commission), with a combined budget of $20 million and 550
lawyers and economists trying to deal with anticompetitive abuses
in a trillion-dollar economy, not to mention an economy where the
200 largest corporations control two-thirds of all manufacturing
assets, is truly a charade." (Quoted in M. J. Green, C. B. Moore
and B. Wasserstein, The Closed Enterprise System (New York,

Grossman, 1972), p. xii. See also M. S. Lewis-Beck "Maintaining economic competition: The causes and consequences of antitrust", in Journal of Politics, vol. 41, 1979.) By 1980, 20 US corporations employed over 100 in-house lawyers each (AT & T 902 and Exxon 384). Du Pont allocated 39 corporate lawyers exclusively for antitrust work.

[67]See A. S. Eichner, The Megacorp and Oligopoly: Micro-Foundations and Macro-Dynamics (Cambridge, Cambridge University Press, 1976). See also Paul Baran and Paul Sweezy, Monopoly Capital (New York, Monthly Review Press, 1966), pp. 69-71.

[68]These operations are detailed in UNCTAD, Fibres and Textiles . . ., op. cit.

[69]OECD, Restrictive Business Practices of Multinational Enterprises: Report of the Committee of Experts on Restrictive Business Practices (Paris, 1977), para. 57.

[70]See UNCTAD, Fibres and Textiles . . ., op. cit., and "The structure and behaviour of enterprises in the chemical industry and their effects on the trade and development of developing countries", study prepared by the UNCTAD secretariat (UNCTAD/ST/MD/23), 1979.

[71]A detailed description of the operational mechanisms of one such cartel in the Japanese machine tool sector was given in a 163-page unfair trade practices petition filed with the Office of the US Trade Representative. (See Wall Street Journal, 3 May 1982.)

[72]New York Times, 26 July 1981.

[73]Business Week, 19 July 1982. According to an article in The New York Times (22 August 1982): "Such 'countertrading' and related transactions account for 30 per cent of world trade these days, and the percentage is growing depite concern that such deals undermine free trade."

[74]General Electric's trading company is supported by 765 distributors, sales representatives in 140 countries, contacts at

[75]Business Week, 19 July 1982.

[76]The political aspects of these relations have recently been spelled out by one of the leading authorities on US corporations: "The giant corporation . . . tends to spend almost as much energy manipulating government policies for its own benefit as it does competing in the marketplace, improving productivity, or planning technological breakthroughs. It seeks governmental favors, subsidies, and privileges. It pleads for relief from 'onerous' burdens like clean air, pure water, industrial safety, and energy conservation reguations. Above all, it expects the government to compensate it for its own mistakes which, given the firm's giant

size, are likely to be of gigantic proportions. The result is, more often than not, government bailouts—whether in the form of protection from import competition or protection from bankruptcy—and such bailouts seem to be becoming standard operating procedure in the US economy." (See Walter Adams, "Mega-mergers spell danger", <u>Challenge</u>, March–April 1982, p. 13.) 120 affiliated companies, and 156 service shops in 63 countries.

[77]<u>The Economist</u>, 14 February 1981. For an economic and legal treatment of State export credits, see "Export credit facilities: An international comparison", <u>Midland Bank Review</u>, autumn 1980.

[78]Boeing, the biggest US industrial exporter, had $3 billion (out of $5 billion) of its 1980 exports financed by the Export–Import Bank. (<u>International Herald Tribune</u>, 20 May 1981.)

[79]In this respect, the vital factor which clinched a $275 million US subway contract for Kawasaki Heavy Industries was a subsidized $126 million loan from the Japanese Export–Import Bank. (<u>Financial Times</u>, 19 March 1982.)

[80]In 1980, governments of DMEs provided $5.5 billion of such subsidized credits, led by France ($2.3 billion), the UK ($1.0 billion), Japan ($566 million) and the US ($315 million). (<u>International Herald Tribune</u>, 30 October 1981.)

[81]For particulars of the range of subsidies and companies involved see the <u>Financial Times</u>, 14 June 1982.

[82]In four high technology sectors, the investments of MITI and the Pentagon were distributed as follows: the former invested (1980) $100 million in fibre optics, $150 million in semiconductors, $320 million in advanced computers and, since 1975, $115 million in lasers. In precisely the same sectors, the Pentagon spent $180 million, $210 million, $250 million, and $130 million. (<u>International Herald Tribune</u>, 2 December 1981.)

[83]<u>International Herald Tribune</u>, 6 June 1982.

[84]The policies of developing countries, whose primary goal is to boost exports, at times generate side effects which benefit the biggest TNCs. In Indonesia, for example, TNCs to which government contracts are awarded are required to buy back an equivalent value of Indonesian goods to be sold abroad. One Japanese executive has said: "This policy wil be of special benefit to us." The reason is that it is primarily the Sogo Shoshas, with their extensive worldwide trading networks, that have the leverage to exploit such an opening. (<u>Financial Times</u>, 22 December 1981.)

[85]Even in certain socialist countries, conspicuously China, FTZs are being established as a device for breaking into the market.

Pepsico, in its ware to dislodge Coca Cola from the top spot in Hong Kong's soft drink market, is constructing a bottling plant in Shenzhen Special Economic Zone which offers fiscl incentives to TNCs hoping to supply Hong Kong from a lower cost base. (Financial Times, 26 May 1982.)

[86]While these may trace their historical origins back to compradorism and the comprador capitalists of the pre-1914 and inter-war periods, the compradors operated in an entirely colonial context (and a quasi neo-colonial one in China) and their relations with the colonial State machinery were at best tenuous. In contrast, modern internal collaborationist oligarchies emanate largely, but not exclusively, from three social groups: the newly ascendant military, the civil service and the indigenous bourgeoisies. Their defining characteristic is their identity with the interests of foreign capital, although their personal gains and roles differ with the historical, cultural and political specificities of capitalism in the developing country concerned. For a far-reaching discussion, see F. Clairmonte and J. Cavanagh, The World in Their Web: the Dynamics of Textile Multinationals (London, Zed Press, 1982).

[87]Referring to the "other-wordly mathematical models" of an important segment of neo-liberal theorists, the Nobel prize winner Wassily Leontief has said: "Page after page of professional economic journals are filled with mathematical formulas leading the reader from sets of more or less plausible but entirely arbitrary assumptions to precisely stated but irrelevant conclusions." (Quoted in The Economist, 26 June 1982.)

[88]Paradoxically, the alleged neo-liberals (and their various sub-formats) are harking back to an idealized free-trade era (1840-1860) while ignoring the march of global capital accumulation that has annihilated the laissez-faire model, and given rise to oligopolies and conglomeration throughout the industrial, agricultural and services sectors.

[89]For a critique of the South-South approach, see Srikant Dutt, "South-South Patterns of Exploitation: India's New Relationship with Developing Countries", Journal of Contemporary Asia, vol. 10, No. 4, 1980.

[90]Bank for International Settlements, Fifty-First Annual Report (Basle, 1981, p. 97).

[91]Describing the mechanisms employed, the Deputy Governor of the Saudi Arabian Monetary Agency stressed that he was "only too aware of the economic interdependence of the Free World . . . Direct lending by OPEC is inefficient because it is unlikely that governments can be as flexible as the commerical banks; and it is difficult for governments to act on a solely commerical basis". It follows that "the problem of recycling is essentially not one of liquidity. OPEC surpluses are recycled naturally (italics

added) back into the financial centers of the industrial world".
(H. E. Sheikh Abdul Latif, "Recycling", Bangkok Bank Monthly
Review, vol. 22, No. 6, June 1981.)

[92]The neo-liberals and their supporters have ceased to look for the
causes of unemployment within the system. Rather, and by no
means surprisingly, GATT's director of economic research suggests
that unemployment is the price to be paid for "freedom". "Le
chomage est, pourrait-on dire, le prix a payer pour la liberte,
et pour les progres que la liberte rend possibles". Such a
contention is not far from an equally vacuous definition of
unemployment as: "le chomage peut en general etre considere
comme le temps que l'on passe a chercher un nouvel emploi". (Jan
Tumlir, "Le chomage: un privilege moderne", Le Temps
Strategique, Geneva, summer 1982.)

[93]The profound inflationary implications of these takeovers have
been admirably elaborated by one of the leading North American
corporate executives, Mr. Edgar Bronfman, chairman of the Seagram
Company, that participated in the biggest ($7.5 billion) takeover
battle in corporate history. "In the takeover battles that we
have all seen recently", he writes, "and which are still going
on, billions of dollars have been borrowed on a short term basis
from the banking system to finance the acquisition of one company
by another. When too many would-be borrowers are seeking credit,
the cost of money goes up. This is especially true when the
Federal Reserve system considers inflation a worse hazard than
recession and is thus loath to increase the money supply—to
print more money." (The New York Times, 29 September 1982.) The
inflationary effects of such massive and continuous TNC
annexations would not have been as strong were it not for certain
fiscal exemptions by the State. As Mr. Bronfman once again
points out: "If the interest on corporate takeover money
borrowed specifically to buy the common stock of another
corporation were not tax deductible, as it now is, such activity
would be sharply curtailed."

[94]Financial Times, 26 January 1982.

The Multinational Corporations and Inequality of Development

ARGHIRI EMMANUEL

I. AN INCOMPLETE RECORD

One of the few points on which the Group of Eminent Persons appointed by the Secretary-General of the United Nations to examine the problem of multinational corporations (MNC) agreed was the penury of 'useful and reliable' information. The majority of members emphasized this in their reports.[1]

Such a situation regarding a subject which has held pride of place in political and economic literature over the past decade is surprising in itself. It ceases to be so when considered in relation to the eminently ideological nature of this discussion which, as such, tends to overlook and even elude the data in favour of the deductions.

Not being a specialist on the subject myself, I could, in writing this article, assess the discrepancy between the inflated nature of the discussion and the meagreness of the facts. For example, the most recent figure I could find for the total 'stock' of foreign investments in the developing countries dates from 1967 and was published in 1973.[2] Moreover, since the majority of the statistics dealing with the activities of the multinational corporations are mere estimates, very considerable discrepancies, which reflect the subjectivity of their authors, are commonplace. Thus, as regards the effects of the expatriation of American capital on employment in the United States, two United Nations estimates give a loss of 400,000 and 1,300,000 jobs respectively, while a similar estimate by the Harvard Business School reports a gain of 600,000!

From **INTERNATIONAL SOCIAL SCIENCE JOURNAL**, Vol. XXVIII, No. 4, 1976, (754-772), reprinted by permission of the publisher.

The champions of the cause

In this speculative field it is as well first of all to distinguish the apologists from the detractors. The formers' argument is simple. The multinationals merely eliminate the distortions caused by the discontinuity of political frontiers. They tend to render the economic space of the world as homogeneous and as unadulterated as that of the neo-classical free-trade models. They tend, therefore, to rationalize the system and maximize its yield.

Since this represents no specific argument in favour of the multinationals it may be said that there is no mystification either. The multinationals do no more than restore, as well as they can, an ideal state of affairs which has been upset by the interventionism of national bureaucracies. They illustrate the original superiority of private enterprise over the management of governments. What is good for General Motors is good for the United States and, a fortiori, for Brazil.[3]

In so far as this approach is coherent and adds nothing whatsoever to the neo-classical traditional argument that the profit motive results in the optimal allocation of factors, there is nothing to add to its equally traditional refutation either.

The right-wing adversaries

With the adversaries things are less simple. First, they must be divided into two major groups. The criticisms of the first spring from a defence of the existing economic system, those of the second from questioning it.

Objectively, the circles constituting the first group form an integral part of the system or even occupy dominant positions in it. As such, they enter either directly or indirectly into conflict with the rival power of the MNCs.

Ideologically, they see in the MNCs a misuse of the system. They put forward the same ideal of competition as the upholders, but unlike them find that the multinationals, owing to the oligopolistic nature, cause even more serious distortions and discontinuities than do the interventions of the nationalist State.

This group includes both international organizations, such as the Organisation for Economic Co-operation and Development (OECD), the World Bank and even the North Atlantic Treaty Organization (NATO), and national States.[4] The major trade union organizations of the advanced countries also fall under this category.

Special mention should be made of the AFL-CIO, which has carried on the most virulent and systematic campaign against the multinationals. Its attitude is the least 'ideological' of all in the sense that it does not encumber itself with any reference to the common good of mankind. It openly concerns itself with the exclusive interests of one section of the 'labour aristocracy' of

the world--the workers of the United States. Here, its analysts
find themselves on solid ground.
Any attempt to show them that they are making a technical
error is vain. It consists of changing standards upon transition
from the initial period, during which the outlay of funds exceeds
income, to the subsequent period when income exceeds new
investments. In speaking of the former, the positive effect on the
balance of trade is invoked; in speaking of the latter, it is the
positive effect on the balance of payments that is put forward.
The artful trick here is isolating the operations of the
multinationals from the rest of the economy. It is true
enough that exports of capital are nothing but exports of unpaid
goods, compensated for by the acquisition of foreign assets.
Consequently, when in the first stage a multinational corporation
sets up in business outside the frontiers of the United States and
sends dollars there, it is obvious that, assuming the monetary
reserves in the remainder of the world remain unchanged, these
dollars will be used to purchase the means of production, failing
which, incidentally, it is difficult to see how the multinational
corporation in question could establish itself abroad. It is
therefore true that, at the time when it leaves American territory,
the multinational corporation creates additional employment in
order to produce the additional exports which are the material
form its 'export of capital' will take.
But, still assuming that reserves remain unchanged, the
subsequent re-entry of dollars by way of dividends and interest
payments can only take place by means of imports of goods not
compensated for by exports from the receiving country.
Consequently, when during the second period--that of the maturing
of the investments--re-entries begin to exceed outgoings, the
effect on the balance of trade (which alone affects the level of
employment) will be negative by that amount although positive where
the balance of payments is concerned. Paradoxical though it may
appear, the period detrimental to the working class is not that
when capital is exported but that when its fruits begin to flow
back into the investing country.
These imports, which are the counterpart of dividends, are not
necessarily made by the multinational corporations themselves.
They do not, therefore, appear on their balance-sheets, with the
result that figures as divergent as 1.3 million jobs less and
600,000 more are obtained. But it is easy enough to understand the
process if we imagine it taken to its logical conclusion, where
American capitalists will have sent all branches of industry abroad
(except those whose products are not transportable), at which
point, having become 'coupon clippers', they will be able to import
any consumer goods they want and pay for them with their
dividends.
The external balance will then merely show imports of goods on
one side and receipts of funds on the other. The proprietors of
General Motors will be no worse off. Their works will be located
in Mexico or Brazil where wages are lower. From these countries
and others they will be able to import their private cars and other
consumer goods, plus, perhaps, the ingredients of the soup for
distribution to the destitute, which they will have to organize for

their former workers. The external accounts of the nation will be balanced, and so will the budget. The dollar will be in a strong position. The workers will, so to speak, be 'marginalized'. They will then be free either to follow General Motors abroad and join the other 'emigrant workers' or take jobs as domestic servants, the employment of whom by the rentier-capitalists concerned will increase in proportion as their remunerations fall.[5]

The AFL-CIO, therefore, sees things clearly from its own point of view. Exports of capital are prejudicial to the American working class. Whether, from the point of view of the 2,000 million inhabitants of the developing countries and of the 1,000 million who are hungry and from that of human progress generally, this possible re-proletarianization of some of the American wage-earners is a negative or positive feature is quite another question.

And those on the left

We now have to consider the second group of adversaries, who are much more numerous. To the extent that, in contradiction with their revolutionary projects, they slide irresistibly towards the attitudes inherent in the system of capitalist relations and end up by perceiving the MNCs as the constituent element of a variant of the system and criticizing it as such for the same reasons and in the same terms as its detractors to the right, they become the most 'ideological' and the most productive of mythology of all. At worst, the issue is not one of after the MNCs what? but of no MNCs at all, not of the destruction of the system with or without the MNCs but of the destruction of the MNC within the system. At the best, the system would have to be destroyed all the same but the only reason for doing so is the impossibility of getting rid of its MNCs. This attitude is not unrelated to the historical constant of a petit-bourgeois opposition to the capitalist system which proceeds from a confused, subconscious basis in the 'Paradise Lost' of pre-capitalist trading relations and periodically breaks out into reactionary campaigns against machinery, urban living, trusts, cosmopolitanism, and so on and whose 'national roads' to socialism are today one of the variables of life's potential hazards.

And yet it needs to be said that, so far as the MNC is concerned, it is not the theoretical attitudes of communist parties which are the most mystifying. On the contrary, by refusing to recognize that the MNC has a specific character and by considering it merely as a geographical extension of State monopoly capitalism, they do not in the least contradict their frankly reformist position towards this type of society, already considered as a variant of the capitalist mode of production. Moreover, since this position is chiefly adopted by the theorists of certain European parties who are increasingly turning aside from the problems of the developing countries and are only concerning themselves with the minor aspects of the problem, so to speak--in other words the aspects directly affecting their respective countries: American penetration on the one hand and drain on national capital on the other--their arguments are of only secondary interest here.[6]

This applies even more to the social-democrat parties, which are openly reformist, and to the liberal theorists, progressives and non-engaged Marxists.

We can also leave aside the attitudes adopted by certain theorists of the East European countries who reconcile scientific abstraction with the judicious pragmatism of their respective governments, in something like the following manner: (a) first, they contribute to the universal pillorying with the routine arguments; (b) next, they declare outright that the MNCs (which, having been proscribed in the capitalist world, have probably become more accommodating) will find opportunities for joint and mutually advantageous operations in socialist countries and, in addition, will enjoy these countries' well-known respect for agreements and the stability of their governments; (c) they explain the contradiction between (a) and (b) by the fact that, in their case, the strategic 'heights' of the economy are well in hand and run no risks. Foreign investors can make money but never dominate them.[7] Since everyone knows that foreign investors only want to make money and have no particular ambitions to dominate the 'heights', this is a perfectly safe statement which reassures one side without worrying the other.

'Ideological' occultation is mainly to be found on the left, in the multitude of small groups claiming to preach revolutionary Marxism which, as always happens in periods when, on account of material circumstances, social movement is slowing down, miss their target and resort to verbiage. In particular I am referring to that infinity of shades of opinion concerning the 'Internationalization of capital'.

To top it all, the very fact that the detractors of the MNCs are recruited in all camps confers on their argument an outstanding respectability, with the result that dissertations proliferate, thus making quite a contribution to the general confusion.[8]

Space does not allow me to examine these innumerable doctrines one by one. Nor does it seem to me to be necessary. Both the specific arguments against the MNCs and the myths overlap with the most widely divergent views of the world. I shall therefore discuss the problem thematically, giving priority to those concerned with development.

II. EXPORTS OF CAPITAL GENERALLY

A distinction should perhaps have been made between the MNC problem and that of exports of capital generally. The former are merely one vehicle for the latter. However, in the case of the least developed countries, private foreign investments are nearly always direct investments in practice, since such countries have no extensive undertakings of their own, and a portfolio investment can only take the form of minority participation or the acquisition of bonds in an existing foreign undertaking which has, consequently, been the result of previous direct investments.

As for direct investments themselves, except for settlers' undertakings which are only a marginal phenomenon today, the present trend towards widening the definition of the MNC makes any distinction regarding the status of the investor pointless. On the other hand, the distinction between exports of capital from developed countries to others on the one hand and movements of capital between the developed countries themselves, on the other, is still very important. On this basis attempts have been made to interpret the present 'internationalization' of capital as a movement new in quality and much superior in quantity to similar movements in the past. So far as quality is concerned, that is a matter of appreciation, and I shall put forward my own analysis later. But quantity is a matter of figures, and, as such, the statement is false and even grossly misleading.

In 1914 the 'stock' of United Kingdom's accumulated assets abroad came to 4,000 million gold sovereigns. Whether one converts this figure on the basis of the value of gold or on that of purchasing power, it comes to about 130,000 million 1974 paper dollars. In 1974 total United States public and private assets of all categories (including short-term export credits) amount to $265,000 million, or in other words just about double in absolute figures. But a comparison in absolute figures between a United Kingdom with 45 million inhabitants in 1914 and a United States of more than 210 million in 1974 has little significance, and in relative terms it turns out that British external assets in 1914 accounted for about double annual national revenue of the period, whereas those of the United States today account for only one-fifth.

If we took into account the economic 'surface' of the countries invested in at these same two dates, the results would be about the same.[9] Whether, therefore, from the point of view of 'overaccumulation of capital' and its need for outlets beyond the frontiers of the 'centre' or from that of aggression to which the 'periphery' is subjected, whether focusing on departure or on the arrival of capital, we find that the present figure of $265,000 million which gives rise to such emotion is laughable, since the United Kingdom was doing ten times better sixty years ago.

If we add the other OECD countries we arrive at a total which bears about the same relation to the 1974 American assets alone as did the assets of the only four investing countries in 1914 (United Kingdom, France, Germany and the United States) to the British assets of that time alone, i.e. about double.

But this would give rise to a consolidation problem, since these countries invest in each other. This consolidation would have the effect of changing the results in favour of my position. Thus, while the United States had 265,000 million dollars' worth of assets in the rest of the world in 1974, the rest of the world (in effect, the rest of the OECD countries) had $187,000 millions' worth of assets in the United States at the same time. This reduces the net assets of the United States from $265,000 million to $78,000 million.[10] This was not the case with the United Kingdom in 1914 when investments in the other direction were negligible.

If we leave aside total assets and deal with direct investments in the developing countries only, which is the true purpose of this article, we shall find that in 1974, out of a total 'stock' of $118,600 million of American direct investments, those which had been made in the periphery amounted to only $28,500 million, including $19,600 million in Latin America, which is not exactly the least developed region, by a long shot. Only $8,900 million remained, therefore, for the really underdeveloped countries--that is, more than 1,500 million people.[11]

But that is not all, for out of the amount $4,700 million is invested in oil which, from every point of view, is a special case and which, incidentally, concerns only a small proportion of the populations of this group of countries. For all other industrial activities, such as mining, manufacturing, etc., therefore, only $4,200 million remains for this group (this is 3.6 per cent of the total and represents less than $3 per inhabitant or $7 per worker, just enough to equip each of them with a good screwdriver).[12]

So far as the direct investments of the OECD countries as a whole are concerned, all that is available is the 1967 figure, as I said earlier. This is $8,200 million for countries other than those of Latin America, not including oil.[13] If we apply to this figure the same coefficient as that represented by the increase in total foreign direct investments between 1967 and 1974, we arrive at an approximate figure of $16,000 million. (Here again I am speaking of accumulated assets and not of flow).

This is an extremely generous estimate in view of the fact that, over the same period, the share accounted for by investments in developed countries was increasing, whereas withdrawals of investments from developing countries were increasing as a result of nationalization. However, it will suffice to compare this figure with American investments in Canada alone, which came to $28,300 million in 1974, to see immediately that the Third World countries, far from having been invaded by foreign capital, have been starved of it.

If we list the countries of the world, first in decreasing order of capital received, from Canada to India via Europe, Latin America and the developing countries of Africa and Asia, and secondly in decreasing order of their GNP per head of the population, we shall find that, apart from a few exceptions, the two lists coincide exactly. So either there is no causal link between foreign capital and underdevelopment, in which case the multinationals cannot be accused of having caused a deadlock at the periphery, or the deadlock occurred not because international capital flowed in but because it has stayed out.

Exports of capital and Marxism

Although, in the present climate of intoxication, this latter conclusion appears paradoxical, it fits in perfectly well not only with the most traditional view of affairs but also with the most orthodox Marxist teaching. Lenin did not feel that he was innovating when he wrote in his Imperialism, the Highest Stage of Capitalism that the effect of exporting capital was to accelerate the development of the countries to which it was sent and slow down the development of the countries from which it came.[14] Before him, Marx had already written in the 'Preface' to the first German edition of Das Kapital that 'the most industrially developed country merely shows to those which follow it on the industrial ladder the picture of their own future', and in his article in the New York Daily Tribute dated 8 August 1853 he explained how the building of the railroad in India would inevitably result in the development of India, whether the British wanted it or not.

By a sort of communicating vessel process, the backward region drained off the surplus from the advanced region. As Rosa Luxemburg pointed out, the cities of northern Italy sent their surplus capital to finance the development of Holland during the sixteenth century. During the seventeenth and eighteenth centuries, Dutch capital contributed to England's take-off. British capital, in turn, took the road to North America and Australia during the eighteenth and nineteenth centuries. Local saturation discharged the surplus of nutritive substances from the top to the lower slopes.

When Britain had already completed her industrial revolution at the beginning of the nineteenth century, continental Europe had not even begun. This did not make it the 'periphery' of Britain: it became a 'Britain' in turn. Marx was not wrong in considering that there was only a time-lag between development and underdevelopment.

What was it that caused such a rapid saturation at the top and the cessation of internal accumulation, causing capital and technology to be poured out on to the external valleys? It was the lack of elasticity in the internal market which, beyond a certain point, discouraged investments. This lack of flexibility was due to the relative stagnation of wages at a level close to the cost of the biological reproduction of labour. The system provisionally avoided grinding to a halt by expatriating its surplus capital. But this was only putting off the evil day, for there was not an inexhaustible number of Indias. And when all the Indias of the world had become Britains, the system would have exhausted the margins of development of the 'productive forces which it is wide enough to contain'.[15]

Something happened towards the end of the nineteenth century and this conventional Marxist picture ceased to reflect reality. This was a radical change in the distribution of power among the classes within the bourgeois parliamentary system in the industrialized countries, which had the effect of finally lifting

the price of manpower out of the swamp of the mere physiological
survival of the worker. In order to appreciate the effect of this
event it suffices to remember that, for thousands of years, the
worker's wage was the most stable economic magnitude which existed.
The purchasing power of the average European worker round about
1830 differed very little from that of the worker in Byzantium,
Rome or the Egypt of the Pharaohs. In the following century and a
half it was multiplied by ten.

There followed a reversal of the conditions for accumulation
at the international level. In the central countries, the domestic
market underwent expansion at breakneck speed. Moreover, since the
mechanism of unequal exchange enabled the overpaid workers of the
centre to take greater advantage of the consumers of the Third
World than of the capitalists of the country which paid them, all
barriers to the capitalization of profit broke down. The trade
union struggle in a way extricated the system from the dead-end
against its will, at least temporarily, by settling the argument
between the two prerequisites of investments: widening the market
without reducing profits.

That being so, capital no longer needs to run off to the
Antipodes; it finds means of accumulation at home, or at least in
the region of the 'centre'.[16] Its movement to less-developed
countries, far from being a continuous, regulating flow, has become
merely casual. Perhaps Marxist theorists were right when they
believed that exports of capital had a levelling effect. The only
thing is that such exports have just not taken place towards a
certain category of countries, except in insufficient quantities.

Those who speak of deadlocks apparently have good reason to
suppose that these quantities are still excessive. In that case,
if they cannot explain why, they should at least tell us how these
countries could develop without these quantities. The United
Kingdom took 200 years about it. During the century preceding the
First World War, her national revenue increased at a rate of 1 3/8
per cent a year.[17] In the absence of the 'short-cut' involving
foreign resources of capital and technology, is there any reason
why the countries in question should advance within the capitalist
system any quicker than Britain did in former times? If not, do
they find acceptable a rate which causes the GNP to double
every fifty years and will ensure that the average developing
country of today will reach the present level of France in the
year 2176?

But perhaps those in favour of 'self-centred' development do
not mean development 'within the capitalist system', and here
arises the major misunderstanding in the controversy. As Bill
Warren points out, there is a constant shift from the conception of
development to that of socially satisfactory development.[19] We
simply forget to make the distinction Marx made between 'the
development of productive forces' and 'their appropriation by the
people'.

It is forgotten that capitalism is not a bad dream but a
social system which has a historical part to play; a system which,
as it developed, gave not only gadgets and pollution but also
widespread literacy and an average life expectancy of seventy years
instead of forty. And that, consequently while awaiting the social

revolution, it is by no means a matter of indifference for people whether they live in India or the United States, no matter what similarity may be recognized between the production relations in these two countries.[20]

III. THE CONCRETE POSSIBILITIES OF DEVELOPMENT

That does not mean to say that, in present historical circumstances, India can become the United States by accelerating her development through foreign financial aid. The reasons why such financing is falling off have already been explained, but the author would go even further. He thinks that in no circumstances can 'Indias' ever become 'United States', even if they wanted to. The United States are the United States only because the others are not. The level of development reached there considerably surpassed the over-all potentialities of the capitalist system on a world scale. In the capitalist sense, they are overdeveloped. Quite naturally, they can only be so because all round them there are sufficient developing countries which are exploitable.

It may perhaps still be possible to generate this extraverted accelerated development in some small country if the little international capital available is concentrated there. This will be because the others do not follow it along the same road. For the developing countries generally, such an attempt would be futile, quite apart from any normative considerations. The only road open to them then is to skip the capitalist stage. It may then be hoped that, if only from the strictly economic point of view, the mobilization of domestic resources and the rationalization of production will advantageously replace the few and increasingly problematic crumbs available to them by way of foreign finance.

All this, however, arises from calling into question the system and not of the MNCs. If it were a matter of socialist development, it would be frankly ridiculous to reproach the MNCs for not acting as the vehicle. And if it is a matter of capitalist development, the only valid criticism would be one making a distinction between the MNC and the national capitalist corporation.

Such a distinction has never been made. In particular, it has never been clearly explained how the nationality of the owner can change the nature of the capital. When people speak of centres of decision they forget to tell us in what way the location of the centres affects the nature of the decisions and why. Two-thirds of all the capital in Canada belongs to foreigners, 80 per cent of whom are Americans. On the other hand, India is the country par excellence where industrialization was carried out almost exclusively by the local bourgeoisie. It is not very clear what the Canadian people--who are among the richst in the world--would stand to win if the 'centres of decision' moved from the skyscrapers of Manhattan to the office blocks of Montreal, or what the people of India--among the most poverty-stricken of the world--would stand to lose further if her capitalists handed over their factories to others holding a Japanese or German passport.

Very much to the contrary, for whenever we find, rightly or wrongly, that in any particular aspect the behaviour of the MNC differs from that of the traditional capitalist undertaking, the specific character of the MNC is generally to its advantage.

Transfer of technology

One of these alleged deviations, and perhaps the most important, is that concerning the notorious problem of 'appropriate' technology. From time immemorial, the entrepreneur has been blamed for wasting human labour by selecting his technology on the basis of the 'paid labour time' and not the 'total labour time' devoted to production. Market forces gave 'to each his due', to the Ghanaian worker his hoe and to the American worker his tractor. Cheap muscles drove out grey matter and machinery from the low-wage countries, while grey matter and machinery took the place of expensive muscle power in the developed countries. The situation reached deadlock precisely because the rarefaction of grey matter and machinery maintained productivity at a low level, thus forcing the cost of muscle power even lower. This lowering of cost in turn rendered grey matter and machinery less profitable. We then though that only deliberate intervention by the State, apart from capitalist rationalism, was capable of breaking the vicious circle and putting the 'inappropriate' tractor into the African plantation; otherwise it was difficult to see how development could ever occur.

Now we are told that the MNCs--the most capitalistic-minded of all capitalist undertakings--have discovered the dodge of locating heavy technology in regions where labour is cheap, or in other words exactly what the Soviet Union did during the early five-year plan and what any socialist planner is supposed to do. And instead of rejoicing at the good news, we are supposed to meditate on the diabolical strategy of the multinational corporations which waste capital (their own) exclusively in order to cause underemployment in the receiving countries.

In order to support the 'appropriate' technology argument (which basically is just a euphemism for 'intermediate' technology), reference is sometimes made to Chinese practice. But, in fact, the basic Chinese principle is the plurality of technologies which is just about the opposite of the 'intermediate' technology suggested by critics, such as E. F. Schumacher. The latter dilutes the available capital among all the production units involved. The former introduces straight away the pioneer technology entailing the highest organic composition in as many units as possible, regardless of the fact that the shortage of capital prevents its immediate spread over the rest of the branch. Macro-economic calculations show that this is the method giving maximum long-term output. However, it is an impossible method in a market economy where competition forbids any disparity between the conditions of production in different undertakings. It is only possible in a planned economy.[21]

The following passage from a text by Mao is very explicit on this point:[22]

> The fact that we are developing small and medium-size industries on a large scale, although accepting that the large undertakings constitute the guiding force, and that we are using traditional technologies everywhere, although accepting that foreign technologies constitute the guiding power, is essentially due to our desire to achieve rapid industrialization.

It appears to me that the 'appropriate' technology is the very thing to be outlawed. An appropriate technology for poor countries can only be a poor technology; an appropriate technology made to measure for underdeveloped countries can only be an anti-development technology.[23]

Rehabilitating the neo-classical theory which had been previously pilloried, certain people complain that the technology introduced into developing countries by the MNCs does not correspond to the resources available there. Nor should it. If it did, the mix of factors would be frozen and the deficiencies reproduced ad infinitum. If 'transfer' is seen as a vehicle of domination, it is forgotten that, if there were no transfer at all, the technological domination of the centre would be even more decisive.

'Autonomous' technology

Sometimes it is not an 'appropriate' technology but a national, so-called 'autonomous' one that is called for. Without going into details on this particular point, it may be said that, apart from questions of political prestige, an 'autonomous' technology is the most disadvantageous product that can exist, since technology is the most under-valued commodity on the international market. Although it is the product of the industrialized countries, it is offered at abnormally low prices. This is due to the fact that the direct or indirect assumption by the state of part of the R and D expenditure over-compensates by a wide margin both the high remuneration of the technology production factors and profits in all forms, even if excessive, of the seller.[24]

'Imitative' technology, particularly in Japan and Italy, had undoubtedly been good business for these countries. Italy, by importing the majority of her technology during the 1950s and devoting only 0.6 per cent of her GNP to R & D, as against 3.09 per cent in the United States and 1.51 per cent in France, achieved a remarkable increase in productivity, and it is estimated that 72 per cent of economic growth between 1954 and 1959 was due to technological progress.

Sometimes, moreover, a qualitative dimension is attached to

this argument, and a certain impoverishment of culture arising from the standardization of consumer goods throughout the world is deplored.[25] Undoubtedly, in addition to the problem of means, there is also trade-off regarding ends. And it may be thought that social revolution will not be content with organizing the production and distribution of the motor-car and television set more rationally but will profoundly modify them so as to adapt them to a less individualized and more human environment and way of life. But it would be utterly absurd to increase, in the meantime, the number of makes of cars and colour-television processes, with all the wastage and duplication involved, under the pretext of escaping from the domination of General Motors and the SECAM, just as it would be childish to keep the wooden plough in order to safeguard the authentic traditions of the people.

The cost of imported technology is another favourite subject for MNC myths. UNCTAD puts forward the figure of $1,500 million as the total annual cost for the Third World as a whole.

Even if this figure is correct, it would only account for about 0.4 per cent of the GNP, whereas expenditure on R & D in the most advanced OECD countries came to about $50,000 million, that is 2 per cent of the GNP of the same year.[26]

But the UNCTAD figure covers a composite statistical category. It includes not only the cost of patents, licences and know-how but also trade marks, royalties, the leasing of films and television programmes and all the revenue of intellectual property generally. It is obvious that a considerable part of this expenditure forms part of the balance of services rather than that of technological transfers.

The local outlet prerequisite

Another specific feature of the MNC which is vaguely considered to generate prejudice but which, if it really exits, is eminently advantageous, is its independence of the domestic market of the receiving country. Since the main problem of capitalism is not to produce but to sell, less traditional capital was attracted by the low wage rates of certain countries than was discouraged by the narrowness of the local market associated with such wages. This lack of capital in turn prevented growth and hence wage increases. The result was deadlock.[27]

In theory the solution was production for exports alone. But except for standardized primary products, such an operation appeared to transcend the fief of the traditional capitalist. In any case, it has never occurred.[28] The MNC, with its own sales network abroad and, even more, its own consumption in the case of a conglomerate, would not be put off by the lack of 'pre-existing' local outlets. It would, according to Gy. Adam, take advantage of both the low wages of the periphery and the high wages of the centre. I have no idea of the relative importance of the phenomenon. Here, as elsewhere, statistical information is lacking. Albert Michalet considers that it is very extensive in quantity and very important from the point of view of quality.[29] All I can say is that, if this is so, this gives us for the first time the possibility of breaking the most pernicious vicious circle which was holding up the development of the Third World. It is rather a matter for rejoicing.

Enclaves and profit repatriation

It is somewhat contradictory to accuse the MNC of being an enclave and a nuisance at the same time. If the MNC becomes a real enclave, it ceases to be a nuisance, since its relations--whether good or bad--with the national economic space are restricted, and if its effects on the environmental economy increase it ceases ipso facto to be an enclave.

Let us take the extreme case of an enclave--a free zone. In exchange for authorization to close off a few acres of beaches and allow goods to transit, the foreigner pays certain dues. This is a net profit, and there is no problem about it.

Now let us suppose that the foreigner asks authorization to set up, in the perimeter covered by the authorization and with his own resources, a workshop for repairing his equipment or even a factory to produce something of no concern to the surrounding power. He offers extra payments in the form of corporation tax, say 50 per cent of the profits. Can there be any good reason for refusing? Would one be concerned with what he was going to do with the other 50 per cent? Next, he asks if he can employ some nationals as workers. I would not mind betting that, not only would one agree, but one would be opposed to his bringing his own workers from the other side of the ocean if some jobs could be entrusted to the local population.

Naturally, this is the point where the unilateral flow of advantages from the enclave to the receiving country ceases. The wages paid are no longer a 'net profit'. Labour power is provided from which the enclave extracts a value higher than its price--a surplus value. But one is an underdeveloped capitalist country, and like all underdeveloped capitalist countries has an underemployment situation. So rather than send workers to the multinational's factory on the other side of the sea, it is much better if the factory is set up on the other side of the road.[30] Lastly, one will obviously be pleased if the enclave purchases from local traders and producers as much as possible of the supplies it needs and pays for them, as it does for the wages, in foreign currency.

The situation becomes more involved if the enclave overlaps with the national economy to a greater extent, i.e. when it ceases to be a real enclave, particularly (a) if it sells part of its production on the domestic market at prices higher than world prices by taking advantage of protective tariffs; (b) if it raises funds locally and appropriates the difference between the interest rate and the profits;[31] or (c) if it exploits natural resources, mineral or other, inside the enclave and exhausts them, paying only an abnormally low ground rent, which is itself determined by the fact that the country is underdeveloped and insufficiently urbanized.

All the above is a matter of calculation--a calculation which makes sense only if, as W. M. Corden suggests, we neglect the relations of the enclave with the outside world and confine ourselves to those with the country containing it. From this point of view, the much-debated question of the repatriation of profits assumes quite another meaning. Under conditions of underemployment which are the common lot of capitalist countries both of the centre and of the periphery, capital, no matter where it is invested, produces 'value added', i.e. the gross total of wages, rents, profits and taxes. The profits and some of the rents can be repatriated; the remainder accrues to the local economy. Except in specific cases such as those mentioned above, it is obvious that the centre suffers a loss of income as compared with the situation where the same capital is invested within its own frontiers, but it is difficult to see what the receiving company loses as compared with a situation where this capital had not come at all.[32]

Complaints about the repatriation of profits are merely a reminder that the total value added is more than the value added minus the profit. This is not only trite; it is contradictory. For one cannot regard the MNC as the supreme evil, while at the same time hoping it will grow and multiply by investing its profits locally. Moreover, there is absolutely no difference either in practice or in theory between repatriation of profits by a foreigner and the expatriation of capital by a citizen, and we have already shown that such expatriation is indeed prejudicial to the country of origin. The fact that, in this case, it is not the centre but the periphery which is exporting makes no difference. It is not as an importer but as an exporter of capital that the peripheral country suffers when the profits of foreign capital are repatriated.

Capital, whether multinational or national, is governed by opportunities for its investment. Since there is a sharp difference between wages in industrialized and developing countries, these opportunities are no longer a decreasing but an increasing function of development. The same capital reinvests its profits in Canada ad infinitum and becomes Canadian; it withdraws them as quickly as possible from Zaire and becomes an enclave there. This has a cumulative effect on the development gap to the very extent that the MNC does not thwart this process; despite its alleged possibilities of 'delocalizing' production in relation to markets, it is less specific than is claimed.

Accommodation invoicing

As has already been noted, criticism of the MNC often deals

with possible abuses. This, from the pen of Marxists, is heart-rending. Marx always emphasized that exploitation is not cheating but the inevitable effect of the mechanics of the system. This is what separates revolution from reform. Fraud can always be eliminated by reform, but the system can only be changed by revolution. However, it may be supposed that there would not have been such an outburst regarding 'fictitious prices' if the spirit of the former had not in fact today overcome the spirit of the latter.

In concrete terms the problem is rather more complex than is thought. There are two chief reasons which may induce an MNC to under- or over-invoice the goods dispatched from one establishment to another: taking advantage of differences in taxation or evading exchange controls.

The second reason may, in fact, be prejudicial to the developing countries since that is where exchange controls are most widespread. But the first generally acts in their favour, since their levels of taxation are much lower than those of the industrialized countries. There is a tendency, therefore, for the one to cancel out the other. Possible abuses are not necessarily actual abuses.

The MNC an instrument of domination

Another feature which is criticized is that the MNC constitutes a one-way conveyor belt for political behests. Since the legal framework of the corporation's hierarchy is based on the laws of property, certain legal prohibitions may be conveyed from the parent company to the subsidiary, but not vice versa. Thus, the laws of the United States may require the headquarters of General Motors to forbid its subsidiary in Brazil to export certain equipment to China, whereas Brazilian law cannot require the local subsidiary to forbid the parent company in the United States to do anything.

First, we are here concerned with the direct intervention of a non-economic factor, and the main loser is the MNC itself. It also presupposes that the MNC is centralized and loyal to its country of origin to an extent that is not proven. On the other hand, there is a multitude of concrete examples to the contrary, the most spectacular of which was the refusal of Exxon-Philippines to refuel the United States Fleet at Subic Bay in 1973 out of respect for the Arab embargo.[33]

Lastly, so far as the balance of power between the MNC and the local government is concerned, it is simply not true that the former is in a stronger position than a national undertaking would be. It seems obvious to me, for example, that, whatever the foreign interferences, Allende would still be alive and in power if he had been content to nationalize Anaconda and had not touched national capital. In the same way I am quite certain that Saudi Arabia would not have been able to nationalize Aramco so easily if its capital had been Arab.[34]

IV. CONCLUSIONS

The majority of critics who take an interest in Third World problems do not represent the MNC as a factor contributing to increased tension--with which, probably, nobody would quarrel--but as a primary, structural force, a factor determining the 'freezing' of the periphery on the one hand and contributing to a corresponding increase in the development of the domination countries on the other. This is unacceptable.

The attitude of writers who base their opinions on revolutionary Marxism is particularly interesting. Having first isolated the MNC as the characteristic evil of the century, they study it concretely as an excrescence of the system. Nevertheless, they continue to see salvation outside the system in planned local development. This contradiction between the analysis and the conclusions makes it possible to agree with the latter while at the same time disagreeing with the former.

For it is either one or the other. Either the economic calculations of the MNC are essentially the same and conducted in the same way as those of any other capitalist undertaking, in which case in order to explain the deadlock in certain countries, it is enough to show how the capitalist optimum differs from the social optimum, even though the very existence of the MNC has a certain amplifying effect; or the MNCs calculations are basically (and not just circumstantially) in contradiction with those of the independent firm, in which case the conclusion cannot be avoided that a simple anti-MNC policy and a return to a free market economy would liberate centrifugal forces.

NOTES

[1]c.f. 'The Impact of Multinational Corporations on Development', United Nations, 1974, E/5500/Rev.1 ST/ESA/6.

[2]'Multinational Corporations in World Development', United Nations, 1973, ST/ECA/190.

[3]This is the viewpoint sometimes expressed by Business Week. It

is also more or less that of Harvard. Lastly, it is also roughly
the one expressed by some members of the Group of Eminent Persons
who insisted on submitting remarks and expressing reservations
individually on the 1975 report.

[4]Particularly those of the industrialized countries. Those of the
others are content to manoeuvre in such a way as to profit from
the guilt complexes of the multinationals to increase their
bargaining power, without ever calling into question the
principle of foreign investments. On the contrary, they make a
virtue of attracting as much of them as possible by means of
increasingly generous 'investment codes'.

[5]Certain features of this imaginary situation are already
appearing today in some of the oil-exporting countries, where
disapproportionately high 'external' revenues exist side by side
with a very low domestic level of employment. Nineteenth-century
Great Britain, moreover, bore the distinctive signs of the
process outlined above. At the beginning of the nineteenth
century the balance of trade was positive and revealed a net
export of capital. Subsequently, there was a radical change in
the situation. There were net imports of capital, particularly
from 1870 onwards, which went on increasing till 1914, with a
negative balance of trade and, as a corollary, a trend towards a
parasitical economy, the stagnation of domestic industry, and an
increase in the number of unemployed or people in unproductive
employment. As recently as 1934, domestic servants accounted for
11.8 per cent of the working population.

In the United States, since the Second World War, the cycle
has, to be sure, been less pronounced, since not only is the
volume of operations concerned, in spite of all the talk about
it, much smaller in relative terms than that of Great Britain in
former times but also, as a result of public international aid of
all sorts combined with a partial accumulation of dollars in the
reserves of the other countries, investment operations are
diluted within a greater volume of other financial movements.
However, a reversal of the trend was already preceptible in 1971,
when the formerly regular balance of trade surplus ceased to
exist, while on the other hand the balance of payments, which had
formerly shown a clear deficit, began to move towards a surplus.

[6]cf. P. Herzog and G. Kebabdjian, _Economie et Politique_, April–May
1974: 'The export of capital is today still not the constitution
of a-national capital but the external effect of
over-accumulation on national bases.'

The theory of over-saturation is more or less shared by
Rowthorn, Hymer, Baran, Sweezy, etc. Albert Michalet asks why,
if that is so, the corporations move the productive process
instead of merely exporting the produce, and the SIFI Group asks
why capital moves from one central country to another when both
are equally affected by over-accumulation.

[7]cf. G. Adam, 'New Trends in International Business', _Acta
Oeconomica_, Vol. 7, 1971, and 'The Big International Firm and the

Socialist Countries', International Colloquy, CNRS. Typical in this connexion was the naive disappointment of participants in the 1974 Europe-Third World Seminar in the Netherlands at the following statement of the Romanian position: 'Romania is not prepared to boycott the MNCs or reduce her relations with them because: (a) such relations are already at a minimum; (b) the MNCs are a reality of the capitalist system; (c) such relations are founded on principles of reciprocity and mutual advantage; (d) Romania is still a developing country.'

Lastly, Richard Barnet points out that 'China . . . has already begun to allow foreign corporations to use its hugh labour pool to manufacture exports', Global Reach, p. 67, New York, 1974.

[8] In the most conservative universities throughout the world, a doctorate thesis criticizing the MNCs does not raise any objection on principle. A revolutionary student can thus remain 'pure' without endangering his chances of getting a degree. The result is that recently the proportion of social science students who choose this subject has become frightening.

[9] Resulting in negligible quantities at both dates so far as the periphery is concerned. But no matter how small the share of the periphery at all times, it is obvious that, in domestic relative terms, the share was much greater in 1914 than today. For, apart from a few exceptional cases such as India and Japan, there was not a shop, a chimney or a mile of railroad in the nowadays developing countries which, in 1914, was not owned by foreign capital. We are a long way from that situation today if only as a result of the various nationalizations which have occurred.

[10] cf. Survey of Current Business, October 1975.

[11] cf. Survey of Current Business, September-October 1975. I differ from current doctrine in considering that the difference, from every point of view, between Argentina and even Mexico and Chile on the one hand and India and Central Africa on the other, is infinitely greater than between the former group of countries and those of the OECD generally. I even consider that difference in the extent to which foreign capital has penetrated is not unrelated to differences in the level of development between the two groups. But the figures given pere show that, even in the case of Latin America, the favourite target of multinational capital, the penetration is much less than is generally thought.

[12] It should be emphasized that this is the value of the accumulated assets and not of the annual flow.

[13] cf. Table 14 in Multinational Corporations in World Development, New York, N.Y., United Nations, 1973.

[14] Complete Works, Vol. 22, p. 263, Paris, Editions Sociales, 1960.

[15]K. Marx, Avant-Propos au Manuscrit de 1859, Pleiade, Vol. I, p. 273 (literal translation).

[16]This is something which was lost sight of by those who find the 'investment codes' too generous and consider it advisable to give the governments of developing countries practical advice on how to avoid overbidding and come to an agreement on dictating their conditions. They forget that capital has not only a choice between one developing country and another but also the choice between expatriating itself and staying put.

They also forget the first 'investment code' ever was the 'Law on concessions' adopted by the U.S.S.R. in 1922 and promulgated by Lenin himself; this not only granted to foreign capital a maximum of the usual advantages (fiscal privilege, repatriation of principal and dividends, etc.) but also granted something which the developing countries of today are particularly unwilling to accept--international arbitration in the case of disputes between the investor and the Soviet Government.

However, in adopting Resolution No. 2626 on 24 October 1970, the United Nations General Assembly was farsighted enough to recommend the developing countries to adopt 'the appropriate measures to attract, encourage and use effectively foreign private capital . . and propose conditions which would encourage continued investments'.

[17]According to Schumpeter, who is not very far from the results of calculations by Bairoch and others.

[18]However, in an ad hoc report of the United Nations experts dated 1951, the situation was described with remarkable simplicity. The developing countries lacked capital and technicians. To provide both, they needed an enormous amount of time, which was not available. The only solution, therefore, was to import them.

[19]cf. 'Imperialism and Capitalist Industrialization', New Left Review (London), No. 81, September-October 1973. Also A. Emmanuel, 'Myths of Development versus Myths of Underdevelopment, op. cit., No. 85, May-June 1974.

[20]This does not mean that development of the productive forces is an end in itself. The end is man. Granting, however, that the development of the productive forces is neither the same thing as, nor the sufficient condition of, social and human progress, it nevertheless remains its necessary condition. Moreover, indirectly and whatever the time-lags, development as such does generate social progress, if only because it makes the existing system ripe for overthrow and replacement by a new one. It is, therefore, unscientific to try to assess development in terms of its direct social effects and deny the existence of the former merely on account of the momentary absence or even negative features of the latter. One cannot dissociate development from its social content, we are told. Very well! Are we then to say that the United States is undeveloped, if it so happens that its social structure appears to us as unsatisfactory? And what about

those who suggest that Cuban society is more human, or less inhuman than that of the United States? Are they supposed to claim that Cuba is also more developed than the United States? Yet it seems to me that in the everyday intercourse nobody, whatever his social philosophy, has ever had a communication problem, when people at large say that the United States is more developed than Cuba. Is that not the proof that the dissociation between 'development of the productive forces' and their 'appropriation by the people' is already being made implicitly , even by those who oppose it explicitly?

[21]cf. C. Bettelheim, Le Probleme de l' Emploi, p. 106, Paris, 1952, (literal translation).

[22]Hu Chi-Hsi, Mao-Tse-Tung et la Construction due Socialisme, p. 85, Paris, Le Seuil, 1975.

[23]'There cannot be', says Boumediene, 'one industry for the under-developed and another industry for the developed'.

[24]In the United States, for example, the Federal Government finances between a half and two-thirds of R & D directly.

[25]Though much more subtly and avoiding carefully any normative statements, Albert Michalet also refers to this 'homogenization'. cf. 'Transfert des Technologies', Tiers Monde, January-March, 1976.

[26]But this is only direct expenditure.If indirect expenditure, particularly the entire educational and cultural infrastructure, libraries, universities, and so on which the private producer of technology enjoys, were included, the cost to society would amount to more than double the sum acknowledged by the statistics.

[27]This is what Rosenstein-Rodan calls the difference between the private and social marginal products, which constitute a decisive barrier to the installation of new industries in a developing region.

[28]Except, they say, in the case of plastic Christmas trees manufactured in non-Christian Japan.

[29]Michalet considers that this is the real syndrome of the internationalization of the capital cycle, and here he is right. No matter what the quantitative extent of the phenomenon, it is an unusual novelty, since it is the work process itself which is affected by it. On the other hand, the circulation stage, internationalized according to Christian Palloix, has in fact to do with trade, and international trade has always existed. It existed even before national trade.
  As for the internationalization of money-capital, either this is a phrase devoid of meaning or it means merely the convertibility of currency. But what the MNCs may be doing in

this field today, with difficulty, laboriously and skating on the thin ice of the law and exchange control regulations, was done a century ago quite openly and without formalities by the man in the street simply by going to his money changer or banker. So if it is considered that overcoming obstacles is a more internationalist situation than one in which there are no obstacles, this is a problem of terminology which is quite beyond me.

[30]It would certainly make no sense to have boats bringing metropolitan workers into the 'enclave' and carrying back on their return trip the 'Gastarbeiter' of the host country. One should certainly be able to persuade the MNC's subsidiary that everybody would be better off if this absurd coming and going ceased and everybody worked where he lived.

[31]There is little chance of this happening in the last developed countries, such as those of Africa south of the Sahara, or if it did the funds would not be for investment but would be squandered on luxuries or find their way to Switzerland, if the MNC did not make use of them.

[32]cf. Robert Gilpin, United States Power and the Multinational Corporation, London, 1975.

[33]For the conflicts between the American MNCs and the State Department, see an interesting article in Politique Aujourd'hui by Joseph D. Collins, January–February 1975. T. Dos Santos notes astutely that ' . . . the very interests of national economies . . . determine an objective determination which places pressure on subsidiary undertaking which are obliged to conform if they do not want to be marginalized'. 'Les Societes Multinationales, une Mise au Point Marxiste', 'L'Homme et la Societe', July–September 1974.

[34]Ambassador William Eberle, in his statement to the National Executive Conference in Washington on 7 February 1974, recalled that there had never been a case where an MNC had won a conflict against a sovereign government of any sort or size. (True enough, but we should add: after the failure of Mossadegh in 1952 and since the fiasco of the Suez gunboat operation in 1956.)

Role of Multinational Corporations in Developing Countries: Policy Makers' Views

S.C. JAIN
Y. PURI

The debate about the multinational corporation and its role in developing countries has been going on for as long as these corporations have been around. Usually, this debate has taken the form of attacks on multinational enterprise. These attacks commonly focus on the economic, social and political ills caused by the multinational corporations in the developing host countries. Elaborating these effects, Louis Wells[1] argues that critics of foreign investment in developing countries are concerned about the cost of such investment and the efficiency of utilization of resources employed by the multinational enterprise. He contends that such an investment can be harmful to the host country if the costs are higher than some ideal investment. Also, the resources are used less efficiently if the national income would have been higher with the same resources deployed in another project. These results are indeed possible due to the protection and subsidy sometimes afforded the foreign investor. Raymond Vernon[2] narrows down the major conflict areas to the choice of products and services supplied and the choice of technologies used by the multinational enterprises in developing countries. He argues that the products and services offered may not serve the national interest. There is also a preference for capital intensive facilities in developing countries which is not consistent with their labor factor costs. Though this bias may be introduced by the host governments themselves who demand the latest technology, the end result is the creation of another source of conflict. The following quote from Vernon[3] highlights the concern: "...one group of leaders in the developing countries tends to see the linkage of the national economy to foreign-owned enterprises as a betrayal of the national interests. Other groups tend to see such links as opportunities for national growth, provided the links

From **MANAGEMENT INTERNATIONAL REVIEW**, Vol 21, 1981, No. 2, (57-65), reprinted by permission of the publisher.

are properly managed and carefully exploited...The interests of
governments and those of foreign-own enterprises in developing
countries are usually compatible in some degree; both sides, at any
rate, usually think they will gain by a continuation of the
relationship. But elements of conflict are always present, in the
sense that one or another would like to acquire more of the
available pie."
The purpose of this study is to present the general feeling that
prevails among the leadership and policymakers in developing
countries. Our contention was that since most of the criticism of
the multinational corporation emerges from the developing
countries, the analysis should be based on probings there. A
questionnaire was developed to study four broad areas of
interaction between the multinational corporation and the
developing country. These four areas are: (1) Contributions made
by the multinational corporations to the economy of the host
developing country; (2) Problem areas that are a source of conflict
and concern; (3) Expectations of the developing countries from the
multinational corporation; and (4) Legitimate responsibilities of
the developing country as a host country.
The results presented here are based on eighty-four usable
questionnaires returned by respondents in thirty-five countries.
The questionnaires were mailed to respondents in seventy-three
countries selected from the list of one hundred and ten countries
as developing countries in the World Tables[4]. Countries with
non-market economies were not included in this study. Considering
that the policymakers were asked to respond to about eighty
questions, the response rate is quite satisfactory.

I. CONTRIBUTIONS OF MULTINATIONAL CORPORATIONS

The decision of a business firm to invest in a foreign country must
be a positive sum game for the investment to be a long-term viable
venture. Both the firm and the host country should derive positive
benefits. The first part of this study focused on the issues
involved here. The questionnaire sought the opinions of the
respondents in the areas of capital usage, technology usage,
employee training in the host country, contributions to the
economic development of the host country, etc. The results have
been summarized in Exhibit 1 (see Annex).
In the area of capital usage, the multinational corporations comes
out with flying colors in the eyes of the host country planners.
Multinational corporations are credited with not only bringing in
foreign money for their investments, but also with helping in
capital formation locally. Additionally, the presence of
multinational corporations in a developing country is instrumental
in attracting capital both from private sources and international
organizations. This is understandable since established
multinational corporations in a country breed confidence among
other investors to favorably consider that country for expansion

possibilities. Usually, once a few multinational corporations
establish themselves in a country, their banks, insurance
companies, accounting firms, and advertising agencies closely
follow them. Thus, coupled with capital inflow, multinational
corporations perpetuate more business into a country. Efficiency
of capital utilization is also perceived as an important
contribution by the host countries. Nurtured in the free
enterprise system with competition to face both at home and abroad,
multinational corporations have to be efficient to operate
profitably. This trait of multinational corporations is duly
appreciated since they set an example for the local firms.
In other areas of contribution, substantial benefits are usually
seen by the host countries. While most were in reasonable
agreement that multinational corporations introduce new products
and processes into host countries in a reasonable time after
development, they lamented about the lack of actual research and
development conducted in host countries. The efficiency of
multinational operations, reflected through new managerial
techniques, training in new processes, and measures adopted to
boost labor productivity, were also widely appreciated by the host
countries. Over time these benefits filter down to local companies
which become more efficient and productive. Multinational
corporations are also seen as aiding in exports and import
substitution. This may sometimes be an obligation that the
corporation must fulfill in order to import required raw materials,
or as a part of their deal to operate in the country. A large
number of host countries perceive the multinational corporation as
an important contributing agent to their economic infrastructure,
but are concerned about the income inequities that such enterprises
usually cause.
Interestingly, multinational corporations do not seem to be
contributing much in the way of promoting political stability,
preserving local culture or enriching consumer life style. This is
interesting since it is their role in the politics and
socio-cultural affairs of developing countries that is usually
questioned. If these companies became the mainstream of the
political and socio-cultural life of a developing country, they are
diatribed for unnecessary interference in local affairs. And, if
they remain aloof, they are castigated as disinterested aliens in
the realities of local life. It is the kind of issue on which no
matter what posture a multinational corporation adopts, it could be
taken to task.

II. PROBLEM AREAS

As noted above, developing host countries do benefit from the
investments of a multinational corporation. But, these benefits
are riddled with concomitand problems. The second part of the
study aimed at understanding these issues.
Exhibit 2 (see Annex) lists the problems associated with the

multinational corporations' operations in developing countries. The fundamental problem which was most frequently mentioned by respondents has to do with the basic orientation of multinational corporations. As profit-making institutions, they have to be concerned with the bottom line which when put in the context of a country does not seem to make sense to host governments. Such issues as long-term vs. short-term profitability, repatriation of profits and control policy which a multinational corporation may pursue in developing countries are a matter of corporate strategy and management style. The multinational corporation views its strategy in a world-wide context and in this process the specific needs and requirements of a country may not be as adequately met as the country would want them to be, and this becomes a subject of discord. Host governments feel that more benefits accrue to the multinational corporation than to the host country.

A second problem has to do with the feeling among policy makers in developing countries that multinational corporations do not become active partners in their economic development efforts. A large proportion of the respondents (45 percent) considered this to be a major problem and half of them labeled it as a problem of average dimension. While not a major problem, over seventy percent of the respondents do not find multinational corporations helping them in balance of payments problems (measured in terms of economic self-sufficiency) and in finding a solution for unemployment. Since, in the earlier part, the host governments do credit the multinational corporations with aiding them with increased exports and import substitution, the concern here is in terms of repatriation of profits and lost reinvestment which have adverse implications for balance of payments and employment creation. In other words, a sizable group of respondents find that multinational corporations fail to the host countries in solving their national problems.

This problem raises two interesting questions: (a) Are multinational corporations really equipped to help a host country in finding solutions to such chronic problems such as employment and other economic problems and can they really get locked up in such issues, and if so to what extent? These questions can be endlessly debated. Conceptually, once a business organization steps out of its immediate area of concern, that is, running a business, the sky is the limit to its involvement in local affairs. The history of the East India company adds credence to such a conceptualization. Will a host country tolerate any such interference from an alien organization in current times? Perhaps it is in realization of such issues that multinational corporations keep aloof from overinvolvement in local affairs.

Presumably, it is predominantly because of this aloofness of the multinational corporations from the political and economic issues of national character that respondents claimed that, overall, multinational corporations benefit more from their enterprises than the host country. Their parent organizations also have been charged with monopolizing the control of their affiliates, and frustrating the development efforts of the host governments.

Interestingly, only seven percent of the respondents though (as a major problem) that multinational corporations make headway through corrupt practices, which in recent years have been debated as a major issue of political and moral character. Their efforts to train nationals for managerial positions was not considered a major problem by a large proportion of the respondents, but they complained that local managers do not get a chance to move to parent or other subsidiaries. This is different than what one would expect since over the years lack of efforts to make the locals self-sufficient has often been mentioned as a matter of concern.

III. HOST COUNTRY EXPECTATIONS

As the previous section indicates, a large number of host nations expressed dissatisfaction, about the benefits accruing the country. As this was to be expected to some extent, a part of the questionnaire was devoted to probing this issue. Since it is the nonconsummation of the expectations that leads to frustration and friction, 'a better understanding of these can help avoid potential conflicts. Exhibit 3 summarizes the expectations of host governments. In the important area of rate of return on investments, over eighty percent of the respondents thought that a return somewhere between 10 percent and 20 percent was reasonable. While about thirteen percent were willing to go along with a return of more than 20 percent, a very small minority considered less than 10 percent return as more appropriate (see Annex).

Almost two-thirds of the respondents felt that between 40 percent to 60 percent of the profits of the local subsidiary should be reinvested in the host country. As a matter of fact, almost 25 percent of the respondents wanted this proportion to be as high as 60 percent or more. In the light of the feelings expressed earlier that multinational corporations do not become partners in economic development, these sentiments are understandable. But, from the point of view of the parent organization, repatriation of profits is important. This often leads to an element of discord. As the exhibit indicates, most host governments were willing to live with tax rates that are similar to or lower than those prevailing in most developed nations.

IV. HOST COUNTRY RESPONSIBILITIES

Generally speaking, there are several policy alternatives that the developing countries can follow in order to make themselves more attractive to the multinationals. A "service" package can be developed that will achieve the desired results. Some of the steps involved here might include items such as:

-- Special tax deals
-- Import protection
-- Special rebates during the initial phases of the project
-- Financing packages designed to make the investment less risky
-- Special administrative facilities and procedures
-- Guarantee of non-discriminatory application of laws
-- Protection against expropriation
-- Informational support to help multinationals easily and cheaply identify profitable opportunities of interest to the host country

This part of the study focused on the responses of the policy makers in this area. The general pattern that appears to emerge is that while the developing countries are willing to provide support and encouragement in terms of services, they are not willing to provide substantial financial benefits to the multinational corporations. The summary of the responses has been included in Exhibit 4 (see Annex).

Most policy makers agreed that an image of stability and reliability is of great importance in attracting foreign investments. But, while about half of them are willing to guarantee no changes in tax rates for a certain period of time, a very small proportion were willing to offer incentives such as sharing the cost of investigating opportunities (23 percent); an incentive package on a perpetual basis (10 percent); local currency loans (13 percent); accelerated depreciation (13 percent); incentives to increase multinational corporations' rate of return (15 percent); etc. Surprisingly, none of the responding developing countries was inclined to offer a "loss rebate" to the extent of depreciation to a multinational corporation that did not make enough money to cover the depreciation. It is clear from these responses that any item that involves paying a direct subsidy to a foreign enterprise is not popular with the policy makers in developing countries. A reason for this might be the political consequences of such policies. Such policies would leave the policy makers open to attacks from their rivals in an election year. Charges of foreign involvement and support of the ruling party in an election year are heard of quite often. The recent investigations leading to revelation of large payoffs made to foreign government officials by the U.S. multinationals have made the policy makers in developing countries very nervous and highly susceptible to renewed attacks of a similar nature, both from within and without the country. One would, therefore, expect to see the kind of responses obtained.

Host countries were inclined to provide informational support such as projects suitable to the conditions of their countries (80 percent); Local market opportunities (70 percent); import substitution possibilities (68 percent); clearly spelled out economic policies (85 percent); analysis of their comparative economic advantages (60 percent), and help the multinational corporations in investigating investment opportunities without financial involvement. In addition, about seventy-four percent of the respondents were willing to adept special administrative measures that would help out the red tape for the multinationals.

Also, a large number of developing countries (63 percent) were
willing to provide information on what components and supplies
needed for new ventures in their countries could be provided by the
existing businesses. As is apparent from these responses, a large
number of policy makers felt enthused about the informational needs
of the multinationals and were willing to help out in this regard.
A part of this desire to help might stem from the realization that
the information systems in most developing nations are not well
developed. Usually there are no private agencies that one can turn
to for help in this area. Almost all the information that is
generated in these countries is collected by the government and is
not freely available to non-governmental establishments.
Therefore, the government is usually the only source of secondary
data. Realizing that a primary data collection exercise for each
informational need of a multinational enterprise will lead to
excessive costs, the governments are willing to take on this
function.

V. CONCLUSIONS

The area of interaction between a foreign enterprise and a host
government has been studied in the past. The focus of this study,
however, is slightly different. Most past studies have approached
this area on an ex-post basis. They have taken a given situation
and tried to analyze it. Here, an attempt has been made to attack
the question on an exante basis. Most of the questions have sought
the opinions of the policy makers. Admittedly, in many situations,
it may take several years before these opinions are actually put
into practice. But, the study helps in pointing out the direction
which policy in the developing countries is likely to take. We
have seen that many areas of conflict remain between the developing
countries and the multinational corporations. But, there appears
to be a realization that multinational corporations are conducive
to growth and that a clear policy in this regard is essential.
Developing countries appear to be willing to support further
investments by the multinational corporations, but there is a clear
cut reluctance to underwrite these ventures in any financial sense.
This is an area where pointing fingers at the accused party would
lead to no benefits. Mutual consultation and a clear understanding
of each other's problems is imperative to future growth. Far more
research is needed to establish how the areas of conflict can be
minimized and how the much needed understanding can be achieved.

NOTES

[1]Louis T. Wells, "More or Less Poverty? The Economic Effects of the Multinational Corporation at Home and in Developing Countries", in Carl H. Madden, editor, The Case for the Multinational Corporation, Praeger Publisher, New York, 1977, pp. 71-72.

[2]Raymond Vernon, "The Power of Multinational Enterprises in Developing Countries", Carl H. Madden, editor, The Case for the Multinational Corporation, Praeger Publisher, New York, 1977, p. 155.

[3]Ibid, p. 165.

[4]World Tables 1976 (Baltimore, MD: University of Baltimore Press, 1977).

Exhibit 1: Contributions of Multinational Corporations in Developing Countries

Contributions	Nature of Response		
	Very Important %	Moderately Important %	Not Important %
A. *Capital Usage*			
Bring in foreign capital	71.0	26.3	2.7
Help in capital intensive investment than local investors	36.9	47.3	15.8
Make more capital in intensive investment than local investors	68.4	31.6	0
Show more efficient use of capital than do local investors	47.5	47.5	5.0
Create a favorable climate for the inflow of other foreign capital (private direct investments)	57.5	40.0	2.5
Create a favorable climate for the approval of loans from international organizations	57.5	37.5	5.0
Create a favorable climate to receive loans from developed countries (foreign aid)	42.5	50.0	7.5
B. *Technology Usage*			
Introduce new products soon after innovation in home country	23.1	51.2	25.7
Introduce new production methods and processes soon after innovation	28.2	48.7	23.1
Conduct research and development directly in problem area locally	7.7	43.6	48.7

122

C. Training			
Train local people in new industrial processes	45.0	47.5	7.5
Introduce new managerial techniques to national managers	50.0	45.0	5.0
Increase labor productivity over that found in domestic companies	45.0	55.0	---
D. Economic Development			
Materially add to the industrial infrastructure	55.0	40.0	5.0
Develop local supply industries	30.0	65.0	5.0
Set an example for national corporations to become more efficient and productive	47.5	52.5	---
Help in increasing exports	47.5	50.0	2.5
Create new markets for products other than their own	30.0	52.5	17.5
Help in import substitution	32.5	50.0	17.5
Promote a more equitable income distribution by providing new jobs	15.0	65.0	20.0
Help in developing natural resources	47.5	37.5	15.0
E. General			
Promote political stability	15.0	52.5	37.5
Tend to preserve the existing socio-cultural setting	12.5	57.5	30.0
Support and promote technical education	27.5	70.0	2.5
Support and promote managerial education	32.5	62.5	5.0
Introduce new products which enrich consumers' life style	25.0	70.0	5.0

Exhibit 2: Problems Associated with MNCs Operations in LDCs

	Nature of Response		
	Major Problem %	Average Problem %	Not a Problem %
A. Capital Usage			
Capital from local sources which deprives domestic companies of needed funds	25.0	45.0	30.0
Use of local capital by MNCs frustrates some government development objectives	15.0	42.5	52.5
Do not serve the best interests through their emphasis on short term profitability	42.5	37.5	20.0
Are more interested in the repatriation of profits than retaining earning for investment in growth	55.0	27.5	17.5
B. Technology Usage			
Tend to use outdated technology	10.2	59.0	30.8
C. Training			
Tend not to give local employees the type of training they need to make the production process work	15.0	42.5	42.5
Are not fair in providing national managers a chance to move to the parent or other subsidiary companies	50.0	45.0	5.0
D. Economic Development			
Do not help most countries to become economically self-sufficient	32.5	50.0	17.5
Force most countries and local-owned industries to become economically dependent on them	22.5	50.0	27.5
Help in planning economic development	45.0	50.0	5.0
Help in solving the unemployment problem	5.0	75.0	20.0

124

Exhibit 2: Problems Associated with MNCs Operations in LDCs

	Nature of Response		
	Major Problem %	Average Problem %	Not a Problem %
Operations in most countries are controlled by parent organizations, which give little consideration to the interests of the latter	50.0	42.5	7.5
Overall, MNCs benefit more than the host country	47.5	37.5	15.0
E. Alignment			
Do not align themselves with new government policy statements which affect their operations	10.0	70.0	20.0
Do not want to work with host countries in establishing new laws	10.0	75.0	15.0
Comply only with the letter of law not its spirit	30.5	47.5	20.0
Are more difficult to control than are local-owned companies	57.5	37.5	5.0
Frustrate government policies	35.0	40.0	25.0
Parent company control over the subsidiary in the host country and need for the government's economic development program is a major source of conflict	55.0	35.0	10.0
Enforce many policies in the name of the parent company which have little relevance in the host country	40.0	45.0	15.0
F. General Policies			
Make headway through corrupt practices	7.5	55.0	37.5
Have a poor impact on local culture	25.0	57.5	17.5
Do very little to promote labor welfare	7.5	62.5	30.0

125

Exhibit 3: Host Government Expectations From Multinational Corporations

(a) Reasonable rate of profit as a percentage of investment which MNCs may earn in DCs:	20 % or more	12.8
	Between 15 % to 20 %	48.7
	Between 10 % to 15 %	33.3
	Less than 10 %	5.1
(b) Percentage of their profits that MNCs should reinvest:	75 % or more	10.3
	Between 60 % to 75 %	15.4
	Between 50 % to 60 %	28.2
	Between 40 % to 50 %	38.5
	Less than 40 %	7.7
(c) Percentage of profits that MNCs ought to pay in taxes to DCs:	60 % or more	—
	Between 50 % to 60 %	10.0
	Between 40 % to 50 %	45.0
	Between 30 % to 40 %	27.5
	Less than 30 %	17.5
(d) Percentage of gross income (profits before taxes) which MNCs ought to spend in DCs on research and development:	5 % or more	31.6
	Between 4 % to 5 %	23.7
	Between 3 % to 4 %	28.9
	Between 2 % to 3 %	13.2
	Less than 2 %	2.6
(e) Percentage of foreign nationals in managerial positions that should be employed by MNCs in DCs:	75 % or more	5.0
	Between 50 % to 75 %	12.5
	Between 25 % to 50 %	15.0
	Less than 25 %	67.5

126

(f) Percentage of foreign nationals in technical positions that should be employed by MNCs in DCs:

75 % or more	10.0
Between 50 % to 75 %	22.5
Between 25 % to 50 %	40.0
Less than 25 %	27.5

(g) Percentage of total net income that MNCs should spend on voluntary public service activities in DCs:

10 % or more	12.5
Between 8 % to 10 %	17.5
Between 6 % to 8 %	20.0
Between 4 % to 6 %	42.5
Less than 4 %	7.5

(h) Voluntary public service activities on which MNCs should spend their money:[1]

Education (technical)	85.0
Housing	60.0
Medical Care	42.5
Education (general)	37.5
Sports and recreation	22.5
Agriculture	5.0
Communications	5.0
Research	5.0
Roads	5.0
Transportation	5.0
Arts	2.5

1 Total responses are over 100 percent due to multiple responses

127

Exhibit 4. *Steps Which Developing Countries May Follow to Interest MNCs*

| | Nature of Response | | |
Steps	Very Important %	Moderately Important %	Not Important %
Project an image of stability and reliability in the eyes of MNCs	87.0	12.5	—
Guarantee *no* changes in the rate of taxation for a certain period of time	45.0	42.5	12.5
Create confidence among the MNCs about their governments as those which live up to their promises	77.5	22.5	—
Invite discussions with MNCs *prior* to fixing rules which will affect business	52.5	37.5	10.0
Circulate proposed regulations to all businesses in their countries before finally setting the laws	47.5	35.0	17.5
Spell out economic policies (at least those aspects which are relevant for MNCs) clearly and in objective terms. An example is the level of tariff protection, if any	85.0	15.0	—
Apply uniform rules to both domestic corporations and MNCs	42.5	37.5	20.0

Exhibit 4: Steps Which Developing Countries May Follow to Interest MNCs

Steps	Nature of Response		
	Very Important %	Moderately Important %	Not Important %
Clearly spell out any exceptions to the law or concessions which must be guaranteed to selected business to avoid a feeling of discrimination among the MNCs	75.0	22.5	2.5
Discover projects suitable to the conditions of their countries (and programs) and make such projects known to MNCs	80.0	20.0	—
Provide the MNCs information on local market opportunities	70.0	25.0	5.0
Determine the requirements for components and supplies of new enterprises which could be provided by existing business and make available this information to MNCs	62.5	32.5	5.0
Analyze their comparative economic advantages and make available this information to MNCs	70.0	27.5	2.5
Bear (or share with a prospective investor, the MNC) the cost of investigating opportunities in their countries	22.5	55.0	22.5
Provide other forms of help to MNCs in their on-the-spot investigation of an opportunity	60.0	40.0	—

Exhibit 4: Steps Which Developing Countries May Follow to Interest MNCs

Steps	Nature of Response		
	Very Important %	Moderately Important %	Not Important %
Help the MNCs in reducing their risks via providing them local currency loans	12.5	47.5	40.0
Provide accelerated depreciation allowance to MNCs on their investments	12.8	53.8	33.4
Give "loss rebates" to the extent of depreciation to MNCs if they do not make enough money to cover the depreciation	—	42.5	57.5
Provide other incentives to MNCs, which may increase the rate of return from their investment	15.0	60.0	24.0
Provide such concessions to MNCs which may reduce their cost of capital	7.5	70.0	22.5
Provide such concessions to MNCs which may reduce their cost of production	17.5	57.5	25.0
Keep "servicing" the MNCs with an incentive package on a perpetual basis rather than providing various incentives as one-shot proposition	10.0	50.0	40.0
Adopt such administrative measures for MNCs which will cut the red tape involved in obtaining government licenses and permits which are considered essential	74.3	23.1	2.6

The Transnational Corporation as an Agent for Industrial Restructuring

SECRETARIAT OF UNIDO

This contribution has three broad positive aspects. First, transnationals can channel finance away from contracting industrial branches in the developed market economies to industries that are expanding in the developing countries. They can also help these industries by investing a larger proportion of their own profits in them. Second, this investment can enhance the capability of a developing country to better utilize its resources. Since most developing countries have an abundant labour force, the investment by transnationals can have an important effect on the domestic economy by generating employment.

An expansion of industrial production unaccompanied by a corresponding increase of industrial employment in most developing countries will not be sufficient to propel the country into a higher stage of development. But where industrial employment has risen, its rate of growth has been an important index of the extent to which industrial growth leads to industrial restructuring and improved international competitiveness. For example, in many newly industrializing developing countries (NICs) -- including Brazil, Mexico, the Republic of Korea and Singapore -- the share of industry in total employment has risen sharply over the past two decades.[1] These countries have developed strong competitive positions in the international markets for a varied range of industrial products.

Finally, since the transnationals have developed well-knit production and marketing structures which can serve as powerful instruments for overcoming protectionist barriers and establishing competitive positions, their investment, if properly controlled, can strengthen the bargaining power of developing countries. In the absence of an adequate policy, however, gains in industrial productivity may be eroded by reductions in the price of the

From **WORLD INDUSTRY IN 1980**, United Nations, 1981, (231-265), reprinted by permission of the publisher.

exports of a developing country or by its inability to gain access to the markets of the developed countries.

While investment by the TNCs in developing countries offers benefits, it may also entail substantial costs. A transnational's investment policies may be designed to exploit "sourcing" opportunities and to profit from fiscal incentives provided by liberal taxation policies. It may not be concerned with the relocation of industrial capacity in accordance with long-term changes in national comparative advantage. It is therefore essential that the Governments of developing countries formulate policies based on a careful assessment of the part transnationals can play in international industrial restructuring.

The first section of this chapter concerns the role of the transnationals as industrial producers and investors. Attention is focused on the contribution they can make to increasing industrial production, employment and exports and to developing links between manufacturing and other sectors of the economy. In the section, an empirical analysis is undertaken to identify the determinants of the investment behaviour of transnationals. Finally, some suggestions are made relating to the implications of this analysis for government policy in developing countries.

I. THE ROLE OF TRANSNATIONAL CORPORATIONS IN WORLD-WIDE INDUSTRIAL RESTRUCTURING

It is now generally recognized that the transnationals have demonstrated a remarkable capacity to integrate diverse economic factors, evolving organizational structures with a high degree of adaptability. Today, according to researchers in this field, "TNCs overwhelmingly dominate not only international investment, but also international production, trade and technology -- so much so that any analysis of the present structure of international economic relations that does not take them into account and, indeed, concentrate its attention on them runs the gravest risk of being unrealistic and irrelevant."[2] Many attempts have been made to estimate the share of the transnationals in world production, investment and trade. According to a United Nations study corporations is about one fifth of world gross national product not including centrally planned economies"[3] (32 per cent of the world's leading transnationals accounted for 14 per cent of global GNP). The transnationals also play an important part in foreign investment. For example, 180 transnationals provided 80 per cent of the United Kingdom's overseas investment, 300 TNCs provided over 70 per cent of the United States' foreign capital flows, and 83 TNCs provided over 20 per cent of the Federal Republic of Germany's foreign investment in the early 1970s.[4] These firms are also assuming increasing importance in foreign trade. According to United States official sources, they accounted for 20 per cent of world exports and for 25 per cent of all manufacturing exports in 1971. United States TNCs accounted for 62 per cent of that

country's exports in that year.[5] Similar figures can be cited for
many other developed market economies such as Sweden and the United
Kingdom.[6] The growth in the investment of the transnationals and
their expanded role in world trade has been facilitated by the
strong ties with international liquid assets and their influence in
international capital markets is now substantial.

Finally, there is a high degree of concentration of technology
in the hands of the transnationals. Thus, during the period
1963-1965, the 100 largest firms (most of them TNCs) in each OECD
country accounted for over 50 per cent of total industrial R and D
expenditure.[7] More recent data show that in the United States the
transnationals provide over 60 per cent of R and D expenditure in
the high-technology industries.[8] It is thus clear that
transnationals are responsible for the bulk of technological
innovations in world industry today.

The preponderant role of the transnationals in the
organization and management of world industrial production and
trade make them an important agent for the restructuring of
manufacturing investment in the developing countries. Their
increasing significance has spurred the growth of counterbalancing
forces in the restructuring process. In many developing
countries -- e.g. Brazil, India and Kenya -- the domestic private
industrial sector is growing. Moreover, public manufacturing
enterprises have become increasingly important. Thus, "public
enterprises accounted for three quarters of total sales of LDC
companies listed in Fortune's (1978) 500 largest non-US
industrials".[9] In the larger, resource-rich and relatively
industrialized developing countries, public manufacturing concerns
have considerable scope for independent action. Even the smaller
developing countries can greatly enhance the role of public
manufacturing enterprise as an agent of industrial restructuring
through the development of effective policies of regional
co-operation.

However, interaction between domestic public and private
enterprises, on the one hand, and the transnationals, on the other,
is unavoidable. Each group possesses resources and has access to
the same decision-makers that are necessary for the achievement of
its operational objectives. Developing countries should therefore
carefully assess their need for the involvement of transnationals
in the process of domestic industrial restructuring and should be
aware of the costs and benefits of this involvement to the national
economy.

There are two principal reasons for the need for increased TNC
involvement. The first relates to the significant differences in
the interindustrial costs of acquiring production technology. In
general, the wider the diffusion of technology in the developed
market economies, the less costly its acquisition will be for the
developing countries. The diffusion of technology varies greatly
among industrial branches. In the pharmaceutical industry,
especially in patented drugs, scientific information may be
specific to individual firms. In the aluminium industry,
scientific information may be widely available, while in cement
plants, technological information is easily accessible to experts
and technicians outside the industry. The terms on which

scientific information and production technology can be acquired by developing countries in the pharmaceutical industry usually involve an expansion of transnational investment in the developing country. This need not be the case in either the aluminium or cement industry, in which licensing arrangements and direct hiring of technical expertise are quite common.

The second reason has to do with the characteristics of international markets which are also likely to be important determinants of the need for co-operation between transnationals and the Governments of developing countries. For standardized products, the international market is relatively accessible. These goods can be distributed through an existing specialized network of trading concerns. For many other mineral and manufactured exports, however, there are powerful market barriers, and the cost of acquiring access to a distributive network may be considerable. In such cases, the transnationals may well provide the means for acquiring market access to industrial producers in developing countries.

The contribution that transnationals can make to industrial restructuring in developing countries is likely to be determined by their organizational objectives and their institutional structures. Industrial restructuring implies a relocation of investment in accordance with changing comparative costs. However, TNCs may not be particularly responsive to input cost reductions in the developing countries and may not direct investment to industrial branches whose production costs are declining. If an industrial activity -- notably food processing and mineral extraction -- is integrated within a larger production complex, a reduction in the input price of one product may not outweigh other considerations that determine the level of investment and the location of the units producing this product. Furthermore, the decision to reduce the input price of a particular industrial branch may be contested by economic actors interested in maintaining its present location or its present level of production. These actors may reduce the price of other inputs within this production process, substitute the cost-reduced input by other inputs, alter the output mix of the industrial branch or pursue a host of other strategies.

A firm's ability to respond to cost reductions and technological changes is related to size, its market share and the rate of growth of the industrial branch (or branches). Most transnationals have a high potential of technological adaptability on these counts. However, they can modify long-term investment opportunities in specific industrial branches by concentrating large amounts of R and D expenditure on inputs that have most recently become comparatively expensive. The resulting innovations ensure that the cost of these inputs shall be reduced, and a comparative cost advantage is created in product lines that abundantly use factors originally considered to be scarce.[10] This reaction can offset the extent of redeployment or the growth of investment in branches in which input costs have been lowered.

Even when the investment of transnationals moves to developing countries in response to changes in international comparative advantages, its impact on the domestic economy need not be entirely beneficial. Different industrial branches provide different possibilities for the Governments of developing countries to combine direct investment, joint venture and licensing agreements; and specific combinations may entail different costs and benefits. In some instances, "breaking open the package" -- i.e. combining joint ventures and licensing arrangements with the operation of TNC subsidiaries -- may result in important gains. Furthermore, the extent to which the organization and policymaking structure of a transnational corporation is centralized may be an important determinant of the ability of its subsidiaries to adapt their policies to the economic strategy of a given developing country. The headquarters office plays a supervisory and co-ordinating role in all TNCS -- indeed, this dominance of headquarters over branch offices distinguishes a TNC from an international holding company.[11] But the extent of centralization varies considerably. Branches and affiliates of transnationals may enjoy a substantial autonomy if they are product-based.[12] (i.e. if executive authority and responsibility is delineated in terms of the production and distribution of specific products). All these factors should be borne in mind by the Governments of developing countries when adopting a policy towards these firms.

It is clear that industrial restructuring in the developing countries requires the increased availability of international capital and technology and easier access to world manufacturing markets. The transnationals can be an important channel for procuring capital and technology and for increasing developing countries' exports. The extent to which this potential has been realized is examined below in an analysis of the existing evidence on the impact of transnational investment on growth, employment creation and export expansion in the developing countries.

II. THE INVESTMENT BEHAVIOUR OF TRANSNATIONAL CORPORATIONS: CONSEQUENCES FOR GROWTH

According to conventional economic theory, foreign investment can make a significant positive contribution to income growth in the host country, provided that there is a scarcity of capital, a high elasticity of substitution between domestic saving and foreign capital and a significant unemployment of labour. At the same time, the beneficial effects on income through increased employment may be offset by a rise in the productivity of the export sector and an increase in foreign-exchange spending for servicing the foreign capital. In general, it is assumed that the inflow of foreign capital is beneficial to host countries. And it is usually assumed that borrowing takes place under competitive conditions and that Governments are sufficiently powerful to offset monopolistic tendencies.

Empirical studies have not fully borne out these theoretical expectations, however. Researchers have found a negative association between the inflow of foreign resources and domestic saving, that frequently the degree of TNC penetration (defined as the ratio of capital stock controlled by transnationals to the total capital stock of the host country) is negatively related to the subsequent level of income growth in the host country. This relationship is described as "particularly strong for less developed countries with a large modernized sector".[13] In other words, the higher the level of TNC involvement in a developing country in a given year, the less probable it is that the country will achieve high rates of growth in the subsequent period. This empirical finding lends support to the "decapitalization thesis". According to this view, TNC operations lead to a reduction of the supply of funds available for investment in the host country. Transnationals may transfer resources out of the host economy by repatriating declared profits or by over-pricing production inputs. This drain of investment resources leads inevitably to a reduction in growth.

The negative effect of transnational penetration on the growth of the developing countries has been explained in terms of its impact on the domestic industrial structure. In particular, when the transnational presence fosters high levels of industrial concentration, which increase income inequalities and lead to a rapid depletion of investment funds in agriculture, it can be argued that such TNC involvement has reached a point of "saturation". In such a case, domestic demand fails to rise sufficiently, import-substitution possibilities become increasingly difficult, and foreign trade opportunities may be limited by protectionist policies of trading partners and the reluctance of transnational subsidiaries to encroach on the markets of sister companies. Hence, profit rates fall, investment levels are reduced, and the high growth rates associated with high levels of domestic and foreign investment do not pertain.

All these possibilities point to the importance of the effect of transnational investment on the industrial structure of the host developing countries. If the TNCs drain a disproportionately high share of investment resources from the developing countries, then policy measures are needed to limit these firms' possibilities of transferring domestic investment resources and to make the domestic deployment of these resources more attractive. The former objective can be achieved most effectively reducing concentration and increasing competition within the manufacturing sector.

Some studies investigating the relationship between transnational penetration and concentration have shown that TNCs predominate in industrial branches with the highest levels of concentration in Brazil, Mexico and some Central American countries.[14] However, there is little systematic evidence on the impact of transnational policies on levels of concentration within specific industrial branches in developing countries. It has sometimes been argued that the TNCs exhibit a strong preference for entering new markets through mergers or take-overs -- particularly in the "low" technology industries[15] -- but it must be stressed that higher levels of concentration in specific industrial branches may be the consequence of factors that have little to do with prevailing forms of ownership. For example, economies of scale or production technologies may lead to wider differences in

concentration levels of different industrial branches than
marketing or financial policies. If the transnationals employ a
more capital-intensive technology than that prevalent among
domestic enterprises in a given industrial branch, then firm
concentration is likely to be pronounced. Evidence of this
phenomenon is mixed, however, as will be shown in the next section.

The tendency of transnationals to transfer investment funds
from host developing economies can also be countered by increasing
linkages between domestic firms and these corporations. Little
systematic research has been devoted to an assessment of the impact
of transnational operations on the performance of domestic
enterprises. In India, there is evidence of extensive
subcontracting, a clear tendency to increase locally purchased
components and an indication that the level of vertical integration
in the TNCs operating in the automotive industry is declining, all
of which would imply greater autonomy for domestic subsidiaries.
Indian imports as a proportion of total components have been
declining: they represented 62.5 per cent of automative
manufacturing output in 1956, but declined to less than 4 per cent
by 1969.[16]

In both Morocco and Peru, the share of procurement from local
firms for in-house manufacturing was considerably lower. This
circumstance is explained by differences in levels of industrial
development and in government policy. Although Morocco and Peru
have higher levels of per capita income than India, the latter has
an advanced and integrated industrial structure. In India, the
Government has followed a policy of encouraging the local
manufacture of components and local procurement -- a policy not
pursued by Morocco or Peru. Moreover, the policy of the Indian
Government -- particularly its licensing procedures and
encouragement of small enterprises -- has precluded transnational
subsidiaries from moving into the manufacture of components. Local
procurement has also been stimulated by the Government's emphasis
on import substitution.

Studies have sometimes emphasized the ability of host
Governments to increase the degree of domestic integration.
"Empirical findings suggest that a main determinant of linkage
creation is host government policy. Measures focusing on the
specifics of the process of the creation of linkages seem to be
more effective if they are implemented in the framework of a broad
industrialization strategy, where actions related to the
stimulation of TNC linkages are guided by the dynamic comparative
advantages of the host country."[17]

Government policy can modify the impact of transnational
investment on a developing economy in other ways, by reducing
levels of industrial concentration and by increasing the domestic
linkages of foreign investment. If successful, these policies can
increase the attractiveness of the domestic economy to foreign
investors by ensuring a high growth of domestic demand. Sustaining
this growth, however, requires that investment be concentrated in
industrial branches with international comparative advantages, and
their development requires the optimum utilization of productive
resources.

Since most developing countries have abundant labour,

sustained growth would entail a substantial long-term expansion in employment. Estimates of total direct employment provided by transnationals -- admittedly subject to a large margin of error -- range from 13 to 30 million.[18] The estimates vary in terms of the definition of foreign control[19] and thus reflect different statistical populations. However, even if the most liberal estimates are accepted, the proportion of total world employment accounted for by TNCs is only 1.3 per cent. In terms of industrial employment, these firms contribute approximately 4.8 per cent of total employment.[20] In developing countries, transnationals have created a total of between 2 to 4 million jobs (representing 0.3 per cent of total employment and 2 per cent of total industrial employment.)[21] It is thus apparent that employment in these firms is mainly concentrated in the developed market economies.

For some developing countries, however -- Brazil, Mexico, Peru, Republic of Korea, Singapore -- transnational employment is a significant proportion of total industrial employment. In some countries these firms accounted for over one fifth of total industrial employment in the mid-1970s. Transnational employment in developing countries seems to be concentrated mainly in the manufacturing sector, although their investment is spread fairly evenly between manufacturing and the extractive industries. Table 1 estimates the proportion of transnational employment in the total employment of industrial branches in four developing countries in various years.

In Mexico and the Republic of Korea, the transnationals accounted for a large proportion of total employment in heavy industries such as chemicals, petrochemicals, electrical machinery and metal products. In Peru -- which is at an earlier stage of industrial development -- this employment was significant in consumer goods industries such as beverages and tobacco. The transnational share of employment in capital-intensive equipment, electrical machinery and metal products was also high.

These estimates relate only to the direct employment effects of TNC investment. Depending on the extent of backward and forward linkages developed by such firms, some indirect employment may be generated.[22] While this employment is relatively limited in the extractive industries, it may be substantial in manufacturing. Thus, for the Republic of Korea, it has been estimated that the indirect employment effect of TNC investment have been substantial; such investment generated 102,000 jobs through backward linkages with domestic producers. In general, indirect employment stimulated by these corporations is likely to be less significant than the indirect employment created by domestic manufacturing enterprises, since the former are larger net importers of both raw materials and capital than local firms.[23] Moreover, the output mix of TNC subsidiaries may not be particularly suitable for generating high employment in some developing countries. Transnationals may also specialize in the production of "luxury" goods. An increase in the production of such goods is less likely to generate a demand for unskilled labour than an expansion of products to meet basic necessities.

The impact of investment on employment is most directly

TABLE 1. SHARE OF TRANSNATIONAL EMPLOYMENT IN INDUSTRIAL BRANCHES
IN SELECTED DEVELOPING COUNTRIES, VARIOUS YEARS

(Percentage)

Industry	Mexico (1970)	Peru (1973)	Republic of Korea (1974)	Singapore (1968)
Food	} 12.9	18.5	2.6	} 19.5
Beverages		23.5		
Tobacco		61.2		
Wood	8.1	11.1	1.9	25.5
Paper	24.8	59.8		
Printing	6.7	1.1		
Leather		33.1		35.9
Chemicals	40.2	37.8	11.5	
Petroleum		59.0	70.3	93.7
Non-metallic	13.0	13.5	10.2	
Basic metallic	} 30.0	48.6	11.7	} 20.0
Metal products		12.8	29.7	
Electrical machinery	75.4	49.2	58.0	65.8
Transport	42.0	40.1	2.7	
Textiles	4.0	18.7	8.1	61.0

Source: United Nations Centre on Transnational Corporations, Transnational Corporation Linkages in
Developing Countries (New York, 1980), pp. 14-17.

influenced by the investor's choice of production technology. Many attempts have been made to compare the relative capital intensity of domestic and foreign firms in developing countries. Technologies employed by transnationals are likely to be rigid since these firms tend to predominate in modern, complex industries with continuous production processes. This rigidity is also enhanced by increased vertical integration between the units of a transnational family, although there is scope for some technological flexibility in processes such as handling, transport and administration. Flexibility may also be incorporated in production processes by using more shifts, increasing the level of subcontracting and using lower-quality material inputs. TNC subsidiaries have been induced to adopt a relatively labour-intensive production technology in many Asian and Latin American countries.

The choice of an industrialization strategy is an important determinant of the effect that transnational investment may have on employment. In particular, an export-oriented industrialization strategy has in many instances -- for example in the Republic of Korea[24] -- had a significant impact on employment. Export-oriented subsidiaries are likely to have more labour-intensive production processes than domestic-oriented firms. However, the linkages of the former firms with the rest of the economy are sometimes weak because their operations are often self-contained and because they tend to import a high proportion of their inputs. Hence the indirect employment generated by export-oriented TNC subsidiaries is likely to be limited.

In most developing countries, an export-oriented industrialization strategy cannot be effectively pursued without co-operation from transnationals, particularly where market barriers are substantial. TNC subsidiaries are often more successful exporters than domestic firms. Therefore, a restructuring of investment in accordance with changing comparative advantages requires the support of these firms. Such restructuring implies that countries concentrate on the production of goods in which they have an international comparative advantage. market barriers and protectionist policies can effectively frustrate this pattern of international specialization. It is therefore essential to explore the potential of the transnational as an instrument for overcoming protectionism and hence for redistributing industrial capacity in accordance with changing comparative advantages.

The transnationals have rapidly increased their level of international involvement during the past decade. The United Nations Centre on Transnational Corporations (UNCTC) has estimated that over the period 1971-1976 the foreign subsidiaries of 251 of these firms grew 25 per cent faster than the parent companies. A large proportion of the exports of the developed market economies are manufactures of transnationals, and there is some evidence that this proportion may be increasing.[25]

The expanded role of these corporations in the export sector of developed market economies has led many researchers to assume that they have also been instrumental in articulating the export-led growth strategy adopted by some newly industrializing economies. Foreign firms have played a dominant part in the organization of international trade in primary commodities in the past. It was expected that they would adapt their structures easily to participate in the drive for expanded manufactured exports in the developing countries. A few countries and areas -- Argentina, Brazil, Colombia, Hong Kong, India, Malaysia, Mexico, Pakistan, the Republic of Korea and Singapore -- currently account for about 60 per cent of the developing countries' manufactured exports.[26] Six -- Brazil, Hong Kong, India, Mexico, the Republic of Korea and Singapore -- account for approximately 57 per cent of the stock of direct foreign investment in the non-OPEC developing world.[27] In many of these countries, transnational subsidiaries account for over 20 per cent of the manufactured exports.

Table 2 gives estimates of the export shares of the United States subsidiaries of transnationals in developing countries. Exports of these TNCs grew at an annual rate of 48 per cent over the period 1966-1974. During the same period total manufactured exports grew at a rate of 60.8 per cent annually.[28] Thus, the share of United States firms in the total manufactured exports from developing countries fell from 10 per cent in 1966 to 8.7 per cent in 1974. The estimates show that United States subsidiaries have been important exporters in Latin America, although their significance has recently declined. They have been far less important exporters in other developing regions, and their share has steadily declined, particularly since 1970, in the exports of developing countries as a whole.

Two components of TNC exports have been growing rapidly, however, over the past decade. First, intra-firm trade has been expanding rapidly. Estimates for the early 1970s indicate that 50 per cent of United States exports are of this type. Corresponding percentages for Canada, Sweden and the United Kingdom are 60, 29 and 39 respectively. Second, tariff provisions for off-shore assembly have encouraged the rapid growth of international subcontracting. United States imports of goods assembled or processed abroad from materials and components originally produced in the United States have grown rapidly. Tariffs on these imports are levied only on the foreign value added. In 1966, their gross value represented 1.6 per cent of developing countries' exports of manufactures to the United States. By 1974, this figure had risen to over 7 per cent. A very few (five) developing countries accounted for 85 per cent of imports permitted into the United States under tariff items 807.00 and 806.30.

Export-oriented transnationals in developing countries are not likely to create domestic linkages and to facilitate restructuring if they are concerned primarily with transferring fairly complex technologies to these countries in order to serve established world markets. "Border industries", such as the electronic industrial complexes of Mexico and Singapore, are relevant examples; they rarely use locally available components. Domestic linkages are also likely to be limited where the subsidiaries transfer only a (labour-intensive) part of the production process to a developing country. Once again, the electronic industry is a good example, in which the rapidly changing technology, the demanding

TABLE 2. SHARE OF UNITED STATES TRANSNATIONAL SUBSIDIARIES IN THE MANUFACTURED EXPORTS OF THE DEVELOPING COUNTRIES, 1966-1974

(Percentage)

Year	Latin America	Africa	Middle East	Other Asia	All developing countries
1966	37.8	—	1.3	7.0	10.0
1967	40.0	2.6	1.1	7.7	11.5
1968	33.0	5.7	0.9	8.2	11.0
1969	29.4	6.0	1.0	6.5	9.2
1970	22.3	6.4	0.9	8.8	10.8
1971	23.7	6.3	1.1	6.0	9.5
1972	22.1	7.2	2.0	4.9	8.5
1973	19.2	5.6	2.2	5.4	8.1
1974	19.2	6.1	2.8	5.8	8.7

Source: D. Nayyar, "TNCs and manufactured exports from developing countries", *Economic Journal*, vol. 88, March 1978, p. 65.

specifications, and requirements of cost minimization reduce the possibility for domestic linkages to practically nothing.

Significant domestic linkages may be created by transnational affiliates that have switched from import-substitution to export-oriented policies in response to changing international comparative advantages. Such firms generally use standardized, mature technologies. They have usually been located in the developing countries for a relatively long period of time and have strong links with local markets and domestic suppliers. In some industrial branches, such as in textiles, footwear and leather manufacturing, comparatively small foreign firms, many of them based in other developing countries, are likely to be as labour-intensive as their local counterparts.

Governments should seek continuously to develop a strategy that attracts transnational investment in the industrial branches in which they retain an international comparative advantage. They should attempt to establish an understanding with TNCs in order to overcome protectionist barriers. These barriers increasingly take the form of administrative controls and are often less applicable to intra-firm trade than to "arms-length' trade. Such an understanding can also help to induce the TNCs to reduce private "non-tariff barriers" -- particularly in the form of restrictive business practices -- which these firms sometimes impose at a heavy cost to developing countries.[29] Similarly, co-operation between the Governments of developing countries and transnationals can improve access to technological resources and marketing and distributive networks.

Such co-operation, however, requires an appreciation of transnational performance and policies. An examination of the policies of TNC affiliates operating in developing countries is presented in the section that follows, and a comparison is made between the policies of these firms and those of domestic enterprises. In particular, an attempt is made to intensify the main determinants of TNC investment in developing countries. It has been argued that an expansion of this investment is a necessary element for industrial restructuring in these countries, but that such an expansion may entail significant costs. Subsequently, these costs are assessed by focusing on the impact of TNC investment growth on the level of industrial concentration in the developing countries. Indirect evidence of the existence of transfer pricing is also presented. Finally, some conclusions are drawn about the implications of this analysis for government policy in developing countries.

III. DETERMINANTS OF TNC POLICIES: AN EMPIRICAL INVESTIGATION

This section is concerned with the main determinants of the growth and profitability of transnationals and the principal factors influencing their investment behaviour. These questions have been widely studied within the context of the theory of the growth of the firm and the theory of investment.[30] Empirical tests of several hypotheses based on these theories have led to many varied explanations of the behaviour of firms' investment and financing. Although foreign investors have attracted considerable attention, in the words of a recent study, "there is still a large grey area of semi-ignorance, illuminated only by fragmentary and scattered evidence from small samples or else provided on a highly aggregated basis".[31] The size of the sample available in the present study is also small, but it is hoped that some of the issues discussed may provide an insight into aspects of TNC policies that could prove useful in assessing their impact on industrialization in the developing countries. Such an assessment is indispensable for international negotiations seeking to evolve an efficient strategy for world industrial restructuring.

The study relies mainly on data gathered from balance sheets and profit-and-loss statements of individual companies. Standardized "analyses of accounts" were available for India and Thailand. For the United Kingdom, documents were procured directly from the companies themselves. Estimates based on company accounts are, of course, subject to wide margins of error. They do not provide wholly satisfactory criteria for evaluating a TNCs performance, particularly when (as is often the case) many of the costs are determined on the basis of the internal transactions of the firm and its affiliates. Moreover, these estimates are generally based on accounting conventions that do not adequately represent the effect of inflation on, for example, the valuation of fixed assets. There are also ambiguities in the method of valuation employed and often errors of omission, particularly in the appropriation of income statement. Items such as wages and purchases of raw material are often absent. Statements on "sources and uses of funds" omit "book" transactions -- i.e. those internal to the company, such as the revaluation of fixed assets and the conversion of debenture stock to ordinary or preference shares. Obviously, these omissions are of particular importance when consolidated statements are being considered, for these require that adjustments be made in fixed assets, current assets and liabilities, and provisions. However, subsidiary accounts could not be procured and the necessary adjustments could not therefore be made.[32]

There are shortcomings and limitations to which such data are subject. However, the existence of a broadly similar framework of presentation and of broadly similar company objectives (most companies seek to maximize profits or growth and the choice of one or the other objective does not lead to significant differences in business strategy)[33] ensures that there is a basic consistency in the figures. Thus, it can be predicted that fixed assets will usually be undervalued in balance sheets. "It is considered almost criminal to overvalue and prudent to undervalue."[34] Accounting conventions remain fairly stable over time and across continents. Thus, many problems that arise in the use and interpretation of accounting data -- the inability to take inflation into account in the valuation of assets, the arbitrary nature of depreciation estimates, conceptual ambiguities in the definition of categories such as "capital employed" and "net worth" -- are in principle amenable to theoretical handling. Estimates of the gross value of foreign investment and of value added created by such enterprises, and explanations of the financial policies that they pursue are usually available only in data of this type. To avoid the use of such data because of the problems inherent in their interpretation and the difficulties of comparison between countries and over time would limit the scope of investigation of TNC behaviour to an aggregate level.

There is a need to gather data of this type from many developing and developed countries over an extended period, and to scrutinize the data in order to develop an appropriate conceptual framework for reconciling their contradictions, improving their estimates and widening the possibility of international (and intertemporal) comparability of the trends that they reveal. These exercises should also involve the transnationals themselves in order to acquire more detailed and specific information. In the developed market economies, such attempts have usually proved fruitful since large firms today provide many more details of their activities than they did two decades ago. Such co-operation, including the development of accurate and realistic estimates of firm performance, is in the interests of all parties.

For the present study, data were compiled from three sources. On the basis of this information three samples were formed comprising transnational corporations in the United Kingdom and subsidiaries in India and Thailand. For the data on British firms, UNIDO sent requests for information to those manufacturers in the United Kingdom that were listed in Fortune's analysis of the 500 largest industrial corporations outside the United States[35] and that were judged not to be affiliates of other TNCs.[36] Firms were asked to supply annual consolidated accounts and financial statements for the period 1975-1979 and annual accounts and financial statements of their subsidiaries operating in developing countries in this period. The firms included in the study are estimated to account for approximately 36 per cent of the net assets of manufacturing companies in the United Kingdom during the period 1975-1977.[37] The companies in the group accounted for 53 per cent of the sales by the 65 largest manufacturers in the United Kingdom.38 Although the accounts of subsidiary firms were not considered in this exercise, there are sound reasons to believe that foreign investment by the companies considered is substantial. This aspect, along with a more detailed description of the United Kingdom sample, is discussed in the appendix to this chapter.

Data for Indian companies were taken from the volume Top 300 Companies, published by the Economic and Scientific Research Foundation of India.[39] This source provides an analysis of accounts of the largest public limited companies in the period 1966-1971; it distinguishes between companies on the basis of ownership. A total of 46 manufacturers were included in the present study. All were in continuous operation during the period 1966-1971 and are subsidiaries or affiliates of foreign companies. The net sales of these 46 companies were equivalent to almost 20 per cent of the net sales of the 300 largest Indian public corporations, suggesting that the group includes many of the large foreign manufacturers in India. In the absence of a proper scientific sample design, it is not possible to assess the "representativeness" of this group. But it is clear that the companies included account for a significant proportion of foreign manufacturing investment,[40] and their policies are likely to be of considerable importance in determining the overall impact of TNC investment on the Indian economy. The firms are located in the chemical, petrochemical, machinery, electrical machinery, food, metal manufacturing and transport equipment industrial branches. The largest group is in the chemical industry.

The third source of data was the Directory of Thailand's 300 Largest Companies, published by Thamasat University.[41] This volume gives the balance sheets, income statements and financial highlights of the 100 largest manufacturing companies in Thailand for the years 1976 and 1977. Information is included on 21 subsidiaries and affiliates of foreign companies located in Thailand.[42] These latter companies were selected as the Thai group of foreign manufacturing firms. Their performance and policies were compared with those of the top 20 national Thai firms. The total sales of the foreign manufacturers in the Thai group accounted for 34.2 per cent of the sales of the 100 largest manufacturing firms in Thailand in 1977. Although it was not possible to estimate the total foreign investment in Thai manufacturing, the Thai firms included are clearly an important component of this investment.

The total sample drawn from three sets of country data comprised 96 firms.[43] For 76 of these firms, data spanning a five-year period were available. Comparability between the national samples was limited because of differences in accounting concepts and in the presentation of financial statements.

An attempt was made to develop a set of common indicators that could be used to assess financial policies and performance. It was decided, however, not to pool the sets of national data of the subsequent analysis, because of the large differences in national environment and policies, the nature of the enterprises in the sample and the periods covered by the national data. Moreover, some measures could not be calculated for all the countries in the overall sample.

The measures calculated are described in some detail in the appendix to this chapter. They represent financial estimates of the growth of individual companies, and of changes in their size and financial policies. Alternate measures of corporate profitability have also been estimated. These variables are defined according to conventional and generally accepted criteria. The first question studied was the relationship between size of firms and the growth of their assets. This investigation was useful for studying the impact of TNC growth on industrial concentration in the host economy. The growth of concentration can be a powerful barrier restricting the process of industrial restructuring in developing countries. The theory of the growth of the firm,[44] which was developed after the Second World War, unlike its neo-classical progenitor treats growth as a strategic choice of management. In certain circumstances, management may prefer a strategy that emphasizes the maximization of growth rather than profits. The two major themes emerging from this literature seem to be the relationship between growth and size of the firm, on the one hand, and between growth and the level of profitability, on the other.

The first theme has been the subject of a number of empirical studies designed to test "The Law of Proportionate Effect" (Gibrat's Law). This Law states that the probability of a firm's growing at any (given) rate is independent of the initial size of the firm. Hence, the Law implies that there is no "optimal" size of the firm.[45] Neither of these assertions are generally supported by the modern theory of the growth of the firm.[46]

Gibrat's Law also implies that the rate of growth of a firm in one period does not influence its rate of growth in the subsequent period. A related hypothesis is that there is an inherent tendency towards increasing concentration (if large and small firms grow at the same rates, large firms will eventually predominate and concentration will occur).

To test the Law of Proportionate Effect for the sample of companies in this study,[47] the following linear regression models were applied to the data,

$$G = a + bS + \varepsilon$$

$$\ln G = a + b \ln S + \varepsilon \,[48]$$

where G is the rate of growth of the firm, measured as the difference between its net assets at the beginning and end of the period, as a ratio of its assets in the first year of the period; S represents the net assets of the firm at the beginning of the period; ε is a disturbance term; a and b are parameters, b indicating the difference in growth for every difference of one unit in size. Thus, if a value of, say, 0.5 was estimated for b, firms that had a size of £1 million at the beginning of the period would be expected to grow at twice the rate of firms that had an opening size of only 500,000. If the value of $b = 0.0001$, on the other hand, it could be concluded that initial size made little difference for growth prospects. The first equation implies that percentage growth changes by the same amount (given by the coefficient b) for any given change in size for all sizes of firms. The logarithmic equation, on the other hand, asserts that the proportional change in percentage growth is the same for any proportional change in size for all firm sizes.

These models were tested in order to acertain whether the growth rates varied in some systematic fashion with the size indicator. Each equation was estimated separately for the British, Indian and Thai data. None of the resultant equations (six) suggested the existence of a conclusive relationship between growth and size.[49] The result implies that no simple linear or log-linear relationship exists between size and growth for the firms in the sample. The findings do not, of course, establish conclusively that Gibrat's Law operates -- growth may have a non-linear relationship with initial size.

Table 3 shows average growth rates for different size classes of the firms in the sample. It is evident that there is some form of association between average growth and firm size. In all three cases, the lowest rate of growth was recorded by firms in the largest size class and, in the data for the Thai and the United Kingdom firms, the average rates of growth in the two smallest size classes exceeded the growth rate for large firms. Moreover, the results were statistically tested for significant differences in the value of the means of different size classes. In most cases statistical comparisons between pairs of means led to the conclusion that they were significantly different.[50] It is thus probable that there is a systematic, though weak, association between size and growth. Larger firms tend in general to grow more slowly than the relatively smaller TNCs.

Differences in the standard deviation of the different size classes were also tested[51] and showed a distinct association between size class and the variability of growth performance. This difference was most marked in the case of the United Kingdom group where the growth of the larger TNCs was considerably less dispersed. In that country group the value of the standard deviation of the average growth rate for the largest size class was less than one third of that found among the smallest firms. It can be concluded, therefore, that the larger firms have a relatively uniform growth performance while growth rates among smaller firms, on the other hand, differ widely. These results can only be regarded as tentative, because in no country group did the value of the standard deviation decline consistently with size class.

For the United Kingdom firms these results are similar to those of Singh and Whittington who found that for a sample of over 200 United Kingdom firms there was a clear association between initial size and the dispersion of growth rates during the period 1948-1960.[52] The same study noted no statistically significant difference in the growth performance of different size companies. However, for the period 1954-1960, firms in the largest size class had an average growth rate that was (statistically) significantly greater than the average growth rate of firms in most other size classes.[53]

It is not possible to tell how many firms within each size class were transnationals in Singh and Whittington's data. But the present finding that the growth rate is smallest in the largest size class for firms in the sample is clearly at variance with studies that provide evidence of increasing levels of concentration. It may be that transnationals as a group grow more rapidly than other companies, but within the group of TNCs and TNC subsidiaries analysed here, the larger firms were clearly not growing more rapidly than the smaller. So far as the TNC subsidiaries are concerned, this finding might give some support to the "decapitalization" thesis according to which beyond a "saturation" point growth in TNC investment tends to fall off. Table 3 may provide some evidence that a saturation level had been attained by the larger TNC affiliates in Thailand and perhaps also in India.[54] Thus, in the case of the Thai and Indian companies, neither proposition associated with the Law of Proportionate Effect -- that (1) average growth rates and (2) their dispersion will be similar for different size classes -- is confirmed by this analysis.

The validity of the Law of Proportionate Effect has also been

TABLE 3. AVERAGE RATES OF GROWTH OF FIRMS IN DIFFERENT SIZE CLASSES

Opening size class	India		Thailand		United Kingdom	
	Mean rate of growth	Standard deviation	Mean rate of growth	Standard deviation	Mean rate of growth	Standard deviation
I. Small	115.8	134.8	36.8	36.2	73.8	74.6
II. Small to medium	57.4	61.0	46.1	48.1	100.2	109.6
III. Medium to large	33.8	39.2	7.2	23.0	30.5	18.8
IV. Large	30.8	39.8	6.5	15.0	9.7	23.9

Source: Data compiled by UNIDO from company balance sheets.

tested by examining the relationship between the size of a firm at
the beginning and end of a time period[55] using the following
regression equation:

$$\log S_{t+1} = a + b \log S_t + \mathcal{E}$$

If b = 1 and the variance of   is in fact constant, this implies
that for all firms irrespective of size the average and the
variance of the logarithms of proportionate growth are the same.[56]
This equation was estimated for the United Kingdom TNCs and the
Indian subsidiaries.[57] The estimate of b for the British TNCs was
0.997, or not significantly different from unity, thus
contradicting the earlier finding[58] that growth was negatively
associated with size. It also contradicts Singh and Whittington's
results, which showed a positive relationship.[59] On the other
hand, Hart found evidence of the validity of the Law of
Proportionate Effect for a sample of British firms.[60] For the
Indian subsidiaries, the value for the regression coefficient was
only 0.89, which was significantly different from zero and
considerably below unity. This result implies that the smaller TNC
subsidiaries were growing at a more rapid rate than the larger
ones, and that the gap between them was closing. The result (or
fit) obtained for the Indian firms was not particularly good and
there is some doubt about the extent to which the estimated
equation correctly represents the distribution of growth rates. In
general, the result was not conclusive enough to reject the
possibility of the operation of the Law of Proportionate Effect.

One important aspect of the results presented in table   3 is
that they show no evidence of increasing concentration. This is
contrary to findings of Prais for the United Kingdom,[61] according
to which the share of the top 100 manufacturing companies increased
from about 20 per cent of net output in 1950 to almost 50 per cent
by 1980.[62]

From Thailand, the distribution of growth rates for size class
in a sample of national firms is presented in table   4. Once
again it is evident that there is a marked (highly statistically
significant) difference between the growth performance of firms in
the smallest size class[63] and other firms. The table cannot
provide any direct evidence on increasing levels of concentration.

Industrial concentration may be studied from both a static and
a dynamic point of view. The former involves the use of an index
of concentration that measures the predominance of the largest
firms in the economy over a period. The dynamic approach studies
the way in which the firms in the industrial sector have changed
ranks as a result of growth. A "transition matrix" has been built
to study the internal mobility of firms in the present sample.

Table   5 shows, for example, that for the United Kingdom
group, 57.1 per cent of the firms in the lowest size class at the
beginning of the period remained in the same size class at the end
of the period, while 42.8 per cent went up by one size class. For
the Indian group 71.4 per cent of the firms in the second highest
size class remained in the same size class; 14 per cent moved up by
one size class, and another 14 per cent went down by one size
class.

TABLE 4. DISTRIBUTION OF GROWTH RATES BY SIZE CLASS, THAI NATIONAL SAMPLE, 1976-1977

Opening size class	Mean growth percentage rate	Standard deviation
I. Small	94.1	144.1
II. Small to medium	5.3	35.6
III. Medium to large	-2.3	11.9
IV. Large	3.3	23.4

Source: Data compiled by UNIDO from company balance sheets.

TABLE 5. TRANSITION MATRIX FOR MEASURING THE MOBILITY OF FIRMS

(Percentage)

Opening size	India I	II	III	IV	Thailand I	II	III	IV	United Kingdom I	II	III	IV
I. Small	20	50	10	20	75	25	—	—	51.7	42.8	—	—
II. Small to medium	—	46.6	40	13.4	20	80	—	—	—	81.8	9.1	9.1
III. Medium to large	—	14.3	71.4	14.3	—	20	60	20	—	—	100	—
IV. Large	—	—	—	100	—	—	50	50	—	—	—	100

Closing size[a]

Change

	-1	0	+1	+2	+3
Proportion of total firms changing size class (India)	2.1	60.8	23.9	6.5	4.3

	-1	0	+1
Thailand	15	70	15

	-1	0	+1	+2
United Kingdom	—	83.3	13.13	3.3

[a] I, small; II, small to medium; III, medium to large; IV, large.

The results shown in table   5 are biased downward in that the
construction of the matrices does not permit firms in the highest
opening size class to move up. The results are biased upward in
that the matrix does not permit firms in the lowest size class to
move down. In the case of the Thai and United Kingdom groups of
firms, this is not an important limitation;[64] the majority of the
firms -- 83 per cent of the United Kingdom TNCs and 70 per cent of
the Thai firms -- did not change size class. There is little
evidence of internal mobility. The present findings are not
irreconcilable with the studies of United Kingdom industry that
have found rising levels of concentration. Specifically, the
present results show that in the case of manufacturing TNCs in the
United Kingdom, although growth rates tend to be inversely related
to size, the difference in the growth performance of firms within
the sample was not sufficient to alter the size distribution. Very
few firms switched size class. It seems, therefore, that the
impact of the higher growth rates of the smaller TNCs on overall
levels of concentration is small.

For the Indian subsidiaries, on the other hand, adjustments in
table   5 would make significant differences. The top three firms
in the highest size class had closing sizes that were over 25 per
cent in excess of their opening sizes. If these firms were to have
moved to a "largest-plus-one" size class, 21 of the 46 firms (i.e.
45.6 per cent)[65] would have gone up by one size class or more.
Thus, although the majority of the firms once more seemed to have
remained in their initial size class, the possibilities of
switching were greater as was the impact of growth rate
differentials on the levels of industrial concentration.

The finding that levels of industrial concentration are most
likely to be affected by differential growth performances among the
Indian firms is also confirmed by a rank correlation analysis. The
value of the Spearman y for firms ranked by opening and closing
size was 0.953 for the Thai group, 0.927 for the United Kingdom
TNCs, but only 0.629 for the Indian firms. The lower the value of
y the greater the relative mobility of firms. Thus, while mobility
was comparatively high among the group of Indian subsidiaries, it
was virtually non-existent for the United Kingdom TNCs and the Thai
firms. It is important to note that for the latter two groups the
estimates of mobility were significantly lower than similar
estimates for national industry. The value of y_s (Spearman) for
the 20 national firms in Thailand was estimated as 0.83. Singh and
Whittington's estimates of y_k for surviving registered (i.e. large)
British firms for a 12-year period ranged between 0.69 and 0.72.[66]
For a 6-year period, their estimates ranged from 0.771 to 0.873.[67]

The results indicate a weak negative relationship between size
and growth. Smaller firms grew at a faster rate in all three
country groups, but their growth performance was more erratic than
that of the larger enterprises. Moreover, except perhaps in the
case of the Indian firms, the difference in growth rates was not
sufficient to lead many firms to switch ranks within the respective
group and was thus not likely to have a pronounced impact on the
level of industrial concentration.

Growth And Profitability

The relationship between growth and size has been shown to be
negative for the firms in the present sample; this finding is
contrary to the predictions of economic theory, which postulate
that there is no relationship between these variables.
Conventional theory postulates that in equilibrium no relationship
will exist between growth and profitability, that all firms will
have achieved their optimum size and will have ceased to grow. If
equilibrium does not exist, the relationship between growth and
profitability will be determined by the causes of disequilibrium
and the speed with which firms adjust to their equilibrium
position.68 The theory regards a firm's growth as dependent on
ability and willingness to grow. Profitability clearly adds to a
firm's potential for growth, and, therefore, in an expanding
economy a positive association between these two variables should
be expected. A firm's willingness to grow, on the other hand, is
likely to be related to its level of profitability in a more
complicated manner. With regard to TNC subsidiaries, there may be
a tendency to transfer profits from the host country to the home
country or to other host countries; hence the observed association
between profits and growth may be a weak one within a given
national sample. Moreover, in the case of a TNC, the willingness
to grow may also depend on demand and labour conditions in a wide
range of industries that it seeks to integrate. Furthermore,
inasmuch as such TNCs are likely to be predominantly
management-controlled rather than owner-controlled firms, the
relationship between growth and profitability may be weak. Some
authors argue that the former type of firm maximizes growth subject
to a "profit-satisfying" constraint. Such firms may, beyond a
certain point, consciously sacrifice higher profits for higher
growth.69
    The following equations were estimated for the firms in the
sample:

$$\text{Growth} = a + b \, X \, (\text{Profitability index}) + \varepsilon$$
$$\text{Growth} = a + b \, X \, (\text{log Profitability}) + \varepsilon$$
$$\text{Log Growth} = a + b \, X \, (\text{Log Profitability}) + \varepsilon^{70}$$

Profitability indices were (a) rate of return of net assets;
(b) net profits to sales; (c) net profits to equity assets. There
were a total of 18 estimates. The "best" estimates are reproduced
in table   6. For the United Kingdom and Indian firms, a
positive relationship between levels of profitability and growth
can be discerned. However, estimated equations clearly do not
provide a good explanation of the relationship between
profitability and growth. The value of R^2 (the coefficient of
determination) is very low, indicating that the estimated curve
does not adequately fit the actual scatter of points on the graph
that related growth to profitability. It is clear that a simple
linear relationship between profitability and growth is not
obtained. The low value of the coefficient of determination may be

TABLE 6. IMPACT OF PROFITABILITY ON GROWTH

Coefficient	India	Thailand	United Kingdom
Independent variable	Net profit to net assets	Net profit to net sales	Log of rate of return on net assets
Value of regression coefficient	2.61[a]	−0.94[b]	1.105[b]
Value of coefficient of determination	0.12	0.18	0.11

Source: Data compiled by UNIDO from company balance sheets.

[a]Significantly different from zero at a 5 per cent confidence level.
[b]Significantly different from zero at a 10 per cent confidence level.

[1]Marris, *op. cit.,* chap. 1.
[2]*Ibid.,* chap. 2.
[3]For specification of these models, see Singh and Whittington, *op. cit.,* pp. 150-153.

accounted for by a significant specification error in the regression models. This may be owing to heteroscedasticity in the variance of the distribution of the errors in the models and/or owing to the fact that the relationship between growth and profitability was not linear. Evidence of differences in the relationship between growth and profitability at different growth rates has been estimated.[71] Hence some non-linearity in this relationship can clearly be discerned.

It may be argued that some of the weakness of the association between growth and profitability discerned here is because the independent variables include amounts payable to the Government as taxation. On the basis of the information available, it was not possible to determine the duration of the payment of this taxation in the case of the Indian and the Thai firms. Some of the taxation may have been deferred and have served as a source of financing growth. For the United Kingdom group, an analysis of the firms' financial statements permitted a reasonably accurate estimate of "profits net of taxation". Size equations were fitted and the equation that related the logarithm approximation of the relationship.[72] It is thus clear that there is a closer relationship between profits net of taxation and growth. Of course, it is <u>net</u> profits that enhance a firm's "ability to grow", and a closer relationship with growth is to be expected, particularly if growth is defined with reference to financial assets as in the present study. It is all the more interesting to note, therefore, that even if the figures on net profits provided by the sources used in this study are accepted, there is no appreciable change in the estimates of the equation relating profitability to growth for either the Indian or the Thai firms.

Results for the Thai firms may be regarded largely as inconclusive because of the shortness of the period under study. Six equations relating profitability indices to growth were estimated for 50 of the largest Indian manufacturing companies for the period 1966-1971. Double-log models provided the best fit.[74] Four of the six equations demonstrated a significant impact of profitability on growth. There is, therefore, some justification for arguing that Indian subsidiaries were either growth-maximizing firms and not dependent on high profit rates for growth, or that they did not use their profits for domestic expansion. For about 46 per cent of the subsidiaries, the rate of growth of net profits exceeded the rate of growth of net assets. Thus, it can be argued that a significant number of the subsidiaries did not employ a large proportion of earnings for domestic expansion.

The results for the United Kingdom TNCs corresponded broadly with Singh and Whittington's estimates of the relationship between profitability and growth for larger firms.[75] They found that there were differences in the relationship between profitability and growth among large and small firms within their sample. In the majority of the cases, they obtained a higher value of R^2 for the smaller firms than for the larger ones.[76] This phenomenon implies that changes in levels of profitability explain a larger proportion of the variation of growth among smaller firms than among larger ones.

The relatively modest estimates for R^2 and for the regression coefficient arrived at in the present investigation suggest that the United Kingdom TNCs -- the largest British firms in existence -- are less constrained by short- and medium-term profitability. Profitability is a longer-term constraint on these firms than on the comparatively smaller firms, which make up the majority in the Singh-Whittington sample. It is not possible, however, to establish the extent to which the TNCs in the present sample are "profit-satisfying" entities and deliberately "sacrifice" profits for maximizing growth, on the basis of the preceding analysis. The lack of association between growth and profitability once again indicates a lack of evidence about increasing industrial concentration -- the firms with the highest potential to grow (as measured by the profitability indices) do not exhibit a growth performance different from the other firms in the present sample.

Thus, growth is not explained by levels of profitability by the preceding method of investigation for the firms in the sample. According to economic theory, variables measuring the level of capacity utilization explain the growth patterns of such firms more adequately. This theory, however, takes a more restricted view of the growth process than that implied by the definition that has been used so far in this study. It is concerned with analysing changes in the level of firms' investment -- defined as changes in fixed assets -- over a period of time. This theoretical framework is used below in an examination of the investment behaviour of the TNCs and subsidiaries in the present sample.

Determinants Of Investment

A theory of investment behaviour concerns factors that induce a firm to increase its demand for capital equipment and that influence the availability of funds for investment purposes. The former may be regarded as a demand function and the latter as a supply function. An adequate investment theory should integrate both demand and supply factors in seeking an explanation for changes in capital expenditure.

In capacity-utilization theories of investment it is postulated that changes in capital stock are strictly proportional to the (positive) rate of change in output. Investment is held to be proportional to the difference between the desired capital stock and existing capital stock at the beginning of a period. The desired capital stock is predicted on the assumption that the current level of sales will continue into the future. This approach assumes that investment varies with output and sales. Some authors have pointed out that in capacity-accelerator theories of investment profits are also adequately accounted for, since they are closely associated with both sales and capital stock. Capacity-acceleration models have been developed by using more complex distribution lags and taking irreversibilities into account. However, the basic framework has remained largely unchanged.

The main alternative to the capacity-utilization theories of investment are the profit theories. These may be divided broadly into two: (a) those that hold that investment depends on present profit rates since these reflect future profits, and (b) those that postulate a linear relationship between profits and sales and hence consider the profit theories to be hypotheses subsidiary to the capacity-utilization theories. Some theories also take market imperfections etc. into account and predict that the investment rate will be restricted mainly to gross profit levels.

The investment behaviour of the firms in the present sample was analysed by fitting a number of single equation regression models to the data. It was not possible to use any but the simplest specifications. The most important drawback of the models was the inability to experiment with a number of distributed lag systems, which may allow a better specification of the relationship between investment and the independent variables included in the model. Moreover, it was not possible to take asset appreciation or other price changes into consideration.

The capacity-utilization models have regressed sales, capital stock and the ratio of sales to capital stock (which is a measure of capital intensity) on investment. In the profit models, profits after taxes, fixed assets and the capital-intensity indictor have been regressed on changes in capital stock. Equations combining the capacity-utilization and profit models have also been estimated. The specifications of the models are along conventional, generally accepted lines.[77] The results are summarized in table 7. for the United Kingdom and the Indian firms, the accelerator models gave better explanations.

For the United Kingdom TNCs the best fit was obtained by the model that relates the ratios of capital stock and capacity utilization to total capital, to investment.[78]

For the Indian data, the best fit was given by a profit model, but only one profit coefficient was significant at a 5 per cent confidence level. Thus, the capital-utilization variables are again judged to be the better estimators of the relationship between investment growth and the economic variables.

The results for the Thai firms were largely inconclusive. The best fit was obtained by models that combined the profit and the capacity-utilization variables; only one regression coefficient was significantly different from zero. This indicates that changes in capacity utilization and profit are not shown to influence the level of investment. It is interesting to note that a better fit for the data on Thai national firms was obtained by the combined models. The fit obtained for the national data was significantly superior to that obtained for the Thai subsidiaries. Moreover, both profit and capacity-utilization estimations were found to have a significant impact on investment.[79] It is thus evident that the investment behaviour of the national firms was adequately explained by the simple combined models, and that profits were an important determinant of the investment decisions of these firms.

The results for the Indian subsidiaries were also at some variance with the studies of Indian national firms. Although capacity-utilization variables were shown to be associated with

TABLE 7. INVESTMENT BEHAVIOUR OF TRANSNATIONAL CORPORATIONS AND
SUBSIDIARIES[a]

Characteristics	India	Thailand	United Kingdom
Largest R^2 obtained for capacity-utilization models	0.80	0.20	0.99
Largest R^2 obtained for profit models	0.84	0.31	0.78
R^2 obtained for combined models (containing both capacity-utilization and profit indicators as independent variables)	0.80	0.35	0.81
Sales coefficient; number of significant coefficient	6	1	3
Capital stock coefficient; number of significant coefficient	8	0	3
Capital-intensity coefficient; number of significant coefficient	8	0	6
Profit coefficient; number of significant coefficient	1	0	0

[a] A small minority of regression coefficients were significant at the 5 per cent level but had the "wrong" (i.e. not predicted by economic theory) sign. These have not been included in the table.

growth in capital stock,[80] financial variables were also important determinants of the investment decision.

For the period 1962-1970, Krishnamurty and Sastry have analysed the behaviour of about 360 Indian firms in a number of industries and have concluded that: "In the capital goods sector the cross section results suggest the importance of financial variables, (but) the accelerator estimators do not seem to have any impact at all".[81] The few significant profit coefficients estimated for the Indian subsidiaries in the present study thus reveal that domestic demand conditions are more important determinants of their investment decisions, and medium-term profitability is a less important determinant than for the national Indian firms. It is important to note that the present estimates of R^2 are invariably higher than those of Krishnamurty and Sastry.[82] This may in part be accounted for by differences in model specifications.

In the case of the Thai subsidiaries, the inability of the models to explain the relationship between investment, on the one hand, and the accelerator and profit variables, on the other, may be because factors external to the Thai economy are the main determinants of the growth of capital stock of these subsidiaries. Such factors could be the level of economic and political stability in other potential host economies, or factors not easily taken into account by these models, such as high levels of intra-firm trade that are effectively camouflaged by transfer pricing.

With regard to the better performance of the capacity-utilization models for the United Kingdom TNCs, it has been argued that in periods of economic expansion, capacity-utilization is more likely to be an important determinant of the decisions to invest than profit variables. In periods of recession, on the other hand, external borrowing becomes difficult, and the ability of a firm to make profits becomes an important determinant of its ability to expand its capital stock.[83] The period 1975-1979 was one of industrial contraction in the United Kingdom. It is interesting to note that during this period a decline in profit rates was not an important constraint on the investment plans of the large TNCs included in this study. Their investment schedules were based on longer-term planning. They could mobilize resources to maintain investment levels, and, clearly, demand conditions were important in determining investment levels.

On the basis of the foregoing analysis, it is possible to state that systematic variations in the growth process of TNCs in the United Kingdom and subsidiaries in India have been identified. For the Thai firms, the results are inconclusive. In none of the three cases, however, was there any systematic association between profit estimators and other variables. An attempt will be made below to identify the determinants of profitability.

Determinants Of Profitability

The theory of the growth of the firm emphasizes the
relationship between profits and the size of the firm. If a
positive relationship can be established or if the dispersion of
profits can be shown to decline systematically with size, then it
can be argued that higher profits provide an incentive for growth.
If there is no systematic variation of profits with size,
profitability will not provide an incentive for expansion. The
evidence on the relationship between size and profitability for
firms included in this study is presented in table   8.   It appears
that there is no clear association between the size of firms and
their profitability -- as measured by the rate of return on net
assets -- for either the United Kingdom or the Indian firms. For
the United Kingdom TNCs, however, if firms of the smallest size are
ignored, a negative association between profitability and size does
emerge. The average profit rate in size class II is significantly
different (statistically) from that of the two larger size classes.
There is no systematic variation in the standard deviation of the
rate-of-return measure by size class in any of the country groups.
For the Thai subsidiaries, there is an apparent positive
association between size and profitability. However, if one
extreme case is eliminated from the largest size class, the average
profit rate for that size class declines to 3.5 per cent, a rate
significantly below that of any other size class. Thus, the
evidence on the relationship between size and profitability is once
again obscured.
The inconclusive character of the results shown in table V.8
is even more clear when account is taken of the inherent limitation
of the measure of profitability that was employed. Differences in
methods of fixed asset evaluation may introduce systematic biases
in the estimation of the profit indictors. Unfortunately, it was
impossible to account for these biases. Furthermore, the small
number of firms included in the individual size classes rendered
the average figures highly dependent on extreme values, as is
illustrated by the Thai firms. In order to deal with this second
difficulty, regression analysis was employed to estimate the
relationship between size and profitability.
The following regression models were used:

$$P = a + bS + \varepsilon$$
$$P = a + b \log S + \varepsilon$$
$$\log P = a + b \log S + \varepsilon \quad ^{84}$$

where

$\underline{P}$ was estimated variously as:

(a) rate of return on net assets
(b) post tax rate of return on equity assets
(c) post tax profits to net sales

TABLE   8.   DISTRIBUTION OF PROFITABILITY BY SIZE CLASS: RATE OF RETURN
ON NET ASSETS

Size class	India (1966-1971)		Thailand (1976-1977)		United Kingdom (1975-1979)	
	Mean rate of return	Standard deviation	Mean rate of return	Standard deviation	Mean rate of return	Standard deviation
I. Small	39.44	26.94	6.13	11.17	11.49	4.30
II. Small to medium	29.03	16.58	9.80	9.90	31.35	19.20
III. Medium to large	31.86	20.80	13.86	16.15	17.03	4.83
IV. Large	25.84	13.44	21.46	40.70	15.40	13.48

Source: Data compiled by UNIDO from company balance sheets.

S = opening size of the firm
$\overline{\mathcal{E}}$ = the disturbance term.

The relationship between profits and size was found to be very weak. There was no association whatsoever in the case of the United Kingdom firms. For the Thai subsidiaries, the logarithmic equation relating net profits as a proportion of net sales to opening size of firms yielded evidence of a significant negative association, indicting some reason to believe that the larger Thai subsidiaries were less profitable than the smaller ones.

A comparison of these results with those for national firms reveals diverse trends. For Thai national firms, no significant association was discerned between opening size and the profitability indices. For a sample of 50 Indian national firms, on the other hand, there was a significant negative association between profits to net assets and opening size. However, the fit obtained by the equation was very weak. Figures were not available for United Kingdom national firms for the same period covered by this investigation. For an earlier 12-year period, Singh and Whittington found no systematic association between size and average profitability, although they did find that larger United Kingdom firms had less variable profit performances.[85] The present study did not find evidence of such a relationship.

The overall conclusion is therefore that size is not a prime determinant of profitability of firms in the present sample. This is thus not a distinguishing characteristic of transnational enterprises and their subsidiaries. Nor do national firms exhibit a marked association between size and profitability.

In line with other research, an attempt was also made to relate profitability to financing patterns.[86] The results are briefly summarized below. For the Thai subsidiaries, net profits to sales were significantly negatively associated with measures of liquidity and gearing.[87] For the Indian data, on the other hand, there was evidence of a significant positive association with both total liquidity and levels of profit retention.[88] Also for the Indian firms, there was a significant positive association between profitability and dividend payments, suggesting that the financing patterns of the Thai and Indian subsidiaries differed significantly. The latter group of firms apparently borrow more "efficiently" and effectively. Profitable Thai subsidiaries tend to rely mainly on internal resources. (It should be stressed that this is a finding derived from indirect evidence. It was not possible to estimate the retention ratio for the Thai firms in the sample.)

The results for the United Kingdom TNCs indicated a weak positive association between profitability and indicators measuring retention.[89] There was also a relatively strong association between profitability and dividend payments, indicating the relative importance of equity resources. No significant association appeared between profitability and measures of external financing, a result not unexpected in a period generally characterized by a trend towards industrial contraction.

The general conclusion is that conventional analysis is not a particularly adequate tool for explaining differences in levels of profitability of subsidiaries and of transnationals.[90] On the other hand, a number of studies of corporate profitability of national Indian firms have shown a significant association between profitability indicators and financing variables, thus supporting conventional theory as an adequate framework for an analysis of profitability variations among national firms in India. For the group of Thai national firms described earlier, the association between profitability and financial variables was found to be very low.

Finally, an attempt was made to determine the persistency of profits. If a firm enjoys monopoly power or possesses superior management resources, it could be expected to remain relatively more profitable over a period of time. Persistency of profitability was estimated by the equation

$$P_1 = a + P_{t-1} + \mathcal{E}$$

where t is the last year of the period and $t - 1$ the first year, and P represents different indicators measuring pre- and post-tax profitability. These equations were fitted to the Indian and United Kingdom groups of firms. For the Indian data, a significant positive relationship was discerned although the fit was poor.[91] For the United Kingdom TNCs, on the other hand, a good fit was obtained[92] and once again there was evidence of a strong positive association. Further, the correlation coefficient (Spearman) for firms ranked by the profitability indices in the first and last years of the period under study was 0.763 for the sample of United Kingdom TNCs and 0.422 for the Indian subsidiaries. It is clear, therefore, that whereas the persistency of profits was comparatively high for the United Kingdom firms, it was moderate for the Indian subsidiaries. A corresponding coefficient for the 50 largest Indian national firms, ranked by profitability in the first and last years of the same time period, was 0.399, or not significantly different from the estimate for Indian subsidiaries. On the other hand, the value of the coefficient of correlation for United Kingdom TNCs was significantly higher than that found in other studies of 364 British manufacturing firms over a 12-year period.[93] Thus, there is a distinction in the persistency of profitability for the United Kingdom and Indian firms. In neither case, however, was the preceding analysis particularly successful in revealing the major determinants of interfirm variations in profitability.

Implications For Host Government Policies

The lack of association between profitability and what are generally regarded as its financial and economic "determinants" may be explained partly by the existence of transfer pricing within TNC systems.

The level of transfer pricing is associated with the extent of the intra-firm trade of a given industrial branch. This in turn is affected by technological intensity, the divisibility of the production process and the need for after-sales servicing.[94] Potential for and incidence of transfer pricing is highest in product areas characterized by high levels of specialization. It is also associated with high economies of scales and significant levels of international integration of production structures. Industries that operate on R and D intensive technologies of production and that maintain a close co-ordination between production and marketing systems use firm-specific products and are usually dominated by TNCs that can "maximize the profitability of possessing special monopolistic advantages by internalizing trade".[95] It has been found that intra-firm trade -- and hence the potential for transfer pricing -- is highest in the technology-intensive industries, such as office machines, plastics and transport equipment. Textiles and apparel have what is described as "an intermediate level of intra-firm trade" attributable mainly to their highly integrated marketing structures. Industrial branches with low levels of intra-firm trade are characterized by the existence of standardized products, a widely diffused technology and a relatively loose international marketing structure. These industries include metals, non-metallic minerals and industrial chemicals. In general, it may be argued that the more generally a product is traded and the less specific it is, the smaller the likely difference will be between "arms-length" and transfer prices. Governments of developing countries need not be overly perturbed by such industries. In other industries, with highly specific products (e.g. pharmaceuticals), differences between arms-length and intra-firm prices have been found to be very extensive.[96] In such cases, it is important to identify factors inducing a TNC to increase this difference, and to take countervailing measures in the interests of the host and home economies.

The neo-classical theory of pricing does not adequately explain the process of transfer pricing within transnationals. Price theory is concerned with explaining behaviour when buyers and sellers seek to maximize profits at each other's expense. In intra-firm transactions, on the other hand, the aim is to maximize profits over the whole spectrum of activities integrated within the TNC system. An important incentive for making use of transfer pricing is provided by international differences in tax and tariff rates, by the operation of multiple exchange-rate systems (which apply relatively costly exchange rates to profit transmissions) and by limits imposed on the legal remittance of profits from host and home countries. Transfer prices may also be used by TNC subsidiaries to increase the share of parent company profits or to appreciate the value of the capital equipment provided by way of equity participation. Obviously, these policies may be at the cost of local shareholders. Local and foreign equity holders may, however, collude and use transfer pricing as a means for foreign accumulation of funds.

While there is no a priori reason to expect that transfer pricing will always be to the detriment of the host developing countries,[97] many analysts have held that "the cards are in fact

stacked heavily against the DCs".[98] Tax rates tend to be higher,
import duties on intermediate inputs tend to be comparatively low,
quantitative restrictions on repatriations of profits are usually
in force, and the socio-economic environment is vulnerable to
external and internal destabilizing pressures. It is therefore
important that developing countries pay some attention to devising
a consistent policy for dealing with problems of transfer pricing.

A first step in this direction could be to estimate the extent
of transfer pricing in specific areas. It has been argued that
this varies considerably between industries. It also varies with
the extent of organizational integration within TNC systems. The
greater the degree of centralized control and the greater the
subordination of subsidiaries to a head office, the greater the
potential for transfer pricing. On the other hand, area-based
TNCs -- as against TNCs that delegate executive responsibility for
product coverage -- are more prone to require subsidiaries to be
fairly autonomous profit-making enterprises. In such cases, the
scope for transfer pricing is likely to be more limited. The
Governments of developing countries should therefore not assume
that transfer pricing is an all-pervasive problem unvarying in
intensity and a necessary and unavoidable consequent of TNC
investment. For example, there is some evidence that despite the
fact that TNCs dominate certain branches of the foodprocuring
industry, they do not usually resort to transfer pricing in this
sector.[99]

On the basis of the foregoing arguments, Governments of
developing countries can adopt a number of means for dealing
effectively with the problem of transfer pricing. Some of these
are listed below:

(a) An attempt may be made to harmonize tax and tariff
structures;

(b) Imports to local subsidiaries may be channelled through a
independent importing agency;

(c) Use may be made of international organizations,
particularly those within the United Nations system, to monitor
prices of important imports and compare them with prices charged by
transnationals;

(d) Encouragement of local participation in the equity of TNC
subsidiaries may also help persuade these firms to adopt internal
restraints or to avoid excessive use of transfer pricing.

(e) Through regional co-operation schemes, the activities of
regionally based TNCs may be jointly monitored and access may be
requested to more detailed information than is currently available
in balance sheets and other financial statements.

These measures are naturally not without cost -- both
administrative and financial -- but they are unlikely to be a major
impediment to increased TNC investment in developing countries. A
number of studies have shown that TNCs are not particularly

responsive to fiscal incentives, and, in any case, taxes on corporate income in developing countries are generally lower than in the developed market economies. Moreover, many developed market economies --including the Federal Republic of Germany, Holland, the United Kingdom and the United States -- have been able to impose fairly stringent controls on transfer prices without in any way affecting the inflow of direct foreign investment.[100] The general economic environment of a country, its growth performance and its prospects are the primary influences affecting TNC investment. This is a finding supported by the analysis of investment behaviour undertaken in this study.

An expansion of TNC investment in developing countries can make a contribution to international industrial restructuring. The Governments of developing countries should pursue policies that facilitate its location in industrial branches in which these countries have a dynamic comparative advantage, in industries with the brightest medium- and long-term growth prospects. Co-operation between TNCs and developing countries can ensure that the costs and benefits of the expansion of these branches shall be equitably shared.

The main findings of the present analysis of investment patterns may be summarized as follows:

1. Growth -- measured in terms of (net) fixed and current assets -- is weakly associated with size in the present sample. This implies that there is some evidence to support the "saturation" thesis which holds that foreign investment falls off after a certain level of foreign participation has been achieved. No evidence has been found to substantiate the claim that TNC investment contributes to increased industrial concentration. Therefore, measures that limit industrial concentration should be applied with equal efficacy to subsidiaries and local firms.

2. Variations in levels of investment are best explained by the "accelerator" theories, which employ sales and capacity-utilization variables. This trend was most clearly evident for the United Kingdom transnationals and the Indian subsidiaries. For the Thai subsidiaries, on the other hand, the models combining accelerator and profit variables provided the "best" fit. Only one profit coefficient was significant, however, and therefore little can be inferred from this result. The closer association between investment and the capacity-utilization variables suggests that the economic conditions prevailing in host economies are likely to be important determinants of the level of TNC investment. In growing economies with high levels of capacity utilization, such investment is likely to expand rapidly. On the other hand, since TNCs and their subsidiaries appear to be less constrained by the availability of finance, government tax concessions and the liberal treatment of TNCs (in terms of permission to retain monopoly control of markets and thus to ensure the continued existence of artificially high levels of profits) is not likely to be particularly useful in attracting foreign investment, particularly in the long term.

The Governments of developing countries and TNC investors have a mutual interest in realizing the full economic potential of host economies. Clearly, the short-term costs incurred by different economic actors may be substantial. The finding that TNC investment levels are related to the rate of output growth and to the degree of market stability (for it is this second factor that induces high levels of capacity utilization) gives reason to expect that TNCs can be persuaded through a process of protracted negotiation to accept lower levels of short-term profitability in order to overcome structural bottlenecks in specific industrial branches in developing countries. The relatively industrialized developing countries with potentially large domestic markets are advantageously placed to persuade TNCs to take a longer-term perspective and to share the cost of industrial consolidation and rationalization within the developing world. This is evident from the present analysis of the investment behaviour of Indian subsidiaries. For the smaller developing countries with limited domestic markets -- such as Thailand -- opportunities in this field are perhaps more limited. It has been shown that short-term profitability is a significant determinant of subsidiary investment in the case of the Thai firms (although it is less significant than in the case of domestic manufacturing enterprises in Thailand). But the size of the domestic market is by no means necessarily limited by the rate of growth of domestic income and population. In the case of Thailand, for example, regional economic co-operation within the Association of South-East Asian Nations framework may be an important determinant of the size of the market in a wide range of industrial branches. "Collective bargaining" with the TNCs under the auspices of ASEAN may be an effective means of enhancing the development impact of foreign investment. Small developing countries -- and many less developed countries -- can make effective use of regional economic programmes in this respect.

3. The preceding analysis failed to show any systematic association between interfirm variations in profitability and growth size or the financial variables that were examined. This is not an entirely unexpected result. Since the mid-1970s a number of authors have opined that TNCs have considerable ability to transfer profits between home and host countries. If this is true, then declared profits may not be an accurate index of actual profitability, and hence the relationship between balance sheet estimates of rates of return and other variables may be obscured. Given the nature of the data available, the present study has not attempted to estimate the profit transfer. But a lack of association between profitability estimates and estimates of financing and investment behaviour may be explained in part by the existence of some elements of transfer pricing. Moreover, the fact that this lack of relationship is found for both the TNCs and the subsidiaries suggests that transfer pricing was not confined to transactions from host to home countries. Some transfer may also take place in the opposite direction, particularly if the home country is experiencing economic difficulties and the subsidiaries of the TNC are located in healthy and rapidly growing economies.

However, as the analysis demonstrates, there are many

effective measures that the Governments of developing countries can take -- both individually and collectively -- to restrict the extent of transfer pricing by transnationals in specific industries.

NOTES

[1] World Bank, World Development Report, 1980 (Washington, D.C., 1980), pp. 146-147.

[2] S. Lall and P. Streeten, Foreign Investment, Transnationals and Developing Countries (London, Macmillan, 1977), p. 4.

[3] United Nations Centre on Transnational Corporations, Multinational Corporations in World Development (New York, 1973), p. 32.

[4] United States Tariff Commission, Implications of Multinational Firms for International Trade and Labour (Washington, D.C., Government Printing Office, 1973), p.7.

[5] Ibid., pp. 7-13.

[6] See Lall and Streeten, op. cit., for a review of the evidence.

[7] OECD, Gaps in Technology and Analytical Report (Paris, 1970), table 23.

[8] United States Tariff Commission, op. cit., chap. 6.

[9] L. P. Jones, "Public enterprises in less developed countries" (Boston, Boston University).

[10] This is demonstrated in the case of the United States. See W. H. Davidson, "Factor endowment, innovation and international trade theory" Kyklos, 1979, pp. 764-774.

[11] C. Tugenhadt, The Multinationals (Harmondsworth, Penguin, 1971), p. 31.

[12] In contrast to TNCs that are area-based.

[13] V. Bornischer, "Multinational corporations and economic growth", Journal of Development Economics, vol. 7, June 1980, pp. 191-210.

[14] See R. S. Newfarmer and S. W. Mueller, <u>Multinational Corporations in Brazil and Mexico</u> (Washington, D.C., United States Senate Sub-Committee on TNCs, 1975), pp. 62 and 185, and L. Wilmore, "Director foreign investment in Central American manufacturing", <u>World Development</u>, 1976, pp. 490-578.

[15] Lall and Streeten, <u>op. cit.</u>, pp. 220-221.

[16] United Nations Centre on Transnational Corporations, <u>Transnational Corporation Linkages in Developing Countries</u> (New York, 1980), p. 41.

[17] <u>Ibid.</u>, p. 43.

[18] These estimates are evaluated in United Nations Centre on Transnational Corporations, <u>Transnational Corporatiom Linkages</u> . . . pp. 7-19. All data in this section (unless otherwise specified) are taken from this report.

[19] If 20 per cent foreign ownership is regarded as the cut-off point between TNC and domestic firms, it would lead to a higher direct TNC employment estimate than a cut-off point of 30 per cent.

[20] Figures are for the late 1970s (mainly 1978). The second estimate assumes that all TNC direct employment is in the industrial sector. United Nations Centre on Transnational Corporations, <u>Transnational Corporation Linkages</u> . . ., p. xl and <u>World Development Report, 1980</u>, pp. 110-11, 146-147.

[21] These estimates exclude China, Cuba, Democratic People's Republic of Korea and Mongolia, but include Viet Nam.

[22] Indirect employment is employment generated in industries associated with the industry in question. For example, increased activity in one industry will mean an increase in that industry's supply requirements, thus leading to an icnrease in employment in supplying or associated industries.

[23] G. L. Reuber, <u>Private Foreign Investment in Development</u> (London, Oxford University Press, 1973), pp. 151-154.

[24] S. Watanabe, "Exports and employment: The case of the Republic of Korea:, <u>International Labour Review,</u> vol. 107, No. 10 (December 1972), p. 495.

[25] United Nations Centre on Transnational Corporations, <u>Transnational Corporation Linkages</u> . . ., p. 43.

[26] Estimates are at current prices.

[27] D. Nayyar, "TNCs and manufactured exports from poor countries", <u>Economic Journal</u>, vol. 88, March 1978, pp. 61-63.

[28]Both estimates are at current prices.

[29]See A. J. Yeats, "Monopoly power, barriers to competition and the patterns of price differentials in international trade", Journal of Development Economics, vol. 5, No. 2 (1978), for evidence that small countries pay more for imported capital equipment than do larger ones.

[30]The major writings in this area are: Edith Penrose, The Theory of the Growth of the Firm (London, Oxford University Press, 1959); R. L. Marris, Economic Theory of Managerial Capitalism (London, Cambridge University Press, 1964); Myron Gordon, The Investment, Financing and Valuation of the Corporation (Illinois, Irwin Press, 1962); O. Williamson, The Economics of Discretionary Behaviour: Managerial Objectives in a Theory of the Firm (Englewood Cliffs, N.J., Yale University Press, 1964); J. Steindl, Random Processes and the Growth of the Firm (London, Allen and Unwin, 1965); P. Hart and S. Prais, "The analysis of business concentration: a statistical approach", Journal of the Royal Statistical Society, Series A, 1956, pp. 150-181; T. Barna, Investment and Growth Policies in British Industrial Firms (London, Cambridge University Press, 1962); H. Simon and G. Bonini, "The size distribution of business firms", American Economic Review, September 1958, pp. 607-617; S. Hymer and B. Pashigan, "Firm size and the rate of growth", Journal of Political Economy, December 1962, pp. 556-569; E. Mansfield, "Entry, Gibrat's Law, innovation and the growth of firms", American Economic Review, December 1962, pp. 1023-1051; A. Singh, Takeovers (London, Cambridge University Press, 1971); J. Palmer, "The profit variability effect of the managerial enterprise", Western Economic Journal, 1973; E. Kuh, Capital Stock Growth: A Microeconometric Approach (Amsterdam, North Holland Press, 19673); A. Singh and G. Whittington, Growth Profitability and Valuation (London, Cambridge University Press, 1968).

[31]Lall and Streeten, op. cit., p. 98.

[32]The annual balance sheets and the flow may contain other defects. See H. Rose, "Disclosure in company accounts" (London, Institute of Economic Affairs, 1965), and F. W. Paish, Business Finance (London, Pitman, 1965). On how some of the problems can be solved, see C. A. Wilk, Accounting for Inflation (London, Sweet and Maxwell, 1960).

[33]See R. Larner, Management Control and the Large Corporation (New York, Johns Hopkins University Press, 1970); P. Holl, "Effect of control type on the performance of the firm in the U.K.", Journal of Industrial Economices, June 1974, pp. 257-271.

[34]Singh and Whittington, op. cit., p. 221.

[35]Fortune, 13 August 1979, pp. 193-207. For a more detailed description of this data, see the appendix to this chapter.

[36] This judgement was formed on the basis of information supplied by the United Nations Centre on Transnational Corporations.

[37] Estimates were based on supplementary information from Government Business Monitor MA3 (London, HM Stationery Office, 1980), table 7, pp. 32-33.

[38] The relatively high proportion of sales of companies covered by the study shows that, in general, it was the larger companies that responded.

[39] V. Sriram and Associates, Top 300 Companies (New Delhi, Economic and Scientific Research Foundation of India, 1979).

[40] The exact figures may be found in the Reserve Bank of India Bulletin.

[41] Faculty of Commerce, Thamasat University, Directory of Thailand's 300 Largest Companies 1977-1978 (Bangkok, Thailand, 1979).

[42] Identified on the basis of company profits given in ibid., pp. 205-240.

[43] Lall and Streeten's sample consisted of 109 Indian and Colombian firms for which data were available for the year 1968-1969. See Lall and Streeten, op. cit., chap. 6, pp. 99-129.

[44] For a review of developments in the theory of the growth of the firm, see Fortune, 13 August 1979, pp. 193-207.

[45] Gibrat's Law suggests that the technology and market demand will not generate an optimal size for a "typical" firm. But this may not necessarily mean that individual firms within an industry do not have optimal induced sizes.

[46] Some economists have countered with the opinion that firms of medium size tend to grow faster than either small or very large firms, while others maintain that a firm's "willingness to grow" beyond a certain size may be reduced because of the nature of the association between growth and profitability.

[47] These specifications are generally used in empirical studies of Gibrat's Law. See Singh and Whittington, op. cit., p. 113.

[48] This equation could be estimated for firms with positive growth rates only.

[49] Neither the regression coefficient nor the coefficient of determination differed significantly

[50] The Welch-Aspin test was used. This test does not assume equal variances of growth rates in different size classes. See A. C. Aspin and B. C. Welch, "Tables for use in comparisons whose

accuracy involves two variances", Biometrika, vol. 36, 1949, pp. 290-296. The following comparisons did not prove to be significantly different: United Kingdom, class III and class IV; India, classes I and IV and III and IV; Thailand, classes I and II and III and IV.

[51]The standard F test for testing significance of differences in variances was applied.

[52]Singh and Whittington, op. cit., p. 80.

[53]Ibid., p. 77.

[54]Bornischer, loc. cit., pp. 191-193.

[55]J. M. Samuels, "Size and growth of firms", Review of Economic Studies, 1965, pp. 183-197.

[56]This is a restricted version of the Law which implies that the frequency distribution of opening size and closing size represents a log-normal surface.

[57]Thai companies were excluded because data extended over only two years.

[58]See pages 247-248.

[59]Singh and Whittington, op. cit., pp. 63-65.

[60]P. E. Hart, "The size and growth of firms", Economica, vol. 28, 1962.

[61]J. Prais, "A new look at the growth of industrial concentration", Oxford Economic Papers, vol. 29, July 1974, pp. 78-85.

[62]Loc. cit., p. 8.

[63]Even if the one firm that tripled its net assets over 1976-1977 is excluded, the mean growth rate of this size class is 30.36 per cent, which is significantly greater than the mean growth rate of all other size classes.

[64]No firm in the Thai group and only one firm in the United Kingdom group in the "highest" size class had net assets in the final yaer in sufficient excess of net assets in the first year of the period to justify being placed in a higher size class.

[65]According to table 5, this proportion is 34.78 per cent.

[66]Although y_k (not y_s) is estimated, Singh and Whittington note "the same pattern of relative mobility is observed when Spearman's y is computed as where y_k is used". Singh and Whittington, op. cit., p. 102.

[67]Singh and Whittington, op. cit., p. 102.

[68]Marris, op. cit., chap. 1.

[69]Ibid., chap. 2.

[70]For specification of these models, see Singh and Whittington, op. cit., pp. 150-153.

[71]But not reproduced.

[72]The fit obtained by these models was superior to that reproduced in table   6, and variations in profitability were found to have a significant impact on the growth performance of the firms. All b estimates in these models had the expected sign.

[73]The best estimate yielded an R^2 of 0.10 and a regression coefficient which, though positive, was significant at a 10 per cent confidence level.

[74]With R^2 ranging from 0.48 to 0.51.

[75]Singh and Whittington, op. cit., pp. 162-168. Their estimates of the coefficient of determination for the period 1954-1960 range from 0.10 to 0.29.

[76]Singh and Whittington, op. cit., pp. 154-157 and p. 163.

[77]They are primarily based on the work of Khu, op. cit.

[78]The two ratio models yield an R^2 of 0.99 and 0.79.

[79]R^2 is 0.79 for the "best" estimated equation: four regression coefficients for profit estimators and five regression estimates for capacity-utilization estimators (four in the combined models, one in "accelerator" models) were significantly different from zero.

[80]K. Krishnamurty and D. N. Sastry, Investment Accelerator and Financial Factor (Delhi, Institute of Economic Growth, 1973), p. 29.

[81]D. N. Sastry, Investment Behaviour in the Capital Goods Industry (Delhi, Institute of Economic Growth, 1973), p. 19.

[82]Krishnamurty and Sastry, op. cit., p. 41.

[83]M. Meyer and E. Kuh, The Investment Decision (Cambridge, Mass., Harvard University Press, 1957), pp. 116-136.

[84]The specification of these models is given in Singh and Whittington, op. cit., pp. 120-124.

[85]Singh and Whittington, op. cit., p. 144.

[86]Lall and Streeten, op. cit., pp. 123-129. Data on advertising expenditure and indicators measuring barriers to entry were not available for inclusion in this analysis.

[87]The value of the coefficient of determination was 0.61 when net profits to sales were regressed on estimates of total gearing, and rose to 0.67 when an aggregate liquidity indicator was added to the equation.

[88]The value of R^2 was 0.54.

[89]The value of R^2 was only 0.17.

[90]These results are not at variance with those of other researchers. One study found relatively few statistically significant regression coefficients in an analysis of the impact of financial policy on profitability levels in a sample of Indian and Colombian subsidiaries.

[91]The average value of R^2 was only 0.201.

[92]The average value of the coefficient of determination was as high as 0.87.

[93]Singh and Whittington, op. cit., p. 139.

[94]S. Lall, The Multinational Corporation (London, Macmillan, 1980), p. 106.

[95]Ibid., p. 139.

[96]C. Vaitsos, Intercountry Income Distribution and Transnationals (Oxford, Clarendon Press, 1974).

[97]The present study finds a lack of association between declared profits and what are usually recognized as variables determining the variation in interfirm profitability for the United Kingdom as well as for the Indian and Thai firms. There is thus indirect evidence of the existence of some transfer pricing in both home and host countries. Many "home" developed market economies -- notably the United States -- have enacted measures to control transfer pricing. See M. C. Duess, Tax Allocations and International Business (New York, The conference Board 1978).

[98]Lall, op. cit., p. 117.

[99]

[100]Ibid., p. 148.

Multinational Enterprises, Employment and Technology Adaptations

SUSUMU WATANABE

Opinions remain split as to whether multinational enterprises (MNEs) have been making sufficient efforts to help the Third World countries which host them to attain their development goals. This is especially true with respect to employment creation and technology choice and adaptation. Consequently, those who are concerned about the slow progress made on the development front often have mixed feelings of expectation and frustration vis-a-vis MNEs. Disappointed critics tend to create, consciously or unconsciously, a hostile public attitude towards these enterprises. This is unfortunate, since MNEs can be one of the major driving forces of economic development as the experience of Singapore, the Republic of Korea, Hong Kong, Brazil, Mexico, etc., demonstrates.

My contentions in this article are: (1) that the extent and pattern of employment and technological adaptation that can be realistically expected of MNEs are more or less narrowly determined once their product and target market have been chosen in the given context of the host country's economic conditions and policy set-up; (2) that they can, however, vary considerably from one industry to another depending on the nature of the product, and also over time as a result of changes in the local context; and (3) that frustrations regarding the MNEs' performance accrue, more often than not, from overestimation of their adaptive capacity and from neglect of the important bearing of the time element on the growth of such capacity.

These points will be elaborated upon in the following pages, after which some suggestions will be made for future policy makers and researchers. For purposes of illustration, reference will occasionally be made to findings of recent field work, but neither a thorough review of the literature nor a comprehensive assessment of employment and technological adaptation by MNEs is intended.[1]

From **INTERNATIONAL LABOUR REVIEW**, Vol. 120, No. 6, Nov.-Dec. 1981, (693-709), reprinted by permission of the publisher.

I. SCOPE FOR TECHNOLOGICAL ADAPTATION

Researchers often compare the technology used by an MNE in a host country with that used in its home country, and then proceed to assess the extent of its efforts at technological adaptation, on the implicit assumption that considerable opportunities exist for such adaptation. In many cases this is unrealistic, for different reasons.

(i) Technological Constraints

In "low-technology" industries producing unsophisticated conventional goods (e.g. non-synthetic textiles, footwear, food, crude metal products), a fair range of technological choice exists.[2] In any country people know these products well and, having manufactured them for generations as a matter of necessity, they are also familiar with the traditional production processes. Imported technologies often find local counterparts with which they can be "married" to produce "intermediate technologies". The Japanese textile industries (e.g. silk reeling) are a good example.[3] The variety of imported technologies itself tends to be large, because different countries of origin have different technologies based on their own traditions. In local markets in developing countries the customers' requirements as regards the quality of the product are likely to be flexible; not only a wide range of income groups need it, but it can function satisfactorily at different quality levels from a technical point of view. This provides the producers with a wide range of technological choice. MNEs may use technologies different from those used by indigenous firms, but not necessarily more capital-intensive. In some cases at least, MNEs' choice of factor proportions is more suitable to the local conditions thanks to their greater access to a wide range of technological alternatives.[4]

In the case of exports to the industrialised world, however, the choice of technology tends to become narrower even in these industries because of a more specific quality requirement.

In modern "high-technology" industries, the tolerance regarding the quality of the product, including parts and components, is usually limited (except in the case of repair shops and replacement parts). The developing countries rarely have a local technological base in these industries. Redesigning of the equipment and plant requires a considerable amount of time and money. Moreover, labour tends to be only a minor cost item.[5] Thus, technological adaptations are largely confined to scaling down of imported technologies to suit the small local market and replacement of machinery with manpower in the peripheral processes (e.g. in-plant transport, packing, etc.).[6] The scaling down of technologies can be achieved, for instance, by application of older vintages of technologies which MNEs used in their home countries some time ago. A typical example is the engine plant of Delta (Toyota) in the Philippines.[7]

Engineers often point out that scaling down of existing technologies is much more difficult than economists imagine. The supply of small-size technologies of older vintages is constrained by the lack of relevant information (e.g. blueprints) and by the high cost of obtaining it.[8] MNEs may be well placed in this respect, because they usually have long experience in their lines of business and consequently have a vast amount of technological information accumulated within the house. Even so, it will not always be easy or possible for them to find old equipment.

Technological constraints on such adaptations in the core processes (as opposed to the peripheral processes) are even greater in the processing industries (e.g. chemicals) and with respect to systems technology (e.g. a telephone exchange) than in the assembly industries such as automobiles and electronics.[9]

Within the assembly industries, the scope for technological adaptation varies between assembly and parts and components manufacturing, and from one type of part or component to another, because of difference in the nature of the product and in quality requirements (transmissions and axles compared with moulded rubber parts, for example).

MNEs are naturally concentrated in those lines of business where competition with local enterprises is either non-existent or quite limited, e.g. because of their superior technology.[10] Where the required technology is very common and the developing countries have comparative cost advantages because of lower labour costs, MNEs tend to resort to international commercial subcontracting[11] rather than to direct investment. These tendencies are intensified by host governments' policies of restricting foreign investment in those lines of business where local suppliers (including foreign subsidiaries) already exist.[12]

Another type of technological adaptation in these modern high-technology industries involves simplification of the product and/or use of local substitutes for imported materials. An important example is the Asian utility vehicles which have been introduced by major car assemblers (Chrysler, Ford, General Motors, Toyota and Volkswagen) in the ASEAN region since the early 1970s. Although the main components are the same as those of these assemblers' passenger cars, they have been redesigned on simplified lines for the local market and they look like large jeeps. Fabricated with more local components and more manual work, these vehicles are much cheaper (over 30 per cent in 1977-78) than the assemblers' smallest standard passenger cars, and they are used as mini-trucks and mini-buses. By 1977 they accounted for 30 per cent (nearly 20,000 units) of the total automobile sales in the Philippines. In the case of Toyota the model was designed in close consultation with its distributors in the Philippines and Indonesia, benefiting from the active participation of those distributors' R and D staff.[13] It may well be that the MNEs' efforts for the development of utility vehicles in this region were initially stimulated by the need for competing with imports from Japan in this relatively promising market. The Filipinos' two

decades of experience with "jeepneys"[14] must have been of some help
in this connection.

For the manufacturers of certain "new" daily consumption
goods and agricultural inputs (including machinery), R and D
efforts for adaptation of the product to local conditions and
discovery of cheap local substitutes for imported materials are
almost indispensable. For instance, Unilever spends considerable
resources for these purposes, both at its headquarters and at its
local plants. The optimum formulation of washing products (e.g.
soap) depends on such factors as the kind of clothing, the kind of
soil, the hardness and temperature of the water and the incidence
of washing machines, while the properties of edible fats such as
margarine have to vary from country to country, depending on local
people's taste, the product's texture, colour and stability at the
ambient temperature, and whether it is used as a spread or for
cooking. Unilever has succeeded in developing technologies to
extract oil from sal, neem, mowrah and rice bran for hard soap in
India. It has also developed technologies to produce edible oil
from previously neglected materials (babassu palm oil in Brazil and
coconut parings oil in Sri Lanka), and research is going on to
develop rice bran oil in Japan and passion fruit seed oil
in Kenya.[15] In Malaysia, where it has its own palm plantations, its
R and D staff, in collaboration with its laboratory in the United
Kingdom, it has recently devised a technology to grow a practically
unlimited number of palm trees from a single piece of tissue from a
parent plant by cloning.[16] Differences in the kind of soil, depth
of soil, pattern of rainfall, etc., often forbid direct
international transfer of agricultural machinery and induce
adaptations to imported equipment.[17]

Adaptations to local conditions of developing countries do not
always mean a relaxation of the quality standard. In Argentina the
greater distances and more difficult topography between
transmitting stations and receivers have necessitated designing of
transistor radios to stricter reception standards than in the
United States. Unfavourable conditions regarding maintenance
service and supply of parts, fuel, lubricants, etc., have raised
some quality standards for diesel engines in India to a level
higher than in developed countries.[18]

A recent survey of 75 American and 18 European MNEs[19]
suggests that host-market-oriented MNEs are generally most likely
to pursue R and D outside their own countries, particularly when
operating in the Third World. They are followed by
world-market-oriented MNEs, while home-market-oriented ones are
least likely to do R and D abroad. This tendency can be explained
by the factors mentioned in the previous paragraphs. It is also
true that in the case of exports the scope for product adaptation
is usually much more limited because importers have more or less
fixed ideas as to the quality standard and design of these
enterprises' products, especially in their home countries.

This brings us to another problem concerning a commonly
applied research method. Some researcher try to assess MNEs'
efforts at technological adaptation by comparing their plants with
indigenous firms in the same industry with respect to their
capital- or labour-intensity, using industrial census or similar

aggregate data. This approach is inadequate. For one thing, the two groups of enterprises are often engaged in different kinds of activities, even where statistically they belong to the "same" industry. For example, many indigenous assemblers of electronic and electrical appliances in Mexico use parts and components supplied by MNEs of various national origins.[20] Production of these parts and components requires modern equipment, while their assembly can be done largely by hand. MNEs will then naturally be more capital-intensive than local enterprises. Moreover, even where the two groups of enterprises are producing similar end-products (e.g. record players), their target market may be different. Many MNEs are under pressure from the host governments to export their products, and they cater for the relatively high-income consumer market, while local firms produce more commonly for the lower-income market. In such a case, the two groups have to satisfy different quality standards. Higher quality requirements usually demand more up-to-date and more capital-intensive technologies, because in modern engineering it is often the machinery that determines the quality of products.

The range of substitutability between labour and capital is usually narrow as long as product quality is held constant, relative factor prices not being the primary determinant of the technology decision in many industries.[21] In Brazilian metal engineering it has been found that the overwhelming determinants of technologies among MNEs are the scale of production and the quality of the product, while labour costs rank "a distant third".[22] A survey of over 300 firms in different industries of West Malaysia discovered that quality of product was by far the most important consideration in the choice of technology, followed by volume of annual production, raw material costs, price of machines, and familiarity with the technology. Labour costs came only after all these factors.[23] These findings are in conformity with my own in Filipino auto parts manufacturing.[24]

(ii) Economic Constraints

The intensity of MNEs' enthusiasm for the development of new products and inputs naturally depends on the expected gain. This, in turn, will be governed by a number of factors: (1) the size of the existing and potential market for the product, (2) the savings in material cost expected from the introduction of a new input, and (3) the required R and D costs.

While, as already mentioned, scaling down of technologies often implies the application of technologies of older vintages, efforts to develop new technologies will require the prospect of a market large enough to make the R and D project economically attractive. For example, Philips developed a simplified village radio in India, but this would have been impossible with a smaller market.[25] Similarly, the utility vehicles in the ASEAN region would have been unfeasible if the target market were confined within the national borders of a single State.

A frequent criticism levied against MNEs is that their global business strategy tends to neglect their host country's needs and development objectives. The experience related to the Asian utility vehicles, however, demonstrates that it can work in such a way as to reduce economic constraints on R and D programmes for poor countries.

Factor (2) can be considered as a technological factor, since its importance depends largely on the nature of the product and raw materials: the need for developing local raw materials and savings in the material cost expected from the introduction of local substitutes are considerable in certain lines of business (cf. the case of Unilever), while they may be negligible in industries based on standard materials, such as steel, which are cheaper when imported from industrialised countries than when produced locally, owing to economies of scale.

The cost of developing a new technology can be reduced considerably where reasonably good research institutes and researchers exist in the host country. This is indeed a major consideration in MNEs' choice of overseas R and D locations.[26] This condition is, however, rarely satisfied in the Third World. Similarly, the scope for the application of locally made--and therefore probably better-adapted-machinery depends partly on the nature of the industry and partly on the stage of development of local capital goods industry. "Low-technology" industries will naturally offer more opportunities for the use of local equipment than "high-technology" ones. The implications of the stage of development of local capital goods industry may be illustrated by the fact that all the necessary equipment used by Unilever for manufacturing detergents is supplied locally in India, while a certain percentage has to be imported in the case of Colombia.[27]

Where these economic and technical conditions are not met, technological adaptations tend to be too costly. Consequently, MNEs quite commonly apply a standard technology or a limited range of "recommended" technologies within their group all over the world. This gives rise to the already mentioned criticism that they do not pay sufficient attention to local needs and development objectives.

In his study of a multinational plastic footwear manufacturer, Boon[28] discovered that uniform quality standards were applied everywhere in the group, and the member companies in different countries were effectively obliged to use machines produced by three makers belonging to the group. All the machines were automatic and as versatile as possible so that they could make all kinds of shoes, sandals and boots. By manufacturing a limited variety of versatile machines, the group reduced its production costs through economies of scale. Use of common machines in the group permitted interplant transfer of managers and machines, and training, management of spare parts, stock-taking, printing of instructions, etc., became easier. Even where the machines were not produced by the member companies, the headquarters issued recommendations as to which should be used. In these cases, its strong negotiating power with some outside machine producers seemed to enable the group to secure considerable discounts.

As Boon notes, such a practice is not necessarily against the host countries' interest. At least part of the cost savings to these enterprises is also beneficial to consumers in the host countries. Besides, in the industries such as footwear, where products are diverse and sensitive to fashion, the use of universal machines is economical, especially for the relatively small markets of most developing countries.

I stressed earlier that the quality requirement and the scale of production are the major determinants in the choice of technology in modern industries. In reality, however, all kinds of modifications are made to imported modern machinery in the Third World, e.g. to slow down its speed for the purpose of coping with the irregular quality of raw or intermediate materials (e.g. cotton spinning in Thailand) and the lack of skill and discipline among workers (e.g. assembly of electrical and electronic appliances in Kenya). Mechanised equipment in metal engineering (e.g. in Manila)[29] is converted into semi-manual, because of the unreliable supply of electricity. When MNEs are operating on a sufficiently large scale, however, they usually try to solve these problems more positively so as to make imported equipment workable, by looking for ways of improving the quality of raw and intermediate materials, training local workers, installing their own generators, etc.

This may be elaborated upon with reference to medium and small enterprises in Mexican metal engineering. In Mexico the apprenticeship system was abolished in 1970, and the employers are usually obliged to pay fairly high statutory minimum wages even to the trainees. Consequently, most medium and small entrepreneurs are unwilling to take on school leavers and train them. The supply of skilled and semi-skilled labour being extremely short, many of them deliberately keep down the scale of their business, while a small minority who are lucky enough to be able to secure sufficient capital substitutes machines for labour to "cope with the problem of labour shortages".[30] Only relatively large firms, including foreign subsidiaries, hire school leavers and train them, partly because they can afford to set up the necessary training facilities and spend time and resources on the formalities needed to enable them to benefit from the Government's training incentive schemes.

In this connection, the following points need to be mentioned. The first is that the existence of masses of jobless people does not mean an abundant supply of labour. Shortage of labour can and does often exist in the ocean of unemployment and underemployment: large numbers of people are simply unemployable in modern industries because of lack of discipline, education and skills. In this respect, Japan was no exception: "One almost feels that Japan's prewar development was limited by the lack of paid labour suitable to large-scale, capital-intensive factories", a deep-seated antipathy to paid (and disciplined) employment being a major explanation for the prevalence of cottage industries.[31] Without doubt a similar statement holds good regarding many parts of the "urban informal sectors" in today's developing countries.

The second point is that the installation of facilities for refining materials, workers' training, power generation, etc., makes MNEs more capital-intensive than other firms which passively adapt themselves to the existing constraints without investing in such facilities. Consequently, MNEs' efforts tend to be evaluated unfavourably, since it is a common practice among economists to assess the degree of their technological adaptation in a labour-surplus economy with reference to the capital-labour ratio. In contrast, the other firms' approach (e.g. slowing down the speed of machinery) is usually considered to be "appropriate". This judgment may be reasonable where demand for the product is highly inelastic with respect to price and/or quality. It would be quite wrong, however, where there is a good chance of expanding the market, either domestic or international, by reducing prices or improving quality. For that matter, it is regrettable that economists and policy makers of or for developing countries do not appreciate the importance of sales efforts, working on the assumption that the extent of the market is more or less constant.

(iii) Institutional Constraints

My earlier remarks on the quality of labour and minimum wage legislation bring me to some by now well publicised institutional obstacles to the application of labour-intensive technologies. Management of machinery is easier than that of a large number of workers where labour unrest and tight restrictions on dismissal prevail. Substitution of machinery for labour is economical where the price of labour is raised by the minimum wage and other labour legislation, while many governments welcome the entry of foreign firms with up-to-date capital-intensive technologies for the sake of national prestige and are offended if foreign firms propose using old-fashioned but more economical labour-intensive technologies.[32]

These problems arise largely because the authorities screening the incoming foreign firms and technologies have criteria other than employment creation, or because the host government is not clear about priorities with respect to different policy objectives. I shall discuss this subject in some detail in section 3 below.

II. PROBLEMS IN ASSESSING EMPLOYMENT EFFECTS

Ideally speaking, an evaluation of the employment effect of an MNE must take account not only of the direct effect but also of the indirect and long-term effects, since it is the total effects that count in the context of development economies.

The direct employment effect is the employment created in the investor's own plant, which is determined by three factors: (1) the labour intensity (labour-output ratio) of the product, (2) the size of the existing market for the product, and (3) the sales

FIGURE 1. MNEs' Indirect Effects

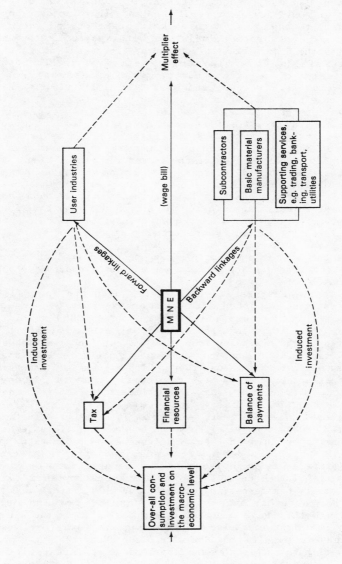

efforts made by the enterprise or its marketing agents, which will expand the extent of the market. As already discussed, the range of choice of technology open to MNEs is, generally speaking, fairly limited. In many cases, moreover, concentration of purchasing power in small groups of population and other factors, internal and external to them, make the market imperfect and the demand for their products rather inelastic with respect to the price.[33] So long as the home market is concerned, therefore, one can tell the scale of direct employment expected on an MNE more or less precisely for a given product. In the case of exports, the situation is different and MNEs' global distribution network can help to expand the market considerably (cf. the case of Volkswagen in Brazil, for example).

The indirect effects are naturally more complicated and difficult to quantify. The diagram depicts major conceivable indirect effects, excluding temporary employment created at the time of the construction of the investor's plant. The solid lines indicate the <u>primary</u> indirect effects that the MNE's operation will immediately generate outside its plant, while the dotted lines indicate the <u>secondary</u> indirect effects on the economy that accrue from the primary effects. An MNE's impact on the tax revenue, the balance of payments and the supply of capital in the country can be significant;[34] but it is practically impossible to evaluate the effects of such changes on employment.

Other conditions remaining constant, the relative importance of direct and primary effects per unit of product is determined by the nature of the product.

At one extreme lie those MNEs which are engaged in export processing of imported materials or assembly of consumer goods imported in the completely knocked down (CKD) form. In these cases, the primary indirect effects are almost negligible, being limited to those arising from their modest linkages with supporting activities (e.g. transport, banking and utilities). More or less the same can be said about those which are engaged in extraction of minerals and production of agricultural products for unprocessed export, although they sometimes stimulate an important development of the communications system (e.g. railways). It must be remembered, however, that, even where the linkage effects are quite limited, the secondary effects can be enormous if masses of people are employed in such export processing and production, creating a sizable effective demand for local industries. This is amply demonstrated by experience in the Republic of Korea, where the growth of local durable consumer goods industries such as automobiles has been stimulated considerably in this way.

At the other extreme is the case of trading companies. Although they have been relatively neglected in the literature on MNEs, the first four places in the overseas investment ranking of Japanese companies in 1980 were occupied by trading companies, in terms of both the total cumulative amount of investment and loans and the number of projects. Most of their investments had been made in joint ventures with other firms in the primary and secondary sectors, but each of them had 16 to 27 trading offices. About half of these offices were set up in the developing world.[35] Even Daieh, the largest retailer in Japan, which was ranked in

only the 82nd place in terms of the amount of overseas investment
and loans, had 13 small-sized purchasing offices abroad, eight of
them in South-East Asia and the People's Republic of China.[36] The
marginal direct employment created at their small purchasing
offices can be accompanied by sizeable indirect effects, resulting
from international commercial subcontracting of labour-intensive
products such as garments, toys, wigs, etc.

Between these two extreme cases, the relative importance of
the direct and indirect effects of MNEs varies considerably.
Forward linkages can be considerable in the case of basic, or
intermediate, material manufacturers; e.g. chemical fertiliser
manufacturing with agriculture, and synthetic textile manufacturing
with the export processing sector of the garment industry. As
already noted, MNEs in certain industries and countries have also
been making efforts to develop local sources of supply of their
inputs. In such cases, considerable employment can be created
through backward linkages.

In countries at an intermediate stage of industrialisation,
assembly industries such as automobiles, electrical and electronic
equipment, and industrial machinery manufacturing are growing.
Multinational assemblers are under pressure from host governments
to subcontract manufacturing of parts and components to local
enterprises, although most of their main subcontractors are also of
foreign origin and include MNEs like Spicer, Lucas, etc.

The actual extent of these primary indirect effects depends,
obviously, on (1) the scale of production, (2) the type of market
(export or local), and (3) the availability of local inputs (i.e.
basic materials, parts and components, and various services).
Without adequate supplies of parts, components and basic materials,
MNEs cannot operate properly, and without growth of user industries
their local market and hence their forward linkage effects cannot
expand. Of course, the opposite is also true: MNEs' growth will
provide a market for subcontractors and basic material suppliers
and facilitate the development of user industries. The main
constraints on over-all industrial expansion have to be determined
carefully case by case. In the metal engineering industry of the
Third World usually skills are in short supply, equipment is poor,
and supplies of basic materials such as steel and copper are
unreliable in terms of quantity, quality and delivery dates.
Consequently, the development of local subcontractors has been
slow, even where the government introduced a programme for
the localisation of, say, the automobile industry a couple of
decades ago.

The primary indirect effect is not necessarily positive. For
example, the entry of a multinational plastic shoe manufacturer may
destroy considerable job opportunities not only in the leather
footwear industry but also in the industries related to it through
backward linkages (tannery and cattle raising).[37] As a matter of
fact, even the direct employment effect can be negative if the
MNE's entry takes the form of a take-over of existing local firms,
and leads to the dismissal of employees as a result of
rationalisation.

An important determinant of the extent of MNEs' technological
and employment effects is the time element: indirect effects

increase over time. The experience of export processing zones in
the Far East tends to refute the fairly commonly held view that
such zones have serious limitations as instruments of economic
development because they lack linkages with the local economy.
These zones generally start as net importers, because local
enterprises cannot yet supply them with materials or parts of
internationally competitive quality and price. With encouragement
from local authorities, however, foreign firms in the export
processing zones commonly help indigenous suppliers to improve
their quality control or manufacturing methods by giving advice or
lending sophisticated test instruments, and rapidly increase their
procurement of local goods. Consequently, some of these zones are
now earning nearly $1,000 million of foreign exchange a year and
providing over 50,000 jobs for local workers. As regards
technology transfer, local engineers, managers or workers have been
sent abroad for training, while expatriate specialists have helped
to train unskilled workers on the job. As a result, many MNEs in
these zones now have large numbers of local technicians, and some
of them are managed entirely by local staff.[38]
      It is true that steel mills, synthetic textile mills or
chemical fertiliser plants have little scope for direct
contribution to employment, but they can expand, in the long run,
opportunities for employment and higher incomes in the user
industries (i.e. metal engineering, garment manufacturing and
agriculture) if they can provide the latter with materials which
are internationally competitive as regards quality and price.
Overemphasis on the use of labour-intensive technology may result
in a loss of international competitiveness and eventually in a
decline in the number of job opportunities or in the rate of their
increase as has been demonstrated in the case of Indonesia's batik
industry[39] or India's garment industry.[40]
      The scope of existing studies is often too narrow with regard
to the time horizon and/or the extent of indirect effects covered.
Moreover, when indirect effects are found to be smaller than
expected, few studies proceed to investigate the causes of the
problem in detail. Just as many authors seem unaware of various
obstacles to technological adaptation, they are inattentive to the
fact that the extent of indirect effects depends on the degree of
development of user and supporting industries and that MNEs can do
little to develop these industries directly. MNEs' limitations in
this respect are clear, for example, from the fact that major local
parts and components suppliers for multinational automobile
assemblers in the Third World are also foreign subsidiaries.

III. POLICY GOALS AND OBSERVERS' EXPECTATIONS

      An odd phenomenon which comes out not infrequently in the
research world is an attempt to evaluate a policy programme or
investment project with reference to objectives which the
responsible authorities had no intention of achieving or considered

only as a secondary objective. A typical example is a research project proposal which came to my attention quite recently. This project was to examine technology transfer effects of export processing zones and seek ways to strengthen the host governments' bargaining power vis-a-vis foreign investors. On the face of it, this is strange, because these zones are usually[41] intended to expand export earnings and to create employment for unskilled labour, especially in economically depressed or stagnant areas. Transfer of technology is rarely a major objective. It is also difficult to understand why outsiders should look for ways of government intervention when the host governments themselves deliberately refrain from it in order to attract investors.[42]

While researchers are examining the degree of labour-intensive technological adaptation by MNEs, local authorities are keen to import technologies for the purpose of, for example, modernising the economy of the defence industry, as has been the case in India. In the case of the automobile engine plant in Manila to which reference has already been made, the local partner at first insisted on Toyota's introducing the up-to-date technology in use at its home plant. Small-size technology of an old vintage was accepted only after a lengthy process of persuasion by Toyota. One of the people involved in these negotiations felt that the long business relationship between the two parties had helped their mutual understanding and that without this it would have been difficult, as is the case in any developing country, to persuade the local partner to accept the old technology.

To quote another example, it is often argued that MNEs should adapt the quality of their products to the needs of the low-income masses of the host countries, since this could increase opportunities for more labour-intensive technologies. Such demand is unrealistic where these enterprises are required by the host governments to export certain portions of their output. Besides, product adaptions in that direction would in many cases threaten the survival of indigenous firms which tend to cater for lower-income consumers' markets: in reality, many host governments rightly or wrongly restrict MNEs' entry in lines of business where, as already mentioned, competition with already existing firms is anticipated.

This kind of gap between local people's and governments' objectives and researchers' and critics' expectations seems to arise partly from the ambiguity in host governments' policy objectives and priorities.

Even where employment and the application of more labour-intensive technologies are repeatedly stressed as major objectives of a development plan, these objectives tend to be lost to view as soon as the plan comes down to sectoral or industry levels. Even if the Ministry of Labour manages to maintain its employment targets, it usually has little influence on the Ministry of Industry, which tends to be far more preoccupied with the modernisation of industries. Thus, employment becomes only a secondary criterion, e.g. in screening technologies and foreign firms. In those rather rare cases where the Ministry of Industry maintains employment as a main criterion, it often faces--and succumbs to--pressure from various interest groups exercised, for example, through parliamentary campaigns.[43]

Actually, contradiction among announced policy objectives may arise even within a single ministry. A classic example is the conflict between employment and higher labour standards (minimum wages, restriction of dismissal and night work, etc.), in the case of the Ministry of Labour.

A combined result of all these is a diversion of goals of sectoral policies from the over-all goals of the development plan, or the emergence of "implicit technology policies" to replace announced "explicit technology policies".[44] Often, the criteria by which the authorities screen incoming technologies and foreign firms are left undefined, their decision being taken discretionally on an ad hoc basis.[45] All these problems have been explored by different authors. Nowhere else do their arguments apply better than with respect to MNEs, and yet this fact has been singularly neglected by researchers and critics of these enterprises.

IV. CONCLUDING REMARKS

The MNEs do not operate in a vacuum any more than do the local firms. Their pattern of behaviour is affected not only by the degree of development of infrastructure and supporting industries but also by all kinds of socio-political factors, including the host governments' policies. The influence of labour legislation has already been mentioned. There is no doubt that MNEs' contribution to the fast absorption of surplus labour in the Republic of Korea and Singapore (as well as in Hong Kong) is in great part due to the less demanding policy of these countries in this domain and the low incidence of industrial disputes. No less important are industrial and trade policies, which influence the degree and pattern of industrial competition. Given all these factors and its product and target market, what could be realistically expected from an MNE is more or less narrowly determined with respect to employment and technological adaptation, especially in high-technology industries. The current controversy over MNEs' performance in these regards arises largely from the confusion concerning the definitions of the product and target market and "technology" (whether it concerns only "core technology" or includes "peripheral technology" and managerial and production skills as well). To some extent it is also a matter of value judgment: some observers consider certain contributions by MNEs "significant", while others do not.

What is of the greatest practical importance, however, is probably the difference in the time horizon adopted by different authors. It is fashionable to argue that MNEs, like any local firm, should apply technologies suitable to the existing local factor endowments (including skills) and socio-economic conditions. Such an argument makes one wonder what the meaning of "economic development" is: does it not imply changes in those conditions? Scholars and policy makers probably have to distinguish between

the following two groups of industries or sectors and treat them
separately: one for immediate employment creation, and the other
for the long-term development of the economy which needs to be
fostered for the future, surmounting the existing obstacles to
their development with positive measures. Most of the MNEs in
high-technology industries seem to belong to the second category.
Joan Robinson has recently written: "The interaction between the
long-run and the short-run consequences of technological
innovations is a complicated subject which requires more study".[46]
This is particularly true with regard to these MNEs.

In this connection, the now emerging discussion on the subject
of MNEs of Third World origin may turn out to be interesting. A
certain number of relatively advanced developing countries have
started exporting machinery to other Third World countries. These
machines are said to be often more suitable to developing countries
than those from industrialised countries because they are cheaper
and less sophisticated.[47] In a similar vein of reasoning, it is
argued that multinationals from these countries, the number of
which appears to be gradually increasing, may develop technologies
of a lower capital-labour ratio than MNEs from industrialised
countries. They may also cause less fear of "dependency" on the
part of the receiving developing countries. On the other hand,
they may be in an inferior position with regard to providing a
continual flow of new technology and especially access to a foreign
market. In the future their weakness in these domains may
decrease. However, MNEs from the Third World are still rare and of
recent behavior. The existing debate about them is largely of a
speculative nature.[48]

No matter what their national origin may be, it would be
unrealistic to expect MNEs to sacrifice their own benefit, in the
long run, for the sake of the economic development of the host
countries (where the two do not go hand in hand). A host
government needs to screen an MNE's entry proposal carefully,
taking due account of its direct and indirect effects.

In many cases, what is crucial is the choice of product and
the target market. Once a decision has been made in this respect,
the range of technological choice becomes limited largely because
the quality standard required of the product is more or less
determined by the nature of the product and/or the target clients'
needs. This is especially true in high-technological modern
industries where MNEs are concentrated. Similarly, the extent and
pattern of MNEs' indirect effects become largely known, given the
product and the target market, the local conditions of related
industries, etc. In order to be able to decide in what
industries and for what target markets MNEs should be permitted,
however, the responsible government officials would require a clear
idea about what their industries should look like in the next 5,
10, and 20 years in the light of the expected demand patterns both
at home and abroad, labour supplies etc.

At the same time, the host government would have to know what
kinds of technologies would be required or preferred to attain the
industrial structure desired in the long run. It must possess an
adequate capacity to appraise the quality of the technologies to be
brought in, which in turn depends largely on its ability to "shop

around". For the development of such local capacity and abilities, constant local R and D efforts are essential. If the responsible government officials are well informed about the technological alternatives available, they should also be able to negotiate with the incoming MNEs to make their production methods more suitable to the local development goals, wherever possible.

Once an MNE has been allowed into a country, the host government can increase its total positive effect by encouraging forward and backward linkages through appropriate policies. A good example is provided by the Philippines, where government-controlled vocational training centres offer plating and other services for small enterprises, which enable the latter to work as subcontractors for multinational automobile assemblers. The Philippines Coconut Authority provided financial assistance for a medium-sized local company which developed coconut fibres into seat pad material with encouragement from these assemblers. This kind of co-operation by host governments and other local institutes seems much more likely to achieve results that government regulations simply demand that MNEs adapt to local conditions and needs.

All this is possible only where there is a stable government and sufficient economic and technological expertise. In these respects there seems to be considerable room for improvement in most of the developing countries.

NOTES

[1] For a survey of literature on this subject, see, for example, Sanjaya Lall: "Transnationals, domestic enterprises, and industrial structure in host LDCs: a survey", in Oxford Economic Papers (Oxford), July 1978, pp. 217-248; Lawrence J. White: "The evidence on appropriate factor proportions for manufacturing in less developed countries: a survey", in Economic Development and Cultural Change (Chicago), Oct. 1978, pp. 42-45; and various papers in James H. Street and Dilmus D. James (eds.): Technological progress in Latin America: the prospects for overcoming dependency (Boulder (Colorado), Westview Press, 1979).

[2] Cf. A. S. Bhalla (ed.): Technology and employment in industry, 2nd ed. (Geneva, ILO, 1981).

[3] See, for example, Shigeru Ishikawa: "Appropriate technologies: some aspects of Japanese experience", in Austin Robinson (ed.): Appropriate technologies for Third World development (London, Macmillan, 1979), p. 90; and Susumu Watanabe: "Intersectoral linkages in Japanese industries: a historical perspective". in Susumu Watanabe (ed.): Technology, marketing and industrialisation linkages between large and small enterprises (New Delhi, Macmillan, forthcoming in early 1982), Ch. II. section 2.

[4] Cf. David J. C. Forsyth and Robert F. Solomon: "Choice of technology and nationality of ownership in manufacturing in a developing country", in Oxford Economic Papers, July 1977. See also ILO: Employment, incomes and equality (Geneva, 1972), pp. 446-452; and Howard Pack: "The substitution of labour for capital in Kenyan manufacturing", in The Economic Journal (Cambridge), Mar. 1 1976, pp. 45-58.

[5] On this subject, see Samuel A. Morley and Gordon W. Smith: "Adaptation by foreign firms to labour abundance in Brazil", in Street and James (eds.), op. cit., pp. 199-225.

[6] Ibid. See also Lall, op. cit.

[7] Cf. Susumu Watanabe: "Technical co-operation between large and small firms in the Filipino automobile industry", in Watanabe (ed.), op. cit.

[8] See C. Cooper et al.: "Choice of techniques for can making in Kenya, Tanzania and Thailand", in Bhalla (ed.), op. cit.

[9] Cf. J. C. Ramaer's statement in Robinson (ed.), op. cit., p. 249.

[10] Sanjaya Lall and Paul Streeten: Foreign investment, transnationals and developing countries (London, Macmillan, 1977), Ch. 2.

[11] Cf. Susumu Watanabe: "International subcontracting, employment and skill promotion", in International Labour Review, May 1972, pp. 425-449

[12] For example, see s. 13 of the Act to promote Mexican investment and regulate foreign investment, dated 9 March 1973, and related discussions in Susumu Watanabe: "Technological linkages through subcontracting in Mexican industries", in Watanabe (ed.), op. cit.

[13] Masaharu Tanaka: "Transportation and an affluent society: the Toyota basic utility vehicle", in The Wheel Extended. A Toyota Quarterly Review (Tokyo, Toyota Motor Sales Co.), Special Issue, 1976, pp. 31-36.

[14] On jeepneys and utility vehicles in the Philippines, see Watanabe, "Technical co-operation . . .", op. cit.

[15] K.H. Veldhuis: "Transfer and adaptation of technology: Unilever as a case study", in Robinson (ed.), op. cit., pp. 219-238, and discussion on this paper, pp. 246-249.

[16] International Herald Tribune (Paris), 26 June 1980, p. 9.

[17] Edwin M. Koloko: "Appropriate technology in appropriate institutions", in African Social Research (Lusaka), June 1979, p. 590.

[18] Simon Teitel: "On the concept of appropriate technology for less industrialised countries", in Technological Forecasting and Social Change (New York), No. 11, 1978, p. 354.

[19] Jack N. Behrman and William A. Fischer: "Transnational corporations: market orientations and R. and D abroad", in The Columbia Journal of World Business (New York), Fall 1980, pp. 55-60.

[20] Findings during my consultancy service to the Government of Mexico, March-April 1980.

[21] Werner Baer: "Technology, employment and development: empirical findings", in World Development (Oxford), Feb. 1976.

[22] Morley and Smith, op. cit.

[23] Cf. Lutz Hoffman and Tan Siew Ee: Industrial growth, employment and foreign investment in Peninsular Malaysia (Kuala Lumpur, Oxford University Press, 1980), pp. 115-117.

[24] Cf. Watanabe, "Technical co-operation . . .", op. cit.

[25] Cf. Robinson (ed.), op. cit. p. 247.

[26] Cf. Behrman and Fischer, op. cit., pp. 59-60.

[27] Veldhuis, op. cit., pp. 224-225.

[28]Gerard K. Boon: Technology and employment in footwear manufacturing (Alphen aan den Rijn, Sijthoff and Noordhoff, 1980), Ch. 6.

[29]I found all these cases during my field work in the past.

[30]Cf. Watanabe: "Technological linkages...", op. cit.

[31]Koji Taira: Economic development and the labour market in Japan (New York, Columbia University Press, 1970), pp. 203 and 7.

[32]On these issues, see Mohammad Sadli: "Application of technology and its employment effects: the experience in Indonesia", in Edgar O. Edwards (ed.): Employment in developing nations (New York, Columbia University Press, 1974), p. 370.

[33]Cf. Watanabe, "Technical co-operation . . .", op. cit., pp. 53-55.

[34]Hoffmann and Ee found that about 45 per cent of all tax collections in West Malaysia came from foreign firms and that their tax contribution was higher than that of their local counterparts not only in absolute but also in relative terms (per unit of output of capital) (Hoffmann and Ee, op. cit., p. 8).

[35]Kaigai Shinshutsu Kigyo Soran (Japanese multinationals: facts and figures for 1981) (Tokyo, Toyo Keizai Shimpo-sha, 1980).

[36]Asahi Shimbun (Tokyo), 16 June 1980, p. 1.

[37]To some extent this negative effect is offset, e.g. because the MNE may create jobs for retailers, while the small local shoemakers sell directly to the end consumers (cf. Boon, op. cit., p. 129).

[38]For supporting evidence, see for example, papers presented at the APO Symposium on Economic and Social Impacts of Export Processing Zones. August 1980 (Tokyo, Asian Productivity Organization), and Linda Lim and Pang Eng Fong: Technology choice and employment creation: a case study of three multinational enterprises in Singapore (Geneva, ILO, 1981; mimeographed Multinational Enterprises Programme Working Paper No. 16; restricted).

[39]Sadli, op. cit., p. 370.

[40]S. K. Subramanian: "Sub-contracting in India", in Susumu Watanabe: International sub-contracting: a tool of technology transfer (Tokyo, Asian Productivity Organization, 1978), p. 95.

[41]There are some exceptions. In India, for example, export processing zones are intended to improve technological standards of indigenous small enterprises and inducement of foreign investment is not their primary objective.

[42] Cf. Byung Gil Van: Survey on duty-free export processing zones in APO member countries. Paper presented at the APO Symposium on Export Processing Zones, Seoul, 1975 (mimeographed), Ch. 2.

[43] The Centre for Studies on Science and Technology, Council of Scientific and Industrial Research,Government of India, is engaged in a research project on this particular issue in India.

[44] See, for example, Amilcar Herrera: "Social determinants of science policy in Latin America: explicit science policy and implicit science policy", in Journal of Development Studies (London), Oct. 1972, pp. 19-37: D. Babatunde Thomas and Miguel S. Wionczek (eds.): Integration of science and technology with development: Caribbean and Latin American problems in the context of the United Nations Conference on Science and Technology for Development (New York, Pergamon Press, 1979).

[45] Literature on this subject is abundant, especially in India. See, for example, Jagdish N. Bhagwati and Padma Desai: India, planning for industrialisation: industrialisation and trade policies since 1951 (London, Oxford University Press, 1970), Ch. 13 in particular: National Council of Applied Economic Research (India): Foreign technology and investment: a study of their role in India's industrialisation (New Delhi, NCAER, 1971), especially pp. 54-55; K.K. Subrahmanian: "Approach to foreign collaboration: a critique of new industrial policy", in Economic and Political Weekly (Bombay), 8 Apr. 1978, pp. 613-617. All these studies suggest that problems dealt with by Myrdal still remain real: see Gunnar Myrdal: Asian drama (New York, Pantheon, 1968), Vol. II. Chs. 15 and 18-20.

[46] Joan Robinson: "Time in economic theory", in Kyklos (Basel), Vol. 33, 1980, Fasc. 2, p. 228.

[47] Cf. Sanjaya Lall: "Developing countries as exporters of industrial technology:, in Research Policy (Amsterdam), No. 9, 1980, pp. 24-52.

[48] See Louis T. Wells, Jr.: "The internationalisation of firms from developing countries", and Stephen J. Kobrin's comments on this paper in Tamir Agmon and Charles P. Kindleberger: Multinationals from small countries (Cambridge (Massachusetts), MIT Press, 1977), pp. 113-165.

Multinational Corporations, Sociocultural Dependence, and Industrialization: Need Satisfaction or Want Creation?

STEPHEN J. KOBRIN

One of the major contributions of the dependence literature is its refusal to disaggregate societal analyses into isolated and self-contained academic disciplines.[1] Dependentistas are concerned with the interpenetration of national economies in terms of productive facilities, technologies, ideologies, political parties, private and government institutions, cultural activities, and consumption patterns.[2] This paper will violate the spirit of that accomplishment by focusing rather narrowly on an aspect of social or cultural dependence.

Specifically, its primary concern will be the role of multinational corporations (MNCs) in transferring consumption patterns of advanced capitalist countries to underdeveloped poor countries and the relationship of that phenomenon to the larger question of dependence. The last point is crucial. The demonstration effect[3] is not dependence per se but rather a potential mechanism for its maintenance. This aspect of sociocultural dependence will be examined in terms of mainstream theories of foreign direct investment and the multinational corporation, and the literature on consumerism in advanced countries.

While dependency theory has been viewed as an alternative development paradigm,[4] Moran has suggested that a dialogue between dependentistas and nondependentistas could be valuable.[5] The evaluation of dependency theory in terms of mainstream research should isolate points of agreement and difference and may shed some new light on both traditions. This study will first briefly review the dependence literature's discussion of the transference of consumption patterns from rich to poor countries and then utilize theories of foreign direct investment (FDI) to look at the role played by MNCs. Next, consumerist capitalism in rich and poor countries will be compared and an attempt made to relate the

From **JOURNAL OF DEVELOPING AREAS**, Vol. 13, No. 2, Jan. 1979, (109-125), reprinted by permission of the publisher.

discussion to the question of dependence. Last, empirical data will be reviewed and conclusions drawn.

I. DEMONSTRATION EFFECT

Many writers consider the transfer of patterns of consumption, taste, and demand from the center (advanced industrial countries) to the peripheral poor countries as an important mechanism for the maintenance of dependent relationships among nominally independent countries.[6] Given the wide disparity in income and wealth, emulation of advanced country middle- and upper-class consumption patterns is possible by only a small minority of the population of the periphery.[7] Thus, concentration of income is postulated as necessary to provide a market for the consumer products of advanced countries.[8]

Furtado believes that "the formation of a social group (whose relative importance varies, but which is always a small minority of the population) with consumption patterns similar to those of countries with higher levels of productivity becomes the basic factor in the transformation of the peripheral countries" (emphasis added).[9] The transfer of tastes, however, occurs without the "corresponding process of capital accumulation and assimilation of technical process" which results in a "transformation of the structure of production and dependence."[10] Others, including Hymer and Hveen, conclude that the demonstration effect or the imposition of patterns of consumption functions as a control mechanism, an indirect means of maintaining dependence.[11]

Multinational corporations are frequently seen as agents of the transfer. Levitt, writing about Canada, which she considers a wealthy dependent country, makes the case in strong terms.

It is argued that MNCs facilitate or even accelerate the process by taking advantage of their superior marketing and communications techniques and responding to their natural interest in creating or expanding markets for their products.[13] In their role as vehicles for the extension of advanced country consumption patterns, they function as a mechanism for enforcing the indirect control associated with dependence.

It would appear that the theory of FDI, and research on MNCs in general, supports the assertion that international corporations have an interest in, and given proper conditions, capabilities which would facilitate, transferring consumption patterns from rich to poor countries. However, the second point, that the transfer results in or aids in maintaining dependency relationships is analytically distinct and must be established separately. Furthermore, if one is to draw policy implications for poor countries, it is crucial to distinguish, or to attempt to distinguish, between dependence and the extension of (consumerist) capitalism to the periphery. If a case for dependence is established, it must be shown that consumerist capitalism, which has concerned authors from Marx to Veblen to Galbraith, is a different phenomenon in the periphery than in the center.

II. MANUFACTURING DIRECT INVESTMENT

This section will attempt to demonstrate that an assertion that MNCs are more likely to transfer high-income consumer products differentiated cn the basis of brand names and advertising from advanced to poor countries than they are to develop products more appropriate to host socioeconomic realities is consistent with mainstream theoretical work on foreign direct investment. It is suggested that this phenomenon, which will be called (for want of a better term) the transfer of consumerist capitalism, does not conflict with the logic of FDI.

The existence of the transfer of consumer capitalism is not, however, a sufficient condition for dependence. To establish the latter, one must demonstrate that it contributes to the maintenance of indirect control by the dominant unit.

Hymer first noted that FDI can better be explained by the theory of industrial organization than by the theory of international capital movements.[14] FDI, a function of imperfections in goods and factor markets, is found in industries characterized by oligopoly. As the foreign investor is inherently at a disadvantage versus host country competitors in terms of knowledge about the local environment (or at least the cost of acquiring it) and the burdens imposed by operating at a distance,[15] direct investment could not exist in a perfectly competitive world. According to Kindleberger, "For direct investment to thrive there must be some imperfection of goods or factors, including among the latter technology, or some interference in competition by government or firms, which separates markets."[16]

The foreign investor must be able to generate, and contain, returns to some advantage over host country competitors which offsets the inherent disadvantages of foreignness and distance. Thus, Caves notes that FDI occurs in industries characterized by either oligopoly with product differentiation where "corporations make °horizontal' investments to produce abroad the same lines of goods they produce at home" or by oligopoly not necessarily differentiated where firms "undertake °vertical' direct investments to produce abroad a raw material or other input to their production process at home."[17] The former is obviously of interest.

Horizontal FDI is likely to take place in markets characterized by differentiated products, by goods market imperfections.[18] Competing products are typically distinguished by "minor physical variations, °brand name' and subjective distinctions created by advertising, or differences in ancillary terms and conditions of sale."[19] Thus, the foreign investor's advantages (which are necessary to provide the monopoly returns needed to offset his disadvantages vis-a-vis host country competitors) are likely to derive from marketing skills including

advertising, promotion, product development and design, and
packaging.

It should be obvious that the argument does not apply to all
manufacturing FDI. The advantage held may well be a function of
technology or management capabilities. One would certainly expect
that capital goods producers would not rely, at least to a very
great extent, on product differentiation and advertising skills.
The point is that the dependency argument that foreign investment
is likely to result in the introduction of products sold on the
basis of marketing skills is consistent with FDI theory. Indeed,
marketing skills developed in advanced countries which provide an
absolute advantage versus local competitors are a requisite for
much horizontal FDI. These marketing skills include the design,
promotion, and distribution of products as well as mass media
advertising.

What can one say about the nature of products sold in poor
countries by MNCs? First, they are likely to be very similar to
those sold in the home country. Horizontal FDI represents an
attempt to diversify geographically with the same or a very similar
line of products. The investor is obviously better off to the
extent that previous product development efforts and marketing
knowledge can be exploited with minor modifications. At the other
end of the spectrum, if products and marketing capabilities are not
transferable, one would have to question the source of the
investor's advantage versus local competitors. Product
diversification across national boundaries would be unlikely.[20]

Second, the product life cycle hypothesis[21] would suggest that
goods sold by advanced country firms, either through export or FDI,
are likely to be developed in response to conditions in the home
country. In the U.S. case it is argued that products have been
developed in response to (1) a shortage or relatively high cost of
labor and (2) relatively high consumer incomes. U.S. innovators
would thus be most likely to come up with products (or processes)
which either appeal particularly to high-income consumers or which
save on expensive labor.[22]

The model, which is described only partially, is based upon
the very realistic assumption that there is not a free flow of
information across national boundaries. That being the case, it is
argued that (1) new product innovation is likely to occur in or
near markets where there is strong potential demand, and (2) an
entrepreneur is more likely to supply risk capital for the
production of new products in his (or her) home markets.[23] Thus,
new products developed in any given market are likely to reflect
the characteristics of that market.

Thus, a second point put forth by dependentistas appears to be
supported by, or at least does not conflict with, existing theory.
One would expect U.S. investors to produce products which are
designed to appeal to a relatively high-income consumer market. In
terms of strategy, one could support a contention that, in general,
they would seek a relatively high-income segment of consumers in a
poor country rather than develop a product designed to appeal to
the lower-income mass.[24] Furthermore, given the choice, investors
should prefer a maldistribution of income which results in a
homogeneous population of very moderate income. That conclusion

does not either imply or disavow that MNCs either consciously foster (oppose) income concentration (redistribution) or prefer a rich elite and a poor mass to a more even distribution with a large middle class resulting from growth.

In summary, it appears that the dependency hypothesis that MNCs transfer consumer capitalism--differentiated products which are designed to be sold to relatively high-income consumers and supported by relatively heavy advertising--is consistent with various theories of the MNC. The next section will more closely examine what has been rather loosely called consumerist capitalism and its relation to dependence.

III. CONSUMERIST CAPITALISM

> In a world of artificially created wants we are, however, entitled to question the rationale of the assumption that an increase in national income and expenditure constitutes an improvement in the welfare of the nation.[25]

Once one backs away from the doctrine of consumer sovereignty, which Levitt obviously does with vengeance, one opens a Pandora's box of metaphysical distinctions between the physiological and psychological, or the internal and the external determination of needs or wants. Regardless of the merits of their arguments, it is clear that the dependentistas were neither the first to raise the lid nor the first to express consternation over the implications for society of the furies which swarmed out.

Marx clearly saw a multidirectional flow between production and consumption. "Production," he wrote, "not only supplies the want with material, but supplies material with a want. . . Production thus produces consumption: first, by furnishing the latter with material; second, by determining the manner of consumption; third, by creating in consumers a want for its products as objects of consumption."[26]

Veblen also had little faith in the independence of production and consumption. He noted that "the idiosyncrasies of the individual consumers are required to conform to the uniform gradations imposed upon consumable goods by the comprehensive mechanical processes of industry."[27] While he, perhaps unfortunately, lived before the age of mass marketing, he nonetheless saw a clear separation between basic needs and artificial, societally induced wants.[28]

The most articulate, and certainly the most vociferous, critic of the industrial capitalist system's tendency to rely on demand created by the productive system (and of mainstream economists' views on the matter) is Galbraith. Following Marx and Veblen, he concludes that production and consumption are not independent; rather "production induces more wants and the need for more production."[29] In what he calls the dependence effect, wants are created either passively by suggestion or emulation or actively through advertising and salesmanship on the part of producers.[30] In his later work, Galbraith tends to concentrate on the active mechanism.

The dependence effect is seen as arising from structural conditions, from the tendencies towards increasing affluence and industrial concentration, and the need for constant increases in production associated with advanced industrial capitalism. The lower propensity to consume resulting from increased affluence would result in difficulties for the system in terms of limits on both overall expansion or growth and the motivation of individuals to "work without any limiting horizon to procure more goods."[31] "Advertising and its related arts thus help develop the kind of man the goals of the industrial system require--one that reliably spends his income and works reliably because he is always in need of more."[32]

Many of the arguments of the dependentistas concerning what has been labelled consumerist capitalism are certainly not restricted to the periphery. In fact, the opposite conclusion, that the phenomenon is a function of industrial capitalism per se, appears as reasonable. Galbraith and others argue that wants are induced by the productive system through marketing (through nonprice competition by firms in oligopolistic industries) which are inappropriate for the societies in which they are sold. The dependence effect results in private consumption at the expense of necessary public spending.

It would appear that one could reasonably argue that what the dependentistas call cultural imperialism (or at least the portion of immediate concern) represents only the extension of capitalist industrialization to poor countries. One would expect, and I have argued extensively elsewhere,[33] that MNCs would be a singularly effective vehicle for the transfer of the institution of industrialization--the social structures and individual values and attitudes associated with it as well as technology--from rich to poor nations.

Thus, while one may or may not prefer to see capitalist industrialization in general, or consumerist capitalism in particular, implanted in poor countries, one cannot assume a priori that either is synonymous with dependence. If the concept of sociocultural dependence, in the limited sense in which it is being used, is to have meaning, one must demonstrate that consumerist capitalism differs in a phenomenological sense in the center and at the periphery.

IV. DEPENDENCE AND THE DEPENDENCE EFFECT

If the concept of dependence is to have analytical value, it must "(1) lay down certain characteristics of dependent economies not found in independent ones and (2) these characteristics must be shown to affect adversely the course and pattern of development of

dependent countries."[34]   The fact that tastes and consumption
patterns of the center are replicated by elites in the periphery,
even if one assumes that MNCs are central agents of that
replication, is not sufficient to demonstrate dependence. As Lall
observes, the tastes of elites are typically alienated from those
of the mass; that is, after all, one of the distinctions between
the two.   Furthermore, one can think of many instances of elite
tastes being dominated by those of another culture, e.g., the
imperial Russian nobility's preference for the French. One must
show that this superficially similar phenomenon (elite taste
alienation) differs substantively in the center and the periphery
and that this difference affects the development of the putatively
dependent states.
     Dependence implies some sort of asymmetrical social
relationship where one unit exercises control over and accumulates
value from another.[35]   Dos Santos provides a good working
definition:

> By dependence we mean a situation in which the economy
> of certain countries is conditioned by the development
> and expansion of another economy to which the former is
> subjected. The relationship of interdependence assumes
> the form of dependence when some countries (the dominant
> ones) can expand and be self-sustaining, while other
> countries (the dependent ones) can do this only as a
> reflection of that expansion.[36]

     Thus dependency implies both a reduction in the capability
to determine policy autonomously (which would be true of
interdependence as well) and an asymmetrical relationship where one
social unit is able to constrain, either directly or indirectly,
the development of another—presumably to the former's net benefit.
It should also be clear that once one moves away from either
autarky or a state of interdependence between two perfectly
balanced entities, dependence will probably be the norm and its
extent a matter of degree rather than kind.[37] Furthermore,
dependence does not require a conscious policy of exploitation; it
may well be structural.[38]
     The question then is how can the establishment of consumerist
capitalism in the periphery either establish or reinforce the
center's ability to exert control? The most obvious answer, that
goods are introduced which are either culturally alien or
inappropriate given societal needs or both, merely describes the
process.   It, in itself, does not imply a state of dependence. It
begs the question of how the mechanism works. Furthermore, the
argument applies to the center as well.
     Similarly, Hveem's argument that inducing a demand for
consumer goods provides a mechanism which insures that individuals
will accept "those tasks in the production and distributive system
allocated them"[39] would not seem to differentiate between center
and periphery. It would appear that to the extent that the
implantation of consumerist capitalism in the periphery—what
Sunkel has called the "overwhelming and systematic promotion and
publicity of conspicuous consumption capitalism (by the

transnational firm)"[40]--contributes to dependence, it does so
because of differences in the nature of the productive system
rather than differences in the phenomenon per se.

In the industrialized countries the development of new
products is likely to be functionally related to internal
production and market conditions. They are likely to be
developed through indigenous R&D efforts and, at least in the U.S.
case, to reflect the existence of relatively affluent consumers and
relatively scarce labor.

While patterns of consumption in advanced industrial countries
may or may not be either artificial or inappropriate, they are a
direct function of product and process technology in those
countries. Consumption of consumer products may divert both funds
and attention from more important needs. However, their
development is typically a result of indigenous R&D efforts and
their production, or rather its growth, results in the indigenous
accumulation of capital.

The situation is quite obviously different in the periphery.
One would have to agree with Furtado that even with foreign direct
investment, there are still discontinuities between consumption and
production. Even if products are produced locally, they (1) may
require production processes inconsistent with factor endowments,
(2) are typically not functionally related to indigenous
technological capacities, and (3) may demand marketing skills which
are beyond the capabilities of host country enterprises.

The first point is heard frequently; consumer durables or
high-income consumer products in general require (or are typically
produced with) more capital-intensive production processes than do
products designed for mass consumption.[41] If relatively
capital-intensive production processes are imported as a result of
consumerist capitalism, then some degree of technological
dependence is likely to follow. It is probable that the host
society will not have the capacity to design, build, modify, or
even to maintain the productive machinery. They will thus be
technologically dependent on an advanced economy, and that
dependence will be exacerbated to the extent that demand for
high-income consumer goods either exists or is created.

It would seem, however, that this issue transcends the
question of cultural dependence. The literature on technology
transfer is complex and vast. Many explanations for the transfer
of inappropriate technology have been advanced,[42] and it is not
clear that consumerist capitalism play the, or even a, leading
role. While the question of factor substitutability has not been
resolved, it is at least possible that these products are not
inherently capital intensive and that a proper framework of
regulation could result in more labor-intensive production
processes.[43]

The discontinuity between production and the capacity for
innovation represents a more powerful link between consumerist
capitalism and dependence. The transfer of the capacity to produce
to the periphery does not necessarily imply a transfer of the
capacity to innovate. MNCs generally centralize the R&D effort,
and the ability to develop or perhaps even to improve products does
not typically exist in the host country. This tendency is

exacerbated by the nature of the products in question.

First, if the products are developed in response to the "needs" of relatively high-income consumers, then it is likely (if one accepts the product life cycle hypothesis) that innovation is likely to occur in the large home markets. Second, the industries of direct concern are likely to be characterized by oligopoly, product and not price competition, the products differentiated via either minor differences or marketing campaigns.

MNCs certainly transfer to their subsidiaries management and technology, which are then diffused through host societies via mechanisms such as the mobility of personnel, rearward and forward linkages, and competitive emulation. However, management and technology also provide foreign investors necessary advantages vis-a-vis local competitors. Thus, a complete transfer of product development capabilities in the sense of a reproduction of the capacity to innovate in the host society at large--and typically, even in the subsidiary itself--is unlikely. By doing so, the MNC would eliminate its competitive advantage versus local firms. One would have to conclude that the periphery is likely to be and remain dependent upon the center as a source of new and improved products. And, if one accepts validity of the demonstration effect, they are likely to be products for which there is a considerable demand among important population segments.

Similarly, to the extent that marketing knowledge and skills are not completely transferred to the host country--and given the argument above there is no reason to expect that they will be--the periphery will remain dependent upon the center. If marketing skills remain proprietary and contained, and the capacity to utilize them effectively is limited in the periphery, consumerist capitalism cannot become a totally indigenous phenomenon--even in the absence of new product innovation. Furthermore, in the industries we are concerned with, one cannot separate product development and marketing; they are really part and parcel of the same process. Product improvements are likely to represent a means for differentiation through advertising rather than a functional product change. Thus, to the extent that marketing skills (broadly defined) remain underdeveloped, the dependence of peripheral countries on the center for products, and for innovation in general, may be reinforced.

One additional question must be explored: the relationship between consumerist capitalism, MNCs, and income distribution. As noted above, one would expect a relationship between consumerist capitalism--the transfer of high-income consumer products--and an inequitable distribution of income in the periphery. However, the issue at hand is dependence. To relate consumerist capitalism and income distribution in the periphery with dependence, one must establish that the introduction of these products, and the creation of the necessary demand, either negatively affects the distribution of income or acts to restrain host country attempts at remedial action.

At this point the question is problematic; much work needs to be done before one can establish a causal hypothesis. Again, we are accepting the likelihood of a correlation: the issue is causality. There are at least two lines of argument. The first would assume that once a pattern of consumption of center products by high-income elites is established, efforts to redistribute income would be inhibited. To the extent that industrialization is based upon foreign investors producing high-income consumer goods, any shrinking of the market would have adverse effects in terms of growth, investment, and employment. There might thus be a tendency to avoid redistribution and to rely on absolute growth in income to alleviate the plight of poorer segments of the population.

One also cannot ignore the <u>comprador</u> or bridgehead elite thesis.[44]   It is not unreasonable to anticipate a mutuality of interest: neither MNCs nor the current elites would benefit from a redistribution, and MNCs may well led support to those who would not at the expense of those who would. The presence of MNCs producing high-income consumer products may thus affect the balance of power between those favoring and those opposing redistribution.

Second, one could make an even stronger argument: that a government pursues policies resulting in an inequitable distribution of income in order to industrialize via foreign direct investment in industries producing high-income consumer goods.   If one believes that the structure of the international economic system is such as to place severe limitations on indigenous industrialization, then the maldistribution of income would certainly be a function of dependence.

Mericle argues that point in the context of the development of the auto industry in Brazil. By 1967 the regime needed to restore real growth to the economy in order to develop a broader political base, and a decision was taken to industrialize via the promotion of automobiles and other expensive consumer durables. He concludes:

> The major economic problem of the consumer durable
> sector was one of insufficient demand. . . The
> government simply created effective demand [by] making
> consumer credit available and following a number of
> policies which contributed to income concentration. By
> transferring effective purchasing power to the upper and
> upper-middle classes, the military simultaneously
> created a market for consumer durables and developed a
> base of political support.[45]

V. THE DATA

It is obvious, given the nature of the subject matter and problems of data availability and quality, that one cannot test a theory of cultural dependence.[46] Rather, the available data will be reviewed in an attempt to determine whether it is consistent with the arguments presented above. Furthermore, the dependence effects of the transfer of consumerist capitalism cannot be operationalized directly. Thus, inferences will have to be drawn from analysis of relationships between consumerism, foreign direct investment, and, to a more limited extent, the distribution of income. The relationships are examined across a group of 48 nonsocialist bloc developing countries which were sovereign, met certain size minimums, and had attracted at least $1 million worth of U.S. manufacturing direct investment as of year-end 1967.[47]

The three concepts are operationalized as follows. The Harvard project's measure of the number of new manufacturing subsidiaries of U.S. multinationals is used as an indicator of FDI.[48] While the measure has its drawbacks, the major one being that it is based upon the number of subsidiaries rather than enterprise size, it also provides an important advantage. The Harvard data can be disaggregated by industry, allowing total FDI in each host country to be subdivided by advertising intensity of industry of the subsidiary, which is obviously germane to this research. Consumerist capitalism is represented by an index combining passenger cars and television sets per 1,000 of population with each equally weighted.[49]

The measure of income distribution utilized is the percentage of income received by the top 20 percent of the population.[50] It should be noted that there are major problems with this indicator. First, it is available for only 32 of the 48 countries included in the analysis, and this subsample is biased towards the more developed countries. Second, while the modal observation is the mid-1960s, there is considerable variation in the time of observations. Third, the observations are not all directly comparable. While most reflect a national sample on a household basis, some countries utilize individuals and/or economically active population as a base. Any findings regarding income distribution must thus be viewed as extremely tentative.

Empirical analysis will proceed by first exploring relationships between consumerism and the level and distribution of income, and then introducing FDI into the analysis. Last, discriminant analysis will be used to investigate differences between countries where the level of consumption is relatively high and those where it is relatively low. Again, theory is not being tested. Rather, the data are being reviewed in an attempt to shed some additional light on the transfer of consumerist capitalism to poor countries and the role MNCs play in that process.

A direct relationship can be established between consumerist capitalism (or at least auto and TV ownership) and the level, but not the distribution, of income. The simple correlation coefficient between the index of consumption and GNP per capita (both measured in 1966) is .82.[51] However, given the limited subsample and the difficulties with the indicator, one cannot draw inferences from the failure to establish a significant relationship between the share of income held by the top 20 percent of the population (Top 20) and consumption.[52]

FDI will now be introduced into the analysis. Because both theory and previous empirical work[53] suggest that the distribution of manufacturing FDI is to a large extent a function of income (larger markets draw more FDI), the number of manufacturing subsidiaries is normalized by Gross Domestic Product (GDP) arising from the manufacturing sector. Thus, the three indicators used are

relative measures: manufacturing FDI, manufacturing   FDI   in
high-advertising intensive industries, and manufacturing FDI in
low-advertising   intensive   industries,   all   per   dollar   of
manufacturing GDP. (Advertising intensity reflects the ratio of
advertising expenditures to   sales.)[54] The three variables,
designated FDI, HIGHADV, and LOWADV, respectively, represent stocks
or the total number of subsidiaries accumulated as of 1966.[55]

Simple correlation   coefficients for the relative measures of
FDI and   indicators of income, income distribution, and consumption
are (with all coefficients significant at .01): for GNP/CAPITA--.34
(FDI), .29 (HIGHADV), and .38 (LOWADV); for Top 20--.44 (FDI), .40
(HIGHADV), and .40 (LOWADV); for CONS--.38 (FDI), .33 (HIGHADV),
and .39 (LOWADV).

FDI (normalized by GDP) is, as one would expect, positively
correlated with both income per capita and consumption. Given
countries of comparable economic size, FDI tends to flow to those
where there is a smaller but wealthier population and/or higher
levels of individual consumption. (Given the high correlation
between consumption and GDP/capita, the relationship between FDI
and   consumption is not surprising.) The moderately   strong
correlation between FDI and income concentration is quite
significant. Again, FDI is normalized by GDP. Thus, given
comparable economic size, FDI tends to flow to those countries
where the top 20 percent of the population has a greater proportion
of the total income.

Results of disaggregating FDI by advertising intensity are not
in accord with expectations; one would have predicted that the
correlation between consumption and HIGHADV would be stronger than
that with LOWADV. However, the results are difficult to interpret.
First, the problems associated with using an indicator of FDI based
upon the number of subsidiaries established may be exacerbated by
disaggregation. There may well be a bias as to size; it may take
fewer low-advertising intensity subsidiaries to produce the same
output. Second, the assumptions behind normalization of FDI by GDP
may not hold after disaggregation by advertising intensive FDI
(i.e., numbers of subsidiaries), the association with consumption
is stronger for the former than for the latter.[56]

The relationship between consumption levels in 1966 and the
change in FDI (in terms of the number of subsidiaries established)
lends credence to this line of argument. Correlations between
changes in FDI and consumption (1966) are: for FDI, .42; for
HIGHADV, .51; and for LOWADV, .34, the last figure significant at
.05, the other two at .01. As can be seen, there is a much
stronger association between the flow of high-advertising intensive
FDI over the nine-year period and consumption levels at the
beginning of the period than there is for low-advertising intensive
FDI.

All the foregoing discussion indicates that controlling for
market size (GDP) FDI is positively associated with higher per
capita incomes, higher levels of consumption, and a greater
concentration of income in the top 20 percent of the population.
Consumption is positively correlated with GNP per capita. Thus,
empirical relationships are consistent with the hypothesis that
foreign direct investment is associated with consumption of

consumer durables by a high-income market segment.

In addition to exploring direct relationships between
indicators of consumption, income, and foreign investment, one can
look at differences between countries where there is a relatively
high level of consumption per capita (again, specifically of
automobiles and television sets) and those where it is relatively
low. One can ask how well indicators of income per capita and FDI
discriminate between the two groups of countries.[57]

Using discriminant analysis, a function—a linear combination
of variables—can be derived which will discriminate between low-
and high-consumption countries based upon GNP per capita and
normalized indicators of low- and high-advertising intensive FDI.[58]

Table 1 contains relevant statistics resulting from the
analysis.

The results are of interest. First, the function derived from
the three independent variables quite accurately discriminates
between low (Group 1) and high (Group 2) consumption countries.
The Chi squared statistic for the derived function, and the
univariate F ratios (considering each independently) for each of
the independent variables are highly significant. The canonical
correlation coefficient is .81, and applying the derived function
to the original data results in the "correct" classification of 94
percent of the cases.[59]

As would be expected, GNP/capita dominates the function with a
standardized coefficient of .88, over twice that of the normalized
indicator of high-advertising intensive FDI. The indicator of
low-advertising intensive FDI is of minor importance with a
coefficient of .13. However, the sign of the latter is negative.
Thus, while both low- and high-advertising intensive FDI are
positively associated with consumption (again, perhaps because both
are positively correlated with income), their effects differ when
one attempts to discriminate between low- and high-consumption
countries. As the function as a whole is negative for Group 1,
low-consumption countries tend to score higher on low-advertising
investment than do high-consumption countries.

It must be noted that the last finding is based upon rather
weak evidence and must be viewed as highly tentative. First, the
coefficient of LOWADV is quite small when compared to both HIGHADV
and GNP/C. Second, while it is significant on a univariate basis,
when one utilizes a stepwise discriminant procedure, the
multivariate F of LOWADV is not large enough to warrant
inclusion.[60]

In summary, it would appear that the data are consistent with
the major propositions advanced above. Consumerism, the
consumption of expensive consumer durables, is associated quite
strongly with higher levels of income per capita in the
nonsocialist developing countries included in the study.[61] FDI is
a function of market size, and, holding market size (GDP) constant,
FDI is positively associated with higher per capita incomes and a
greater concentration of income among the top 20 percent of the
population. While the differences between high- and
low-advertising intensive FDI are much less clear, it appears that
there is some basis for postulating a relationship between levels
of consumption and advertising intensity of FDI.

TABLE 1

RESULTS OF DISCRIMINANT ANALYSIS

INDEPENDENT VARIABLES	UNIVARIATE F RATIO	STANDARDIZED DISCRIMINANT COEFFICIENT
GNP/C	65.9	0.88
HIGHADV	11.4	0.41
LOWADV	11.0	-0.13

For the Discriminant Function:

		Centroids	
Chi^2	Canonical Correlation	Group 1	Group 2
46.38	0.81	-0.73	0.87

(Significant at .001)

VI. CONCLUSIONS

The application of mainstream theory to the problems posed by dependentistas appears to be valuable: it can help to isolate critical points of contention.   Both traditional theory and dependency   analysis   would   predict   the   same   behavior   by geographically   diversified   MNCs engaged   in   the   production of consumer products.   They will tend to transfer products which have been developed in response to conditions in advanced countries (with minimal modifications), which are differentiated   on   a nonprice basis, and which are supported by intensive advertising and marketing. Given the need for higher income consumers, under conditions of low per capita income they will prefer (ceteris paribus) markets where income is concentrated to those where it is not.

It would appear, however, that many of the dependentistas' arguments apply to the extension of industrial capitalism to Third World countries rather than to the dependent relations which result. Again, complaints about the rise of large enterprises with considerable market power, the difficulties in societal control of corporations, the creation of artificially induced wants, and the failure of materialism are heard as frequently in the center as in the periphery. More specifically, many of the dependentistas' concerns relate to the replication of capitalist industrialization in the form it has taken in the center.

Furthermore, many of the problems   of dependence are a function of integration into an interdependent   international economic system and affect center and periphery alike. As noted above, once one moves from the idealized extremes of either autarky or interdependent relationships among perfect equals, asymmetrical relationships result. While dependence is a reality, it is also a matter of degree.

There are, however, major differences between the periphery and the industrialized center.   While integration into the international economic system restricts any subunit's freedom of action, conditions may exist in the periphery which make independent decision making especially difficult.

Given a discontinuity between production and consumption, mechanisms such as the transfer of what we have called consumerist capitalism do have different effects in the periphery. They do serve to increase the reliance of poor countries upon the advanced for research and development, for productive technologies, and for managerial techniques. By doing so, they exacerbate reliance on exogenous capabilities, and under certain conditions they may inhibit the development of indigenous resources. The net result is to increase the cost of achievement of alternative objectives and patterns of development.

We will conclude by briefly discussing policy implications. First, it is clear that if a society rejects capitalist development per se, dependence is relevant only as either a reason for or an obstacle to an alternative. However, the choice is not simply revolution or dependent development.   Once the implications of

dependence are understood, actions can be taken to lower the costs
and increase the benefits of integration into the international
economic system.   Contrary to the assertions of the earlier
dependentistas, political   independence has and does make a
difference. Poor countries are becoming increasingly sophisticated
in   their dealings with the West, especially in the areas of the
determination of conditions for entry and regulation of MNCs.
While this is more evident in the extractive sector, where control
over natural resources provides an undeniable advantage, control is
being exercised over manufacturing enterprise.[62]

The question is not whether objectives of MNCs and host
countries conflict. The objectives of most participants in economic
transactions conflict. Rather, the important issues are whether a
sufficient overlap exists   to allow a   mutually advantageous
agreement, and whether the relative strengths of the parties are
conducive to negotiation.   One cannot expect equal relations
between   unequal   actors.   One   can   expect   that increasing
sophistication and knowledge on the part of nations in the
periphery, including a more complete understanding   of their
relationship with the center, will help reduce the costs and
increase the benefits derived from such a relationship.

APPENDIX: COUNTRY LIST

Greece

Spain*

Turkey*

Algeria

Congo (Kinshasa)

Ethiopia

Ghana

Kenya*

Libya

Morocco

Nigeria

South Africa*

Sudan

Tanzania*

Tunisia*

United Arab Republic*

Zambia*

Costa Rica*

Dominican Republic

El Salvador*

Guatemala

Honduras*

Jamaica*

Mexico*

Nicaragua

Panama*

Argentina*

Bolivia

Brazil*

Chile*

Columbia*

Ecuador*

Peru*

Uruguay*

Venezuela*

Iran

Lebanon*

Cambodia

Ceylon*

India*

Indonesia*

South Korea*

Malaysia*

Pakistan*

Philippines*

Taiwan*

Thailand*

South Vietnam

*Countries for which income distribution data is available.

NOTES

[1] There is by now a vast and growing literature on dependence or neocolonialism that reflects a variety of viewpoints and approaches. See Robert I. Rhodes, ed., _Imperialism and Underdevelopment: A Reader_ (New York: Monthly Review Press, 1970) for a collection of earlier readings and Adrian Foster-Carter, "From Rostow to Gunder Frank: Conflicting Paradigms in the Analyses of Underdevelopment," _World Development_ 4 (March 1976): 167-80, for a more recent view.

[2] Osvaldo Sunkel, "Big Business and Dependencia: A Latin American View," _Foreign Affairs_ 50 (April 1972): 519.

[3] Thomas E. Weisskopf, "Capitalism, Underdevelopment, and the Future of the Poor Countries," in _Economics and World Order_, ed., Jagdish N. Bhagwati (New York: Free Press, 1972), p. 47.

[4] Foster-Carter, "Conflicting Paradigms," p. 167.

[5] Theodore H. Moran, "Multinational Corporations and Dependency: A Dialogue for _Dependentistas_ and _Non-dependentistas_," mimeographed (Washington, DC: Johns Hopkins University, School of Advanced International Studies, 1975).

[6] Helge Hveem, "The Global Dominance System," _Journal of Peace Research_ 4 (1973): 333; Stephen Hymer, "The Multinational Corporation and the Law of Uneven Development," in _Economics and World Order_, ed. Bhagwati, p. 114.

[7] Weisskopf, apitalism, Underdevelopment, p. 47.

[8] The statement merely acknowledges that MNCs will seek a market for their products, and that under certain conditions it is likely to be a high-income segment of the population of a poor country. It does not imply either acceptance or rejection of the argument that MNCs create or maintain unequal patterns of income distribution. That is an empirical question which cannot be settled given the available data.

[9] Celso Furtado, "The Concept of External Dependence in the Study of Underdevelopment," in _The Political Economy of Development and Underdevelopment_, ed. Charles K. Wilber (New York: Random House, 1973), p. 119.

[10] Ibid., pp. 119-20. Also, Harry R. Targ, "Global Dominance and Dependence, Post-Industrialism and International Relations Theory," _International Studies Quarterly_ 20 (September 1976): 471.

[11] Hveem, "Global Dominance System," p. 333; Hymer, "Multinational Corporations," p. 131.

[12] Kari Levitt, _Silent Surrender_ (New York: St. Martins Press, 1970), p. 22.

[13]Hveem, "Global Dominance System," p. 333; Hymer, "Multinational Corporations," p. 125; Weisskopf, "Capitalism, Underdevelopment," p. 50.

[14]See Charles P. Kindleberger, American Business Abroad (New Haven: Yale University Press, 1969), p. 11. For the purposes of this paper we can define FDI as equity investment sufficient to provide some degree of managerial control extended across national frontiers.

[15]A direct investor must accept the loss of diversification benefits which accompany portfolio investment if he is to concentrate assets to the point where managerial control is achieved. Since the managerial control implies a cost in terms of increased investment risk, it must then be utilized to gain increased returns. Its exercise, across distances and in unfamiliar environments, however, entails costs a comparable local investor would not face.

[16]Kindleberger, American Business Abroad, p. 13.

[17]Richard E. Caves, "International Corporations: The Industrial Economics of Foreign Investment," Economica 38 (February 1971), p. 1.

[18]Caves, "International Corporations," p. 5; Kindleberger, American Business Abroad, p. 14.

[19]Caves, "International Corporations," p. 5.

[20]Ibid., p. 3. Automobiles, television and radio receivers, household appliances, and packaged consumer products are presentative of the types of products of concern.

[21]For an introduction, see Louis T. Wells, Jr., ed., The Product Life Cycle and International Trade (Boston: Harvard University, Graduate School of Business Administration, Division of Research, 1972).

[22]Ibid., p. 6.

[23]Ibid.

[24]There are, of course, obvious exceptions; Coca-Cola, for example, sells a mass product worldwide.

[25]Levitt, Silent Surrender, p. 22.

[26]Karl Marx, A Contribution to the Critique of Political Economy (Chicago: Charles Kerr, 1904), p. 280.

[27]Thorstein Veblen, The Theory of Business Enterprise (New York: Charles Scribner's Sons, 1923), p. 11.

[28]Veblen notes that "unproductive consumption of goods is honorable, primarily as a mark of prowess and human dignity," Theory of the Leisure Class (New York: Mentor Books, 1953), p. 61.

[29]John K. Galbraith, The Affluent Society (Cambridge, MA: Riverside Press, 1958), p. 159.

[30]Ibid., p. 158.

[31]Galbraith, The New Industrial State (New York: Signet Books, 1968), p. 219.

[32]Ibid.

[33]See Stephen J. Kobrin, "Foreign Direct Investment, Industrialization and Social Change," Journal of Conflict Resolution 20 (September 1976): 497-522.

[34]Sanjaya Lall, "Is Dependence a Useful Concept in Analyzing Underdevelopment?" World Development 3 (1975):800.

[35]Hveem, "Global Dominance System," p. 300.

[36]Theotonio Dos Santos, "The Structure of Dependence," American Economic Review 60 (May 1970): 231.

[37]Cohen notes that "dependence is a matter of degree rather of degree rather than kind: Economies are more or less dependent, rather than absolutely dependent or not." Benjamin J. Cohen, The Question of Imperialism (New York: Basic Books, 1973), p. 191.

[38]Knorr disagrees. "We insist that there is no neocolonialism unless there is an effective use of power for deliberately establishing and maintaining an exploitative relationship." Klaus Knorr, The Power of Nations (New York: Basic Books, paperback ed., 1971), p. 255.

[39]Hveem, "Global Dominance System," p. 333.

[40]Sunkel, "Big Business and Dependencia," p. 528.

[41]While the argument that luxury consumption products require capital-intensive production processes is made quite often, little empirical evidence supports the allegation. Furthermore, even if—as we would suspect is the case—luxury consumption products are produced with relatively capital-intensive production processes, the association does not prove causality. The products and their production may be distinct entities; one may be able to produce them with a variety of factor proportions. Thus, there may well be two separate policy issues at hand: whether one wants to allow the sale of luxury products affordable by only a minority of the population, and whether one

wants to control the capital intensity of their production process. Thus, an objection to the transfer of "inappropriate" production technology alone may not justify prohibiting the sale of final products.

[42]The question of the appropriateness of technology transferred has received a great deal of attention. One can develop a reasonable prima facie argument that much productive technology imported by foreign investors (and others) is inappropriate given factor proportions and the technical capabilities found in the host country. However, the issue is considerably more complex; the interests of investors and the host society may well diverge. Investors may be cnocerned with a shortage of an industrial labor force, training costs, and with utilizing past experience, all of which may lead them to a solution which is less than optimal from a societal point of view. See Louis T. Wells, Jr., "Economic Man and Engineering Man: Choice of Technology in a Low Wage Country." Public Policy (Summer 1973), for a good discussion of the issue.

[43]We recognize that dependentistas would argue that regulation requiring more labor-intensive production processes is unlikely given a mutuality of interest between foreign investors and elites in the host country.

[44]For a discussion of the bridgehead elit concept see Johan Galtung, "A Structural Theory of Imperialism," Journal of Peace Research 8 (1971): 81-117.

[45]Kenneth S. Mericle, "The Brazilian Motor Vehicle Industry: Its Role in Brazilian Development and Its Impact on United States Unemployment," mimeographed (Cambridge, MA: M.I.T., Sloan School of Management, 1975).

[46]Measurement of socioeconomic concepts, on an aggregate basis and across a relatively large number of poor countries, involves severe conceptual and practical difficulties. One must thus question the accuracy, validity, and importantly, the comparability of the raw data. See John Gillespie and Betty A. Nesvold, "An Introduction to Macro Cross-National Research," in Quantitative   Analysis: Conflict   Development   and Democratization ed. idem (Beverly Hills: Sage Publications, 1971).

[47]Only countries that met size minimums--a population of over 1 million and a GNP of at least $500 million--were included to insure comparability of national units. The date, 1967, was selected for the cross section because of data availability. The Harvard Business School made data through 1975 available while this analysis was in progress; however, the only complete compendium of FDI in poor countries is for year-end 1967. Stock of Private Direct Investments in Developing Countries End 1967 (Paris: Organization for Economic Cooperation and Development, 1972).

[48]The Harvard Business School's Multinational Enterprise Study reports data on foreign subsidiaries of 187 major U.S. manufacturing enterprises. A subsidiary is defined as a company in which a parent owns at least 5 percent of the equity. For this study, industries which were either part of the extractive sector or involved in the processing of raw or primary materials (e.g., oil refineries and steel mills) were eliminated and the remaining subsidiaries classified by advertising intensity of industry. See James W. Vaupel and Joan P. Curhan, The Making of Multinational Enterprise (Boston: Harvard University, Graduate School of Business Administration, Division of Research, 1969) for more information.
FDI has proven difficult to quantify. The most common indicator, book value, is a static balance of payments concept which includes reinvestment as well as new investment. Neither it nor the indicator used in this study are really satisfactory; neither captures what is meant by FDI. However, the fact that the author has previously found a strong correlation between the Harvard project's indicator (new subsidiaries established) and the book value of U.S. manufacturing investment as of year-end 1967 lends some confidence to the analysis.

[49]The sources for socioeconomic variables used in the study are Charles L. Taylor and Michael C. Hudson, World Handbook of Political and Social Indicators, 2d ed. (New Haven, CT: Yale University Press, 1972); The United Nations Statistical Yearbook (New York: United Nations, various issues); World Tables 1976 (Baltimore: Johns Hopkins University Press for World Bank, 1976).

[50]Income distribution data were obtained from Sahil Jain, Size Distribution of Income (Washington, DC: World Bank, 1975).

[51]All coefficients are significant at .01 or better unless otherwise noted.

[52]Top 20 is missing for 57 percent of the African countries, 23 percent of the Asian countries, and 22 percent of the Latin American countries included in the analysis. The uneven distribution of missing values is important because both the index of consumption and Top 20 are significantly correlated with region. (Four regions—Europe, Africa, Latin America, and Asia are specified via a set of four 0-1 dummy variables.) The link is most probably income per capita, which at least one study has suggested is related nonlinearly to income distribution. See Montek S. Ahluwalia, "Inequality, Poverty, and Development," Journal of Development Economics 3 (1976):1-36.

[53]See Kobrin, "The Environmental Determinants of Foreign Direct Investment: An Ex-Post Empirical Analysis," Journal of International Business Studies 7 (Fall-Winter 1976): 29-42.

[54]The Harvard Project obtained data on the advertising expenditure to sales ratio from <u>Newsfront</u>, March 1966, and then dichotomized industries on that basis.   See Vaupel and Curhan, <u>Multinational Enterprise</u>, p. 5.

[55]Total numbers of subsidiaries in each classification through 1966 and 1975 are reported as follows:

	1966				1975		
LOWADV	HIGHADV	TOTAL	FDI	LOWADV	HIGHADV	TOTAL	FDI
777(57)	575 (43)	1352	(100)	1226 (57)	914 (43)	2140	(100)

[56]Normalization of FDI by GDP is justified by the need to control for market size, its primary determinant.   However,given that the relationship between low- and high-advertising intensive FDI and market size is not homogenous (low-advertising intensive FDI tends to flow into large markets), normalization can distort comparisons of relationships with third variables.

	Total FDI	LOWADV	HIGHADV
Consumption	.52	.50	.54

(All coefficients are significant at the .01 level.)

[57]Countries were divided into two groups based upon scores on the indicator of consumption. The point of division was the nearest natural breakpoint to the median. There are 26 cases in Group 1 (low consumption) and 22 in Group 2.

[58]Discriminant analysis   provides   a means for distinguishing statistically   between   two (or more) groups of cases.   A discriminant   function--a   weighted   linear   combination of   previously selected   independent   or   discriminating variables--maximizes the   separation of   the groups.   The Discriminant Subprogram of the Statistical Package for the Social Sciences is used in this analysis.

[59]It must be noted that judging the accuracy of a discriminant function on the basis of its ability to classify correctly cases which were used to derive that function is problematic at best. Given a sufficient number of cases, one would prefer to utilize a portion of the cases to derive the function and the remainder to check its accuracy.

[60]Utilizing a stepwise discriminant analysis which calculated an F ratio for each variable given those variables already included in the function resulted in a two variable function composed of GNP/C and HIGHADV. (F to enter was set at 1.5.) Their coefficients were .90 and .17 respectively, and the canonical correlation coefficient was.78.

[61]While consumerism is positively correlated with development, there is no indication of a convergence to a uniformly high

level of   per capita   expenditure   in   advanced   industrial
societies.   On the contrary, previous research has indicated an
increase in the variation of this indicator at   higher levels of
industrialization.   See Stephen   Kobrin, "Industrialization and
Variation   in   Social   Structure: An   Empirical   Test   of   the
Convergence Hypothesis," <u>Proceedings of the Industrial Relations
Research Association</u> (Madison, WI: IRRA, 1976), pp. 177-86.

[62]For an analysis of   entry controls imposed by poor   countries on
FDI see Richard D. Robinson, <u>Natural Control Of Foreign Business
Entry</u> (New York: Praeger, 1976).

Multinational Corporations, the Industry Technology Cycle and Development

STEPHEN P. MAGEE

I. INTRODUCTION

This paper develops a technology cycle for industries which
parallels Vernon's (1966) cycle for individual products. The
industry cycle emerges from a new appropriability theory of the
creation of commercial information (technology) by multinational
corporations.[1] We also consider the implications of the cycle for
technology imports by less developed countries (LDCs).

The appropriability theory is a natural outgrowth of the
industrial organization approach to international direct investment
developed by Hymer (1960), Vernon (1966), and Caves (1971) as well
as the views of Arrow (1962), Demsetz (1969), and Johnson (1970) on
the creation and appropriability of the returns from private market
investments in information. The appropriability theory suggest
that multinational corporations are specialists in the production
of information which is less efficient to transmit through markets
than within firms; that multinational corporations produce
sophisticated technologies because appropriability is higher for
these technologies than for simple ones; that the large proportion
of skilled labor employed by the multinationals is an outgrowth of
the skilled-labor intensity of the production process for both the
creation and the appropriability of the returns from information;
that the relative abundance of skilled labor in the developed
country dictates that they have a comparative advantage in creating
and exporting new information; that there are diminishing returns
to information in the short run; and that output growth in each
industry ultimately becomes information saving, i.e. the share of
value added which goes to scientists and engineers in the

From **JOURNAL OF WORLD TRADE LAW**, Vol II, Jul-Aug., 1977, (297-321),
reprinted by permission of the publisher.

development of new information ultimately declines.

The hypothesis proposed in this paper is that the structure of industry and the creation of technology are jointly determined endogenous variables. The presence of a monopoly or oligopoly, ceteris paribus, encourages research and development (R and D) and other investments in innovation because appropriability costs are lower for these industry structures. In turn, a major innovation encourages an increase in optimum firm size, so that industry structure becomes more concentrated. This two-way causation between new information and industry structure is developed in the paper.

In section II of the paper we consider some of the economic issues in the private market creation of information: the motivations, risks and the payoff. Section III summarizes the appropriability theory of information creation and applies it to the multinational corporation (MNC). Five distinct types of information (i.e. technology) are created during the life cycle for an individual product and these are described. Section IV provides the transition which must be made from Vernon's (1966) product cycle to the industry cycle developed here. The analysis enumerates six economic factors causing innovation and concentrated industry structures to be correlated. Section V describes the three stages in the life of each industry: stage I is the invention stage; stage II the innovation stage and stage III the standardization stage. Industry structure, the information created, production, markets, appropriability and the mechanisms of trade are described in each stage. Examples of 36 young, medium and old industries are provided. Section VI gives empirical evidence on the cost of technology imports into an LDC (Colombia) and derives a measure of the social cost of using the patent system (without government action) to create new information. Section VII concludes the paper with seven specific (normative) policy proposals for increasing technology exports to LDCs which are built upon the (positive) appropriability theory and the industry technology cycle.

A word of caution is in order. Readers should be aware that the content of a stage theory is inductively derived but economically grounded in a dynamic process while the timing of the stages (when each will start) is an empirically inspired tautology for the products or industries from which the theory is built. The virtue of stage theories is that past regularities in economic behaviour can be labeled and analysed. Such labelling is helpful if it permits us to identify behavioral determinants of the stages and to predict future behavior, particularly of industries which were not used in developing the theory.

II. PRIVATE MARKET CREATION OF INFORMATION

The creation of new information is a special problem in the area of public goods analysis. Information is a durable good in that present resources must be devoted to its creation and its existence results in a stream of future benefits. However, it is also a public good in that once it is created, its use by the party who discovers it does not preclude its use by second parties. But, in the case of privately created information, use by second parties reduces the private return on information created by the first party. This is the "appropriability problem" (see Arrow (1962)), To the extent that noninventors succeed in "stealing" and selling technology, society benefits in the short-run (because of the lower price) but the supply of future information shrinks. Johnson (1970) has examined this public goods nature of information. He notes that either the government can create the information and provide it freely to private markets or the legal system can be used to permit private firms to capture the returns on their information by creating temporary monopolies (through the patent system) or by allowing other restrictions on free trade in information (through trade secrets).

Since these returns are difficult to observe, we must measure them indirectly. We expect that the returns on the book value of capital in industries creating new information should be higher than the returns in other industries. These monopoly profits are a natural outgrowth of the protection afforded new ideas by patent systems. A regression of monopoly profits in 19 two-digit U.S. Standard Industrial classification (SIC) industries on research and development as a percent of sales yields a relationship between variables which is nearly significant at the ten per cent level (t-statistics in parentheses):

$$(1) \quad MP = 4.47 + .57 \ R \ \& \ D \qquad \overline{R}^2 = .15$$
$$ (6.84) \ (1.71) \qquad F_{1,17} = 2.94$$

MP   monopoly profits (profits less 5 per cent of book value) as a per cent of industry sales (source Scanlon, 1972).

R & D   research and development expenditures as a per cent of industry sales in 1969 (source: National Science Foundation, 1973).

The equation asserts that every 1 percentage point increase in the ratio of R and D sales increases normalized "monopoly profits" by .57 per cent. Since R and D expenditures have a long pay-off period, we expect monopoly profits to be related to past rather than present R and D expenditures. However, since data on the stock of past R and D expenditures is not available, we use the flow of R and D expenditures to act as a proxy for the stock since the two are correlated. The other problem with equation (1) is that the use of sales to normalize both variables biases the R and D coefficient toward 1. Since all normalizing variables will be positively correlated across industries, the author knows no easy way around this problem.

It should be noted that the monopoly profits being earned in industries creating new ideas need not reflect distortions in the use of economics resources. The monopoly profits may simply reflect normal rates of returns on past investments in the creation of new information. Some observed investments will have extraordinarily high rates of return (such as the often criticized high monopoly profits earned by pharmaceutical companies in the creation of Librium and Valium). However, these high rates are offset by the unobserved investments in scientists and engineers which result in negative returns. Efficiency dictates that firms should invest in R and D until their expected patent-induced monopoly returns equal the returns on other risk-equivalent investments. If MNCs do this, the technology-importing country criticisms of monopoly profits earned by MNCs on their technology creation alone are not justified on economic grounds.

On the other hand, many concentrated industries got that way because of investments by member firms in barriers to entry. Since both investments in barriers to entry and new technology are rewarded by monopoly profit streams, it is difficult to assess the proportions of monopoly profits allocable to each of the two (sometimes unobservable) inputs. For this reason, the long-run prices paid for information by technology importers overstate the cost of generating the technology alone.

The problem is further complicated by the fact that without the barriers to entry, private firms might not create the information at all. Barriers to entry investments must be split into those necessary for appropriating technology returns and those which are not (again, a near impossibility). Thus, the long-run costs to society for privately created technology is the R and D cost plus the cost of making the returns appropriable to private parties. Any excess above this price is a payment by technology consumers for "barriers to entry investments" which are unrelated to appropriability. It is this component of the purchase price which is both wasteful and redistributive.

III. INFORMATION, MULTINATIONALS AND THE APPROPRIABILITY THEORY

Each product goes through a life cycle with a lot of new information created in the early stages and less created as the product matures. Investments must be made in information for the discovery of new products, for their development, for the creation of their production functions, for the creation of their markets and for appropriability.

First, investments are required to discover new products. While an increasing proportion of total R and D is done within large corporate organizations, many new ideas are still developed by small independent inventors. The share of patents in the United States obtained by corporations increased from 19 per cent in 1908 to 59 per cent in 1955.[2] By 1973, the number was 70 per cent, leaving 30 per cent of new patents in the hands of noncorporate inventors.[3] Enos (1962, p. 304) found that almost all of the major inventions in the development of thermal and catalytic cracking processes in the petroleum industry were made by people who were not attached to major firms (although some were closely associated with the oil industry). Mueller (1962) found that most of Dupont's major new products and processes were not discovered by Dupont scientists: 15 out of 25 of the inventions were discovered outside of the firm and were purchased by Dupont. It is the author's impression that invention is not the focus of MNC activity: their R and D efforts are focused on innovation, which encompass the next four types of information.

The second activity requiring large expenditures on scientists and engineers is in product development: i.e. applied research, product specification, pilot plants and prototypes. Mansfield (1974) discusses product development and finds that it frequently required five to ten years for major products. These undertakings are the activities engaged in by multinational corporations at the beginning of each product's life cycle. MNCs develop a comparative advantage in moving products through Vernon's (1966) life cycle. MNCs are large because it is more efficient to transfer information on development from product to product within the firm rather than through the market. This explains the tendency of multinational corporations to carry more product lines than national firms.[4] Information on avoiding mistakes is usually more costly to transmit through the market than intrafirm. Also, the public-goods nature of such information dictates that firms expand to internalize the externality of such information.

The third piece of information required in the product cycle is the creation of the production function. Economists frequently assume that engineers or that technicians provide such functions. However, for a given price structure for inputs, the creation of the production function is determined like other processes: by the supply and demand for information. Factor price structures differ between the developed countries (DCs) and the LDCs. This affects which portions of the production function will be developed in each stage of the cycle. Early in Vernon's (1966) cycle, products are produced in the United States and other DCs. Given the relatively high cost of unskilled-labor intensive than would be desired later in the production process. Production isoquants[5] are "created" in segments covering only the empirically relevant price ranges; the classic production isoquant which spans the entire region in capital-labor space with costless substitution of factors (as taught in all elementary economic sources) is a fiction. When a capital-intensive production function is taken from the DCs to the LDCs, the firm substitutes relatively cheap unskilled labor for other factors. However, the degree of substitution is limited by the past investments which the firm has made in developing unskilled-labor intensive production techniques. Such investments are frequently small. There are several reasons why such production technologies have not been developed. The abundance of cheap unskilled labor in LDCs is not empirically relevant when production functions are being created: production occurs in LDCs so late in the cycle that discounting gives their relative factor price structures a small weight.

Another point is that industry structures become more competitive through the cycles as patents lapse so that the production function becomes "frozen" or standardized at a less

unskilled labor intensive level than is socially desirable for LDC
production (i.e. the unskilled labor intensive ends of the
production isoquants are not developed at all). The reason for the
freeze is that increased industry competition erodes the private
market appropriability of the private returns from developing the
unskilled-labor intensive production techniques.

Fourth, investments in information must be undertaken to
create product markets. One interpretation of the multinational
corporation is that they act like large retail stores in selling
new technologies and new information.[6] Let us develop a framework
for this theme. Information is closer to an "experience" good
rather than a "search" good.[7] This distinction in the advertising
literature explains why large retail stores have become important
in pre-screening for consumers. For example, if a person wishes to
buy a very high quality consumer product, he is more likely to go
Saks Fifth Avenue than to a bargain basement discount store.
"Experience goods" are those whose value to the purchaser cannot be
established upon visual inspection. "Search goods" are those whose
physical attributes can be examined and successfully compared with
the claims of advertisers before purchase.

Multinational corporations specialize in the development,
production and marketing of an important experience good, new
information. They build their trademarks and reputations by
establishing a predictable level of the quality of the technology
they produce for consumers of new information.

Finally, there is an important fifth piece of information
which every multinational firm must have before it embarks on
developing a particular product. This is appropriability, and it
has been largely overlooked by many experts on the multinational
corporation (although Caves and several writers have alluded to it
but without pursuing fully its implications).[8]

There is considerable variation across products and processes
in the extent to which a private firm can appropriate the returns
from an investment in new information. For complicated ideas and
technologies, it is relatively difficult for interlopers to steal
the idea. For simple ideas, there is a larger sample of potential
entrants who can steal the idea and reduce the appropriability of
the idea to the innovator. This is one reason for the lack of R
and D in highly competitive industries. Loss of appropriability is
analogous to depreciation: complicated ideas have slow
depreciation rates while simple ideas have high ones. Differential
private appropriability leads to social underinvestments by private
firms in simple and unskilled-labor technologies.

Coase (1960), in his classic article on the problem of public
goods, points out that externalities can be efficiently handled by
private parties (rather than the government) if the legal system
clearly establishes property rights. One implication of his paper
is that governmental agencies are not required in order to provide
the optimum level of public goods, such as new information.
However, the difficulty with the Coase (1960) argument is that the
legal costs to private firms of appropriating the returns to their
investments may be so high that only the government can provide
certain types of information efficiently, e.g. unskilled-labor
intensive technologies.

The transactions and legal costs of establishing property rights for even sophisticated technologies are frequently high. The ultimate irony is that private expenditures by individuals and firms to prevent the loss of appropriability are also public goods. The first firm in an industry may expend large sums to establish proprietary rights, and establish legal precedents for property rights to complicated technologies used in the industry. Since subsequent innovators do not share in these investments but benefit from the appropriability protection they provide, they will take a free ride on these legal investments. Thus, appropriability investments will be low unless industry structure becomes concentrated so that entrants end up paying their share of the appropriability costs. Initially monopolistic or cartelized industries are less plagued by this problem since their collusion on price and other matters provides a useful framework in which to share the costs of private appropriability. The LDCs are at a disadvantage on this score since their comparative advantage is in products with competitive market structures. Since they have no institutional framework within which firms in their industries can share the costs of appropriability, R and D is discouraged.

There is another argument why multinational corporations have biased their research away from simple, unskilled-labor technologies. The appropriability of these types of information is lower than for sophisticated technologies. The rational monopolist or collusive oligopoly will prevent or delay the production of a randomly discovered unskilled-labor technology (which has low appropriability) if it is highly substitutable with an existing technology which has a higher private present value (which has high appropriability). The empirical importance of this serious problem in the private market creation of new information should be investigated.

There is ample evidence that the transactions costs of protecting new ideas are not trivial. This is true for even the most efficient vehicles for creating information, the multinational corporations. Carley (1974) documents many problems in an article entitled "Multinational Firms Find Patent Battles Consume Time, Money". He cites difficulties by 3-M and the controversy between Eastman Kodak and Polaroid in a patent battle in Britain, the difficulties of major American steel companies in an infringement suit brought by Austrian steel makers, the court battle by several large U.S. oil companies in the United Kingdom over a patent for off-shore drilling techniques and the infringement suit brought by General Electric against a Japanese firm over industrial diamonds. An official for the French electrical products maker, Compagnie Generale d'Electricite, noted that one of their biggest difficulties is that if they are involved in litigation over a single patent in several countries, they cannot be sure of getting the same decision from all of the courts. As a result, the company is forced to make costly variations in the patent on the same invention or process from country to country (making the descriptions wider or narrower) because of the local laws. Whenever a patent or licensing agreement is found invalid in one country, this upsets licensing agreements that the company has worked out in other countries.

IV. FROM THE PRODUCT CYCLE TO THE INDUSTRY CYCLE

Vernon's (1966) product cycles suggested that the life of each product can be broken into three distinct stages: the new product, the maturing product and the standardized product. He suggested that the locus of production would move from the originating DC in the first stage to the LDCs in the third stage. Three considerations suggested why production would begin in the DCs for new products. On the demand side, high unit-labor costs generate demand for labor-saving investment goods and high incomes generate demand for sophisticated and differentiated new consumer products which save on household labor. On the supply side, the research intensity of new products is high and the relatively large endowments of skilled labor (scientists, engineers, etc.) dictate that DCs have a comparative advantage in creating new products. Finally, demand and supply interact since rapid changes in new products require swift and frequent communication between producers and consumers.

In Vernon's stage II, production expands from the originating DC to other DCs as foreign markets grow, as (other DC) import barriers rise, as international transportation costs become a larger proportion of the product price and as the production process becomes more standardized. In Vernon's stage III, the standardized product stage, production shifts to the LDCs since little interaction is needed between producers and consumers, small inputs of research and development are required, and as the production technologies become routinized through assembly lining so that more unskilled labor can be utilized in the production process.

In support of this theory, Vernon (1972, p. 98) gives several examples of innovations stimulated in the United States by a scarcity of either artisans or the high cost of unskilled labor: rifles with interchangeable parts, railway automatic signal blocks, automatic bottle-making machinery and drip-dry shirts. He cites the automobile and frozen foods as innovations stimulated by consumer demands for high-income consumer products.

How do we make the transition from Vernon's product cycle to an industry technology cycle? The idea that industries may also go through cycles is suggested by Nelson's (1962) review of evidence that patents for a given industry tend to follow an S-curve over long periods of time. This Nelson relationship between the total number of patents and the age of an industry is shown in Fig. 1. The steeply rising part of the curve suggests that a major breakthrough may have occurred in one product in the industry which stimulates the demand for new components. The new information implicit in the development of a major new product will have complementary applicability to other products in the same industry. At any point in time, we know that the marginal returns on additional information, just like the marginal returns on any other input, will fall until the (present value of the) marginal revenue product of the last unit of information just equals the marginal cost of that information. This applies to flows of information in

the short run. In the long-run, the marginal return on the <u>stock</u>
of information created in the industry will eventually hit
diminishing returns. This is consistent with the levelling off of
the total numbers of patents shown in Fig. 1 as the industry
continues to age. In the accelerating parts of the curve, factor
productivity is increasing, observed technological change will be
high and the effects of learning by doing will all be important
considerations for the industry sales declines after some point.
This observation is supported by the data: the simple correlation
between R and D investments as a percentage of sales and industry
age in 1967 for 29 U.S. three-digit SIC industries is -.34.[9]

More importantly, the appropriability theory suggests that
industry structure <u>itself</u> is an endogenous variable which varies
systematically through time. Industry structure and R and D have a
two-way interaction: concentrated industry structures encourage R
and D; but also, promising inventions encourage investments in
product innovation (development, production functions, marketing
and appropriability), the returns on which are more appropriable if
the firm grows large. The implication is that <u>young industries are
concentrated and have high R and D while older ones are competitive
and spend less on R and D</u>. There are three ways that new products
and new ideas can spread from the country developing and
discovering them to the rest of the world. Exporting could occur;
or, the firm developing the product could produce and market in
the host country itself; or it can license the rights to production
to a firm in the host country. Vernon (1966) points out why
exporting will occur in stage 1 in his cycle. However, it is not
necessary that the world-wide dissemination of new products and new
technologies occur within the firm such as multinational
corporations. It could occur through licensing whereby production
moves abroad but is not controlled by the innovating firm. We
summarize next five reasons why technologies are transferred within
firms: <u>these arguments are key to the industry technology cycle
and to the size of multinationals being positively correlated with
information creation</u>.

Appropriability is the <u>first</u> reason why firms which develop
new products become large. Innovating firms expand to internalize
the externality which new information creates, namely the public
goods aspect of new information. <u>Second</u>, there is a tendency for
new products to be experience goods and for standardized products
to be search goods. Optimum firm size is usually larger for
domestic retailers of nonbrand name experience goods. By analogy,
subsidiaries of multinational corporations are more likely than
licensing arrangements. <u>Third</u>, sales of many high technology
products must be accompanied by sales of service information. The
firm's optimum size is expanded because of service subsidiaries,
e.g. IBM's servicing of computers. <u>Fourth</u>, the number of products
produced by information-creating firms is large because of product
complementarities within each of the four types of information
(development, production, marketing and appropriability). There
are also complementaries <u>among</u> the four types of information
themselves coupled with their more inexpensive transmission
intrafirm. <u>Fifth</u>, for new and differentiated products, the spread
between the buyer and seller valuation of new information is higher

228   Stephen P. Magee

than when the products are older and more standardized. This again suggests that market transactions costs are relatively higher earlier in the cycle, lower late in the cycle so that optimum firm size will fall through the industry cycle.

These five reasons explain why new technologies are correlated with concentrated industry structures and why international trade in technology occurs within large MNCs rather than through licensing agreements and why older industries are more competitive and less innovative. The correlation between concentration and R and D early in an industry's life and competition with less R and D late in each industry's life is now explained (although the direction of causation is not). The empirical evidence showing that firm size and hence industry concentration is negatively related to the average age of the industry has been shown elsewhere.[10]

V. THE STAGES OF THE INDUSTRY TECHNOLOGY CYCLE

The three stages of Vernon's (1966) product cycles were: new product, maturing product and standardized product. The three stages of the industry technology cycle developed here are a bit different: the first stage is invention, the second is innovation and the third is standardization. The first stage in the industry technology cycle involves the invention itself, which occurs before the product is observable commercially. The second stage of the technology cycle includes Vernon's first two stages; that is, innovation here covers both the new product (as it is developed in the originating country) and the maturing product (as production is disseminated to other DCs). The third stage of the technology cycle and the product cycle coincide: the standardized product and the standardized industry.

Several aspects of the technology cycle are discussed in this section: industry structure, the types of information created, the skill intensities and other characteristics of production, the nature of markets, aspects of appropriability and the efficiency of the mechanisms by which information is traded.

Table 1 describes the three stages in the industry technology cycle and summarizes some of the arguments in the previous sections. Industry structure may not be defined early in the invention stage since the industry and the products to be invented may not exist. On the other hand, the industry may exist but the invention defining a breakthrough may not have occurred. A contrived example of the latter would be "road vehicles". This would be horse-drawn buggies before automobiles and both after, say, 1900.

Toward the end of the invention stage, the large number of auto firms would decrease and optimum firm size would increase as large scale development of the automobile, the production function and markets necessitated large information investments. Finally, as autos become standardized, world proliferation of production and international trade makes the industry less concentrated and more competitive.

Consider next the types of information created; i.e. the four types of information discussed in the previous section. In the invention stage, investments are made in information to create the new product. In the innovation stage, the product must be developed, its production function must be created and its markets must be developed. There is little or no information created in the standardization stage. Mansfield (1974) estimates that for all products which succeed, 10 per cent of total R and D investments are devoted to invention and 90 per cent to innovation. R and D may be low in the standardization stage either because no appropriability scheme exists which allows private investors to capture the social return or because the social return itself is too low to justify private investments in R and D.

The production characteristics of each industry vary from the first to the third stages. As in Vernon's (1966) cycle, the skilled-labor intensity of production is highest in the initial stage and lowest when the product becomes standardized. The capital intensity of industries creating new products is relatively low because of the absence of heavy equipment in the invention stage. However, through the cycle, the capital intensity of production increases. Optimum plant sizes start small and increase until stage 3. Technological change is not measurable in the invention stage (since the major industry product does not exist yet), is high in the innovating stage, and eventually declines for older and more competitive industries. Much of the literature treats technical change as if it were manna from heaven. However, the framework here views technical change as the economic return on investments in information. The skill required for managers is lower in the first (invention) and third stages relative to the second stage (in the innovating stage, the organizational skill required to develop products, create the production functions, supervise market development and coordinate appropriability is high).

The markets for each industry vary throughout the cycle. In the first stage, the inventor's markets for new products and recently invented technologies are large innovating firms such as multinational corporations. In the second stage, the multinational corporations develop and sell the products primarily through their own sales outlets to final consumers or users. However, in the third stage, in which the industry products are standardized and competition is high, most of the sales from the producers are to market specialists, i.e. wholesalers. It is difficult to generalize because of high variance but there is a tendency for the advertising intensity of goods to vary from experience-differentiated goods in the innovating stage to search-standardized goods in the third stage. There is greater variation in buyer-seller evaluation of the products in the first two stages (because of product differentiation) but less in the third stage (because of the homogeneous nature of the products).

Appropriability is an important key to the creation of new information. It is high for many product inventions because of the patent system. However, appropriability declines in the innovation

MULTINATIONAL CORPORATIONS

TABLE 1

THE INDUSTRY TECHNOLOGY CYCLE

	I. Invention	II. Innovation	III. Standard-ization
Industry Structure (Optimum firm size)	competitive (small)	concentrated (large)	competitive (medium to small)
Information Created	new product	product development production function markets	
Information intensity	high	high	low
R and D investments	10%	90%	0
Production Skilled labor intensity	high	decreasing	low
Capital intensity	low	increasing (assembly line)	high
Optimal plant size	small	increasing	large
Observed technical change	—	high but declining	low
Skilled managerial intensity	low	high	low
Markets Purchasers of the information/goods	innovators	final users	wholesalers
Advertising-type good	—experience (differentiated)—search (standardized)		
Variance in buyer-seller valuation	high	high	low
Appropriability Ease of appropriability	highest	high but declining	low
Private social mechanism	patents	patents/trade secrets	trade secrets/ collusion

stage because of the difficulty of protecting the private rights to
returns on new information on product development, new production
processes and the development of new markets. Appropriability is
especially low for homogeneous, standardized and simple products in
competitive industries. The private social mechanism used most
frequently in protecting appropriability are patents in the
invention stage, patents and trade secrets in the innovation stage
and either trade secrets (e.g. Coca-Cola formula) or outright
collusion in the standardization stage (although there tends to be
so little information created in the third stage that hypothesizing
appropriability schemes is futile).

Finally, the most efficient mechanism for trade in information
in the first stages is the market because of the saleability of
patents. In the innovation stage, information is traded largely
within firms, such as multinational corporations. Finally, in
standardized industries, there is a return to the market (in
trading what little information is created).

Consider those industries falling into the innovation and
standardization stage. Since the industries to be listed in both
groups are those already listed as SIC industries in the United
States, we have no observations for the invention stage. Table 2
shows a listing of 36 four-digit SIC industries in the United
States in 1967 which fall into three age brackets.[11] Notice that
the younger industries are R and D intensive (pharmaceuticals,
optical, surgical, photographic and electronics) the older ones are
typically not (fur, shoes, cut stones and leather) and the
middle-age industries are mixed (design intensive textiles,
abrasives, steel, and welding).

VI. THE PRICE OF NEW TECHNOLOGY

The patent system confers limited monopoly powers on the
sellers of new technologies. The price paid for technology is the
monopoly rent portion of the product price. This can be illustrated
in Fig. 2. Consider a technological breakthrough resulting in the
creation of a new product or service whose demand, marginal revenue
and marginal cost curves are represented by D, MR and MC in Fig. 2.
If private markets develop the ideas and if the rights to the
breakthrough are fully protected legally by patents or trade
secrets, output of the product will be Q_m, the price will be P_m,
monopoly profits will be B, and the gain to society will equal the
sum of B and the consumer's surplus triangle, A. If the government
develops the same product and distributes the information freely,
absence of the legally sanctioned monopoly and the presence of many
competitive firms will drive market output to the competitive level
Q_c, the price to P_c, and the gain to society equals the consumer's
surplus areas, A + B + C. With government free dissemination of
the information, welfare is higher than under patent protected
creation of the information by area C. These points are developed
in some detail in Johnson (1970).[12]

TABLE 2

Average Age of 36 Industries in 1967

Less than 20 years		20 to 30 years		Over 30 years	
Sic No.	Name	Sic No.	Name	Sic No.	Name
2833	Medical Chemicals & Botanical products	2256	Knit Fabric Mills	2371	Fur goods
2834	Pharmaceutical Preparations	2335	Women's Dresses	3111	Leather Tanning & Finishing
		2396	Automotive Fabric Trimmings & Apparel findings	3141	Shoes (Non-rubber)
3811	Engineering & Scientific & Research Instruments	2819	Miscellaneous Industrial Inorganic Chemicals	3161	Luggage
3831	Optical Instruments & Lenses	2861	Gum & wood chemicals	3171	Handbags & Purses
3841	Surgical & Medical Instruments	2891	Adhesives & chemicals	3241	Cement, hydraulic
3843	Dental Equipment & Supplies	3291	Abrasive Products	3274	Lime
3851	Ophthalmic Goods	3293	Gaskets & Insulations	3281	Cut Stone & Stone Products
3534	Elevators & Escalators	3312	Blast Furnaces & Steel Mills		
3536	Hoist, cranes & monorails	3441	Fabricated Structural Steel		
3541	Metal-cutting machine tools	3623	Electric Welding Apparatus		
3651	Radio & TV sets	3953	Marking Devices		
3674	Semiconductors, etc.	2241	Narrow Fabric Mills		
3861	Photographic equipment	3322	Malleable Iron Foundaries		
		3552	Textile Machinery		

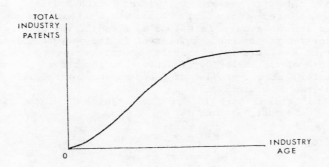

Figure 1. Relationship Between the Total Number of
Patents and the Age of an Industry

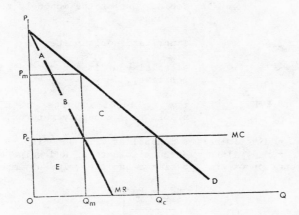

FIGURE 2.

Price of Technology's Relationship with Product Price

We do not have direct estimates of the areas in Fig. 2. We already know from equation (1) that there is a weak though detectable statistical relationship between monopoly profits and the creation of new information. Vaitsos (1974) provides indirect evidence via the monopoly profits on pharmaceutical imports into Colombia. While he does not provide marginal cost data, he does have the price paid by Colombia for its imports relative to the "world price". Since the latter is an average of prices charged in all countries, it must exceed world marginal cost. But we have no estimates of marginal costs, so we will assume that marginal cost equals the world price measured by Vaitsos (which equals P_c in Fig. 2). The imported price into Colombia corresponds to P_m, D represents import demand in Colombia, B equals the price paid by Colombia for the new technology inherent in the pharmaceuticals and C equals the social cost of having patent protected monopoly distribution of the technology (rather than government purchase of the technology at a cost flow of B per period for the life of the patent and free dissemination).

The traditional formula for the social cost of the monopoly restriction on output, area C, is

$$C = .5 \left[\frac{P_m - P_c}{P_m} \right]^2 e_d M$$

(2)

C — social cost of the monopoly restriction on output

P_m, P_c — import and world prices

e_d — elasticity of import demand (defined as positive).

$M = (B + E)$ — the value of imports (cost at world prices plus monopoly returns).

We know that a discriminating monopolist will set his price so that $e_d = P_m/(P_m - P_c)$. Thus, we can eliminate e_d and write the social cost as a function of the two prices and the value of imports:

$$(3) \qquad C = .5 \left[\frac{P_c - P_c}{P_m} \right] M$$

and monopoly profits, B, are a function of the value of imports and prices

$$(4) \qquad B = \left[\frac{P_m - P_c}{P_m} \right] M$$

Notice that the social cost of exiting patent distributed technology is always one-half the monopoly profits for linear

TABLE 3

MONOPOLY PROFITS AND THE SOCIAL COST OF PATENT RESTRICTIONS ON
OUTPUT FOR PHARMACEUTICAL IMPORTS INTO COLOMBIA

Product	Percentage excess of Colombian price over world price (1)	Thousands of $		
		Value of imports (2)	Monopoly profits (3)	Social cost (4)
Oxytetracycline	310	333	252	126
Chlortetracycline	400	544	435	218
Streptomycin Sulfate	19	127	20	10
Penicillin G	67	869	348	174
Other Antibiotics	72	1382	580	290
Triaminicinolone, Dexamethasone, Prednis. & Desoxycorticosterone acetate	449	1474	1209	605
Testosterone Cyclopentyl- propicnate	246	291	1209	104
Total		5020	3051	1527

Sources: Column (1) is from Vaitsos (1974); (2) was provided by Frank Reid and comes from the National Dept. of Statistics, Bogata, Colombia; let $V = (1)/((1)/100 + 1)$, so that $(3) = (2) \cdot V/100$; $(4) = .5 (2) V/100$.

demand functions (the marginal revenue curve is one-half the distance from the price axis to the demand curve).

The percentage excess of Colombian prices over world prices, the value of imports (area B + E in Fig. 2), monopoly profits (B) and the social costs (C) are shown in Table 3 for pharmaceutical imports into Colombia. Notice the $3 m. out of the $5 m. paid for these imports, or 60 per cent, payment for the technology. If the Colombian government paid the drug companies $3 m. per period, and distributed freely the technology to create the products at world prices, Colombian welfare would increase by $1.5 m. The payment of $3 m. is actually an upper bound which is the proper amount only if all of the monopoly profits are allocable to past R and D expenditures. The "technology payment" is too high by that part of the monopoly profits which are due to monopoly power unrelated to technology creation. In this case, less than $3 m. could be paid without affecting the supply of future information.

The evidence for Colombia suggests that the elasticity of demand for knowledge-intensive goods may be lower in developing countries than in the rest of the world (this contrasts with Johnson's (1970, p. 41) speculation that they would be higher). If this is true generally, then developing countries pay more than their pro-rata share of the costs of the development of knowledge. While international price discrimination permits a higher level of expected returns (and hence greater creation of private information) than would be the case if one world price were charged, an adverse international redistribution seems to result from international price discrimination.

VII. POLICY MEASURES FOR MORE EFFICIENT "TRANSFERS OF TECHNOLOGY" TO THE LDCS

We noted earlier that an increasing proportion of technology has been developed by corporate entities. The United States is an important source of technology transferred to the LDCs: the U.S. share of patents granted by LDCs to technology exporters remained steady at around 40 per cent from 1964 to 1972 (UNCTAD, 1975a, p. 39, Table 9). Thus, any consideration of policies directed at increasing technology flows to LDCs must consider the response of both U.S. and other DC based multinational corporations.

The philosophy which should guide all LDC technology policy should be the following: developers of new technology, whether foreign or domestic, should be provided with efficient legal mechanisms to permit them to reap the social rewards of their investments in new information. If innovators are hampered by bureaucratic entanglements and if their perception of the correlation between their efforts and their expected returns is small, then private markets will undersupply the technologies desired.

The conflict between the pricing of existing technologies and the creation of future technologies is analogous to the question of

nationalization. It is clear that any country which nationalizes a
foreign held firm increases its short-run welfare (since profits on
the existing operation are transferred from foreigners to the
domestic government) but reduces its future welfare (there is a
reduction in future investment by foreigners in the country). The
same is true of technology. Countries cutting the prices they pay
for existing technology (increased restrictions on profits,
repatriation, etc.) gain in the short-run but they reduce the
future supply of new information to the country. Given the short
lives of many LDC governments, short-run calculations will lead to
an excessive tax on the flow of existing technology. A careful
calculation must be made by technology importers on this welfare
trade-off between the price paid for existing technologies and the
expectational effects of the current price on the supply of future
technology. The LDCs should adopt the following criterion.

> The LDCs as a whole should tax present technology
> imports, i.e. reduce the price paid, until the marginal
> decrease in monopoly profits paid to current technology
> suppliers equals the present value of the marginal loss
> in consumer's surplus on future technologies.

We consider next eight of the many policy proposals for
increased transfer of technology to the LDCs discussed in three
UNCTAD documents (1975a, 1975b, and 1975c).

1. Increased Use of Utility Models

One proposal which would increase the type of technologies
appropriate for LDCs would be to switch their existing patent laws
away from traditional DC-type patents toward "utility models". A
"utility model" is a simple patent, of short duration (usually
three years) is easier to obtain than the traditional patent and
applies to both products and processes. A number of the LDCs
already use utility models and they have been successfully used in
two DCs which have had rapid technological change -- Japan and West
Germany.[13]

2. Majority Ownership of Foreign Affiliates

One of the most serious restrictions which LDCs impose upon
multinational corporations attempting to set up subsidiaries in
their countries (through either mergers or takeovers) is that
foreign ownership must not exceed fifty per cent. For example, in
India, foreign equity holdings cannot exceed forty per cent without
approval from the relevant authorities. Similar restrictions exist

in Argentina, Mexico, and the Andean group countries.[14] These
restrictions are generally justified by the phrase that such
foreign control of ownership can be allowed only in cases which the
action "conforms with national interest". While these restrictions
may achieve other goals, the LDCs should be aware that they impose
severe limitations on technology transfers. UNCTAD support of
these restrictions is, in my view, a mistake.

The LDCs might benefit greatly if they permitted majority
foreign ownership (at least fifty-one per cent). This would still
allow equity holders in the LDCs to capture nearly half of the
rents on the technology while at the same time overcoming the
severe "appropriability" problem which is a key to much foreign
direct investment in high technology industries.[15] MNCs have a
legitimate fear that if they do not control at least 51 per cent of
the operation, the other party to the agreement might "steal" the
technology, sell it in third markets and reduce the worldwide
return on a given technology.

3. Limitations on R and D in LDC Subsidiaries

Two restrictions on LDC research and development documented in
the UNCTAD study (1975c, p. 34-35) are the limitation by
multinationals on R and D done in LDC subsidiaries or affiliates
and in "grant-back" provisions for R and D done in LDCs, i.e. that
the host country must provide the parent with the results of
subsidiary R and D on a unilateral and frequently unrenumerated
basis. This allows modifications and adaptations of sophisticated
R and D to developing countries to revert to the parent. This is
socially wasteful since it prohibits LDC subsidiaries from
transforming sophisticated ideas into forms more useful to the
LDCs. However, it is explainable since the appropriability of the
latter is low. The parent realizes that the simpler technology may
undercut its profits on the more sophisticated technology. There
is no easy solution to this problem.

A partial solution would be a special provision for R and D
done in subsidiaries or by licensees of multinational corporations:
that all such technologies would be patentable as a utility model;
that the parent would have three years in which to exploit all
revenues from the new technology; and, that the revenues on such
new technologies would be split equally between the
subsidiary/licensee and the parent.

The danger of this proposal is it would cut the existing
transfer of technology to the developing countries. On the other
hand, the provision would guarantee the parent that it would gain
half of all revenues from the R and D developed by the licensee.
If the MNC parent failed to exploit the potential revenues from an
LDC developed technology, the LDC subsidiary has recourse through
the legal provisions for "failure to work" a patent: after an
appropriate interval, the licensee can exploit the new technology.
(The legal instrument by which this is done is the "compulsory

license" (see UNCTAD (1975a, p. 10). It authorizes the subsidiary to perform acts without authorization of the parent which would otherwise be excluded by the patent privilege.)

4. Territorial Restrictions

One of the most criticized restrictions on the use of technology by importers is the requirement by multinationals that the technology (or products embodying it) not be exported from the host country. An UNCTAD study (1975a, p. 21, Table 1) of 2640 contracts for technology imports into 12 LDCs showed that 47 per cent of the contracts contained such territorial restrictions. An UNCTAD study (1975b, p. 19, Table 7) of ten technology importing LDCs showed that in the median country, 83 per cent of the technology contracts contained restrictive export clauses (i.e. either a total prohibition or prior approval required for exports of the technology from the recipient). The two economic motivations are appropriability (the technology exporters fear the loss of the private returns to the new ideas) or price discrimination (maximizing profits by differential pricing in separated markets). Empirical work is needed in this area to determine which of the two causes is dominant. If appropriability is the concern, increased international legal guarantees for technology exporters would reduce the likelihood that their ideas would be stolen with freer trade in technology. If price discrimination is the motivation, the question is more complicated. If price discrimination is eliminated by new legal mechanisms which prohibit market separation by (economically artificial) legal boundaries, welfare will improve in technology importing countries with low import elasticities (because of a decrease in the price they pay for technology) and fall in countries with high elasticities (because of an increase in the price they pay). The supply of all future information will fall since the total profits of technology exporters are reduced when price discrimination is eliminated. The Vaitsos (1974) evidence suggests that LDCs may have lower import price elasticities for technology than other demanders.

Thus, <u>elimination of territorial restrictions would shift rents to the LDCs from the DCs on existing technologies</u> (this is at variance with Johnson's (1970) conjecture). Whether this welfare gain would offset the welfare loss from a lower total world supply of future technology is an open question.

5. Tied Purchases

A provision imposed on many technology importers is that the purchase of the technology be accompanied by an agreement to purchase raw materials, spare parts, intermediate products and capital equipment from the technology supplier. An UNCTAD study (1975b, p. 16, Table 5) showed that in four out of the five importing countries, 66 per cent or more of the contracts required tied purchase provisions. Again, this is simply another monopolistic profit maximizing technique. In terms of Fig. 2, the technology importer should never pay more for a new technology (including rents lost through excessive prices for such tied purchases) than the sum of areas A + B. The tied purchase agreement is a vehicle for the technology exporter to extract as much as possible of the consumer surplus in area A. Without a tied sale, area A would accrue to the technology importer. If the technology exporter succeeds in extracting all of area A, there is no economic gain to the importing region. The governments of the LDCs are attempting to prevent foreigners from capturing this much of the consumer surplus by their forced tied sales and other techniques.

6. Package Licensing

Package licensing is a serious abuse of the patent system by technology exporters. An exporter can lump together two technologies, one of which has a patent which expires many years away and the other of which lapses soon. By making a long term contractual arrangement for the sale of both, the technology exporter is able to continue its monopoly pricing of the older technology past that time when society has legally deemed it should become a pure public good. We see no easy way of dealing with this problem (since a technology which has not yet lost its appropriability through normal erosion is, by definition, difficult to steal). Outright prohibition will help but MNCs can escape many restrictions by covert tied sales. Further study of this problem is needed for an adequate solution.

7. Excessive Pricing

A frequent complaint of technology importers is that the prices charged are "excessive". Again, this is a very general accusation which covers the previous three types of problems already discussed. In effect, technology exporters are attempting to extract the entire area under the demand curve. If they were completely successful in doing this, note in Fig. 2 that the technology exporter could capture all of areas A + B + C, and the quantity of technology transferred would equal that under free dissemination of technology. However, all but a fraction of the

economic benefits of the new technology are captured by the
exporter rather by the importer. Ironically, in this case the
amount of technology transferred exceeds the amount transferred
under single-price monopoly sale but the gain to the importing
region is less. The LDC obtains almost no welfare from the
technology import. The only way around this problem is for
importing country governments to play an active (though not
burdensome) role in negotiating technology imports. For example,
Mexico's law provides that a contract shall not be registered "when
the price or counter-service is out of proportion to the technology
acquired or constitutes an unwarranted or excessive burden on the
country's economy".[16]

The Japanese approach to the technology question might serve
as a useful model for the LDCs. The Japanese government has been
particularly active in working with Japanese businessmen in
obtaining foreign technology on the most favorable terms possible
for Japan. However, such a policy requires an enlightened
government and the danger is that cumbersome and slow-witted
bureaucracies are likely to add more inefficiency to the process
than they are able to save by obtaining technology on more
favorable terms.

The last consideration suggests the dangers of excessive
restrictions by LDC governments. While Mexico was cited as an
example of a country which has an active policy of preventing
discriminatory pricing by MNC exporters of technology, it also has
a long list of restrictive practices which many foreign
businessmen would shun: one UNCTAD study (1975b, p. 38) lists
eleven different conditions under which technology may not be
imported into Mexico. Mexico's welfare might be improved by a
reduction in this list. Mexico may be an example of the
bureaucrat's dream: "if more regulation is better, then too much
regulation is just right".

REFERENCES

Aliber, R., 1970, "A theory of direct foreign investment," in: C.
P. Kindleberger, ed., The international corporation (The M.I.T.
Press, Cambridge, Mass.).

Arrow, K. J., 1962, "Economic welfare and the allocation of
resources for invention", in: The rate and direction of
inventive activity; economic and social factors -- A report of
the National Bureau of Economic Research, New York (Princeton

University Press, Princeton, N.J.).

Bhagwati, J., 1972, R. Vernon's, Sovereignty at bay: The multinational spread of U.S. enterprises" (a review), Journal of International Economics 2, 455-459.

Brock, W. A. and S. P. Magee, 1975, "The economics of pork-barrel politics", Center for Mathematical Studies in Business and Economics, University of Chicago, Report No. 7511, February.

Carley, W. M., 1974, "Multinational firms find patent battle consume time money, Wall Street Journal, June 24, 1 and 17.

Caves, R., 1971, "International corporations: The industrial economics of foreign investment", Economics, 38, 1-27.

Caves, R., 1974, "Industrial organization", in: J. H. Dunning, ed., Economic analysis and the multinational enterprise (Praeger, New York).

Coase, R., 1960, "The Problem of Social Cost", Journal of Law and Economics, 3, 1-44.

Demsetz, H., 1969, "Information and efficiency: Another viewpoint", Journal of Law and Economics 12, 1-22.

Enos, J. L., 1962, "Invention and innovation in the petroleum refining industry", in National Bureau of Economic Research, The rate and direction of inventive activity: economic and social factors (Princeton University Press: Princeton), 299-321.

Helleiner, G. K., 1975, "The role of multinational corporations in the less developed countries' trade in technology", World Development, 3, 161-189.

Hufbauer, G. 1970, "The impact of national characteristics & technology on the commodity composition of trade in manufactured goods", in : R. Vernon ed., The technology factor in international trade -- Universities -- National Bureau Conference Series (Colombia University Press, New York).

Hymer, S. H., 1960, The international operation of national firms: A study of direct foreign investment, Ph.D. dissertation, M.I.T. (published in 1976 by the M.I.T. Press, Cambridge, Mass.).

Johnson, H. G., 1970, "Multinational corporations and international oligopoly: The non-American challenge", in: C. P. Kindleberger, ed., The international corporation (The M.I.T. Press, Cambridge, Mass.).

Kindleberger, C. P. 1974, "Size of firm and size of nation", in: J. H. Dunning, ed., Economic analysis and the multinational enterprise (praeger, New York).

Magee, S. P., 1977, "Technology and the appropriability theory of the multinational corporation," forthcoming in The New International Economic Order; edited by Jagdish Bhagwati (M.I.T. Press, Cambridge).

_____, 1977a, "Application of the dynamic limit pricing model to the price of technology and international technology transfer", forthcoming in a Supplement to the Journal of Monetary Economics.

Mansfield, E., 1974, "Technology and technological change", in J. H. Dunning, ed., Economic analysis and the multinational enterprise (Praeger, New York).

Mueller, W. F., 1962, "The origins of the basic inventions underlying DuPont's major product and process innovations, 1920 to 1950", in National Bureau of Economic Research, The rate and direction of inventive activity: economic and social factors (Princeton University Press: Princeton, 323-358.

National Bureau of Economic Research, 1962, The rate and direction of inventive activity: economic and social factors (Princeton University Press: Princeton, N.J.).

National Science Foundation, 1973, Research and Development in industry, 1973 (U.S. Government Printing Office, Washington).

Nelson, R., 1962, Introduction, in: The rate and direction of inventive activity: Economic and social factors -- A report of the National Bureau of Economic Research, New York (Princeton University Press, Princeton, N.J.).

Nelson, P., 1970, "Information and consumer behaviour", Journal of Political Economy, 78, 311-239.

Rodriquez, C., 1975, "Trade in technological knowledge and the national advantage", Journal of Political Economy, 83, 121-135.

Scanlon, P. D., 1972, "FTC and Phase II: the 'McGovern papers'," Antitrust Law and Economics Review, 5, 19-36.

Telser, L., 1976, "Comment", Journal of Law and Economics, 19, 337-340.

United Nations Conference on Trade and Development, 1975a, The role of the patent system in the transfer of technology to developing countries (United Nations, New York). TD/B/AC,11/19/Rev.1.

_____, 1975b., Major issues arising from the transfers of technology to developing countries, (United Nations, New York), TD/B/AC.11/10/Rev.2.

_____, 1975c, An international code of conduct on transfer of technology, (United Nations, New York), TD/B/C.6/AC.1/2/Supp.I/Rev.1.

United States Department of Commerce, 1974, Statistical abstract of the U.S., 1974 (U.S. Government Printing Office, Washington).

Vaitsos, C., 1974, Intercountry income distribution and transnational enterprises (Clarendon, Oxford).

Vernon, R., 1966, "International investment and international trade in the product cycle", Quarterly Journal of Economics 80, 190-207.

_____, 1971, Sovereignty at bay (basic Books, New York).

____, 1972, Manager in the international economy (Prentice-Hall, Englewood Cliffs, N.J.).

NOTES

[1] See Magee (1977). By "appropriability", we mean the ability of private originators of ideas to obtain for themselves the values of the ideas to society. The appropriability theory asserts that multinational corporate product development is guided by careful calculations of the likelihood of loss of the returns on new information to emulators.

[2] See UNCTAD (1975a, p. 39, Table 10).

[3] See U.S. Department of Commerce (1974, p. 541).

[4] See Vernon (1971, p. 285, note 4).

[5] A production isoquant is a locus of points along which factor inputs (capital, labor, etc.) vary but output is constant.

[6] See Magee (1977).

[7] See Nelson (1970).

[8] A new theory of direct investment and the multinational corporations is built upon appropriability in Magee (1977). The next section derives the industry cycle from this theory.

[9] See Magee (1977) and footnote 11 in this paper for the sources of the data for all statistical results reported in the text.

[10] See Magee (1977, Fig. 4).

[11] Industry age is measured by the average age of all of the seven-digit TSUSA (Tariff Schedules of the United States Annotated) products in that industry in 1967. Product age equals 1967 less the year when the product was first listed as a

separate category in the U.S. trade statistics (see Hufbauer (1970) who constructed the "first-trade-date" statistics). The industries shown in Table 2 were picked from a sample of 137 four-digit SIC industries for which industry age data was available.

[12]See Magee (1977a) for a dynamic model of pricing new technologies and the effects of government policies on technology transfer in such a framework.

[13]See UNCTAD (1975a, p. 4 and 19) and UNCTAD (1975b, p. 37).

[14]See UNCTAD (1975a, p. 15).

[15]See Magee (1977).

[16]See UNCTAD (1975a, p. 26).

Technology Transfer, Regional Co-operation and Multinational Firms

DIMITRI GERMIDIS

Convincing proof has been given in recent years of the strategic role played by the technology variable in the development process in countries of the Third World.

In the case of these countries "technology" means mainly imported technology, or what is more commonly called "technology transfer".

In the long run transferred technology by itself is only of value to the recipient countries if they are capable of combining the separate elements they receive so as to form a national stock of know-how co-ordinated by a policy for science and technology, and if they have the industrial capacity to use it.

As multinational firms are the leading channel for transferring technology to the developing countries, they bear a heavy responsibility for the way in which the technology they transfer is assimilated and adapted by the host countries and hence for developing the latter's scientific, technological and industrial potential.

The criticisms of multinational firms[1] for not trying seriously to adapt their technologies (but not their products) to conditions in host countries, to decentralise R & D effectively and to observe the right priorities for national development in host countries can only throw doubt on the ultimate objectives of their "world-wide" strategies, or in other words their view of the world.

As regards the developing countries, two points may be made. First, the policies followed so far for transfering technology and the policies for science and technology have been individualistic and sometimes even isolationist, so that they have favoured current methods of transferring technology. Indeed, there has been very little effective concertation (apart from the various attempts to work out "codes of behaviour" which are far from being followed

From **TRANSFER OF TECHNOLOGY BY MULTINATIONAL CORPORATIONS**, 1977, (24-36), reprinted by permission of the publisher, OECD, Paris.

universally) and still less has there been true horizontal
co-operation between these countries.

Secondly, most attempts at regional integration have had
little success in reaching their targets and many of them have
failed lamentably. One of the main reasons for their failure is
that technology has almost always been regarded as a variable
outside the scope of integration or, which is worse, as a given
constraint which one cannot alter, and in both cases people have
been content to make subsequent measurements of profitability as a
residual factor resulting from the industrialisation process.

But what would happen if one reversed this traditional
approach?

Let us suppose that technology occupied a strategic position
in the regional integration process and so became its driving
force. Science and technology policies would be co-ordinated,
there would be regional co-operation in R & D together with
exchanges of technologies and measures to adapt them, and there
would be supervision of technology transfers which was better than
chauvinistic and sometimes even xenophobe reflexes, etc. There
would then be prospects for establishing a degree of regional
autonomy in technology which fitted into the overall pattern.

Would multinational firms not then be inclined, or at least be
obliged or tempted, to develop regionalised strategies for areas
demarcated by the developing countries concerned, and at the same
time to make maximum use in their activities of the scientific,
technological and industrial potentials of the area? Is that not
the only way of deliberately aligning development targets for a
region (and thereby the targets of the countries composing it) with
the targets of the multinational firms, which for planning purposes
would then become active promoters of development?

But before seeking answers to all these questions we must
begin by noting a number of points concerning the effects of
current practice in transferring technology on the regional
integration of developing countries.

I. PRESENT METHODS OF TRANSFERRING TECHNOLOGY: DO THEY TEND TO UNDERMINE THE STRUCTURES OF DEVELOPING COUNTRIES AND ISOLATE THEM?

It is not our purpose here to list exhaustively all the
methods for transferring technology.[2] We would only point out
in passing that for the purpose of this paper technology transfer
takes place mainly through:

   i)   direct investment, whether within a country or between
        countries, and imports of capital equipment
        incorporating technology;

  ii)   visits by individuals from one country to another, the
        employment of foreign experts, consultancy agreements

and exchanges of information and staff under
international programmes for technical co-operation;
and

iii) licensing contracts covering patents and know-how.

The first negative aspect of the transfer of technology to
developing countries is its excessive cost to the recipient
countries.

This high cost has been widely condemned both by isolated
research workers and by research establishments and international
organisations,[3] while argument about the justification for their
structures (or at least of their extent) has led to a discussion
which is still open on how to fix (if this is possible) a "fair
price"[4] for transferring technology.

Thus the first adverse effect for developing countries as a
direct result of current practices in transferring technology is
the heavy financial burden in foreign exchange which they have to
bear and which is a mortgage on their future options because it
unduly increases their debt service. Moreover, investigation into
the opportunity cost of these practices can provide us with some
initial evidence that they undermine the economic structures of the
countries which acquire the technology.

In spite of all the fuss and publicity about the idea of
"intermediate technology", its application has not yet gone beyond
the stage of a few isolated experiments.

A transferred technology usually remains as it was designed
for developed countries, irrespective of the stage it has reached
(e.g. whether it is new or second-hand).

With particular reference to technology transferred by
multinational firms by setting up subsidiaries or concluding
licensing agreements, it has been shown that such technology
assumes an almost universal form irrespective of the particular
conditions in host countries and that its power to propagate itself
in the latter is negligible.[5] The result is to accentuate the dual
character of the economic structures of developing countries, so
here we have a second force undermining these structures as a
result of the practices followed in transferring technology.

Subcontracting may be defined as the system whereby a
manufacturer replaces his own production by the production of
another firm (in another country) which has to comply strictly with
the economic and technical specifications he lays down while he
remains responsible for marketing, and this is another channel for
transferring technology. The practice is of special importance,
because many people including leaders of developing countries
regard it as the open sesame to industrialisation and of course to
modern technology and the international market, as well as a means
of absorbing the unemployment which is rife in most of these
countries.

Without looking very far (e.g. in South-East Asia where the
case of Singapore, despite its special features, may serve as a
model), one may point to the case of Tunisia which openly proclaims
its desire to become an international subcontracting centre and, to
a lesser degree, of Morocco which does so less unreservedly.

The size of the trade flows generated by international subcontracting indicates how much this activity has grown in recent years.

For example in the United States, which was the first country to embark on international subcontracting, the share of developing countries in American imports of articles regarded as products of subcontracting[6] increased from 6.4% in 1966 to 21.4% in 1969, 30.3% in 1972 and nearly 36% in 1973.[7] Indeed this subcontracting by the Americans has driven European and Japanese firms to follow suit.

But while subcontracting undeniably helps to relieve unemployment, it is only a temporary measure and makes the economies of developing countries more vulnerable if economic conditions change. As regards transfers of technology, they only take place when subcontracting agreements are the first step towards setting up joint ventures, apart from technical assistance given (sometimes) by the principal firm to enable the subcontractor to comply with the required standards.

Otherwise international subcontracting leads in most cases to accentuating the "enclaves" and to dismembering the national economy, so making its dual character more pronounced.

It is also argued that international subcontracting enables developing countries to exploit their comparative advantages,[8] so helping to establish relations of mutual benefit between them and developed countries. However, this argument is only valid in the context of the traditional international division of labour, roundly condemned by the countries of the Third World which blame it for their continued dependence on the industrialised countries.

But even if it is agreed that international subcontracting creates mutually advantageous relations between countries at different levels of economic development, they are not permanent and are created on the initiative and for the benefit (mainly) of industrialised countries. In addition and what is worse, international subcontracting helps to isolate the developing countries, because not only does it not strengthen regional solidarity and still less integration, but it often drives them to compete with one another and thereby worsen the terms (especially financial) of subcontracting itself.

The unfavourable effects on developing countries of including restrictive clauses in the various contracts for acquiring technology are too well known to need repeating here.[9]

It should be noted that such clauses (the main ones concern tied purchases, restrictions on exports and volume of production, and a guaranteed status quo to the advantage of the seller in the event of a change in customs, fiscal or exchange control regulations) may have most serious effects, not only on the host country's technological dependence, but also on the structure of its production costs and competitive strength, as well as on the development of mutual advantageous relations and trade between developing countries which are necessary for any attempt at regional integration.

To conclude this section we find that, while the channels for transferring technology to developing countries are becoming much more numerous, they do nothing (and sometimes are even a hindrance) to strengthen the links between developing countries in the same

area and they often accentuate certain characteristics of
underdevelopment, of which in our view the most important is that
these countries maintain dual economic structures.

II. REGIONALISATION OF STRATEGIES OF MULTINATIONAL FIRMS AND REGIONAL INTEGRATION

While the practice of supplying turn-key factories (or
factories already on stream or even complete with market) is
increasing, especially rich oil-producing countries whose
scientific and technological potential is weak, (to varying
degrees), one of the leading methods of transferring technology to
developing countries is still to set up subsidiaries of
multinational firms.

It is found that by nature multinational firms take a global
and even a world-wide view and operate on the basis of world-wide
strategies.

Nevertheless there is a tendency to forget that their
strategies are acquiring an increasingly regional basis,[10] the
region involved taking the form of a trading community (e.g. the
E.E.C., the Andean Group and the ASEAN countries) or (especially)
of geographical units of different sizes (Latin America, Europe,
the Middle East, Africa, etc.).

In the first case the choice of region is due much more to a
defensive reaction to legal, economic, political and other
constraints imposed by the new regional grouping than to
rationalising the firms' activities, but at any rate both motives
co-exist, with one or other of them predominating according to the
situation.

In the second case, which is much more common, the region is
chosen on the basis of commercial criteria laid down by the
multinational firm and which it thinks may maximise its profits.
The firm carves up the world, but it is not at all certain that a
region thus demarcated will suit the interests and aspirations of
the developing countries concerned. The result will in any case be
a de facto regionalisation imposed by the will of the firm alone.
However, one must not mistake the nature of this "regionalisation"
of the strategies of multinational firms, even if it obliges them
to set up new organisational structures in which regional
management takes the place of their former "international
departments", thereby putting an end to planning of the "top-down"
type and bringing in planning of the "bottom-top" type in which the
subsidiaries take the initiative in proposing developing plans.
What the multinational firms are doing is in fact to decentralise
their structures and some of their activities and, while this will
make their operations more effective, it will not specifically (or
at least not necessarily) be the answer to a regional development
problem. What is worse, it will sometimes (e.g. in the case of R &
D work) be a sham decentralisation involving simply a brain drain
inside the host country. Thus decisions on the value, nature and

place of investment projects, the technology to use, the type of product, the marketing networks, etc. are taken almost exclusively by the multinational firms, which never lose sight of the world scene.

The basic question is whether these firms would behave differently, if the developing countries resolved to club together or simply to co-operate seriously in a regional grouping decided on by themselves. In this case what would be the role of "technology", which is considered (whether it is transferred or the region acquires some degree of technological independence) to be the strategic variable and driving force in such regionalisation?

The results of the various attempts which the developing countries have made so far to link together their economies on a regional basis might be summed up by saying that some are dead, some stillborn and some abortive, while others are simply still vegetating; in other words undeniable failure.

On the other hand the weakness or simply the non-existence of national enterprises of regional stature, the lack of industries which supply one another, the lack of a scientific and technological infrastructure and the harmonisation of protectionist measures (or prospects of harmonising them) create a most favourable climate for the activities of multinational firms, which are thus presented with an area which is a logical outlet for their development. Seen in historical perspective, multinational firms are the legitimate offspring of what are mistaken for common interests with the developing countries.

Thus a multinational firm becomes the pivot of a strategy for regional growth (on a pattern imposed by multinational firms and serving their interests) by acting as a financial intermediary or pole of industrialisation.

This apparently paradoxical situation may be better understood by taking a concrete example such as the Arab countries which possess surplus oil capital.[11] These countries are unenthusiastic about the capacity of the other Arab countries to absorb capital, although the latter are a wide market which has several times been the epi-centre of attempts at regional integration. Thus the oil-producing countries find themselves in a "tragic dilemma". On the one hand they are jealous of their financial wealth which they know may dry up in the long run, while on the other hand, being under pressure from the masses and aware of an economic awakening in the Arab world, they cannot refuse to make their contribution towards industrialising the other countries. Egypt's position marks it out to play an increasingly important part as a client for capital and a growth pole for the region, and the reopening of the Suez Canal together with the establishment of customs-free industrial zones along it are the beginning of a policy whose implications are both regional and world-wide.

In view of these interacting forces and of the lack of regional financial institutions, multinational firms will act as instruments for transforming capital from surplus countries into specific projects, either agricultural or industrial, and the surplus earnings from oil will flow through multinational banks before coming to rest in Egyptian, Syrian or North-West African territory.

A second type of integration may be envisaged which is brought about, not by market forces, but by production and development and is based on programmes for investing in industries which cannot reach their optimum size inside their national frontiers. Here multinational firms will have to be executive agents and institutions in the service of the regional development authorities. The optimum allocation of resources will be made through multinational decision-making centres and no longer through multinational firms, while the latter, instead of assuming the strategic role of co-ordinating their activities on a world scale, become instruments for transferring technology within the region under a regional development plan, and they may even take part in working out this plan by conducting a continuous dialogue with the regional authorities with a view to reconciling interests which might conflict by seeking satisfactory compromises.

All this can only work well when there is a supranational regional authority, which has so far been lacking in all attempts at regional integration.

Consequently this ideal situation in which integration is brought about by the producers is far from materialising and will not be easy to achieve in the near future.

Again, the possibility of fitting multinational firms into a pattern of national planning or subjecting them to their requirements has to be dismissed out of hand owing to the nature of these firms since, if a multinational firm pursued a "national" policy, it would no longer be "multinational".

Having regard to these two basic facts, one can only aim at a form of regional technical co-operation which could lead gradually to regional integration through production and development and hope that this would contribute to redefining the nature and strategies of multinational firms.

III. REGIONAL TECHNOLOGICAL CO-OPERATION

Regional concertation and co-operation between the developing countries are necessary, not only to enable them to resist pressure from the industrialised world, but also to rationalise their development, and are made quite indispensable by the present interplay of forces which will decide the new international division of labour.

In May 1975 the Agence Tunisienne de Cooperation organised a seminar on technical co-operation between developing countries at which the following three major objectives were assigned to horizontal co-operation:

- to promote and strengthen economic integration;

- to encourage independence in science and technology;

- to co-ordinate policies for the international transfer of

technology.

Although this list confuses objectives with instruments, it shows a definite awareness of the importance of technology as a factor in economic integration.

In the first place regional co-operation, which might range from exchanging information on the terms and conditions for importing technology to establishing technology transfer centres[12] on a regional basis, would undeniably strengthen the position of countries in the region in their negotiations with owners of technology.

In the same way a form of regional co-operation might be envisaged which aimed at training negotiators, evaluating alternative technologies and unpackaging the technological package.[13]

Moreover, if such horizontal co-operation were matched by vertical co-operation between the two groups of countries (buyers and sellers of technology), there would be considerably increased possibilities of really improving on the present situation. For example, preferential terms might be negotiated for the developing countries for their purchases of various types of patents, licenses and know-how, and the industrialised countries might adopt policies of subsidising sales of technology rights to developing countries as an integral part of their development aid policies.

In this way the de facto protection against the abuses seen in transfers of technology might be made more effective and at all events more of a spur to development than a legal armoury which, when used to excess (like any other form of protectionism), could aggravate technological under-development in the region concerned.

The objectives of regional co-operation might also include adapting imported technologies, because they could be adapted profitably in an economic area which was large and relatively homogeneous. The resources in such an area could then be pooled and a specific technology could be developed with the aid of a production infrastructure which existed already or was in any case potentially available (depending on the stage and nature of regional co-operation), and with the aid of the marketing outlets. It might also usefully be noted that when advanced regional co-operation reached the integration stage, it would become profitable to introduce, without adaptation, techniques evolved by developed countries.

The question of joint regional efforts to make it profitable to adapt technology leads directly to the question of regional co-operation in R & D.

Nowhere is the disparity between developed and developing countries so pronounced as in R & D, as over 90 per cent of all R & D in the world is done by developed countries with market economies.[14]

R & D is expensive, especially for some industries such as the pharmaceutical industry, while its results, considered from the point of view of their value for application by industry and therefore as innovations, are uncertain. Often R & D cannot be done by a single enterprise (apart from large multinational firms) or even a single country.

It follows that owing to the small size of the developing countries' own enterprises and the relative, and sometimes even absolute, poverty of these countries, the only way to develop R & D is through regional co-operation. By pooling a region's financial, technical and human resources its member countries could attain objectives which they could not hope to attain by going it alone. Moreover, the resulting co-ordination of effort would make their R & D work less fragmentary and avoid overlapping, so helping to rationalise the use of the resources available.

A still unpublished OECD report on the transfer of technology in the pharmaceutical and fine chemicals industry[15] in the less developed OECD countries (Greece, Ireland, Portugal, Spain, Turkey and Yugoslavia) points out (and makes the corresponding recommendations) that the main scope for co-operation between them in that industry lies in R & D undertaken jointly by their own pharmaceutical firms on the basis of their respective strengths and weaknesses (raw materials, processes, human resources, etc.).

While the development of R & D is undeniably the key to creating a scientific and technological infrastructure, can it be maintained that, mutatis mutandis, international subcontracting is the key to creating an industrial infrastructure which is capable of marketing via a country's own industrial fabric the products of research laboratories, i.e. of producing them at a profit and distributing them?

Of all the different subcontracting relationships[16] easily the most important are subcontracting to obtain missing or additional capacity and subcontracting to achieve economics.

However, both types are based on an entirely traditional concept, because they are purely Ricardian forms of specialisation which reflect only one aspect of the international division of labour practised in the past, whereby work whose technological content was small or standardised was relegated to the periphery, while R & D and new industrial products were kept at the centre. Although this dichotomy may bring temporary relief (by creating jobs and bringing in foreign exchange) to the developing countries, it leaves them completely dependent on the developed countries.

Regional co-operation and the resulting rationalisation of industrial activity could considerably strengthen the position of the developing countries when they ask, as part of the new international division of labour, for a dividing line to be drawn between industrial activities which is not a vertical line between industries, but a horizontal line between the work of designing products and techniques and the work of making the goods. In other words, to speak more in United Nations terms, the South asks the North to transfer to it a number of activities so as to organise a vast self-contained trading area on either side of the demarcation line. Within this area the organisation and purpose of international subcontracting would have to be thoroughly reviewed, and this is an avenue to be explored and a hypothesis to be tested.

This last idea prompts us to ask the following leading question: What will be the role and nature of multinational firms in this regional perspective, assuming that most of the controls over the region will gradually be taken over by the regional authorities?

While all that is still to be worked out, there can be no doubt that the profit motive will continue to be the right driving force behind multinational firms, except that <u>optimum profit</u> should be pursued instead of maximum profit. In this case the optimum profit will be made either because a firm voluntarily foregoes a part of its profit margin in order to help in achieving regional development objectives, or as a result of confrontation between the two strategies, the "minmax" and the "maxmin", pursued respectively by the firm and the region. It will then be the resultant of an interplay of forces, in which case the closer is the regional co-operation, the nearer the point of equilibrium will come to the optimum profit.

Can one imagine multinational firms changing gradually into regional firms[17] serving the development of a region, while the latter acquires increasing participation rights[18] in their capital and management?

Will the multinational firms not tend to become more and more <u>service industries</u> as a result of this trend combined with the ability of some developing countries, including the oil countries with large financial resources due to the money-oil cycle, to buy up some of the foreign-owned assets in them? By changing in this way the multinational firms would capitalise their skills (management methods, technology and access to international markets) and their international information and feedback network which are mainly responsible for their success.[19]

Thus the multinational firms, which began by being "ethnocentric", might gradually change into world-wide federations or confederations or confederations of local or regional firms.

For purposes of methodology it should be noted that in investigating the prospects for multinational firms in a region which aspires to bring about integration through technology, one must first make a study of:

- the reasons why firms are multinational which belong to the region and invest in it (whether by new investment, buying up, joint ventures, etc.);

- how industrial concentration takes place in the region. In this connection the main question is whether it is dominated by mergers between regional firms or by firms outside the region (e.g. the role of American or Japanese multinational firms in Europe);

- international subcontracting: the type of subcontracting, technical assistance agreements, industries concerned, nationality of subcontracting enterprises, etc.;

- the patterns of international trade within the region, its transport systems, etc. in order to gauge whether centripetal or centrifugal tendencies are the stronger, as this may be an important precondition for deciding whether to establish a multinational firm;

- lastly, the banking system and financing circuits in the

region.

Under the influence of prevailing international competition the industrialised countries will in most cases have to reorganise their industrial production and the developing countries will have to start industries of their own.

In the industrialised countries the public authorities are making great efforts to prepare to restructure and redeploy their production facilities in accordance with a new international division of labour. Each country's economy must find its niche in the world economic system. Markets are becoming international, products are becoming standardized and technology is tending to become homogeneous. Concentration in a world-wide framework means changing the scene of world competition, but not stopping or altering it, and technology is becoming even more of a key to the multinational firms' monopolistic or oligopolistic power, as the case may be.

The developing countries are increasing their demands for continued access to the technology of the major multinational groups, while aspiring to become technologically independent, and the idea of regional association or integration has emerged as an attempt to create units comparable in size to the major developed markets.

In such regions a competitive technology should evolve, because it will be based on mass production, but at present it seems difficult to achieve economic integration, a step which in any case must be prepared with the greatest care.

The most suitable course today would seem to lie in regional technological co-operation, to which should be added genuine vertical co-operation between developing countries and industrialised countries. By this means it would perhaps be possible to avoid serious setbacks in years to come.

NOTES

[1]D. Germidis "Le transfert international des technologies: Les F.M.N. face aux pays d'accueil en voie de developpement" (International Technology Transfers: multinational firms and the developing host countries), Revue "Options., Mediterraneennes", No. 27, Paris 1975.

[2]For a critical analysis of these methods see, among other studies:
- Antonio Marques Dos Santos, "Les mecanismes actuels du transfert de technologie" (Present-day mechanisms for transferring technology), to appear in "Actuel Developpement"; and
- Pierre Gonod, "Cles pour le transfert de technologie"

(Principles of technology transfer), Institut de Developpement Economique, I.B.R.D., Washington, August 1974.

[3]The pharmaceutical industry is still in the front rank of the most expensive sellers of technology and resorts to over-pricing in selling it. A recent OECD report on the "Transfer of Technology for Pharmaceutical Chemicals" by A.C. Cilingiroglu (October 1974) stated (on the evidence of United States Senate reports) that some ingredients were over-priced by 1,000 per cent or even 5,000 per cent!

With regard to quite a different technology policy, namely "Technical co-operation", a report by the OECD Development Centre (in preparation) by S. Kassapu estimates the cost of a research worker (in man/months) at $25,000, $70,000 or $100,000 depending on whether he is a native of the country or a technical assistance officer under a bilateral or multilateral co-operation agreement. Even if in the two last cases it is not the developing country which pays for the research workers, the problem of the opportunity cost of "technical co-operation" to the assisted country is most serious.

[4]Dimitri Germidis, "De la denonciation des couts excessifs a la recherche d'un juste prix dans le transfert international de technologie" (From condemning excessive costs to seeking a fair price for international transfers of technology), Report to the Seminar held by the Association Francaise de Sciences Economiques, Lille 1974, to appear in the Association's annals, Paris 1974. Dimitri Germidis and Christine Brochet, "The Price of technology transfer", Special Study, OECD Development Centre, Paris 1975.

[5]Cf. Dimitri Germinis, "Transfer of technology by multinational corporations and the absorptive capacity of the developing countries: a synthesis", Volume I of this study.
Also Francis Stewart in "Technological dependence in the Third World", a report submitted to a Seminar on "Science, Technology, and Development in a changing world", Paris, April 1975, which deals with cases of "non-transfer" of technology.

[6]Articles under numbers 807.00 and 806.30 of the United States tariff lists which, under the customs regulations, may be imported on payment only of the tax on the value added abroad.

[7]Michael Sharpston "International Subcontracting", IBRD, Staff Working Paper No. 181, September 1974.

[8]Sergio Zampetti, "La sous-traitance internationale et les pays en voie de developpement" (International subcontracting and the developing countries), Problemes Economiques, No. 1,331 of 18th July, 1973, p. 18.

[9]D. Germidis and C. Brochet, "The price of technology transfer in developing countries", op. cit., p. 23 et seq.

[10] See among other studies: W.A. Dymsza "Multinational Business Strategy", McGraw-Hill Inc., New York, 1972.

[11] Elias Gannage, "Capitaux et Developpement avec reference aux Pays Arabes" (Capital and development with reference to the Arab countries), Revue Proche-Orient, Etudes Economiques, May-October, 1975.

[12] See the Note by the Secretary-General of UNCTAD on "A strategy for strengthening economic co-operation among developing countries", TD/B/557, 24th June, 1975.

[13] Most of these objectives were included in the OAS Pilot Project on Technology Transfer (see Informe Final, PPTT/34, June 1975).

[14] "Reviewing the International Order (RIO)", Interim Report (June 1975), Annex L by Bouwcentrum International Education, Rotterdam.

[15] Op. cit.

[16] S. Zampetti, in his article "La sous-traitance internationale et les pays en voie de developpement", op. cit., distinguishes:
   a) subcontracting to obtain missing or additional capacity, of which use is made when production capacity is not sufficient to deal with an abnormal rush of orders;
   b) subcontracting specialised work, whereby a manufacturer hands over, usually as a permanent arrangement, certain operations to a subcontractor who has specialised machinery and equipment or has developed special techniques;
   c) marginal subcontracting, which is done when the orders a manufacturer receives are too small or infrequent to warrant additional investment;
   d) subcontracting to achieve economies, when a manufacturer asks a subcontractor to carry out certain operations for processing or manufacturing certain components, mainly because the latter's production costs are much lower.

[17] UNIDO, "Regional Co-operation in Industry", monograph No. 18, New York, 1971.

[18] P.N. Rosenstein-Rodan in "Multinational investment in the framework of Latin America integration" in Multinational Investment in the Economic Development and Integration of Latin America, IDB, Washington, 1968, p. 28, maintains that the degree of a host country's participation must vary, at least at the start, inversely with the degree of importance of the investment concerned to the country's economy.

[19] Andre Van Doun, "Comment amplifier le dialogue entre F.M.N. et P.V.D.?" (How can the dialogue be extended between multinational firms and developing countries?), Memorandum submitted to the World Conference of the Society for International Development, Abidjan, August 1974.

Transnational Enterprises and International Development: A New Focus in the Perspective of Industrial and Technological Cooperation

MIKOTO USUI

I. THE ORTHODOX VIEW REGARDING TRANSNATIONAL ENTERPRISES (TNEs)

Much of the literature on the behaviour of TNEs and industrial organisation problems in the market environment characterised by small numbers impresses us with the existence of various ad hoc models, formal and informal, case-study information, anecdotal observations, vague notions of business psychology, etc., which can only be displayed in a smorgasbord style. The neo-classical black box of the profit-maximising firm in a competitive market can be turned into some formal oligopoly models but, for the sake of formal elegance, such models have to tack on relatively simple behavioural rules, ignoring the ways in which actual firms make actual decisions in particular markets. Under these circumstances one might be tempted to dismiss a generalization about the oligopolist behavioural rules and preference schemes as a matter of taste. This state of affairs is unfortunate since many of the important policy issues arise in international markets dominated by a finite number of large, well-established enterprises.

One of the important policy issues concerns the choice of particular forms of cooperation aimed at transfer of technology. This choice problem is viewed in terms of "unpackaging" possibilities: i.e. separation of technology acquisition from direct foreign investment. The major alternatives considered are:

a) Licensing agreements;

b) Ad hoc technical aid agreements, including ad hoc management contracts;

From **TRANSFER OF TECHNOLOGY BY MULTINATIONAL CORPORATIONS**, 1977, (10-23), reprinted by permission of the publisher, OECD, Paris.

c) Turnkey contracts;

d) "Product-in-hand" contracts, including long-term
   management contracts;
e) Joint ventures with major financial control vested
   locally (including some combination of the above);

f) Joint ventures with major financial share in the hand
   of foreign firms;

g) 100% affiliate of foreign firms.

Now, without reviewing the full corpus of formal oligopoly
theory, one could easily recognise the inappropriateness of the
profit maximisation principle -- at least its static formulation
applicable to a relatively competitive market -- in dealing with
the problem of oligopolitically structured industries. The
behaviour of large, dominant TNEs can certainly be more readily
explained by a general multiple-objective function which includes
"profit" only as one of its maximanda. Other important maximanda
are, as often contended, at least three: growth (of sales or
market share), security (against rivals and political hazards), and
control (which may include both control of the external environment
and control of intrafirm hierarchy of decision authority).[1] The
firms cannot necessarily maximise all these multiple objectives but
usually seek an appropriate combination of satisfactory values in a
given situation.

The emphasis on the objective of "control" readily points to
the importance of direct investment or "control by ownership" in
the olopolists' preference scheme. Many point out that licensing
and other technical cooperation agreements, and even management
contracts, have seldom been first priority choices for most
multinationally oriented firms. Nevertheless, E.B. Lovell's
enquete of 191 U.S. firms showed that no more than 50% of the firms
declared clearly their preference of direct (100%) affiliates or
joint ventures while 42% of them expressed their preparedness to
continue their policy of licensing.[2]

Indeed, the bulk of direct foreign investment has so far been
carried out by large firms operating in discernibly
oligopolistically structured markets. The Fortune list of the 500
largest firms would practically exhaust the universe of U.S. direct
overseas investors. However, definitional esoterics apart, not all
"transnational enterprises" are "majors" or "insiders" of the
oligopolistic arena. There are a number of "minors", "outsiders"
and "new-comers" which may be said to be peripheral to the
closed-circuit, self-reinforcing strategy of dominant oligopolists.
These outsiders, if vulnerable to an appreciable degree of
competition, can weave themselves into the oligopolist arena,
establishing themselves in some viable positions. These are
certainly to be counted as among TNEs.

II. "MAJORS" AND "MINORS" IN THE DEVELOPMENT SCENE

Vernon present some evidence suggesting that moves into new regions either to manufacture or extract raw materials will be led often by firms with the most to gain or the least to lose from upsetting the prevailing division of world market shares in a given industry.[3]

The TNEs involved in the first stage surge of industrial ventures in the oil-exporting countries in the Near and Middle East seem to have been predominantly "outsiders" in the industries considered.

Our quick review shows that the involvement of the largest chemical companies (such as Du Pont and Bayer) appear to be an exception to this rule, which occurred more recently and may be linked not only to their desire to match rival chemical companies but also to a fear of being "held to ransom" for feedstock by American "oil" majors.

The first aluminum smelters ("Alba" in Bahrain and "Arak" in Iran) were established with minority participation of Kaiser (17% equity, together with General Cable 17%, British Metal 17%, etc.) and Reynolds (25% equity) respectively. Only in 1975 did a "major" like Alcan become involved in project negotiations. The recent massive expansion plans of automobile assemblies and General Motors' involvements (45% equity with full management control) were preceded by the earlier (abortive) ventures of American Motors and Chrysler-Rootes' Hillmans under licensing agreements in Iran.

Three of the first four chemical ventures in Saudi Arabia and Kuwait were joint ventures of "oil" companies and not "chemical" majors. These oil-based TNEs, as well as chemical-based TNEs involved in Iran and Qatar, did not then belong to the largest 15 (chemical and oil) companies in chemicals.[4]

Certainly, to draw a line between majors and minors for a given industry and at a given point of time is merely a matter of expedient. The minors themselves may be susceptible to further sub-divisions, such as major minors and minor minors; insider-miners and outsider-miners, already well-established and new entrants in the scene of transnational operations, etc. Also, the ranking of firms in terms of size of annual sales cannot immediately speak for the relative maturity of firms' transnational operations. While we consider in this context generally those fields of industry which are characterised by advanced technology, proprietary technology, highly differentiated products, intensive use of capital, oligopolistically structured markets in a world-wide perspective, etc., the organisational structure and the state of play of the oligopolist game would greatly vary from one field of industry to another. However, our point is that many of the TNEs first attracted to the Middle East seem to have had relatively little experience in handling production, management and marketing problems in the region; not very self-contained in exercising their "control" objective; not among the dominant oligopolists if countable already as "insiders"; more quickly responsive to joint-venture and other types of opportunities emerging in the periphery of the established market shares. The majors—minors dichotomy would be rather uncomfortably simplistic without a fine-grain typology of TNEs mapped out more systematically. Leaving such an empirical elaboration as a future research task, let us see for the moment what sort of theoretically reasonable generalisations could be deduced from this dichotomy which is at least less simplistic than the notion of "the TNE in general".

III. SOME THEORETICAL CONSIDERATIONS

In theory, smaller firms operating in the periphery of larger oligopolists, or firms less advanced and less diversified in their multinational operations, may be expected to be preoccupied more with larger, well-establishing TNEs. They would certainly have active interest in achieving their long-run security position and increasing their shares in world-wide markets. But they could not afford to sacrifice too much of their immediate cost-profit consideration for that purpose. Their technology, if important for their survival, may have a rather transitory value due to competitive pressure; or else, only part of their crucial technological assets may be their own property, the rest being acquired from other firms; their R and D capacities may also be so limited that they have to seek reliable partners to cope with the pressure of continual technological changes.[5]

Relatively small or new entrants in the MNE circle may have only limited financial means of their own, permitting them to accept only partial equity participation in joint venture proposals. When substantial equity participation is called for (often by host countries), they would rather do it together with other collaborators in their home countries or elsewhere, at least to disperse risks. Limits to their own individual technological strengths would also favour the idea of multiple-participant projects. If acting individually, they would more readily respond to the proposition of licensing and other technical cooperation of more or less limited scope, than to the full turnkey or "product-in-hand" type of proposition. Within certain limits, they could take "management contracts" to the extent that their managerial and organisational know-how and links to supplementary contractors and procurement sources prove adequate for the scale and complexity of the project in question.

Thus, not only industries differ significantly in their structural characteristics, but the firms therein will differ with respect to the modalities with which they are willing to make their technology available. The "unpackaging" strategy of technology acquisition would not only be difficult but could be futile for products which call for the special institutionalised marketing facilities of international firms, and where these firms are highly integrated and few in number, with an established pattern of market separation. If these "majors" would not accept anything less than the creation of a 100% affiliate, what could be an alternative open for the host country? Some minors or outsiders may then see an opportunity of cutting into this potential market (if the country's domestic market is large enough) and offer help, if not all the way to the product-in-hand stage, and if somewhat more slowly and inefficiently than majors could do. If the host country domestic market is not large enough, the collaborating minors might succeed in tapping their home country markets to some extent if the backfire of the majors remained weak.

An important issue for the outsider TNEs themselves would be the reaction of majors to the anticipated possibilities of their own markets being disrupted. It can happen that a new export joint venture will have to compete with another TNEs existing 100% affiliate. Despite the latter's preference in principle, he may choose to enter a joint venture if he foresees no possibility of excess capacity in his direct affiliate, or if he expects that the average cost of production of a joint venture will be lower than the marginal cost of the existing affiliate.[6] This consideration leads us to the thumb-marked problem of entry in oligopolistic competition.

An interesting theory in this respect stresses information cost or the fact that the firm's ability to monitor and respond to the action of rivals, both real and potential, is limited by considerations of both bounded rationality and information costs.[7] (Another important consideration is the cost of forming, monitoring and enforcing informal collusive agreements with rivals.) The larger the information costs, the less likely will a firm be able to identify and to respond to the threat of potential entrants. The information costs are affected by the notion of proximity -- geographical closeness of one firm to another, similarity of products and technologies, links to particular financial institutions, etc. The information costs will be high for monitoring the opportunities emerging in regions unfamiliar to the firm, and still higher if such opportunities are individually small and scattered over different countries. Thus, "majors" are not omniscient; still less so are "minors" but they are larger in number. However, as a given region becomes densely packed by various industrial activities, informations costs per bit of information will decrease and the firm will react more quickly to the action of rivals in that region. This theoretical speculation seems to be borne out by the recent pattern of involvement of TNEs in the Near and Middle East region.

Organisations with complex hierarchies and centralised decision making are likely to respond more slowly to changes in local conditions than organisations with a less hierarchical and more decentralised structure. This aspect may also be responsible for the relatively slow involvement of major TNEs.

IV. TRANSNATIONAL ENTERPRISES IN AN EVOLUTIONARY PERSPECTIVE

Apart from such cross-sectional comparative characteristics, there is need for investigating the "evolutionary" aspects of majors-minors relationships. For example, the recent thinking about top management strategy for overseas activities often stresses the shift from "control by ownership" to "control without ownership". At least among the aggressive proponents of this idea, "management contract" is not merely the second-best choice in foreign investment strategy, but, more progressively is said to be a challenge to the traditional capital-geared notion of management. Certainly, the importance of this new function of "selling management" instead of "capital mobilisation and allocation" would depend on the state of development of the structure of the given industry and the degree of maturation of its natural market.[8]

Minors cannot just emerge "from nowhere", but one could see their emergence, from the "evolutionary" point of view, as a consequence of the maturity of a given industry. The Schumpeterian process of "automation and innovations" is accompanied by an accumulation of managerial and technological resources within leading firms. But an important point that is often missed in this Schumpeter-Burnham type of scenario is that this centralised accumulation can trigger off, beyond a certain threshold, the new process of structural spilling and spinning, whereby a variety of specialised firms emerge, including such new trades as engineering contractors and management consultants. This process is prompted by the maturation of the natural markets facing the leading firms, which induces selective and adaptive applications of the accumulated resources, rather than a further concentrated accumulation of the resources.[9]

To the extent that this scenario is relevant for the emergence of various newcomers in international operations, our majors-minors dichotomy is somewhat "overdrawn", neglecting sequential aspects of the structural evolution of industrial division of labour among different classes of TNEs. Minors, particularly smaller, relatively highly specialised firms, are not likely to have emerged as "rivals" to larger, well-integrated firms from the outset. But, rather, many of the former may have evolved as offshoots of the latter, maintaining occasional subcontractor-type relationships with the latter. The rapid ramification of this process and its secondary offshoots can, however, give rise not only to competition in the periphery of large olipolists but also scope for "backfiring" or at least "aggressive gleaning" into the olipoly territory.

The evolution pattern varies from industry to industry, indeed. But generally it would make much difference whether the "leading" firms continue to lead in new innovations despite the spilling and spinning process they have generated around them. If their markets do not mature very quickly and majors themselves see more gains in leading the "diffusion" of innovations than in new innovations, then, chances are that the majors-minors relationship will entail more of an element of rivalry than complementarity.

For example, in the field of chemicals, many of the majors have highly diversified operations, quickly phasing out of old products and shifting on to newer products and newer technologies. Thus, such majors, as Du Pont, do not actively seek joint venture partnerships on already relatively standardised products, and as far as their new innovations successfully feed on newly growing markets, they could tolerate minors' encroachment, giving rise to an evolutionary, but stable process of division of labour between majors and minors. But certainly this sort of stability notion does not seem to apply to, for example, the automotive industry of today as yet; despite the existence of significant scope for technical standardisation, the overall rate of innovation of this industry has been slow and often impugned for its "defensive" characteristics. This situation may change significantly only after the current energy-saving and anti-pollution drive has succeeded in generating a new wave of innovations; majors will then be preoccupied with the new markets awaiting new kinds of automobiles, leaving those for standard vehicles of older vintages in the hands of minors.

V. IMPLICATIONS FOR THE HOST-COUNTRY CHOICE

In embarking on industrial ventures calling for massive foreign technological assistance and market outlets, the host-country preferences will be envisaged in two different perspectives: one related to the objective of "unpackaging" and the other concerns the differential responsiveness of "major" and "minor" TNEs. The latter point of view can further be elaborated so as to cover not only the responsiveness in time but also the responsiveness to the host-country development objectives and aspirations.

The low equity involvement of TNEs in Algeria and the absence of TNE involvement in Iraq may be associated with the current ideological aversion to foreign capital involvement, but another reasonable explanation can be found in the governments' policy favourable to the promotion of relatively unsubstituting development, which does not call for TNE's expertise and facilities for tapping export markets. (It is to be recalled, also, that there was relatively little TNE involvement in the earlier phase of industrialisation of Iran.) It seems that Algeria and Iraq continue to seek alternatives to equity-TNE participation, such as turnkey plants; and they further try to combine the notion of "unpackaging" with TNE commitments in purely technical aid contracts of the "product-in-hand" type, as opposed to "key-in-hand" terms for plant sales. For relatively tightly oligopolistic industries and especially when ventures are to be export-oriented, much difficulty will be foreseen in finding capable foreign collaborators willing to accept such a proposition without equity participation and control over key management decisions. The expansion plan of a nationalised facility formerly owned by Renault in Algeria has met only grudging responses from several automobile TNEs.

The "unpackaging" theme has been, and will remain, the first preference of most other industrialising nations, too. Nevertheless, in countries like Saudi Arabia, the Gulf States and Iran, a more flexible sentiment appears to prevail now for the TNE equity participation. Certainly, the choice of collaboration modalities depends on the very nature of technology being sought. When a given venture implicates the notion of creating a newcomer TNE and thus entering into rivalry with insider TNEs, the equity participation of foreign collaborators may even be regarded as the necessary stake for long-term partnerships.

The choice of modalities is in practice tantamount to the choice of partners. Obvious as it is, many developing countries seem thus far to have confined the evaluation of projects involving TNEs to financial, engineering and socio-economic plausibilities, without going very systematically into the evaluation of possibly collaborative TNEs. Very few countries have industrial licensing and registration laws requiring information on foreign collaborators. Indeed, a certain amount of hear-say about foreign firms' performance and conduct in overseas ventures is circulating informally. Nevertheless, an active intelligence work by national (or regional) planning organisations would be desirable for a full assessment of the prospects of success for ventures involving TNEs. The particular TNE characteristics to be examined should include, among others:

a) the state of play in the oligopoly game in which the candidate TNE might be involved on a world-wide basis;

b) the institutional ability to manage export-oriented operations in the presence of local partners, and the access to other technological and marketing resources than those held within the particular TNE;

c) previous experience and/or preparedness in providing flexible teaching services for local partners on technical and managerial operations;

d) R and D capabilities and structures, including cross-licensing practice, which would be relevant for living through future technological competition in a world-wide perspective.

The experience in the Near and Middle East with some of the TNEs which arrived there early is said to have often been disappointing. Operations under culturally and economically foreign conditions would in any event require a substantial learning process on the part of participating TNEs. Erroneous expectations in this respect often produced sharp disappointment at poor financial results being achieved in early phases of operation. Export joint ventures could make the transfer-pricing problem more serious than local-market ventures, since shipping and trading operations remain for some time in the hands of foreign partners and are likely to involve different access strategies for different markets. The question of suspicion apart, there generally seems to be a tendency for export-oriented joint ventures to have a shorter life than import-substitution joint ventures;[10] reasons for discontinuities may vary from case to case, but this tendency seems to have helped nourish the fairly commonly-held contention that "multinationals would never export from joint ventures".

It is difficult to say whether "majors" will do a better job than "minors" due to the former's late entry in the region. Industry majors do have world-wide networks into which Middle Eastern ventures could fit. But they may or may not respond immediately to such opportunities. Moreover, well-established, large TNEs may tend to be less responsive than smaller TNEs to the host developing country requirements in terms of development of local skills and know-how. The strategy of large TNEs for training, "de-nationalising" and rotating locally-recruited high-skill personnel within their respective intra-corporate circuits is fairly well evidenced.[11] It is also often pointed out that large TNEs, which have many years of relatively smooth international growth, have developed a "tribe" of administrators rather than aggressive, innovative, real managers; and that the tribal TNE management and technicians seem good at applying their know-how but not so good at teaching local personnel. The moral pressure towards a "Code of Conduct", which is now rapidly mounting in international fora for development, will need some time until it can visibly affect the rules of operations of tribal TNE managements.

Collaborations with smaller, less dominant TNEs will generally be technically less efficient, more costly and time-consuming in achieving the projected results. But they may be less constrained by their own internal build-up, and possibly eager to innovate in their international business strategy. It would be worthwhile to say, if only on a speculative basis, that the chances are that the relatively inefficiency of smaller, newly-rising TNEs will be compensated for by their greater responsiveness to the host-country thrust towards industrial and technological advancement. Of course, this presupposed that the host country sees in them an opportunity for accelerating its own efforts to build up its domestic technological and industrial capabilities. The crux of the technology transfer policy issues lies in how to ignite local participation in the ongoing innovation process underlying the particular industry in which the country chooses to get involved and to allocate more resources and design better policies to accelerate the evolution of indigenous capabilities suitable for that participation. The "unpackaging" preoccupation, coupled with an underestimation of the magnitude of this self-help task, could only lead to abortive results, strewn with confusions and conflicts.

VI. TOWARDS A REAL INTERNATIONALISATION OF INTERNATIONAL VENTURES

The unique pattern of involvement of Japanese industrial firms in transnational operations, led by leading general-purpose trading companies, suggests that the existence of a well-developed, self-contained TNE is not the necessary condition for the creation of an international venture. Also, ad hoc consortia of relatively large, but not yet "multinational", Japanese firms for new international ventures may support the notion of a "reserve army" of TNEs, which could offer a large assortment of technological and operational know-how, were an adequate central management available. This notion need not be conditional to the existence of "Zaibatsu"-type structures. The reserve army may be internationally mixed, as in the case of the Marcona Group for the steel complex of Petromin, Saudi Arabia (Marcona 40%, and Esthel, Nippon Steel and others 10%), the Khuzestan Agro-industrial complex negotiated in Iran (with Chase Investment, Diamond Agatel, Mitsui, Hawaiian Agronomic, each 15%), the aluminum smelter plant "Alba" in Behrein (Kaiser, General Cable, British Metal, each 17%), etc.

The RIO report[12] stresses the possibility of a "real internationalisation of some transnational enterprises", which could be owned, controlled and managed by an "international development authority". The case in point is the considerations underlying the existing proposals regarding the seabed resource exploitation. The same philosophy is being stretched to the idea of experimenting an international pharmaceutical corporation as a counterthrust against the prevailing private majors.

The feasibility of such rather "extremist" propositions depends on:

a) the real political will of the developing countries arguing for "solidarity" and regional cooperation;

b) the availability of a central managerial and organisational authority; and

c) the possibility of mobilising adequate technological and productive capabilities from the "reserve army" of TNEs.

It is yet to be seen if the IBRD Group and various Regional Development Banks and Funds, as well as some sort of consortia of national development corporations, could take initiatives in creating sufficiently de-nationalised top-management complexes corresponding to requirement b) above. The adequacy of a mosaic of technical capabilities drawn from the reserve army of TNEs needs also an in-depth assessment. It would be worthwhile to see more clearly how far the pure "technocracy" (including the one to be released from within the private reserve-army industrial forces) could be stretched to ensure the technical and economic viability of such counterthrust operations in the face of the prevailing private oligopolists. A serious exploration along this line might be useful at least to clear part of the mythology of the "New

International Economic Order".

Indeed, the question of "political will" remains the most intractable question. Reverting to the actual behaviour of TNEs in the Near and Middle East region, these enterprises themselves are in no position to promise the sort of trade and development cooperation that is desired by some exponents of Arab regional integration. They may have few qualms about the chance of improving their world market shares and thus disrupting the positions of majors, and they may thus be capable of "integrating" world markets to some extent. But as one TNE gains an advantage in one country, other TNEs are tempted to match this in other countries. If this continues, countries in the region will soon end up competing with one another in giving favourable energy costs and financing TNE ventures. With smaller, quickly responsive TNEs, this trend may even grow more palpable than when majors are involved. Export diversification of newly industrialising countries is generally bound to imply greater competition and conflict among these countries. The political will to take advantage of opportunities for "collective self-reliance" would certainly be essential for the developing countries successfully to tap the resources of the reserve army of TNEs. Otherwise, TNEs, no matter whether they are majors or minors, would simply be made a scapegoat to deflect attention from the growing competition among the developing countries themselves.

Much has been said about "triangular" projects, which could bring together the oil money and the OECD technology for development opportunities in less developed countries. A number of ventures combining the oil money with TNE equity or technical aid have been announced in Egypt, Sudan, Jordan, Guinea, Pakistan, etc. The number of triangular projects are apparently still small, though growing, and their scope has so far been confined to investments in oil-related areas, including industry, through the recently established intergovernmentally owned regional companies, such as the Arab Mining Company and the Arab Petroleum Investment Company. Observers in the region seem to feel that the complexities of negotiating such arrangements will cause a much greater lag in their realisation than in the case of bilateral ventures in the oil-exporting countries. The initial enthusiasm for triangular ventures might give way to a more traditional set of bilateral transactions which would imply triangular "flows" of resources but not triangular management of ventures. It is also yet to be seen if triangular ventures will cover industrial fields for which international markets are important. Still another interesting question is whether such ventures can be instrumental in the advancement towards a multilateral joint decision-making practice (or at least a more productive art of "consultation") on matters relating to the demand and supply schedules of industry of international significance.

Needless to say, parallel to the advancement of developing countries towards collective self-reliance, the governments of the technology-supplier, too, should see an important task for them to share. Contributing to multilateral development financing institutions is just part of this task. One cannot neglect the significance of those bilateral intergovernmental agreements between the home country governments of TNEs and their host country governments. Most of these agreements are essentially designed to secure raw materials, provide trade outlets and credit facilities and strengthen the competitiveness of the participating firms. they can thus serve as a broad political framework of guarantee against the cooperation risks of their TNEs. Monitoring such bilateral agreements and encouraging mutual adjustments for global implications can certainly be an important task for the OECD.

Many observers note that some countries, such as Japan, are administratively better equipped to monitor the proposals and projects of their TNEs, than other home countries. The relative intensity of a particular country's TNE activities in a given region is naturally an important factor accounting for this difference. A massive increase in TNE involvement, in terms of project responsibility, if not so much in terms of financial commitment, can give rise to some political risk. The cumulative problems of TNEs will then become a problem to be jointly solved by several home-country governments concerned.

Presumably, collective action need not be extended to all industries, but priority may well be given to those required in catering for the basic necessities of developing society: food, clothing and housing. If not to speak of agriculture and forestry products, there will technically be greater scope for real internationalisation of industrial ventures in a certain range of basic and intermediate manufactures which can be internationally standardised and can enjoy significant economies of sale. On the other hand, the final products which are susceptible to taste variations and discontinuous production processes may well have greater leeway for each country's initiative-taking and competitive diversification. At least on the part of TNE managements, those specialised in basic material technology (e.g. synthetic fibres, resins and various chemical compounds) appear to have less confused views about their future involvement in development cooperation than those specialised in final product lines (e.g. weaving and plastics fabrication).

NOTES

[1] Recall the now classical textbook references on this subject: especially J. Schumpeter, K.W. Rothschild, M. Reder, W.J. Baumol, etc.

[2]E.B. Lovell, "Appraising Foreign Licensing Performance", in S.P. Sethi and J.N. Smeth, ed., Multinational Business Operations, California 1973. Also see the report on the forum for licensors organised at the International Technology Fair, Oslo, 28th October to 1st November 1974: M. Delapierre, La Vente Internationale de la Technologie: l'Optique de la Firme, OECD Development Centre, Industry and Technology Occasional Paper No. 6, 1975.

[3]See Raymond Vernon, "The Location of Economic Activity" in J. Dunning ed., Economic Analysis and the Multinational Enterprises, George Allen and Unwin, 1974.

[4]The OECD Development Centre has undertaken a modest study on the recent MNE involvement in the region. The results will soon be issued under the Industry and Technology Occasional Paper series: Prospects for Industrial Joint Ventures in the Oil-Exporting Countries of the Middle East and North Africa, by L.G. Franko. Some of the region-specific observations in the following draw on Franko's report.

[5]These point are alluded to, especially in relation to the controversy over corporate innovation policy and in an attempt to see some implication of it for the developing country technology buyers, in M.Usui, Oligopoly, R and D and Licensing -- A Reflection Towards a Fair Deal in Technology Transfer, OECD Development Centre, Industry and Technology, Occasional Paper No. 7, 1975.

[6]Lawrence G. Franko, Joint Venture Survival in Multinational Corporations, Praeger, N.Y., 1971.

[7]See a brief review by Paul L. Joskow, in his "Form Decision-Making Process and Oligopoly Theory", in American Economic Review, May 1975, pp. 270-279.

[8]See, for example, Peter P. Gabriel, "The New Concepts of Foreign Investment", in McKinsey ed., The Arts of Top Management as well as the same author's The International Transfer of Corporate Skills, Harvard Univ. Graduate School of Business Administration, Boston, 1967.

[9]Much attention has been paid to this type of offshoot of the evolution process and its implications for development in the Technology and Industrialisation Programme of the OECD Development Centre. The first phase of research, examining various types of industrial engineering service and consultancy organisations based in OECD countries, has been under way and is expected to reach a concluding stage within this year.

[10]See for exaple, L.G. Franko, Joint Venture Survivals in Multinational Corporations, 1971 and the Colombo Plan (Information Bureau), The Special Topic: Joint Ventures, Wellington, New Zealand, Nov.-Dec., 1973.

[11]This has been confirmed in the several countries covered by the OECD Development Centre project on multinational enterprises and host-country technology absorptive capacities. See also, J.D. Peno, Jr., The Multinational Firm -- The Utilisation and Development of Host-Country High-Level Manpower, Michigan State University, Doctoral Dissertation, 1975.

[12]The Interim Report of the "Reviewing the International Order" project (coordinator: Jan Tinbergen), prepared during the second general meeting held 17th-20th June 1975, Rotterdam.

The Transnational Corporations in a New Planning Process

ARTURO NUNEZ DEL PRADO

During the last few years, events of the greatest importance have taken place which have significantly altered the world picture, and of course the Latin American one too. The author therefore considers it an appropriate time to reflect on some aspects of the prevailing form of development, and especially the role played by the transnational corporations in this context.

The way in which these phenomena are interpreted, the defence mechanisms employed by the countries, the strategies formulated in this respect and the plan of action adopted will have consequences of tremendous significance for the future of the region. The author draws attention to the role of planning in carrying out these demanding tasks, above all if it is desired to try to cope with the prevailing conditions not just on an emergency basis but also from a longer-term prospective. Planning is the most suitable instrument for conducting economic and social activity in general and regulating the market in particular, and the imperfections from which the latter suffers demand not only active State participation but also new forms of co-ordination and participation for the agents of the economic and social system, breaking away from the usual limitation to the traditional distributive struggle.

In the last section of the article, the author outlines a possible change in the basic methodology of planning with a view to reappraising and selecting the participation of transnational corporations in the development of Latin America: he sustains that planning at the enterprise level, in the case of a mixed economy, would give rise to a fresh conception of the planning process particularly appropriate for the present time and would help to strengthen the region's bargaining power.

From **CEPAL REVIEW**, Aug. 1981, (33-50), reprinted by permission of the publisher.

I. GOVERNMENTS FACE TO FACE WITH THE NEW LATIN AMERICAN SITUATION: PASSIVITY OR ACTION?

Once again the region is being shaken by external forces which are aggravating the already difficult internal situations of the countries. While it is true that Latin American development has been characterized by continual adaptation to conditioning factors which have been changing with the course of time and by the constant modification of the domestic apparatus to suit such changes, the current phenomenon seems to go deeper and is certainly more complex. Anyone who thinks about the future can see that the 1980s could witness the consolidation within the framework of modern capitalism of forms or styles of growth and development different from those of the recent past.[1] Judging by the factors which gave rise to it, the process initiated in recent years enables us to gauge the depth and extension of this phenomenon. The features of the crisis which the world is experiencing mean that the very roots of the economic systems are feeling the impact of this and will have to embark on a transformation in the strict sense of the word rather than a mere readaptation to the new circumstances.

This is a crucial time which calls for the closest analysis of what is happening and the course which is being followed: a time which makes it essential to appraise the scenarios that would be formed in line with the tendencies which appear to be taking shape. Failure to take such action could lead to much more pressing situations.

If we examine the main elements affecting the Latin American economies it is easy to see that a form of evolution has been initiated which is quite different from that which characterized most of the preceding decade. Although a great deal has already been written on this matter, it does not seem superfluous to stress that the more general crisis of the world economic system is undoubtedly one of the factors which is most influencing the readjustment and restructuring of the economic systems of the region. The central countries themselves are suffering from disturbances in the functioning of their economies, and although they obviously possess greater defence mechanisms than the countries of the region for facing this crisis, in one way or another they are being seriously perturbed by it and are surviving the new situation only with difficulty. Both on the side of the real supply and demand of goods and that of financial flows, changes are to be observed at this moment which not only affect the context and frames of reference but also alter the very substance of the functioning of capitalism in the economic systems where it has become established. Hence, it is clear that the world scene is in a process of transformation and a qualitatively and quantitatively different situation is taking shape which has direct and more serious implications for the Latin American economies.

A decisive influence in the eruption of the crisis, but not in its creation, has been the upheaval in the energy sector and the multiplication of oil prices almost by twenty. The origin of this phenomenon must of course be sought not only in the problem of the oil and gas reserves and the political and economic agreements of producers, but also in the behaviour of the production units which are at the head of the industrialized economic systems. The energy problem is today one of the severest conditioning factors for the economic, social and political processes of the future. The saying that in the past the process of industrialization was carried out on the basis of oil at a couple of dollars a barrel is a dramatic truth which, in the light of present circumstances, reflects the profound nature of the change which is taking shape. The multiplication of oil prices by twenty is inevitably bound to cause far-reaching changes in the very essence of the processes of accumulation, production and consumption, and especially in the generation of technology.

The majority of the countries of the region are suffering not only from the consequences of the original earthquake, but also the after-effects caused by the action of the centres, who, in their urgent efforts to defend themselves as best they can from the results of this situation, are passing on its consequences to the countries with the weakest defence mechanisms. The most visible forms of this particular transfer of negative effects are prices, and above all the 'manipulation' of the domestic markets for consumer goods, inputs and capital goods and the terms and destination of finance, associations with domestic private enterprises, etc. By way of example, it should be borne in mind that for the developing countries as a whole the 'manufactures bill' was higher than the oil bill in the period 1970-1978.[2]

Moreover, within the economies of the region the contradictions inherent in the prevailing forms of development were getting worse. The terms 'vulnerable', 'exclusive' and 'concentrative' applied to Latin American development are clearly reflected in a number of indicators and analyses which it is not necessary to refer to at greater length at this point, although in order to back up the propositions which will be put forth below it seems desirable to outline their most obvious symptoms.

Despite the significant growth achieved by the region until recently in various activities under the prevailing form of development, a serious appraisal of the volume, content and distribution of this growth leads to conclusions that call for reflection. On the one hand, if we look at the growth rate of the per capita product, we may see that between 1970 and 1979 it grew by a little over 30%, that is to say, in almost a decade the per capita income has risen from 650 to 860 dollars at 1970 prices.[3]

Certainly, this is a rate of expansion with which we cannot be over-satisfied. But if in addition we consider the main beneficiaries of economic progress, we see from various studies and many other indications that generally speaking it was the richest sectors which gained. Consequently, the spread of growth does not seem to have reached in an equal manner to the lower strata of the region's population. Various estimates of the number of persons who may be classified as extremely poor (30% to 40% of the population) confirm this judgment. The prevailing form of development has not been capable of solving this problem: indeed, it is precisely the most privileged section of the income

distribution pyramid which appears to have enjoyed the benefits.
This contrast alone is sufficient to lay this form of development
open to question and suggest that another orientation of the
economic activity of the region should be proposed.

If, in addition, we consider that the form of development
which has been characteristic of the region has demanded growing
external indebtedness, then the objections to this form become even
more obvious. Thus, between 1970 and 1979 Latin America's
external debt more than doubled in constant terms.[4] It is clear
that this type of development, in the present energy context,
involves large and increasing injections of external finance for
most of the non-oil-exporting developing countries, forming a kind
of self-perpetuating spiral.

Although the information on the stock of capital continues to
be very scanty, there are some indications that the product/capital
ratio has gone down significantly.[5] The available data show that
the gross investment coefficient has risen from a little over 21%
in 1970 to almost 27% in 1976.[6] In other words, within the form of
development under consideration growth seems to be becoming more
expensive at an unusually high rate, which means that a larger
number of units of capital are needed to generate a single unit of
product.[7] If the consumption structures of the various social
groups are considered and that of the upper strata is compared with
those of the rest of the population (to say nothing of that
characteristic of the sector sunk in absolute poverty), the
questioning of and opposition to the prevailing forms of
development are seen to be perfectly legitimate.[8]

When it is borne in mind that a considerable part of society
does not have access even to the items most essential for their
subsistence, can there be any justification for a situation where
the useful life of a product is artificially reduced by the
appearance of new models which frequently have no real novelty but
their design? Is it reasonable that in the case of certain
articles the container and packing are worth more than the
contents? Can there be any justification, in view of the reigning
inequality, for a situation where the compulsive acquisition of
non-essential goods becomes a growth factor for a by no means
insignificant part of the economic system? We could go on asking
such questions, but the real point is that the contradictions which
they reflect assume even more disquieting dimensions when
projected into the medium and long term. What level of imports
will be needed to sustain this form of development? How big will
the external debt be, and what proportion of exports will be needed
to cover its servicing? What export effort must be made to cover
this type of gap?

Whether in terms of diagnosis or as a function of prospective
analyses, the external and internal conditioning factors have
promoted the initiation of a process of adjustment in the
functioning of the economies of the region. The fundamental issue
to be examined is where the active trends and the forces of inertia
are leading, what courses are being approved, and who is deciding
the directions which will characterize Latin American development
in the future.

There can be no doubt that the set of problems facing the

region, including the oil-exporting countries, calls for mature
reflection on possible strategies to tackle the future in such a
way as to get round the obstacles which cannot be surmounted or
circumvent them as painlessly as possible. The adoption of this
type of strategy makes it essential to select different forms of
development.

Up to a few years ago, the discussion on alternative forms or
styles of development gave rise to interpretations with a high
ideological content. In reality, while the topic succeeded in
arousing the interest of academic centres and research institutes
it was not the subject of examination and debate within
governmental organizations, or at least not with the aim of
correcting the tendencies which economic and social activity
seemed to be following.

The new conditions through which the world economy is passing
and the internal problems faced by the governments of the region
give reason to foresee even greater difficulties with which the
economies of Latin America will have to struggle. In view of the
magnitude of the problems hanging over the developing world, this
seems not only a favourable opportunity but also a time of urgent
necessity for reflection and appraisal of the various available
options. Whether we like it or not, the very weight of the
prevailing problems has opened the door to a debate on forms or
styles of development which had up to now been pushed to one side
because it was attributed to radical political motives or
excessively theoretical concerns.

If this is not done, then the relocation of the region in the
world context and the functioning of the Latin American economies
will be adapted to the interests of the countries of the developed
world and their strongest economic units, which are facing the
crisis from a position of obvious advantage rather than to the
needs of the Latin American masses and the governments which are
genuinely concerned for them. There is no reason to assume that in
a more dramatic situation these two kinds of interests will
converge, unless the governments of the region take the initiative,
clearly face up to this crucial moment, assume the leadership in
this situation and present a solid negotiating position.

In this connexion, it should be noted that the successive
stages of generation, ripening and maturity of the crisis, together
with the reactions of the developed world and the attempts of the
developing countries to find an answer to this, are by no means
foreign to the activities of the transnational corporations.

In the following chapter, some considerations regarding
alternative forms of development will be outlined.

II. THE TRANSNATIONAL CORPORATIONS AND THE CHANGE IN THE FORM OF DEVELOPMENT

Although each country of the region has been affected by
particular combinations of internal and external factors, the

direct presence of indirect influence of transnational corporations
must form one of the central aspects of any analysis of Latin
American development.

Just as the weight of this type of economic unit has been a
determining factor in shaping the previous form of development, it
also appears as one of the principal factors in the transformation
which has now been begun. The transnational nature of their
activities gives them enormous advantages not only for relocating
themselves in a substantially different framework, but also for
taking initiatives which signify positions of real privilege for
them. It may be said that they are facing the forthcoming changes
on the basis of a more global and longer-term view than that which
is to be observed among most of the governments of the region,
which are mostly struggling with serious conjuctural problems which
limit their horizons.

If we take into account their economic and political power at
both the external and internal levels, the information at their
disposal, and the fact that their pursuit of a single objective
means that they are hampered by fewer restrictions, the
transnational corporations are seen to have clear advantages
compared with most of the governments with which they are
negotiating. As already noted, governments have to reconcile
political, social, economic and technical rationales in their
activities and must also grapple with contradictions, all of which
goes to make up a situation full of severe restrictions. Thus, it
is difficult for governments to reconcile the objectives of
economic growth stability, social justice and independence of
decision (especially if political pluralism is added to all this)
with conjunctural and short-term perspectives.

In this context, the initiative does not exactly lie with the
public sectors, and this different situation means that the
transnational corporations are able to face the transition through
action which reflect policies based on a broad and long-term view
of their activities. The position of the governments is very
different, as they must respond to the transition mainly through
resort to defensive and tardy reactions to the appearance of
foreseeable phenomena. They have to administer rather than conduct
economic and social activity, and on occasions they are obliged to
give full liberty of action and facilities to foreign capital, thus
forming an alliance between the public sector, national enterprises
and foreign capital which reproduces precisely those styles of
development which are being questioned.[9]

It is against the background of this situation of imbalance,
due mainly to the failure to take advantage of the effective
bargaining power available to governments, that this kind of
readjustment of the components of the economic systems is taking
place during the present period of crisis and the transition which
lies before us. In effect, a change is beginning to take place in
the forms of development, and in this change significant weight is
being exerted by the decisions and behavior of the transnational
corporations and their allies in the countries, while the action of
governments is limited, as already noted, to unsystematic reactions
rather than a deliberate policy fitting within a strategy in
keeping with the importance of the phenomenon through which the

region is living.

The transnational corporations have clearly seen that in view of the new general economic context the previous form of development no longer provides the same conditions of dynamism as in the past. Generally speaking, and leaving aside part of fiscal expenditure, the nucleus or motor driving the growth of their activities was the purchasing power of the top strata of the income distribution pyramid, particularly in the countries with the highest degree of industrialization.

In the face of this phenomenon, certain features of the behaviour of the transnational corporations indicate that their basic strategy also pursues the objective of expanding the market for their products by reaching consumers of lower purchasing power. This appraisal becomes particularly evident if we observe the structure of consumption, for if we analyse some of the characteristics of the market for final goods we see that it now displays some features which make it different from the situation prevailing until a few years ago.

Although such characteristics as the extravagant variety of products made available to the population with the highest purchasing power continue to predominate, and the wild round of renewal fashions and models persists, both backed up by truly overwhelming publicity campaigns,[10] we may note a greater effort to reach also the markets immediately below that represented by the richest 20% of the population.

The relative cheapening of a number of types of consumer goods such as transistor radios, stereo equipment, digital watches, television sets, electronic calculators, etc., together with the massive introduction of disposable articles, are clear examples of a tendency towards the mass marketing of certain products which will give the entrepreneurs involved another level of dynamism for their activities and a different context for securing their objectives. Various factors would appear to be of influence in this different treatment of markets between the elite, the middle groups and even the low-income groups, which is shaping a different background and changing the forms of development of the countries.

Of course the growing number and greater variety of countries of origin of the transnational enterprises which are entering the region or selling their products in it has led to some degree of competition, which in its turn has had some influence in the price reductions referred to. Obviously, the effects of scale and in general the fulfilment of what is known as the product cycle have as their results lower costs and generally also lower real prices, while it is also necessary to take into account the practice of presenting as 'new' in developing countries products which are already past their first youth in the developed countries.

At all events, however, the foregoing do not seem to be the only causes of this type of expansion and change in the destination markets. Cost-benefit evaluations by the entrepreneurs, or the production of really new articles or the lowering of the prices of old ones through efforts which go beyond increases of scale and are designed to win broader markets, could constitute another factor to be considered.

With the passage of time, the richer stratas have undoubtedly become more demanding. Today it is more difficult than before to introduce into everyday consumption products which do not really represent an authentic novelty and whose consumption does not provide any significant new satisfaction. The almost irresistible urge observed some time ago to acquire appliances which originally worked manually or mechanically but then progressed to automatic, electrical or electronic operation is no longer to be observed with the same vigour, except in the case of goods which, as already noted, constitute real technological progress and provide real new satisfaction. The renewal of models -- particularly in clothing, where this may even run counter to the laws of functionality -- is an expedient which is used with disquieting persistence and aggresivity, with the aim of creating artificial 'obsolescence'.

The ever-expanding publicity campaigns where use is made of insinuations or even demonstrations which go beyond the bounds of the ethical, warping the authentical behaviour of consumers, form another element which shows how far these firms are having to go to secure the expansion of their markets and thus guarantee other sources of dynamism to increase their sales and profits. The policy of consumer credit, which has reached an excessive level in some countries, is another complementary mechanism in market management. At the same time, however, in proportion as technology advanced and an extraordinary range of products was placed at the disposal of consumers, part of the richest sector became rather reluctant to continue with their buying mania, although not because of considerations of purchasing power. In the final analysis, the capacity for enjoyment also has a limit, in the form of the time available for enjoying the products acquired. Although the time devoted to cultural development has given way to another type of entertainment, such as the consumption of different types of services, these also take up time and make it necessary to exercise a choice, thus generating forms of behaviour which reflect a refusal to accept 'sophisitications' which represent only apparent or insignificant degrees of progress.

The magnitude of the technological effort made and the amount of financial resources invested gain easier rewards, in terms of profits, when, as already noted, real innovations are made. The cheapening of older products seems to have been considered as a complementary alternative resulting from a deliberate policy on the part of the producers and generators of technology, quite separate from decisions of governments.

The question now arises in the countries of the region: who is taking these decisions to modify the structure of consumption? What direct role is being played by the public sector in shaping this new situation? In most cases it can be said that government bodies have not had any direct intervention in the adoption of decisions in this sphere, and their action has been limited to influencing the course of these events through their handling of the short-term situation, mostly with a short-term perspective. A decision which involves the incorporation of the intermediate and even the lower strata into the consumption of products which are not always essential is of very great importance, especially when it is borne in mind that this type of decision has fundamental implications for the industrialization processes of the countries, with their role sequel of direct and indirect, positive and negative, controllable and uncontrollable effects. Of course any expansion of the consumer base, especially if it originates in the reduction of prices, leads to a reaction which is in principle positive, but it remains to be seen first what type of products are going to reach the broad masses of the population, and what is the quid pro quo for these market expansions. How will they affect the population which receives them, and what part of the available resources will be absorbed by this new increasing growth? What does this form of growth mean in terms of attention to the needs of the extremely poor section of the population? What is the new industrial structure which will be built up through this form? What effects will it have on employment and income distribution? How much more or less dependent on external financing is this new type of economy likely to be?

Obviously, it is not possible to answer these questions without first of all clarifying the phenomenon and seeing where these trends lead in the framework of the economic and social activity of each particular country. The above is intended only to draw attention to a change which already seems to have started and which may become uncontrollable, as happened with elite consumption. This is all the more true when one considers that the objectives pursued by a private economic unit, particularly if it is transnational, do not always coincide with the needs of the countries and especially of the broad masses in them: indeed, they frequently diverge from these needs or even contradict them completely.

III. THE BASIC OPTIONS

In the face of the situation described, one option is obviously to use the market as the means of solving the fundamental problems of the functioning of economic and social activity. This is an option which, in its own way and with the consequences already suffered by the region, has helped to reproduce the type of concentrative, exclusive and vulnerable growth already referred to.

There is no doubt that the imperfect mechanism of the market is indeed a form of settling the incompatibilities, maladjustments and imbalances typical of the Latin American economies, but unfortunately it does so with results and final balances which are far from being satisfactory in the light of any appraisal which includes economic and social criteria seen from the general viewpoint of the community. In practice, the imbalance between the insufficient capacity to absorb labour displayed by the economic system and the relatively abundant supply of such labour results in disquieting levels of unemployment. The maladjustments between the supply and demand of goods are corrected by the market through price rises. The disparity between the financing needs of a type of development which is increasingly expensive in terms of investments and intermediate goods and the capacity for generating exportable surpluses is reflected in growing deficits and external indebtedness, and this generally leads to the adoption of extreme and urgent measures to export, even at the cost of adversely affecting domestic consumption.

The different weights of the agents involved, whether they be consumers of economic units, mean that the unrestricted play of the market mechanism suffers from such a degree of imperfection that its advantages turn out to be only apparent and its results are frequently negative. There is no need to enlarge on the list of its disadvantages; since this is not a new matter, it is enough to ask ourselves whether, in the present crisis, it will permit the solution of the gravest problems and the assignment of proper attention to social problems, when it did not do so in less severe and less complex situations.

It hardly seems necessary to say that the long-term view, which is so neglected by those who participate in the taking of decisions, once again shows itself to be essential, and this time in a more urgent manner than before. It is worth noting that short-term views, and even medium-term ones, are not capable of assimilating the real significance of the change which looms ahead of us. In practical terms, what is involved is the construction of different economic systems and different societies, and a limited time horizon does not permit us, in the present context, to gain a clear idea of the possible final situations that will result. Moreover, the appraisal criteria characteristic of the short term are not only insufficient but may even be misleading. How can we evaluate decisions which may have great importance in the future in the light of short-term and even transitory parameters? Can the play of the markedly imperfect market forces ensure at one and the same time a growing and better distributed income, greater sobriety in consumption, and the allocation of resources to items which the community really needs in terms of essential goods and services? What long-term view does this type of market have, unless it is simply that of profitability? At a time when the allocation of resources should be carefully examined in order to ensure that priority is given to the most pressing needs, is it reasonable that publicity and propaganda should be the factors generating needs, instead of the needs generating production?

Every time that crises and upheavals which affect the countries of the region in a profound and extensive manner loom over us, planning is rehabilitated as a form of government management of the economic systems. It should not be assumed from this, however, that in this other option the problems can be solved without difficulty. As long as needs are greater than availabilities, that is to say, as long as the problem of shortages continues to prevail, the difficulties will continue. The basic question to be considered is therefore what type of needs, and whose needs, deserve priority attention, and this brings us to reflect on alternative forms which make the sacrifices and opportunities more equitable and provide greater possibilities of growth. The problem of running economic activity is not a trivial matter and lies at the very heart both of the form of development and of the long-term options.

Whether we like it or not, the forms of development which

prevailed until recently will have to undergo changes. The
line these will follow is relatively foreseeable if the fundamental
problems are left to the unrestricted play of market forces,
whereas the planning alternative, in contrast, involves the
assumption of broad responsibilities: identifying the most
important outlines of the type of society which it is desired to
attain, establishing the primary characteristics of the form of
development consistent with this object, and proposing the
mechanisms of participation which this society will have at the
different levels of decision-making.

Quite apart from the various ideologies and concepts of
economic, social and political activities, planning as a practice
and as a method is essential if we are to defend ourselves more
effectively during crises and gain a proper place for ourselves
with vision and foresight in the complex set of international
economic relations, and above all if we are to respect the
principle of equity in the distribution of the fruits of growth.
As already noted, the achievement of these objectives involves
recognition of the need for planning, in all its temporal, spatial,
sectoral and institutional dimensions.

The main responsibility for running economic and social
activities lies with governments, and it is their responsibility to
appraise the course and evolution of future development and make
the necessary corrections if this course, as often happens in the
region, does not lead to the desired situations, particularly for
the most under-privileged sectors. This responsibility is even
more obvious when it is observed that moves are being made in
circles other than those of government which are likely to affect
future development and modify its forms.

It was already noted above that the transnational corporations
and the domestic economic units controlled by them or assimilated
to them are taking steps, with particular and often alien criteria,
which could lead the course of development in the region towards
destinations not yet appraised from a long-term perspective. The
criteria regarding the activation of economic processes, the
reduction of inflationary pressures and balancing of the balance of
payments have generally been established within a narrow time
horizon, using measures of a traditional nature which, in the final
analysis, favour that sector of the population whose purchasing
power is most vigorously manifested in the play of the market
forces. Thus, the incompatibility between the objectives of the
private economic circles (especially the transnational
corporations) and the more genuine needs of the mass sectors of the
region is not brought out in its true dimensions. It would be very
different if the presence and activities of this type of economic
unit were weighed in the light of these needs and with perspectives
which also included the medium and long term.

It is indispensable to identify the main features of the
situations which would be created if the question of the form of
development were left to the decision-making centres which have
been taking the initiative up to now. If this were done, it would
provide us with qualitative and quantitative indications of the
type of society which is being created and we would be able to
appraise the potential magnitude of the inequalities and

imbalances. This would permit the proposal of strategies leading to different situations, if the considerations of equity of distribution merit a weighting which, if not paramount, is at least comparable with that given to purely economic considerations.

Even in the case of those countries which have been most reluctant to plan their economies, sooner or later the circumstances will convince them that some form of planning will be necessary in order to tackle the crisis and adjust their forms of development in the light of the external restrictions and the persistence of domestic problems. In some cases because of social sensibility, and in others because of the pressures and demands of those who can no longer bear to continue in extreme poverty, forces could emerge which also demand another style of growth or another type of development dynamics, adding their influence to that arising from the inadequacies and contradictions of the forms of development currently prevailing.

IV. REAPPRAISAL OF TRANSNATIONAL CORPORATIONS IN THE CONTEXT OF PLANNING

Latin America in the 1980s, a document prepared by the CEPAL Secretariat, clearly states the need to appraise the activities of these agents from the point of view of planning, as a way of expanding the negotiating power of governments. The present article takes up some of the proposals made in that document. Although the considerations set forth below concern various agents of the economic and social system, this study is directed in particular towards the phenomenon of the transnational corporations, in view of the decisive influence which this type of economic unit has had on the development of the region so far and the determining role which it could play in the future. It must be borne in mind from the start that the transnational enterprises also engage in planning, in their own manner, and not only are their decisions based on detailed and timely data on economic, social and political aspects of the countries where they are operating or have the intention of establishing themselves, but also their broad geographical and temporal view of business gives them the advantageous position already referred to. If the instruments at the disposal of the modern State are organized and applied as a function of plans, development strategies or planned economic policies, then they can approach the negotiations with these corporations from a more solid position. Even in those cases where planning is already institutionalized, reappraisal of the role of the transnational corporations in the light of the new circumstances could be beneficial.

In the final analysis, what is necessary is to analyse the way in which the transnational corporations could contribute to the fulfilment of a political plan or project and also, of course, to decide which activities are not in keeping with the lines of the latter. In essence, this is the basic scheme for a new appraisal not only of their investments but also of their entire area of influence.

The reappraisal of the transnational corporations in the context of a planning process would make it possible to identify first of all those sectors and activities where their collaboration is considered appropriate and even indispensable; next, the areas reserved for the activity of national firms, whether public or private; and finally those areas where the activities of the transnational corporations would run counter to the main lines of the options decided upon by the countries. A reappraisal based on this type of criteria, appropriate to the planning process, would make possible better selection of the transnational corporations and their activities; it would create a suitable field for new dealings with foreign capital and would also make possible more stable agreements with these economic units. For their part, the transnational corporations which make a real contribution to the achievement of the objectives of the type of integrative development proposed will be more inclined to make their conditions more flexible, and the legitimate nature of their presence would undoubtedly modify the negotiating positions.

For governments, the fact of their knowing the implications of the presence of transnational corporations for the main variables in play in a planning process would not only increase their information on the repercussions of this type of economic units but would also mean that they could properly appraise the positive and negative consequences of their presence, thus imparting greater accuracy, a broader perspective and a sounder basis to the process of decision-making in this area.

It has already been stated that the operations of the transnational corporations have been decisive in shaping the present style of development and can also be decisive during the critical period through which the region is passing. Hence, a different type of appraisal of and negotiation with them is essential in order properly to fulfil the accepted principle that it is necessary to maximize the benefits represented by their presence and minimize the costs involved in it. As a guiding criterion, this represents the first step in a new relationship with the transnational corporations. At all events, in order to determine with some degree of accuracy how to maximize the benefits and minimize costs, it is essential first of all to prepare a list of quantitative and qualitative objectives to be achieved over various periods, followed by an outline of the various alternative policies that could lead to the achievement of this. These two tasks are routine fundamental steps in planning processes. On the basis of them it is then possible to go more deeply into the diagnosis designed to clarify the present behaviour of the transnational corporation and identify the main components of the strategies and plans connected with this type of economic unit. The appraisal of their presence and possible future participation in the context of a planning process naturally offers possibilities for a new type of negotiations between governments and transnational corporations.

When a government clearly perceives the most important delayed and immediate, direct and indirect effects which the participation of transnational corporations is likely to have on a set of economic and social variables, its real negotiating capacity automatically acquires a different scope and it is in a much better position to appraise the implications of each concession and each demand. Thus, knowing what the immediate or potential influence will be on employment and wages, the balance of payments, taxes, the use of credit, internal activities on the side of inputs and sales, etc. -- all specified for different time-spans within a gradual process of improvement -- would permit a really strict appraisal of the effects of this type of economic unit. Up to now, many of these aspects have only been given superficial qualitative appraisal, and most often the factors which have predominated in the negotiations are related with aspects which are very important for contingent situations, but are of minor significance for development.

An appraisal methodology like that suggested above would lead to the selection of transnational corporations whose activities and behaviour were compatible with the new form of development which it is hoped will take shape in the region. The capacity to discriminate in favour of those enterprises which are in line with the form of development finally selected can only be properly carried out when the respective appraisal fits in with one of the basic stages of planning process.

Moreover, as already noted, the rules of the game will be clearer for the transnational corporation itself, and its presence will become more legitimate when its activities effectively contribute to the achievement of the objectives pursued by a country. Volumes of investment, scales of production, amortization policies and policies on the reinvestment and repatriation of profits will have another frame of reference which would probably lead to the corporations making their negotiating positions more flexible, while the true problems of the countries would be seen more and it would be easier to distinguish between the interests of economic groups and those of the national masses.

In reappraising the transnational corporations it would seem useful to contemplate all three of the traditional perspectives of planning: the short medium and long term. By doing this, it will be possible to establish what their implications are in terms of the variables pertaining to each of these time horizons. The entry of a particular transnational corporation may satisfy short-term requirements, but it may come into conflict with longer-term needs. Moreover, while conjunctural requirements are generally easier to satisfy, at the same time they are more fleeting and frequently spurious. In contrast, those connected with the structural background, apart from being reflected better in longer-term perspectives, are not always even contemplated by the typical short-term criteria because the short-term is much more conditioned by contingent pressures, and different weight is given in it to the different aspects and effects of foreign investment.

It is self-evident that attempts to appraise transnational corporations from the point of view of plans and strategies which aim at more sober forms of development are likely to encounter strong reactions from the groups which are associated with the very forms it is desired to change. The resistance of the economic

groups connected with the transnational corporations to their
inclusion in other schemes which would alter the distribution and
appropriation of the surplus will undoubtedly constitute a
difficult barrier for any attempt to correct the situation, and
these corporations will accuse those who are trying to reorient
development of interventionism and transgression of the laws of the
market.

Although it is difficult to oppose the idea of promoting a
form of development which is more rapid but less extravagant, more
efficient but less unjust, it will not come as a surprise to anyone
that the groups which are benefiting from the exaggerated consumer
society will use all their economic and political power to hinder a
new form of development. It is foreseeable that attempts in this
direction will give rise to violent reactions, but it can also be
foreseen that the search for a form of development which is less
extravagant and has a higher social content will receive by no
means insignificant support even from entrepreneurial groups, to
say nothing of the support from those sectors which are more deeply
affected by the imbalances and weaknesses of the styles of
development which are being questioned. In the discussion of these
topics, it will be of really crucial importance that the analysis
should concentrate on the essential features of what the
transformation of its development model will mean for a society.[11]

It may be noted, in this connexion, that this matter gives
rise to discussions which enter the ideological sphere, and it is
very likely that the real positions against the correction of the
situation will be disguised with fallacious arguments and
surrounded by dark and mysterious warnings of dire consequences.
Of course the economic, social and political implications of
changes of this type require not only a clear diagnosis in each
country, but also a firm political decision to seize the initiative
precisely in the present period of crisis, and not afterwards, when
the courses will already have been set and the new economic
relations consolidated. Choosing planning as a basic instrument
for the management of the economy by the government not only
strengthens the tendency towards a desirable course of development
but also opens up new possibilities for negotiation with foreign
capital and, in particular, with the transnational corporations.
Neglecting to lead society in a particular direction not only means
eluding an essential responsibility but also implies overlooking an
effective capacity for negotiation which, in varying degrees, the
countries of the region have significantly increased in recent
years. Merely by way of illustration, think of the potential
negotiating capacity which the State enterprises of each country
would have if they acted together in accordance with a plan or in
the light of a planned economic policy.

In advocating a different form of negotiation with foreign
enterprises, within the framework of a process of planning and with
the aim of achieving a new type of development, there arises a
basic issue which must be defined: the demarcation of areas or
activities in which the participation of transnational corporations
would be permitted, and of areas which are reserved for national
public or private capital. In this demarcation it seems vital to
introduce the criterion of whether the activities are essential or

not, so that foreign investment is limited to those activities which really help to make the form of development more equitable and less vulnerable. It is worth stressing that these proposals involve the idea of a gradual process which begins by identifying the most important and crucial aspects and goes on, with the passage of time and the accumulation of experience, to cover a larger number of aspects.

The negotiating capacity of the countries will be increased in proportion as there is an increase in the degree of generalization of those positions which stress the most essential and transcendental issues in their policies with regard to foreign capital. If this is not done, the result could be the proliferation of 'consumer paradises' as the result of policies which welcome all types of foreign investment with open arms.

Once the sectors, activities or projects where the participation of this type of enterprise is considered appropriate have been demarcated, the negotiations with them should not be restricted solely to the topics covered by most of the laws and regulations on the treatment of foreign investment. Thus, in addition to the traditional concern with the establishment of regulations on taxes, permits, reinvestments, repatriation of profits, etc., it seems advisable to introduce also clauses on minimum export quotas and maximum import levels, on the employment of labour, on the use of domestic credit, etc. When their administration permits, clauses should also be included on prices, qualities and quantities of products. Naturally, the introduction of these other variables into the negotiations means that differential treatment must be given to the different categories of transnational corporations, but in spite of the greater complexity involved, the magnitude of the investments in question and the importance of their compliance with the basic objectives of the new development policies make it advisable to spare no effort to overcome these difficulties.

In advocating specific treatment for each transnational corporation, we have in mind the larger projects: those activities which call for special attention because of the size of the investment involved or the weight they can assume in the economic process. In speaking of the treatment of foreign capital in general terms we are only typifying a global position or characterizing a certain philosophy with regard to the entry of such capital: in contrast, the actual negotiations involve factual and detailed considerations.

While the transnational corporations form a category with common features they are nevertheless very heterogenous and of different origins, while the projects or activities which the countries wish to promote are themselves of great diversity. In the face of these two types of heterogeneity it is difficult to see how general laws or regulations could permit the 'optimization' of negotiations with foreign capital.

Perhaps global regulations could be reserved for investments or projects of smaller scale, but for those of greater importance it is necessary to leave open the possibility of ad hoc negotiations capable of taking account of the special features involved so that it is possible to obtain from the transnational corporations a contribution which is really in keeping with the most genuine objectives of the countries.

In this way it can be ensured that the participation of the transnational corporations is in line with a kind of open competition which permits the appraisal of the way in which each enterprise complies with the specifications and criteria previously laid down by the host country in order to select the corporations which best satisfy the requirements. The emergence of new transnational corporations and their interest in entering the region mean that the countries would have some possibility of choice in the matter.

Apart from this consideration, the negotiating position of the countries would also be strengthened by looking into the possibilities of negotiating with medium-sized enterprises in the central countries and in the most advanced Latin American countries, and moreover the scales and forms of operation of these companies might be more compatible with the special features of the economies of the region. At all events, the search for other alternatives and the establishment of conditions to orient the negotiations and agreements towards the achievement of a new type of development seem to be fundamental tasks which must be faced during the period of transition in order to take advantage of and increase the effective negotiating capacity of the region.

The considerations and proposals set forth above involve significant changes in the process of planning, particularly as regards the main techniques and methodologies. In the next section we will sketch some of the main modifications needed to the basic instruments in order to permit a more integral appraisal of the transnational corporations.

V. PLANNING AT THE ENTERPRISE LEVEL AND THE APPRAISAL OF AND NEGOTIATIONS WITH TRANSNATIONAL CORPORATIONS

For some time past, judgments have been expressed on the problems affecting the planning processes in the region. A number of causes which might account for their main limitations have been observed, and as a result three well-defined areas may be distinguished which typify the diagnoses regarding their present state.

On the one hand, it is indicated that there is a set of factors related to the political sphere, that is to say, the question of to what extent the plans really represent a commitment on the part of those holding the real power. When it is admitted that the adoption of decisions does not come within the lines of the plan or is even contrary to them, we are admitting that the plan does not reflect the intentions and does not incorporate the interests of the political authorities and the groups supporting them. In reality, no plan can go beyond what the real centres of decision are willing to carry out. When it is pointed out that the economic policy diverges from the lines of the plan, in reality what is being indicated is the type of dichotomy which separates the intentions of those who prepare the plans from the actions of those who carry out the policy.

On the other hand, there is another set of causes related with the organization of the planning systems and the participation of the various bodies, entities and agents of the economic and social system. The difficulties encountered by the operative organisms in taking into account the categories specific to planning in the conjunctural management of the economy, and the problems which the planners have in incorporating on a flexible and timely basis the political restrictions and alterations which inevitably arise in the everyday functioning of the economy suitably summarize the essence of the problems which affect planning from this point of view. At all events, the different level of concern and the unequal size of the variables handled by the two groups explain a type of fundamental maladjustment which short-term planning and the so-called operational plans have not been able to solve.

Finally, there is a third area, related with the information and planning methodologies and techniques usually used in Latin America. While there has been significant progress in this field, generally speaking the instruments used still do not seem to fit in adequately with the complex tasks involved in a planning effort. The different rationales implicit in the economic, social and political processes have not found in the types of models used a suitable mechanism of comparison and appraisal capable of generating alternatives in which these rationales become coherent or at least do not contradict each other. Moreover, the instruments in question have suffered from rigidities which have prevented them from responding adequately to the conduct and behaviour of the different agents of the economic and social system. It may be noted in passing that such limitations have also become obvious, in different measures and forms, in centrally managed economies with great planning experience. However, it should be noted that the models based on numerical experimentation are those which have shown the greatest capacity for taking account of the special features and complexities of real events and properly reflecting the intentions behind the different types of plans.[12]

A different conception of planning is set forth below which could smooth out a number of the difficulties which planning has encountered in the region. It is interesting to note in this connexion the possibility provided by this alternative for appraising transnational corporations in a integral manner and negotiating with them on a more solid basis.

The fundamental change lies in the definition of the element or basic category to be planned. Up to now, planning has been mainly at the level of economic aggregates. At most, the classical macroeconomic variables such as the product, consumption, investment, etc., have been broken down into some subcategories, while the conventional economic sectors have been broken down into particular activities in order to avoid working with excessively heterogeneous conglomerates. There do not appear to be any serious objections either at the conceptual level or in the field of practical application, however, to the possibility of using the enterprise as the basic category of the planning process.

This possibility has been opened up for some time now by electronic computation. Planning by enterprises or by economic units seems to be a suitable response to the needs for better government management of economic and social activity and, in particular, for a fuller appraisal of the transnational corporations.

For the medium-sized or small countries, where 50, 100 or 150 enterprises are responsible for a high proportion of total production and marketing, planning at the enterprise level does not present any impracticable tasks or major complexities. It has been verified in Latin America that it is possible to work with models containing several hundred equations, which in turn means the use of highly disaggregated matrices.

For the larger countries, planning at the enterprise level can constitute an efficient alternative when planning by states, provinces or regions, where likewise 100 enterprises or so can represent a large part of economic activity, traditional planning by economic aggregates being retained at the national level.

If the characteristics of a particular country appear to present obstacles to the proposed change, one possibility would be to introduce this system gradually, selecting the leading enterprises in each sector which, by their direct weight or indirect influence, condition the functioning of economic activity. Thus, a distinction could be drawn in each sector between the public enterprises, the leading domestic and foreign private enterprises, and the rest. The knowledge of economic activity which the planning offices would have after a strict examination of the activities of the leading enterprises would make it possible to reconcile economic planning and policy with less difficulty.

An effort in this direction would make it possible to gain both periodic and continual knowledge of the operations of these enterprises, their investments, production, imports, exports, hiring of staff, credits, taxes, profits, etc. When one considers the difficulties involved in planning by economic aggregates, precisely because of the need to estimate these aggregates, the advantages of planning at the enterprise level can be clearly appreciated.

Planning by economic aggregates generally use the space of one year as its time unit. It is difficult to reconcile short-term planning, whose time unit is one month, with a three- or five-year plan. This is to a large extent the reason for the gulf between planners and those working in more operational bodies of the public sector. Planning at the enterprise level would give planners an extraordinary amount of information on the conjunctural situation, would facilitate their contact and participation in short-term decisions, and the timeliness and specific nature of the information continually collected would make it possible to bring plan and reality closer in two respects: on the one hand by enabling the plan to incorporate in a timely manner real events which had not been foreseen in it, and on the other, by orienting the real functioning of economic activity along the lines laid down in the plan.

This represents a change in the methodological conception of

planning which would undoubtedly have repercussions on the actual
organization of the work of a planning office. It could become a
qualitative leap forward of great significance if solutions were
found to the problems of working with massive information,
designing new accounting systems and, in general, modifying the
routines and ways of obtaining information. It is precisely in
this respect that the first objections have been levelled at this
proposal for planning at the enterprise level. The so-called
statistical secrecy provided for in the business law of most
countries and the difficulties of continuously following up dozens
of enterprises have been suggested as possible obstacles. These
are not insuperable barriers however, and it would be perfectly
possible to tackle them if there was determination to progress
along these lines. It would be easy to continue listing the
features of planning at the enterprise level and enumerating its
advantages,[13] but this is not the moment to do so, since the aim is
simply to give some idea of its main outlines so as to propose its
use in the appraisal of transnational corporations.

   There does not seem to be any need to give more illustrations
of the way in which the presence of the transnational corporations
would be appraised if the basic planning element were the
enterprise. Each of these economic units would receive explicit
consideration and treatment in this new methodology of planning at
the enterprise level. In this way, it would be possible to see
clearly and in detail what direct and indirect, immediate and
delayed effects their operations would have on the present and
future economic system under various hypotheses; what their
positive and negative effects would be; what variables they would
decisively influence; what the interrelations between this type of
enterprise and those forming the rest of the system would be, etc.
The comparison of transnational corporations among themselves and
with the other public and private units, and knowledge of their
cost structures, their expansion programmes and the role they play
in the field of economic relations would undoubtedly make possible
an integral appraisal of their real and potential behaviour.

   The negotiating capacity of a government which had identified
in detail the various types of repercussions and the magnitude of
their effects would assume very different levels of solidity and
accuracy from those characteristics of partial appraisals. In this
different conception of planning at the enterprise level, new
elements of judgment would emerge, some of them favouring the
transnational corporations and others working against them. At all
events, a larger amount of available information cannot but
guarantee better appraisal, and this would contribute to different
treatment of foreign capital based on a variety of criteria and
judgments with greater time and space coverage and, undoubtedly,
with greater accuracy and scope.

NOTES

[1]The concept of form or style of development used in this article is in line with the approach described by Anibal Pinto in "Styles of development in Latin America", CEPAL Review, No. 1, first half of 1976.

[2]See CEPAL, Latin American development in the 1980s (E/CEPAL/G. 1150), p. 69.

[3]CEPAL estimates prepared by the Latin American Economic Projection Centre.

[4]Ibid.

[5]See CEPAL, Long-term trends and prospects of Latin American development (E/CEPAL/1076), April 1979, table 5.

[6]It should be noted that this indicator only provides an order of magnitude as regards the ratio of the two variables. The difficulties in counting up and valuing the various capital goods and in estimating their depreciation are limitations which must be borne in mind.

[7]It might be held that the lag between investment and production is a point to be held against this appraisal, but only extremely high rates of growth of the product in the coming years could partially invalidate this statement, and even so there would still be valid grounds for discussion regarding the type of product generated.

[8]See Raul Prebisch, "Socio-economic structure and crisis of peripheral capitalism", CEPAL Review, No. 6, second half of 1978.

[9]Peter Evans, A triplice alianca, Rio de Janeiro, Zahar Editores, 1980.

[10]See Carlos Filgueira, Consumo y estilos de desarrollo, CEPAL, March 1979 (CEPAL/DS/VP/190).

[11]See Jorge Graciarena, "Power and development styles", CEPAL Review, No. 1, first half of 1976.

[12]See the article by Oscar Varsavsky, "Modelos matematicos y experimentacion numerica in Oscar Varsavsky and Alfredo E. Calcagno (compilers), America Latina: Modelos Matematicos, Santiago, Chile, Editorial Universitaria, 1971.

[13]In the CEPAL/CTC Joint Unit on Transnational Corporations, research has been initiated with a view to proposing methodological alternatives for the explicit and disaggregated consideration of transnational corporations in planning processes.

The Role of Multinationals in the NIEO

ROLF JUNGNICKEL
GEORG KOOPMANN

The establishment of a New International Economic Order has been the subject of intensive consultations in the international institutions for some time now. The industrialized countries are confronted with demands which have the aim of a drastic redistribution of the wealth and incomes to the benefit of the developing countries and a fundamental restructuring of the inherited international division of labour. The Third World intends thereby to raise its share of industrial production from currently 7 p.c. to 25 p.c. in the year 2000.

To achieve this objective, the old order governing international economic relations on the basis of the market mechanism is to be superseded by a new one in which considerably more use is to be made of direct regulatory intervention in the production structure of the world economy.[1] This move towards international economic _dirigisme_ is mirrored by the role assigned to the multinational enterprises.

I. DEMAND FOR CONTROLS

The various resolutions adopted so far show however significant differences in content. The declarations which was issued in February 1975 by the Raw Materials Conference in Dakar still referred in general terms to "anarchic exploitation" of the developing countries by the multinational enterprises and looked on the latter as an essential cause of the instability of the international monetary system and the consequent disadvantages for

From **INTERECONOMICS**, March 1976, (80-83), reprinted by permission of the publisher.

the Third World. The "Declaration for the Establishment of a New
International Economic Order", which was adopted by the Sixth UN
Special General Assembly, and the Second UNIDO Conference likewise
called for nationalization of foreign enterprises in accordance
solely with national law, i.e. passing over the provisions
of international law. Finally the control over the multinational
enterprises was one of the principal items of the "Programme of
Action" adopted at the Sixth UN Special General Assembly. The aim
of the developing countries in this respect is to evolve a Code of
Conduct designed to

--prevent interference in the domestic affairs of the host country;

--preclude restrictive practices -- especially in foreign
trade -- and allow for the revision of existing agreements;

--ensure transfer of technology and management know-how on
favourable terms;

--encourage the reinvestment of profits and "regulate" the transfer
of profits from developing countries.

II. MORE CONCILIATORY ATTITUDE

The resolution adopted by the Seventh UN Special General Assembly
by a consensus of industrialized and developing countries generally
reflects a more conciliatory attitude to the multinational
enterprises. It contains demands for their stricter control only
in the general form of a reference to previous UN resolutions.
Further to that the industrialized countries are urged to promote
private investments which are of service to the technological and
industrial advancement of the developing countries.
        The wish for stricter control of the multinational enterprises
is understandable in view of the undeniable occurrences of economic
exploitation and political tutelage, and also justified because the
multinational enterprises and the developing countries pursue
differing interests. Direction of the multinational enterprises is
for this reason necessary in order to enhance the usefulness of
their activities from the point of view of development policy.
        The developing countries appear however to set out from the
premise that they themselves or, prompted by them, the governments
of the industrialized countries can at their discretion bring about
the transfer of capital, technology and management and marketing
know-how within the compass of multinational enterprises through
appropriate decisions. In this they overrate the influence of the
governments of the wester industrialized countries with their
market-economy orientation, and misunderstand the private-economy
character of the multinational enterprises which do not set out to
act as development aid institutions but want to make a profit, at
least in the longer term. The developing countries thereby put

their own aim of increased industrialization, to which the
multinationals can make a substantial contribution, in jeopardy.

III. CONTRIBUTION TO INDUSTRIALIZATION

In view of the paucity of the resources in the developing countries
there would be only limited scope for the establishment of new
industries if the cooperation of multinational enterprises were not
forthcoming, and it would involve high alternative costs, for the
services which the multinationals transfer as a factor package
would have to be obtained each by itself from other sources. In
practice this would probably prove impossible or much more
expensive in many cases. It can certainly not be assumed that
public development aid is capable of taking on all the functions
performed by the multinational enterprises.
   Utilization of the activities of multinational enterprises for
the industrialization process does not necessarily imply that
national capital and management are debarred. On the contrary, the
multinationals show increasing willingness to invest in the form of
joint ventures, i.e. of letting native partners participate in
their operations. Joint "fade-out" ventures have been set up in
several countries, like some Andes Pact states for instance, in
which the capital and management are transferred step by step,
according to a fixed schedule, from the multinationals to native
hands.
   The multinationals are most willing to enter into joint
ventures with national enterprises for investments with a domesic
market orientation (including projects designed to supply
integration areas) and relatively little interlocking with the
group operations in other countries. Insofar as the production is
oriented towards the world market or involves specialized work for
group companies abroad, it is important that the multinational
enterprises should be allowed a substantial measure of at least de
facto control to facilitate the necessary coordination of their
world-wide interests.

IV. ADVANTAGES OVER ALTERNATIVES

It is because of their world-wide interests that the multinational
enterprises seem to be particularly well suited to the
establishment of export-oriented industries in developing countries
and to improve their integration with the international division of
labour. The multinational enterprises have an advantage over
alternative operators by virtue of the know-how on production
techniques concentrated in their hands and their extensive
distribution networks -- especially for setting up labour-intensive

industries, but also for processing raw materials and thus for meeting one essential demand which arises in connection with the New International Economic Order.

The multinational enterprises can also make a major contribution to raising the technological level in developing countries, i.e. to the technology transfer, for most of the technological know-how in the market-economy countries is concentrated in private enterprises. In many cases it is their technology which gives the multinational enterprises such a strong competitive basis.[2] The widest possible control over the use of their technology is therefore the precondition of continual technology transfers within the compass of the multinational enterprises. An "appropriate" and transferable renumeration must also be ensured for the medium term. Both these considerations will have to find a place in the desired Code of Conduct for Technology Transfer. They do not rule out supervision of the technology transfer by the developing countries in order to prevent transfer of "wrong" technologies and excessive costs.

The activities of the multinational enterprises have evidently not always yielded the indicated positive results in the past. The developing countries are attributing this in the main to the conduct of the multinational enterprises and the policies of the industrialized countries in their support. This view is reflected by the various resolutions on the establishment of a New International Economic Order.

V. MISTAKEN DEVELOPMENTS IN THE PAST

They ignore however that the developing countries have often themselves encouraged the mistaken developments which have taken place. In many cases their policy in regard to foreign capital had no clear aim at all, or else objectives were pursued by corrupt governments which were inconsistent with the needs of the economy as a whole. In quite a few cases, moreover, an overdrawn policy of import substitution has given rise to uneconomical productions which were unnecessary or even harmful under development aspects but, protected by high tariff walls, provided substantial profits for the investor.

For these reasons there is still considerable scope for improvements in the elaboration of a consistent policy towards the multinationals by the developing countries. It would have been a reasonable and necessary function of UN Programmes of Action to evolve guidelines for such a policy.

Direction of multinational enterprises in accordance with development-political aims can only achieve its purpose -- to improve the cost-benefit relationship in favour of the developing countries -- if it

--accepts the private-economic character of the multinational enterprises, i.e. their profit and growth aspiration, and

--makes purposeful use of the special capability of the multinationals for cost-saving coordination of economic activities in different countries.

VI. IMPROVEMENTS FOR THE FUTURE

Justice must be done in the practical elaboration of this policy to three considerations above all: First, the "rules of the game" for the activities of multinational enterprises must be clear and binding for a fairly long period. They must cover

--definitions and priority ratings for the criteria on which investment projects are to be judged (effect on employment, balance of payments repercussions, etc.);

--identification of areas in which foreign investments are are unwanted;

--rules for national participation in foreign enterprises;

--provisions for profit transfer, capital repatriation, local borrowing, pre-production imports, etc.

Plain and abiding rules of this kind have a considerable positive effect on the propensity to invest and at the same time strengthen the bargaining position of the developing countries, for foreign investors tend to be more willing to put up with restrictions and alter their modes of conduct if they come upon constant institutional parameters.

Since clear rules must be laid down for the investments by multinational enterprises, the terms on which enterprises may be nationalized are also of vital importance. In this context it may be regarded as an important step that the developing countries at the Seventh UN Special General Assembly no longer insisted on a right of nationalization irrespective of the international law. It is true that nationalization problems have so far played no major role in the most important investment countries in the Third World in particular[3], and that the multinational enterprises affected in individual cases certainly often mean something different by respect for international law than do the host countries. The fact remains however that a general tendency towards national -- and thus possibly arbitrary -- determination of the compensation in the event of expropriation would probably impede investments especially in the politically least stable countries.

Secondly, any direction of multinational enterprises should be flexible in operation. Joint ventures with national firms for instance will be the more difficult to pursue the more closely the foreign establishments are integrated into a world-wide division of labour between group enterprises (e.g. through production of primary and intermediate products for another group enterprises).

Similar observations apply to demands to secure the largest possible national share in production: To remain internationally competitive, export-oriented investment projects must as a rule rely much more on foreign supplies of accessories than do enterprises which confine themselves largely to supplying the domestic market of the investment country. Distinctions of this kind should be taken into consideration for a rational policy towards the multinational enterprises which aims at enhancing the investments and their benefit to the developing countries.

VII. DEMANDS ON ECONOMIC POLICY

Another important prerequisite for efficient operation of multinational enterprises in the development process is, thirdly, a steady general economic policy with clear development priorities, favouring expansion of the markets and improving the conditions for production. It will be all the easier for the multinational enterprises to take their place in the framework of the national development plans as has been demanded time and again in the various resolutions, the more consistently the work of planning if carried out. Moreover, the willingness of multinational enterprises to reinvest their profits in developing countries and bring in more capital and technology depends decisively upon their expectations concerning the development of the markets. This is clearly brought out by various studies of the motives for investments in developing countries.

Besides, the distribution of the investments over the various countries reveals clearly that the investors prefer the larger and dynamic markets. A policy orientated towards market expansion therefore tends to promote at the same time the propensity to invest and the integration of the foreign enterprises with the national economy. Efforts to strengthen the economic integration between developing countries on a regional or sub-regional level assume increasing importance in this context. The small and least developed developing countries in particular cannot achieve a substantial market expansion except by closer cooperation.

A matter of concern is also the improvement of the production conditions, especially by selective infrastructural measures. If foreign enterprises engage in developing countries only in the final manufacturing stages or in assembly work, the reason is often to be found in inadequate infrastructural facilities in the country in which they have made investments. The developing countries are hampered in taking remedial action by their limited resources. They depend, also in this respect, upon active support by public and private development aid institutions -- a point which has been emphasized in the UN resolutions.

The governments of the home countries of the multinational enterprises would additionally take appropriate measures in favour of private investments in developing countries. They should also consider the least developed countries and match the assistance to

the development benefit of the investment project. The developing
countries on their side must accept that in an economic system
bearing the stamp of the market economy the governments of the
multinationals' home countries cannot dictate to private
enterprises which of them should invest how much in which other
countries and with which technology.

VIII. STARTING POINTS FOR A CODE OF CONDUCT

These demands are starting points for the evolvement of codes of
conduct for multinational enterprises and the transfer of
technology. Such a code of conduct for governments and enterprises
should not however lead to the installation of an international
bureaucracy which would find its scope for dealing with concrete
disputes in any case limited by the sovereignty claims of the
affected states. It would for this reason have to confine itself
to formulating general principles; it could nevertheless foster a
disposition to adapt modes of conduct on a basis of mutuality and
to create thereby better preconditions for a reconciliation of
interests.
     A Code of Conduct cannot however be a substitute for a
national policy towards multinational enterprises. The practical
elaboration and implementation of the measures must be the task of
the developing countries themselves. A rational policy however
presupposes the availability of comprehensive information about
modes of conduct and alternatives to the multinational enterprises.
The Information Centre on Multinational Enterprises which was
recently set up at the UN and the projected Technology Transfer
Information System can undertake important functions in this
respect. If the developing countries see at the same time to the
creation of an investment climate which keeps the inherent risk and
uncertainty within tolerable limits and leaves scope for
enterpreneurial decisions, the multinational enterprises will be
able to contribute significantly to the improvement of the
developing countries' participation in the international division
of labour.

NOTES

[1]Cf. Alfons Lemper, Die "alte" and die "neue" Ordung (The "old" and the "new" order), in: WIRTSCHAFTSDIENST, 55th year (1975), No. 5, p. 235ff. On the most important documents connected with the New International Economic Order cf. the compilations in: Federal Ministry for Economic Cooperation, Materialien zur Entwicklungspolitik, Nos. 45, 49, 51, and the Federal Government's second report on development policy, November 1975, appendix 6-8.

[2]On the question of the special advantages of multinational enterprises over local competition and other multinationals cf. Georg Koopmann, Warum gibt es multinationale Unternehmen? (Why are there multinational enterprises?), in: Dietrich Kebschull, Otto G. Mayer (eds.), Multinationale Unternehmen -- Anfang oder Ende der Weltwirtschaft? (Multinational enterprises -- Beginning or end of the international economy?), Frankfurt 1974, p. 41f.

[3]Cf. United Nations, Permanent Sovereignty over National Resources, Report to the Secretary General, A/9716, September 20, 1974, Annex, p. 1ff.

Transnational Corporations and Science and Technology in the NIEO

UNCTAD

I. INVESTMENT AND TECHNOLOGY: INTERNATIONAL MARKETS AND SELF RELIANCE

The international markets for investment and technology are characterized by imbalances in the bargaining strengths of, on the one hand, enterprises in developing countries which are for the most part buyers and, on the other, enterprises in developed countries -- many of them large transnational corporations -- which are for the most part sellers. The developing countries have for historical reasons been highly reliant on those markets, and, in general, have lagged behind in the development of their own capacities for business organization and for scientific and technological advance.

Transnational corporations have acquired considerable market power vis-a-vis the Governments and enterprises of developing countries. This has been due in part to their command over resources of various kinds -- finance, management, marketing networks and skills, technology and "know-how" generally; in part to their ability to combine and deploy such resources across the world; and in part because transnational corporations, particularly those enjoying monopolistic positions, have generally integrated their subsidiaries and affiliates into the company as a whole, rather than as autonomous enterprises. Transnational corporations have been able to take advantage of their strong bargaining positions in a variety of ways -- on occasion by interfering in the political affairs of the host country -- and the relationships between transnational corporations and host countries have often involved patterns of growth and industrialization that cause the

From TOWARDS THE NEW INTERNATIONAL ECONOMIC ORDER: ANALYTICAL REPORT ON DEVELOPMENTS IN THE FIELD OF INTERNATIONAL ECONOMIC CO-OPERATION SINCE THE SIXTH SPECIAL SESSION OF THE GENERAL ASSEMBLY, U.N., 1982, reprinted by permission of the publisher.

benefits of investment and associated activity to be distributed inequitably and that limit the ability of developing countries to pursue self-reliant development.

Host countries have a strong interest in ensuring that transnational corporations behave as autonomous enterprises: for example, ensuring that an affiliate's growth and diversification are not curtailed in the interests of the parent company when such growth is to the benefit of the affilliate and the host country; that it is not obliged to purchase materials from the parent when cheaper sources are available; that it is not prevented from extending and deepening its linkages with domestic suppliers; that the affiliate is not prevented from exporting its output for the purpose of protecting its parent company's position; and that it is not prevented because of the retention of control in the hands of the parent company from employing nationals in management and from using local engineering and design capabilities. The host Government may also have a longer-term perspective than the transnational corporation.

On the other hand, transnational corporations, being commercial enterprises, undertake their activities in order to make profits, taking due account of the risks involved. If their various capabilities are to be harnessed, transnational corporations must be able to earn an adequate rate of return on their investments and enjoy a reasonable degree of security. Stability is important in order for the relationship between company and country to be mutually advantageous; at the same time, fairness is needed to ensure stability.

Experience shows that in order for the capabilities of transnational corporations to be mobilized for the development of the host country, systematic efforts are required to ensure that the division of benefits between the company and the country is equitable and mutually advantageous, and that the activities of transnational corporations result in a strengthening -- rather than a stunting -- of domestic and especially technological capacities. Indeed, increased self-reliance, in the sense of being able autonomously to set goals, make decisions and implement them, is essential both for strengthening the countervailing power of the host country and to ensure that the transnational corporation acts in accordance with the interest of the host country.

The enormous strides made in the countries with developed economies in the field of science and technology constitute another and partly overlapping set of capabilities that must be harnessed effectively to accelerate the development, including the technological transformation, of developing countries. The access of developing countries to this potential has been inadequate in scale and has been on unfavourable terms and conditions. This has been partly because developing countries have lagged in establishing and strengthening their own capacities to absorb, adapt and diffuse scientific and technological advances acquired from abroad and to generate new scientific and technological advances of their own. The technological transformation required to generate genuine development has therefore taken place on only a very small scale.

To remove imbalances and distortions in the international

market for investment and scientific and technological knowledge, action is required to reduce monopolistic behaviour and impediments to the flow of information generally, and to build up the bargaining power and infrastructure of developing countries; these tasks are closely interrelated, for increased self-reliance will bring with it greater bargaining power in the international market. Such action needs to be blended with measures to tap more fully the development potential of transnational corporations and foreign scientific and technological advances.

The basic texts on the new international economic order reflect the pervasive role, negative and positive, that transnational corporations have played in the development and international economic relations of developing countries, and the strategic importance of the application of science and technology to development. The declaration (resolution 3201 (S-VI)) included among its principles the "regulation and supervision of the activities of transnational corporations by taking measures in the interest of the national economies of the countries where such transnational corporations operate on the basis of the full sovereignty of those countries" (para. 4 (g)) and "giving to the developing countries access to the achievements of modern science and technology, and promoting the transfer of technology and the creation of indigenous technology for the benefit of the developing countries in forms and in accordance with procedures which are suited to their economies" (para. 4 (p)).

Similarly the programme of action (resolution 3202 (S-VI)) contained provisions on the encouragement of foreign investment, the transfer of technology, and the regulation of and control over the activities of transnational corporations. The Charter of Economic Rights and Duties of States (resolution 3281 (XXIX)) also set out principles covering permanent sovereignty, the regulation and exercise of sovereignty over foreign investment, the regulation and supervision of the activities of transnational corporations, and nationalization and principles covering the transfer of technology and creation of indigenous technology and infrastructure. Moreover, resolution 3362 (S-VII) on development and international economic co-operation contained a number of proposals designed to improve the functioning of the technology market and to augment the capacities of developing countries; it also called for a strengthening of the contribution of the United Nations system in the application of science and technology for development, and for the convening of a United Nations conference on science and technology for development.

II. PARTICIPATION IN AND CONTROL OVER
TRANSNATIONAL CORPORATIONS

Developing countries have taken a variety of policy measures designed to exercise authority over the activities of transnational corporations in order to bring them in line with national development objectives. This has been particularly evident in the industrial sector, especially in the production of capital goods, which is generally technology-intensive and where the tendency of affiliates of transnational corporations to integrate with the parent has often been found inimical to the extension of intersectoral linkages in the national economy and of technological capabilities such as engineering services.

Some host Governments have excluded transnational corporations from direct investment in all or some sectors and activities regarded as being of key strategic importance for the economy. In some cases, the goods have been produced by domestic enterprises, with the aid of input, such as technology, acquired from abroad under contractual arrangements. On occasion, this has not proved possible and the goods have had to be imported.

In other cases, the Government has sought to reconcile direct foreign investment with national objectives by means of measures aimed at ensuring that the affiliate of the transnational corporation behaves as an autonomous enterprise. Various instruments have been used to that end. Some operate on the parameters affecting the decisions of the affiliate of the transnational corporation. However, instruments that set the framework for company decisions have tended to be less effective as a means of bringing about affirmative action, such as expanding output or local content, to the extent that this is not considered to be in the strategic interest of the transnational corporation. Some developing countries have, therefore, also sought to exercise control by having nationals (in some case private firms, in others state enterprises, and sometimes a combination of the two) participate in the ownership, and hence in the decisions, of the foreign affiliate. Increasingly, transnational corporations have been prevailed upon to operate through joint ventures rather than wholly-owned affiliates, as they generally prefer. Nevertheless, they have often been in a sufficiently strong bargaining position (for example, because of a dominant position in the technology or in the market for the product) either to resist such participation, or to retain control over decisions through their control over management or through special contractual provisions.

The control attained by national entities through participation in ownership has frequently proved symbolic rather than genuine. Indeed, in some cases government participation in equity has yielded financial benefits to the transnational corporation without causing it to lose its influence over the operations. But experience also shows that the right measures applied in favourable circumstances can give the host country a real measure of control.

For these reasons Governments have found a dual approach necessary, involving both the settling of the parameters of a framework governing company decisions and participation in the decision-making process itself by domestic entities, including state enterprises. Transnational corporations have made increasing efforts to adapt to these policies in the manner sought by the host country, but the process is far from being advanced.

Host Governments have also become increasingly sophisticated as regards the distribution of the financial costs and benefits of investments of transnational corporations. Many Governments have adjusted their investment requirements, and their laws and regulations generally, in order to ensure that the rate of return earned by the foreign investor is not in excess of the minimum acceptable to it; at the same time, it has been found that frequent changes in government policies tend to undermine investors' confidence and deter new investments since foreign investors may value stability more than generous terms which may subsequently be withdrawn.

Host Governments have been increasingly aware of the fact that transnational corporations command a host of techniques for disguising and withdrawing profits, and many have sought to be comprehensive in their coverage of the various channels of profit remission and to monitor enterprises, concentrating on the largest transnational corporations. Efforts have also been made to prevent abusive transfer pricing. However, the Government's ability to monitor observance of the rules laid down depends critically on an adequate system of reporting by transnational corporations and on its capacity for verifying information received. Information on practices of transnational corporations and pricing policies is hard to find in published sources but could be a subject for exchange of information among Governments. This area accordingly calls for increased attention.

III. TRANSFER AND DEVELOPMENT OF TECHNOLOGY

Although the internationalization of production by transnational corporations has resulted in an expansion of the geographic area over which modern production techniques are deployed, it has not resulted automatically in an effective transfer of technology to host countries. The transnational corporation has a strong incentive not to disclose the technology used and thereby foster its diffusion, adaptation and mastery by the host country if that puts in jeopardy its source of market power. This tends to limit the spillover of its technology to the host country.

Many developing countries have used instruments of control and participation to counteract this tendency and the dependence of the affiliate on the parent for proprietary and non-proprietary technology by requiring transnational corporations to form joint ventures with domestic enterprises having technological capacity, and by instituting rules and regulations designed to increase research and development and training by the affiliate, localization of staff, and links between the affiliate and local scientific and research institutions. Moreover, these countries have found it necessary to set guiding parameters for imports of technology in certain branches in order to ensure that involvement by transnational corporations results in genuine transfer and absorption, and to prevent the use of technology that is inappropriate to the conditions of the host countries.

In preference to technology transfer through direct foreign

investment, a large number of developing countries have sought to acquire the technology through license or direct purchase and to separate it from the other elements of direct foreign investment, such as finance, management and marketing. They have also sought to disaggregate the various components of the technology which, though usually offered for sale as a bundle, may often be bought separately. Such a policy enlarges the scope for competitive bidding and for increasing the local component of the technology; it may not only represent savings in costs and in foreign exchange, but also foster local capabilities for manufacture of the equipment and components embodying the technology, strengthen national expertise and develop consultancy services. This consideration is of key importance for a number of countries, particularly those at a relatively advanced level of industrial development.

These policies have not always provided a ready answer to the problem of obtaining effective transfer and development of technology. For one thing, their scope has been restricted. In cases where a transnational corporation is confident of the superiority of its product it may be able to ensure that its technology is used only by an affiliate under its control or is sold only in the form of a complete system and not as individual components. By the same token, where engineering contractors with the skills to recombine various components are themselves dependent on the technology supplier, the incentive to require input for other sources may be weak or lacking. Some countries have, accordingly, placed great emphasis on the development of domestic capabilities in consultancy services.

Licensing has not always resulted in greater absorption and diffusion. The transnational corporation may be able in certain circumstances to maintain its control by means of restrictive conditions placed on the technology license, which may be so restrictive as to make the licensee a dependency of the licenser in all but name -- without any of the licenser's capital being placed at risk -- and seriously to limit the possibilities for local subcontracting and purchasing, and thus to hold up domestic technological development. Moreover, licensees in developing countries are often unable to resist the application of overly restrictive conditions because of their small size and limited access to information. They may also be unwilling to fend off attempts to limit the diffusion of the technology purchase, in order to safeguard their own competitive position.

By and large, developing countries have not looked to affiliates of transnational corporations to act as the main channel of technology transfer and have recognized that it is up to the country itself to advance its technological transformation by creating the conditions to adapt, absorb and develop the input of technology in its development process. The establishment and growth of infrastructure for research and development with effective linkages to the productive structure has been given increasing importance. Governments have also played an increasingly prominent role in ensuring a sufficient and growing demand for domestically produced technology.

Host countries have generally been concerned not only to secure a genuine transfer of technology from transnational corporations but also to minimize the cost of purchase. The pricing of technology raises particular difficulties, because research and development costs of new techniques tend to be high relative to the costs of production of the goods to which they give rise. This, together with the fact that the buyer often does not know the value of the technology until it has been acquired, introduces an extraordinarily wide range of bargaining possibilities. In these circumstances, custom and precedents have great importance, and access to information about comparable experience elsewhere is invaluable. However, such information may not be readily available, partly because of the practice of including confidentiality clauses in agreements covering not only the details of proprietary technology but also disclosure of the terms and conditions governing technology transfer. Co-operation among developing countries in this regard can be particularly useful. Some advance has been made, fostered to a degree by organizations of the United Nations system, but there would appear to be considerable scope for further progress.

The experience with government policies shows that adequate knowledge of the implications of alternative approaches is a prerequisite for successful government action, and that the availability of technical expertise to the Government, including the ability to collect and evaluate information, is critical in this context. Successful intervention also depends on the host country's bargaining power, which in turn hinges, inter alia, on the size and potential for its market. Regulation is therefore no substitute for the efforts of domestic enterprises to absorb technology and know-how, to keep abreast of innovations in their respective fields and to develop their own research and development capabilities. Moreover, technology policies need to be integrated with policies regarding scientific and technological education and with industrialization programmes. A number (though still small) of developing countries have formulated technology plans as an integral part of their over-all development plans, embracing essential responsibilities such as budgeting, management, co-ordination, stimulation and execution of technological activities, and covering specific requirements at the sectoral and intersectoral levels for the assessment, transfer, acquisition, adaptation and development of technology. In order to be viable, such planning should reflect short-term, medium-term and long-term strategies, including the determination of technological priorities, mobilization of natural resources, dissemination of the existing national stock of technology, identification of sectors in which imported technology would be required and determination of research and development priorities for the improvement of endogenous technologies. In particular, it must involve deliberate policies to initiate or accelerate the process of substituting domestic technology for imported.

The strengthening of domestic capabilities and bargaining power necessitates, as emphasized in the basic documents of the new international economic order, not only financial assistance and incentives at the national level, but also international programmes, including advisory services of various kinds, assistance in establishing and developing information systems and improving access to information regarding inventions, processes, patents, agreements, company structure, etc. This consideration has been reiterated in Economic and Social Council resolution 1980/60 of 24 July 1980, in which the Council recommended that the individual and collective self-reliance of developing countries should be enhanced, _inter alia_, by strengthening their negotiating capacity in their dealings with transnational corporations, particularly in the fields of financing and investment, science and technology, management, production and marketing, and by improving their capacity to regulate and accordingly to monitor the activities of transnational corporations. A number of organizations and other entities of the United Nations system have developed such activities, but there is ample room for expansion, as well as for efforts to ensure that they are mutually supportive in meeting the needs and priorities of developing countries.

IV. "RULES OF THE GAME"

Commercial transactions take place within a certain framework of rules, established by custom, administrative action and law. The nature of these rules, their coverage and mechanisms of enforcement influence significantly the efficiency and equity of the commercial transactions. Hence a significant component of efforts to establish the new international economic order has been the negotiation of new legal norms designed to provide a new setting for the functioning of the investment and technology markets so as to enhance their contribution to the development process.[1] These have been sought in order to limit abuses of market power by transnational corporations and by other sellers of technology and patents and to enhance their contribution to development, while protecting the legitimate interests of such entities with a view to mutually advantageous, and hence sustainable, relations.

While, as explained below, some advance has been made in the formulation of new "rules of the game" regarding transnational corporations and technology, a number of important stumbling blocks remain to be overcome. Among these are the extent to which the "rules" are to have a legal significance, and the extent to which they are to be directed at constraining the behaviour of the suppliers of investment and technology and to what extent that of Governments of developing countries. In any event, it may be noted that new "rules of the game" are not a substitute for action at the national level but rather a complement to such action.

1. Transnational Corporations

In accordance with section V of the Programme of Action on the establishment of a New International Economic Order, the United Nations Commission on Transnational Corporations has been drawing up a code of conduct. This code is expected to contain comprehensive and generally acceptable standards regarding the behaviour of transnational corporations and the treatment of transnational corporations by home and host Governments. These standards would require transnational corporations, <u>inter alia</u>, to respect national sovereignty, adhere to economic and social objectives, respect human rights, and abstain from interference in internal political affairs and intergovernmental relations. In addition to these general principles, specific standards would deal with the behaviour of transnational corporations regarding ownership and control, balance of payments and financing, transfer pricing, taxation, competition, restrictive business practices, transfer of technology and consumer and environmental protection. Regarding restrictive business practices, the code would refer to the Set of Multilaterally Agreed Principles and Rules for the Control of Restrictive Business Practices (TD/B/CONF/10) to be adopted by the General Assembly,[2] and regarding the transfer of technology it would refer to the code of conduct which is currently under negotiation. In the matter of employment and labour, the standards would refer to the Tripartite Declaration of Principles concerning Multinational Enterprises and Social Policy which was adopted by the International Labour Organisation in November 1977. The Commission is also developing standards regarding disclosure of information by transnational corporations to the public, Governments and trade unions and other representatives of employees, and a special intergovernmental group has started work on reporting standards. With respect to the treatment of transnational corporations by Governments, the code can be expected to set out appropriate norms in such areas as nationalization and compensation, jurisdiction, non-discrimination and national treatment. While there is a consensus that the resulting instrument should be effective, the question of legal character of the code remains unresolved. In any event, the effectiveness of the code will depend on the extent to which all Governments undertake a commitment towards its application at the national and international levels, and particularly towards the establishment of an international implementation machinery, including measures for intergovernmental co-operation. A system of periodic reviews of the application of the code and of consultations among Governments for all issues related to transnational corporations could contribute to the resolution of difficulties and to the maintenance of the consistency of the rules while, at the same time, permitting an evolution of those rules.

The strengthening of the legal framework of host countries in reference to transnational corporations is also an important objective of this work. Progress in that direction depends on the establishment of generally acceptable rules to serve as a yardstick

for evaluating the performance of transnational legislation.
Regardless whether the purpose of a given instrument is primarily
to prevent negative effects or to channel foreign direct investment
into desired directions, and regardless whether the level of
control and encouragement is national or international, it has been
found important that the legal and regulatory framework be kept
reasonably clear and stable. Reasonable stability does not, of
course, mean an indefinite freezing of laws and rules, but rather a
conscious effort to avoid abrupt discontinuities to the extent
feasible.

On the recommendation of the Commission, the Economic and
Social Council adopted Council resolution 1980/60 in which it
affirmed that the code of conduct should, inter alia, be effective,
comprehensive, generally accepted and universally adopted;
associate effectively the activities of transnational corporations
with the efforts to establish the new international economic order
and their capabilities with the developmental objectives of
developing countries; reflect the principle of respect by
transnational corporations for the national sovereignty, laws and
regulations of the countries in which they operate, as well as the
established policies of those countries and the right of States to
regulate and accordingly to monitor the activities of transnational
corporations; foster the contributions that transnational
corporations can make towards the achievement of developmental
goals and established objectives of the countries in which they
operate, particularly developing countries; and proscribe
subversion, interference in the internal affairs of countries and
other inadmissible activities by transnational corporations which
aim to undermine the political and social systems of the countries
in which they operate.

2. Technology

As called for in the Programme of Action on the new
international economic order, a United Nations Conference on an
International Code of Conduct on the Transfer of Technology was
convened under the auspices of UNCTAD. The over-all purpose of
the code is the establishment of a general and universal legal
framework for an adequate transfer and development of technology
with a view to strengthening the scientific and technological
capabilities of all countries, particularly the developing
countries.

More specifically, the code seeks (a) to establish general and
equitable standards on which to base the relationships between
parties to transactions in the field of transfer of technology and
Governments concerned, taking into consideration their legitimate
interests, and giving due recognition to the special needs of
developing countries for the fulfilment of their economic and
social development objectives; (b) to promote mutual confidence
between parties as well as their Governments; (c) to encourage

transfer of technology transactions, particularly those involving developing countries, under conditions where bargaining positions of the parties to the transactions are balanced in such a way as to avoid abuse of a stronger position and thereby to achieve mutually satisfactory agreements; (d) to facilitate and increase the international flow of technological information, particularly on the availability of alternative technologies, as a prerequisite for the assessment, selection, adaptation, development and use of technologies in all countries, particularly in developing countries; (e) to facilitate and increase the international flow of proprietary and non-proprietary technology for strengthening the growth of the scientific and technological capabilities of all countries, in particular developing countries, so as to increase their participation in world production and trade; (f) to increase the contributions of technology to the identification and solution of social and economic problems of all countries, particularly the developing countries, including the development of basic sectors of their national economies; (g) to facilitate the formulation, adoption and implementation of national policies, laws and regulations on the subject of transfer of technology by setting forth international norms; and (h) to promote adequate arrangements as regards unpackaging in terms of information concerning the various elements of the technology to be transferred, such as that required for technical, institutional and financial evaluation of the transaction, thus avoiding undue or unnecessary packaging.

The substantive provisions of the draft code fall into two broad categories: (a) those concerning the regulation of transactions involving transfer of technology and of the conduct of parties who enter into such transactions; and (b) those relating to possible or desirable measures by Governments, at the national level, or at the bilateral, multilateral, subregional, regional or interregional levels, concerning transfer of technology. The first category of provisions, establishing certain generally agreed and universally applicable standards, aims at determining which practices and arrangements involving transfer of technology are to be deemed undesirable and under what conditions; identifying and clarifying obligations as well as rights of parties to transfer of technology transactions; and defining the extent of the freedom of the parties to choose the law and forum for the settlement of their disputes. The second category of provisions relating to possible or desirable State and inter-State action in the field of transfer of technology comprises measures related to the regulation of transactions involving transfer of technology by particular States; measures concerning transfer of technology and related transactions that will be applied only where the acquiring country is a developing country; and measures concerning international co-operative activities of State, on a bilateral, multilateral, regional or interregional basis, to assist in transfer of technology and in the growth of the technological capabilities of developing countries.

Those two main categories of provisions of the draft code of conduct differ from each other in significant aspects, although both are intimately related and may best be understood as complementary and, to a degree, interdependent. Provisions under the first category embody mutually agreed standards applicable to all transfer of technology transactions. Those under the second category deal with desirable or permissible action which countries may wish to take either on account of their national policies relating to the acquisition of technology or because they deem such action appropriate in order to assist developing countries, in view of the special conditions prevailing in the latter.

While there is consensus that the code must apply universally and to all parties including branches, subsidiaries and affiliates, joint ventures or other legal entities regardless of the economic and other relationships between and among them, the question of the extent of the application of the chapter regulating restrictive practices to enterprises belonging to the same concern remains unresolved and is one of the main issues outstanding in the present negotiations. An important component of the draft code of conduct is the international institutional machinery to be set up to monitor the application and implementation of its provisions. It will provide for a review conference some years after the adoption of the instrument for the purpose of reviewing all the aspects of the code. A fundamental counterpart to the code negotiations is the action to be undertaken at the national level to implement policies and regulations with respect to transactions involving transfer of technology consistent with the objectives and principles of the code of conduct.

3. Industrial Property

In accordance with General Assembly resolution 3362 (S-VII), efforts have been exerted to ensure that the current revision of the Paris Convention for the Protection of Industrial Property, which is being undertaken by a Diplomatic Conference under the auspices of the World Intellectual Property Organization, should meet, in particular, the special needs of developing countries. This is the first time in the history of the Convention that the special interests of the developing countries are being explicitly taken into account. The developing countries are pressing for the establishment of a fair balance between, on the one hand, the broader needs of development -- particularly the promotion of the effective industrial exploitation of inventions and the recognition by patent granting countries of the need to prevent abuses which might result from the exclusive rights conferred by the industrial property system -- and the rights of patent holders, on the other.

The Diplomatic Conference on the Revision of the Paris Convention has held one session (Geneva, 4 February to 4 March 1980) at which it agreed to new rules of procedure which give developing countries a greater say, as compared to the rules in force on previous revision. The proposals before the Conference include two elements commanding a wide measure of agreement which are of interest to the developing countries. One of these provides for effective rules to enable developing countries to exercise the right to grant non-voluntary licenses where the patented invention is not sufficiently worked by the patent holder. The other envisages a new article in the Convention which would strengthen the commitment of member States collectively to contribute to the development of developing countries by means of industrial property. It is expected that the Conference will be reconvened during 1981 in order to complete its work.

V. OUTFLOW OF SKILLED PERSONNEL

In resolution 3362 (S-VII), the General Assembly stated that "since the outflow of qualified personnel from developing to developed countries seriously hampers the development of the former, there is an urgent need to formulate national and international policies to avoid the 'brain drain' and to obviate its adverse effects" (sect. III, para. 10).

Significant progress has been made in identifying the nature and magnitude of the problem, and a basis has been laid for the elaboration of concrete measures, in the context of UNCTAD resolution 102 (V)[3] on development aspects of the reverse transfer of technology. In that resolution it was recognized that the problem of reverse transfer of technology is a multifaceted one, encompassing social, economic and development issues as well as political, civil and human aspects; that in order to have a balanced understanding of the issues and to improve the policy responses, there is a need for studying the experience of countries belonging to different geographical areas; and that there is a need for a comprehensive approach to reverse transfer of technology. The next phase of work will need to be directed at formulating a comprehensive plan of action and strategies for its implementation, including in particular the co-operative exchange of skills among developing countries.

VI. VIENNA PROGRAMME OF ACTION ON SCIENCE AND TECHNOLOGY FOR DEVELOPMENT

In accordance with section III, paragraph 7, of resolution 3362 (S-VII), the United Nations Conference on Science and Technology for development was held at Vienna from 20 to 31 August 1979. The Conference was, inter alia, conceived as an integral part of the establishment of a new international economic order, and one of its objectives was to adopt concrete decisions on ways and means of applying science and technology in establishing a new international economic order, and as a strategy aimed at economic and social development within a defined time-frame.

A principal achievement of the Conference, as well as of its preparatory process, was to heighten national awareness of the importance of science and technology as an instrument of development in developing countries, cutting across the spectrum of development in an intersectoral and multidimensional matrix, and the need to bridge the technological gap between the developed and developing countries. The principal focus of the Vienna Programme of Action on Science and Technology for Development[4] adopted by the Conference and endorsed by the General Assembly in its resolution 34/218 of 19 December 1979 encompasses strengthening the scientific and technological capacities of developing countries; restructuring the existing pattern of international scientific and technological relations and strengthening the role of the United Nations in the field of science and technology and the provision of increased financial resources.

Among the numerous recommendations contained in the Programme of Action special mention may be made of the establishment of a United Nations Financing System for Science and Technology for Development beginning with an Interim Fund, designed to provide additional financial resources required to strengthen scientific and technological capacities of the developing countries and, as a part of the restructuring process, to support programmes and activities designed to supplement the efforts of developing countries in the field of science and technology. A pledging conference for the Interim Fund was held in March 1980 and resulted in firm and anticipated pledges of $45.7 million. On this basis, the Interim Fund, which is administered by UNDP, became operational in May 1980. Project requests already received far exceed the resources pledged, and it is essential that resources available to the Fund be augmented as soon as possible, to give practical substance to the agreement reached in Vienna and endorsed by the General Assembly in its resolution 34/218 that the target for voluntary contributions for the two-year period 1980 and 1981 should be no less than $250 million.

An intergovernmental group of experts, with the support of the Director-General for Development and International Economic Co-operation, has been charged with the responsibility of preparing the detailed structure and framework of the long-range financing system that would succeed the Interim Fund. In determining the nature and level of the resources of the financing system, a number of considerations would be taken into account, including the asymmetry of technological capacity between developed and developing countries, the need for predictability, continuity, and a substantial increase in the flow of resources, particularly of untied resources for the scientific and technological development of the developing countries.

One of the principal functions of the Inter-Governmental Committee, which is open to all Member States and is to assist the General Assembly in the area of policy making and in co-ordinating science and technology activities within the United Nations system, is to prepare an operational plan for carrying out the Vienna Programme of Action and to identify priorities with a view to facilitating operational planning at the national, subregional, regional, interregional and international levels. The activities in respect of which the Committee will give policy guidance include, among others, the provision of advisory services to developing countries to strengthen their endogenous capacities, the acquisition of foreign technology, and the establishment of an international technological information network, with a view to helping developing countries to achieve national and collective self-reliance.

The General Assembly, in its resolution 34/218, gave fresh recognition to the fundamental and pervasive role of science and technology in the development process and reaffirmed the paramount importance of the application of science and technology for development in establishing a new international economic order and in achieving the goals and objectives of the third United Nations Development Decade. This points up, among other things, the importance of improved international co-operation for the transfer of technology and the need to bring the negotiations on the code of conduct to a speedy conclusion and effective implementation. The valuable conceptual breakthroughs provided by the Programme of Action on the application of science and technology for development also require adequate follow-up. In addition, there is the need to monitor and assess new and advanced scientific and technological developments which may adversely affect the development process.

International action in the coming years should lay particular stress on marshalling the science and technology resources of the world, in a concerted manner, towards the objective of creating and strengthening endogenous science and technology capacities in developing countries. It also should accord greater importance to strengthening in particular the research and development capacities of developing countries, including measures directed towards reducing the research and development gap between the developed and developing countries. Notwithstanding the unsuccessful attempts initiated by the international development strategy for the Second United Nations Development Decade, strenuous efforts seem necessary to achieve a consensus regarding quantified targets in the field of science and technology, particularly as regards contributions from developed countries. These targets can usefully be considered in conjunction and in the light of their consistency with both over-all and sectoral growth rates in the context of the implementation of the new international development strategy.

NOTES

[1] Parallel to these efforts, work has proceeded on equitable rules and principles for the control of restrictive business practices, which pertain to services as well as goods, and are also intended to provide new "rules of the game" for business enterprises. See chap. III above.

[2] See chap. IV above. The key section of the Set is the Principles and Rules for enterprises, including transnational corporations, which describe in detail the restrictive business practices from which enterprises should refrain. The Set also contains principles and rules for States relating, inter alia, to the adoption and improvement of appropriate legislation and the implementation of judicial and administrative procedures.

[3] See TD/268, part one, sect. A.

[4] Report of the United Nations Conference on Science and Technology for Development, Vienna, 20-31 August 1979 (United Nations publication, Sales No. E.79.I.21 (A/CONF.81/16 and corrigenda), chap. VII.

PART II
STATISTICAL INFORMATION AND SOURCES

Main purpose of this section is to provide a current bibliography of data sources and statistical data for various indicators of international development, as they relate to special needs of the developing countries. An attempt is made to provide the reader with an overview of global trends, based on an analysis of the country data, as it is sometimes difficult to form any such general impression when faced with a general body of highly detailed data.

I. BIBLIOGRAPHY OF INFORMATION SOURCES

AFRICAN STATISTICAL YEARBOOK, UN

Presents data arranged on a country basis for 44 African countries for the years 1965-1978. Available statistics for each country are presented in 48 tables: population; national accounts; agriculture, forestry, and fishing industry; transport and communications; foreign trade; prices; finance; and social statistics: education and medical facilities.

ASIAN INDUSTRIAL DEVELOPMENT NEWS, UN, Sales no. E.74.II.F.16

In four parts: (a) brief reports on the ninth session of the Asian Industrial Development Council and twenty-sixth session of the Committee on Industry and Natural Resources; (b) articles on multinationals and the transfer of know-how, acquisition of technology for manufacturing agro-equipment, fuller utilization of industrial capacity; (c) report of Asian Plan of Action on the Human Environment; and (d) statistical information on plywood, transformers, and transmission cables.

Banks, Arthur S., et al., eds.
ECONOMIC HANDBOOK OF THE WORLD: 1981. New York; London; Sydney
and Tokyo: McGraw-Hill Books for State University of New York
at Binghamton, Center for Social Analysis, 1981.

Descriptions, in alphabetical order, of all the world's independent
states and a small number of non-independent but economically
significant areas (such as Hong Kong). Data are current as of
1 July 1980 whenever possible. Summary statistics for each country
include: area, population, monetary unit, Gross National Product
per capita, international reserves (1979 year end), external
public debt, exports, imports, government revenue, government
expenditure, and consumer prices. Principal economic institutions,
financial institutions, and international memberships are listed
at the end of each description.

BULLETIN OF LABOUR STATISTICS. Quarterly, with supplement 8
times per year. Approx. 150 p.

Quarterly report, with supplements in intervening months, on
employment, unemployment, hours of work, wages, and consumer
prices, for 130-150 countries and territories. Covers total,
nonagricultural, and manufacturing employment; total unemployment
and rate; average nonagricultural and manufacturing hours of
work per week, and earnings per hour, day, week, or month; and
food and aggregate consumer price indexes.

COMPENDIUM OF SOCIAL STATISTICS, 1977. 1980, UN, Sales No. E-F.
80.XVII.6.

Contains a collection of statistical and other data aimed at
describing social conditions and social change in the world.
In four parts. Part 1 includes estimates and projections for
the world, macroregions, and regions. Part 2 comprises data
for countries or areas that represent key series describing social
conditions and social change. Part 3 consists of general
statistical series for countries or areas. Part 4 is devoted
to information for cities or urban agglomerations. Includes
a total of 151 tables, covering population, health, nutrition,
education, conditions of work, housing and environmental
conditions, etc. Provides an overall view of the world social
situation and future trends.

DEMOGRAPHIC YEARBOOK, 1978. (ST-ESA-STAT-SER.R-7) 1979, UN,
Sales No. E-F.79.XIII.I.

--Vol. 1. viii, 463 p. This volume contains the general tables
giving a world summary of basic demographic statistics, followed
by tables presenting statistics on the size distribution and
trends in population, natality, fetal mortality, infant and
maternal mortality, general mortality, nuptiality, and divorce.
Data are also shown by urban/rural residence in many of the tables.
--Vol. 2: Historical supplement.

DEVELOPMENT FORUM BUSINESS EDITION.   DESI/DOP, UN, Palais des
Nations, CH-1211 Geneva 10, Switzerland.   24 times a yr.   16 p.

A tabloid-size paper, published jointly by the United Nations
Department of Information's Divison for Economic and Social
Information and the World Bank. Presents articles on all aspects
of the development work of the United Nations, with emphasis
on specific development problems encountered by the business
community. Contains notices referring to goods and works to be
procured through international competitive bidding for projects
assisted by the World Bank and the International Development
Association (IDA). It also includes a Supplement of the World
Bank, entitled "Monthly Operational Summary", and a similar
supplement of the Inter-American Development Bank (IDB), once
a month, which provide information about projects contemplated
for financing by the World Bank and IDB, respectively.

DEVELOPMENT FORUM GENERAL EDITION

A tabloid-size paper, published jointly by the United Nations
Department of Public Information's Division for Economic and
Social Information and the World Bank, having as objective the
effective mobilization of public opinion in support of a number
of major causes to which the United Nations is committed. Presents
articles reporting on the activities of various UN agencies
concerned with development and social issues (health, education,
nutrition, women in development). Includes a forum for
nongovernmental organizations (NGO's) and book reviews.

DEVELOPMENT AND INTERNATIONAL ECONOMIC CO-OPERATION: LONG-TERM
TRENDS IN ECONOMIC DEVELOPMENT. Report of the Secretary-General.
Monograph.   May 26, 1982.

Report analyzing world economic development trends, 1960's-81,
with projections to 2000 based on the UN 1980 International
Development Strategy, and on alternative low and medium economic
growth assumptions. Presents data on GDP, foreign trade,
investment, savings, income, population and labor force, housing,
education, food and energy supply/demand, and other economic
and social indicators.

DIRECTORY OF INTERNATIONAL STATISTICS: VOLUME 1.   1982 Series.
Sales No. E.81.XVII.6

Vol. 1 of a 2-volume directory of international statistical time
series compiled by 18 UN agencies and selected other IGO's. Lists
statistical publications, and machine-readable data bases of
economic and social statistics, by organization and detailed
subject category. Also includes bibliography and descriptions
of recurring publications, and technical descriptions of
economic/social data bases.

VOLUME 2:   INTERNATIONAL TABLES.   Sales No. E.82.XVII.6, Vol. II

Presents analytical summary of major income and product accounts for approximately 160 countries, by country and world region.

ECONOMIC AND SOCIAL PROGRESS IN LATIN AMERICA: 1980-81 REPORT. 1981, IDB.

Provides a comprehensive survey of the Latin America economy since 1970, with particular emphasis on 1980 and 1981. Part One is a regional analysis of general economic trends, the external sector, the financing of development from internal and external sources, regional economic integration, and social development trends (women in the economic development of Latin America). Part Two contains country summaries of socioeconomic trends for 24 States members of IDB. Statistical appendix includes data on population, national accounts, public finance, balance of payments, primary commodity exports, external public debt, and hydrocarbons.

ECONOMIC AND SOCIAL SURVEY OF ASIA AND THE PACIFIC, 1977. The International Economic Crises and Developing Asia and the Pacific. 1978, UN, Sales No. E.78.II.F.1.

In two parts: (a) review of recent economic developments and emerging policy issues in the ESCAP region, 1976-1977; and (b) the impacts of the international economic crises of the first half of the 1970's upon selected developing economies in the ESCAP region and the market and policy response thereto. Topics discussed include: the food crisis; the breakdown of the international monetary system; fluctuations in the international market economy comprising the primary commodities export boom, the associated inflation and the subsequent recession, and, finally the sharp rise in the price of petroleum.

ECONOMIC AND SOCIAL SURVEY OF ASIA AND THE PACIFIC, 1979. Regional Development Strategy for the 1980's. 1981, UN, Sales No. E.80.II.F.1.

Analyzes recent economic and social development in the UN ESCAP region, as well as related international developments. Focuses on economic and social policy issues and broad development strategies. In two parts: (a) recent economic developments, 1978-1979, covering the second oil price shock economic performance of the developing countries of the ESCAP region, inflation, and external trade and payments; and (b) findings of a two-year study dealing with regional developmental strategies, covering economic growth, policies for full employment and equity, energy, technology, implementation systems, international trade, shipping, international resource transfers, and intraregional cooperation.

ECONOMIC SURVEY OF ASIA AND THE FAR EAST, 1973. 234 p. (also issued as Economic Bulletin for Asia and the Far East, vol. 24, no. 4), 1974, UN, Sales No. E.74.II.F.1.

Contains a general summary followed by Part One, which covers: education and employment--the nature of the problem; population, labor force and structure of employment and underemployment in the ECAFE [ESCAP] region; the role of location--assumptions underlying the education policies of developing countries in the ECAFE region; momentum and direction of expansion of education; structuring the flow of workers into the modern science of education for self employment--the traditional and informal sectors; and the search for new policies--a review of current thinking. Part Two covers: current economic developments--recent economic developments and emerging policy issues in the ECAFE region, 1972/73; and current economic developments and policies in 28 countries of the ECAFE region.

ECONOMIC SURVEY OF LATIN AMERICA. Series.

Series of preliminary annual reports analyzing recent economic trends in individual Latin American countries. Each report presents detailed economic indicators, including GDP by sector, agricultural and industrial production by commodity, foreign trade, public and private sector finances, and prices. Also includes selected data on employment and earnings.

THE ECONOMIST. THE WORLD IN FIGURES. Third edition. New York: Facts on File, Inc., 1980.

Compendium of figures on economic, demographic, and sociopolitical aspects of over 200 countries of the world. The first part is a world section with information on population, national income, production, energy, transportation, trade, tourism, and finance. The second part is organized by country (grouped by main region), containing statistics on location, land, climate, time, measurement systems, currency, people, resources, production, finance and external trade, and politics and the economy. The data, from many sources, cover through 1976. Country name and "special focus" indices.

FACTS OF THE WORLD BANK. Monthly (current issues).

A compilation of figures on World Bank lending, giving cumulative amounts and amounts for the current fiscal year of commitments by number of projects and by sector, as well as for each country by region. Also gives figures on sales of parts of Bank loans and IDA credits and on World Bank borrowings by currency of issue, original and outstanding amounts, and number of issues.

IMF SURVEY. Biweekly.

Biweekly report on international financial and economic conditions; IMF activities; selected topics relating to exchange rates, international reserves, and foreign trade; and economic performance of individual countries and world areas.

MAIN ECONOMIC INDICATORS: HISTORICAL STATISTICS, 1960-1979.
1980, OECD, Sales No. 2750 UU-31 80 20 3.

Bilingual: E-F. Replaces previous editions. Base year for
all indicators is 1970. Arranged in chapters by country, the
tables cover the period 1960 to 1979, and are followed by short
notes describing some major characteristics of the series, and,
where applicable, indicating breaks in continuity. Note:
Supplements the monthly bulletin Main Economic Indicators.

MONTHLY BULLETIN OF STATISTICS. Monthly.

Monthly report presenting detailed economic data including
production, prices, and trade; and summary population data; by
country, with selected aggregates for world areas and economic
groupings, or total world. Covers population size and vital
statistics; employment; industrial production, including energy
and major commodities; construction activity; internal and external
trade; passenger and freight traffic; manufacturing wages;
commodity and consumer prices; and money and banking. Each issue
includes special tables, usually on topics covered on a regular
basis but presenting data at different levels of aggregation
and for different time periods. Special tables are described
and indexed in IIS as they appear.

POPULATION AND VITAL STATISTICS REPORT. Quarterly.

Quarterly report on world population, births, total and infant
deaths, and birth and death rates, by country and territorial
possession, as of cover date. Also shows UN population estimates
for total world and each world region.

QUARTERLY BULLETIN OF STATISTICS FOR ASIA AND THE PACIFIC.
Quarterly.

Quarterly report presenting detailed monthly and quarterly data
on social and economic indicators for 38 ESCAP member countries.
Includes data on population; births and deaths; employment;
agricultural and industrial production; construction;
transportation; foreign trade quantity, value, and direction;
prices; wages; and domestic and international financial activity.

1978 REPORT ON THE WORLD SOCIAL SITUATION. 1979, UN, Sales No.
E.79.IV.1.

Deals with the global issues of population trends and employment;
growth and distribution of income and private consumption; the
production and distribution of social services; and changing
social concerns. A supplement reviews the patterns of recent
governmental expenditures for social services in developing
countries, developed market economies, and centrally planned
economies.

STATISTICAL INDICATORS FOR ASIA AND THE PACIFIC.   Quarterly.

Quarterly report presenting selected economic and demographic indicators for 26 Asian and Pacific countries. Covers, for most countries, population size, birth and death rates, family planning methods, industrial and agricultural production, construction, transport, retail trade, foreign trade, prices, money supply, currency exchange rate, and GDP.

STATISTICAL YEARBOOK, 1979/80.   1981, UN, Sales No. E/F.81.XVII.1.

A comprehensive compendium of the most important internationally comparable data needed for the analysis of socioeconomic development at the world, regional and national levels. Includes tables (200) grouped in two sections: (a) world summary by regions (17 tables); and (b) remaining tables of country-by-country data, arranged in chapters: population; manpower; agriculture; forestry; fishing; industrial production; mining and quarrying; manufacturing; construction; development assistance; wholesale and retail trade; external trade; international tourism; transport; communications; national accounts; wages and prices; consumption; finance; energy; health; housing; science and technology; and culture. For this first time, this issue contains three new tables on industrial property: patents, industrial designs, and trademarks and service marks. Note: This issue is a special biennial edition, covering data through mid-1980, and in some cases for 1980 complete.

STATISTICAL YEARBOOK FOR ASIA AND THE PACIFIC, 1978.   1979, UN, Sales No. E-F.79.II.F.4.

Eleventh issue. Contains statistical indicators for the ESCAP region and statistics for period up to 1978 available at the end of 1978 for 34 countries and territories members of ESCAP, arranged by country, covering, where available: population; manpower; national accounts; agriculture, forestry, and fishing; industry; consumption; transport and communication; internal and external trade; wages, prices, and household expenditures; finance; and social statistics.

STATISTICAL YEARBOOK FOR LATIN AMERICA, 1979.   1981, UN, Sales No. E/S.80.II.G.4.

In two parts. Part 1 presents indicators of economic and social development in Latin America for 1960, 1965, 1970 and 1975-1978, including: population; demographic characteristics; employment and occupational structure; income distribution; living levels; consumption and nutrition; health; education; housing; global economic growth; agricultural activities; mining and energy resources; manufacturing; productivity; investment; saving; public financial resources; public expenditure; structure of exports and imports; intra-regional trade; transport services; tourist services; and external financing. Part 2 contains historical series in absolute figures for the years 1960, 1965 and 1970-1978

on population; national accounts; domestic prices; balance of
payments; external indebtedness; external trade; natural resources
and production of goods; infrastructure services; employment;
and social conditions.

SURVEY OF ECONOMIC AND SOCIAL CONDITIONS IN AFRICA, 1980-81 AND
OUTLOOK FOR 1981-82: SUMMARY

Examines growth in GDP, agricultural and industrial production,
trade and balance of payments, resource flows, energy
production/consumption, and selected other economic indicators,
1979-80, with outlook for 1981-82 and trends from 1960's.

TECHNICAL DATA SHEETS

Provides up-to-date information about projects as they are approved
for World Bank and IDA financing. In addition to a description
of the project, its total cost, and the amount of Bank financing,
each technical data sheet describes the goods and services that
must be provided for the project's implementation and gives the
address of the project's implementing organization. On the
average, 250 such sheets will be issued annually. Requests for
sample copies are to be addressed to: Publications Distribution
Unit, World Bank, 1818 H St., N.W., Washington, D.C. 20433,
U.S.A.

UNESCO STATISTICAL YEARBOOK, 1978-79, 1266 p. 1980, UNESCO.

Composite: E/F/S (introductory texts). Presents statistical
and other information for 206 countries on education; science
and technology; libraries; museums and related institutions;
theater and other dramatic arts; book production; newspapers
and other periodicals; film and cinema; radio broadcasting; and
television. In this edition, the summary tables relating to
culture and communications, previously given in the introduction
to each of the corresponding chapters, have been grouped together
in a separate chapter.

World Bank. ANNUAL REPORT, 1982. 1982, WBG.

Presents summary and background of the activities of the World
Bank Group during the fiscal year ended 30 June 1982, covering:
the International Bank for Reconstruction and Development (IBRD);
the International Development Association (IDA); and the
International Finance Corporation (IFC). Chapters cover: brief
review of Bank operations in fiscal 1982; a global perspective
of the economic situation; Bank policies, activities and finances
for fiscal 1982; 1982 regional perspectives; and Executive
Directors. Lists projects approved for IBRD and IDA assistance
in fiscal 1982 by sector, region and purpose. Also reviews trends
in lending by sector for 1980-82 and includes statistical annex.

WORLD BANK COUNTRY STUDIES. Series.

Series of studies, prepared by World Bank staff, on development issues and policies, and economic conditions in individual developing countries. Studies may focus on specific economic sectors or issues, or on general economic performance of the country as a whole.

The World Bank.
WORLD DEVELOPMENT REPORT, 1978. August 1978.

First volume in a series of annual reports designed to provide a comprehensive, continuing assessment of global development issues. After an overview of development in the past 25 years, the report discusses current policy issues and projected developments in areas of the international economy that influence the prospects of developing countries. Analyzes the problems confronting policy makers in developing countries, which differ in degree and in kind, affecting the choice of appropriate policy instruments, and recognizes that development strategies need to give equal prominence to two goals: accelerating economic growth and reducing poverty. Reviews development priorities for low-income Asia, sub-Saharan Africa, and middle-income developing countries.

The World Bank.
WORLD DEVELOPMENT REPORT, 1979. Washington, D.C.

Second in a series of annual reports designed to assess global development issues. Focuses on development in the middle income countries, with particular emphasis on policy choices for industrialization and urbanization. Part one assesses recent trends and prospects to 1990 and discusses capital flows, and energy. Part two focuses upon structural change and development policy relevant to employment, the balance between agriculture and industry, and urban growth. Part three reviews development experiences and issues in three groups of middle income countries: semi-industrialized nations; mineral primary-producing countries; and predominantly agricultural primary-producing countries. Maintains that progress toward expanding employment and reducing poverty in developing countries lies not only in internal policy choices but also in a liberal environment for international trade and capital flows.

The World Bank.
WORLD DEVELOPMENT REPORT, 1980. New York: Oxford University Press for the World Bank, 1980.

Third in a series of annual reports. Parts one examines economic policy choices facing both developing and developed countries and their implications for national and regional growth. Projects, to the year 2000 but particularly to the mid to late 1980's, growth estimates for oil-importing and oil-exporting developing countries; and analyzes the fundamental issues of energy, trade, and capital flows. Part two focuses on the links between poverty, growth, and human development. It examines the impact of

education, health, nutrition, and fertility on poverty; reviews
some practical lessons in implementing human development programs;
and discusses the trade-offs between growth and poverty and the
allocation of resources between human development and other
activities. Stresses the views that growth does not obviate
the need for human development and that direct measures to reduce
poverty do not obviate the need for economic expansion. Concludes
that world growth prospects have deteriorated in the past year,
but higher oil prices have impoved the outlook [for the first
half of the 1980's] for the fifth of the developing world's
population that lives in oil-exporting countries; however, the
four-fifths that live in oil-importing countries will experience
slower growth for the first half of the decade. Includes a
statistical appendix to part one; a bibliographical note; and
a very lengthy annex of World Development Indicators.

The World Bank.
WORLD DEVELOPMENT REPORT, 1981.   New York: Oxford University
Press for the World Bank, 1981.

With the major focus on the international context of development,
examines past trends and future prospects for international trade,
energy, and capital flows and the effects of these on developing
countries. Presents two scenarios for the 1980's, one predicting
higher growth rates than in the 1970's and one lower. Analyzes
national adjustments to the international economy, presenting
in-depth case studies. Concludes that countries pursuing
outward-oriented policies adjusted more easily to external shocks.
Contends that whichever scenario prevails, income differentials
will increase between the industrial and developing countries.
Low income countries have fewer options and less flexibility
of adjustment, therefore requiring continued aid from the more
affluent countries. Advocates policies to channel increased
resources to alleviate poverty.

The World Bank.
WORLD DEVELOPMENT REPORT, 1982.

The Report this year focuses on agriculture and food security.
As in previous years there is also a section on global prospects
and international issues, as well as the statistical annex of
World Development indicators.

The World Bank.
WORLD TABLES 1980:   FROM THE DATA FILES OF THE WORLD BANK.   Second
edition.   Baltimore and London: Johns Hopkins University Press
for the World Bank, 1980.

A broad range of internationally comparable statistical information
drawn from the World Bank data files. Includes historical time
series for individual countries in absolute numbers for most
of the basic economic indicators for selected years (1950-77
when available); also presents derived economic indicators for
selected periods of years and demographic and social data for

selected years. Although the number of social indicators is
fewer than those in the 1976 edition the quality of the data
has been improved through the use of more uniform definitions
and concepts, greater attention to population statistics, and
better statistics on balance of payments and central government
finance. Includes an index of country coverage.

WORLD ECONOMIC OUTLOOK: A SURVEY BY THE STAFF OF THE INTERNATIONAL
MONETARY FUND. 1980, IMF.

An in-depth forecast of the world economy in 1980 and a preliminary
summary for 1981. Chapters discuss: a profile of current
situation and short-term prospects; global perspectives for
adjustment and financing; industrial countries; developing
countries--oil-exporting and non-oil groups; and key policy issues.
Appendixes include country and regional surveys; technical notes
on the world oil situation, estimated impact of fiscal balances
in selected industrial countries, and monetary policy and
inflation; and statistical tables.

WORLD ECONOMIC OUTLOOK: A SURVEY BY THE STAFF OF THE INTERNATIONAL
MONETARY FUND. [1982 ed.] 1982, IMF.

A comprehensive analysis of economic developments, policies,
and prospects through June 1981 for industrial, oil exporting
and non-oil developing countries. It highlights persistent
imbalances in the world economy, high inflation, rising
unemployment, excessive rates of real interest, and unstable
exchange rates. Appendix A includes supplementary notes providing
information on selected topics in greater depth or detail than
in the main body of the report: country and regional surveys;
medium-term scenarios; fiscal development; monetary and exchange
rate development; world oil situation; growth and inflation in
non-oil developing countries; developments in trade policy; and
commodity price developments and prospects. Appendix B presents
statistical tables on: domestic economic activity and prices;
international trade; balance of payments; external debt;
medium-term projections; and country tables.

The World Bank.
WORLD BANK ATLAS. Fourteenth edition. 1979. Annual.

Presents estimates of gross national product (GNP) per capita
(1977), GNP per capita growth rates (1970-77), and population
(mid-1977), with population growth rates (1970-77) for countries
with populations of one million or more in three global maps;
a computer-generated map shows GNP per capita (1977) by major
regions. Six regional maps give the same data for 184 countries
and territories, as well as preliminary data for 1978. The base
years 1976-78 have been used for the conversion of GNP for both
1977 and 1978. A Technical Note explains in detail the methodology
used.

The World Bank.
WORLD DEVELOPMENT INDICATORS. June 1979. 71 pages.

A volume of statistics prepared in conjunction with and
constituting the Annex to the World Development Report, 1979
to provide information of general relevance about the main features
of economic and social development, reporting data for a total
of 125 countries whose population exceeds one million. Countries
are grouped in five categories and ranked by their 1977 per capita
gross national product (GNP) levels. The volume contains 24
tables covering some 110 economic and social indicators. The
choice of indicators has been based on data being available for
a large number of countries, the availability of historical series
to allow the measurement of growth and change, and on the relevance
of data to the principal processes of development.

The World Bank.
WORLD ECONOMIC AND SOCIAL INDICATORS. Quarterly (current issues).

Presents most recent available data on trade, commodity prices,
consumer prices, debt and capital flows, industrial production,
as well as social indicators and select annual data (by countries
where applicable). Each issue contains an article on topics
of current importance. Strategies for improving the access to
education of the disadvantaged rural poor by serving areas out
of range of existing schools are discussed and programs in four
projects financed by the World Bank are described.

WORLD ECONOMIC OUTLOOK: A SURVEY BY THE STAFF OF THE INTERNATIONAL
MONETARY FUND. Annual. April 1982. (Occasional Paper No. 9)

Annual report on economic performance of major industrial and
oil exporting and non-oil developing countries, 1970's-81 and
forecast 1982-83, with some projections to 1986. Includes analysis
of economic indicators for selected industrial countries, world
economic groupings, and world areas, primarily for IMF member
countries. Covers domestic economic activity, including prices,
GNP, and employment; international trade; balance of payments;
and foreign debt. Also includes financial indicators for selected
industrial countries, including government budget surpluses and
deficits, savings, money supply, and interest rates.

WORLD ECONOMIC SURVEY. 1978, UN, Sales No. E.78.II.C.1.

Provides an overview of salient developments in the world economy
in 1977 and the outlook for 1978. Focuses on policy needs for
improving the tempo of world production and trade. Examines
in detail the course of production and trade and related variables
in the developing economies, the developed market economies,
and the centrally planned economies.

WORLD ECONOMIC SURVEY 1979-80. 1980, UN, Sales No. E.80.II.C.2.

A survey of current world economic conditions and trends, with chapters on salient features and policy implications; the growth of world output, 1979-80; the accelerating pace of inflation; world trade and international payments; world economic outlook, 1980-1985; and adjustment policies in developing countries. Annexes cover external factors and growth in developing countries--the experience of the 1970's; supply and price of petroleum in 1979 and 1980; and prospective supply and demand for oil.

YEARBOOK OF NATIONAL ACCOUNTS STATISTICS, 1980.   Annual.   1982.

Annual report presenting national income and product account balances for approximately 170 countries, and for world areas and economic groupings, selected years 1970-79, often with comparisons to 1960 and 1965.   Data are compiled in accordance with the UN System of National Accounts (SNA) for market economies, and the System of Material Product Balances (MPS) for centrally planned economies.   SNA data include GDP final consumption expenditures by type; production, income/outlay, and capital formation accounts, by institutional sector; and production by type of activity.   MPS data include material and financial balances, manpower and resources, and national wealth and capital assets.

STATISTICAL NEWSLETTER.   Quarterly.

Quarterly newsletter on ESCAP statistical programs and activities, and major statistical developments in ESCAP countries.   Includes brief descriptions of meetings, working groups, upcoming international statistical training programs, and regional advisory services; and an annotated bibliography of recent ESCAP and UN statistical publications.

DIRECTORY OF UNITED NATIONS INFORMATION SYSTEMS.   IOB for UN, 1980.

Vol. 1:   Information Systems and Data Bases.   This volume gives particulars of United Nations family organizations and their information systems, together with the practical details, such as the address to contact for information, the conditions of access, the type of services that can be obtained.   Details are provided on where to obtain bibliographies, indexes and other publications which are frequently available in several languages. The information systems covered include libraries, referral centres, clearing-houses, data banks, statistical information systems and other data collections, computerized or manual.
Vol. 2:   Information Sources in Countries.   Gives information by country, to facilitate contact between users and organizations' systems and services.   More than 2,500 addresses in 167 countries are given.   The addresses include organizations' offices, centres contributing information or serving as contact points to the various systems, and depository libraries where the publications or organizations can be found.   Information is given on the publications and papers of the different organizations held in depository libraries and in United Nations Information Centres, and on the related services provided.

II. STATISTICAL TABLES AND FIGURES

This section focuses attention on some of the major economic and social indicators from a global and developing country perspective. It's aim is to highlight some generalizations made in the first part of this book as pointers to needed policies. The limited extent to which statistical information is cited in this book is solely for illustrative purposes. Most of the statistical information in the following pages have been reproduced from the following sources:

WORLD TABLES 1980: FROM THE DATA FILES OF THE WORLD BANK, Baltimore: Johns Hopkins University Press for the World Bank, 1980, (Reprinted by permission of the World Bank and Johns Hopkins University Press).

WORLD ECONOMIC AND SOCIAL INDICATORS, October 1978. Report No. 700/78/04. Washington, D.C.: WORLD BANK.

GLOBAL INDICATORS

TABLE 1. SOCIAL INDICATORS BY INCOME GROUP OF COUNTRIES

INDICATOR	DEVELOPING COUNTRIES EXCLUDING CAPITAL SURPLUS OIL EXPORTERS						(ADJUSTED COUNTRY GROUP AVERAGES)		
	LOW INCOME			LOWER MIDDLE INCOME			INTERMEDIATE MIDDLE INCOME		
	1960	1970	MOST RECENT ESTIMATE	1960	1970	MOST RECENT ESTIMATE	1960	1970	MOST RECENT ESTIMATE
GNP PER CAPITA (IN CURRENT US $)	67.4	107.4	162.0	136.1	239.6	398.6	225.6	410.9	817.9
POPULATION									
GROWTH RATE (%) – TOTAL	2.2	2.4	2.4	2.7	2.7	2.6	2.7	2.7	2.5
– URBAN	5.3	4.7	4.7	4.7	4.4	9.8	5.4	4.9	5.1
URBAN POPULATION (% OF TOTAL)	10.4	14.0	14.8	17.7	21.6	26.1	33.7	41.4	46.1
VITAL STATISTICS									
CRUDE BIRTH RATE (PER 1000)	47.5	46.9	45.2	47.1	45.5	42.6	44.6	41.2	38.2
CRUDE DEATH RATE (PER 1000)	26.1	21.7	18.2	21.4	16.1	12.7	18.6	13.5	11.1
GROSS REPRODUCTION RATE	2.9	3.1	3.1	3.4	3.2	3.3	3.0	2.8	2.6
EMPLOYMENT AND INCOME									
DEPENDENCY RATIO – AGE	0.8	0.9	0.9	0.9	0.9	0.9	0.9	0.9	0.9
– ECONOMIC	1.0	1.1	1.1	1.3	1.4	1.4	1.6	1.6	1.5
LABOR FORCE IN AGRICULTURE (% OF TOTAL)	65.4	62.0	59.3	70.4	65.9	62.5	62.8	54.5	47.0
UNEMPLOYED (% OF LABOR FORCE)	4.7	4.0	3.1	6.3	8.4	5.3	6.1	6.0	5.8
INCOME RECEIVED BY – HIGHEST 5%	24.5	23.3	20.3	25.1	23.1	25.5	31.5	27.0	19.3
– LOWEST 20%	4.6	5.1	6.5	4.8	4.9	4.8	4.4	3.9	5.7
HEALTH AND NUTRITION									
DEATH RATE (PER 1000) AGES 1-4 YEARS	43.6	33.0	33.0	9.3	6.8	7.5	8.5	3.6	2.7
INFANT MORTALITY RATE (PER 1000)	129.0	121.3	102.8	84.6	79.9	58.4	88.6	65.8	55.0
LIFE EXPECTANCY AT BIRTH (YRS)	39.2	43.8	46.0	45.0	50.8	53.2	51.1	57.0	59.1
POPULATION PER – PHYSICIAN	21790.7	15219.9	13235.9	16767.4	11977.3	10586.0	3299.7	2549.2	2412.7
– NURSING PERSON	8472.3	5215.0	4830.9	4078.2	1921.9	1683.8	3394.0	2205.1	1502.1
– HOSPITAL BED	1386.7	1267.8	1236.2	1037.6	815.3	793.1	721.8	629.2	507.1
PER CAPITA PER DAY SUPPLY OF:									
CALORIES (% OF REQUIREMENTS)	89.8	91.5	94.5	85.1	93.3	102.3	94.4	101.8	103.9
PROTEIN (GRMS) – TOTAL	50.5	51.6	53.9	47.4	53.0	56.9	54.4	58.7	60.6
– FROM ANIMALS & PULSES	14.9	14.4	16.4	17.7	18.1	18.8	21.8	22.1	23.0
EDUCATION									
ADJ. ENROLLMENT RATIOS – PRIMARY	37.4	48.4	59.0	60.7	74.0	92.7	77.8	95.3	99.9
– SECONDARY	4.8	10.3	13.9	12.7	12.7	22.6	14.5	26.7	29.4
FEMALE ENROLLMENT RATIO (PRIMARY)	34.6	39.0	43.3	45.6	75.0	77.5	65.8	87.8	87.6
ADULT LITERACY RATE (%)	24.4	32.0	33.8	41.0	60.0	63.0	49.8	57.8	62.3

TABLE 1. Social Indicators by Income Group of Countries (Continued).

(ADJUSTED COUNTRY GROUP AVERAGES)

DEVELOPING COUNTRIES EXCLUDING CAPITAL SURPLUS OIL EXPORTERS

INDICATOR	LOW INCOME			LOWER MIDDLE INCOME			INTERMEDIATE MIDDLE INCOME		
	1960	1970	MOST RECENT ESTIMATE	1960	1970	MOST RECENT ESTIMATE	1960	1970	MOST RECENT ESTIMATE
HOUSING									
PERSONS PER ROOM - URBAN	2.5	2.0	2.8	2.6	2.5	2.2	2.3	2.2	1.6
OCCUPIED DWELLINGS WITHOUT WATER	62.2	69.8	..	68.7	64.6	67.8	74.6	64.2	58.9
ACCESS TO ELECTRICITY (%) - ALL	..	..	..	17.3	23.3	40.4	28.4	49.6	71.9
- RURAL	..	..	..	..	..	..	5.6	26.7	34.1
CONSUMPTION									
RADIO RECEIVERS (PER 1000 POP.)	4.5	14.4	23.1	11.9	62.3	70.4	48.8	96.2	102.6
PASSENGER CARS (PER 1000 POP.)	1.3	2.5	3.0	3.0	6.5	8.6	4.2	7.5	11.1
ENERGY (KG COAL/YR PER CAPITA)	62.0	83.4	104.8	99.6	220.1	265.2	258.7	489.2	586.2
NEWSPRINT (KG/YR PER CAPITA)	0.2	0.4	0.3	0.6	0.8	0.8	1.1	1.8	2.4

INDICATOR	DEV'G CTRIES. EXCL. CAP. SURP. OIL EXP. UPPER MIDDLE INCOME			HIGH INCOME			CAP. SURP. OIL EXP.			INDUSTRIALIZED COUNTRIES		
	1960	1970	MOST RECENT EST.	1960	1970	MOST RECENT EST.	1960	1970	MOST RECENT EST.	1960	1970	MOST RECENT EST.
GNP PER CAPITA (IN CURRENT US $)	401.2	817.1	1648.7	689.4	1564.2	2911.1	1054.3	2858.9	5710.5	1417.4	3096.8	5297.7
POPULATION												
GROWTH RATE (%) - TOTAL	1.6	1.3	1.5	2.1	3.1	2.9	4.5	2.4	2.7	0.9	0.9	0.9
- URBAN	3.3	3.4	2.8	4.5	3.9	3.5	..	5.8	6.8	1.6	1.3	1.3
URBAN POPULATION (% OF TOTAL)	43.4	51.1	53.1	63.0	82.1	88.6	24.6	20.0	39.0	66.1	70.5	73.8
VITAL STATISTICS												
CRUDE BIRTH RATE (PER 1000)	26.2	28.5	20.8	41.7	37.4	33.6	48.3	49.4	45.0	21.3	20.0	18.7
CRUDE DEATH RATE (PER 1000)	10.4	9.1	8.9	9.6	8.3	8.0	21.2	22.8	14.7	9.7	9.0	8.8
GROSS REPRODUCTION RATE	1.7	1.8	1.8	2.3	2.5	1.8	..	3.5	3.3	1.3	1.3	1.2

TABLE 1. Social Indicators by Income Group of Countries (Continued)

(ADJUSTED COUNTRY GROUP AVERAGES)

INDICATOR	DEV'G CTRIES. EXCL. CAP. SURP. OIL EXP. UPPER MIDDLE INCOME			CAP. SURP. OIL EXP. HIGH INCOME			CAP. SURP. OIL EXP.			INDUSTRIALIZED COUNTRIES		
	1960	1970	MOST RECENT EST.	1960	1970	MOST RECENT EST.	1960	1970	MOST RECENT EST.	1960	1970	MOST RECENT EST.
EMPLOYMENT AND INCOME												
DEPENDENCY RATIO - AGE	0.7	0.7	0.6	0.8	0.6	0.6	0.9	0.9	0.9	0.5	0.6	0.4
- ECONOMIC	1.3	1.7	1.6	1.2	1.2	1.2	1.8	1.7	1.7	0.9	0.9	0.8
LABOR FORCE IN AGRICULTURE (% OF TOTAL)	48.5	42.5	36.3	26.1	17.8	21.0	54.7	44.5	29.0	19.8	13.2	10.0
UNEMPLOYED (% OF LABOR FORCE)	7.4	3.3	4.0	9.0	5.4	5.1	7.4	2.0	3.0	2.1	1.5	1.9
INCOME RECEIVED BY - HIGHEST 5%	32.5	28.2	21.3	18.9	16.1	..	13.3	..	..	19.3	14.0	15.5
- LOWEST 20%	4.2	3.8	4.7	5.8	6.6	..	10.1	..	..	4.2	7.0	5.7
HEALTH AND NUTRITION												
DEATH RATE (PER 1000) AGES 1-4 YEARS	4.8	2.9	1.9	..	1.3	..	..	3.6	3.6	1.2	0.9	0.8
INFANT MORTALITY RATE (PER 1000)	74.4	51.3	37.9	44.9	27.8	23.2	45.4	134.3	80.3	27.7	17.0	15.0
LIFE EXPECTANCY AT BIRTH (YRS)	64.6	67.3	68.4	66.2	64.0	68.2	..	44.9	52.9	69.5	71.4	72.5
POPULATION PER - PHYSICIAN	1625.8	967.5	718.2	1117.5	888.9	756.9	9833.7	6323.4	1260.0	895.2	825.6	656.0
- NURSING PERSON	1690.7	1279.6	1028.5	1165.0	605.9	683.5	5140.0	2856.8	460.0	279.6	194.6	167.1
- HOSPITAL BED	209.9	180.4	185.8	170.0	162.5	170.0	1093.2	727.5	230.0	96.1	86.0	81.9
PER CAPITA PER DAY SUPPLY OF:												
CALORIES (% OF REQUIREMENTS)	104.5	114.4	111.5	106.3	107.2	113.6	83.9	90.3	104.9	118.7	118.7	119.5
PROTEIN (GRMS) - TOTAL	75.5	84.9	77.8	78.5	79.2	89.9	53.6	57.0	65.1	90.3	94.1	94.8
- FROM ANIMALS & PULSES	27.0	29.0	27.5	33.0	40.1	48.0	11.0	14.8	18.2	49.7	55.0	54.9
EDUCATION												
ADJ. ENROLLMENT RATIOS - PRIMARY	94.6	97.9	95.7	104.4	120.1	107.6	18.2	47.1	145.0	106.7	104.3	103.3
- SECONDARY	22.7	36.6	46.7	18.1	40.1	46.2	3.1	12.4	47.0	59.5	79.1	79.8
FEMALE ENROLLMENT RATIO (PRIMARY)	89.7	87.9	86.1	100.2	100.0	102.0	3.5	31.6	40.4	111.4	104.6	104.0
ADULT LITERACY RATE (%)	51.4	67.8	66.1	81.8	86.2	87.2	25.2	17.1	..	98.0	99.0	99.0
HOUSING												
PERSONS PER ROOM - URBAN	1.4	1.2	..	1.1	..	..	..	1.9	..	0.8	0.7	0.9
OCCUPIED DWELLINGS WITHOUT WATER	59.1	75.3	67.1	57.1	20.0	..	..	69.0	..	7.2	3.1	4.3
ACCESS TO ELECTRICITY (%) - ALL	50.6	47.4	59.8	79.3	91.0	..	..	24.0	..	97.3	98.9	99.1
- RURAL	26.9	..	..	57.0	58.0	..	..	..	..	91.4	95.2	94.8
CONSUMPTION												
RADIO RECEIVERS (PER 1000 POP.)	76.3	137.2	200.4	170.7	174.3	185.6	13.8	17.5	18.4	277.1	359.7	379.3
PASSENGER CARS (PER 1000 POP.)	11.2	29.2	42.3	14.1	41.3	54.4	7.6	16.6	113.7	90.7	233.3	266.5
ENERGY (KG COAL/YR PER CAPITA)	676.2	1426.1	1618.7	798.4	1755.1	2467.6	302.5	1003.1	1419.4	2624.7	4575.2	4997.3
NEWSPRINT (KG/YR PER CAPITA)	1.4	1.9	2.3	3.5	8.7	6.6	0.2	0.2	0.1	16.4	22.3	22.2

TABLE 2. SOCIAL INDICATORS BY GEOGRAPHIC AREAS (DEVELOPING COUNTRIES)

(ADJUSTED COUNTRY GROUP AVERAGES)

INDICATOR	EUROPE			LATIN AMERICA & CARIBBEAN			N. AFRICA & MIDDLE EAST		
	1960	1970	MOST RECENT ESTIMATE	1960	1970	MOST RECENT ESTIMATE	1960	1970	MOST RECENT ESTIMATE
GNP PER CAPITA (IN CURRENT US $)	496.6	1018.0	2070.3	362.0	626.8	1015.6	307.7	579.0	1290.3
POPULATION									
GROWTH RATE (%) - TOTAL	1.0	0.8	0.9	2.5	2.7	2.6	2.7	2.9	3.0
- URBAN	3.8	2.8	2.1	4.2	4.1	4.2	6.4	4.5	5.1
URBAN POPULATION (% OF TOTAL)	32.1	40.7	38.7	48.3	54.3	58.5	33.8	39.6	44.3
VITAL STATISTICS									
CRUDE BIRTH RATE (PER 1000)	23.3	20.5	19.2	40.9	39.0	36.8	48.3	47.2	45.7
CRUDE DEATH RATE (PER 1000)	10.5	9.0	9.0	14.1	10.9	9.2	22.6	18.0	15.3
GROSS REPRODUCTION RATE	1.4	1.3	1.3	2.7	2.6	2.6	2.3	3.4	3.4
EMPLOYMENT AND INCOME									
DEPENDENCY RATIO - AGE	0.6	0.6	0.4	0.9	1.0	0.9	0.9	1.0	1.0
- ECONOMIC	1.0	1.1	1.0	1.6	1.5	1.7	1.6	2.0	1.9
LABOR FORCE IN AGRICULTURE (% OF TOTAL)	47.9	31.8	27.4	48.3	41.0	36.9	52.6	43.4	42.9
UNEMPLOYED (% OF LABOR FORCE)	3.0	4.0	6.0	7.6	6.2	8.8	6.3	3.4	4.1
INCOME RECEIVED BY - HIGHEST 5%	21.8	24.5		37.1	30.4	31.7	24.0	25.0	21.0
- LOWEST 20%	5.4	3.9	3.9	3.9	3.5	2.0	4.4	4.2	5.2
HEALTH AND NUTRITION									
DEATH RATE (PER 1000) AGES 1-4 YEARS	4.7	2.8	1.7	10.6	7.7	6.6	..	6.0	..
INFANT MORTALITY RATE (PER 1000)	60.4	39.7	34.5	77.4	67.3	56.2	127.8	111.6	97.8
LIFE EXPECTANCY AT BIRTH (YRS)	65.8	68.6	69.1	55.8	60.6	62.5	45.5	50.3	52.8
POPULATION PER - PHYSICIAN	1004.0	821.3	694.4	2058.1	1866.8	1796.9	5690.8	5760.2	4724.7
- NURSING PERSON	1343.2	653.9	339.2	4542.1	3389.5	2804.5	3286.6	2564.7	2383.1
- HOSPITAL BED	190.5	168.0	170.5	444.1	392.3	405.6	670.8	661.6	700.0
PER CAPITA PER DAY SUPPLY OF: CALORIES (% OF REQUIREMENTS)	109.3	118.0	118.0	97.6	103.2	105.5	80.9	91.0	96.0
PROTEIN (GRMS) - TOTAL	85.9	90.7	90.0	63.7	59.8	60.7	54.5	58.3	63.1
- FROM ANIMALS & PULSES	27.0	29.0	33.0	29.0	28.0	28.2	17.5	15.0	15.6
EDUCATION									
ADJ. ENROLLMENT RATIOS - PRIMARY	105.0	102.1	104.3	85.0	101.7	105.1	51.5	75.6	80.5
- SECONDARY	25.5	50.5	49.2	15.0	27.6	36.0	10.3	20.4	22.2
FEMALE ENROLLMENT RATIO (PRIMARY)	98.9	99.4	100.4	85.6	98.3	98.1	30.8	50.2	52.3
ADULT LITERACY RATE (%)	64.9	75.0	88.2	61.4	74.6	75.7	17.7	26.9	40.6
HOUSING									
PERSONS PER ROOM - URBAN	1.4	1.5	1.4	1.9	1.3	2.1	1.8	2.3	3.0
OCCUPIED DWELLINGS WITHOUT WATER	67.0	63.3	59.5	65.5	67.0	66.4	62.2	77.1	90.5
ACCESS TO ELECTRICITY (%) - ALL	51.4	46.3	57.9	44.4	54.2	53.1	40.1	31.0	39.1
- RURAL	18.1	20.9	33.8	9.3	12.5	12.6			

TABLE 2. Social Indicators by Geographic Areas (Developing Countries), Continued

(ADJUSTED COUNTRY GROUP AVERAGES)

INDICATOR	AFRICA SOUTH OF SAHARA 1960	1970	MOST RECENT ESTIMATE	SOUTH ASIA 1960	1970	MOST RECENT ESTIMATE	EAST ASIA AND PACIFIC 1960	1970	MOST RECENT ESTIMATE
GNP PER CAPITA (IN CURRENT US $)	94.9	137.0	207.4	54.1	88.2	131.4	141.8	290.0	568.3
POPULATION									
GROWTH RATE (%) - TOTAL	2.2	2.4	2.6	2.2	2.6	2.1	3.0	2.8	2.3
- URBAN	5.6	6.0	6.0	5.2	4.1	4.3	5.4	5.0	5.2
URBAN POPULATION (% OF TOTAL)	9.1	12.5	13.5	7.8	9.8	12.4	28.1	27.1	38.1
VITAL STATISTICS									
CRUDE BIRTH RATE (PER 1000)	48.8	48.1	47.1	47.4	45.8	45.1	42.3	40.7	32.0
CRUDE DEATH RATE (PER 1000)	26.7	23.7	21.2	26.4	21.4	17.3	19.2	12.4	8.7
GROSS REPRODUCTION RATE	2.9	3.1	3.0	3.2	3.0	2.9	3.0	2.5	2.3
EMPLOYMENT AND INCOME									
DEPENDENCY RATIO - AGE	0.9	0.9	0.9	0.8	0.8	0.8	0.9	0.9	0.7
- ECONOMIC	1.1	1.1	1.1	1.5	1.4	1.2	1.4	1.4	1.3
LABOR FORCE IN AGRICULTURE (% OF TOTAL)	79.8	75.0	73.1	61.8	60.8	63.0	67.9	59.5	48.4
UNEMPLOYED (% OF LABOR FORCE)	5.1	4.6	5.1			11.0	5.1	5.1	4.1
INCOME RECEIVED BY - HIGHEST 5%	28.2	26.4	25.7	24.6	23.2	18.6	22.7	20.5	19.8
- LOWEST 20%	5.2	3.9	5.7	4.6	5.2	7.8	5.5	5.8	6.6
HEALTH AND NUTRITION									
DEATH RATE (PER 1000) AGES 1-4 YEARS								3.4	2.0
INFANT MORTALITY RATE (PER 1000)	153.9	129.6	127.5	136.2	124.3	104.0	61.2	31.1	27.4
LIFE EXPECTANCY AT BIRTH (YRS)	36.9	41.5	43.4	40.6	45.2	48.1	52.5	59.1	61.6
POPULATION PER - PHYSICIAN	31866.1	24906.5	21616.5	9920.9	8519.2	7412.6	3429.3	2268.9	2208.9
- NURSING PERSON	4558.4	3088.7	2496.5	14566.1	9168.6	8339.3	3096.6	1935.5	1165.5
- HOSPITAL BED	1234.7	819.9	799.9	2885.8	1998.5	1908.0	1270.8	921.7	662.1
PER CAPITA PER DAY SUPPLY OF:									
CALORIES (% OF REQUIREMENTS)	89.6	90.7	91.9	89.1	97.6	96.0	90.0	99.4	106.5
PROTEIN (GRMS) - TOTAL	56.6	59.0	60.6	47.8	53.2	50.8	48.1	53.4	55.6
- FROM ANIMALS & PULSES	19.2	19.8	23.1	15.0	16.0	15.5	19.0	22.1	22.1
EDUCATION									
ADJ. ENROLLMENT RATIOS - PRIMARY	27.7	42.4	50.0	36.9	47.9	55.2	95.0	105.7	110.0
- SECONDARY	1.9	5.6	6.9	9.1	15.5	20.0	17.3	26.9	51.1
FEMALE ENROLLMENT RATIO (PRIMARY)	21.7	37.4	43.2	22.2	53.8	44.5	88.5	102.0	104.7
ADULT LITERACY RATE (%)	9.8	17.4	18.4	16.0	20.0	21.0	47.7	66.4	72.6
HOUSING									
PERSONS PER ROOM - URBAN	2.7	2.4	1.7				2.5	2.3	
OCCUPIED DWELLINGS WITHOUT WATER							83.7	69.5	60.3
ACCESS TO ELECTRICITY (%) - ALL							22.6	40.7	50.5
- RURAL							12.0	20.1	23.4

GLOBAL INDICATORS

TABLE 3. COMPARATIVE SOCIAL INDICATORS FOR DEVELOPING COUNTRIES (BY GEOGRAPHIC AREA AND COUNTRY)

AREA AND COUNTRY	POPULATION & VITAL STATISTICS				EMPLOYMENT AND INCOME			HEALTH & NUTRITION			EDUCATION (MOST RECENT ESTIMATE)		
	POP. GROWTH RATE % (65-75)	URBAN POP. % OF TOTAL	CRUDE BIRTH RATE (/000)	CRUDE DEATH RATE (/000)	LABOR IN AGR. % OF TOTAL	INCOME RECD BY HIGHEST 5% HH	INCOME RECD BY LOWEST 20% HH	LIFE EXPECT. YRS AT BIRTH	CALORIE SUPPLY %/CAP REQD.	PROTEIN SUPPLY GR/DAY /CAP	PRIMARY SCHOOL ENROLL % RATIO	FEMALE ENROLL. RATIO PRIMARY	ADULT LITERACY RATE % OF TOTAL
EUROPE													
CYPRUS	0.6	42.2	22.2	6.8	34.0	12.1	7.9	71.4	113.0	86.0	71.0	72.0	85.0
GREECE	0.6	64.8	15.4	9.4	34.0	18.7	6.3	71.8	132.0	102.0	106.0	104.0	82.0
MALTA	0.2	94.3	17.5	9.0	6.0	..	..	69.6	114.0	89.0	109.0	109.0	87.0
PORTUGAL	0.3	28.8	19.2	10.5	32.5	56.3	7.3	68.7	118.0	85.0	116.0	94.0	70.0
ROWANIA	1.2	43.0	19.7	9.3	36.0	..	..	69.1	118.0	90.0	109.0	109.0	98.0
SPAIN	1.0	59.1	19.5	8.3	23.0	18.5	6.0	72.1	135.0	94.1	115.0	115.0	94.0
TURKEY	2.6	42.6	39.4	12.5	52.5	28.0	3.5	56.9	113.0	75.7	104.0	94.0	55.0
YUGOSLAVIA	0.9	38.7	18.2	9.2	39.0	25.1	6.6	68.0	137.0	97.5	97.0	93.0	85.0
ALL COUNTRIES - MEDIAN	0.8	42.8	19.4	9.3	34.0	18.6	6.5	69.4	118.0	89.5	107.5	99.0	85.0
LATIN AMERICA & CARIBBEAN													
ARGENTINA	1.4	80.0	21.8	8.8	15.0	21.4	5.6	68.3	129.0	107.1	108.0	109.0	93.0
BAHAMAS	3.6	57.9	22.4	5.7	7.0	20.7	3.4	66.7	100.0	87.0	135.0	..	93.0
BARBADOS	0.4	3.7	21.6	8.9	18.0	19.8	6.8	69.1	133.0	82.5	117.0	116.0	97.0
BOLIVIA	2.7	34.0	44.0	19.1	65.0	36.0	4.0	46.8	77.0	48.5	74.0	65.0	40.0
BRAZIL	2.9	59.1	37.1	8.8	37.8	35.0	3.0	61.4	105.0	62.1	90.0	90.0	64.0
CHILE	1.9	83.0	27.9	9.2	19.0	31.0	4.8	62.6	116.0	78.3	119.0	118.0	90.0
COLOMBIA	2.8	70.0	40.6	8.8	39.0	27.2	5.2	60.9	94.0	47.0	105.0	108.0	81.0
COSTA RICA	2.8	40.6	31.0	5.8	36.4	22.8	5.4	69.1	113.0	60.8	109.0	109.0	89.0
DOMINICAN REPUBLIC	2.9	45.9	45.8	11.0	53.8	26.3	4.3	57.8	98.0	45.4	104.0	105.0	51.0
ECUADOR	3.4	41.6	41.8	9.5	43.5	..	..	59.6	93.0	47.4	102.0	100.0	69.0
EL SALVADOR	3.4	39.4	42.2	11.1	55.0	38.0	2.0	65.0	84.0	50.3	75.2	69.0	63.0
GRENADA	1.0	..	27.4	6.8	30.8	..	..		89.0	57.0	99.0	..	85.0
GUATEMALA	3.2	37.3	42.8	13.7	56.0	35.0	5.0	54.1	91.0	52.8	62.0	56.0	47.0
GUYANA	2.1	40.0	32.4	5.9	30.9	18.8	4.3	67.9	104.0	58.0	114.0	114.0	85.0
HAITI	1.6	23.1	35.8	16.3	77.0	..	..	50.0	90.0	39.0	70.0	37.0	20.0
HONDURAS	2.7	31.4	49.3	14.6	60.3	28.0	2.5	53.5	90.0	56.0	90.0	88.0	53.0
JAMAICA	1.7	37.1	32.2	7.1	26.9	30.2	2.2	69.5	118.0	68.9	111.0	112.0	86.0
MEXICO	3.5	63.3	42.0	8.6	41.0	27.9	3.4	64.7	117.0	66.9	112.0	109.0	76.0
NICARAGUA	3.6	48.0	48.3	13.9	48.0	42.4	3.1	52.9	105.0	68.4	85.0	87.0	57.0
PANAMA	3.2	49.6	36.2	7.1	30.0	22.2	4.6	66.5	105.0	61.0	124.0	120.0	82.2

TABLE 3. COMPARATIVE SOCIAL INDICATORS FOR DEVELOPING COUNTRIES (BY GEOGRAPHIC AREA AND COUNTRY)   Continued

AREA AND COUNTRY	POPULATION & VITAL STATISTICS				EMPLOYMENT AND INCOME			HEALTH & NUTRITION			EDUCATION (MOST RECENT ESTIMATE)		
	POP. GROWTH RATE % (65-75)	URBAN POP. % OF TOTAL	CRUDE BIRTH RATE (/000)	CRUDE DEATH RATE (/000)	LABOR IN AGR. % OF TOTAL	INCOME REC'D BY HIGHEST 5% HH	INCOME REC'D BY LOWEST 20% HH	LIFE EXPECT. YRS AT BIRTH	CALORIE SUPPLY %/CAP REQ.	PROTEIN SUPPLY GR/DAY /CAP	PRIMARY SCHOOL ENROLL RATIO %	FEMALE ENROLL. RATIO PRIMARY	ADULT LITERACY RATE % OF TOTAL
PARAGUAY	2.6	37.4	39.8	8.9	49.0	30.0	4.0	61.9	118.0	74.5	106.0	102.0	81.0
PERU	2.9	55.3	41.0	11.9	40.0	28.8	3.1	55.7	100.0	61.7	111.0	106.0	72.0
TRINIDAD & TOBAGO	1.0	25.1	27.3	5.9	13.5	..	..	69.5	114.0	66.0	111.0	111.0	90.0
URUGUAY	0.4	80.6	20.4	9.3	13.2	19.0	4.4	69.8	116.0	98.1	95.0	94.0	94.0
VENEZUELA	3.3	75.7	36.1	7.0	21.0	21.8	3.6	66.4	98.0	63.1	96.0	96.0	82.0
ALL COUNTRIES - MEDIAN	2.7	43.7	36.2	8.9	37.8	27.9	4.0	63.0	104.0	61.7	105.0	105.0	81.0
NORTH AFRICA & MIDDLE EAST													
ALGERIA	3.3	39.9	48.7	15.4	42.8	..	..	53.3	88.0	57.2	77.0	72.0	35.0
BAHRAIN	3.3	78.1	49.6	18.7	..	..	..	44.5	..	..	..	..	..
EGYPT	2.4	44.6	37.8	14.0	43.9	21.0	5.2	52.4	113.0	70.7	72.0	55.0	40.0
IRAN	2.9	43.0	45.3	15.6	41.0	29.7	4.0	51.0	98.0	56.0	90.0	67.0	50.0
IRAQ	3.3	62.0	48.1	14.6	51.0	35.1	2.1	52.7	101.0	60.4	93.0	63.0	26.0
JORDAN	3.4	42.0	47.6	14.7	19.0	..	..	53.2	90.0	65.0	83.0	77.0	62.0
KUWAIT	7.7	88.0	45.4	..	2.0	..	..	64.0	..	..	90.0	86.0	55.0
LEBANON	2.8	60.1	39.8	9.9	17.8	26.0	4.0	63.3	101.0	67.9	132.0	125.0	68.0
LIBYA	4.2	30.5	45.0	14.7	19.5	13.3	10.1	52.9	117.0	62.0	145.0	135.0	27.0
MOROCCO	2.4	40.1	46.2	15.7	50.0	20.0	4.0	53.0	108.0	70.5	61.0	44.0	28.0
OMAN	3.1	5.0	49.6	18.7	48.0	..	..	47.0	..	..	44.0	..	20.0
QATAR	10.5	85.0	..	..	..	..	..	..	..	..	112.0	..	21.0
SAUDI ARABIA	1.9	17.9	50.2	24.4	61.0	..	..	42.0	86.0	56.0	34.0	27.0	15.0
SYRIAN ARAB REP.	3.1	46.2	45.4	15.4	49.9	17.0	5.0	56.0	104.0	66.7	102.0	81.0	40.0
TUNISIA	2.3	47.0	40.0	13.8	37.4	..	..	54.1	102.0	67.4	95.0	75.0	55.0
UNITED ARAB EMIRATES	13.1	80.0	..	..	..	..	..	..	..	..	75.0	..	21.0
YEMEN ARAB REP.	1.7	7.0	49.6	20.6	73.0	..	..	37.0	83.0	58.3	25.0	6.0	10.0
YEMEN PEOP. DEM. REP.	3.1	35.3	49.6	20.6	42.9	..	..	44.8	84.0	57.0	78.0	48.0	27.1
ALL COUNTRIES-MEDIAN	3.1	43.8	46.9	15.6	42.9	21.0	4.0	52.8	101.0	62.0	83.0	70.5	28.0
AFRICA SOUTH OF SAHARA													
BENIN PEOP. REP.	2.7	13.5	49.9	23.0	47.5	31.4	5.5	41.8	87.0	56.0	44.0	28.0	20.0
BOTSWANA	2.1	10.7	45.6	23.0	83.0	28.1	1.6	43.5	85.0	65.0	85.0	93.0	25.0
BURUNDI	2.0	3.7	48.0	24.7	86.0	..	..	39.0	99.0	62.0	23.0	17.0	10.0
CAMEROON	1.9	28.5	40.4	22.0	82.0	..	..	41.0	102.0	59.0	111.0	97.0	6.0
CENTRAL AFRICAN EMPIRE	2.2	35.9	43.4	22.5	91.0	..	..	41.0	102.0	49.0	79.0	53.0	15.0

TABLE 3. COMPARATIVE SOCIAL INDICATORS FOR DEVELOPING COUNTRIES
(BY GEOGRAPHIC AREA AND COUNTRY)   Continued

AREA AND COUNTRY	POPULATION & VITAL STATISTICS				EMPLOYMENT AND INCOME			HEALTH & NUTRITION			EDUCATION (MOST RECENT ESTIMATE)		
	POP. GROWTH RATE % (65-75)	URBAN POP. % OF TOTAL	CRUDE BIRTH RATE (/000)	CRUDE DEATH RATE (/000)	LABOR IN AGR. % OF TOTAL	INCOME RECD BY HIGHEST 5% HH	INCOME RECD BY LOWEST 20% HH	LIFE EXPECT. YRS AT BIRTH	CALORIE SUPPLY % /CAP REQD.	PROTEIN SUPPLY GR/DAY /CAP	PRIMARY SCHOOL ENROLL RATIO %	FEMALE ENROLL. RATIO PRIMARY	ADULT LITERACY RATE % OF TOTAL
CHAD	2.0	13.9	44.0	24.0	90.0	21.5	7.7	38.5	75.0	60.2	37.0	20.0	15.0
CONGO PEOP. REP.	2.3	38.0	45.1	20.8	56.0	..	..	43.5	98.0	44.0	153.0	140.0	50.0
EQUATORIAL GUINEA	1.3												..
ETHIOPIA	2.5	11.2	49.4	25.8	85.0	..	..	41.0	82.0	58.9	23.0	14.0	7.0
GABON	1.5	32.0	32.2	22.2	58.0	45.3	3.2	41.0	98.0	49.3	199.0	197.0	12.0
GAMBIA	2.3	14.0	43.3	24.1	79.6	..	..	40.0	98.0	64.0	32.0	21.0	10.0
GHANA	2.6	32.4	48.8	21.9	52.0	..	..	43.5	101.0	53.4	60.0	53.0	25.0
GUINEA	2.8	19.5	44.6	22.9	84.1	..	..	41.0	84.0	42.7	28.0	..	7.0
IVORY COAST	4.1	34.3	45.6	20.6	80.0	30.9	9.0	43.5	113.0	64.5	86.0	64.0	20.0
KENYA	3.4	13.0	48.7	16.0	84.0	20.2	3.9	50.0	91.0	59.6	109.0	101.0	40.0
LESOTHO	2.2	3.1	39.0	19.7	90.0	..	..	46.0	109.0	67.6	121.0	144.0	40.0
LIBERIA	3.3	27.6	43.6	20.7	72.0	61.7	5.3	43.5	87.0	39.0	62.0	44.0	15.0
MADAGASCAR	2.9	14.5	50.2	21.1	83.0	41.0	5.2	43.5	105.0	57.0	85.0	80.0	40.0
MALAWI	2.5	6.4	47.7	23.7	86.0	29.5	5.7	41.0	103.0	68.4	61.0	48.0	25.0
MALI	2.2	13.4	50.1	25.9	88.7	..	..	38.1	75.0	64.0	22.0	16.0	10.0
MAURITANIA	2.6	23.1	44.8	24.9	85.0	..	..	38.5	81.0	63.2	17.0	9.0	10.0
MAURITIUS	1.4	48.3	25.1	7.8	30.3	31.0	4.5	65.5	108.0	55.8	80.0	78.0	80.0
MOZAMBIQUE	2.2	55.0	43.3	21.4	73.0	..	..	41.0	94.0	41.0	46.0	..	..
NIGER	2.7	9.4	52.2	25.5	91.0	23.0	6.0	38.5	78.0	62.1	17.0	12.0	5.0
NIGERIA	2.5	26.0	49.3	22.7	62.0	..	..	41.0	88.0	46.3	49.0	39.0	25.0
RWANDA	2.8	3.8	50.0	23.6	93.0	..	..	41.0	90.0	51.3	58.0	54.0	23.0
SENEGAL	2.7	38.8	47.6	23.9	73.0	..	..	40.0	97.0	67.1	43.0	33.0	10.0
SIERRA LEONE	2.3	15.0	44.7	20.7	73.0	36.8	3.2	43.5	97.0	50.9	35.0	28.0	15.0
SOMALIA	2.4	28.3	47.2	21.7	77.0	36.2	1.1	41.0	79.0	55.1	58.0	41.0	50.0
SUDAN	2.2	13.2	47.8	17.5	66.5	20.9	5.1	48.6	88.0	60.4	40.0	27.0	15.0
SWAZILAND	3.2	14.3	49.0	21.8	83.0	..	..	43.5	89.0	..	103.0	102.0	50.0
TANZANIA	2.8	7.3	47.0	20.1	83.1	33.5	2.3	44.5	86.0	47.1	57.0	46.0	49.0
TOGO	2.7	15.0	50.6	23.3	75.0	..	..	41.0	96.0	52.1	98.0	68.0	12.0
UGANDA	3.1	8.4	45.2	15.9	86.0	20.0	6.2	50.0	90.0	54.0	44.0	43.0	25.0
UPPER VOLTA	2.2	12.1	48.5	25.8	89.0	..	..	38.0	78.0	59.2	14.0	11.0	7.0
ZAIRE	2.7	26.4	45.2	20.5	77.0	..	..	43.5	85.0	32.0	88.0	87.0	15.0
ZAMBIA	2.9	36.3	51.5	20.3	52.0	23.0	3.8	44.5	89.0	58.8	88.0	86.0	43.0
ALL COUNTRIES—MEDIAN	2.5	14.8	47.4	22.1	82.5	30.9	4.5	41.0	90.0	57.0	58.0	47.0	15.0

TABLE 3. COMPARATIVE SOCIAL INDICATORS FOR DEVELOPING COUNTRIES (BY GEOGRAPHIC AREA AND COUNTRY)   Continued

AREA AND COUNTRY	POPULATION & VITAL STATISTICS				EMPLOYMENT AND INCOME			HEALTH & NUTRITION			EDUCATION (MOST RECENT ESTIMATE)		
	POP. GROWTH RATE % (65-75)	URBAN POP. % OF TOTAL	CRUDE BIRTH RATE (/000)	CRUDE DEATH RATE (/000)	LABOR IN AGR. % OF TOTAL	INCOME RECD BY HIGHEST 5% HH	INCOME RECD BY LOWEST 20% HH	LIFE EXPECT. YRS AT BIRTH	CALORIE SUPPLY %/CAP REQ.	PROTEIN SUPPLY GR/DAY /CAP	PRIMARY SCHOOL ENROLL RATIO %	FEMALE ENROLL. RATIO PRIMARY	ADULT LITERACY RATE % OF TOTAL
SOUTH ASIA													
AFGHANISTAN	2.2	14.3	51.4	30.7	52.9	..	..	40.3	83.0	61.5	23.0	7.0	14.0
BANGLADESH	2.3	8.8	49.5	28.1	78.0	16.7	7.9	45.0	93.0	58.5	73.0	51.0	23.0
BURMA	2.2	22.3	39.5	15.8	67.8	14.6	8.0	50.1	103.0	58.0	85.0	81.0	67.0
INDIA	2.2	20.6	37.0	17.0	69.0	25.0	4.7	49.5	89.0	48.0	65.0	52.0	36.0
NEPAL	2.1	4.8	42.9	20.3	94.4	..	..	43.6	95.0	50.0	59.0	10.0	19.2
PAKISTAN	2.9	26.0	47.4	16.5	54.8	17.3	8.4	49.8	93.0	54.0	51.0	31.0	21.0
SRI LANKA	2.0	24.3	28.2	7.9	55.0	18.6	7.3	67.8	97.0	48.0	77.0	77.0	78.1
ALL COUNTRIES-MEDIAN	2.2	20.6	42.9	17.0	67.8	17.3	7.9	49.5	93.0	54.0	65.0	51.0	23.0
EAST ASIA & PACIFIC													
CHINA REP.	2.6	51.1	23.0	4.7	35.0	13.3	8.8	68.6	111.0	68.0	104.0	..	82.0
FIJI	2.2	38.5	25.0	4.3	43.3	19.0	5.1	70.0	..	..	111.0	110.0	75.0
INDONESIA	2.3	18.2	42.9	16.9	69.0	33.7	6.8	48.1	98.0	43.8	81.0	75.0	62.0
KOREA	2.1	48.5	28.8	8.9	44.6	18.1	7.2	68.0	115.0	75.7	109.0	109.0	92.0
LAO P.D.R.	2.7	15.0	44.6	22.8	85.0	..	..	40.4	94.0	58.0	57.0	47.0	20.0
MALAYSIA	2.7	30.2	31.7	6.7	45.2	28.3	3.5	59.4	115.0	56.5	93.0	91.0	60.0
PAPUA NEW GUINEA	2.5	12.9	40.6	17.1	83.0	..	..	47.7	98.0	48.2	59.0	44.0	31.0
PHILIPPINES	2.9	29.8	43.8	10.5	52.6	28.8	5.5	58.5	87.0	50.0	105.0	103.0	87.0
SINGAPORE	1.7	90.2	21.2	5.2	2.8	..	..	89.5	122.0	74.7	111.0	108.0	75.0
THAILAND	3.1	16.5	37.6	9.1	76.0	22.0	5.6	58.0	107.0	50.0	78.0	75.0	82.0
VIET NAM	2.6	21.5	36.9	6.7	67.0	..	..	58.0	100.0	52.7	91.0	..	97.8
WESTERN SAMOA	1.9	..	..	..	..	..	..	..	..	..	..	..	..
ALL COUNTRIES-MEDIAN	2.6	29.8	36.9	8.9	52.6	22.0	5.6	58.5	103.5	53.6	93.0	91.0	75.0

COMPARATIVE ECONOMIC DATA

TABLE 4. Selected Economic Development Indicators: Population and Production
(Average annual real growth rates)

Income group/ region/country	Population				Gross domestic product				GDP per capita			
	1950-60	1960-65	1965-70	1970-77	1950-60	1960-65	1965-70	1970-77	1950-60	1960-65	1965-70	1970-77
Developing countries	2.2	2.4	2.5	2.4	4.9	5.0	6.4	5.7	2.7	3.1	3.8	3.2
Capital-surplus oil-exporting countries	2.3	3.2	3.7	4.1	..	..	11.0	6.7	..	..	7.2	3.0
Industrialized countries	1.2	1.2	0.9	0.8	3.8++	5.3	4.9	3.2	2.5++	4.0	4.0	2.4
Centrally planned economies	1.7	1.8	1.6	1.4	..	6.2+	7.7+	6.4+	..	4.8+	6.7+	5.6+
A. Developing countries by income group												
Low income	2.0	2.4	2.4	2.2	3.8	3.8	5.3	4.0	1.8	1.4	2.8	1.7
Middle income	2.4	2.5	2.5	2.5	5.3	6.1	6.6	6.0	2.8	3.5	4.0	3.4
B. Developing countries by region												
Africa south of Sahara	2.3	2.5	2.5	2.7	3.6	5.0	4.9	3.7	1.3	2.4	2.3	0.9
Middle East and North Africa	2.4	2.6	2.7	2.7	5.1	6.4	9.4	7.1	2.6	3.7	6.5	4.3
East Asia and Pacific	2.4	2.6	2.5	2.2	5.2	5.5	8.0	8.0	2.8	2.8	5.4	5.7
South Asia	1.9	2.4	2.4	2.2	3.8	4.3	4.9	3.2	1.8	1.9	2.4	1.0
Latin America and the Caribbean	2.8	2.8	2.7	2.7	5.3	5.2	6.1	6.1	2.4	2.3	3.3	3.4
Southern Europe	1.5	1.4	1.4	1.5	6.1	7.5	6.5	5.3	4.5	6.0	5.0	3.8
C. Developing countries by region and country												
Africa south of Sahara												
Angola	1.6	1.5	1.6	2.3	..	5.9	3.2	-9.4	..	4.3	1.6	-11.5
Benin	2.2	2.5	2.7	2.9	..	3.1	2.7	2.7	..	0.6	0.0	-0.1
Botswana	1.7	1.9	1.9	1.9	2.9	4.2	9.8	15.7	1.2	2.2	7.8	13.5
Burundi	2.0	2.3	2.4	1.9	-1.3	2.8	5.8	2.3	-3.2	0.5	3.3	0.4
Cameroon	1.4	1.7	1.9	2.2	1.7	2.9	7.3	3.4	0.3	1.2	5.3	1.2
Cape Verde	3.1	3.1	2.7	2.1	..	..	..	..	..	..	..	..
Central African Republic	1.4	2.2	2.2	2.2	2.6	0.5	3.5	3.1	1.1	-1.7	1.3	0.9
Chad	1.4	1.8	1.9	2.2	..	0.5	1.6	1.2	..	-1.3	-0.3	-0.9
Comoros	3.0	3.2	3.3	3.8	..	9.5	3.2	-1.5	..	6.1	-0.1	-5.2
Congo, People's Republic of the	1.6	2.1	2.2	2.5	1.1	2.7	3.4	3.9	-0.5	0.6	1.2	1.4
Equatorial Guinea	1.5	1.7	1.9	2.2	..	13.8	2.0	-3.0	..	11.8	0.1	-5.0
Ethiopia	2.1	2.3	2.4	2.5	3.9	5.1	3.7	2.6	1.7	2.7	1.2	0.1
Gabon	0.2	0.5	0.7	0.9	11.5	3.9	5.3	9.1	11.3	3.3	4.6	8.1

TABLE 4. COMPARATIVE ECONOMIC DATA (Continued)

Income group/ region/country	Population				Gross domestic product				GDP per capita			
	1950-60	1960-65	1965-70	1970-77	1950-60	1960-65	1965-70	1970-77	1950-60	1960-65	1965-70	1970-77
Gambia, The	2.0	3.3	3.2	3.1	1.3	5.2	4.3	8.2	-0.7	1.9	1.1	4.9
Ghana	4.5	2.7	2.1	3.0	4.1	3.3	2.5	0.4	-0.4	0.6	0.4	-2.5
Guinea	2.2	2.7	3.0	3.0	:	3.9	3.0	5.4	:	1.2	0.0	2.4
Guinea-Bissau	0.2	-1.1	-0.2	1.6	:	:	:	:	:	:	:	:
Ivory Coast	2.1	3.7	3.8	6.0	3.6	10.1	7.4	6.5	1.5	6.1	3.5	0.5
Kenya	3.3	3.4	3.5	3.8	4.0	3.6	8.6	4.8	0.7	0.2	4.9	1.0
Lesotho	1.5	1.8	2.2	2.4	4.4	8.7	2.1	8.0	2.8	6.7	-0.1	5.5
Liberia	2.8	3.1	3.2	3.4	10.5	3.1	6.4	2.7	7.4	0.0	3.1	-0.6
Madagascar	1.8	2.1	2.3	2.5	2.3	1.4	4.9	-0.7	0.5	-0.7	2.5	-3.2
Malawi	2.4	2.7	2.9	3.1	:	3.3	4.5	6.3	:	0.6	1.5	3.1
Mali	2.1	2.5	2.4	2.5	3.2	3.2	2.9	4.7	1.0	0.7	0.5	2.1
Mauritania	2.2	2.5	2.6	2.7	:	9.9	4.6	2.2	:	7.2	2.0	-0.5
Mauritius	3.3	2.7	1.9	1.3	0.1	5.4	-0.3	8.2	-3.0	2.7	-2.2	6.8
Mozambique	1.4	2.1	2.3	2.5	3.1	2.3	8.3	-3.7	1.7	0.2	5.9	-6.1
Namibia	:	2.4	2.6	2.8	:	:	:	:	:	:	:	:
Niger	2.3	4.0	2.7	2.8	:	6.6	-0.3	1.2	:	2.5	-2.9	-1.5
Nigeria	2.4	2.5	2.5	2.6	4.1	5.3	4.5	6.0	1.6	2.7	1.9	3.3
Réunion	:	3.3	2.5	1.8	:	:	:	:	:	:	:	:
Rhodesia	4.1	4.2	3.7	3.3	:	3.2	6.1	3.2	:	-0.9	2.4	-0.1
Rwanda	2.3	2.5	2.7	2.9	1.0	-2.9	8.5	5.2	-1.2	-5.3	5.6	2.2
Senegal	2.2	2.4	2.5	2.6	:	3.6	1.3	2.8	:	1.1	-1.2	0.2
Sierra Leone	1.8	2.1	2.3	2.5	3.6	4.3	3.9	1.5	1.8	2.1	1.6	-1.0
Somalia	2.0	2.4	2.5	2.3	12.8	-0.5	3.4	1.2	10.6	-2.8	0.9	-1.1
South Africa	3.0	2.5	2.7	2.7	2.9	6.6	5.9	4.0	-0.1	4.0	3.1	1.2
Sudan	1.9	2.2	2.4	2.6	5.5	1.5	1.3	5.4	3.5	-0.7	-1.0	2.7
Swaziland	2.0	2.3	2.1	2.5	8.4	13.6	6.3	6.2	6.3	11.0	4.1	3.7
Tanzania, United Republic of	2.2	2.6	2.8	3.0	6.0	5.2	5.9	5.2	3.7	2.6	3.1	2.1
Togo	2.2	2.7	2.7	2.6	1.3	8.4	6.7	4.0	-0.9	5.8	3.9	1.4
Uganda	2.8	3.8	3.7	3.0	3.3	5.7	5.9	0.5	0.5	1.8	2.2	-2.4
Upper Volta	1.9	1.6	1.6	1.6	1.6	2.7	3.3	0.5	-0.3	1.0	1.6	-1.0
Zaire	2.3	1.9	2.1	2.7	3.4	3.7	4.3	1.0	1.1	1.7	2.2	-1.7
Zambia	2.4	2.8	2.9	3.0	5.6	5.4	2.8	2.8	3.1	2.6	-0.1	-0.2

TABLE 4. COMPARATIVE ECONOMIC DATA (Continued)

Income group/ region/country	Population				Gross domestic product				GDP per capita			
	1950-60	1960-65	1965-70	1970-77	1950-60	1960-65	1965-70	1970-77	1950-60	1960-65	1965-70	1970-77
C. Developing countries by region and country (cont.)												
Middle East and North Africa												
Algeria	2.1	2.0	3.7	3.2	6.5	0.8	8.1	5.4	4.4	-1.2	4.2	2.2
Bahrain	3.5	4.2	2.9	7.1	:	:	:	10.7[d]	:	:	:	3.2[d]
Egypt, Arab Republic of	2.4	2.5	2.1	2.1	3.3	7.6	3.2	6.4	0.9	4.9	1.1	4.2
Iran	2.5	2.7	2.8	3.0	5.9	9.2	12.6	7.4	3.3	6.3	9.5	4.3
Iraq	2.8	3.1	3.2	3.4	9.9	7.7	4.1	8.1[e]	6.9	4.5	0.9	4.7[e]
Jordan	3.2	3.0	3.2	3.3	:	:	:	7.0[f]	:	:	:	3.6[f]
Lebanon	2.6	3.0	2.8	2.5	:	:	:	:	:	:	:	:
Morocco	2.7	2.5	2.9	2.7	2.0	4.2	5.7	6.4	-0.7	1.7	2.8	3.6
Syrian Arab Republic	2.7	3.1	3.3	3.3	:	8.8	5.6	9.6	:	5.4	2.3	6.2
Tunisia	1.8	1.9	2.1	2.0	:	5.2[c]	4.9	8.5	:	3.3[c]	2.8	6.4
Yemen, Arab Republic of	2.0	2.1	1.5	1.9	:	:	:	8.4	:	:	:	6.4
Yemen, People's Democratic Republic of.	1.9	1.9	1.9	1.9	:	:	:	6.8[d]	:	:	:	4.8[d]
East Asia and Pacific												
Fiji	3.1	3.3	2.3	1.8	2.8	3.7	7.4	5.0	-0.3	0.3	5.0	3.1
Hong Kong	4.5	3.7	1.3	2.0	9.2	11.7	8.0	8.0	4.5	7.7	6.6	5.9
Indonesia	2.1	2.2	2.2	1.8	4.0	1.6	7.5	8.0	1.9	-0.6	5.2	6.1
Korea, Republic of	2.0	2.6	2.2	2.0	5.1	6.7	10.3	9.9	3.1	4.0	7.9	7.8
Malaysia	2.5	2.9	2.9	2.7	3.6	6.8	5.9	7.8	1.0	3.7	2.9	4.9
Papua New Guinea	1.8	2.3	2.4	2.4	4.8	6.4	5.7	5.0	2.9	4.0	3.3	2.5
Philippines	2.7	3.0	3.1	2.7	6.5	5.2	5.2	6.3	3.6	2.2	2.1	3.5
Singapore	4.8	2.8	2.0	1.6	:	5.5	13.0	8.6	:	2.6	10.7	6.9
Solomon Islands	2.6	2.6	2.6	3.5	10.7	3.7	2.5	5.4	7.9	1.1	-0.1	1.8
Taiwan	3.5	3.0	2.4	2.0	7.6	8.9	9.2	7.7	4.0	5.8	6.7	5.6
Thailand	2.8	3.0	3.1	2.9	5.7	7.4	8.4	7.1	2.8	4.2	5.1	4.0
South Asia												
Afghanistan	1.5	2.2	2.2	2.2	:	1.7	2.3	4.5	:	-0.4	0.2	2.2
Bangladesh	2.4	2.8	3.0	2.5	:	4.6	3.4	2.3	:	1.8	0.4	-0.1

TABLE 4. COMPARATIVE ECONOMIC DATA (Continued)

Income group/ region/country	Population 1950-60	1960-65	1965-70	1970-77	Gross domestic product 1950-60	1960-65	1965-70	1970-77	GDP per capita 1950-60	1960-65	1965-70	1970-77
Bhutan		1.9	2.1	2.3			2.3	3.6				1.4
Burma	1.9	2.1	2.2	2.2	6.3	4.4	5.0	3.1	4.3	2.2	0.1	1.0
India	1.9	2.3	2.4	2.1	3.8	4.0	2.2	2.6	1.9	1.7	2.6	0.4
Nepal	1.2	1.9	2.2	2.2	2.4	2.7	2.2	2.8	1.2	0.8	0.0	0.7
Pakistan	2.3	2.7	2.9	3.1	2.4	7.2	6.9	3.8	0.1	4.4	3.8	0.7
Sri Lanka	2.6	2.5	2.3	1.7	3.9	4.0	5.8	2.9	1.3	1.5	3.4	1.1
Latin America and the Carribean												
Argentina	1.9	1.5	1.4	1.3	2.8	3.0	4.5	2.8	0.9	1.4	3.1	1.5
Bahamas	3.6	4.8	4.4	2.7							7.8	
Barbados	0.9	0.3	0.3	0.5	5.9	4.5	7.9	2.0	4.9	4.1	7.6	1.4
Belize	3.1	2.8	2.8	0.9				6.0				5.0
Bolivia	2.1	2.5	2.6	2.7		5.0	4.8	5.9		2.5	2.1	3.1
Brazil	3.1	2.9	2.9	2.9	6.9	4.0	8.0	9.9	3.7	1.1	5.0	6.8
Chile	2.2	2.3	1.9	1.7	4.0	4.9	3.6	0.1	1.8	2.6	1.7	-1.8
Colombia	3.1	3.3	2.8	2.1	4.6	4.7	5.9	5.7	1.5	1.4	2.9	3.6
Costa Rica	3.7	3.7	3.2	2.5		5.3	6.9	6.0		1.5	3.6	3.3
Dominican Republic	2.9	2.9	2.9	3.0	5.8	4.6	6.6	8.0	2.8	1.6	3.6	4.9
Ecuador	2.9	3.0	3.0	3.0			5.8	9.2			2.7	6.0
El Salvador	2.8	3.4	3.5	3.1	4.4	6.7	4.3	5.3	1.5	3.2	0.7	2.1
Honduras	3.3	3.5	2.8	3.3	3.1	4.9	4.2	3.2	-0.2	1.4	1.4	-0.1
Jamaica	1.5	1.6	1.2	1.7	8.1	3.7	5.1	0.0	6.5	2.1	3.9	-1.7
Mexico	3.2	3.3	3.3	3.3	5.6	7.4	6.8	4.9	2.4	3.9	3.5	1.5
Netherlands Antilles	1.7	1.7	1.4	1.2								
Nicaragua	2.9	3.0	3.0	3.3	5.2	10.4	4.1	5.8	2.2	7.2	1.1	2.4
Panama	2.9	3.1	3.1	3.1	4.9	7.9	7.8	3.5	1.9	4.7	4.6	0.4
Paraguay	2.6	2.6	2.7	2.9	2.7	4.5	4.3	7.0	0.1	1.9	1.6	4.0
Peru	2.6	2.9	2.9	2.8	4.9	7.1	4.3	4.5	2.2	4.1	1.4	1.7
Puerto Rico	0.6	1.6	1.3	2.8	5.3	8.1	7.0	3.6	4.7	6.5	5.6	0.7
Trinidad and Tobago	2.8	3.0	1.1	1.2		4.7	3.3	2.2		1.6	2.2	1.0
Uruguay	1.4	1.2	1.0	0.2	1.7	0.6	1.9	1.6	0.3	-0.6	1.0	1.3
Venezuela	4.0	3.6	3.3	3.4	8.0	7.4	4.9	5.6	3.8	3.7	1.6	2.2

TABLE 4. COMPARATIVE ECONOMIC DATA (Continued)

Income group/ region/country	Population				Gross domestic product				GDP per capita			
	1950-60	1960-65	1965-70	1970-77	1950-60	1960-65	1965-70	1970-77	1950-60	1960-65	1965-70	1970-77
C. Developing countries by region and country (cont.)												
Southern Europe												
Cyprus	1.5	0.6	0.8	0.7	4.0	3.7	8.1	1.0	2.5	3.0	7.2	0.3
Greece	1.0	0.5	0.6	0.7	6.0	7.7	7.2	4.6	5.0	7.2	6.6	3.9
Israel	5.3	3.9	3.0	2.8	11.3	9.8	8.7	5.0	5.6	5.6	5.5	2.2
Malta	0.5	-0.6	0.5	0.3	3.3	0.3	9.0	11.4	2.7	0.9	8.5	11.1
Portugal	0.7	0.2	-0.2	0.8	4.1	6.4	6.4	4.6	3.4	6.1	6.6	3.7
Spain	0.8	1.0	1.1	1.0	6.2	8.0	6.3	4.7	5.3	7.5	5.1	3.6
Turkey	2.8	2.5	2.5	2.5	6.3	5.3	6.3	7.3	3.4	2.8	3.7	4.6
Yugoslavia	1.2	1.1	0.9	0.9	5.6	6.6	6.2	6.2	4.4	5.4	5.2	5.2
D. Capital-surplus oil-exporting countries												
Kuwait	6.2	11.1	9.6	6.2	..	4.7[h]	5.7	-0.1	..	-5.8	-3.5	-6.0
Libyan Arab Republic	2.7	3.8	4.2	4.1	..	..	..	..	..	..	..	..
Oman	2.0	2.5	2.7	3.2	..	5.7	39.7	6.8	..	3.2	36.0	3.5
Qatar	2.4	7.1	0.9	10.3	..	..	..	..	..	..	..	..
Saudi Arabia	2.0	2.5	2.8	3.0	..	..	9.1	12.7	..	..	6.1	9.4
United Arab Emirates	2.4	9.3	13.7	16.7	..	..	..	12.5[l]	..	..	..	-2.1[l]
E. Industrialized countries												
Australia	2.3	2.0	1.9	1.7	4.7[f]	5.3	6.2	3.3	2.3[f]	3.2	4.2	1.6
Austria	0.2	0.6	0.5	0.2	5.6	4.3	5.1	4.0	5.4	3.7	4.6	3.8
Belgium	0.6	0.7	0.4	0.3	3.1[i]	5.2	4.8	3.7	2.5[j]	4.5	4.4	3.4
Canada	2.7	1.9	1.7	1.2	4.0[j]	5.8	4.8	4.7	1.3[j]	3.8	3.0	3.4
Denmark	0.7	0.8	0.7	0.4	3.6[j]	5.1	4.5	2.8	2.9[j]	4.3	3.7	2.4
Finland	1.0	0.6	0.2	0.4	4.9	5.0	5.1	3.4	3.9	4.4	4.9	3.0
France	0.9	1.3	0.8	0.7	4.8	5.9	5.3	3.8	3.8	4.5	4.5	3.1
Germany, Federal Republic of	1.0	1.3	0.6	0.2	7.3[j]	4.8	4.5	2.4	6.3[j]	3.5	3.9	2.2
Iceland	2.1	1.8	1.2	1.3	..	7.1	1.1	4.6	..	5.2	-0.2	3.2
Ireland	-0.5	0.3	0.5	1.2	4.0	4.0	5.3	3.4	..	3.7	4.7	2.3
Italy	0.7	0.7	0.7	0.7	5.5[k]	5.0	6.1	2.9	4.8[g]	4.3	5.4	2.2

TABLE 4. COMPARATIVE ECONOMIC DATA (Continued)

Income group/ region/country	Population				Gross domestic product				GDP per capita			
	1950-60	1960-65	1965-70	1970-77	1950-60	1960-65	1965-70	1970-77	1950-60	1960-65	1965-70	1970-77
Japan	1.3	1.0	1.1	1.2	8.0[l]	10.1	12.4	5.0	6.6[l]	9.0	11.2	3.7
Luxembourg	0.6	1.1	0.4	0.8	..	3.3	3.6	2.3	..	2.2	3.2	1.5
Netherlands, The	1.3	1.4	1.2	0.9	4.7	4.9	5.7	3.2	3.3	3.5	4.4	2.3
New Zealand	2.2	2.1	1.4	1.7	..	5.0	2.6	2.9	..	2.9	1.2	1.2
Norway	0.9	0.8	0.8	0.6	3.4[l]	5.1	4.8	4.8	2.5[l]	4.3	3.9	4.1
Sweden	0.6	0.7	0.8	0.4	3.4	5.3	3.9	1.7	2.7	4.6	3.1	1.3
Switzerland	1.3	2.1	1.1	0.2	4.6	5.2	4.2	0.2	3.2	3.0	3.1	0.0
United Kingdom	0.4	0.7	0.3	0.1	2.8	3.2	2.5	1.9	2.3	2.4	2.2	1.7
United States	1.7	1.5	1.1	0.8	3.3	4.7	3.2	2.8	1.5	3.2	2.1	1.9
F. Centrally planned economies[k]												
Albania	2.8	3.0	2.8	2.5	..	..	..	..	..	..	..	..
Bulgaria	0.8	0.8	0.7	0.6	..	7.0	8.6	7.5	..	6.2	7.8	6.9
China	1.9	2.0	1.8	1.6	..	..	..	..	..	..	..	..
Cuba	2.6	2.1	1.9	1.6	..	..	..	..	..	..	..	..
Czechoslovakia	1.0	0.7	0.3	0.7	..	..	6.6[a]	5.2	..	..	6.3[a]	4.5
German Democratic Republic	-0.6	-0.3	0.0	-0.2	..	2.7[l]	5.5[l]	5.1[l]	..	5.9	5.5	5.3
Hungary	0.7	0.3	0.4	0.4	..	4.5	6.8	6.2	..	4.2	6.4	5.8
Korea, Democratic People's Republic of	0.8	2.8	2.8	2.6	..	..	..	..	..	..	..	..
Mongolia	2.2	2.8	3.1	3.0	..	..	..	..	..	..	..	..
Poland	1.8	1.3	0.6	1.0	..	6.0	6.0	8.7	..	4.6	5.4	7.6
Romania	1.2	0.7	1.4	0.9	..	8.8	7.7	10.7	..	8.0	6.2	10.1[m]
Union of Soviet Socialist Republics	1.8	1.5	1.0	0.9	..	6.6	8.2	6.1	..	5.0	7.1	5.5[m]

+ Weighted average of the country growth rates; GDP in US dollars were used as weights; these are not strictly comparable to other group averages.   ++ 1955-60.   a. 1966-70.   b. 1967-70.
differences in national accounting system   l. Based on NMP index (1960=100) constructed from 1975 constant price series.   m. 1970-76.

TABLE 4. COMPARATIVE ECONOMIC DATA (Continued)

	Gross production							
	Agriculture				Manufacturing			
	1950-60	1960-65	1965-70	1970-77	1950-60	1960-65	1965-70	1970-77
Developing countries	3.9	2.8	3.4	2.7	4.9	7.6	7.5	7.4
Capital-surplus oil-exporting countries	..	..	2.2	4.4	..	..	..	..
Industrialized countries	2.3+	2.0	2.2	2.1	6.1+	5.9	5.8	2.8
Centrally planned economies	..	..	3.2+	2.4+	..	8.0+	8.3+	7.4+
A. Developing countries by income group								
Low income	..	1.6	4.1	2.2	..	8.4	3.3	5.2
Middle income	4.5	3.1	3.0	3.0	4.7	7.5	7.9	7.2
B. Developing countries by region								
Africa south of Sahara	4.8	2.6	2.4	1.3	..	8.3	6.0	5.6
Middle East and North Africa	..	1.3	3.6	2.8	..	10.0	0.9	12.1
East Asia and Pacific	4.8	4.6	3.4	4.1	..	4.8	11.9	11.6
South Asia	3.2	1.1	4.7	2.1	6.4	8.8	3.5	4.3
Latin America and the Caribbean	..	3.5	2.8	3.3	4.0	5.6	0.7	5.8
Southern Europe	4.4	3.2	3.2	3.1	8.4	11.4	9.3	6.1
C. Developing countries by region and country								
Africa south of Sahara								
Angola	..	3.2	2.0	-3.4	..	..	..	..
Benin	3.3	1.9	5.2	1.5	..	..	..	..
Botswana	..	2.4	0.4	4.5	..	..	..	..
Burundi	-1.5	1.7	1.7	2.0	..	..	..	..
Cameroon	3.7	7.2	4.4	1.8	..	..	10.7*	6.2
Cape Verde	..	..	..	..	..	..	..	..
Central African Republic	..	-1.2	3.3	2.1	..	4.1	8.1	6.0
Chad	..	0.9	-0.3	0.2	..	..	2.0^b	5.7
Comoros	..	..	..	..	..	..	..	..
Congo, People's Republic of the	..	0.0	2.9	2.8	..	3.4	7.7	2.3
Equatorial Guinea	..	4.8^c	-3.1	-4.9	..	..	..	..
Ethiopia	4.1	1.8	1.9	-0.1	..	..	..	..
Gabon	..	3.2^c	1.9	1.3	..	..	..	..

TABLE 4. COMPARATIVE ECONOMIC DATA (Continued)

| | Gross production | | | | | | | |
| | Agriculture | | | | Manufacturing | | | |
	1950-60	1960-65	1965-70	1970-77	1950-60	1960-65	1965-70	1970-77
Gambia, The	0.4	7.1	-0.3	1.7		3.1	8.9	4.3
Ghana	7.0	3.5	3.8	-0.4	4.6	10.8	12.5	-1.9
Guinea	2.7	1.9	3.5	0.0				
Guinea-Bissau								
Ivory Coast	9.3	11.3	3.7	4.5		14.2	8.0	7.5
Kenya	4.7	2.9	1.1	3.0				
Lesotho		0.1	1.5	2.0				
Liberia	2.6	3.0	3.0	2.3			14.1	5.5
Madagascar	3.9	4.1	1.6	2.7				1.2
Malawi		3.8	3.4	3.8				10.6
Mali	1.8	2.3	3.2	2.7			4.0	9.2
Mauritania		3.4	2.2	-3.3			35.1	2.9
Mauritius		3.1	-1.4	2.6				
Mozambique		0.8	4.4	-1.8				
Namibia								
Niger	5.5	5.2	0.6	0.4	5.0	14.6	8.8	8.6
Nigeria	5.1	2.1	1.7	1.7		11.1	10.4	8.1
Réunion								
Rhodesia		2.9	0.0	3.9	5.0	6.2	7.5	3.8
Rwanda		-1.6	8.4	3.6				
Senegal	4.8	4.1	-4.5	5.0		0.4	1.2	8.2
Sierra Leone	0.3	4.7	2.2	2.0			2.7	3.6
Somalia		2.7	1.9	0.0				
South Africa	4.1	1.5	3.9	2.2	5.0	8.4	6.7	3.2
Sudan	-0.4	5.4	6.0	2.3				
Swaziland		4.6	7.0	3.6		17.1c	21.9	7.3
Tanzania, United Republic of	6.9	2.9	3.0	1.2				
Togo	9.3	31.3	1.4	-5.5			6.7	11.3
Uganda	6.9	1.4	4.2	0.8				
Upper Volta	-0.2	7.2	2.2	1.0			3.8b	7.1
Zaire	1.0	-2.2	2.3	1.9			0.3	1.1
Zambia		1.2	1.9	4.7		12.1	8.6	1.7

TABLE 4. COMPARATIVE ECONOMIC DATA (Continued)

	Gross production							
	Agriculture				Manufacturing			
	1950-60	1960-65	1965-70	1970-77	1950-60	1960-65	1965-70	1970-77
C. Developing countries by region and country (cont.)								
Middle East and North Africa								
Algeria	-0.5	-2.2	4.1	0.4	..	..	..	..
Bahrain	..	..	1.6	4.0	..	..	..	..
Egypt, Arab Republic of	3.4	3.6	3.5	0.7	8.8	20.0	3.8	6.3
Iran	2.1	2.7	4.1	4.2	..	9.5	13.4	16.0
Iraq	1.5	4.0	4.0	-2.3	..	..	..	..
Jordan	..	20.7	-15.3	-1.6	..	..	..	..
Lebanon	5.0	9.1	0.7	-0.5	..	..	..	..
Morocco	3.0	5.1	4.1	-2.0	5.2	3.3	5.8	6.5
Syrian Arab Republic	2.1	10.8	-1.7	9.8	6.3	9.2	4.8	8.3
Tunisia	4.5	3.6	-0.5	5.6	..	2.9	4.8	5.6
Yemen, Arab Republic of	..	1.2	-4.3	3.1	..	..	..	..
Yemen, People's Democratic Republic of	..	2.6	1.2	3.8	..	..	..	..
East Asia and Pacific								
Fiji	..	11.2[c]	3.3	-0.4	..	..	5.4	3.0
Hong Kong	..	0.9	-0.3	-10.3	..	12.4	18.6	4.0
Indonesia	2.0	3.9	3.3	3.1	..	1.0	7.9	12.5
Korea, Republic of	5.5	6.3	3.1	4.9	16.4	13.9	25.6	23.5
Malaysia	0.9	5.2	6.4	4.3	..	..	11.5	12.6
Papua New Guinea	..	4.2	2.8	3.1	9.7[k]	..	..	..
Philippines	3.3	2.8	3.2	5.8	..	6.2	4.4	5.2
Singapore	..	1.4	15.8	1.0	..	7.7	15.8	11.2
Solomon Islands	..	1.4	0.9	1.9	..	..	..	..
Taiwan	4.8	4.8	2.9	3.1	15.4	13.6	21.0	13.3
Thailand	3.8	6.6	3.1	4.7	6.4	10.8	10.2	11.8
South Asia								
Afghanistan	..	1.6	1.0	4.0	..	..	8.0	9.3
Bangladesh	..	3.1	3.1	1.8	..	5.8	7.4	5.7

TABLE 4. COMPARATIVE ECONOMIC DATA (Continued)

| | Gross production | | | | | | | |
| | Agriculture | | | | Manufacturing | | | |
	1950-60	1960-65	1965-70	1970-77	1950-60	1960-65	1965-70	1970-77
Bhutan	2.5	..	..	..	..	..	..	..
Burma	3.2	3.1	3.1	1.6	..	5.6	1.7	4.4
India	..	0.5	4.9	2.1	6.6	9.0	2.8	4.6
Nepal	..	0.9	1.7	1.2	..	..	..	..
Pakistan	..	4.6	5.9	2.6	..	12.1	9.4	2.6
Sri Lanka	2.3	3.6	2.1	2.4	-0.9	6.1	5.6	2.7
Latin America and the Carribean								
Argentina	..	3.0	3.0	3.3	0.4	3.9	6.1	3.0
Bahamas	..	..	..	..	..	..	..	..
Barbados	..	3.6	-2.5	-2.7	..	..	1.6[a]	6.5
Belize	..	13.7	5.4	2.6	..	..	..	..
Bolivia	4.5	4.1	4.2	4.4	1.3	7.0	3.4	7.1
Brazil	2.9	3.2	2.7	4.4	9.1	3.7	10.4	9.6
Chile	..	2.2	2.5	1.7	5.7	6.7	1.5	-4.4
Colombia	..	2.8	3.6	3.9	6.5	5.7	6.2	6.5
Costa Rica	..	3.4	5.6	3.5	..	9.2	8.0	8.1
Dominican Republic	..	-2.7	5.9	2.0	5.0	1.5	11.4	8.8
Ecuador	..	5.8	3.0	3.5	..	..	7.2	10.6
El Salvador	..	2.9	0.4	3.3	5.7	17.0	5.0	8.3
Honduras	2.9	4.5	5.3	1.3	7.0	3.0	4.9	5.6
Jamaica	2.9	3.2	-1.3	1.1	7.6	7.6	3.0	0.6
Mexico	5.4	5.9	2.0	2.1	7.0	9.6	8.4	5.9
Netherlands Antilles	1.1	1.2	3.1	9.7	..	..	..	..
Nicaragua	..	13.0	1.2	5.0	10.7	12.6	9.6	..
Panama	..	4.3	6.5	3.5	..	12.6	9.6	1.2
Paraguay	3.6	4.9	2.4	4.6	..	3.5	5.9	3.1
Peru	..	2.4	2.3	0.7	7.3	9.7	6.7	5.8
Puerto Rico	..	..	..	..	..	..	..	..
Trinidad and Tobago	0.3	2.8	1.4	-0.5	..	..	6.1	-1.1
Uruguay	..	2.3	3.1	0.4	3.2	1.0	2.4	2.7
Venezuela	..	5.6	5.7	2.2	13.0	9.5	3.6	5.6

TABLE 4. COMPARATIVE ECONOMIC DATA (Continued)

	Gross production							
	Agriculture				Manufacturing			
	1950-60	1960-65	1965-70	1970-77	1950-60	1960-65	1965-70	1970-77
C. Developing countries by region and country (cont.)								
Southern Europe								
Cyprus	3.8	7.7	5.4	0.8	..	2.5	10.1	1.4
Greece	4.7	6.5	2.4	3.8	7.9	7.9	8.7	7.7
Israel	12.0	8.1	5.8	4.9	11.6	13.6	11.6	6.1
Malta	..	2.7	6.7	0.4	..	..	..	1.2
Portugal	2.1	3.7	1.1	-1.1	6.7	8.7	8.9	7.9
Spain	2.9	2.6	3.3	3.4	8.8	12.6	10.1	10.1
Turkey	4.7	2.9	4.0	3.7	8.6	12.7	11.6	10.1
Yugoslavia	6.2	2.5	3.1	4.6	10.4	11.7	6.1	8.2
D. Capital-surplus oil-exporting countries								
Kuwait	..	..	3.0	1.5	..	..	..	..
Libyan Arab Republic	3.9	7.2	-2.0	11.4	..	..	..	..
Oman	..	..	2.8	2.1	..	..	..	..
Qatar	..	..	..	..	..	..	..	4.0
Saudi Arabia	..	2.8	2.9	2.8	..	..	11.9	..
United Arab Emirates	..	..	..	..	..	..	..	..
E. Industrialized countries								
Australia	3.8	0.5	3.6	1.9	6.3	6.1	4.9	1.3
Austria	4.7	0.7	3.6	1.9	7.5	4.5	6.4	3.3
Belgium	1.3	0.7	4.3	0.9	4.1	6.3	6.0	2.6
Canada	2.5	5.0	-1.2	2.8	3.5	6.3	4.9	3.7
Denmark	1.5	0.8	-1.1	1.2	3.5	6.9	4.6	1.8
Finland	3.4	2.4	1.4	1.4	6.4	6.2	7.5	3.3
France	3.2	2.7	1.6	1.3	6.8	5.5	9.6	2.8
Germany, Federal Republic of	3.3	0.8	3.7	0.4	9.8	5.7	6.5	1.6
Iceland	..	..	..	3.2	..	..	..	..
Ireland	2.2	0.3	3.2	3.9	3.0	6.6	7.1	4.1
Italy	2.2	3.0	2.4	1.0	9.3	6.3	7.3	3.0

TABLE 4. COMPARATIVE ECONOMIC DATA (Continued)

| | Gross production | | | | | | | |
| | Agriculture | | | | Manufacturing | | | |
	1950-60	1960-65	1965-70	1970-77	1950-60	1960-65	1965-70	1970-77
Japan	2.4	3.2	3.3	2.1	18.3	11.5	16.3	2.9
Luxembourg	1.3	0.7	4.5	0.9	4.4	1.8	4.5	0.0
Netherlands, The	2.9	0.1	6.6	3.0	5.9	6.2	7.4	2.1
New Zealand	3.0	3.0	2.2	1.0	..	..	..	..
Norway	0.6	-0.8	0.8	1.6	4.8	5.8	4.2	2.2
Sweden	-0.2	0.3	0.7	2.5	3.0	7.4	4.9	2.0
Switzerland	1.1	-0.9	2.5	1.9	6.0	5.1	5.8	-1.0
United Kingdom	2.7	3.1	1.1	0.8	3.5	3.4	3.0	0.5
United States	1.8	1.7	1.5	3.1	3.4	6.3	3.8	3.3
F. Centrally planned economies								
Albania	..	..	4.2	3.4	..	..	..	..
Bulgaria	..	..	1.5	1.6	..	11.0	11.0	8.4
China	..	..	2.5	3.0	..	..	..	..
Cuba	..	..	4.0	0.0	..	..	..	..
Czechoslovakia	..	..	3.8	2.9	..	4.5	6.8	6.7
German Democratic Republic	..	..	1.2	3.6	..	5.7	6.4	6.3
Hungary	..	..	2.7	3.7	..	7.7	5.9	6.2
Korea, Democratic People's Republic of	..	..	2.1	6.7	..	..	..	..
Mongolia	..	..	-2.0	2.3	..	..	..	..
Poland	..	..	1.6	1.3	..	8.7	8.9	10.7
Romania	..	..	-0.4	6.9	..	..	..	..
Union of Soviet Socialist Republics	..	..	4.1	1.8	..	8.4	8.6	7.2

c. 1961-65. d. 1973-77. e. 1970-75. f. 1972-77. g. 1951-60. h. 1962-65. i. 1952-60. j. 1953-60. k. GDP data are not strictly comparable to those of other countries because of

PART III

RESOURCE BIBLIOGRAPHY

This bibliography is entirely restricted to publications in English language and covers the literature since 1970. In a bibliography of this nature, it is essential that the material be as contemporary as possible, while at the same time it was thought desirable to provide a balanced weight of materials discussed over the last decade.

With respect to classification of the material, a bibliographic subject index by item number has been provided at the end of this section.

First part of this bibliography entitled, DEVELOPMENT (GENERAL) has been classified for the general reader, according to the following categories. This classification is arbitrary, however, much cross indexing has been done in the bibliographic subject index following this section of the book.

A. Problems, Issues and Trends;
B. Analytical Methods;
C. Strategies and Policies; and
D. Country Studies.

Many of the annotations in this section have been compiled from the Journal of Economic Literature, World Bank Publications, IMF-IBRD Joint Library Periodicals, Finance and Development, U.N. Documents and Publisher's Book Promotion Pamphlets.

I. BOOKS

DEVELOPMENT (GENERAL)

01   Abraham, M. Francis
A B   PERSPECTIVES ON MODERNIZATION: TOWARD A GENERAL THEORY
      OF THIRD WORLD DEVELOPMENT
      Washington, D.C.:   University Press of America, 1980.

02   Adelman, Irma and Morris, Cynthia Taft
B   ECONOMIC GROWTH AND SOCIAL EQUITY IN DEVELOPING COUNTRIES
      Stanford, Calif.: Stanford University Press, 1973.

      A quantitative investigation of the interactions among
      economic growth, political participation, and the
      distribution of income in noncommunist developing nations.
      The study is based on data (presented in the earlier
      study, Society, politics, and economic development) from
      74 countries which is given in the form of 48 qualitative
      measures of the [countries] social, economic, and political
      characteristics, and it includes the use of discriminant
      analysis in an examination of the forces tending to
      increase political participation and the use of a stepwise
      analysis of variance technique in analyzing the
      distribution of income.

03   Albin, Peter S.
A B   PROGRESS WITHOUT POVERTY; SOCIALLY RESPONSIBLE ECONOMIC
      GROWTH
      New York: Basic Books, 1978.

      Examines the relationship among important social
      tendencies, growth processes, and growth policies and
      argues for the return of the growth economy, with the
      caveat that social objectives and policy directions be

reformulated to avert ecological disaster and to improve economic welfare. Using a dualistic imbalance framework, explores the style and impact of unbalanced growth in modern industrial capitalism, focusing on educational policy, income distribution, and the control of technology, poverty, and urban decay. Concludes with policy recommendations for a program of social and technical advance that is geared to the intelligent management of a growth economy and the renovation of its distributive mechanisms. An appendix presents a dualistic-imbalance model of modern industrial growth.

04   Alexander, Robert J.
A B C   A NEW DEVELOPMENT STRATEGY
         Maryknoll, N.Y.: Orbis Books, 1976.

Focusing on the demand side of the development equation, this monograph concerns itself with an economic development strategy of import substitution where industries are established to manufacture products for which a home market has already been created by imports. Analyzing the effect on development of this assured demand, and exploring the limit to which this strategy can be used, the author, looks in detail at the prerequisites for the use of this method (substantial imports and protection for newly created industries) and discusses the priorities for private and public investment in this phase. Contends that this process provides a basis for developing countries to decide which projects should be undertaken first and which can be postponed until later.

05   Alvarez, Francisco Casanova
A C   NEW HORIZONS FOR THE THIRD WORLD
         Washington, D.C.: Public Affairs Press, 1976.

Presents the factors leading to approval of the Charter of Economic Rights and Duties of States by the United Nations General Assembly on 12 December 1974. Shows that the charter, with the main objective of overcoming the injustice prevailing in economic relations between nations and [elimination of] the dependence of Third World countries on industrial nations, owes its origin and adoption to President Luis Echeverria of Mexico. Argues that the developing nations remain essentially colonized and dependent entities of the industrialized world. Concludes that the future world will be less unjust and less ridden with anxiety, more secure and better able to care for its own if we respect the principles of the charter.

06   Anell, Lars and Nygren, Birgitta
A B C   THE DEVELOPING COUNTRIES AND THE WORLD ECONOMIC ORDER
         New York: St. Marin's Press, 1980.

Explores the possible form, functioning, and enforcement
of a New International Economic Order (NIEO). Provides
an account of the demands of developing countries for
a better allocation of the world's resources and considers
the early cooperation between developing and developed
countries, particularly resolutions passed at various
U.N. General Assembly sessions. Also analyzes and comments
on the central NIEO demands. Among the possible actions
the authors suggest developing countries could take are:
(1) force industrialized countries to increase the flow
and quality of aid by threatening trade discrimination;
(2) establish a list of honest consultancy firms and
a file of information on technology procurement; and
(3) feel free to steal patents from big corporations
and make use of copyrights without compensation.

07   Angelopoulos, Angelos T.
A C   FOR A NEW POLICY OF INTERNATIONAL DEVELOPMENT
          New York: Praeger, 1977.

08   Angelopoulos, Angelos T.
A C   THE THIRD WORLD AND THE RICH COUNTRIES;
          PROSPECTS FOR THE YEAR 2000
          Translated by N. Constantinidis and C. R. Corner
New York: Praeger, 1972.

An examination and projection of the gap in incomes between
the developed and underdeveloped countries of the world.
The author brings data on and discusses the indicators
of poverty, the population explosion in the developing
world, the main causes of economic backwardness, the
"myth" of development aid, the need for a new international
development strategy, various strategies of development
financing, precipitating factors in the emergence of
the Third World, economic growth and forecasts of world
income in the year 2000, and the possibilities of China
becoming the spokesman for the Third World.

09   Arkhurst, Frederick S., ed.
B C D   AFRICA IN THE SEVENTIES AND EIGHTIES;
          ISSUES IN DEVELOPMENT
          New York and London: Praeger in cooperation with the
          Adlai Stevenson Institute of International Affairs, 1970.

Eleven experts in various fields express their views
in a symposium "Africa in the 1980's" which met in Chicago
in early 1969 under the auspices of the Adlai Stevenson
Institute of International Affairs. The purpose...was
to attempt to draw a portrait of Africa in the 1980's
on the basis of the experience of the past decade and,
also, on the basis of current trends in the area of
politics, economic development, population, agriculture,
trade, education and law - all viewed as composite and
interactive factors in the development process.

10   Arndt, H. W., et al.
A B C   THE WORLD ECONOMIC CRISIS: A COMMONWEALTH PERSPECTIVE
            London: Commonwealth Secretariat, 1980.

            Report of a group of experts from Commonwealth countries
            on obstacles to structural change and sustained economic
            growth, with recommendations for specific measures by
            which developed and developing countries might act to
            reduce or eliminate such constraints. Focuses on the
            implications of the world economic crises - inflation,
            slowdown of economic growth, and staggering disequilibria
            in balance of payments - for the developing countries
            of the Third World. Stresses the need for collective
            action in view of the interdependence of the world economy.

11   Bairoch, Paul
A C D   THE ECONOMIC DEVELOPMENT OF THE THIRD WORLD SINCE 1900
            Translated from the fourth French edition by Cynthia
            Postan
            Berkeley: University of California Press, 1975.

            The author covers a wide range of factors important to
            development, namely population, agriculture, extractive
            industry, manufacturing industry, foreign trade, education,
            urbanization, the labor force and employment, and
            macroeconomic data. Particular attention is devoted
            to the development of agriculture. Comparison is drawn
            between the economic progress of Third World countries
            and developed countries at a similar stage of
            industrialization. Twenty-four countries were selected
            for the analysis, representing 80 percent of the population
            of the Third World. These include seven countries from
            each of Africa, Latin-America, and Asia respectively,
            and three countries from the Middle East.

12   Bairoch, Paul and Levy-Leboyer, Maurice, eds.
A B   DISPARITIES IN ECONOMIC DEVELOPMENT SINCE THE INDUSTRIAL
            REVOLUTION
            New York: St. Martin's Press, 1981.

            Collection of thirty-five previously unpublished essays
            presented at the 7th International Economic History
            Congress in Edinburgh in August 1978. Main theme deals
            with disparities in economic development. Concerns
            differences in income at micro-regional and international
            levels. In four parts: (1) discussing economic
            disparities among nations (two papers on international
            disparities: ten on the Third World and five on the
            developed world); (2) covering regional economic
            disparities (eight essays on northern, western, and central
            Europe; three on France; two on Southern Europe and one
            on the Third World); (3) detailing relations between
            regional and national disparities (two papers); and (4)
            discussing the methodological aspects of measurement
            of economic disparities (two papers).

13   Baldwin, Robert E.
B C   ECONOMIC DEVELOPMENT AND GROWTH
            New York, London, Sydney and Toronto: John Wiley and
            Sons, Inc., 1972.

            This short text seeks to provide "an analysis of economic
            development that in terms of breadth and sophistication
            lies between the usual elementary and advanced approaches
            to the development topic." It is organized around three
            themes, i.e., what the nature of growth problem is, what
            the main theories of growth and development are, and
            what the main policy issues facing less developed countries
            are. Therefore, the chapters deal with the characteristics
            of poverty, various classical development theories
            relatively more recent contributions to development theory,
            national and sectoral policies for growth, and issues
            in the financing of development.

14   Bauer, P.T.
B C   DISSENT ON DEVELOPMENT.   STUDIES AND DEBATES IN DEVELOPMENT
            ECONOMICS
            Cambridge, Mass.: Harvard University Press, 1972.

            A collection of previously published articles, essays,
            and book reviews, some of which have been rewritten and
            expanded, dealing with various theoretical and empirical
            issues in economic development. Part One ("Ideology
            and Experience") examines general problems of concept
            method, analysis, historical experience and policy in
            economic development, such as the vicious circle of
            poverty, the widening gap, central planning, foreign
            aid, Marxism, etc. Part Two ("Case Studies") features
            five of the author's studies on developing countries,
            particularly Nigeria and India. Part Three ("Review
            Articles") brings book reviews on such well known books
            as W. Arthur Lewis' The Theory of Economic Growth, Benjamin
            Higgins' Economic Development, Walt W. Rostow's The Stages
            of Economic Growth, Thomas Balogh's The Economics of
            Poverty, and other volumes by Gunnar Myrdal, John Pincus,
            Harry G. Johnson, E.A.G. Robinson, B.K. Madan and Jagdish
            Bhagwati.

15   Bauer, P.T.
A B   EQUALITY, THE THIRD WORLD AND ECONOMIC DELUSION
            Cambridge, Mass.: Harvard University Press, 1981.

            Critique of methods and finding of contemporary economics,
            particularly development economics, arguing that there
            is a hiatus between accepted opinion and evident reality.
            All but four chapters are extended and/or revised versions
            of previously published articles. In the three parts:
            equality, the West and the Third World, and the state
            of economics. Criticizes economics and especially
            development economics for disregard of personal qualities

and social and political arrangements as determinants
of economic achievement and for ignoring the role of
external contracts in extending markets. Notes that
the benefits of mathematical economics have been bought
at the cost of an uncritical attitude, which has led
to inappropriate use and in some cases to an emphasis
on form rather than substance.

16   Berry, Leonard and Kates, Robert W., eds.
A C   MAKING THE MOST OF THE LEAST
        New York: Holmes and Meier Publishers, 1979.

The poverty faced by Third World countries today seriously
challenges the stability of the world order. The
contributors look torward the restructuring of the present
economic order by establishing "harmonious linkages"
between the industrialized and nonindustrialized worlds.
A welcome addition to the literature on economic
development.

17   Bhatt, V. V.
A B C   DEVELOPMENT PERSPECTIVES: PROBLEM, STRATEGY AND POLICIES
        Oxford; New York: Sydney and Toronto: Pergamon Press,
        1980.

Discusses the dynamics of the socioeconomic system in
terms of the cumulative and cyclical changes in economic
institutions, ideologies, and technology. Stresses the
importance of: upgrading traditional technology and
adapting modern technology to given situations; the
financial system, since it affects savings and shapes
the pattern of resource allocation; and upgrading of
agricultural organization and technology. Sets forth
as necessary for the development process: the stability
of the international currencey and the international
monetary system, which the author proposes be linked
to prices of primary products; the shaping of the
international monetary-financial-trade system to be
consistent with LDC's development strategy; and viewing
the process of socioeconomic development as an integral
part of nation-building and of building the international
community.

18   Brown, Lester R.
A C   THE GLOBAL ECONOMIC PROSPECT: NEW SOURCES OF ECONOMIC
        STRESS
        Worldwatch Paper no. 20
        Washington, D.C.: Worldwatch Institute; New York, 1978.

Considers the relationship between the expanding global
economy and the earth's natural systems. Discusses the
increase in fuel costs, suggesting that the world is
running out of cheap energy; diminishing returns in grain
production and to fertilizer use; overfishing; global

inflation; capital shortages; unemployment; and the
changing growth prospect. Concludes that future economic
policies must shift from growth to sustainability; not
advocating abandonment of growth as a goal, but with
concern for carrying capacities of biological system.
Fisheries, forests, grasslands, and croplands, require
development of alternative energy sources and population
policies consistent with resource availability.

19   Chenery, Hollis and Syrquin, Moises
A B C   PATTERNS OF DEVELOPMENT, 1950-1970
        Assisted by Hazel Elkington
        New York and London: Oxford University Press, 1975.

Examines principal changes in economic structure that
normally accompany economic growth, focusing on resource
mobilization and allocation, particularly those aspects
needed to sustain further growth. These aspects are
treated in a uniform econometric framework to provide
a consistent description of a number of interrelated
types of structural change and also to identify systematic
differences in development patterns among countries that
are following different development strategies. The
major aim of the research is to separate the effects
of universal factors affecting all countries from
particular characteristics. The authors use data for
101 countries in the period 1950 to 1970. Countries
are grouped into three categories: large country, balanced
allocation; small country, industry specialization.
Chapter 5 compares the results obtained from time-series
data with those observed from cross-sectional data.
Results are obtained from regression techniques, where
income level and population are treated as exogenous
variables. The demographic variables show how the movement
of population from rural to urban areas and lowering
of the birth rate and death rate have influenced demand
and supply of labor. A technical appendix discusses
the methods used, the problems encountered, and all the
regression equations specified in this study.

20   Chenery, Hollis B., et al., eds.
A B C   STUDIES IN DEVELOPMENT PLANNING
        Cambridge, Mass.: Harvard University Press, 1971.

Attempts to bring together the contributors' varied
backgrounds in both field work and the use of quantitative
techniques and show how modern methods can be used in
operational development planning.

21   Chodak, Szymon
A B   SOCIETAL DEVELOPMENT: FIVE APPROACHES WITH CONCLUSIONS
        FROM COMPARATIVE ANALYSIS
        New York: Oxford University Press, 1973.

A sociologist analyzes the development and change of societies using five different conceptual approaches, attempting to view the processes of development in society from a multidimensional synthesizing perspective. These five approaches are called: "Evolutionary Theories," "Development - The Growing Societal Systemness," "Development and Innovation in the Search for Security," "Economic and Political Development," and "Modernization." The author gives references to the societal development which has taken place in various parts of the world and under different political systems.

22   Colman, David and Nixson, Frederick
A B C   ECONOMICS OF CHANGE IN LESS DEVELOPED COUNTRIES
         New York: Wiley, Halsted Press, 1978.

Analyzes the changes that are occurring in the less-developed countries (LDC's); considers the problems generated by change; and examines the agents of change. Emphasizes the internal (rather than the international) aspects of development and focuses on economic inequality within LDC's and the impact on the development process in agriculture and industry of different income distributions. Although recognizing the impact of transnational corporations on the nature and characteristics of development within the LDC's, the authors argue that it is the LDC government that is responsible for the economic policies pursued. Also outlines the concepts and measurement of development, and reviews the literature on economic theorizing about development. A final chapter discusses inflation and migration in LDC's. Authors note that too often policy recommendations ignore political acceptability and recommend that the economist should cooperate with the political scientist in the study of inflation and with the sociologist in the study of rural urban migration.

23   Corbet, Hugh and Jackson, Robert, eds.
A B C   IN SEARCH OF A NEW WORLD ECONOMIC ORDER
         New York and Toronto: Wiley, Halsted Press, 1974.

Focuses on the reform of the international commercial systems for further liberalizations of world trade. Papers are grouped into four categories: (1) introduction, (2) general factors affecting negotiations, (3) outside issues of significance, (4) issues on the agenda.

24   Fields, Gary S.
A B C D POVERTY, INEQUALITY, AND DEVELOPMENT
         New York and London: Cambridge University Press, 1980.

Focuses on the distributional aspects of economic
development and explores the impact of the rate and type
of growth on poverty and inequality in poor countries.
Findings show that in general growth reduces poverty,
but a high aggregate growth rate is neither necessary
nor sufficient for reducing absolute poverty or relative
inequality. Uses case studies of distribution and
development in Costa Rica, Sri Lanka, India, Brazil,
the Phillippines, and Taiwan to examine which combinations
of circumstances and policies led to differential
performance. Concludes that a commitment to developing
to help the poor does not guarantee progress, but it
helps a great deal. In its absence, the flow of resources
to the haves, with only some trickle down to the have-nots,
will be perpetuated.

25   Finger, J. M.
A B D   INDUSTRIAL COUNTRY POLICY AND ADJUSTMENT TO IMPORTS FROM
DEVELOPING COUNTRIES
World Bank Staff Working Paper no. 470, July 1981.

A background study for World Development Report 1981.
Reviews and interprets recent analyses of the policies
established by industrial countries in response to
increasing imports from developing countries.

26   Finger, Nachum
A C D   THE IMPACT OF GOVERNMENT SUBSIDIES ON INDUSTRIAL
MANAGEMENT: THE ISRAELI EXPERIENCE
New York: Praeger, 1971.

27   Fitzgerald, E. V.
A B   PUBLIC SECTOR INVESTMENT PLANNING FOR DEVELOPING COUNTRIES
New York: Holmes and Meier, 1978.

28   Florence, P. Sargant
A B C   ECONOMICS AND SOCIOLOGY OF INDUSTRY: A REALISTIC ANALYSIS
OF DEVELOPMENT
Baltimore, Md.: Johns Hopkins University Press, 1969.

29   Frank, Andre Gunder
A B C   CRISIS IN THE THIRD WORLD
New York: Holmes and Meier, 1981.

30   Frank, Andre Gunder
A B   DEPENDENT ACCUMULATION AND UNDERDEVELOPMENT
New York and London: Monthly Review Press, 1979.

Explains underdevelopment by an analysis of the production
and exchange relations of dependence. Distinguishes
the three main stages or periods in this world embracing
process of capital accumulation and capitalist development:
mercantilist (1500-1770), industrial capitalist (1770-
1870), and imperialist (1870-1930). Analyzes each period

in terms of history, trade relations between the metropolis and the periphery, and transformation of the modes or relations of production, and the development of underdevelopment in the principal regions of Asia, Africa, and the Americas.

31   Frank, Charles R., Jr., and Webb, Richard C., eds.
A B D   INCOME DISTRIBUTION AND GROWTH IN THE LESS-DEVELOPED COUNTRIES
        Washington, D.C.: Brookings Institution, 1977.

Fourteen previously unpublished essays representing part of the results of a project undertaken jointly by the Brookings Institution and the Woodrow Wilson School of Public and International Affairs at Princeton University, dealing with the relation between income distribution and economic growth in the developing countries. The first two articles present an overview of income distribution policy and discuss the causes of growth and income distribution in LDC's, respectively. The next nine examine the relation between income distribution and different economic policies and factors, including: industrialization, education, population, wage, fiscal, agricultural, public works, health and urban land policies.

32   Gant, George F.
A B   DEVELOPMENT ADMINISTRATION - CONCEPTS, GOALS, METHODS
        Madison, Wisconsin: The University of Wisconsin Press, 1979.

Growth and modernization in the less developed countries (LDC's) during the past three decades has frequently depended upon the state's ability to plan and manage a range of developmental activities. Gant's study of development administration looks at some of the issues that could be of concern to managers in LDC's: in particular, coordination, budgeting, the selection of personnel, training, etc. He also delves into the administrative side of certain specific governmental concerns, such as family planning and education, drawing on examples from a number of Asian countries. This is not a book which goes into much technical detail. Nor does it tell one how to design an efficient administrative setup. Primarily for the general reader interested in an overview of these topics.

33   Garbacz, Christopher
A B D   INDUSTRIAL POLARIZATION UNDER ECONOMIC INTEGRATION IN LATIN AMERICA
        Austin, Texas: Bureau of Business Research, Graduate School of Business, The University of Texas, 1971.

The author discusses the problem of increased disparities in the levels of regional economic development that tend to come about as a result of economic integration. The political and economic implications of industrial polarization are studies within the context and experience of the Central American Common Market and the Latin American Free Trade Association. Finally, the author considers the problem in the light of the planned Latin American Common Market, discussing the various measures that could be taken as well as the implications for the future.

34   Garzouzi, Eva
A B C   ECONOMIC GROWTH AND DEVELOPMENT: THE LESS DEVELOPED
        COUNTRIES
        New York: Vantage Press, 1972.

Essays to consolidate into one readable text the whole of the economics of growth and development. Part I discusses the meaning and theories of economic development, outlines historical patterns of development, and summarizes the impact of capital, agriculture, industry, monetary and fiscal policies, international trade, and foreign aid on economic growth. Part II presents comparative analyses of developing regions, including Latin America, the Middle East and North Africa, Africa south of the Sahara, and Southeast Asia.

35   Geithman, David T., ed.
A B C D   FISCAL POLICY FOR INDUSTRIALIZATION AND DEVELOPMENT IN
          LATIN AMERICA
          Gainesville: University Presses of Florida.

Collection of 10 previously unpublished papers (and related comments) presented at the Twenty-First Annual Latin American Conference held in February 1971. Central theme of the conference was the analysis and evaluation of the interaction among fiscal problems, fiscal tools, and fiscal systems in the industrializing economies of Latin America.

36   Ghai, D. P.
A B C   THE BASIC-NEEDS APPROACH TO DEVELOPMENT: SOME ISSUES
        REGARDING CONCEPTS AND METHODOLOGY
        ILO, Geneva, 1977.

Contains five papers which discuss issues which arise in the formulation of criteria and approaches for the promotion of employment and the satisfaction of the basic needs of a country's population. Presents the first results of the research and conceptual work initiated by the ILO to help countries implement the basic needs-oriented strategy recommended by the World Employment Conference in 1976.

37   Gianaris, Nicholas V.
A B C   ECONOMIC DEVELOPMENT: THOUGHT AND PROBLEMS
         North Quincy, Mass.: Christopher Publishing House, 1978.

         Part one examines the process of development, the
         historical perspective, mathematical models, and modern
         theories of development; part two considers domestic
         problems of development, specifically land and other
         natural resources, human resources (particularly the
         role of education), capital formation and technological
         change, the allocation of resources, and the role of
         government and planning; part three discusses the
         international aspects of development (foreign trade,
         aid, investment, and multinationals) and current issues
         such as environmental problems, the status of women,
         income inequalities, and discrimination.

38   Giersch, Herbert, ed.
A B C D INTERNATIONAL ECONOMIC DEVELOPMENT AND RESOURCE TRANSFER:
         WORKSHOP 1978
         Tubingen, Germany: J. C. B. Mohr, 1979.

         Twenty-four previously unpublished papers from a workshop
         held in June 1978 at the Institut fur Weltwirtschaft,
         Kiel University. Contributions organized under ten
         headings: Rural Industrialization, Employment and Economic
         Development; Choice of Techniques and Industries for
         Growth and Employment; Agricultural Patterns and Policies
         in Developing Countries; Hypotheses for the Commodity
         Composition of East-West Trade; The Relationship Between
         the Domestic and International Sectors in Economic
         Development; Patterns of Trade in Services and Knowledge;
         Changes in Industrial Interdependencies and Final Demand
         in Economic Development; Public Aid for Investment in
         Manufacturing Industries; Institutional and Economic
         Criteria for the Choice of Technology in Developing
         Countries; and Problems of Measuring the Production and
         Absorption of Technologies in Developing Countries.

39   Gierst, Friedrich and Matthews, Stuart R.
A B C   GUIDELINES FOR CONTRACTING FOR INDUSTRIAL PROJECTS IN
         DEVELOPING COUNTRIES
         New York: United Nations Publications, 1975.

         Designed to serve public and private organizations in
         developing countries as a guide in preparing contracts
         concerned with industrial investment projects. Examines
         various stages involved in the preparation of an industrial
         project and discusses the basic types of contacts involved
         (i.e. those with financial institutions, with consultants
         and with contractors).

40   Gill, Richard T.
A B C   ECONOMIC DEVELOPMENT: PAST AND PRESENT

Third Edition. Foundations of Modern Economics.
Englewood Cliffs, N.J.: Prentice-Hall, 1973.

Third edition of an introductory textbook with revisions
of the discussions. The Green Revolution, two-gap analysis
of foreign aid, Denison-Jorgenson-Griliches studies of
factors affecting United States economic growth and
Leibenstein's "X-efficiency" concept have been added.
Statistical tables have been updated to include figures
on Chinese economic growth. Six chapters cover: 1)
General factors in economic development, 2) Theories
of development, 3) Beginnings of development in advanced
countries, 4) Growth of the American economy, 5) Problems
of underdeveloped countries, and 6) Development in China
and India.

41   Goulet, Denis
A B C   THE CRUEL CHOICE: A NEW CONCEPT IN THE THEORY OF
          DEVELOPMENT
          Cambridge, Mass.: Center for the Study of Development
          and Social Change, Atheneum, 1971.

This work is intended to probe moral dilemmas faced by
economic and social development. Its central concern
is that philosophical conceptions about the "good life"
and the "good society" should be of more profound
importance in assessing alternative paths to development
than economic, political, or technological questions.
The theoretical analysis is based on two concepts:
"vulnerability" and "existence rationality." Vulnerability
is defined as exposure to forces that can not be
controlled, and is expressed in the failure of many
low-income countries to attain their development goals,
as well as in manifestations of mass alienation in certain
societies where prosperity has already been achieved.
Existence rationality denotes those strategies used by
all societies to possess information and to make practical
choices designed to assure survival and satisfy their
needs for esteem and freedom. These strategies vary
with a country's needs and are conditioned by numerous
constraints.

42   Griffin, Keith
A B C   INTERNATIONAL INEQUALITY AND NATIONAL POVERTY
          New York: Holms & Meier, 1978.

Nine essays, seven previously published between 1970
and 1978. Challenges the classical assumption that
unrestricted international intercourse will reduce
inequality and poverty. Argues that forces creating
inequality are automatic, and not due to malevolence
of developed nations or corporations, but that the motor
of change in the contemporary world economy is technical
innovation. Since the advances tend to be concentrated

in the developed countries where they are applicable
to their technology, rich countries are able to extract
supra-normal profits and rents from the poor countries
through trade. The high level of factor earnings in
rich countries attract the most valuable financial and
human resources of the poor countries through induced
international migration. Divided into two parts, part
one deals with international inequality and discusses:
the international transmission of inequality; multinational
corporations; foreign capital, domestic savings, and
economic development; emigration, and the New International
Economic Order. The essays in part two focus on national
poverty, discussing the facts of poverty in the Third
World, analyzing models of development, and assessing
the Chinese system of incentives.

43   Griffin, Keith B. and Enos, John L.
A B C   PLANNING DEVELOPMENT
         Reading, Mass.; Don Mills, Ontario; Sydney; London; and
         Manila: Addison-Wesley, 1971.

         Part of a series intended to serve as guidebooks on
         development economics, this book deals with practical
         problems of planning and economic policy in underdeveloped
         countries. Consists of four parts: 1) the role of
         planning, 2) quantitative planning techniques, 3) sector
         policies, and 4) planning in practice with reference
         to Chile, Columbia, Ghana, India, Pakistan and Turkey.

44   Hagen, Everett E.
A B C   THE ECONOMICS OF DEVELOPMENT
         Revised Edition. The Irwin Series in Economics.
         Homewood, Ill.: Irwin, 1975.

         Revised edition with two new chapters added, one dealing
         with the earth's stock of minerals and economic growth,
         and the other on the relationships between economic growth
         and the distribution of income. Chapters on population
         and economic planning have been extensively revised,
         with the former focusing on the relationship of food
         supply to continued world growth. Additional changes
         include: reorganization of the discussion of growth
         theories; a considerably augmented discussion of
         entrepreneurhsip; and a reorganization of the chapters
         on import substitution versus export expansion and external
         finance.

45   Helleiner, G. K., ed.
B C   A WORLD DIVIDED: THE LESS DEVELOPED COUNTRIES IN THE
         INTERNATIONAL ECONOMY
         Perspectives on Development, no. 5
         New York; London and Melbourne: Cambridge University
         Press, 1976.

Twelve papers discussing the new policies and instruments needed if the interests of poor nations are to be met. Within the realm of trade, consideration is given to the possibility of increased cooperation through: supply management schemes; bargaining capacity and power; closer ties with other less developed countries; and the development of alternative marketing channels and joint sales efforts. Relations between the less developed countries and transnational firms is then considered with special attention given to the factors affecting the bargaining position of the countries. Issues in international finance and monetary policy are: the borrowing of Eurodollars by less developed countries, internationally agreed upon principles for an honorable debt default, and interests of less developed countries in a new international monetary order. Another paper considers means by which a self-reliant but poor country can seek to conduct its economic affairs in the face of a most inhospitable and uncertain international environment. The concluding paper considers the implication of the new mood in the less developed countries for future international organisation.

46   Hermassi, Elbaki
A C D THE THIRD WORLD REASSESSED
       Berkeley: University of California Press, 1980.

47   Horowitz, Irving Louis, ed.
A B C EQUITY, INCOME, AND POLICY: COMPARATIVE STUDIES IN THREE
       WORLDS OF DEVELOPMENT
       New York and London: Praeger, 1977.

Ten previously unpublished papers by sociologists and economists on the multiple ideologies of development and the drive toward equity congruent with different social systems. Six essays address the problems of the "First World," i.e. those types of societies dominated by a free market and an open society, where the main problem would seem to be how to maintain growth and development while providing distributive justice. Two papers look at the "Second World" of socialism; these assume the central role of state power as imposing its will to produce equity. The remaining papers consider the Third World, examining in particular income distribution in Tanzania and economic equality and social class in general.

48   Jalan, Bimal
A B C ESSAYS IN DEVELOPMENT POLICY
       Delhi: S. G. Wasani for Macmillan of India, 1975.

A common theme of the 11 essays (some previously published) is the explicit reference to political philosophies involved in the choices of means and objectives of

development and social change. Essays include: discussion
of self-reliance objectives; trade and industrialization
policies; distribution of income; the project evaluation
manual of Professors Little and Mirrlees; UNIDO guidelines
for project evaluation; criteria for determination of
appropriate terms of aid assistance; the definition and
assessment of performance in developing countries; the
history of the United Nations Capital Development Fund,
the World Bank, and the International Development
Association; and an analysis of the principal
recommendations of the Pearson Commission Report (1969).

49   Jumper, Sidney R.; Bell, Thomas L. and Ralston, Bruce A.
B C   ECONOMIC GROWTH AND DISPARITIES: A WORLD VIEW
        Englewood Cliffs, N.J.: Prentice-Hall, 1980.

The authors emphasize understanding of real world
differences in levels of human development, rather than
sophisticated analytical procedures. In seven parts:
geographical concepts; the factors influencing variations
in levels of development; world food supplies; minerals;
factors affecting intensity of manufacturing development;
the service industries; and a summary of the role of
geographers in facing these development problems.

50   Kahn, Herman
A B C   WORLD ECONOMIC DEVELOPMENT: 1979 AND BEYOND
        With the Hudson Institute.
        Boulder: Westview Press, 1979.

Examines economic prospects focusing on the period
1978-2000, and particularly the earlier part of the period.
In two parts, part one presents the general historical
framework, concepts, and perspectives on economic growth
and cultural change. Part two examines the major trends
and problems of the real world, focusing on the elements
of change and continuity in both the advanced and
developing economies. Rejects attempts by some to stop
the world and argues for and suggests strategies for
rapid worldwide economic growth, for Third World
industrialization, and for the use of advanced (or at
least appropriate) technology.

51   Kasdan, Alan R.
A B C   THE THIRD WORLD: A NEW FOCUS FOR DEVELOPMENT
        Cambridge, Mass.: Schenkman Publishing, 1973.

52   Kindleberger, Charles P. and Herrick, Bruce
B   ECONOMIC DEVELOPMENT
        Third Edition. Economics Handbook Series.
        New York; London; Paris and Tokyo: McGraw-Hill, 1977.

Textbook that survey[s] the present panorama of
international poverty, the applications to it of economic
analysis, and the policies for improvement that the
analysis implies. This edition which has been completely
rewritten and updated, includes new chapters on:
population, urbanization, collective international action,
employment, income distribution, and the theories of
economic development.

53   Leipziger, Danny M., ed.
A B C BASIC NEEDS AND DEVELOPMENT
       Foreword by Paul P. Streeten
       Cambridge, Mass.: Oelgeschlager, Gunn & Hain, 1981.

Five previously unpublished essays discuss the potential
contribution of the basic needs approach to developmental
theory and practice. Michael J. Crosswell gives his
views in two essays on a development planning approach
and on growth, poverty alleviation, and foreign assistance.
Maureen A. Lewis discusses sectional aspects of the
linkages among population, nutrition, and health. Danny
M. Leipziger writes about policy issues and the basic
human needs approach. Martha de Melo presents a case
study of Sri Lanka focusing on the effects of alternative
approaches to basic human needs. The authors are all
economists.

54   Leontief, Wassily, et al.
A B C THE FUTURE OF THE WORLD ECONOMY: A UNITED NATIONS STUDY
       New York: Oxford University Press, 1977.

Investigates the interrelationships between future world
economic growth and availability of natural resources,
pollution, and the impact of environmental policies.
Includes a set of alternative projections of the
demographic, economic, and environmental states of the
world in the years 1980, 1990, and 2000 with a comparison
with the world economy of 1970. Constructs a multiregional
input-output economic model of the world economy.
Investigates some of the main problems of economic growth
and development in the world as a whole, with special
accent on problems encountered by the developing countries.
The findings include: (1) target rates of growth of
gross product in the developing regions...are not
sufficient to start closing the income gap between the
developing and the developed countries; (2) the principal
limits to sustained economic growth and accelerated
development are political, social and institutional in
character rather than physical; (3) the necessary increased
food production is technically feasible, but dependent
on drastically favorable public policy measure; (4)
pollution is not an unmanageable problem.

55   Lin, Ching-Yuan
A C D   DEVELOPING COUNTRIES IN A TURBULENT WORLD: PATTERNS
           OF ADJUSTMENT SINCE THE OIL CRISIS
           New York: Praeger, 1981.

           Examines national authorities' policy reactions to changes
           in the world economy since 1973, to determine whether
           differences in national economic performances can be
           explained in terms of differences in their policy
           reactions.   Investigates global patterns of absorption,
           production, and adjustment since the oil crisis; global
           expenditure flows before and after the crisis; and
           international bank transactions and world trade.   Reviews
           the experiences of developing countries during the period,
           focusing on non-oil countries.   Finds that collectively
           the non-oil developing countries experienced a much milder
           contraction of domestic demand and real ouput than the
           more developed countries after the disturbances in 1973-75,
           although individual experiences varied; however, inflation
           remains persistent.   Argues that most developing countries
           did not pursue demand management policies early enough
           to counteract sharp changes in external demand.

56   Madhava, K. B., ed.
A B C D   INTERNATIONAL DEVELOPMENT, 1969:   CHALLENGES TO PREVALENT
           IDEAS ON DEVELOPMENT
           Dobbs Ferry: Oceana for Society for International
           Development, 1970.

           Contains the proceedings of the 11th World Conference
           of the Society for International Development held in
           1969 in New Delhi.   The theme "Challenges to Prevalent
           Ideas on Development" was carried out through roundtable
           discussions centering on: the redefinition of goals;
           foreign aid;   manpower, education, and development;
           population communication; social communication; political
           and social-cultural requisites; and challenges to theorists
           and strategists.

57   May, Brian
A C D   THE THIRD WORLD CALAMITY
           London and Boston: Routledge & Kegan Paul, 1981.

           Assessment of social conditions, politics, economics,
           and cultural barriers in the Third World, with particular
           reference to India, Iran, and Nigeria.   Contends that
           the "chronic socio-economic stagnation" that characterizes
           these countries is not attributable to Western imperialism,
           maintaining that fundamental change in Third World
           countries was and is blocked by psychological and cultural
           facts.   Compares relevant factors in Europe and in the
           three countries to show the constraints that block
           significant socioeconomic change.

58   McGreevey, William Paul, ed.
A B C   THIRD-WORLD POVERTY: NEW STRATEGIES FOR MEASURING
          DEVELOPMENT PROGRESS
          Lexington, Mass.:   Heath, Lexington Books, 1980.

Five previously unpublished papers on the problems of
measuring progress in alleviating poverty in the Third
World, originally part of a series of seminars (1976-79)
sponsored by the Agency for International Development.
Editor McGreevey reviews the development progress from
both a human capital and poverty alleviation standpoint;
Gary S. Fields looks at absolute-poverty measures (i.e.,
those not depending on income distribution considerations);
Harry J. Bruton considers the use of available employment
and unemployment data in assessing government poverty
policy, and G. Edward Schuh and Robert L. Thompson discuss
measures of agricultural progress and government commitment
to agricultural development.   The fifth paper by Nancy
Birdsall is a summary of discussion in two seminars on
time-use surveys and networks of social support in LDC's.
The authors find in part that: (1) existing data are
inadequate to judge progress; (2) the best data gathering
method is multipurpose household surveys; and (3) networks
of social support are important (and unmeasured) means
of income transfer between households.

59   McHale, John and McHale, Magda C.
A B C   BASIC HUMAN NEEDS: A   FRAMEWORK FOR ACTION
          New Brunswick, N.J.:   Rutgers University, Transaction
          Books, 1978.

60   Meadows, Dennis L., ed.
A B C   ALTERNATIVES TO GROWTH--I: A SEARCH FOR SUBSTAINABLE
          FUTURES: PAPERS ADAPTED FROM ENTRIES TO THE 1975 GEORGE
          AND CYNTHIA MITCHELL PRIZE AND FROM PRESENTATIONS BEFORE
          THE 1975 ALTERNATIVES TO GROWTH CONFERENCE, HELD AT
          THE WOODLANDS, TEXAS
          Cambridge, Mass.:   Lippincott, Ballinger, 1977.

Seventeen previously unpublished interdisciplinary papers
on the transition from growth to a steady-state society,
i.e., a society with a constant stock of physical wealth
and a constant stock of people.   In four parts: the
relation between population and food or energy; economic
alternatives; the rationales, mechanisms, and implications
of various long-term planning proposals; and analysis
of the determinants, nature, and implications of current
paradigms, norms, laws, and religion.

61   Melady, Thomas Patrick and Suhartono, R. B.
A B   DEVELOPMENT -- LESSONS FOR THE FUTURE
          Maryknoll, New York: Orbis Books, 1973.

Investigation of what determines, economically, which
countries are developing, based on examination of
characteristics of nations agreed to be undergoing this
experience. The study examines such facets of development
as the nonhomogeneity of the developing countries; factors
affecting economic growth, the sectoral aspect of growth
(industry and agriculture), measurements of the phenomenon,
and the applicability of economic theory in this work;
and the effects of economic development on man and his
role in society.

62   Morawetz, David
A B D TWENTY-FIVE YEARS OF ECONOMIC DEVELOPMENT, 1950 TO 1975
      Johns Hopkins University Press for IBRD, 1977.

Assesses development programs of developing countries
and global development targets adopted by international
organizations over the past 25 years. Chapters cover:
a) changing objectives of development; b) growth in GNP
per capita, population and the gap between rich and poor
countries; c) reduction of poverty, including employment,
income distribution, basic needs, nutrition, health,
housing and education; d) self-reliance and economic
independence; and e) conclusions, hypotheses, and
questions.

63   Morgan, Theodore
B C   ECONOMIC DEVELOPMENT: CONCEPT AND STRATEGY
      New York and London: Harper & Row, 1975.

Textbook in economic development with emphasis on policy,
its appropriate definition, its targets, and its
improvement of application. Diverts focus from GNP and
average income growth rates and into issues such as income
distribution, nutrition, disease, climate, and population
increases and their effects on development. Surveys
existing theoretical literature. Discusses development
planning and the importance of the statistical foundation
of decision-making, and planning techniques such as
cost-benefit analysis. Provides sporadic data for
less-developed countries, mostly for the post-World War
II period, on various national variables.

64   Ramati, Yohanan, ed.
A B C ECONOMIC GROWTH IN DEVELOPING COUNTRIES--MATERIAL AND
      HUMAN RESOURCES: PROCEEDINGS OF THE SEVENTH REHOVOT
      CONFERENCE
      Praeger Special Studies in International Economics and
      Development
      New York and London: Praeger in cooperation with the
      Continuation Committee of the Rehovot Conference, 1975.

Collection of 49 papers presented in September 1973.
The papers are grouped into five sections following the

structure of the conference. Part I includes papers setting the framework to analyze natural and human resources as factors in development and problems of planning and the quality of life. Part II includes papers on resources, technology, and income distribution. Part III deals with external constraints on development. Part IV examines planning and implementation. Part V contains the very brief closing addresses by Simon Kuznets and Abba Eban. Participants included 99 experts and policy makers for developing countries in Africa, Latin America, and Southeast Asia.

65   Rubinson, Richard, ed.
A B   DYNAMICS OF WORLD DEVELOPMENT
       Political Economy of the World-System Annuals, vol. 4
       Beverly Hills and London: Sage, 1981.

Twelve previously unpublished papers, almost all by sociologists, presented at the Fourth Annual Political Economy of the World-System conference at Johns Hopkins University, June 1980. Papers are based on the assumption that the world's history is the history of capitalist accumulation; and that capitalist development is the development of a single...modern world-system. Papers cover: development in peripheral areas; development in semiperipheral states; development and state organization; cycles and trends of world system development; theooretical issues; and dynamics of development of the world economy.

66   Sachs, Ignacy
A C   THE DISCOVERY OF THE THIRD WORLD
       Cambridge, Mass., and London: M. I. T. Press, 1976.

Focusing on a redefinition of development theory, discusses the role of ethnocentrism and domination by European and Western ideas in such areas as science, technology, and economics. Argues that discussions regarding economic development strategies attempt to apply Western theories and ignore the fact that Third World growth, unlike capital-intensive European growth, must be based on the use of labor. Proposes a general development theory to bridge the gap between European theory and Third World practice and discusses problems such as economic surplus and economic aid. Recommends that the U.N. assess Western nations and funnel the money to Third World nations on a "no-strings" basis.

67   Shafei, Mohamed Z.
A B   THREE LECTURES ON ECONOMIC DEVELOPMENT
       Beirut, Lebanon: Beirut Arab University, 1970.

The first lecture focuses on the characteristics of developing countries. The second traces the process

of economic development in the U.A.R. (Egypt) since 1952.
The third is on the foreign assistance needs of developing
countries.

68   Singer, H. W.
A C   THE STRATEGY OF INTERNATIONAL DEVELOPMENT: ESSAYS IN
      THE ECONOMICS OF BACKWARDNESS
      Edited by Sir Alec Cairncross and Mohinder Puri
      White Plains, N.Y.: International Arts and Sciences
      Press, 1975.

A collection of 13 papers by the author, all published
in past years, dealing with some of the central problems
of economic development and development policy. Papers
cover such issues as gains distribution among borrowing
and investing countries, dualism, international aid,
trade and development, employment problems, income
distribution, science and technology transfers, etc.
Introduction to the author's work and career by editor
Sir Alec Cairncross.

69   Singer, Hans W. and Ansari, Javed A.
A   RICH AND POOR COUNTRIES
      Baltimore and London: Johns Hopkins University Press,
      1977.

Examines the changes that are required if the relationship
between rich and poor countries is to make a more effective
contribution to the development of the poor countries.
Part one describes the structure of international economy
and the nature of development process. Part two discusses
the importance of the international trade sector to
development in the poorer countries and reviews the trade
policies of the rich and poor countries. Part three
deals with the role of aid in the development process;
and part four is concerned with international factor
movement. Stresses the need for the formulation of an
international development strategy...by the rich countries
(both old and new), providing assistance in an increasing
flow of resources through trade, aid capital and the
transfer of skills and technology to the poor countries.
Argues that such a strategy first must provide for some
discrimination in international trade in favor of poor
countries to provide more resources and secondly to enable
the importation of more appropriate technologies.

70   Spiegelglas, Stephen and Welsh, Charles J., eds.
A B   ECONOMIC DEVELOPMENT; CHALLENGE AND PROMISE
      Englewood Cliffs, N.J.: Prentice-Hall, 1970.

A collection of 33 reprinted readings, each representing
an outstanding contribution, controversial issue, or
synthesis of ideas in economic development. Major sections

include: an   introduction;   nature   and   techniques   of
planning;   strategy   and   policy;   and   trade   or   aid.   The
selection   of   topics   in   these   sections   reflects   recent
increased   emphasis   on   practical   development   problems,
particularly   on   human   resources   development   and   the   need
to   create   exportable   manufactured   goods.   A   matrix   showing
how   each   selection   fits   into   the   scheme   and   sequence
of   the   seven   widely   used   development   textbooks   is   included.

71   T. N. Srinivasan
A B C D DEVELOPMENT, POVERTY, AND BASIC HUMAN NEEDS: SOME ISSUES
World Bank Reprint Series, 76
IBRD, 1977.

Reprinted   from   Food   Research   Institute   Studies,   vol.
XVI,   no.   2   (1977),   pp.   11-28.   Deals   with   the   raising
of   standard   of   living   of   the   poorest   sections   of   the
population   in   developing   countries.   Discusses   aid
problems,   distributional   aspects   of   economic   growth,
employment   goals,   and   the   new   perceptions   of   development.

72   Stein, Leslie
A C D   ECONOMIC REALITIES IN POOR COUNTRIES
Sydney, London and Singapore: Angus and Robertson, 1972.

This   book   surveys   the   problems   of   growth   faced   by   the
developing   countries   of   the   world.   The   first   part   of
the   book   describes   the   economic   and   social   characteristics
of   Third   World   countries   and   presents   some   theories   of
development,   including   Baran's   Marxian   view,   W. W. Rostow's
non-Marxist   alternative,   balanced   growth   theory,   and
Myrdal's   view   which   considers   non-economic   as   well   as
economic   factors   of   growth.   Succeeding   chapters   discuss
population   growth,   problems   of   education,   the   role   of
agriculture   and   industrial   development,   obstacles   to
trade,   and   government   plans   which   have   been   used   in
developing   countries.   Designed   for   use   as   a   text   or
for the layman.

73   Streeten, Paul
A B D   DEVELOPMENT PERSPECTIVES
New York: St. Martin's Press, 1981.

A   combination   of   17   previously   published   articles   and
7   new   chapters,   in   five   parts: concepts,   values,   and
methods   in   development   analysis;   development   strategies;
transnational   corporations;   the   change   in   emphasis   from
the   growth   approach   to   the   basic   needs   approach;   and
two   miscellaneous   chapters   on   taxation   and   on   Gunnar
Myrdal.   Newly   written   chapters   cover: the   results   of
development   strategies   for   the   poor,   alternatives   in
development,   the   New   International   Economic   Order,   the
basic   needs   approach,   human   rights   and   basic   needs,   the

search for a basic-needs yardstick (with Norman Hicks), and transnational corporations and basic needs.

74   Thomson, W. Scott, ed.
A C   THE THIRD WORLD: PREMISES OF U.S. POLICY
       San Francisco: Institute for Contemporary Studies, 1978.

75   Tinbergen, Jan
A B   THE DESIGN OF DEVELOPMENT
       The Johns Hopkins University Press, 1958.

       Formulates a coherent government policy to further development objectives and outlines methods to stimulate private investments.

76   Todaro, Michael P.
A B C ECONOMIC DEVELOPMENT IN THE THIRD WORLD: AN INTRODUCTION TO PROBLEMS AND POLICIES IN A GLOBAL PERSPECTIVE
       London and New York: Longman, 1977.

       In four parts: Part one discusses the nature of underdevelopment and its various manifestations in the Third World, and parts two and three focus on major development problems and policies, both domestic (growth, income distribution, population, unemployment, education, and migration) and international (trade, balance of payments, and foreign investment). The last part reviews the possibilities and prospects for Third World development.

77   Todaro, Michael P.
A B   DEVELOPMENT PLANNING: MODELS AND METHODS
       Series of undergraduate teaching works in economics, Volume V.
       London, Nairobi, and New York: Oxford University Press, 1971.

       This is the last in a series of undergraduate teaching works in economics developed at Makere University, Uganda. This book is an introduction to development planning, with emphasis on plan formulation rather than implementation.

78   United Nations Department of Economic and Social Affairs
       THE INTERNATIONAL DEVELOPMENT STRATEGY: FIRST OVER-ALL REVIEW AND APPRAISAL OF ISSUES AND POLICIES. REPORT OF THE SECRETARY-GENERAL
       New York: United Nations, 1973.

       Deals with the issues and policies in the field of economic and social development...of prime concern in the first two years of the Second United Nations Development Decade. Emphasis is upon changes in the following areas: priorities of objectives, techniques of production, trade and aid relationships, and the external environment in which economic and social development takes place.

79   United Nations Department of Economic and Social Affairs
A C   SHAPING ACCELERATED DEVELOPMENT AND INTERNATIONAL CHANGES
New York: United Nations Publications, 1980.

Contains views and recommendations of the UN Committee for Development Planning relating to the international development strategy for a third UN development decade. Chapters cover general premises and basic objectives; priority areas for action; means and implementation; and key goals and needed changes.

80   United Nations Department of Economic and Social Affairs
A C   DEVELOPMENT IN THE 1980'S: APPROACH TO A NEW STRATEGY; VIEWS AND RECOMMENDATIONS OF THE COMMITTEE FOR DEVELOPMENT PLANNING
New York: United Nations Publications, 1978.

Reviews development issues for the 1980's with a discussion of the current situation and preliminary comments relating to a development strategy for the 1980's. Discusses economic cooperation among developing countries, covering trade, economic integration and other arrangements for economic cooperation.

81   United Nations Industrial Development Organization
A B C INDUSTRIALIZATION FOR NEW DEVELOPMENT NEEDS
New York: United Nations Publication, 1974.

Emphasizes the reshaping of industrial development in the light of new development needs that the pervasive problems of unemployment, maldistribution of income, and poverty in general have brought to the fore in the developing countries.

82   UNRSID
A B C THE QUEST FOR A UNIFIED APPROACH TO DEVELOPMENT
UNRSID: 1980.

Provides background information on UNRSID's efforts to formulate a unified approach to development analysis and planning, an approach which would bring together all the different aspects of development into a set of feasible objectives and policy approaches. Chapters cover: styles of development--definitions and criteria; strategies; the findings of the Expert Group; an assessment by Marshall Wolfe, former Chief of the Social Development Division of UN ECLA; and an annex containing the final report on the project by the UN Commission for Social Development, covering questions of diagnosis, monitoring, indicators, and planning and capicitation.

83   Uri, Pierre
A B C   DEVELOPMENT WITHOUT DEPENDENCE
New York: Praeger for the Atlantic Institute for
International Affairs, 1976.

Monograph on foreign aid. Contends that the aid programs
of the 1950's and 1960's were lopsided and failed to
address the needs of the truly poor. According to Bundy,
the author argues that although effective transfer of
resources and skill remains a vital part of the need...such
nation-to-nation aid...can only help to foster the very
feelings of dependence...that are the deepest grievance
of the developing world. Discusses control of population
growth, the role and necessary scale of official foreign
aid, stabilization of the raw materials market so as
to assist consumers and producers alike, and the types
of industries the developing countries should strive
to build as a part of a rational world division of labor.
Examines the control and regulation of multinational
corporations and, focusing on Latin America, the extent
to which regional cooperation can be developed. Recommends
that development planning be based on future population
growth and distribution.

84   Varma, Baidya Nath
A B C   THE SOCIOLOGY AND POLITICS OF DEVELOPMENT: A THEORETICAL
STUDY
International Library of Sociology Series
London and Boston: Routledge & Kegan Paul, 1980.

The author critically examines theories of development
and presents his own theory. Considers general criteria
used for evaluating the modernization process; describes
a model for a general paradigm of modernization; surveys
other models encompassing ideological, social scientific,
anthropological and activistic theories; and discusses
theoretical problems of planning and national
reconstruction. Summarizes views of theorists in various
social science disciplines and features of modernization
in terms of guidance provided for economic, political,
educational, and bureaucratic decision-making in a
developing country. Concludes that both the socialist
and capitalist systems of modernization are viable models
for Third World countries.

85   Vogeler, Ingolf and De Souza, Anthony R., eds.
A C   DIALECTICS OF THIRD WORLD DEVELOPMENT
Montclair: Allanheld, Osmun, 1980.

Collection of previously published (some revised) papers
designed for use by students of economics, political
science, and development. Representing a variety of
ideas and arguments relevant to Third World
underdevelopment, the readings discuss climate and

resources, cultural traditions, European colonialism (i.e., plantation agriculture), population, tourism, and imperialism. An appendix provides "awareness" exercises.

86   Wallman, Sandra, ed.
A B   PERCEPTIONS OF DEVELOPMENT
New York: Cambridge University Press, 1977.

87   Ward, Richard J.
A C   DEVELOPMENT ISSUES FOR THE 1970'S
New York and London: Dunellen, 1973.

An assessment of key issues and problems which emerged from the Decade of Development and which will continue to absorb the attention of students of development in the present decade. The author, former Chief of Planning of the U.S. Agency for International Development, presents much data which has not been previously released and which is unavailable elsewhere. The book is divided into three parts: "Food and Human Welfare," "Development Problems for This Decade," and "Planning Programs and Strategies." The chapters specifically discuss such issues as labor absorption in agriculture, means of population control, the burden of debt service, the role of foreign aid, big-push development, etc.

88   Waterston, Albert
A B   DEVELOPMENT PLANNING; LESSONS OF EXPERIENCE
The Johns Hopkins University Press, 1979.

Analyzes the success of the development planning experience in over 100 countries in Asia, Africa, Europe, and the Americas. In two parts. Part 1 describes and analyzes the problems associated with the implementation of planning programs, the provision of basic data, the role of national budget, and administrative obstacles. Part 2 contains an extensive and comparative discussion of the experience of the countries under review in setting up organizations and administrative procedures for preparing and implementing development projects; the distribution of planning functions, types of central planning agencies, and subnational regional and local planning bodies.

89   Watts, Nita, ed.
A B   ECONOMIES OF THE WORLD
New York: Oxford University Press.

The purpose of this new series is to provide a brief review of economic development during the post-war period in each of a number of countries which are of obvious importance in the world economy or interesting because of peculiarities of their economic structure or experience, or illustrative of widespread economic development

problems. The series will be of interest to economists
in universities, and in business and government.

90   Wilber, Charles K., ed.
A B   THE POLITICAL ECONOMY OF DEVELOPMENT AND UNDERDEVELOPMENT
        New York: Random House, 1973.

Emphasis in approach and content is on political economy
in the sense of attempting to incorporate such noneconomic
influences as social structures, political systems, and
cultural values as well as such factors as technological
change and the distribution of income and wealth. Readings
are radical in that they are willing to question and
evaluate the most basic institutions and values of society.
Divided into eight groups concerned with methodological
problems, historical perspective, trade and imperialism,
agricultural and industrial institutions and strategies,
comparative models of development, the human cost of
development, and indications for the future.

91   Worsley, Peter
A C   THE THIRD WORLD
        Chicago: University of Chicago Press, 1972.

92   Wriggins, W. Howards and Adler-Karlsson, Gunnar
A C   REDUCING GLOBAL INEQUALITIES
        New York: McGraw-Hill, 1978.

Two papers, plus an introduction on the role that
developing countries themselves take to reduce the gap
between rich nations and poor and to eliminate mass poverty
within their own societies. W. Howard Wriggins, U.S.
ambassador to Sri Lanka and formerly professor of political
science at Columbia University, analyzes the various
bargaining strategies open to developing countries such
as developing commodity or regional coalitions, or a
variety of threats to developed countries. The future
is likely to see continued efforts at coalition building,
but also periodic outbreaks of irregular violence against
local opponents, neighbors, or Northern centers of power.

93   Zuvekas, Clarence, Jr.
A B C   ECONOMIC DEVELOPMENT: AN INTRODUCTION
        New York: St. Martin's Press, 1979.

Text written from an interdisciplinary perspective
stressing policy and empirical findings rather than an
overall development theory. Aims at balance between
theory and policy, including historical development and
empirical evidence. After discussing the terminology
of and the obstacles to development, the author examines
population growth, trade and development, and the role
of government. Also covers: the problems of agriculture

and industry, income distribution, employment, mobilization
of domestic and foreign savings, manipulation of trade
to the advantage of the developing country, and with
the limits to growth controversy. Presumes acquaintance
with basic macro and micro theory.

ROLE OF MULTI-NATIONAL CORPORATIONS IN THIRD WORLD DEVELOPMENT

94   Agmon, Tamir and Kindleberger, Charles P., eds.
MULTINATIONALS FROM SMALL COUNTRIES
Cambridge, MA and London: MIT Press, 1977.

Seven papers and related comments presented at conference
sponsored by the Center for International Studies and
the Sloan School of Management held at the Massachusetts
Institute of Technology on January 8-9, 1976. Papers
include: Jurg Niehans on Switzerland and its benefits
from multinationals; Sune Carlson on Sweden and company
policies for international expansion; Gilles Y. Bertin
on France as a host to small-country investment; Helen
Hughes on Australia and technology transfer; Louis T.
Wells, Jr., on internationalization of firms from LDC's;
Carlos F. Diaz-Alejandro on Latin American foreign direct
investment; and Tamir Agmon and Donald R. Lessard on
financial factors and the international expansion of
small-country firms.

95   Akinsanya, Adeoye A.
THE EXPROPRIATION OF MULTINATIONAL PROPERTY IN THE THIRD
WORLD
New York: Praeger, 1980.

Analyzes expropriatory measures taken by twelve developing
nations and examines the role of law in the economic
relations among nations. Describes the international
legal rules governing expropriation of foreign property;
explores the motives behind expropriation; discusses
specific nationalization measures taken by Third World
countries in Africa, Asia, Latin America, the Caribbean,
and the Middle East; discusses the differing views on
expropriation; and considers the effect on future foreign
private investment in the developing countries. Findings
indicate that both right-wing and left-wing regimes in
the Third World expropriate alien-owned investment; that
expropriation measures are motivated by economic,
political, and nationalistic reasons; that views with
respect to compensation are not uniform; that there seems
to be a positive correlation between expropriation and
the destabilization of expropriating governments; and
that economic nationalism and expropriations of
multinational investments in the developing countries
is likely to grow.

96   Anderson, Michael H.
          TRANSNATIONAL ADVERTISING AND THE "NEW WORLD INFORMATION
          ORDER"
          Sydney: Transnational   Corporation   Research   Project,
          University of Sydney, 1980.

          Monograph on the role of transnational advertising in
          the world economy. Discusses the "New World Information
          Order" controversy about the dominance of world
          communication by the developed Western nations; presents
          an overview of the transnationalization of American
          advertising by a few large agencies; and suggests how
          developing nations might cope with these transnational
          agencies through development of their own national
          advertising policies and associated strategies to implement
          cooperative relations with other nations.

97   Apter, David E. and Goodman, Louis W.
          MULTINATIONAL CORPORATIONS AND SOCIAL CHANGE
          New York: Praeger, 1976.

98   Balasubramanyam, V. N.
          MULTINATIONAL ENTERPRISES AND THE THIRD WORLD
          London: Trade Policy Research Centre, 1980.

          Monograph analyzing the role of private multinational
          entities in the economic development of Third World
          countries through the transfer of technology and management
          know-how from the developed countries. Conclusions stress
          equitable benefit-sharing by foreign private investors
          and the developing countries.

99   Baranson, Jack
          AUTOMOTIVE INDUSTRIES IN THE DEVELOPING COUNTRIES
          Baltimore, MD: Johns Hopkins University Press, 1969.

          Comparison of commerical strategies and operational
          methods, focusing on the role of international
          corporations, the adaptation problems of their affiliates,
          and the impact of economic policy on market structure.

100   Baranson, Jack
          NORTH-SOUTH TECHNOLOGY TRANSFER: FINANCING AND INSTITUTION
          BUILDING
          Mt. Airy, MD: Lomand Publications, 1981.

101   Bhagwati, Jagdish N., ed.
          THE NEW INTERNATIONAL ECONOMIC ORDER: THE NORTH-SOUTH
          DEBATE
          Cambridge, MA: MIT Press, 1977.

          Papers prepared at a 1975 workshop at the Massachusetts
          Institute of Technology that sought to examine specific
          proposals which could form the concrete content of a

reformed world economy. The wide range of international
economic issues, the distinguished panel of international
and development economists, and the lively and informed
disagreements among them make this book a useful survey
of the dominant international economic issues today.
The papers are grouped under: (a) resource transfers;
(b) international trade; (c) world and food problems;
(d) technology transfer and diffusion; and (e) a panel
discussion of North-South issues.

102   Biersteker, Thomas J.
       DISTORTION OR DEVELOPMENT? CONTENDING PERSPECTIVES ON
       THE MULTINATIONAL CORPORATION
       Cambridge, MA and London: MIT Press, 1981.

       Evaluates two alternative, contending theoretical
       perspectives on the consequences of investment in
       underdeveloped countries by multinational corporations.
       The first, the dependency theory offered by critics of
       multinational investment, assumes that feasible
       alternatives to multinationals exist, and the second,
       the neoconventional approach, assumes that such
       alternatives do not exist. Discusses balance of payments
       and patterns of consumption, displacement of indigenous
       production, technology transfer, social structures, and
       income inequality in the light of each theory. Nigeria
       is presented as a case study of the consequences of
       multinational investment in an underdeveloped economy,
       emphasizing the manufacturing sector. Some conclusions
       are that many multinationals contribute to a net outflow
       of capital from the country, but also they contribute
       to the transfer of skills and knowledge employed by
       domestic enterprises. Multinational enterprises tend
       to employ more capital-intensive technologies than domestic
       firms. A major conclusion suggests that extreme
       multinational investment can create obstacles to the
       achievement of development objectives in LDC's.

103   Black, Robert and Blank, Stephen
       MULTINATIONALS IN CONTENTION: RESPONSES AT GOVERNMENTAL
       AND INTERNATIONAL LEVELS
       Conference Board, 1978.

104   Carlsson, Jerker
       TRANSNATIONAL COMPANIES IN LIBERIA
       Scandanavian Institute of African Studies, 1977.

105   Cartagena de Acuerdo
       THE ROLE OF TRANSNATIONAL ENTERPRISES IN THE PROCESS
       OF LATIN AMERICAN INTEGRATION

       Contains conclusion and recommendations of a round table
       organized by UNCTAD with the cooperation of the Acuerdo
       de Cartagena, UNDP and the UN Center for Transnational
       Enterprises, Lima, 12-16 June 1978.

106   Cartagena de Acuerdo
       TRANSNATIONAL ENTERPRISES AND LATIN AMERICAN INTEGRATION

       Contains text of a speech presented at the round table
       mentioned immediately above.

107   Casson, Mark
       ALTERNATIVES TO THE MULTINATIONAL ENTERPRISE
       New York: Holmes & Meier, 1979.

       Explores alternative institutional arrangements for the
       transfer of technology among countries, focusing upon
       the separation of control of production processes by
       multinational companies importing that technology into
       the plants they establish. Argues that the interests
       of the proprietor of the technology and the interests
       of the host country must be harmonized through a negotiated
       contractual arrangement and suggests that the time is
       right for the revival of the concept of an international
       market for proprietary technology. Outlines the basic
       issues and empirical evidence on multinational enterprise
       (MNE)--host-country relations; reviews the fundamentals
       of the theory of resource allocation; explains the
       rationale for the MNE's and analyzes their role in trade
       and capital movements; appraises the costs and benefits
       of foreign direct investment; and evaluates licensing,
       subcontracting, and other forms of arm's-length contractual
       arrangements. Recommends changes in the international
       patent system to promote these alternatives.

108   Chudson, Walter A. and Wells, Louis T., Jr.
       THE ACQUISITION OF TECHNOLOGY FROM MULTINATIONAL
       CORPORATIONS BY DEVELOPING COUNTRIES
       New York: UN, 1974.

       Constitutes part of the documentation supplied to the
       Group of Eminent Persons to Study the Impact of
       Multinational Corporations on Development and on
       International Relations, appointed by the UN
       Secretary-General in 1972. Also supplements the report
       Multinational Corporations in World Development. The
       study examines the multinational corporation as a vehicle
       for supplying technology to developing countries, comparing
       it with certain alternatives and considering the issues
       that arise and possible solutions.

109   Cohen, Benjamin I.
       MULTINATIONAL FIRMS AND ASIAN EXPORTS
       New Haven and London: Yale University Press for the
       Economic Growth Center, Yale, 1975.

       A study of the effects of exports by multinational
       corporations on the economic welfare of the host countries.
       Provides a critique of current economic theories of foreign

investments that have promoted as conventional wisdom
the assumption that developing countries benefit from
such export activities by foreign firms. Presents the
results of a survey of United States and Japanese firms,
as well a local firms, in Singapore, South Korea, and
Taiwan. These countries were responsible for over
one-third of total manufacturing exports of all developing
countries in the early seventies. The author finds that
the economic benefits of foreign firms are negligible
if compared with local firms producing and exporting
the same commodities. Briefly discusses the noneconomic
benefits of foreign investment and suggests desirable
tax policies toward foreign firms to be undertaken by
the host countries. Numerous statistics and data for
the 1960's and up to 1971.

110   Committee for Economic Development
       TRANSNATIONAL CORP. AND DEVELOPING COUNTRIES: NEW POLICIES
       FOR A CHANGING WORLD ORDER
       The Committee, 1981.

111   Connor, John M.
       THE MARKET POWER OF MULTINATIONALS: A QUANTITATIVE ANALYSIS
       OF U.S. CORPORATIONS IN BRAZIL AND MEXICO. FOREWORD BY
       WILLIARD   F.   MUELLER.   PRAEGER   SPECIAL   STUDIES   IN
       INTERNATIONAL BUSINESS, FINANCE, AND TRADE
       New York and London: Praeger, 1977.

       Using the theory of industrial organization as a framework,
       focuses on the determinants of market power and profit
       performance   of   affiliates   of   U.S.   multinational
       corporations (MNC's) in Brazil and Mexico. The study
       is limited to the manufacturing sector, and data were
       derived from 197 responses to survey questionnaire
       commissioned in 1973 by the U.S. Senate Subcommittee
       on Multinational Corporations. The respondents represented
       about 70 percent of U.S. foreign direct investment in
       the two countries. The findings confirm that profits
       are largely affected by the competitive environment and
       they demonstrate more "similarities than differences
       in the industrial market structures of Brazil, Mexico,
       and the United States"; further, they support the theory
       that foreign direct investment reflects the oligopolistic
       characteristics of the country from which the MNC's
       originate. Reviews previous work and considers public
       policy alternatives.

112   Craig, John G.
       MULTINATIONAL   CO-OPERATIVES   AN   ALTERNATIVE   FOR   WORLD
       DEVELOPMENT
       Western Producer Prairie Books, 1976.

113   Curzon, Gerard and Curzon, Victoria, eds.
       THE   MULTINATIONAL   ENTERPRISE   IN   A   HOSTILE   WORLD:
       PROCEEDINGS OF A CONFERENCE HELD IN GENEVA UNDER THE

AUSPICES OF THE GRADUATE INSTITUTE OF INTERNATIONAL STUDIES, L'INSTITUT UNIVERSITAIRE D'ETUDES EUROPEENNES, AND THE CENTER FOR EDUCATION IN INTERNATIONAL MANAGEMENT. IN COLLABORATION WITH LAWRENCE G. FRANKO AND HENRI SCHWAMM Toronto: Macmillan of Canada/Maclean-Hunter Press; London: Macmillan, 1977.

Seven previously unpublished papers presented at a conference held in 1975, concerned with the case for controlling multinational firms and how this might be done. Also includes comments, a general summary of the conference proceedings, and an introduction by the editors. Papers include: "Alternative Policy Prescriptions and the Multinational Enterprise," by John H. Dunning and Martin Gilman; "European Multinational Enterprises in the Integration Process," by Lawrence G. Franko; "The Competition Policy of the European Community," by Dennis Thompson; "Restrictive Practices by Multinational Corporations," by H. Ralph Windle; "The Possibilities and Limitations of an International and Interregional Anti-trust Policy," by Jurgen Poeche; "The Multinational Enterprise, the Nation State and Regional Groupings," by Rainer Hellmann; and "The External Relations of Multinational Companies," by Eric Gabus.

114   Dar, Usha
THE EFFECTS OF MULTINATIONAL ENTERPRISES ON EMPLOYMENT IN INDIA (WORKING PAPER NO. 9)
ILO, 1979.

115   Dunning, John H.
INTERNATIONAL PRODUCTION AND THE MULTINATIONAL ENTERPRISE
London; Boston and Sydney: Allen & Unwin, 1981.

Fifteen previously published essays written by the author during the years, 1973-80 and revised and/or expanded for this volume; five articles have co-authors. Reviews recent advances in the theory of multinational enterprise and analyzes some of the ways in which its activities affect and interact with government policies.

116   Evans, Peter
DEPENDENT DEVELOPMENT: THE ALLIANCE OF MULTINATIONAL, STATE, AND LOCAL CAPITAL IN BRAZIL
Princeton, N.J.: Princeton University Press, 1979.

Analyzes the forces that maintain the alliance of multinational corporations, the state, and local capital to accumulate industrial capital in Brazil. Uses material gathered in interviews over a five year period with 150 corporate executives, combined with business publications, and other data to examine patterns of investment and business behavior. Explores the bases for conflict and cooperation among segments of the Brazilian elite and

of representatives of international capital. Maintains
that Brazilian industrial development must be understood
in the framework of the capitalist world economy. Argues
that this "dependent development" does not represent
a break with past U.S. history.

117   Feld, Werner J.
MULTINATIONAL ENTERPRISES AND U.N. POLITICS: THE QUEST
FOR CODE OF CONDUCT
Pergamon, 1980.

118   Frank, Isaiah
FOREIGN ENTERPRISE IN DEVELOPING COUNTRIES: A SUPPLEMENTARY
PAPER OF THE COMMITTEE FOR ECONOMIC DEVELOPMENT. FOREIGN
ENTERPRISE IN DEVELOPING COUNTRIES SERIES
Baltimore and London: Johns Hopkins University Press,
1980.

Examines the relationship between developing countries
and multinational corporations by focusing upon the
reactions of company officers to the main concerns
expressed by host countries about the operations and
impact of transnational enterprises.   Part one outlines
tha tension between transnational corporations and host
countries and the size and scope of direct private
investment in the developing world.   Part two presents
the result of in-depth interviews with officers of 90
multinationals headquartered in the United States, Japan,
Australia, and eight countries in Western Europe about
fields of investment, types of arrangements, transfers
of technology, host-country policies, home-country
policies, and international programs. part three consists
of the project summary and conclusions, a principal one
being that transnationals "must increasingly recognize
that Third World governments are committed to the goal
of fulfilling the social and economic needs of their
people," and this requires business constraints as well
as inducements; also concludes that, given reasonably
stable and equitable conditions, transnational corporations
can make major contributions to Third World development
goals.

119   Freeman Orville
MULTINATIONAL COMPANY: INSTRUMENT FOR WORLD GROWTH
Praeger, 1981.

120   Ghatak, Subrata
A B   TECHNOLOGY TRANSFER TO DEVELOPING COUNTRIES: THE CASE
OF THE FERTILIZER INDUSTRY
Greenwich, Conn.: JAI Press, 1981.

121   Gunter, Hans
ILO RESEARCH ON MULTINATIONAL ENTERPRISES AND SOCIAL
POLICY: AN OVERVIEW (WORKING PAPER NO. 15)
ILO, 1982.

122   Hammeed, K.A.
A B C   ENTERPRISE: INDUSTRIAL ENTERPRENEURSHIP IN DEVELOPMENT
            Beverly Hills, Calif.:   Sage, 1974.

123   Hawkins, Robert G., ed.
            THE   ECONOMIC   EFFECTS   OF   MULTINATIONAL   CORPORATIONS.
            RESEARCH IN INTERNATIONAL BUSINESS AND FINANCE, VOLUME
            1
            Greenwich, Conn.:   JAI Press, 1979.

            First   volume   of   an   annual   series,   comprising   eight
            previously   unpublished   papers   plus   related   comments   on
            the economic impacts of multinational corporations (MNC's),
            originally   presented   at   a   conference   sponsored   by   the
            New   York   University   Graduate   School   of   Business
            Administration   held   in   December   1976.   Includes: Stephen
            P.   Magee   on   jobs   and   MNC's;   Duane   Kujawa   on   labor
            relations;   Thomas G.   Parry on competition in MNC relations
            with   host   countries;   Donald   R.   Lessard   on   internal
            financial transfers; Arthur W. Lake on technology transfer;
            Richard   W.   Moxon   on   technology   cost   and   adaptation   in
            LDC's;   James   Riedel   on   economic   dependence   and
            entrepreneurial   opportunities;   and Carlos F.   Diaz Alejandro
            on   international   markets   for   exhaustible   resources.   The
            authors   conclude   (with   reservations)   that   MNC   activity
            is a "positive sum game" in almost all instances.

124   Hellinger, Douglas A. and Hellinger, Stephen H.
            UNEMPLOYMENT   AND   THE   MULTINATIONAL: A   STRATEGY   FOR
            TECHNOLOGICAL CHANGE IN LATIN AMERICA. FOREWORD BY BARBARA
            WARD
            Port   Washington,   N.Y.   and   London: National   University
            Publications, Kennikat Press, 1976.

            Concentrates   on   "the   technological   adaptations   required
            to   significantly   reduce   the high   levels   of   joblessness
            that   exist   today   in   Latin   America   and   the   role   of   the
            multinational   corporation   (MNC)   in   this   endeavor."   After
            examining   the   labor-absorbing   potential   of   various   sectors
            and   labor-intensive   technological   possibilities,
            productivity   and   the   appropriation   of   technologies   are
            discussed.   Investigates   the   past,   present,   and   future
            activities   by   MNC's   to   generate   employment   and   the
            relationship   between   Latin   governments   and   MNC's,   the
            employment   problems,   and   technology.   Concludes   that
            Latin American countries should utilize their most abundant
            resource-labor-through   the   use   of   labor-intensive
            production, leading to an enlargement of domestic markets,
            through more equal income distribution.

125   Holland, Susan S., ed.
B C   CODES OF CONDUCT FOR THE TRANSFER OF TECHNOLOGY: A CRITIQUE
            New   York: Council   of   the   Americas   and   Fund   for
            Multinational Management Education, 1976.

Five papers that set out some of the key issues and
questions being discussed concerning codes of conduct
for technology transfer between developed and developing
countries. Following an exploration of the background
of these codes and an examination of the changing nature
of the technology transfer process, two papers look and
the concerns of developing countries and the feasibility
of many of the code regulations they wish to enact. A
final paper presents the partial findings from a research
project on the lack of understanding of the different
parties of each other's objectives and views.

126   IDRC
C D   ANDEAN PACT TECHNOLOGY POLICIES
      Ottawa: IDRC, 1976.

This publication describes basic policy decisions made
to achieve the development of an integrated technology
policy for the six Andean Pact countries which would
fulfill specific economic and social needs and provide
technological autonomy for the region. Topics covered:
foreign direct investment; technology transfer; trademarks;
patents; licensing agreements; royalties; and industrial
property.

127   ILO
      MULTINATIONALS' TRAINING PRACTICES AND DEVELOPMENT
      ILO, 1980.

This report presents the findings of a research project
on the training practices of multinational enterprises
and their impact on development. It provides examples
of the training programs by about 15 parent enterprises
and their subsidiaries in developing countries. It
presents the results of an inquiry among ILO training
experts in six developing countries based on interviews
and surveys addressed to managers of multinationals,
government officials and training institutions, employers
and union circles. It examines the question of the impact
of this training on development in case studies for
three developing countries in Africa, Asia and Latin
America. It also looks at the problems and future
possibilities for cooperation between multinational
enterprises and local training bodies.

128   ILO
      SOCIAL AND LABOUR PRACTICES OF MULTINATIONAL ENTERPRISES
      IN THE PETROLIUM INDUSTRY
      ILO, 1977.

Reviews general policy, employment and training, wages
and basic conditions of work and labor relations in
selected petroleum companies and their subsidiaries
operating in the Americas, Africa, Asia, Europe and the
Middle East.

129   ILO
        EMPLOYMENT   EFFECTS   OF   MULTINATIONAL   ENTERPRISES   IN
        DEVELOPING COUNTRIES
        ILO, 1981.

        Analyzes   foreign   investment   and   the   direct   employment
        (volume,   trends,   distribution   and   structure)   of
        multinational   enterprises   (MNEs)   in   developing   countries
        of   Asia,   Africa   and   Latin   America.   It   also   discusses
        the   indirect   employment   effects   of   MNEs   in   these   countries;
        employment   provided   by   MNEs   in   Free   Trade   Zones;   and
        government   policies   and   technology,   choice   by   MNEs   as
        important   interrelated   determinants   for   the   enterprises;
        employment   effects.   For   the   companion   volume   Employment
        Effects   of   Multinational   Enterprises   in   Industrialised
        Countries.

130   Irish, Donald P.
        MULTINATIONAL   CORP   IN   LATIN   AMERICA: PRIVATE   RIGHTS   AND
        PUBLIC RESPONSIBILITIES
        Ohio University, 1977.

131   Iyanda, Olukunle and Bello, Joseph A.
        EMPLOYMENT EFFECTS OF MULTINATIONAL ENTERPRISES IN NIGERIA
        ILO, 1979.

132   Jackson, Richard A.
        MULTINATIONAL   CORPORATION   AND   SOCIAL   POLICY: SPECIAL
        REFERENCE TO GENERAL MOTERS IN SOUTH AFRICA
        Coun Rel and Intl, 1974.

133   Kaplinsky, R.
        EMPLOYMENT   EFFECTS   OF   MULTINATIONAL   ENTERPRISES: A   CASE
        STUDY OF KENYA
        ILO, 1979.

134   Kindleberger, Charles P., ed.
        THE INTERNATIONAL CORPORATION
        Cambridge, Mass.:   M.I.T. Press, 1970.

135   Konz, Leo Edwin
        THE   INTERNATIONAL   TRANSFER   OF   COMMERCIAL   TECHNOLOGY:
        THE ROLE OF THE MULTINATIONAL CORP
        Armo, 1980.

136   Kumar, Krishna
        MULTINATIONALS FROM DEVELOPING COUNTRIES
        Lexington Books, 1981.

137   Kumar, Krishna
        TRANSNATIONAL   ENTERPRISES: THEIR   IMPACT   ON   THIRD   WORLD
        SOCIETIES AND CULTURES
        Boulder, Colo.:   Westview Press, 1980.

        This   is   a   collection   of   reprinted   journal   articles

organised under three headings: 'Impact on Social Classes
and Inequality', 'Impact on Knowledge Stytems, and 'Impact
on Consumption Patterns and Values'. The editor provides
an overview chapter in which he disclaims any intention
of setting the book's subject within a theoretical
framework, confining himself instead to a review of 'those
impacts which have been stressed in the growing literature
on transnational enterprises'. In the selection, his
own interest in cultural and mass-communications issues
shows through rather clearly, whereas social-structural
aspects are very thinly covered indeed despite the
inclusion of an edited version of Sunkel's influential
paper and interesting contributions by Sklar, Lim and
Emmanuel.

138   Kumar, Krishna and McLeod, Maxwell G., eds.
        MULTINATIONAL FROM DEVELOPING COUNTRIES
        Lexington, Mass., and Toronto: Heath, Lexington Books,
        1981.

Eleven previously unpublished papers, several originally
presented at a 1979 international conference on the
East-West Culture Learning Institute and some written
expressly for this volume. Papers cover multinational
enterprises from several Third World nonsocialist nations
in Africa, Asia, and Latin America, including studies
of the ASEAN region, Hong Kong, India, South Korea,
Indonesia, Nigeria, Taiwan, and Latin America.   Studies
are both theoretical and analytical and attempt to clarify
the kinds of firms, the sectors in which they operate,
their competitive assets vis-a-vis other firms in host
nations, the relationship between the parent-firm and
its subsidiaries or joint ventures, the kinds of host
developing nations, and developing countries' policies
toward multinationals from other developing countries.
Finds that most LDC multinationals are from relatively
industrialized LDCs with a sizeable indigenous industrial
sector and a growing entrepreneurial class.   The
investments have usually been in the less industrialized
LDCs.

139   Lall, Sanjaya
        DEVELOPING COUNTRIES IN THE INTERNATIONAL ECONOMY: SELECTED
        PAPERS
        London: Macmillan Press; distributed in the U.S. by
        Humanities Press, Atlantic Highlands, N.J., 1981.

Eight papers, two previously unpublished, written over
the past eight years, on conceptual and empirical aspects
of development as related to multinational corporations.
Two essays on conceptual issues include a critique of
dependence theories and a discussion of the limitations
of orthodox welfare economics for analyzing development
problems.   Other papers cover: international investment,
technology transfer, and exports by developing countries.

140   Lall, Sanjaya and Streeten, Paul
         FOREIGN   INVESSTMENT,   TRANSNATIONALS   AND   DEVELOPING
         COUNTRIES
         London: Macmillan Press; Boulder, Colo.:   Westview Press,
         1977.

         Noting a growing dissatisfaction with conventional tools
         of development economics and the difficulty of defining
         "welfare," this three-part study analyzes in sober (if
         not   sombre)   general   qualitative   terms   the   nature   of
         transnational   manufacturing   firms   (TNC's)   and   their
         implications for the welfare of the host LDC.   Part two
         deals with description of and findings of empirical UNCTAD
         studies of the balance of payments and income effects
         of a sample of foreign investments in the manufacturing
         sector of six countries: Jamaica, Kenya, India, Iran,
         Colombia, and Malaysia.   The last part discusses policy
         measures for host governments, outlining the difficulties
         in formulating and implementing policy.   Recommends the
         continued use of "the Little-Mirrlees method" of project
         evaluation   (social   cost   benefit   analysis),   but   notes
         that   it   suffers   from   practical   (data)   and   conceptual
         limitations and can only be a part of a larger package.
         Argues further that some influences of the TNC's are
         favorable,   while   others   are   negative   and   that   it   is
         important that there be an awareness of the former.   Most
         host governments are trying to improve their bargaining
         position relative to TNC's, but unless there is a drastic
         change in the internal structure of the host countries,
         the undesirable effects will continue to be felt as these
         countries   become   more   clearly   integrated   into   the
         international structure of production and trade.

141   Lall, Sanjaya
         THE MULTINATIONAL CORPORTION
         Holmes & Meier Publishers, N.Y., 1980.

         Both   books   offer   a   convenient   package   of   reference
         materials for researchers on the role of multinationals
         in the world economy and the manner in which they operate.
         Lall   also   takes   a   closer   look   at   the   workings   of
         international pharmaceutical firms.

142   Lall, Sanjaya
         THE   INDIRECT   EMPLOYMENT   EFFECTS   OF   MULTINATIONAL
         ENTERPRISES IN DEVELOPING COUNTRIES
         ILO, 1979.

143   Langdon, Steven W.
         MULTINATIONAL CORPORATIONS IN THE POLITICAL ECONOMY OF
         KENYA
         New York: St. Martin's Press, 1981.

         Investigates   the   social   and   economic   impact   of   the
         multinationals on Kenya, which extended to foreign firms

a central place in its development plans during the late
1960s and early 1970s. Compares local and multinational
firms in the soap production and shoe manufacturing
industries and tests these conclusions against interview
results from the country's other active large
multinationals. Tests the arguments of economic dependency
theory against reliance on the multinationals in
development planning. Concludes that dependency on
multinationals has widened inequalities, slowed employment
growth, and damaged local enterprise.

144   La Palombara, Joseph and Blank, Stephen
       MULTINATIONALS CORPORATIONS AND DEVELOPING COUNTRIES
       Conference Bd, 1980.

145   Lim, Linda and Pang Eng Fong
B C D TECHNOLOGY CHOICE AND EMPLOYMENT CREATION: A CASE STUDY
       OF THREE MULTINATIONAL ENTERPRISES IN SINGAPORE
       Geneva: ILO, 1981.

       Analyzes the experience of three multinational enterprises
       (MNEs) in the electronics industry in Singapore (1
       European, 1 American, 1 Japanese) relevant to technology,
       employment and linkages, and technology choice and
       employment creation.

146   Masini, Jean
       MULTINATIONALS IN AND DEVELOPMENT IN BLACK AFRICA: IVORY
       COAST
       Praeger, 1980.

147   May, Herbert K.
       MULTINATIONAL CORP IN LATIN AMERICA
       Unipub, 1977.

148   Molineau
       MULTINATIONAL CORP AND INTERNATIONAL INVESTMENT IN LATIN
       AMERICA: A SELECTED BIBLIOGRAPHY
       Ohio University, 1977.

149   Moran, Theodore H.
       MULTINATIONAL CORP AND THE POLITICS OF DEPENDENCE: COPPER
       IN CHILE
       Princeton University Press, 1975.

150   Moxon, Richard W.
       OFFSHORE PRODUCTION IN THE LESS DEVELOPED COUNTRIES--A
       CASE STUDY OF MULTINATIONALITY IN THE ELECTRONICS INDUSTRY
       BULLETIN NOS. 98-99
       New York: New York University, Graduate School of Business
       Administration, Institute of Finance, 1974.

       Analytical framework for understanding a particular
       industry's (electronics) practice of importing products

and components formerly purchased or manufactured in the United States from U.S. subsidiaries established in less developed countries; and for assessing the implications of these activities for the companies and nations involved. Analyzes the elements in the decision to engage in offshore production and the implications of such activities for the U.S. companies, the American economy, and the developing countries. Concludes that the great majority of the electronic companies with offshore plants are "very satisfied" that the greatest success is for standardized products requiring large amount of unskilled labor; risks of losing an offshore facility must be offset against benefits.

151   MULTINATIONALS: NEW APPROACHES TO AGRICULTURE AND RURAL DEVELOPMENT
       Unipub, 1982.

152   Mutharika, B.W.T.
       TOWARD MULTINATIONAL ECONOMIC COOPERATION IN AFRICA
       New York: Praeger, 1972.

153   Negandhi, Anant R., ed.
       FUNCTIONING OF THE MULTINATIONAL CORPORATION: A GLOBAL COMPARATIVE STUDY
       New York; Oxford; Toronto and Paris: Pergamon Press, 1980.

       Twelve previously unpublished papers examine the critical issues and often conflicting goals of the multinational corporations and nation states. Part one consists of an introduction by the editor, Professor of International Business at the University of Illinois at Urbana-Champaign. Part two examines the origins and implications of the New International Economic Order with respect to multinational corporations and explores the nature and intensity of transfer-pricing practices used by the MNCs. Part three compares the strategies, policy-making and organizational adaptability of American, Japanese, and European MNCs to the policies and demands of developed, developing, and Communist countries. Part four discusses the background, training, and outlook of the MNCs' managers and outlines an agenda for future research.

154   Newfarmer, Richard S.
       TRANSNATIONAL CONGLOMERATES AND THE ECONOMICS OF DEPENDENT DEVELOPMENT
       JAI Press, 1980.

155   Odle, Maurice A.
       MULTINATIONAL BANKS AND UNDERDEVELOPMENT
       Pergamon Press, 1981.

156   OECD

INTERNATIONAL INVESTMENT AND MULTINATIONAL ENTERPRISES:
RESPONSIBILITY OF PARENT COMPANIES FOR THEIR SUBSIDIARIES
OECD, 1980.

Presents a comparative analysis on the legal situation
in OECD Member countries regarding the responsibility
of parent companies for their subsidiaries. Also includes
the questionnaire used for the survey and the replies
received from 20 countries.

157   OECD
       INTERNATIONAL INVESTMENT AND MULTINATIONAL ENTERPRISES:
       MID-TERM REPORT ON THE 1976 DECLARATION AND DECISION
       OECD, 1982.

A progress report on the implementation of OECD countries
of guidelines adopted for multinational enterprises and
principles concerning the national treatment of enterprises
under foreign control and concerning the use of investment
incentives and disincentives.

158   Okolie, Charles Chukwuma
B C   LEGAL ASPECTS OF THE INTERNATIONAL TRANSFER OF TECHNOLOGY
       TO DEVELOPING COUNTRIES
       New York and London: Praeger, 1975.

Examines the obstacles to the transfer of technology
and resources to developing countries and suggests ways
of improving the transfer. The study, an outgrowth of
work done by the United Nations Institute for Training
and Research, discusses the legal and moral problems
of international technology transfer, relevant aspects
of international law, United States attitude to the
transfer, the role of Soviet corporations and the legal
norms for Soviet transfer of technology, and the role
of the multinational company in the transfer of technology.

159   Parry, T.G.
A B C THE ROLE OF TRANSNATIONAL CORPORATIONS IN THE DEVELOPING
       ESCAP REGION. CAER PAPER NO. 10
       Kensington, New South Wales: University of New South
       Wales, Centre for Applied Economic Research, 1980.

A general statement on activities (problems and benefits)
of transnational corporations in the developing countries
of the countries making up the Economic and Social
Commission for Asia and the Pacific (ESCAP). Contains
some tables comparing the transnational corporation (TNC)
activities in selected Latin American and African countries
as well. Concludes that the nature of gains from TNCs
depends on host government policies, form of involvement,
TNC policies, and the industry involved. Believes that
there is considerable scope for increasing the level
and host country share of gains.

160   Perlmutter, Howard V. and Sagafi-Jejad, Tagi
B C   INTERNATIONAL   TECHNOLOGY   TRANSFER: GUIDELINES,   CODES
       AND A MUFFLED QUADRILOGUE
       Oxford; Sydney and Paris: Pergamon Press, 1981.

       First in a three-volume series on technology transfer,
       discusses this process between advanced countries and
       less industrialized countries. Proposes guidelines or
       codes of conduct for international technology transfer,
       emphasizing the need to establish some mandatory code
       authority, which would accelerate the reduction in the
       gap between the advanced market economies and the LDCs
       and the attainment by the latter of basic needs and minimal
       standards of living. Analyzes the views, perceptions,
       attitudes, and feelings of persons representing supplier
       countries, supplier firms, recipient countries, and
       recipient firms in developing an international control
       structure that would benefit all four groups. Records
       some major themes that underlie the mistrust among the
       four groups.

161   Pinelo, Adalberto J.
       THE MULTINATIONAL CORP AS A FORCE IN LATIN AMERICAN
       POLITICS
       Praeger Press, 1973.

162   Possas, Mario Luiz
       EMPLOYMENT EFFECTS OF MULTINATIONAL ENTERPRISES IN BRAZIL
       ILO, 1979.

163   Renninger, John P.
       MULTINATIONAL COOPERATION FOR DEVELOPMENT IN WEST AFRICA
       Elmsford, N.Y.: Pergamon Press, 1979.

164   Rosenblatt, Samuel M., ed.
A B C TECHNOLOGY   AND   ECONOMIC   DEVELOPMENT: A   REALISTIC
       PERSPECTIVE
       Boulder, Colo.: Westview Press; in cooperation with
       the International Economic Studies Institute, 1979.

       Five previously unpublished papers focused on technology's
       role in the development process and the problem of
       technological transfer. The editor cites a concensus
       of the authors on the recognition that: (1) the solutions
       found in technology for LDC's are limited; (2) the latest
       technology is not invariably inappropriate nor the most
       basic invariably appropriate; (3) that adaptations of
       the technology and adaptation of their economic and social
       policies to the technology is a responsibility of the
       LDC's; (4) transnational enterprise is neither hero nor
       villain but a necessary if unfortunate conveyor of
       technology; (5) "goodwill, incentives,...[or]political
       decisions can[not] substitute for the basic disciplines
       of competitive economic forces in the developing countries
       themselves" in the transfer of technology.

165   Sagafi-Jejad, Tagi; Moxon, Richard W.; and Perlmutter,
B C   Howard V.
        CONTROLLING   INTERNATIONAL   TECHNOLOGY   TRANSFER: ISSUES,
        PERSPECTIVES AND POLICY IMPLICATIONS
        New York: Pergamon Press, 1981.

166   Science Council of Canada
A C   MULTINATIONALS AND INDUSTRIAL STRATEGY: THE ROLE OF WORLD
        PRODUCT MANDATES
        Ottawa: author, 1980.

        Examines the experience of four Canadian subsidiaries
        of   multinational   corporations--Black   and   Decker,
        Westingtinghouse,   Garrett   Manufacturing,   and   Litton
        Industries--in the use of "world product mandating,"
        a strategy that uses the international market power of
        multinational firm to sell a specific product or product
        line manufactured by a single subsidiary on a world-wide
        basis.   Discusses the benefits of a product mandate to
        the   Canadian   economy   in   terms   of   increased   output,
        profitability,   and   employment   for   these   subsidiaries,
        as   well   as   possible   cost   reductions   for   products
        manufactured   for   the   domestic   market.   Suggests   that
        world product mandates promise a "more secure and stable
        economic   future   for   branch   plants   in   Canada"   than
        continuation   of   the   traditional   subsidiary   or
        rationalization on a continental basis and discusses
        policy instruments to promote this objective.

167   Seya, Pierre Thizier
        TRANSNATIONAL CAPITALIST IDEOLOGY AND DEPENDENT SOCIETIES:
        IVORY COAST
        Stanford University, 1981.

168   Sigmund, Paul E.
        MULTINATIONALS   IN   LATIN   AMERICA: THE   POLITICS   OF
        NATIONALIZATION. A TWENTIETH CENTURY FUND STUDY
        Madison and London: University of Wisconsin Press, 1980.

        Examines the history of nationalization of U.S. corporate
        enterprises   during   the   1960s   and   1970s   in   five   major
        Latin   American   countries--Mexico,   Cuba,   Chile,   Peru,
        and Venezuela--and considers their implications for the
        future of foreign investment and for U.S. relations with
        the Third World.   Identifies the political and economic
        conditions   underlying   nationalization;   evaluates   the
        arguments both for and against nationalization; analyzes
        the management of nationalized industries; and discusses
        the costs and benefits of nationalization and alternatives
        (e.g., joint venture and regulation of investments by
        screening). Points out that the structure of international
        economic relations has been substantially modified since
        1973   and   that   both   Latin   American   governments   and
        multinational   corporations   have   learned   from   the
        experiences of nationalization.   Concludes that the trend

toward nationalization in Latin America may well have
climaxed and that multinationals may have learned how
to accomodate to the new environment. Also suggests
that "the new equilibrium" calls for reconsideration
of the role of the U.S. in promoting and protecting foreign
investment in developing countries.

169   Singh, V.B.
MULTINATIONAL CORPORATIONS AND INDIA
International Publication Service, 1974.

170   Skully, Michael T., ed.
A MULTINATIONAL LOOK AT THE TRANSNATIONAL CORPORATION
Sydney: Dryden Press, 1978.

171   Solomon, Lewis D.
MULTINATIONAL CORPORATIONS AND THE EMERGING WORLD ORDER
Port Washington, N.Y., and London: Kennikat Press,
National University Publications, 1978.

Examines world economic and social order in an effort
"to   encourage   a   rethinking   of...social   questions,
specifically   a   transnational   social   order   based   on
multinational corporations." Analyzes the general nature
of   multinational   corporations   and   problems   for
industrialized   nations   attributable   to   the   activities
of such firms including "the obselescence of significant
portions of...economic theories regarding a competitive
market and the Keynesian fiscal and monetary stabilizers;
the   possibility   that   foreign   direct   investment   by
multinational firms may have adversely affected the balance
of   payments   position   and   created   currency   instability
for   various   nation-states;   and   the   rapid   rise   of
transnational   commercial   banking   and   an   unregulated
Eurodollar market." Also discusses the impact of the
firms on developing nations and the Industry Cooperative
Programme of the Food and Agriculture Organization of
the United Nations as a synergistic organization linking
multinational   agribusiness   corporations   and   the   food
needs of developing nations.

172   Stauffer, Robert B.
TRANSNATIONAL   CORPORATIONS   AND   THE   POLITICAL   ECONOMY
OF DEVELOPMENT: THE CONTINUING PHILIPPINE DEBATE. RESEARCH
MONOGRAPH NO. 11
Sydney: Transnational   Corporations   Research   Project,
University of Sydney, 1980.

Examines the Philippine debate on TNC-Philippine relations,
first analyzing the position of transnational corporations
(TNCs) in the contemporary world, the role of state
authority in the world political economy, and its
relationship to the spread of the TNC's power. Reviews
Philippine literature on TNCs and analyzes interviews
with   26   academics,   government   officials,   and

representatives of the business community. Finds that despite a strong committment by the Philippine government to close cooperation with TNCs , a strong debate.

173   Stewart, Frances
A B C   TECHNOLOGY AND UNDERDEVELOPMENT
            Boulder, Colo.: Westview Press, 1977.

174   Stopford, J.M.
            EMPLOYMENT EFFECTS OF MULTINATIONAL ENTERPRISES IN THE
            UNITED KINGDOM
            ILO, 1979.

175   Strharsky, Harry and Riesch, Mary
            TRANSNATIONAL CORP AND THE THIRD WORLD
            CDC, 1975.

176   Tanchoco-Subido, Chita
            EMPLOYMENT EFFECTS OF MULTINATIONAL ENTRPRISES IN THE
            PHILIPPINES

177   Subrahmanian, K.K.
            MULTINATIONALS AND INDIAN EXPORTS
            South Asia Books, 1979.

178   Szyliowicz, Joseph S.
A B C   TECHNOLOGY AND INTERNATIONAL AFFAIRS
            New York: Praeger, 1981.

179   Tavis, Lee A.
            MULTINATIONAL MANAGERS AND POVERTY IN THE THIRD WORLD
            University of Notre Dame Press, 1982.

180   Thomas, D. Babatunde
B C D   IMPORTING TECHNOLOGY INTO AFRICA: FOREIGN INVESTMENT
            AND THE SUPPLY OF TECHNOLOGICAL INNOVATIONS
            New York: Praeger, 1976.

181   Thomas, D. Babatunde and Wionczik, Miguel S., eds.
B C D   INTEGRATION OF SCIENCE AND TECHNOLOGY WITH DEVELOPMENT:
            CARIBBEAN AND LATIN AMERICAN PROBLEMS IN THE CONTEXT
            OF THE UNITED NATIONS CONFERENCE ON SCIENCE AND TECHNOLOGY
            FOR DEVELOPMENT. PERGAMON POLICY STUDIES, NO. 22
            New York; Oxford; Toronto and Sydney: Pergamon Press,
            1979.

            Nineteen previously unpublished papers by nongovernmental
            participants plus a summary statement on the science and
            technology (S&T) problems of LDC's in the West, most
            originally presented at a conference sponsored by the
            Institute of Social and Economic Research, University
            of the West Indies, and the Institute of Development
            Studies, University of Guyana, held at Florida
            International University (Miami) in April 1978. Considers

the problems in building S&T capability, infrastructure and technology transfer, and technological problems in the Caribbean. Also examines S&T policies in Latin American and preparatory work for the then forthcoming U.S. conference held in August 1979. Concludes in part that: (1) building the needed technology is a long-term proposition; (2) we need to investigate the impact of multinationals on technology transfer; (3) priority should be given to policies to harness nonproprietary technology for development; and (4) new methods are needed for the integration of scientific and technological development goals.

182   Tomlinson, James W.C.
A B   THE JOINT VENTURE PROCESS IN INTERNATIONAL BUSINESS:
C D   INDIA AND PAKISTAN
        Cambridge, Mass.: MIT Press, 1970.

183   Torneden, Roger L.
        FOREIGN DISINVESTMENT OF U.S. MULTINATIONAL CORPORATIONS
        Praeger, 1975.

184   Toyne, Brian
        HOST COUNTRY MANAGERS OF MULTINATIONAL FIRMS: AN EVALUATION
        OF VARIABLES AFFECTING THEIR MANAGERIAL THINKING PATTERNS
        Arno, 1980.

185   Tuomi, Helena
        TRANSNATIONAL CORP, ARMAMENTS AND DEVELOPMENT
        Gower, 1982.

186   Turner, Lois
        MULTINATIONAL COMPANIES AND THE THIRD WORLD
        Hill & Wang, 1973.

187   TRANSNATIONAL BANKS: OPERATIONS, STRATEGIES AND THEIR
        EFFECTS IN DEVELOPING COUNTRIES
        UN, New York, 1981.

        Examines the nature, structure and operations (local and international) of transnational banks and their effects on host, particularly developing, countries. Topics covered: international strategies of 21 transnational banks; policies of 21 transnational banks towards developing countries; credit flows to developing countries; negotiating capacity of developing countr ies for external borrowing from transnational banks; and lending preferences of foreign and national financial institutions.

188   TRANSNATIONAL CORPORATIONS IN THE BAUXITE/ALUMINUM INDUSTRY
        UN, New York, 1981.

        Provides an overall analysis of the production and market characteristics of the bauxite/aluminum industry; discribes the involvement of transnational corporations in the

industry; discusses the strategies and operations of
transnational corporations; examines the policy trends and
prospects of the developing countries; and outlines the
future possible role of transnational corporations in
the industry.

189   UN
B C   AN INTERNATIONAL CODE OF CONDUCT ON TRANSFER OF TECHNOLOGY.
REPORT BY THE UNCTAD SECRETARIAT
UN, New York, 1975.

Part One contains an analytical description of the main
issues to be considered in the preparation of any draft
outline of an international code of conduct in transfer
of technology: objectives and principles; scope of
application of the code; ownership and control; relations
among suppliers; restrictive practices related to the
acquisition of technology for production; practices
relating to distribution; pricing and costs of technology;
development of national technologies and scientific
capabilities; and special preferences for developing
countries. Part Two discusses various considerations
relevant to the formulation of the code: legal nature
and possible form; approaches to formulation; machinery
for implementation; and applicable law and settlement
of disputes.

190   UN
B C   DRAFT INTERNATIONAL CODE OF CONDUCT ON THE TRANSFER OF
TECHNOLOGY AS OF 10 APRIL 1981
UN, New York, 1981.

Contains text of a Draft International Code of Conduct
on the Transfer of Technology. Prepared by UNCTAD, it
deals with national regulation of transfer of technology
transactions; guarantees, responsibilities, obligations;
special treatment for developing countries; international
collaboration; international institutional machinery;
and applicable law and settlement of disputes.

191   UN
TRANSNATIONAL CORPORATIONS IN FOOD AND BEVERAGE PROCESSING
UN, New York, 1981.

Explores the nature of the food-processing investments
of transnational corporations in developing countries,
the impacts of these activities on the development
potentials of the host countries, and the policies evolved
by host countries to improve the performance of
transnational corporations and others in the related
industries. Annexes cover: estimates of activities of
the food-processing industry by countries; factors
affecting entry into food-processing industries; data
on leading food-processing firms and their industry

participation; and classification of food-processing industry activities.

192   UN
TRANSNATIONAL CORPORATION LINKAGES IN DEVELOPING COUNTRIES: THE CASE OF BACKWARD LINKAGES VIA SUBCONTRACTING
UN, New York, 1981.

Focusing on the formation of linkages between transnational corporation affiliate and domestic corporations in the manufacturing sector, this report examines ways in which such linkages can initiate and stimulate production activities of domestic corporations in developing countries. Using the automotive industry as an example of linkages in the manufacturing sector, this report is a compilation of existing literature and case studies conducted in India, Peru and Morocco.

193   UN
TRANSNATIONAL CORPORATIONS IN WORLD DEVELOPMENT: A RE-EXAMINATION
UN, New York, 1978.

Reviews the growth of transnational corporations in the 1970s, in light of the quest for a new international economic order. Chapters cover: (a) the international setting; (b) main trends in policies towards transnational corporations; (c) patterns and trends in transnational corporation activities; (d) emerging relationships, including changing terms and conditions between transnationals and host countries; and (e) the search for new directions. Tabular appendixes cover: selected regulations, policies and arrangements related to transnational corporations; development statistics; foreign content of more than 400 major industrial corporations; and illustrative cases of renegotiation.

194   UN
ACTIVITIES OF TRANSNATIONAL CORPORATIONS IN SOUTHERN AFRICA: IMPACT ON FINANCIAL AND SOCIAL STRUCTURES. REPORT OF THE SECRETARIAT
UN, New York, 1978.

In three parts: (a) summary of recent developments in southern Africa relevant to transnational corporate activities, including patterns of transnational investment during the last year, a brief assessment of internal political and economic events, and relevant policies of home countries; (b) activities of transnational corporations in the banking and financial sectors; and (c) employment practices of transnational investors and their impact on social patterns within the context of local laws and customs.

195   UN

USERS GUIDE TO THE INFORMATION SYSTEM ON TRANSNATIONAL
CORPORATIONS: A TECHNICAL PAPER
UN, New York, 1980.

Coverage includes: (a) nature of information needs; (b)
structure of the system; (c) components and areas of
information; and (d) use of the system and procedures
for meeting requests.

196   UN
THE IMPACT OF MULTINATIONAL CORPORATIONS ON DEVELOPMENT
AND ON INTERNATIONAL RELATIONS
UN, New York, 1974.

Contains the report of the UN Secretary-General and the
text it transmits, and the report of the Group of Eminent
Persons to Study the Impact of Multinational Corporations
on Development and on International Relations, to the
Economic and Social Council (session LVII, 1974). The
report of the Group is in three parts: Part One is a
general evaluation and analysis of the role of
transnational corporations in development, of their impact
in developing countries, especially in relation to the
question of political intervention and consideration
of the international action and machinery that the Group
believes to be an indispensable corollary to national
and regional action. Part Two examines the issue of
control and ownership, implications for finance,
technology, employment and labor, consumer protection,
and other specific issues. Part Three contains comments
by individual members of the Group. The Group had the
help of consultants and of the Secretariat report
Multinational Corporations in World Development.

197   UN
TRANSNATIONAL CORPORATIONS AND THE PROCESSING OF RAW
MATERIALS: IMPACT ON DEVELOPING COUNTRIES
UN, New York, 1978.

Discusses the transnational corporation practices in
natural-resource utilization in developing countries,
focusing on minerals industries.

198   UN
TRANSNATIONAL CORPORATIONS IN THE COPPER INDUSTRY
UN, New York, 1981.

Provides an overall analysis of the production and market
characteristics of the copper industry and the present
and potential role of transnational corporations in this
regard. Coverage includes strategies and operations
of transnational corporations; policies of the developing
countries; and some issues in the negotiating process.

199   UN
       SURVEY OF RESEARCH ON TRANSNATIONAL CORPORATIONS
       UN, New York, 1977.

       Contains brief review of general characteristics and
       substantive coverage of current research on transnational
       corporations, followed by annexes which include: (a)
       research directory providing information on 810 projects
       (planned, completed, in progress); (b) research
       bibliography containing 512 references; and (c) researcher,
       institution, country, principal subject, and general
       subject.

200   UN
       NATIONAL   LEGISLATION   AND   REGULATIONS   RELATING   TO
       TRANSNATIONAL CORPORATIONS
       UN, New York, 1978.

       Includes a general review and analysis of the main features
       of national laws and regulations relating to transnational
       corporations of selected developing, eastern European
       and developed market economy countries. Also considers
       provisions relating to regional and other multinational
       agreements in this context. Presents summaries of the
       laws and regulations in tabular annexes which constitute
       the bulk of the report.

201   UN
       MEASURES   STRENGTHENING   THE   NEGOTIATION   CAPACITY   OF
       GOVERNMENTS   IN   THEIR   RELATIONS   WITH   TRANSNATIONAL
       CORPORATIONS: TECHNOLOGY   TRANSFER   THROUGH   TRANSNATIONAL
       CORPORATIONS
       UN, 1979.

       Defines and analyes the conflicts resulting from the
       present mechanisms by which technology is transferred
       from transnational corporations (TNCs) to the developing
       countries. Presents three different views of technology
       transfer through TNCs and discusses the search for the
       major negotiable issues; technology costs; restrictive
       practices; the unbundling of the technology package;
       the appropriateness of TNC technology transfer; the scope
       and nature of TNC research and development activities
       in developing countries; and subcontracting and personnel
       training.

203   UN
       MEASURES   STRENGTHENING   THE   NEGOTIATING   CAPACITY   OF
       GOVERNMENTS   IN   THEIR   RELATIONS   WITH   TRANSNATIONAL
       CORPORATIONS: REGIONAL   INTEGRATION   CUM/VERSUS   CORPORATE
       INTEGRATION
       UN, New York, 1982.

       Chapters cover: the meaning of integration within the
       system of transnational corporations; the role of

transnational corporations in regional integration among
the least developed countries; and empirical evidence
on roles and power relations between transnational
corporations, local private groups, and government policies
in the processes of the regional integration of the least
developed countries.

204   Villamil, Jose J., ed.
        TRANSNATIONAL CAPITALISM AND NATIONAL DEVELOPMENT: NEW
        PERSPECTIVES ON DEPENDENCE. HUMANITIES STUDIES IN
        DEVELOPMENT SERIES
        Atlantic Highlands, N.J.: Humanities Press, 1979.

        Fourteen essays, 11 previously unpublished, written by
        members of the Dependence Cluster at the Institute of
        Development Studies at the University of Sussex, on the
        impact of the changing world economy on countries of
        the periphery, particularly in light of the growing
        dominance of a relatively small number of large
        transnational corporations. In four parts: the papers
        in part one investigate some theoretical issues related
        to changes in the world system and the theories that
        interpret these changes, those in part two deal with
        transnational structures and processes, and those in
        part three focus on the impact of capitalist development
        and the role of the state. The final section considers
        alternativees to dependent capitalist growth.

205   UNIDO
        UNIDO ABSTRACTS ON TECHNOLOGY TRANSFER: STUDIES AND REPORTS
        ON THE DEVELOPMENT AND TRANSFER OF TECHNOLOGY (1970-1976)
        UN, New York, 1977.

        Presents a selective compilation of abstracts of documents
        issued by UNIDO on the subject of transfer of technology.
        Includes only abstracts from 1970 onwardd using major
        descriptors in the computer program. In two parts: (a)
        subject index, by title, arranged alphabetically be
        descriptors; and (b) bibliographical abstracts.

206   Wallender, Harvey W., III
A B   TECHNOLOGY TRANSFER AND MANAGEMENT IN THE DEVELOPING
C D   COUNTRIES: COMPANY CASES AND POLICY ANALYSES IN BRAZIL,
        KENYA, KOREA, PERU, AND TANZANIA
        Cambridge, Mass.: Harper & Row, Ballinger, 1979.

        Focuses on the problems related to seeking, receiving,
        and using technology by user firms in developing countries.
        Reviews prevailing theories of the transfer of technology
        and examines the management behavior of developing country
        firms in using technology through the analysis of case
        studies and environmental analyses prepared by a study
        team's inquiry into 67 consulting projects in Brazil,
        Peru, Korea, Tanzania, and Kenya and a survey of 405

similar projects in 43 other developing countries. Concludes that the major abstacle in the technology transfer process is at the receiving end, primarily the weakness in local managerial capabilities to handle technology--to diagnose needs, to devise solutions, and to seek assistance, when necessary, in implementing solutions.

207   Watanabe, Susumu
MULTINATIONAL ENTERPRISES AND EMPLOYMENT-ORIENTED "APPROPRIATE" TECHNOLOGIES IN DEVELOPING COUNTRIES
ILO, 1980.

208   Wells, Louis T.
A B C   TECHNOLOGY AND THIRD WORLD MUTINATIONALS
Geneva: International Labor Office, 1982.

209   Widstrand, Carl, ed.
MULTINATIONAL FIRMS IN AFRICA
Uppsala: Scandinavian Institute of African Studies and Stockholm: Almquist and Wiksell, 1975.

II. SELECTED PERIODICAL ARTICLES

210   Abumere, S.I.
Multinationals, location theory and regional development: case study of Bendel State of Nigeria. REGIONAL STUDIES (OXFORD) 12, No. 6:651-64, 1978.

Examines the spatial pattern formed by foreign private investments in Bendel State of Nigeria, and discusses some explanatory factors for this as well as the concomitant political and regional development implications.

211   Agmon, Tamir and Seev Hirsch
Multinational corporations and the developing economics: potential gains in a world of imperfect markets and uncertainty. OXFORD BULLETIN OF ECONOMICS AND STATISTICS (OXFORD) 41:333-44, Nov. 1979.

In this paper it is argued that countries whose factor and product markets are underdeveloped and whose market mechanism is fragile have more to gain from the presence of the MNCs than countries with highly developed and established markets.

212   Aharoni, Yair
"On the Definition of a Multinational Corporation." QUARTERLY REVIEW OF ECONOMICS AND ABUSINESS 11 (Autumn 1971): 27-37.

213   Alam, Ghayur and Langrish, John
       Non-multinational firms and transfer of technology to
       less developed countries. WORLD DEVELOPMENT (OXFORD)
       9:383-87, April 1981.

       The authors describe a comparison of nonmultinationals
       with multinationals in 47 transfers of technology from
       the UK to India.

214   AMERICAN CHAMBER OF COMMERCE JOURNAL (MANILA) 54:2, 4,
       10, May 1978. Impact of multinationals on Philippine
       economy positive on balance.

       Excerpts from a speech by Froilan Bacungan, Director
       of the University of the Philippines Law Center.

215   Banks, F.E.
       "Multinational Firms and African Economic Development."
       JOURNAL OF WORLD TRADE LAW (May-June 1975).

216   Barang, Marcel
       Drawing the teeth of the TNCs. SOUTH: THE THIRD WORLD
       MAGAZINE (LONDON) No. 9:11-12, July 1981.

       Looks at the recommendations of studies by the UN Centre
       of Transnational Corporations andd the Economic and Social
       Commission for Asia and the Pacific (ESCAP) on monitoring
       and regulating TNCs in the two countries.

217   Batra, Raveendra N. and Ramachandran, Rama
       Multinational firms and the theory of international
       trade and investment. AMERICAN ECONOMIC REVIEW (NASHVILLE)
       70:278-90, June 1980.

       The authors conclude that international economic policies
       pursued by one nation make waves in other nations even
       in a small country world where relative prices are
       determined in world markets, with each nation taking
       the terms of trade as constant.

218   Batra, Raveendra and Hadar, Josef
       Theory of the multinational firm; fixed versus floating
       exchange rates. OXFORD ECONOMIC PAPERS (LONDON) N.S.,
       31:258-69, July 1979.

       The authors study the economic behavior of multinational
       firms, including the impact of changes in exchange rates
       under fixed and floating regimes.

219   Behrman, Jack N. and Fischer, William A.
       Transnational corporations: market orientations and R&D
       abroad. COLUMBIA JOURNAL OF WORLD BUSINESS (NEW YORK)
       15:55-60, Fall 1980.

220   Berrie, T.W.
       Multinational companies in the development of nuclear
       power. ECONOMIST INTELLIGENCE UNIT. MULTINATIONAL BUSINESS
       (LONDON) No. 1:24-41, 1981.

221   Bhatt, R.S.
       Problems of transnational corporations. INDIA QUARTERLY
       (NEW DELHI) 34:1-16, Jan./March 1978.

222   Biermann, Herbert
       Imitation and innovation process initiated by technology
       transfer through multinational companies. ECONOMICS
       (TUBINGEN) 23:52-74, 1981.

223   Blond, David
       The future contribution of multinational corporations
       to world growth; a positive appraisal. BUSINESS ECONOMICS
       (WASHINGTON) 13:80-95, May 1978.

224   Bornschier, Volker
       Multinational corporations, economic policy and national
       development in the world system. INTERNATIONAL SOCIAL
       SCIENCE JOURNAL (PARIS) 32, No. 1:158-72, 1980.

225   Bornschier, Volker
       Multinational corporations and economic growth; a
       cross-national test of the decapitalization thesis. JOURNAL
       OF DEVELOPMENT ECONOMICS (AMSTRDAM) 7:191-210, June 1980.

226   Bornschier, Volker and Jean-Pierre Hoby
       Economic policy and multinational corporations in
       development: the measurable impacts in cross-national
       perspective [main findings of a research project at the
       University of Zurich]. SOCIAL PROBLEMS (SOC STUDY SOCIAL
       PROBLEMS) 28:363-77, April 1981.

227   Bradley, Gene E. and Bursk, Edward C.
       "Multinationalism and the 29th Day." HARVARD BUSINESS
       REVIEW 50 (January-February 1972): 37-47.

228   Brandt, William K. and Hulbert, James M.
       Pitfalls in planning for multinational operations. LONG
       RANGE PLANNING (OXFORD) 13:23-31, Dec. 1980.

229   Buckley, P.J.
       A critical review of theories of the multinational
       enterprise. AUSSENWIRTSCHAFT (ST. GALLEN) 36:70-87, March
       1981.

230   Chudnovsky, Daniel
       The challenge by domestic enterprises to the transnational
       corporations' domination; a case study of the Argentine
       pharmaceutical industry. WORLD DEVELOPMENT (OXFORD)
       7:45-58, Jan. 1979.

231   Cieslik, Jerzy
       Transnational corporations and transfer of management
       techniques to developing countries. ECONOMIC PAPERS
       (WARSAW) NO. 11:34-43, 1980.

232   Clairmonte, F.F.
       United States food multinationals: lessons for the third
       world. JOURNAL COMTEMPORARY ASIA 11, NO. 1:62-90, 1981.

233   Clark, Norman
       The multi-national corporation; the transfer of technology
       and dependence. DEVELOPMENT AND CHANGE (THE HAGUE) 6:5-21,
       Jan. 1975.

       The modern multinational corporation has come to exert
       a dominant influence on most aspects of political, economic
       and social life in many underdeveloped countries. The
       article stresses that an extremely important factor
       governing the ability of the large foreign corporation
       to achieve this position is its possession of and
       favourable access to modern technology.

234   Courtney, William H. and Leipziger, Danny M.
       Multinational corporations in LDCs; the choice of
       technology. OXFORD BULLETIN OF ECONOMICS AND STATISTICS
       (OXFORD) 37:297-304, Nov. 1975.

       The focus of this paper is on affiliates of US-owned
       parent MNCs, where the affiliates operate in LDCs and
       in developed countries.

235   Dasgupta, Subhendu
       Transnational corporations in electric power sector.
       1947-1967; continuity of linkages. ECONOMIC AND POLITICAL
       WEEKLY (BOMBAY) 16:1189-1204, July 11, 1981.

       Relates to the power sector in India between 1947 and
       1967.

236   Datta, Arun K.
       The impact of multinationals on economic sovereignty
       of less developed countries. ECONOMIC AFFAIRS (CALCUTTA)
       24:17-25, Jan./Apr. 1979.

237   Davidow, Joel
       Multinationals, host governments and regulation of
       restrictive business practices. COLUMBIA JOURNAL OF
       WORLD AFFAIRS (NEW YORK) 15:14-19, Summer 1980.

238   DEVELOPMENT AND CHANGE (THE HAGUE) 7:195-205, April 1976.
       The Latin American position on transnationals; rules
       of conduct that shall be observed by transnational
       enterprises (TNEs).

"Aide-memoire submitted by the Latin American group, composed of experts from 24 Latin American and Caribbean countries, to the US Government during the third preparatory meeting of the working group on transnational enterprises of the meeting of foreign ministers, Washington, D.C., Jan. 1975."

239   Diaz Alejandro, Carlos F.
The less developed countries and transnational enterprises. YALE UNIVERSITY. ECONOMIC GROWTH CENTER. CENTER DISCUSSION PAPER (NEW HAVEN)No. 298:1-29, Sept. 1978.

Concludes that, on the whole suitably directed by responsible host country planning and channeled selectively, TNEs can contribute to achieving specific developmental targets by supplying clearly defined services and expertise.

240   Doz, Yves
Multinational strategy and structure in government controlled businesses. COLUMBIA JOURNAL OF WORLD BUSINESS (NEW YORK) 15:14-25, Fall 1980.

241   Drucker, Peter F.
"Multinationals and Developing Countries: Myths and Realities." FOREIGN AFFAIRS 53 (October 1974): 121-34.

242   Ebel, Karl H.
Socio-econonomic aspects of multinational mineral mining. INTERNATIONAL LABOUR REVIEW (GENEVA) 113:53-65, Jan./Feb. 1976.

"Capital concentration and technological know-how have combined to make mineral mining increasingly the affair of large multinational enterprises, often to the concern of governments of the producer countries and of national and international trade union organisations."

243   Eels, Richard
"Do Multinational Corporations Stand Guilty as Charged?" BUSINESS AND SOCIETY REVIEW/INNOVATION (Autumn 1974).

244   Erdilek, Asim
Can the multinational corporation be incorporated into the general equilibrium theory of international trade and investment. SOCIAL AND ECONOMIC STUDIES (MONA, JAMAICA) 25:280-90, Sept. 1976.

"The purpose of this paper is to answer this question and to critically examine some of the attempts at incorporating the MNC into general equilibrium analysis."

245   Ewing, David W.
"MNCs [Multiantional Corporations] on Trial." HARVARD BUSINESS REVIEW 72 (May-June 1972): 130-42.

246   FAR EASTERN ECONOMIC REVIEW (HONG KONG) 103:33-50, Jan. 12, 1979. Asia and the multinationals.

247   Farooqi, Muhammad A.
        Multinational corporation in the Third World; boon or bondage? PAKISTAN HORIZON (KARACHI) 30:27-42, First quarter 1977.

248   Frank, Isaiah
        Multinational corporations; the view from the West. DEVELOPMENT FORUM BUSINESS EDITION (GENEVA) NO. 63:1-2, Sept. 30, 1980.

        This article, the first of two, is from the summary and conclusions of a   entitled 'Foreign enterprise in developing countries,' written by Isaiah Frank and sponsored by the Committee for Economic Development.

249   Freeman, O.L.
        Multinational companies and developing countries; a social contract approach. INTERNATIONAL DEVELOPMENT REVIEW 16, NO. 4:17-19, 1974.

250   Freeman, Orville L. and Persen, William
        Multinational Corporations; hope for the poorest nations. FUTURIST (WASHINGTON) 14:3-11, Dec. 1980.

        The authors suggest that the multinational companies can bring desperately needed economic development to poor nationas.

251   Gabriel, Peter P.
        "MNCs in the Third World: Is Conflict Unavoidable?" HARVARD BUSINESS REVIEW 72 (July-August 1972): 93-102.

252   Galloway, Jonathan F.
        Labor and the multinational challenge. STANFORD JOURNAL OF INTERNATIONAL STUDIES (STANFORD) 11:102-21, Spring 1976.

        "Examines some aspects of the development of relations between international business and international labor."

253   Gereffi, Gary and Evans, Peter
        Transnational corporations, dependent development, and state policy in the semiperiphery: a comparison of Brazil and Mexico. LATIN AMERICAN RESEARCH REVIEW (CHAPEL HILL) 16, No. 3:31-64, 1981.

254   Ghoshal, Animesh
        The choice of techniques in multinational investment: causes and consequences. INDIAN JOURNAL OF ECONOMICS (ALLAHABAD) 61:35-46, July 1980.

255   Gillis, Malcolm
       Multinational corporations and a liberal international
       economic order; some overlooked considerations. HARVARD
       INSTITUTE FOR INTERNATIONAL DEVELOPMENT, DEVELOPMENT
       DISCUSSION PAPER (CAMBRIDGE, MASS.) No. 39:1-22, May
       1978.

256   Girvan, Norman
       The impact of multinational entrprises on employment
       and income in Jamaica; preliminary report. INTERNATIONAL
       LABOR OFFICE. WORLD EMPLOYMENT PROGRAMME RESEARCH.
       COMPENDIUM OF WORKING PAPERS ON MULTINATIONAL FIRMS.
       WORKING PAPERS (GENEVA) No. WP 8:1-44, April 1976.

257   Goldberg, Ray
       The role of the multinational corporation. AMERICAN
       JOURNAL OF AGRICULTURAL ECONOMICS (LEXINGTON) 63:367-74,
       May 1981.

       Attempts to evaluate the role of the multinational
       corporation in achieving economic efficiency and equity
       in international agricultural trade 'and development.
       With discussion by Terutomo Ozawa, p. 393-95.

258   Goldsbrough, David J.
       International trade of multinational corporations and
       its responsiveness to changes in aggregate demand and
       relative prices. STAFF PAPERS, INTERNATIONAL MONETARY
       FUND (WASHINGTON) 28:573-99, Sept. 1981.

259   Gopalakrishnan, Chennat
       Multinational corporations, nation-states and ocean
       resource management: the impact of the world's 200-mile
       economic zone on multinational and national development.
       AMERICAN JOURNAL OF ECONOMICS AND SOCIOLOGY (NEW YORK)
       38:253-60, July 1979.

260   Griffith-Jones, S.
       Growth of multinational banking, the Euro-currency market
       and their effects on developing countries. JOURNAL
       DEVELOPMENT STUDIES 16:204-23, Jan. 1980.

261   Gustafsson, Hans
       New family of transnationals. DEVELOPMENT FORUM BUSINESS
       EDITION (GENEVA) No. 53: p. 6, April 30, 1980.

       Describes the development of multinational enterprises
       in the newly industrialized developing countries.

262   Hartmen, David
       Multinational corporations, taxation, and the income
       distribution in host countries. HARVARD INSTITUTE OF
       ECONOMIC RESEARCH, DISCUSSION PAPER SERIES (CAMBRIDGE,
       MASS.) No. 593:1-14, Dec. 1977.

Presents a model of impact of the multinational firms. The firms are assumed to operate abroad. It is shown that increasing the tax rates may result in losses to capital and gains to labor in the host country.

263   Hassan, M.F.
The role of the multinational corporation in land development in Latin America. RIVISTA INTERNAZIONALE DI SCIENZE ECONOMICHE E COMMERCIALI (MILAN) 27:448-68, May 1980.

264   Hawkins, Robert G. and Macaluso, Donald
The avoidance of restrictive monetary policies in host countries by multinational firms. JOURNAL OF MONEY, CREDIT AND BANKING (COLUMBUS, OHIO) 9:562-77, Nov. 1977.

"This study attempts to add to the evidence on MNCs' avoidance of restrictive monetary policies in host countries. It utilizes available aggregate data on capital spending and financial sources of U.S. foreign affiliates in six major industrial host countries.

265   Heenan, David A. and Keegan, Warren J.
The rise of third world multinationals. HARVARD BUSINESS REVIEW (BOSTON) 57:101-09, Jan./Feb. 1979.

266   Helleiner, G.K.
"Manufactured Exports from Less Developed Countries and Multinational Firms." ECONOMIC JOURNAL 83 (March 1973): 21-47.

267   Herman, B.
"A Case of Multinational Oligopoly in Poor Countries: Oil Refinery Investment in East Africa." JOURNAL OF DEVELOPMENT ECONOMICS (June 1975).

268   Hill, John S. and Still, Richard R.
Cultural effects of technology transfer by multinational corporations in lesser developed countries. COLUMBIA JOURNAL OF WORLD BUSINESS (NEW YORK) 15:40-51, Summer 1981.

269   Hill, Roy
Are multinationals aliens in the Third World? INTERNATIONAL MANAGEMENT 36:11-16, Jan. 1981.

Developing countries have a more confident relationship with multinational firms; but the advent of new advanced technology could generate friction.

270   Hirschey, Robert C. and Caves, Richard E.
Research and transfer of technology by multinational enterprises. OXFORD BULLETIN OF ECONOMICS AND STATISTICS (OXFORD) 43:115-30, May 1981.

The authors formulate and test a statistical model to explain the interational dispersion of R&D and transfer of technology by US multinationals.

271   Ikle, Max
"International Monetary Policy: Multinational Firms and the Currency Crisis." INTERECONOMICS (December 1971), pp. 369-71.

272   Imoisili, Imonitie C.
Key success factors in multinational and indigenous companies in Nigeria; a comparative analysis. COLUMBIA JOURNAL OF WORLD BUSINESS (NEW YORK) 13:40-53, Fall 1978.

"The article is based on the results of a survey of the management practice and organizational effectiveness of eighteen large business organizations (indigenous companies as well as American and European multinational subsidiaries) operating in Nigeria."

273   INTER-AMERICAN ECONOMIC AFFAIRS 25 (Autumn 1971): 55-65. "How Will Multinational Firms React to the Andean Pact's Decision 24?"

274   Ivanov, I.
Multinationals: what kind of new world? WORLD MARX REVIEW 21:117-27, July 1978.

275   Iyanda, Olukunle and Bello, Joseph A.
Employment effects of multinational enterprises in Nigeria. INTERNATIONAL LABOR OFFICE. MULTINATIONAL ENTERPRISES PROGRAMME. WORKING PAPER (GENEVA) No. 10:1-16, 1979.

276   Jenkins, Rhys
The export performance of multinational corporations in Mexican industry. JOURNAL OF DEVELOPMENT STUDIES (LONDON) 15:89-107, April 1979.

Seeks to throw some light on the export behaviour of subsidiaries of foreign firms operating in Mexico in comparison with locally-owned firms.

277   Jimenez de Lucio, Alberto
Transnational corporations and the industrialization of the LDCs. EUROPEAN COMMUNITIES. COMMISSION, COURIER (BRUSSELS) No. 60:75-76, March/April 1980.

278   Jimenez de Lucio, Alberto
The East, the South and the transnational corporations CEPAL REVIEW (SANTIAGO DE CHILE) p. 51-61, Aug. 1981.

279   Jo, Sung-Hwan
The impact of multinational firms of employment and incomes; the case study of South Korea. INTERNATIONAL

LABOR   OFFICE.   WORLD   EMPLOYMENT   PROGRAMME   RESEARCH.
COMPENDIUM OF WORKING PAPERS ON MULTINATIONAL FIRMS.
WORKING PAPERS (GENEVA) No. WP 12:1-100, July 1976.

280   Johnson, Harry G.
"The Multinational Corporation as a Development Agent."
COLUMBIA JOURNAL OF WORLD BUSINESS (May-June 1970).

281   Jungnickel, Rolf and Koopman, Georg
"Multinational Corporations: The Role of Multinationals
in the NIEO." INTERECONOMICS (March 1976), pp. 80-83.

282   Kassalow, Everett M.
Aspects of labour relations in multinational companies;
an overview of three Asian countries. INTERNATIONAL
LABOUR REVIEW (GENEVA) 117:273-87, May/June 1978.

Examines the impact of multinationals on the labour
relations systems and practices in the Philippines,
Malaysia and Singapore.

283   Katrak, Homi
Multi-national monopolies and monopoly regulations. OXFORD
ECONOMIC PAPERS (OXFORD) N.S., 32:543-66, Nov. 1980.

284   Khilji, Faizullah
Multinational corporations and restrictive business
practices; the case of Pakistan. PAKISTAN DEVELOPMENT
REVIEW (ISLAMABAD) 14:416-30, Winter 1976.

Content: Introduction. Domestic operations; dominant
firm and the control of industry. Domestic operations;
'the transfer of technology'. International operations;
division of markets and trade cartels. Regulation and
control.

285   Kirkpatrick, Colin and Nixson, Frederick
Transnational corporations and economic development.
JOURNAL OF MODERN AFRICAN STUDIES (LONDON) 19:367-99,
Sept. 1981. Economic development.

286   Knoppers, A.T.
"The Multinational Corporation in the Third World."
COLUMBIA JOURNAL OF WORLD BUSINESS (July-August 1970).

287   Kobein, Stephen J.
Multinational corporations, sociocultural dependence
and industrialization; need satisfaction or want creation?
JOURNAL OF DEVELOPING AREAS (MACOMB, ILL.) 13:109-25,
Jan. 1979.

288   Kojima, Kiyashi
Giant multinational corporations; merits and defects.

HITOTSUBASHI JOURNAL OF ECONOMICS (TOKYO) 18:1-17, Feb. 1978.

Concludes that the biggest defect of the giant multinationals comes from the fact that their behaviour and performance are justified merely from the point of growth of the firm. The author offers new guidelines for the conduct of multinationals.

289   Kopits, George F.
Taxation and multinational firm behavior; a critical survey. STAFF PAPERS, INTERNATIONAL MONETARY FUND (WASHINGTON) 23:624-73, Nov. 1976.

The paper intends to synthesize and evaluate the investigation, particularly that of a quantitative nature, undertaken thus far to answer two fundamental questions. Do taxes influence the decisions of the multinational enterprise? If they do, what are the direction and strength of the response of those decisions to tax changes at home or abroad?

290   Krause, Walter
"The Implications of UNCTAD III for Multinational Enterprise." JOURNAL OF INTERAMERICAN STUDIES AND WORLD AFFAIRS 15 (February 1973): 46-59.

291   Kuin, Pieter
"The Magic of Multinational Management." HARVARD BUSINESS REVIEW 50 (November-December 1972): 89-97.

292   Kumar, Krishna, ed.
Transnational enterprises: their impact on Third World societies and cultures. (WESTVIEW SPECIAL STUDIES IN SOCIAL, POLITICAL AND ECONOMIC DEVELOPMENT), 1980.

293   Lall, Sanjaya
Multinationals and market structure in an open developing economy; the case of Malaysia. WELTWIRT-SCHAFTLICHES ARCHIV (KIEL) 115, No. 2:325-50, 1979.

294   Lall, Sanjaya
Financial and profit performance of MNCs in developing countries; some evidence from an Indian and Colombian sample. WORLD DEVELOPMENT (OXFORD) 4:713-24, Sept. 1976.

Presents detailed information on the financing patterns and profit performance of a sample of multinational and other manufacturing firms in India and Colombia.

295   Lall, Sanjaya
Medicines and multinationals: problems in the transfer of pharmaceutical technology to the third world. MONTHLY REVIEW 28:19-30, March 1977.

296   Lall, Sanjaya and Senaka Bibile
        The political economy of controlling transnationals;
        the pharmacueutical industry in Sri Lanka (1972-76).
        WORLD DEVELOPMENT (OXFORD) 5:677-97, Aug. 1977.

        "Analyses the experience of Sri Lanka in reforming the
        structure of production, importation and distribution
        of pharmaceuticals, a sector dominated by transnational
        companies."

297   Lall, Sanjaya
        The indirect employment effects of multinational
        enterprises in developing countries. INTERNATIONAL LABOR
        OFFICE. MULTINATIONAL ENTERPRISES PROGRAMME. WORKING
        PAPER (GENEVA) No. 3:1-62, 1979.

298   Lall, Sanjaya
        Transnationals, domestic enterprises, and industrial
        structure in host LDCs: a survey. OXFORD ECONOMIC PAPER
        30L217-48, July 1978.

299   Lall, Sanjaya
        Transnationals, domestic enterprises, and industrial
        structure in host LDCs [less developed countries]: a
        survey. OXFORD ECONOMIC PAPER 30:217-48, July 1978.

300   Langon, Steven
        Technology transfer by multinational corporations in
        Africa; effects on the economy. AFRICA DEVELOPMENT (DAKAR)
        2:95-114, April/June 1977.

        "The focus of analysis is primarily the MNC transfer
        of manufacturing technology; and evidence is drawn heavily,
        though not exclusively, from Kenya.

301   LaPalombara, J. and Blank, S.
        Multinational corporations and developing countries.
        JOURNAL INTERNATIONAL AFFAIRS 34:119-36, Spring 1980.

302   Lazar, Arpad Von
        "Multinational Enterprises and Latin American Integration
        A Sociopolitical View." JOURNAL OF INTER-AMERICAN STUDIES
        11 (January 1969): 111-28.

303   Lecraw, Donald J.
        Technological activities of less-developed-country-based
        multinationals. AMERICAN ACADEMY OF POLITICAL AND SOCIAL
        SCIENCE, ANNALS (PHILADELPHIA) 458:163-74, Nov. 1981.

304   Lee, Wayne Y. and Kanwal S. Sachdeva
        The role of the multinational firm in the integration
        of segmented capital markets. JOURNAL OF FINANCE, PAPERS
        AND PROCEEDINGS (NEW YORK) 32:479-92, May 1977.

305   Leonard, J.J.
Multinational corporations and politics in developing
countries; review article. WORLD POLITICS 32:454-83,
April 1980.

306   Lim, Linda Y.C. and Pang Eng Fong
Vertical linkages and multinational enterprises in
developing countries. WORLD DEVELOPMENT (OXFORD)
10:585-95, July 1982.

Presents a case study of three multinational firms in
the export-oriented electronics industry in Singapore
which shows that under certain conditions multinational
firms can lead in creating local vertical linkages.

307   Litvak, I.A. and Maule, C.J.
Transnational corporations in the Banana industry; with
special reference to Central America and Panama. UNITED
NATIONS. ECONOMIC COMMISSION FOR LATIN AMERICA. DIVISION
OF ECONOMIC DEVELOPMENT. CEPAL/CTC JOINT UNIT. WORKING
PAPER (SANTIAGO) No. 7:1-123, Aug. 1977.

308   Long Frank
Is size a disadvantage in dealing with transnational
corporations? INTER-AMERICAN ECONOMIC AFFAIRS (WASHINGTON)
33:61-75, Spring 1980.

Attempts to determine whether the small size of a country
is necessarily a handicap in dealing with transnational
corporations, and presents a case study of foreign
investment policies in Guyana.

309   Magee, Stephen P.
Multinational corporations, the industry technology cycle
and development [some emphasis on the implication for
technology imports by less developed countries]. JOURNAL
WORLD TRADE LAW 11:297-321, July/August 1977.

310   Mahmood, Mir Annice
A note on multinational corporations and technology
transfer agreements. PAKISTAN DEVELOPMENT REVIEW
(ISLAMABAD) 17:355-64, Autumn 1978.

311   Mamalakis, Markos J.
Minerals, multinationals, and foreign investment in Latin
America (Review article). JOURNAL OF LATIN AMERICAN
STUDIES (LONDON) 9, Pt 2:315-36, Nov. 1977.

"The studies listed below analyze manifold aspects...of
mineral exploitation, multinationals and foreign
investment."

312   Markusen, James R.
Multinationals and the gains from trade: a theoretical

analysis based on economies of multi-plant operation. UNIVERSITY OF STOCKHOLM. INSTITUTE FOR INTERNATIONAL ECONOMIC STUDIES, SEMINAR PAPERS No. 160:1-40, Oct. 1980.

313   Meller, Patricio and Alejandra Mizala
U.S. multinationals and Latin American manufacturing employment absorption. BOSTON UNIVERSITY, CENTER FOR LATIN AMERICAN DEVELOPMENT STUDIES. DISCUSSION PAPER SERIES No. 46:1-29, May 1981.

314   Moran, Theodore H.
Multinational corporations and dependency; a dialogue for dependentistas and non-dependentistas. INTERNATIONAL ORGANIZATION 32:79-100, Winter 1978.

Concentrates on three assertions about the relations between multinational corporations and host countries in the Third World that frequently appear in the dependencia literature.

315   Morgenstern, Richard D. and Muller, Ronald
Multinational versus local corporations in LDC's: an econometric analysis of export perforamnce in Latin America. SOUTHERN ECONOMIC JOURNAL (Jan. 1976).

316   Morley, Samuel A. and Gordon W. Smith
Limited search and the technology choices of multinational firms in Brazil. QUARTERLY JOURNAL OF ECONOMICS 91:263-87, May 1977.

The choice of technique is not so limited as it is often portrayed to be and the failure of firms to adapt may well be the result of their limited search in a permissive environment rather than technical factors.

317   Morley, Samuel A. and Gordon W. Smith
The choice of technology; multinational firms in Brazil. ECONOMIC DEVELOPMENT AND CULTURAL CHANGE 25:239-64, Jan. 1977.

The authors seek answers to three basic questions: (1) To what extent have multinational firms adapted their production techniques in order to employ more labor and less capital in Brazil? (2) If adaptation has occured, what are the principal reasons for it? (3) Could the Brazilian government have induced foreign firms to seek more labor-intensive techniques than the ones they chose?

318   Murray, F. T.
Multinationals at the crossroads. BUSINESS AND SOCIAL REVIEW No. 14:82, Summer 1975.

319   Nair, B. N.
Multinationals: need for policy. YOJANA 18:9-10, Sept. 1974.

320   Nayyar, Deepak
        Transnational corporations and manufactured exports from
        poor countries. ECONOMIC JOURNAL 88:59-84, March 1978.

        Attempts to determine the scale of transnational
        participation in LDC exports of manufactures, and offers
        some observations on the economic implications for poor
        countries if they seek to promote manufactured exports
        through foreign firms.

321   Ness, Walter L.
        Brazil: local equity participation in multinational
        enterprises. LAW AND POLICY IN INTERNATIONAL BUSINESS
        6:1017-58, 1974.

322   Nye, Joseph S., Jr.
        Multinational corporations in world politics. FOREIGN
        AFFAIRS 53:153-75, Oct. 1974.

323   O'Brien, P.
        New multinationals: developing-country firms in
        international markets. FUTURES 12:303-16, August 1980.

324   Ozawa, Terutomo
        Japan's multinational enterprise: the political economy
        of outward dependency. WORLD POLITICS 30:517-37, July
        1978.

        Attempts to explain the essential differences between
        the foreign investment patterns of Japan and Western
        countries and to examine how a multitude of supportive
        functions are being mobilized or newly arranged by both
        government and industry to assist the overseas expansion
        of individual Japanese firms.

325   Panglaykim, J.
        MNC and the new international environment and ASEAN.
        INIDONESIAN QUARTERLY 8:53-75, Jan. 1980.

326   Panikar, P. G. K.
        Multinational enterprise in pharmaceutical industry and
        less developed countries. INDIAN ECONOMIC JOURNAL
        26:20-33, Jan./March 1979.

327   Park, Sung Jo
        Economic and social dualism, and Japanese multinationals.
        CULTURES ET DEVELOPPEMENT 9, No. 2:335-54, 1977.

        Concludes that the industrialization strategy of East
        and Southeast Asian countries excellently suits the scheme
        of Japanese multinationals. In the Japanese case, the
        verticalization of interface relations provides for a
        more important rationale of dependence theory.

328   Paul, Samuel
       Transnational   corporations   and   developing   countries;
       some issues in industrial policy.   ECONOMIC AND POLITICAL
       WEEKLY 14:1315-30, Aug. 1979.

329   Possas, Mario Luiz
       Employment effects of multinational enterprises in Brazil.
       INTERNATIONAL   LABOR   OFFICE.   MULTINATIONAL   ENTERPRISES
       PROGRAMME. WORKING PAPER No. 7:1-135, 1979.

330   Powelson, Joh P.
       The balance sheet on multinational corporations in less
       developed   countries.   CULTURES   ET   DEVELOPPEMENT   9,   No.
       3:413-32, 1977.

       Reviews and evaluates thirteen major criticisms leveled
       against   the   activities   of   multinational   corporations
       which have caused a hardening of the attitudes of
       governments in less developed countries.

331   Rose, Sanford
       Why the multinatioianl tide is ebbing.   FORTUNE 96:111-20,
       Aug. 1977.

       Some kinds of American corporations are still powerhouses
       abroad, but the author believes that the basic attractions
       of overseas investment have vanished.

332   Sachdev, Jagdish C.
       Dilution of ownership in multinational concerns.   LONG
       RANGE PLANNING 10:33-39, Oct. 1977.

333   Sau, Ranjit
       Technology growth and transnational corporations in India.
       INDIAN ECONOMIC JOURNAL 26:13-19, Jan./March 1979.

334   Schachter, Gustav, B. C. Cohen and F. N. Schachter
       Policies for multinational corporations.   INTERECONOMICS
       (Sept. 1975).

335   Schatz, Sayre P.
       Assertive pragmatism and the multinational enterprise.
       WORLD DEVELOPMENT 9:93-105, Jan. 1981.

       Proposes a simple conceptual framework regarding the
       literature on the impact of MNE's on developing host
       countries, specifying three approaches along a continuum.

336   Schollhammer, Hans
       Long-range planning in multinational firms.   COLUMBIA
       JOURNAL OF WORLD BUSINESS (Sept.-Oct. 1971).

337   Scott, Christopher D.
       Transnational corporations and the food industry in Latin
       America: an   analysis   of   the   determinants   of   investment

and divestment. WOODROW WILSON INTERNATIONAL CENTER
FOR SCHOLARS, LATIN AMERICAN PROGRAM. WORKING PAPERS
No. 64:1-69, 1980.

338   Senbet, Lemma W.
International capital market equilibrium and the
multinational firm financing and investment policies.
JOURNAL OF FINANCIAL AND QUANTITATIVE ANALYSIS 14:455-80,
Sept. 1979.

339   Shawky, Hany A. and David A. Ricks
Captial budgeting for multinational firms: a theoretical
analysis. SOUTHERN ECONOMIC JOURNAL 47:703-13, Jan.
1981.

340   Shin, Myungsoon
Do developing countries also profit? Critical analysis
on the role of multinational corporations in developing
countries. KOREA AND WORLD AFFAIRS 3:46-66, Spring 1979.

341   Siddharthan, N. S.
Industrial houses, multinationals and industrial policy.
ECONOMIC AND POLITICAL WEEKLY 14:1197-1203, July 21,
1979.

Attempts to test the hypothesis that the different firms
belonging to the two business houses of Birla and Tata,
operating in different market structures, behave
differently with regard to growth of assets and profits.
The paper also presents certain findings on the growth
and profitability of multinational firms in the engineering
industries and analyzes their implications for industrial
policy.

342   Streeten, Paul
Multinationals revisited: review article. FINANCE AND
DEVELOPMENT 16:39-42, June 1979.

343   Teece, David J.
The multinational enterprise: market failure and market
power considerations. SLOAN MANAGEMENT REVIEW 22:3-17,
Spring 1981.

Develops a conceptual framework to examine the relative
efficiency properties of multinational firms.

344   Teece, D. J.
Technology transfer by multinational firms; the resource
cost of transferring technological know-how. ECONOMIC
JOURNAL 87:242-61, June 1977.

The domain of this study is the transfer of the capability
to manufacture a product or process from firms in one
country to firms in another.

345   Tharp, Paul A. Jr.
       Transnational enterprises and international regulation;
       a survey of various approaches in international
       organizations.   INTERNATIONAL   ORGANIZATION   30:47-73,
       Winter 1976.

       The author discusses four models of regulation; the free
       market model, the EEC Model, the multinational consortium
       approach and the development community approach.

346   Tomassini, Roberto
       Complimentarity agreements of LAFTA and the participation
       of transnational corporations; the cases of office machines
       and electronic products.   UNITED NATIONS.   ECONOMIC
       COMMISSION FOR LATIN AMERICA.   DIVISION OF ECONOMIC
       DEVELOPMENT.   CEPAL/CTC JOINT UNIT.   WORKING PAPER No.
       3:1-60, July 1977.

347   Turner, Louis
       There's no love lost between multinational companies
       and the Third World.   BUSINESS AND SOCIETY
       REVIEW/INNOVATION (Autumn 1974).

348   Turner, Louis
       Multinationals, the United Nations and development.
       COLUMBIA JOURNAL OF WORLD BUSINESS (Sept.-Oct. 1972).

349   Turner, Terisa
       Multinational corporations and the instability of the
       Nigerian state.   REVIEW OF AFRICAN POLITICAL ECONOMY
       No. 5:63-79, Jan./April 1976.

       Analyzes operations of foreign capital in Nigeria, and
       the way in which they undermine the stability of the
       state.   In the second part of her paper she shows how
       conflicts over oil policy were crucial to the overthrow
       of the Gowon regime, conflicts which are not likely to
       be resolved by its successor.

350   Ulmer, Melville J.
       Multinational corporations and Third World capitalism.
       JOURNAL OF ECONOMIC ISSUES 14:453-71, June 1980.

       Suggests that, in general, the operations of multinational
       corporations are in the interests of Third world countries,
       and it is in the interest of the U.S. to encourage their
       activities.

351   United Nations.   Economic Commission for Latin America.
       Division of Economic Development.
       The transnational corporations among the one thousand
       largest enterprises in Brazil.   (Principal indicators
       at the level of individual enterprises) CEPAL/CTC JOINT
       UNIT.   WORKING PAPER (SANTIAGO) No. 5:1-14, July 1977.

352   United Nations. Economic and social council. Commission on transnational corporations.
Transnational corporations in world development: a re-examination. March 20, 1978.

353   Van Auken, Philip M. and R. Duane Ireland
The social accommodation process between multinational corporation and host country; guidelines for effectiveness. BAYLOR BUSINESS STUDIES 10, N.S.:53-64, Aug./Oct. 1979.

This paper offers a conceptual framework which can aid the MNC in adapting to the host country environment.

354   Vernon, Raymond
Multinational enterprises in developing countries; an analysis of national goals and national policies. HARVARD INSTITUTE FOR INTERNATIONAL DEVELOPMENT, DEVELOPMENT DISCUSSION PAPER No. 4:1-75, June 1975.

355   von Mehren, Robert B. and Martin E. Gold
Multinational corporations; conflicts and controls. STANFORD JOURNAL OF INTERNATIONAL STUDIES 11:1-41, Spring 1976.

Considers some of the types of tensions and conflicts which the existence and operations of multinational corporations create.

356   Watanabe, Susumu
Multinational enterprises and employment-oriented "appropriate" technologies in developing countries. INTERNATIONAL LABOR OFFICE. MULTINATIONAL ENTERPRISES PROGRAMME. WORKING PAPER No. 14:1-24, 1980.

357   Weigel, Dale R.
Multinational approaches to multinational corporations. FINANCE AND DEVELOPMENT 11:27-29, Sept. 1974.

358   Weinstein, Franklin B.
Multinational corporations and the Third world; the case of Japan and Southeast Asia. INTERNATIONAL ORGANIZATION 30:373-404, Summer 1976.

The article is a case study of Japanese MNC's in Southeast Asia. The author doubts the likelihood that the poor countries will be able to harness MNC's for their development.

359   Wells, Louis T., Jr.
Social cost-benefit analysis for MNC's. HARVARD BUSINESS REVIEW 53:40-48, March-April 1975.

360   Widjaja, Albert
Impact of multinational corporations on social and political conditions in Indonesia. ASIA PACIFIC COMMUNITY

No. 8:44-57, Spring 1980.

361   Wilkins, Mira
       Multinational oil companies in South America in the 1920's.
       BUSINESS HISTORY REVIEW 48:414-46, Autumn 1974.

362   Winiecki, Jan
       Japan's imports and exports of technology policy. STUDIES
       IN   COMPARATIVE   INTERNATIONAL   DEVELOPMENT   14:45-62,
       Fall/Winter 1979.

363   Wohlmuth, Karl
       Collective self-reliance and the control of transnational
       corporations in developing countries with comments on
       Sri Lanka's open-door policy. ASIAN ECONOMIES p. 33-63,
       S 1981.

364   Wright, Peter and others
       The developing world to 1990:   trends and implications
       for multinational business. LONG RANGE PLANNING 15:116-25,
       August 1982.

365   Yamazaki, Kiyoshi and Noritake Kobayashi
       Toward Japanese-type multinational corporations. JAPANESE
       ECONOMIC STUDIES 5:41-70, Summer 1977.

366   Yannopoulos, G. N. and J. H. Dunning
       Multinational enterprises and regional development; an
       exploratory paper.   REGIONAL STUDIES 10, No. 4:389-99,
       1976.

       Concerned with the role of the multinational enterprises
       in the spatial allocation of resources within nations.

367   Yoshihara, Hideki
       Japanese multinational enterprises; a view from outside.
       KOBE ECONOMIC & BUSINESS REVIEW 25:15-35, 1979.

III. SPECIALIZED PUBLICATIONS
(REPORTS, DOCUMENTS AND DIRECTORIES)

368   Administration for Development: A Comparative Perspective
       on the Middle East and Latin America, edited by Jack W.
       Hopkins, contains six papers presented at a meeting on
       the above theme, held at Indiana University in May 1976.
       Copies are available from the School of Public and
       Environmental Affairs, Indiana University, Bloomington,
       Indiana 47401, USA.

369   Agricultural Development and the Rural Poor, edited by
       Guy Hunter, is based on an international seminar in 1978
       sponsored by the Overseas Development Institute. The meeting

considered the need for a radical review of both the
policies and implementation of agricultural development
in the Third World. Copies are available from ODI Sales,
Montagu House, Huntingdon, Cambridgeshire, United Kingdom.

370   Black Africa--A Comparative Handbook, by Donald G.
Morrison, offers country profiles for the 32 independent
black African nations. In addition, the reference provides
comparative profiles in the fields of demography, ecology
and pluralism, social and economic development, political
development, security systems and stability, international
linkages, and urban and ethnic patterns. The document
is available from the Free Press, 866 Third Avenue, New
York, New York 10022, USA. Maps and bibliographies are
included for each country profile.

371   Criteria for Evaluation of Development Projects Involving
Women was prepared by the Subcommittee on Women in
Development of the Committee on Development Assistance,
American Council of Voluntary Agencies for Foreign Service.
The criteria are set forth and then tested against six
sample development projects. The booklet is available
from the Technical Assistance Information Clearing House,
ACVAFS, 200 Park Avenue South, New York, New York 10003.

372   The Development of Development Thinking is the theme
of the OECD Development Centre's Liaison Bulletin--1977/1.
The report contains papers and discussion summaries of
the First Inter-Regional Meeting on Development Research,
Communication and Education, organized by the OECD
Development Centre and Institute of Development Studies
in 1976. "New Development Strategies," "Collective
Self-Reliance," and "Inter-Regional Co-operation" are
the major subject areas. Copies are available from OECD
Publications, 2, rue Andre-Pascal, 75775 Paris Cedex
16, France, or from any OECD sales agent.

373   Development Planning in Ecuador, by R. J. Bromley, presents
a picture of Ecuador in the first half of 1976 against
a background of historical trends and with short-term
projections into the future. Copies are available from
Grant & Cutler Ltd., 11 Buckingham Street, London WC2N
6DQ, England.

374   Development Studies--United Kingdom Research Register
1976, edited by G. E. Gorman, is a guide to current
development studies research in Great Britain. The 450
projects listed represent a wide range of institutions
and agencies involved in development research. Copies
are available from IDS Communications, Institute of
Development Studies, University of Sussex, Brighton,
Sussex BN1 9RE, United Kingdom.

375   Directory of Activities of International Voluntary Agencies
in Rural Development in Africa (Third Edition) contains

description of thirty-seven agencies and their rural
development projects in Africa. Copies may be obtained
from the Voluntary Agencies Bureau, Social Development
Division, U.N. Economic Commission for Africa, P.O. Box
3001, Addis Ababa, Ethiopia.

376   Directory of Economic and Social Development Research
and Training Units in OECD Member Countries/1976--No.
3-4 describes some 300 economic and social development
research and training institutions in OECD Member
Countries. All information is valid as of January 1977.
Copies of the Directory are available from any OECD Sales
Office or from OECD Publications, 2, rue Andre-Pascal,
75775 Paris Cedex 16, France.

377   Directory of Financial Aids for International Activities
contains information on 231 sources of grants to
individuals for study abroad. The guide includes
geographic, subject, type, and level of eligibility
indexes. Copies are available from the Office of
International Programs, University of Minnesota, 201
Nolte West, Minneapolis, Minnesota 55455.

378   A Directory of Institutional Resources: U.S. Centers
of Competence for International Development describes
the resources and services of U.S. universities that
are involved in overseas development programs. The
directory is available from TA/PPU/EUI, Room 2669, Agency
for International Development, U.S. Department of State,
Washington, D.C. 20523.

379   A Directory of Non-Commercial Organisations in Britain
Actively Concerned with Overseas Development and Training
is the third edition prepared by the British Overseas
Development Institute. Some 200 agencies are described
in the new edition. Copies are available from ODI Sales,
Montagu House, High Street, Huntingdon, Cambs. PE18 6EP,
England.

380   Directory of Social Research and Training Units--Africa
was prepared by the OECD Development Centre. The document,
with introductions in French and English, contains a
descriptive listing of institutions in some thirty-seven
African countries. Also included are a subject index,
index of directors and list of institution periodicals.
Copies of the document are available from OECD
Publications, 2, rue Andre-Pascal, 75775 Paris Cedex
16, France.

381   A Directory of Social Science Research and Training
UNITS--Latin America updates a previous listing prepared
by the OECD Development Centre. The directory contains
descriptive summaries of institutions classified by country
and also provides an alphabetical list of institutions,

index of directors, subject index, and periodical guide.
It is available from OECD Publications, 2, rue Andre
Pascal, 75775 Paris Cedex 16, France.

382   The Directory of United Nations Information Systems and
Services lists all the information activities of the
United Nations system. It contains details on more than
100 information sources, and covers subjects ranging
from human rights to industry. Also listed are some
2500 addresses of local offices of organizations and
information centers in 155 countries. Copies are available
to organizations, universities and libraries from the
Director, IOB Secretariat, Palais des Nations, CH-1211
Geneva 10, Switzerland.

383   Dissertation Abstracts Relating to International
Agricultural and Rural Development, Volumes I, II, II
and IV, compiled by N. S. Peabody, III contain abstracts
of participants in Cornell University's Program in
International Agriculture. Single copies are available
from the New York State College of Agriculture and Life
Sciences, Cornell University, Ithaca, New York 14850.

384   Education and Training for Public Sector Management in
Developing Countries, edited by Laurence D. Stifel, James
S. Coleman, and Joseph E. Black, contains nine papers
on various aspects of training for development
administration. Copies may be obtained from The
Rockefeller Foundation, 1133 Avenue of the Americas,
New York, New York 10036.

385   Employment in Developing Countries, by Edgar O. Edwards,
is based on a Ford Foundation study. The report discusses
the nature of the employment problem, environmental factors
which limit the choice of employment programs, and various
strategies for handling the problem, including program
options for donor agencies. The document is available
from the Ford Foundation, Office of Reports, 320 East
43rd Street, New York, New York 10017.

386   The European Community and the Third World describes
in depth all the European Community programs on behalf
of the developing countries. The booklet is available
from the Commission of the European Communities, Rue
de la Loi 200, 1049 Brussels, Belgium, or any Community
press/information offices around the world.

387   Family Farms in Rural Development: A Comparative Study
of Japan and Developing Countries in Asia, by Masakatsu
Akino, Kazushi Ohkawa, and Saburo Yamada, is available
from the International Development Center of Japan, Daini
Shuwa Toranomon Bldg., 20 Sakuragawa-cho, Nishikubo,
Shiba, Minato-ku, Tokyo 105, Japan.

388   Financial Resources for Industrial Projects in Developing
         Countries gives information on some 200 industrial
         development financing institutions in 100 countries,
         and on international banking and aid-giving institutions.
         The directory was compiled by the Investment Cooperative
         Programme Office of UNIDO. The document is available
         from this office, UNIDO, P.O. Box 707, A-1011, Vienna,
         Austria.

389   Glossary of Institutions Concerned with Latin America,
         2nd Edition, is a reference guide to some 244
         international, regional, governmental and private
         institutions concerned with Latin America and the
         Caribbean. The Glossary is available from the Information
         Centre, Canadian Association for Latin America, 42 Charles
         Street East, Toronto, Canada M4Y 1T4.

390   Government Finance Statistics Yearbook--1977, prepared
         by the International Monetary Fund, provides current
         data on the finances of IMF member governments. Material
         for each country is organized in three parts: the
         statistical tables, institutional tables, and where
         information is available, a derivation table followed
         by a statement on the coverage of the central government
         statistics. Copies of the Yearbook are available from
         the International Monetary Fund, Washington, D.C. 20431.

391   A Guide to the Economic Appraisal of Projects in Developing
         Countries is a publication of the British Ministry of
         Overseas Development. The Guide is designed to provide
         a practical basis for the economic appraisal of projects
         financed by the public sector and for screening private
         sector projects subject to public sector approval. Copies
         are available from Her Majesty's Stationery Office, 49
         High Holborn, London WC1V 6HB, England.

392   Higher Education and Social Change--Volume 2, edited
         by Kenneth W. Thompson, Barbara R. Fogel, and Helen E.
         Danner, contains twenty-five case studies and seven special
         reports on higher institutions in the Third World and
         their approaches to development problems. The publication
         is available from Praeger Publishers, New York, Washington
         and London.

393   The Integration of Women in Development: Why? When?
         How?, by Ester Boserup and Christina Liljencrantz, explains
         how and why women's participation in development presents
         special problems, and makes proposals for resolving these
         problems. The booklet is designed for decision makers,
         leaders and training personnel concerned with the role
         of women in development. Copies are available from Room
         CN-300, United Nations Development Programme, New York,
         New York 10017.

394   International Directory of Women's Development Organizations contains information on 600 local and national women's organizations around the world, with emphasis on those in developing countries. The Directory was compiled by Franziska P. Hosken under auspices of the U.S. Agency for International Development. The guide is designed to provide basic contacts for communication among women's organizations, resource groups, and the international development community. Copies are available from Women in Development, U.S. Agency for International Development, Washington, D.C. 20523.

395   Knowledge and Power: The Global Research and Development Budget, by Colin Norman, notes the disparities in research and development expenditures around the world, and stresses, the need to mobilize Third World R & D capacities. The publication is available from the Worldwatch Institute, 1776 Massachusetts Avenue, N.W., Washington, D.C. 20036.

396   A Management Approach to Project Appraisal and Evaluation with Special Reference to Non-Directly Productive Projects, by N. Imboden, is addressed to officials concerned with the management of development programs. The book is based on the premise that appraisal/evaluation frameworks must be adapted in the socio-economic situation of a given country. It is available from OECD Publications, 2, rue Andre-Pascal, 75775 Paris Cedex 16, France, or from any OECD Sales Office.

397   National Objectives and Project Appraisal in Developing Countries, by Hartmut Schneider, analyzes whether and how national objectives are or might be taken into account in making project appraisals in developing countries. Major subject headings are: (1) Interrelations between national objectives; (2) Linking project appraisal to national objectives; and (3) Towards a new framework for project appraisal. Copies of the study are available from OECD Publications, 2, rue Andre-Pascal, 75775 Paris Cedex 16, France.

398   On the Strategy of Industrialization in Developing Countries and Experiences in Economic and Social Development in Socialist Countries (Parts I and II) contains papers presented at the 14th International Summer Seminar sponsored by the University of Economic Science "Bruno Leuschner" in Berlin in 1977. Both documents are available from the Institute for the Economy of Developing Countries, University of Economic Science "Bruno Leuschner", Hermann-Duncker-Strasse 8, 1157 Berlin, German Democratic Republic.

399   The Process of Development in the Middle East: Goals and Achievements is a summary of the 30th Annual Conference

of The Middle East Institute, held in Washington, D.C.,
October 15-16, 1976. Copies are available from The Middle
East Institute, 1761 N Street, N.W., Washington, D.C.
20036.

400   Promotion of Small-Scale Industries in Developing
Countries, by Dr. Karl Wolfgang Menck is a report published
by HWWA--Institut fur Wirtschaftforschung--Hamburg. It
contains 57 abstracts of books and articles which are
concerned with various aspects of promotion of small-scale
industries. Copies are available from HWWA--Institut
fur Wirtschaftsforschung--Hamburg, Public Relations,
Neuer Jungsfernstein 21, 2000 Hamburg 36, Germany.

401   Public Administration Training for the Less Developed
Countries, edited by Irving Swerdlow and Marcus Ingle,
reports on a conference sponsored by the Maxwell School
of Citizenship and Public Affairs, held at Syracuse
University, New York, April 18-19, 1974. The panels
discussed such topics as "Agricultural Administration
Training," "Public Administration and Public Enterprises,"
"Criteria for Improving Public Administration Training,"
"Urban and Rural Works Programs," and "Public Management
and Development Assistance." Copies of the document
may be obtained from the Maxwell School of Citizenship
and Public Affairs, Syracuse University, Syracuse, New
York 13210.

402   The 1978/79 Publications List of Third World Publications
contains over 300 titles of pamphlets, books and teaching
materials about the Third World. The listing is free
from Third World Publications, Ltd., 151 Stratford Road,
Birmingham B11 1RD, England.

403   Register of Development Research Projects in Africa notes
226 current development research projects in 21 African
countries, classified by country and institution. It
contains project descriptions as well as indexes of
researchers, institutions and financial sponsors. The
OECD Development Centre prepared the Register, and is
also working on similar volumes for Latin America and
Asia. For more information contact the OECD Development
Centre, 94, rue Chardon Lagache, 75016 Paris, France.

404   Register of Research Projects in Progress in Development
Studies in Selected European Countries was prepared by
the Centre for Development Studies of the University
of Antwerp at the request of The European Association
of Development Research and Training Institutes. Copies
are available from the Centre, St. Ignatius Faculties,
University of Antwerp, 13 Prinsstraat, 2000 Antwerp,
Belgium.

405   Report to Congress on Women in Development, prepared

by the Office of Women in Development of the U.S. Agency for International Development, assesses the impact of U.S. development aid programs on the integration of women into the developing economies of countries receiving assistance. The report contains five parts: Summary and evaluation; Introduction; Specific projects in Africa, Asia, Latin America, and the Near East plus activities in the area of population; data section; and description of AID programs in the area of women in development. Copies are available from Office of Women in Development, Room 3243 NS, Agency for International Development, U.S. Department of State, Washington, D.C. 20523.

406   Resources for Development: Organizations and Publications, edited by David A. Tyler, notes agencies and publications in the U.S., Africa, Asia and Latin America that would be useful to Peace Corps field workers in coordinating their programs with other local development efforts. Copies are available from the Office of Multilateral and Special Programs, Action/Peace Corps, 806 Connecticut Avenue, N.W., Washington, D.C. 20525.

407   The Role of Rural Women in Development is based on a conference sponsored by the Agricultural Development Council, held in Princeton, New Jersey, December 2-4, 1974. The report summarizes the meeting and lists the participants and major papers presented. Copies are available from the Agricultural Development Council, 1290 Avenue of the Americas, New York, NY 10019.

408   Rural Development Planning in Zambia: Objectives, Strategies and Achievements, by Joachim Luhring, is a socioeconomic analysis with special reference to problems of administration and regional planning. The monograph is available from the African Training and Research Centre in Administration for Development (CAFRAD), P.O. Box 310, Tangier, Morocco.

409   Social Development and the International Development Strategy is a brief paper prepared by the staff of the United Nations Research Institute for Social Development. Copies may be obtained from the Institute, Palais des Nations, 1211 Geneva 10, Switzerland.

410   Social and Economic Development Plans--Microfiche Project is a cumulative catalogue listing the holdings of Inter Documentation Company AG on social and economic development plans around the world. About 1400 plans from over 180 countries are included. Copies of the catalogue and other catalogues of IDC's microfiche projects are free on request from Inter Documentation Company AG, Poststrasse 14, 6300 Zug-Switzerland.

411   Systems Approaches to Developing Countries contains the

proceedings of the First IFAC/IFORS (International
Federation of Automatic Control and International
Federation of Operational Research Societies) Symposium
on the topic, held in May 1973, in Algiers, Algeria.
The sixty-six papers in the book were written by
authorities representing twenty countries. The papers
present the systems engineering approach for the following
applications: Management and Development Policies;
Agriculture and Food; Power Generation; Water and Pollution
Control; Urban Planning, Transport and Communications;
Gas, Oil and Cement Industries; Methodology; Education
and Health; Human Resources; and International Cooperation
and Development. The document is available from the
Instrument Society of America, Publications Department,
400 Stanwix Street, Pittsburgh, Pennsylvania 15222.

412   Third World Deficits and the "Debt Crisis," prepared
by the North-South Institute, is a comprehensive analysis
of the debt problem of developing countries with
suggestions for action in debt relief. Copies of the
booklet are available from the North-South Institute,
185 Rideau Street, Ottawa, Canada K1N 5X8.

413   The United States and the Developing Countries is a report
of the Atlantic Council Working Group on the United States
and the Developing Countries. The report reviews U.S.
development policy and suggests some guidelines for future
action. Copies are available from Westview Press, Inc.,
1898 Flatiron Court, Boulder, Colorado 80301.

414   The University Center for Cooperatives has issued a new
Directory of International Training Programs, a listing
of programs which it is offering at the University of
Wisconsin. Copies are available from the University
Center for Cooperatives, 524 Lowell Hall, 610 Langdon
Street, Madison, Wisconsin 53706.

415   Women and World Development, edited by Irene Tinker and
Michele Bo Bramsen, contains twelve essays prepared
as background papers for the American Association for
the Advancement of Science Seminar on Women in Development,
held in Mexico City, June, 1975. Also included are the
Proceedings of the Seminar. Copies are available from
the Overseas Development Council, 1717 Massachusetts
Avenue, N.W., Washington, D.C. 20036.

416   The World Directory of Social Science Institutions:
Research, Advanced Training, Documentation and Professional
Bodies has been updated by Unesco. For copies write
to Unesco, 7 Place de Fontenoy, 75700 Paris, France.

IV. BIBLIOGRAPHIC SUBJECT INDEX

INCOME DISTRIBUTION, 31

INDIA, 114, 169, 177, 182, 235, 294

INDONESIA, 360

INDUSTRIAL POLICY, 25, 328, 341

INDUSTRIAL PROJECTS, 39

INDUSTRIALIZATION, 81, 122, 277, 287, 298, 320

INDUSTRY, 28

INEQUALITIES, 92

INTERNATIONAL DEVELOPMENT, 7, 56, 68

INTERNATIONAL ECONOMY, 45

INVESTMENT, 27, 338, 339

IVORY COAST, 146, 167

ISRAEL, 26

JAMAICA, 256

JAPAN, 362, 365, 367

KENYA, 133, 143

LABOR POLICY, 128, 252, 282

LATIN AMERICA, 33, 35, 105, 106, 130, 147, 148, 161, 168, 238, 263, 302, 307, 311, 315, 337, 361

LIBERIA, 104

MANAGEMENT, 184, 231, 291

MARKETING POWER, 111, 343

MEXICO, 111, 253, 276

MINERAL MINING, 242

MODERNIZATION, 1

MONOPOLIES, 283

MULTINATIONAL BANKING, 260

MULTINATIONAL CORPORATIONS & DEVELOPMENT, 94, 97, 98, 99, 101, 103, 104, 105, 107, 110, 112, 113, 115, 118, 119, 123, 127, 134, 136, 137, 138, 139, 140, 141, 143, 144, 146, 147, 148, 153, 155, 157, 159, 163, 169, 171, 172, 175, 177, 183, 185, 188, 192, 193, 194, 196, 199, 203, 209, 210, 211, 212, 214, 215, 217, 219, 221, 223, 224, 225, 226, 227, 228, 229, 232, 239, 240, 241, 243, 244, 245, 247, 248, 249, 250, 251, 255, 256, 257, 258, 259, 261, 262, 263, 265, 267, 269, 272, 273, 274, 278, 280, 281, 284, 285, 286, 287, 288, 289, 290, 292, 294, 296, 297, 301, 302, 304, 305, 306, 307, 308, 309, 311, 312, 318, 319, 321, 322, 323, 325, 326, 327, 330, 331, 332, 334, 335, 336, 337, 340, 342, 345, 346, 347, 348, 349, 350, 351, 352, 353, 354, 355, 357, 358, 359, 360, 361, 363, 364, 365, 366, 367

NATIONALIZATION, 95, 168

NIGERIA, 131, 272, 275, 349

NUCLEAR POWER, 221

OIL CRISIS, 55

PAKISTAN, 182

PANAMA, 307

PARENT COMPANIES, 156

PHILIPPINES, 172, 176, 214

POLITICS, 84, 90, 161

POVERTY, 3, 24, 42, 58, 71, 179

PROCESSING, 191, 197

PART IV

DIRECTORY OF INFORMATION SOURCES

I. UNITED NATIONS INFORMATION SOURCES

AUDIO MATERIALS LIBRARY
United Nations, Department of Public Information, Radio and Visual
Services Division, United Nations Plaza, New York, NY 10017.

COMPREHENSIVE INFORMATION SYSTEM ON TRANSNATIONAL CORPORATIONS
United Nations, Information Analysis Division, Centre of
Transnational Corporations, 605 Third Avenue, New York, NY 10017.

BIBLIOGRAPHY ON TRANSNATIONAL CORPORATIONS
United Nations, Centre on Transnational Corporations, Information
Analysis Division, 605 Third Avenue, New York, NY 10017.

CORPORATE PROFILE SYSTEM
United Nations Centre on Transnational Corporations, Information
Analysis Division, United Nations, New York, NY 10017.

SURVEY OF RESEARCH ON TRANSNATIONAL CORPORATIONS
United Nations, Centre on Transnational Corporations, Information
Analysis Division, 605 Third Avenue, New York, NY 10017.

UNITED NATIONS BIBLIOGRAPHIC INFORMATION SYSTEM
United Nations, Department of Conference Services, Dag Hammarskjold
Library, United Nations Plaza, New York, NY 10017.

UNBIS DATA BASE
United Nations, Department of Conference Services, Dag Hammarskjold
Library, United Nations Plaza, New York, NY 10017.

INTEGRATED STATISTICAL INFORMATION SYSTEM
United Nations, Department of International Economic and Social
Affairs, Statistical Office, New York, NY 10017.

UNITED NATIONS VISUAL MATERIALS LIBRARY
United Nations, Department of Public Information, Radio and Visual
Services Division, United Nations Plaza, New York, NY 10017.

WORLD STATISTICS IN BRIEF
United Nations, Department of International Economic and Social Affairs, Statistical Office, New York, NY 10017.

DOCUMENTATION CNETRE OF THE INTERNATIONAL INSTITUTE FOR LABOUR STUDIES
International Labour Office, International Institute for Labour Studies, Case postale 6, 4 route des Morillons, 1211 Geneva 22, Switzerland.

II. BIBLIOGRAPHY OF BIBLIOGRAPHIES

ANNOTATED BIBLIOGRAPHY OF COUNTRY SERIALS is a listing of periodicals, annuals and other serials containing information of economic, business or trade interest. The listing is organized on a regional and country basis. Copies are available from the Documentation Service, International Trade Centre UNCTAD/GATT, 1211 Geneva 10, Switzerland.

BASIC-NEEDS APPROACH: A SURVEY OF ITS LITERATURE, edited by M. Rutjes, contains a brief analysis of the concept of basic needs, its targets, its strategy and implications, followed by a concise bibliography related to the topic. Copies may be obtained from the Centre for the Study of Education in Developing Countries, Badhuisweg 251, The Hague, The Netherlands.

DEVELOPMENT PLANS AND PLANNING - BIBLIOGRAPHIC AND COMPUTER AIDS TO RESEARCH, by August Schumacher, is arranged in three parts. The first contains more than 100 selected bibliographies on development plans and planning, the second is concerned with a new source of empirical materials for the development planner - the automated documentation centre, and the third analyzes recent work on computer aids for the research library. The publication is available from Seminar Press Ltd., 24-28 Oval Road, London NW1, England.

BIBLIOGRAPHY ON DEVELOPMENT EDUCATION lists books, manuals, resource materials, magazines, and articles in the field of development education. The listing was prepared by the Dutch Central Bureau of Catholic Education. Copies are available from the Central Bureau of Catholic Education, G. Verstijnen, Secretary Foreign Department, Bezuidenhoutseweg 275, The Hague, Netherlands.

BIBLIOGRAPHY OF GERMAN RESEARCH ON DEVELOPING COUNTRIES, prepared by the German Foundation for International Development, is divided into two sections: Part A contains an index of research institutes, author index, subject-matter index, and a geographical index. Part B contains specific information on each of the studies listed. The text is in German with explanatory notes in German, English, French and Spanish. Copies may be obtained from the Deutsche Stiftung fur Internationale Entwicklung (DSE), Endenicher Strasse 41, 53 Bonn, Federal Republic of Germany.

BIBLIOGRAPHY OF SELECTED LATIN AMERICAN PUBLICATIONS ON DEVELOPMENT is a listing of over 200 titles in Latin American development literature, including subject and author indexes. The document was prepared by the Institute of Development Studies Library. Copies are available from the Librarian, Institute of Development Studies, University of Sussex, Brighton BN1 9RE, England.

CANADIAN DEVELOPMENT ASSISTANCE: A SELECTED BIBLIOGRAPHY 1950-70, compiled by Shirley B. Seward and Helen Janssen, covers Canada's foreign aid programs and policies from 1950 to 1970. Copies are available from the Distribution Unit, International Development Research Centre, P.O. Box 8500, Ottawa, Canada KIG 3H9.

DEVINDEX CANADA is a bibliography of literature on social and economic development in Third World countries, which originated in Canada in 1975. Copies may be obtained from the International Development Research Centre, Box 8500, Ottawa, Canada KIG 3H9.

The UNESCO Division of Scientific Research and Higher Education has compiled **A DIRECTORY AND BIBLIOGRAPHY ON THE THEME "RESEARCH AND HUMAN NEEDS"**, listing organizations, journals, newsletters, reports and papers, information services and data banks. The bibliographical section includes headings such as food and nutrition, health, housing and sanitation, environment, energy, technology. For copies contact "Research and Human Needs", Division of Scientific Research and Higher Education, UNESCO, Place de Fontenoy, 75007 Paris, France.

GUIDE TO CURRENT DEVELOPMENT LITERATURE ON ASIA AND THE PACIFIC is published every two months by the Library and Documentation Centre of the Asia Pacific Development Information Service. For more information write to the Centre, United Nations Asian and Pacific Development Institute, P.O. Box 2-136, Sri Aydudhya Road, Bangkok, Thailand.

Hald, Marjorie W.
A SELECTED BIBLIOGRAPHY ON ECONOMIC DEVELOPMENT AND FOREIGN AID, rev. ed., Santa Monica, CA: The Rand Corporation, 1958.

Hazelwood, Arthur
THE ECONOMICS OF "UNDERDEVELOPED" AREAS: AN ANNOTATED READING LIST OF BOOKS, ARTICLES, AND OFFICIAL PUBLICATIONS. London: Oxford University Press for the Institute of Colonial Studies, 1954. 623 titles.

THE ECONOMICS OF DEVELOPMENT: AN ANNOTATED LIST OF BOOKS AND ARTICLES PUBLISHED 1958-1962. London: Oxford University Press, for the Institute of Commonwealth Studies, 1964.

INTERNATIONAL BIBLIOGRAPHY, INFORMATION DOCUMENTATION (IBID) provides bibliographic details and annotations necessary to identify the full range of publications prepared by the United Nations and its related agencies, plus those of ten organizations outside the UN system. IBID is published quarterly by Unipub. Available from Unipub, Box 433, Murray Hill Station, New York, New York 10016, USA.

THE 1978/79 PUBLICATIONS LIST OF THIRD WORLD PUBLICATIONS contains over 300 titles of pamphlets, books and teaching materials about the Third World. The listing is available from Third World Publications, Ltd., 151 Stratford Road, Birmingham B11 1RD, England.

A list of 200 books on **NORTH-SOUTH WORLD RELATIONS** has been compiled by the Developing Country Courier. The listing is organized by subject and region. For copies write to the Courier, P.O. Box 239, McLean, Virginia 22101, USA.

United States Agency for International Development
A PRACTICAL BIBLIOGRAPHY FOR DEVELOPING AREAS. Washington, D.C., 1966. 2 vols. (Vol. 1 - A selective, annotated and graded list of United States publications in the social sciences. 202 pp.) (Vol. 2 - A selective, annotated and graded list of United States publications in the physical and applied sciences. 332 pp.)

PUBLIC ADMINISTRATION--A SELECT BIBLIOGRAPHY, prepared by the British Ministry of Overseas Development Library is the second supplement to the 1973 revised edition. Copies may be obtained from Eland House, Stag Place, London SW1E 5DH, England.

PUBLIC ADMINISTRATION--A SELECT BIBLIOGRAPHY, prepared by the Library of the British Ministry of Overseas Development, is a supplement to the revised edition which appeared in 1973. It includes material published in the period 1972-1975 with 1,600 references. Copies may be obtained from the Library, British Ministry of Overseas Development, Eland House, Stag Place, London SW1E 5DH, England.

The OECD Development Centre has gathered together in the catalog **PUBLICATION AND DOCUMENT, 1962-1979** all the books and documents it has published since its establishment in 1962 up to August 1979. Copies available from OECD Development Centre, 94 rue Chardon Lagache, 75016 Paris, France.

REGISTER OF RESEARCH PROJECTS IN PROGRESS IN DEVELOPMENT STUDIES IN SELECTED EUROPEAN COUNTRIES was prepared by the Centre for Development Studies of the University of Antwerp at the request of the European Association of Development Research and Training Institutes. Copies are available from the Centre, St. Ignatius

Faculties, University of Antwerp, 13 Prinsstraat, 2000 Antwerp, Belgium.

Re Qua, Eloise and Statham, Jane
THE DEVELOPING NATIONS: A GUIDE TO INFORMATION SOURCES CONCERNING THEIR ECONOMIC, POLITICAL, TECHNICAL AND SOCIAL PROBLEMS. Detroit: Gale Research Company, 1965.

The East African Academy has published two new bibliographies. **SCIENCE AND TECHNOLOGY IN EAST AFRICA** contains more than 5,000 titles about research in the agriculture, medical technological, and related fields in East Africa, with short summaries on the problems and progress of research in these areas. **TANZANIA EDUCATION SINCE UHURU: A BIBLIOGRAPHY--1961-1971** was compiled by Dr. George A. Auger of the University of Dar es Salaam. Both publications are available from the East African Academy, RIPS, P.O. Box 47288, Nairobi, Kenya.

SELECTIVE ANNOTATED BIBLIOGRAPHY ON BRAZILIAN DEVELOPMENT has been prepared by the SID Sao Paulo Chapter. This first issue contains only references that have appeared in 1975. Copies are available from the Society for International Development, Sao Paulo Chapter, Caixa Postal 20.270-Vila Clementino, 04023-Sao Paulo-S.P. Brazil.

A SELECTED ANNOTATED BIBLIOGRAPHY: INDIGENOUS TECHNICAL KNOWLEDGE IN DEVELOPMENT, compiled by Liz O'Keefe and Michael Howes, is contained in the January 1979 IDS BULLETIN. This issue of the BULLETIN is devoted to the importance of indigenous technical knowledge in rural areas. Single copies of the BULLETIN are from the Communications Office, Institute of Development Studies, University of Sussex, Brighton N1 9RE, United Kingdom.

SELECTED BIBLIOGRAPHY OF RECENT ECONOMIC DEVELOPMENT PUBLICATIONS covers a period of one year, from July 1977 to June 1978 and contains two main sections, one for general and theoretical works, the other for literature related to regions and countries. For copies write to the Graduate Program in Economic Development, Vanderbilt University, Nashville, Tennessee 37235, USA.

International Bank for Reconstruction and Development; Economic Development Institute
SELECTED READINGS AND SOURCE MATERIALS ON ECONOMIC DEVELOPMENT. A list of books, articles, and reports included in a small library assembled by the Economic Development Institute, Washington, D.C., 1961.

SOCIAL AND ECONOMIC DEVELOPMENT PLANS - MICROFICHE PROJECT is a cumulative catalogue listing the holdings of Inter Documentation Company AG on social and economic development plans around the world. About 1400 plans from over 180 countries are included. Copies of the catalogue and other catalogues of IDC's microfiche projects are free on request from Inter Documentation Company AG, Poststrasse 14, 6300 Zug-Switzerland.

Powelson, John
A SELECT BIBLIOGRAPHY ON ECONOMIC DEVELOPMENT.   Boulder, Colorado:
Westview Press, 1979.

THIRD WORLD BIBLIOGRAPHY AND RESOURCE GUIDE features a wide range
of material on Third World issues. It is designed for students
and general readers. Copies may be obtained from the Development
Education Library Project, c/o OSFAM/Ontario, 175 Carlton Street,
Toronto, Canada.

The United Nations Asian and Pacific Development Institute has
prepared a **SPECIAL BIBLIOGRAPHY ON ALTERNATIVE STRATEGIES FOR
DEVELOPMENT WITH FOCUS ON LOCAL LEVEL PLANNING AND DEVELOPMENT**
in connection with a UNAPDI meeting, held in Bangkok, October
31 - November 4, 1978. Copies are available from the APDI Library
and Documentation Centre. UNAPDI, P.O. Box 2-136, Sri Ayudhya
Road, Bangkok, Thailand.

Vente, Role and Dieter Seul
MACRO-ECONOMIC   PLANNING: A   BIBLIOGRAPHY.   Nomos
Verlagsgesellshaft, Baden-Baden, 1970.

Volunteers in Technical Assistance (VITA) has published its 1979
CATALOGUE OF BOOKS, BULLETINS AND MANUALS. The listing contains
VITA documents related to appropriate technology, as well as
materials published by other development organizations around
the world. Copies are available from VITA, 2706 Rhode Island
Avenue, Mt. Ranier, Maryland 20822, USA.

DEVELOPMENT--A BIBLIOGRAPHY, was compiled by Vaptistis-Titos
Patrikios (Rome: FAO, 1974) and updates the first edition,
published in 1970, to cover the 1970/73 period. Contains eight
sections relating to development: theories and problems;
perspectives of the Third World countries; population and food
production; aid, trade and international cooperation; agriculture;
manpower and employment; education; and environment. A ninth
section lists bibliographies.

III. DIRECTORY OF PERIODICALS

ACTUEL DEVELOPPEMENT, English Digest Edition, Paris.

AFRICA, London, Africa Journal, Ltd.

AFRICA INSTITUTE, Pretoria, Africa Institute.

AFRICA QUARTERLY, New Delhi, India Council for Africa.

AFRICA RESEARCH BULLETIN, Exeter, Eng. Africa Research, Ltd.

AFRICA, SOUTH OF THE SAHARA, London, Europa Publications.

AFRICA TODAY, New York, American Committee on Africa.

AFRICAN AFFAIRS, London, Journal of the Royal African Society.

AFRICAN DEVELOPMENT, London.

AFRICAN DEVELOPMENT BANK, Annual Report, Ibadan.

AFRICAN ENVIRONMENT, Dakar, United Nations Environmental Program.

AFRICAN STATISTICAL YEARBOOK, Addis Ababa, Economic Commission for Africa.

AFRICAN STUDIES REVIEW, Stanford, Boston, East Lansing, African Studies Association.

AFRICAN URBAN STUDIES, East Lansing, Mich., African Studies Center.

AGENDA, Washington, D.C., U.S. Agency for International Development.

APPROPRIATE   TECHNOLOGY,   London,   Intermediate   Technology
Publications, Ltd.

APPROTECH, Ann Arbor, Mich., International Association for the
Advancement of Appropriate Technology for Developing Countries.

ARTHA VIJNANA, Poona, Gokhale Institute of Politics and Economics.

ASIA AND THE WORLD MONOGRAPHS, Taipei, Asia and the World Forum.

ASIA YEARBOOK, Hong Kong, Far Eastern Economic Review.

ASIAN AFFAIRS, London, Royal Central Asian Society.

ASIAN DEVELOPMENT BANK, Annual Report, Manila.

ASIAN REGIONAL CONFERENCE OF THE INTERNATIONAL LABOR ORGANIZATION,
Proceedings, Geneva, ILO.

ASIAN SURVEY, Berkeley, Institute of International Studies.

BANGLADESH DEVELOPMENT STUDIES, Dhaka, Bangladesh Institute of
Development Studies.

BANGLADESH ECONOMIC REVIEW, Dhaka, Bangladesh Institute of
Development Economics.

BULLETIN OF INDONESIAN ECONOMIC STUDIES, Canberra, Dept. of
Economics, Australian National University.

CEPAL REVIEW, Santiago, Chile.

CANADIAN JOURNAL OF AFRICAN STUDIES, Montreal, Loyola College.

COMMUNITY DEVELOPMENT JOURNAL, Manchester, U.K., Oxford University
Press.

DEVELOPING ECONOMIES, Tokyo, The Institute of Asian Economic
Affairs.

DEVELOPMENT, Rome, Society for International Development.

DEVELOPMENT CENTER STUDIES, OECD, Paris.

DEVELOPMENT AND CHANGE, Beverly Hills, Calif.: Sage Publications.

DEVELOPMENT CO-OPERATION, Paris, OECD.

DEVELOPMENT DIGEST, Washington, D.C., U.S. Agency for International
Development.

DEVELOPMENT DIALOGUE, Uppsala, Sweden, Dag Hammarskjold Foundation.

EASTERN AFRICA ECONOMIC REVIEW, Nairobi, Oxford University Press.

ECONOMIC DEVELOPMENT AND CULTURAL CHANGE, Chicago, University of Chicago Press.

ETHIOPIAN JOURNAL OF DEVELOPMENT RESEARCH, Addis Ababa, Institute of Development Research.

FAR EASTERN ECONOMIC REVIEW, Hong Kong.

FINANCE AND DEVELOPMENT, Washington, D.C.

IDS BULLETIN, Institute of Development Studies, University of Sussex, U.K.

IMPACT OF SCIENCE ON SOCIETY, Paris, UNESCO.

INDIAN JOURNAL OF INDUSTRIAL RELATIONS, New Delhi, India.

INDUSTRY AND DEVELOPMENT, Vienna, UNIDO.

INTERNATIONAL DEVELOPMENT REVIEW, Rome, Society for International Development.

INTERNATIONAL LABOR REVIEW, Geneva, ILO.

INTERNATIONAL STUDIES QUARTERLY, San Francisco.

JOURNAL OF AFRICAN STUDIES, Los Angeles, UCLA African Studies Center.

JOURNAL OF DEVELOPING AREAS, Macomb, IL, Western Illinois Univ.

JOURNAL OF DEVELOPMENT ECONOMICS, Amsterdam, North Holland Publishing Co.

JOURNAL OF DEVELOPMENT STUDIES, London, U.K.

JOURNAL OF ECONOMIC DEVELOPMENT, JOURNAL OF INTERNATIONAL AFFAIRS, New York, Columbia University.

JOURNAL OF MODERN AFRICAN STUDIES, New York, Cambridge University Press.

LATIN AMERICAN RESEARCH REVIEW, Chapel Hill, North Carolina.

MODERN ASIAN STUDIES, New York, Cambridge University Press.

MONOGRAPH, DEVELOPMENT STUDIES CENTER, AUSTRALIAN NATIONAL UNIVERSITY.

MONOGRAPH, OVERSEAS DEVELOPMENT COUNCIL, Washington, D.C.

ODI REVIEW, Overseas Development Institute, London, U.K.

OXFORD ECONOMIC PAPERS, Oxford, U.K.

PAKISTAN DEVELOPMENT REVIEW, Karachi, Pakistan.

PUBLIC ADMINISTRATION AND DEVELOPMENT, Sussex, U.K., Royal Institute of Public Administration.

THIRD WORLD QUARTERLY, London, Third World Foundation for Social and Economic Studies.

WORLD BANK STAFF WORKING PAPER, IBRD, Washington, D.C.

WORLD DEVELOPMENT, Pergamon Press, N.Y.

NOTE:

For more information on relevant periodicals please consult:

1. **DIRECTORY OF UNITED NATIONS INFORMATION SYSTEMS**

2. **REGISTER OF UNITED NATIONS SERIAL PUBLICATIONS**

Public by **Inter-Organization Board for Information Systems,** IOB Secretariat, Palais des Nations, CH-1211 Geneva 10, Switzerland.

IV. RESEARCH INSTITUTIONS

INTERNATIONAL (GENERAL)

AFRICAN INSTITUTE FOR ECONOMIC DEVELOPMENT AND PLANNING
United Nations Economic Commission for Africa, Dakar, Senegal.

AFRO-ASIAN ORGANIZATION FOR ECONOMIC CO-OPERATION
Chairo Chamber of Commerce Building, Midan el-Falsky, Cairo,
Egypt.

ASIAN ASSOCIATION OF DEVELOPMENT RESEARCH AND TRAINING INSTITUTES
P.O. Box 2-136, Sri Ayudhya Road, Bangkok, Thailand.

ASIAN DEVELOPMENT CENTER
11th Floor, Philippines Banking Corporation Building, Anda Circle,
Port Area, Manila, Philippines.

ASIAN INSTITUTE FOR ECONOMIC DEVELOPMENT AND PLANNING
P.O. Box 2-136, Sri Ayudhya Road, Bangkok, Thailand.

ATLANTIC INSTITUTE FOR INTERNATIONAL AFFAIRS
120, rue de Longchamp, 75016 Paris, France.

CARIBBEAN STUDIES ASSOCIATION
Inter-American University of Puerto Rico, P.O. Box 1293, Hato
Rey, Puerto Rico 00919.

CENTRE FOR STUDIES AND RESEARCH IN INTERNATIONAL LAW AND
INTERNATIONAL RELATIONS
The Hague Academy of International Law, The Hague, Netherlands.

CENTRE FOR THE CO-ORDINATION OF SOCIAL SCIENCE RESEARCH AND
DOCUMENTATION IN AFRICA SOUTH OF THE SAHARA
B.P. 836, Kinshasa XI, Zaire.

CLUB OF ROME
Via Giorgione 163, 00147 Roma, Italy.

COMMITTEE ON SOCIETY, DEVELOPMENT AND PEACE
Oecumenical Centre, 150, route de Ferney, 1211 Geneve 20, Suisse.

COUNCIL FOR ASIAN MANPOWER STUDIES
P.O. Box 127, Quezon City, Philippines.

COUNCIL FOR THE DEVELOPMENT OF ECONOMIC AND SOCIAL RESEARCH IN AFRICA
B.P. 3186, Dakar, Senegal.

EAST AFRICAN ACADEMY RESEARCH INFORMATION CENTRE
Regional Building of East African Community, Ngong Road (rooms 359-60), Nairobi, Kenya.

EASTERN REGIONAL ORGANIZATION FOR PLANNING AND HOUSING
Central Office: 4a, Ring Road, Indraprastha Estate, New Delhi, India.

EASTERN REGIONAL ORGANIZATION FOR PUBLIC ADMINISTRATION
Rizal Hall, Padre Faura Street, Manila, Philippines.

ECONOMIC DEVELOPMENT INSTITUTE
1818 H Street, N.W., Washington, D.C. 20433, U.S.A.

EUROPEAN FOUNDATION FOR MANAGEMENT DEVELOPMENT
51, rue de la Concorde, Bruxelles, Belgique.

EUROPEAN INSTITUTE FOR TRANSNATIONAL STUDIES IN GROUP AND ORGANIZATIONAL DEVELOPMENT
Viktorgasse 9, 1040 Vienna, Austria.

EUROPEAN INSTITUTE OF BUSINESS ADMINISTRATION
Boulevard de Constance, 77 Fontainebleau, France.

EUROPEAN RESEARCH GROUP ON MANAGEMENT
Predikherenberg 55, 3200 Kessel-Lo, Belgique.

INSTITUTE OF INTERNATIONAL LAW
82, avenue de Castel, 1200 Bruxelles, Belgique.

INTERNATIONAL AFRICAN INSTITUTE
210, High Holborn, London WC1V 7BW, United Kingdom.

INTERNATIONAL ASSOCIATION FOR METROPOLITAN RESEARCH AND DEVELOPMENT
Suite 1200, 130 Bloor Street West, Toronto 5, Canada.

INTERNATIONAL CENTRE OF RESEARCH AND INFORMATION ON PUBLIC AND CO-OPERATIVE ECONOMY
45, quai de Rome, Liege, Belgique.

INTERNATIONAL CO-OPERATION FOR SOCIO-ECONOMIC DEVELOPMENT
59-61, rue Adolphe-Lacombie, Bruxelles 4, Belgique.

INTERNATIONAL INSTITUTE FOR LABOUR STUDIES
154, rue de Lausanne, Case Postale 6, 1211 Geneve, Suisse.

INTERNATIONAL INSTITUTE FOR STRATEGIC STUDIES
18, Adam Street, London WC2N 6AL, United Kingdom.

INTERNATIONAL INSTITUTE OF ADMINISTRATIVE SCIENCES
25, rue de la Charite, Bruxelles 4, Belgique.

INTERNATIONAL MANAGEMENT DEVELOPMENT INSTITUTE
4, Chemin de Conches, 1200 Geneve, Suisse.

INTERNATIONAL SCIENCE FOUNDATION
2, rue de Furstenberg, 75006 Paris, France.

INTERNATIONAL SOCIAL SCIENCE COUNCIL
1, rue Miollis, 75015 Paris, France.

INTERNATIONAL STATISTICAL INSTITUTE
Prinses Beatrixlaan 428, Voorburg, Netherlands.

INTERNATIONAL TRAINING AND RESEARCH CENTER FOR DEVELOPMENT
47, rue de la Glaciere, 75013 Paris, France.

LATIN AMERICAN CENTRE FOR ECONOMIC AND SOCIAL DOCUMENTATION
Casilla 179-D, Santiago, Chile.

ORGANIZATION FOR ECONOMIC CO-OPERATION AND DEVELOPMENT
Chateau de la Muette, 2, rue Andre Pascal, 75775 Paris Cedex 16, France.

REGIONAL ECONOMIC RESEARCH AND DOCUMENTATION CENTER
B.P. 7138, Lome, Togo.

RESEARCH CENTRE ON SOCIAL AND ECONOMIC DEVELOPMENT IN ASIA--INSTITUTE OF ECONOMIC GROWTH
University Enclave, Delhi 7, India.

SOCIETY FOR INTERNATIONAL DEVELOPMENT
1346 Connecticut Avenue, N.W., Washington, D.C. 20036, USA.

SOUTHEAST ASIAN SOCIAL SCIENCE ASSOCIATION
Chulalongkorn University, c/o Faculty of Political Science, Bangkok, Thailand.

UNITED NATIONS INSTITUTE FOR TRAINING AND RESEARCH
801 United Nations Plaza, New York, NY, USA.

UNITED NATIONS RESEARCH INSTITUTE FOR SOCIAL DEVELOPMENT
Palais des Nations, 1211 Geneve, Suisse.

AUSTRALIA

AUSTRALIAN INSTITUTE OF INTERNATIONAL AFFAIRS
P.O. Box E181, Canberra, ACT 2600.

INSTITUTE OF ADVANCED STUDIES
The Australian National University, P.O. Box 4, Canberra ACT 2600.

STRATEGIC AND DEFENSE STUDIES CENTER
Research School of Pacific Studies, Australian National University, P.O. Box 4, Canberra ACT 2600.

AUSTRIA

AUSTRIAN FOUNDATION FOR DEVELOPMENT RESEARCH (OFSE)
Turkenstrasse 3, 1090 Vienna, Austria.

VIENNA INSTITUTE FOR DEVELOPMENT
Karntner Strasse 25, 1010 Vienna, Austria.

BANGLADESH

BANGLADESH INSTITUTE OF DEVELOPMENT STUDIES
Adamjee Court, Motijheel Commercial Area, Dacca 2.

BELGIUM

CATHOLIC UNIVERSITY OF LOUVAIN
Center for Economic Studies, Van Evenstraat 2b, 3000 Louvain, Belgium.

FREE UNIVERSITY OF BRUSSELS
Department of Applied Economics, Avenue F-D Roosevelt 50, 1050 Brussels, Belgium.

UNIVERSITY OF ANTWERP
Centre for Development Studies, 13 Prinsstratt, 2000 Antwerp, Belgium.

BRAZIL

BRAZILIAN INSTITUTE OF ECONOMICS
Fundacao Getulio Vargas Caixa Postal 4081-ZC-05, Rio de Janeiro, Brazil.

PROGRAMME OF JOINT STUDIES ON LATIN AMERICAN ECONOMIC INTEGRATION
Caixa Postal 740, Rio de Janeiro, Brazil.

BULGARIA

SCIENTIFIC RESEARCH CENTRE FOR AFRICA AND ASIA
Academy of Social Science, ul. Gagarin 2, Sofia 13, Bulgaria.

INSTITUTE FOR INTERNATIONAL RELATIONS AND SOCIALIST INTEGRATION
Bulgarian Academy of Sciences, Boul. Pencho Slaveicov, 15, Sofia, Bulgaria.

CANADA

CANADIAN ASSOCIATION OF AFRICAN STUDIES
Geography Department, Carleton University, Ottawa, K1S 5B6.

CANADIAN COUNCIL FOR INTERNATIONAL CO-OPERATION
75 Sparks Street, Ottawa 4, Ontario.

CANADIAN INSTITUTE OF INTERNATIONAL AFFAIRS
Edgar Tarr House, 31 Wellesley Street East, Toronto 284, Ontario.

CENTRE FOR DEVELOPING-ASIA STUDIES
McGill University, Montreal.

INSTITUTE OF INTERNATIONAL RELATIONS
University of British Columbia, Vancouver 8.

INTERNATIONAL DEVELOPMENT RESEARCH CENTRE
60 Queen Street, P.O. Box 8500, Ottawa K1G 3H9.

REGIONAL DEVELOPMENT RESEARCH CENTER
University of Ottawa, Ottawa 2, Ontario.

CHILE

CATHOLIC UNIVERSITY OF CHILE
Institute of Economics, Avda. Libertador Bernardo O'Higgins, No. 340, Santiago, Chile.

CATHOLIC UNIVERSITY OF CHILE
Center for Planning Studies (CEPLAN), Avda. Libertador Bernardo O'Higgins, No. 340, Santiago, Chile.

UNIVERSITY OF CHILE
Planning Centre (CEPLA), Avda. Libertador Bernardo O'Higgins, No. 1058, Santiago, Chile.

COLOMBIA

UNIVERSITY OF ANTIOQUIA
Economic Research Centre, Apartado Aereo 1226, Medellin, Colombia.

CZECHOSLOVAKIA

INSTITUTE OF INTERNATIONAL RELATIONS
Praha 1 - Mala Strana, Nerudova 3, Czechoslovakia.

DENMARK

INSTITUTE FOR DEVELOPMENT RESEARCH
V. Volgade 104, DK-1552 Kobenhavn.

CENTRE FOR DEVELOPMENT RESEARCH
9, NY Kongensgade, 4K-1472 Copenhagen K, Denmark.

FRANCE

UNIVERSITY OF PARIS, INSTITUTE OF ECONOMIC AND SOCIAL DEVELOPMENT
STUDIES
58 Boulevard Arago, 75013 Paris, France.

INSTITUTE FOR RESEARCH INTO THE ECONOMICS OF PRODUCTION
2 rue de Rouen, 92000 Nanterre, France.

INTERNATIONAL CENTRE OF ADVANCED MEDITERRANEAN AGRONOMIC STUDIES
Route de Mende, 34000 Montpellier, France.

INSTITUTE FOR ECONOMIC RESEARCH AND DEVELOPMENT PLANNING
B.P. 47, 38040 Grenoble Cedex, France.

GERMANY, FEDERAL REPUBLIC OF

INSTITUTE FOR DEVELOPMENT RESEARCH AND DEVELOPMENT POLICY
Ruhr-Universitat Bochum, 463 Bochum-Querenburg, Postifach 2148,
Federal Republic of Germany.

INTERNATIONAL INSTITUTE OF MANAGEMENT
Wissenschaftszentrum Berlin, Criegstrasse 5-7, Berlin 33, D-1000.

GERMAN ASSOCIATION FOR EAST ASIAN STUDIES
Rothenbaumchaussee 32, 2 Hamburg 13.

GHANA

INSTITUTE OF AFRICAN STUDIES
University of Ghana, P.O. Box 73, Legon, Accra.

HUNGARY

INSTITUTE FOR WORLD ECONOMICS OF THE HUNGARIAN ACADEMY OF SCIENCES
P.O. Box 36, 1531 Budapest, Hungary.

INSTITUTE FOR ECONOMIC AND MARKET RESEARCH
P.O. Box 133, Budapest 62, Hungary.

INDIA

CENTRE FOR THE STUDY OF DEVELOPING SOCIETIES
29, Rajpur Road, Delhi 6, India.

INDIA INTERNATIONAL CENTRE
40 Lodi Estate, New Delhi 110003, India.

INDIAN COUNCIL FOR AFRICA
Nyaya Marg, Chankyapuri, New Delhi 21, India.

INDIAN COUNCIL OF WORLD AFFAIRS
Sapru House, Barakhamba Road, New Delhi 110001, India.

INDIAN INSTITUTE OF ASIAN STUDIES
23/354, Azad Nagar, Jaiprakash Road, Andheri, Bombay 38, India.

INDIAN SCHOOL OF INTERNATIONAL STUDIES
35, Ferozeshah Road, New Delhi 1, India.

INSTITUTE OF ECONOMIC GROWTH
University of Enclave, Delhi 7, India.

MADRAS INSTITUTE OF DEVELOPMENT STUDIES
74, Second Main Road, Gandhinagar Adyar, Madras 20, India.

INDONESIA

NATIONAL INSTITUTE OF ECONOMIC AND SOCIAL RESEARCH
Leknas, UC, P.O. Box 310, Djakarta, Indonesia.

ISRAEL

DAVID HOROWITZ INSTITUTE FOR THE RESEARCH OF DEVELOPING COUNTRIES
Tel-Aviv University, Ramat-Aviv, Tel-Aviv.

AFRO-ASIAN INSTITUTE FOR CO-OPERATIVE AND LABOUR STUDIES
P.O. Box 16201, Tel-Aviv.

ISRAELI INSTITUTE OF INTERNATIONAL AFFAIRS
P.O. Box 17027, Tel-Aviv 61170.

JAPAN

INSTITUTE OF DEVELOPING ECONOMIES
42 Ichigaya-Hommura-cho, Sinjuku-ku, Tokyo 162, Japan.

JAPAN CENTER FOR AREA DEVELOPMENT RESEARCH
Iino Building, 2-1-1 Uchisaiwai-cho, Chiyoda-ku, Tokyo, Japan.

KENYA

INSTITUTE FOR DEVELOPMENT STUDIES
University of Nairobi, P.O. Box 30197, Nairobi.

KOREA

INDUSTRIAL MANAGEMENT RESEARCH CENTRE
Yonsei University, Sodaemoon-ku-Seoul.

INSTITUTE OF OVERSEAS AFFAIRS
Hankuk University of Foreign Studies, 270 Rimoon-dong, Seoul.

INSTITUTE OF THE MIDDLE EAST AND AFRICA
Rom. 52, Dong-A Building, No. 55, 2nd-ka, Sinmoonro, Congro-ku, Seoul.

MEXICO

CENTRE FOR ECONOMIC RESEARCH AND TEACHING
Av. Country Club No. 208, Apdo. Postal 13628, Mexico 21, D. F.

NEPAL

CENTRE FOR ECONOMIC DEVELOPMENT AND ADMINISTRATION (CEDA)
Tribhuvan University, Kirtipur, P.O. Box 797, Kathmandu, Nepal.

NETHERLANDS

CENTRE FOR LATIN AMERICAN RESEARCH AND DOCUMENTATION
Nieuwe Doelenstraat 16, Amsterdam 1000, Netherlands.

INSTITUTE OF SOCIAL STUDIES
Badhuisweg 251, P.O. Box 90733, 2509 LS The Hague, Netherlands.

FREE UNIVERSITY, DEPARTMENT OF DEVELOPMENT ECONOMICS
De Boelelaan 1105, Amsterdam 1000, Netherlands.

CENTRE FOR DEVELOPMENT PLANNING
Erasmus University, Postbus 1738, Rotterdam, Netherlands.

DEVELOPMENT RESEARCH INSTITUTE
Hogeschoollaan 225, Tiburg 4400, Netherlands.

NEW ZEALAND

NEW ZEALAND INSTITUTE OF INTERNATIONAL AFFAIRS
P.O. Box 196, Wellington, New Zealand.

NEW ZEALAND INSTITUTE OF ECONOMIC RESEARCH
26, Kelburn Parade, P.O. Box 3749, Wellington, New Zealand.

NIGERIA

INSTITUTE OF AFRICAN STUDIES, UNIVERSITY OF NIGERIA
University of Nigeria, Nsukka, Nigeria.

NIGERIAN INSTITUTE OF INTERNATIONAL AFFAIRS
Kofo Abayomi Road, Victoria Island, G.P.O. Box 1727, Lagos,
Nigeria.

NIGERIAN INSTITUTE OF SOCIAL AND ECONOMIC RESEARCH
Private Mail Bag No. 5, U.I. University of Ibadan, Ibadan, Nigeria.

NORWAY

INTERNATIONAL PEACE RESEARCH INSTITUTE
Radhusgt 4, Oslo 1, Norway.

NORWEGIAN AGENCY FOR INTERNATIONAL DEVELOPMENT (NORAD)
Planning Department, Boks 18142 Oslo Dep., Oslo 1, Norway.

THE CHR. MICHELSEN INSTITUTE (DERAP)
Fantoftvegen 38, 5036 Fantoft, Bergen, Norway.

PAKISTAN

DEPARTMENT OF INTERNATIONAL RELATIONS
University of Karachi, Karachi-32, Pakistan.

PHILIPPINES

ASIAN CENTER
University of the Philippines, Palma Hall, Diliman D-505, Quezon
City, Philippines.

ASIAN INSTITUTE OF INTERNATIONAL STUDIES
Malcolm Hall, University of the Philippines, Diliman, Quezon
City, Philippines.

INSTITUTE OF ECONOMIC DEVELOPMENT AND RESEARCH
School of Economics, University of the Philippines, Diliman,
Quezon City, Philippines.

POLAND

RESEARCH INSTITUTE FOR DEVELOPING COUNTRIES
Rakowiecka 24, Warsaw, Poland.

CENTRE OF AFRICAN STUDIES
University of Warsaw, Al. Zwirki i Wigury 93, 02-089 Warsaw,
Poland.

SINGAPORE

INSTITUTE OF ASIAN STUDIES
Nanyang University, Jurong Road, Singapore 22.

INSTITUTE OF SOUTH-EAST ASIAN STUDIES
Campus of University of Singapore, House No. 8, Cluny Road,
Singapore 10.

SRI LANKA

MARGA INSTITUTE
P.O. Box 601, 61 Isipathana Mawatha, Colombo 5, Sri Lanka.

SUDAN

INSTITUTE OF AFRICAN AND ASIAN STUDIES
Faculty of Arts, University of Khartoum, P.O. Box 321, Khartoum,
Sudan.

SWEDEN

INSTITUTE FOR INTERNATIONAL ECONOMIC STUDIES
Fack S-104 05, Stockholm 50, Sweden.

STOCKHOLM SCHOOL OF ECONOMICS, ECONOMIC RESEARCH INSTITUTE
Box 6501, 11383 Stockholm, Sweden.

UNITED KINGDOM

CENTRE FOR SOUTH-EAST ASIAN STUDIES
University of Hull, Hull HU6 7RX.

CENTRE OF AFRICAN STUDIES
University of Edinburgh, Adam Ferguson Building, George Square, Edinburgh 8.

CENTRE OF LATIN AMERICAN STUDIES (CAMBRIDGE)
University of Cambridge, History Faculty Building, West Road, Cambridge CB3 9ES, England.

CENTRE OF LATIN AMERICAN STUDIES (OXFORD)
Oxford University, St. Antony's College, Oxford OX2 6JF, England.

CENTRE OF WEST AFRICAN STUDIES
University of Birmingham, P.O. Box 363, Birmingham B15 2TT.

INSTITUTE FOR THE STUDY OF INTERNATIONAL ORGANISATION
University of Sussex, Stanmer House, Stanmer Park, Brighton BN1 9QA, England.

INSTITUTE OF DEVELOPMENT STUDIES
University of Sussex, Falmer, Brighton BN1 9QN, England.

INSTITUTE OF LATIN AMERICAN STUDIES
University of London, 31 Tavistock Square, London WC1, England.

INSTITUTE OF LATIN AMERICAN STUDIES (GLASGOW)
University of Glasgow, Glasgow.

ROYAL INSTITUTE OF INTERNATIONAL AFFAIRS
Chatham House, St. James' Square, London SW1Y 4LE, England.

UNITED STATES

AFRICAN STUDIES CENTER (BOSTON)
Boston University, 10 Lenos Street, Brookline MA 02146.

BROOKINGS INSTITUTION
1775 Massachusetts Avenue, N.W., Washington, D.C. 20036.

CENTER FOR ASIAN STUDIES
Arizona State University, Tempe, AZ 85281.

CENTER FOR COMPARATIVE STUDIES IN TECHNOLOGICAL DEVELOPMENT AND SOCIAL CHANGE
University of Minnesota, Minneapolis, Minnesota 55455.

CENTER FOR DEVELOPMENT ECONOMICS
Williams College, Williamston, MA 01267.

CENTER FOR INTERNATIONAL AFFAIRS
Harvard University, 6 Divinity Avenue, Cambridge, MA 02138.

CENTER FOR INTERNATIONAL STUDIES
Massachusetts Institute of Technology, Cambridge, MA 02139.

CENTER FOR LATIN AMERICAN STUDIES, ARIZONA STATE UNIVERSITY
Arizona State University, Tempe, AZ 85281.

CENTER FOR LATIN AMERICAN STUDIES, UNIVERSITY OF FLORIDA
University of Florida, Room 319 LACH, Gainesville, FL 39611.

CENTER FOR RESEARCH IN ECONOMIC DEVELOPMENT
506 East Liberty Street, Ann Arbor, MI 48108.

CENTER FOR STRATEGIC AND INTERNATIONAL STUDIES
Georgetown University, 1800 K Street, N.W., Washington, D.C.
20006.

CENTER OF INTERNATIONAL STUDIES, PRINCETON UNIVERSITY
Princeton University, 118 Corwin Hall, Princeton, NJ 08540.

HARVARD INSTITUTE FOR INTERNATIONAL DEVELOPMENT
Harvard University, 1737 Cambridge Street, Cambridge MA 02138.

INSTITUTE FOR WORLD ORDER
1140 Avenue of the Americas, New York, New York 10036.

INSTITUTE OF LATIN AMERICAN STUDIES
University of Texas at Austin, Sid. W. Richardson Hall, Austin,
TX 78705.

STANFORD INTERNATIONAL DEVELOPMENT EDUCATION CENTER
P.O. Box 2329, Stanford, CA 94305.

UNIVERSITY CENTER FOR INTERNATIONAL STUDIES
University of Pittsburgh, Social Sciences Building, Pittsburgh,
PA 15213.

WORLD FUTURE SOCIETY
4916 St. Elmo Avenue, Bethesda Branch, Washington, D.C. 20014.

UNIVERSITY OF HAWAII
Centre for Development Studies, Department of Economics, Porteus
Hall, 2424 Maile Way, Honolulu, Hawaii 96822.

URUGUAY

LATIN AMERICAN CENTRE FOR HUMAN ECONOMY
Cerrito 475, P.O. Box 998, Montevideo, Uruguay.

VENEZUELA

UNIVERSITY OF ZULIA
Department of Economic Research, Faculty of Economic and Social
Sciences, Maracaibo, Venezuela.

YUGOSLAVIA

INSTITUTE FOR DEVELOPING COUNTRIES
41000 Zagreb, Ul. 8 Maja 82, Yugoslavia.

RESEARCH CENTRE FOR CO-OPERATION WITH DEVELOPING COUNTRIES
61 109 Ljubljana, Titova 104 P.O. Box 37, Yugoslavia.

INSTITUTE OF WORLD ECONOMICS AND INTERNATIONAL RELATIONS OF THE
ACADEMY OF SCIENCES OF THE U.S.S.R.
Yaroslavskaya Ul. 13, Moskva I-243.

Appendix

COUNTRIES BY INCOME GROUP
(based on 1976 GNP per capita in 1976 US dollars)

INDUSTRIALIZED COUNTRIES

Australia
Austria
Belgium
Canada
Denmark
Finland
France
Germany, Fed. Rep. of
Iceland
Ireland
Italy
Japan
Luxembourg
Netherlands
New Zealand
Norway
South Africa
Sweden
Switzerland
United Kingdom
United States

DEVELOPING COUNTRIES BY INCOME GROUP
(Excluding Capital Surplus Oil Exporters)

High Income (over $2500)

American Samoa
Bahamas
Bermuda
Brunei
Canal Zone
Channel Islands
Faeroe Islands
French Polynesia
Gabon
Gibraltar
Greece
Greenland
Guam
Israel
Martinique
New Caledonia
Oman
Singapore
Spain
Venezuela
Virgin Islands (U.S.)

Upper Middle Income ($1136-2500)

Argentina
Bahrain
Barbados
Brazil
Cyprus
Djibouti
Fiji

French Guiana
Guadeloupe
Hong Kong
Iran
Iraq
Isle of Man
Lebanon
Malta
Netherlands Antilles
Panama
Portugal
Puerto Rico
Reunion
Romania
Surinam
Trinidad & Tobago
Uruguay
Yugoslavia

Intermediate Middle Income ($551-1135)

Algeria
Antigua
Belize
Chile
China, Rep. of
Colombia
Costa Rica
Dominica
Dominican Republic
Ecuador
Ghana
Gilbert Islands
Guatemala
Ivory Coast
Jamaica
Jordan
Korea, Rep. of
Macao
Malaysia
Mauritius
Mexico
Namibia
Nicaragua
Paraguay
Peru
Seychelles
St. Kitts-Nevis
St. Lucia
Syrian Arab Rep.
Trust Territory of the Pacific
   Islands
Tunisia
Turkey

Lower Middle Income ($281-550)

Angola
Bolivia
Botswana
Cameroon
Cape Verde
Congo, P.R.
El Salvador
Equatorial Guinea
Grenada
Guyana
Honduras
Liberia
Mauritania
Morocco
New Hebrides
Nigeria
Papua New Guinea
Philippines
Rhodesia
Sao Tome & Principe
Senegal
St. Vincent
Sudan
Swaziland
Thailand
Tonga
Western Samoa
Zambia

Low   Income   ($280   or   less)

Afghanistan
Bangladesh
Benin
Bhutan
Burma
Burundi
Cambodia
Central African Empire
Chad
Comoros
Egypt
Ethiopia
Gambia, The
Guinea
Guinea-Bissau
Haiti
India
Indonesia
Kenya
Lesotho
Madagascar
Malawi

Maldives
Mali
Mozambique
Nepal
Niger
Pakistan
Rwanda
Sierra Leone
Solomon Islands
Somalia
Sri Lanka
Tanzania
Togo
Uganda
Upper Volta
Viet Nam
Yemen Arab Rep.
Yemen P.D.R.
Zaire

**CAPITAL SURPLUS OIL EXPORTING
DEVELOPING COUNTRIES**

Kuwait
Libya
Qatar
Saudi Arabia
United Arab Emirates

CENTRALLY PLANNED COUNTRIES

Albania
Bulgaria
China, People's Rep. of
Cuba
Czechoslovakia
German Dem. Rep.
Hungary
Korea, Dem. Rep. of
Lao People's Dem. Rep.
Mongolia
Poland
U.S.S.R.

Index

About the Editor

Pradip K. Ghosh is President of the World Academy of Development and Cooperation, Washington, D.C. and Adjunct Associate Professor and Visiting Fellow at the Center for International Development at the University of Maryland, College Park. He is the author of *Thinking Sociology* and *Land Use Planning,* and editor of the International Development Resource Books series for Greenwood Press.